D1446959

Articles on American Slavery

An eighteen–volume set collecting nearly four hundred of the most important articles on slavery in the United States

Edited with Introductions by
Paul Finkelman

State University of New York,
Binghamton

A Garland Series

Contents of the Series

VOL. 18

Comparative
Issues
in Slavery

Edited with an Introduction
by Paul Finkelman

Garland Publishing, Inc.
New York & London
1989

Library of Congress Cataloging-in-Publication Data

Comparative issues in slavery /edited with an
introduction by Paul Finkelman.

p. cm.—(Articles on American slavery; vol. 18)

Includes bibliographical references.

ISBN 0–8240–6798–3 (alk. paper)

1. Slavery—United States History. 2. Slavery—
Southern States—History. 3. Slavery—America—
History. 4. Slavery—America—History.
I. Finkelman, Paul. II. Series.

E441.C66   1989

306.3'62'0973—dc20   89–23467

Printed on acid-free, 250-year-life paper.

Manufactured in the United States of America

Design by Julie Threlkeld

General Introduction

Few subjects in American history have been as compelling as slavery. This should not surprise us. Slavery affected millions of Americans, north and south. Afro-Americans, Euro-Americans, and Native Americans were involved in the system. All antebellum Americans were affected, directly or indirectly, by slavery. Slavery especially affected Americans from 1861 until well after Reconstruction. As Lincoln noted in his famous second inaugural address: "The slaves constituted a peculiar and powerful interest. All knew that this interest was somehow the cause of the war."

The goal of this series is to reprint the key articles that have influenced our understanding of slavery. This series includes pioneering articles in the history of slavery, important breakthroughs in research and methodology, and articles that offer major historiographical interpretations. I have attempted to cover all major subtopics of slavery, to offer wide geographic representation and methodological diversity. At the same time, I have resisted the temptation to reprint highly technical articles that will make sense only to specialists in certain fields. For example, I have not included a number of important slavery related articles on economics, law, theology, and literary criticism (to offer just a few examples) because they appeared to be beyond the interest of most generalists.

I have used articles from a wide variety of scholarly journals. I have also used essays and articles in edited volumes, as long as the main focus of those volumes was not slavery, abolition, or black studies. It is my hope that such books are readily available to scholars and students and will show up through card catalogues or on-line catalogue searches. For the same reason I have not reprinted chapters from books about slavery, which are often found in anthologies. With a few exceptions, I have not reprinted articles that later became chapters of books on the same subject. In a few cases I have strayed from this general rule of thumb. I have also generally avoided essay reviews of books, unless the essays go well beyond the common book review or even essay review format. I have also tried to avoid certain famous historiographical controversies that resulted in large numbers of essays being collected and published. With some exceptions, therefore, I have not included the many articles attacking the "Elkins" thesis or Fogel and Engerman's Time on the Cross. Students and scholars interested in these two enormously important scholarly works, and the criticism of them, will find a great deal on both in their card catalogues. Finally, I have also excluded articles from Encyclopedias and dictionaries. These editorial decisions mean that many famous essays and articles will not be found in these volumes. Indeed, a few very important scholars are not represented because all of their work has been in books that are directly on the subject of slavery. Finally, some important articles were left out because we were unable to secure permission from the copyright holders to reprint them in this series.

This project was made easier by the hard work and dedication of Carole Puccino and Leo Balk at Garland Publishing, Inc. A project of this magnitude would not be possible without the help of a number of other scholars, who read lists of proposed articles and discussed the whole problem of slavery with me. I am especially grateful for the help and suggestions of Catherine Clinton, Robert Cottrol, Jill DuPont, Seymour Drescher, Linda Evans, Ronald Formasano, John Hope Franklin, Kermit L. Hall, Robert Hall, Graham Hodges, Michael P. Johnson, Charles Joyner, Alan Kulikoff, Greg Lind, David McBride, Randall Miller, Alfred Moss, James Oakes, Albert J. Raboteau, Judith Schafer, Robert Sikorski, John David Smith, Jean Soderlund, Margaret Washington, William M. Wiecek, Julie Winch, Betty Wood, and Bertram Wyatt-Brown. Two SUNY-Binghamton students, Marci Silverman and Beth Borchers, helped me with much of the bibliographic work on this project. Carol A. Clemente and the inter-library loan staff at SUNY-Binghamton were absolutely wonderful. Without their patience, skills, and resourcefulness, I would have been unable to complete these volumes.

—Paul Finkelman

Contents

Introduction

Antebellum southern masters often referred to slavery as "our peculiar institution." Kenneth Stampp used this phrase for the title of what remains the best one-volume history of antebellum slavery.[1] Slavery itself was not, of course, "peculiar" in the sense that it was unique or unusual. In his important and provocative study of comparative bondage, *Slavery and Social Death*, anthropologist Orlando Patterson demonstrated that

> There is nothing notably peculiar about the institution of slavery. It has existed from before the dawn of human history right down to the twentieth century, in the most primitive of human societies and in the most civilized. There is no region on earth that has not at some time harbored the institution. Probably there is no group of people whose ancestors were not at one time slaves or slaveholders.[2]

From the perspective of Patterson's analysis, a free society is far more "peculiar" than a slave one.

Patterson was both right and wrong in his judgment on the peculiarity of slavery in the United States. Certainly slavery has been found in almost every society throughout history. There is nothing "peculiar" about the enslavement of humans by other humans. Significantly, defenders of slavery, from 1787 until 1865, argued in ways not dissimilar from Patterson, that slavery was a natural and common status for some people and that the greatest societies in the world were based on slave labor.

At the Constitutional Convention South Carolina's Charles Pinckney argued that "If slavery be wrong, it is justified by the example of all the world." He cited the case of Greece, Rome, and other ancient states; the sanction given by France, England, Holland, and other modern states. In all ages one half of mankind have been slaves."[3] More than sixty years later Edmund Ruffin would argue that "Slavery has existed from as early time as historical records furnish any information of the social and political condition of mankind. There was no country, in the most ancient time of its history, of which the people had made any considerable advance in industry or refinement, in which slavery had not been previously and long established, and in general use." In ancient times "there was nothing but the existence of slavery to prevent any race or society in a state of nature from sinking into the rudest barbarism. And no people could ever have been raised from that low condition without the aid and operation of slavery...." Ruffin asserted that slavery had allowed the creation of "admirable works of art in Greece and Rome" and "also the marvelous triumphs of intellect among these successive masters of the then known world."[4]

But, if slavery itself was not "peculiar," there is something quite "peculiar" about slavery in the Americas, and especially in the United States. Unlike slavery in the ancient world, medieval Europe, Africa, or Asia, American slavery was racially based. This was especially true in the southern United States, where, in most states, any visible evidence of African ancestry created a presumption of enslavement. Indeed, David Brion Davis notes that by depending solely on the enslavement to Africans "the Iberians [and by extension the British, French, and Dutch who settled what became the United States] deserve the dubious credit for gradually *restricting* bondage, for the first time in history, to peoples of African descent, and thereby broadening the category of 'nonenslaveable peoples.'"[5] Thus Davis persuasively demonstrates that American slavery was "peculiar," if for no other reason than that it alone, in the history of mankind, was racially based.

Southern commentators on slavery not only recognized this important distinction, but considered it a great virtue of their culture. In 1858 Senator James Henry Hammond of South Carolina argued that every society needed a class of people

> To do the menial duties, to perform the drudgery of life. That is, a class requiring but a low order of intellect and but little skill. . . . It constitutes the very mud-sill of society and of political government; and you might as well attempt to build a house in the air, as to build

either the one or the other, except on this mud-sill.

Hammond argued that the South was uniquely blessed because it had such a class of Afro-American slaves.

Fortunately for the South, she found a race adapted to that purpose to her hand. A race inferior to her own, but eminently qualified in temper, in vigor, in docility, in capacity to stand the climate, to answer her purposes.[6]

Hammond went on to claim that racially based slavery made democracy in the South possible, because it removed the lowest class of society from the political process. "Our slaves do not vote. We give them no political power." In contrast, Hammond argued that northern society was essentially unstable because white workers were forced to take the jobs that slaves did in the South. Yet, he taunted his northern counterparts in the Senate: "Yours are white, of your own race; you are brothers of one blood. They are your equals in natural endowment of intellect, and they feel galled by their degradation." More importantly, they were allowed to vote, and that meant they might someday take over the society, overthrowing the educated and the elite. Hammond argued that in the South this could never happen, because all whites were equal, and that thus all whites had an interest in maintaining the status quo.[7]

Modern historians have tended to agree with some of Hammond's analysis. Edmund Morgan, in *American Slavery, American Freedom*, has argued that republican government developed in Virginia because planters were willing to give political power to poor whites in order to keep blacks enslaved.

Slavery in the United States was different from slavery in the rest of the New World in a variety of other ways. It was the only slave system that perpetuated itself through natural increase of slaves. Indeed, the birth rate of slaves in the United States was only slightly below that of southern whites. The United States also was the only democratic republic to maintain a slave system in the New World. It was also the only revolutionary nation to do so. In Latin America the colonial rebellions led to emancipation. In the

United States the revolt against colonialism led to a proslavery Constitution. Unlike other New World slave societies, in the United States slavery became not only concentrated, but legal, in a specific geographic region. This may have had profound implications for emancipation. Unlike much of the New World, slaves and blacks were a distinct minority in the United States. Similarly, unlike most of Latin America and the Caribbean, no independent free black society emerged in the United States to serve as a buffer between slaves and masters. With the exception of Haiti, only the United States required massive bloodshed—a great civil war—to end slavery. Only in the United States did the slave owners ultimately rebel against a central government to keep their slaves. The American Civil War—a revolt of masters—may be the most peculiar aspect of slavery in the United States.

There are other aspects of the peculiar nature of slavery in the United States that remain disputed questions. Was the United States the only "capitalistic" slave society in the New World, or indeed, in human history? How did English common law affect slavery in the United States? Did the Protestant heritage of the United States create a peculiar and unique slave society? Was American slavery crueler or less cruel than its Latin-American and Caribbean counterparts; how did it compare with slave systems in other places and times?

Questions like these, and answers to them, come from comparative approaches to slavery. Comparative history is always difficult. It requires, from the scholar, an expertise in two or more areas of history. It requires a careful approach to subtle differences between cultures. Comparative historians must constantly be aware that they may compare the wrong things, or different things.

The articles in the volume all compare some aspect of slavery in the United States to some other slaveholding culture. Excluded from this volume is the extremely valuable literature that focuses mostly or entirely on slavery in another culture.

—Paul Finkelman

Notes

1. Kenneth M. Stampp, *The Peculiar Institution: Slavery in the Antebellum South* (New York: A.A. Knopf, 1956).

2. Orlando Patterson, *Slavery and Social Death: A Comparative Study* (Cambridge: Harvard University Press, 1982) vii.

3. Max Farrand, *Records of the Federal Convention of 1787*, 4 Vols. (New Haven: Yale University Press, 1966) 2:371.

4. Edmund Ruffin, *The Political Economy of Slavery* (1853) reprinted in Eric McKitrick, *Slavery Defended: The Views of the Old South* (Englewood Cliffs, N.J.: Prentice-Hall, 1963), 69–70, 75–76.

5. David Brion Davis, *Slavery and Human Progress* (New York: Oxford University Press, 1984) 30.

6. James Henry Hammond, "'Mudd-Sill' Speech," March 4, 1858, reprinted in McKitrick, *Slavery Defended*, 122–23.

7. *Ibid.*, 123.

Further Reading*

Berlin, Ira, and Ronald Hoffman, eds.	*Slavery and Freedom in the Age of Revolution* (Charlottesville: University of Virginia Press, 1983).
Bowman, Shearer Davis.	"Antebellum Planters and Vormatz Junkers in Comparative Perspective," *American Historical Review* 85 (1980) 779–808.
Davis, David Brion.	*The Problem of Slavery in the Age of Revolution* (Ithaca: Cornell University Press, 1975).
Davis, David Brion.	*The Problem of Slavery in Western Culture* (Ithaca: Cornell University Press, 1966).
Davis, David Brion.	*Slavery and Human Progress* (New York: Oxford University Press, 1984).
Deglar, Carl.	*Neither Black Nor White: Slavery and Race Relations in Brazil and the United States* (New York: Macmillan Co., 1971).
Dormar, Evsey D.	"The Causes of Slavery or Serfdom: A Hypothesis," *Journal of Economic History* 30 (1970) 18–32.
Elkins, Stanley.	*Slavery: A Problem in American Institutional and Intellectual Life*, 3rd ed. (Chicago: University of Chicago Press, 1976).
Engerman, Stanley.	"Economic Adjustments to Emancipation in the U.S. and the British West Indies," *Journal of Interdisciplinary History* 13 (1982) 191–220.
Finley, M.I.	*Ancient Slavery and Modern Ideology* (New York: Viking Press, 1980).

---

* Publisher's Note: We were unable to obtain permission from the copyright holders to reprint some of the articles on this list.

Foner, Laura, and Eugene D. Genovese. *Slavery in the New World: A Reader in Comparative History* (Englewood Cliffs, N.J.: Prentice-Hall, 1969).

Fox-Genovese, Elizabeth, and Eugene D. Genovese. *Fruits of Merchant Capital: Slavery and Bourgeois Property in the Rise and Expansion of Capitalism* (New York: Oxford University Press, 1983).

Frederickson, George M. *White Supremacy: A Comparative Study in American and South African History* (New York: Oxford University Press, 1981).

Genovese, Eugene D. *From Rebellion to Revolution: Afro-American Slave Revolts in the Making of the Modern World* (Baton Rouge: Louisiana State University Press, 1979).

Herskovits, Melville. *The Myth of the Negro Past* (New York: Harper and Row, 1941).

Hoetink, H. *Slavery and Race Relations in the Americas: An Inquiry into Their Nature and Nexus* (New York: Harper and Row, 1973).

Horwitz, Donald. "Color Differentiation in the American Systems of Slavery," *Journal of Interdisciplinary History* 3 (1973) 509–41.

Kolchin, Peter. *Unfree Labor: American Slavery and Russian Serfdom* (Cambridge: Harvard University Press, 1987).

Klein, Herbert. *Slavery in the Americas: A Comparative Study of Virginia and Cuba* (Chicago: Quadrangle Books, 1971).

Mintz, Sidney W., ed. *Slavery, Colonialism, and Racism* (New York: W.W. Norton and Co., 1974).

Patterson, Orlando. *Slavery and Social Death* (Cambridge: Harvard University Press, 1982).

Rice, C. Duncan. *The Rise and Fall of Black Slavery* (New York: Harper and Row, 1976).

Tannenbaum, Frank.   *Slave and Citizen* (New York: Alfred A. Knopf, 1946).

Williams, Mary.   "The Treatment of Negro Slaves in the Brazilian Empire: A Comparison with the United States of America," *Journal of Negro History* 15 (1930) 315–36.

Wright, Gavin.   "Capitalism and Slavery on the Islands: A Lesson from the Mainland," *Journal of Interdisciplinary History* 17 (1987) 851–70.

Comparative
Issues
in Slavery

Labor Forces and Race Relations:
A Comparative View of the
Colonization of Brazil and Virginia

RICHARD R. BEEMAN

University of Pennsylvania

The adaptation of Portuguese and English political and religious institutions to new environments, the paths of land settlement, the rates of migration, and countless other social, political, geographic, and demographic differences helped contribute to the distinctive development of each of the New World colonies in Brazil and Virginia. But the initial stages of the English and Portuguese experiences, though separated in time by nearly three-quarters of a century, paralleled one another in one important, negative respect: although both Brazil and Virginia would ultimately yield handsome profits, neither colony during the first century of existence was capable of producing the instant wealth of a Cuzco or Tenochtitlán.[1] Moreover, the ways in which the Portuguese and the English initially went about making a profit from their western colonies—lands that did not immediately yield either the material or the human resources that they had anticipated—were, at least in the first two decades of those colonies' existence, strikingly similar. Both nations first entrusted the job of colonization to a relatively small band of private adventurers, and in both cases those individuals proved unable to

[1] I am concerned here primarily with the first century of colonization in Brazil and Virginia and, therefore, given the patterns of English and Portuguese settlement, will focus on Portuguese efforts in the northeast of Brazil and on English colonization on the eastern coastal plain of Virginia.

1

recruit a labor force capable of turning their respective colonies into profitable enterprises. At this juncture—which coincided roughly in both colonies with the time in which private enterprise was replaced by royal control—the economic policies pursued in Brazil and Virginia began to diverge. The Portuguese were to make a series of decisions with regard to the economic organization of their colony, and in particular with regard to the recruitment of a labor force to carry out that organization, that would drastically change the character of their western colony. The English, although faced with much the same conditions the Portuguese had faced three-quarters of a century before, were, for a variety of reasons, unable to follow the Portuguese example in solving their own labor problem in Virginia. Those decisions on the recruitment of a labor force and, even more important, the timing of those decisions would ultimately help shape the differing characters of the cultures of Brazil and Virginia.[2]

The Portuguese and English Models for Colonization

The composition, motives, and expectations of the English and Portuguese colonists in America were far removed from the realities of the New World. That they were so unrealistic was almost wholly due to the lack of any comparable examples of colonization. Both Portugal and England drew on the two most familiar examples, but neither was adequate to the task of building permanent and profitable colonies in the initially hostile environment of Brazil and Virginia. The first—the launching of an overseas commercial enterprise—was based on Portugal's fantastically successful trading ventures in West Africa and India and on England's increasing interest in similar markets in India and eastern Europe. The second—a military expedition designed to exploit the existing physical and human resources of the New World as

[2] Sigmund Diamond, "From Organization to Society: Virginia in the Seventeenth Century," *American Journal of Sociology*, LXIII (1958), 457-75 and Diamond, "An Experiment in Feudalism: French Canada in the Seventeenth Century," *William and Mary Quarterly*, XVIII (1961), 1-34, has stressed the critical importance of labor supply and labor discipline in the early development of both Virginia and French Canada. This focus on economic organization can, I think, prove helpful in explaining the initial stages of social and political development, as well as economic development, in all of the North and South American colonies.

2

swiftly as possible—was drawn from the astounding tales of Spain's success in the New World, tales of gold and silver and of passive natives willingly giving their labor to their European conquerors.[3] The important thing about both of these earlier ventures is that neither of them anticipated the need for a European labor force. The Europeans foresaw the need for military boldness and entrepreneurial skill, but it would be many decades before they would become reconciled to the fact that the environments of both Brazil and Virginia were not suited to a purely extractive enterprise, but rather necessitated hard, sustained labor on the part of the European colonists themselves.[4]

[3] A number of historians have suggested other possible models. Edmund S. Morgan, in an article which has helped to stimulate much of my thinking on this subject, "The Labor Problem at Jamestown, 1607-18," *American Historical Review*, LXXVI (1971), 595-611, has suggested that, in addition to the mounting of a military expedition, many Englishmen thought they were traveling to settle wastelands or to build a society resembling England. Charles M. Andrews, *The Colonial Period of American History* (New Haven, 1934), I, 53-77, describes the English enterprise as one composed of a land-hungry lower class anxious to found a colony of permanent settlement and a courageous and innovative "merchant-capitalist" class that provided the actual leadership for the venture. I would not deny that these motives were present in the minds of some, but, in my judgment, the commercial and military motives were paramount. David B. Quinn, *The Elizabethans and the Irish* (Ithaca, 1966), 106-22, argues that the English plan for the occupation of Ireland, a plan that envisioned the elimination of the Irish aristocracy and the exploitation of the Irish laboring classes, served as an important model for some of the organizers of the Virginia enterprise. Mr. Quinn's argument is a persuasive one and perhaps deserves more attention than I have given it. The Irish example does not, however, conflict with those that I have suggested. The English plan for the subjugation of Ireland, like the Virginia plan, was drawn in large part from the experience of the Spanish in Mexico and Peru. Another plausible reason for the English effort in the New World—the longstanding desire to find a passage to the Pacific—has also been given too little attention in these pages. There is no question that some prominent members of the Virginia Company, such as Sir Thomas Smith, were deeply involved in the search for a western passage. In this effort, too, commercial and military techniques were of overriding importance.

[4] In particular, the resources that Europeans were most interested in—gold, silver, copper, and precious stones—were sadly lacking. The Indians of Virginia wore some copper jewelry, but most of the copper had been obtained from other Indian cultures far to the northwest. Similarly, the Indians of Brazil possessed a few gold and silver trinkets, but these would serve only to give the Portuguese settlers a false impression of the land. Not until two centuries after the discovery of Brazil would the Portuguese finally locate any important sources of gold, and those mines were 250 miles to the west of the original settlements, in the province of Minas Gerais. Nancy Oestreich Lurie,

3

Portugal had been the first European nation to embark on voyages of exploration into unknown lands and waters. Beginning in 1418, when Prince Henry the Navigator organized a voyage to Porto Santo, the Portuguese had undertaken an impressive series of explorations down the west coast of Africa. By 1487, they were headed up the east coast of Africa, and finally, in 1497, Vasco da Gama succeeded in establishing the long sought-after sea route to India.[5] Portugal used these discoveries to her commercial advantage almost immediately. By 1449, she had set up trading posts along the west coast of Africa and was trading corn, cloth, and horses for African slaves and gold. In 1505, Francesco de Almeida was granted viceregal authority over the new found lands of India. He immediately entered into diplomatic alliances aimed at securing for Portugal a monopoly over the valuable Indian spice trade. By the second decade of the sixteenth century, Alfonso de Albuquerque, with the help of Portuguese naval power, was turning Almeida's diplomatic successes into concrete, commercial gains. At the time of Albuquerque's death in 1515, the Portuguese had secured the valuable ports of Goa, Calicut, Malacca, and Ormuz and had earned lucrative commercial concessions from the rulers of western India, Ceylon, Bengal, Burma, and Siam. By their initiative in overseas expansion and by their willingness to use military power to impose their wishes on recalcitrants, the Portuguese earned profits estimated at one million cruzados per year from the Indian spice trade, with some ships realizing profits of roughly one hundred times the total cost of the voyage from Portugal to India.[6]

The East was so profitable in fact that the Portuguese were not at first particularly anxious to found colonial settlements in the West. When Pedro Alvares Cabral stumbled across the land of

---

"Indian Cultural Adjustment to European Civilization," in James M. Smith, ed., *Seventeenth Century America: Essays in Colonial History* (Chapel Hill, 1959), 4-46; Charles C. Willoughby, "The Virginia Indians in the Seventeenth Century," *American Anthropologist*, IX (1907), 70-73; Charles R. Boxer, *The Golden Age of Brazil, 1695-1750: Growing Pains of a Colonial Society* (Berkeley, 1962), 30-60; and João Antonil, *Cultura e Opulencia do Brasil* (Lisbon, 1711; São Paulo, 1923), 205-61.

[5] A land route to India had been discovered by the Portuguese as early as 1488. H. V. Livermore, *A History of Portugal* (Cambridge, 1947), 188-92, 220-21, 229-32.

[6] *Ibid.*, 232-38.

Brazil in 1500, Portugal was just beginning to reap the enormous rewards of the trade with India; the land and the people that Cabral had discovered did not seem promising enough to divert Portuguese investment.[7]

Pedro Vaz Caminha, chronicler of Cabral's voyage to India via Brazil, issued a guarded prediction that pearls might be found in Brazil, but this was probably based more on his recently acquired knowledge that Christopher Columbus had found pearls during his third voyage than it was on any concrete evidence of the existence of such precious stones in Brazil. Cabral's crew did discover some small Indian villages and some apparently friendly natives. At least they appeared friendly. Unfortunately, on the seventh day of Cabral's stay in Brazil, a group of Indians, their faces beaming with friendly smiles, proceeded to beat on the head with clubs, and then eat, a member of Cabral's advance scouting party. The whole scene occurred in full view of the ship's crew.[8] This would prove to be only the first of many dispiriting encounters between the Portuguese and the aboriginal inhabitants of Brazil. Although not all of the Indians of Brazil proved consistently hostile to the Portuguese settlers, their behavior toward outsiders was erratic enough to make them less than ideal partners in the building of a new colony.[9]

[7] There has been considerable debate among historians as to whether Cabral discovered Brazil by accident or whether he was consciously planning to stake out a Portuguese claim in the New World. For a review of the historiographical problem and a careful statement of the facts pointing to the conclusion that Cabral's landing was accidental, see W. B. Greenlee, ed., *The Voyage of Pedro Alvares Cabral to Brazil and India* (London, 1937), xlvi-lxvii.

[8] Letter of Pedro Vaz de Caminha to King Manuel, May 1, 1500, *ibid.*, 9; Robert Southey, *History of Brazil* (London, 1810), I, 15.

[9] The most numerous and powerful Indian culture of northeastern Brazil, the Tupí-Guaraní, was an extremely loose confederation of separate tribal units bound together only by a common linguistic stock. Considerable data have been gathered on the Tupí-Guaraní communities, but the most important fact for this study is that the members of nearly every Tupí-Guaraní village literally detested the members of every other Tupí-Guaraní village, with each village carrying out interminable warfare against the others. This intense hostility among the Indian tribes was the product both of a struggle for political supremacy and of the desire for captives with which to satisfy their ritualistic needs for human sacrifices. Robert H. Lowie, "The Tropical Forest Tribes," in Julian Steward, ed., *Handbook of South American Indians* (Washington, D. C., 1948), III, 1-47; and Alfred Metraux, "The Tupinamba," in Steward, III, 97-116.

5

Cabral discovered the brazilwood tree—the source of an important dyestuff for the European textile industry—during his brief stay in the land he called Terra do Vera Cruz, but the reddish dye obtained from the brazilwood could hardly justify a major investment in the hostile environment of the New World when the silks and spices of India yielded superior returns.[10] When Cabral sailed from Brazil he left behind two convicts. The two unfortunates immediately "began to weep, and the men of the land comforted them and showed that they pitied them."[11] A few decades later when the Portuguese sovereign compared the magnificence of New Spain and Peru with the unpromising character of his possession in the New World, there would be still more cause for weeping.

The Portuguese crown, because it was interested in exploitation and not in colonization, waited over three decades, until 1533, before drawing up a plan of settlement for Brazil. This 33-year hiatus is roughly comparable to the period separating England's initial experiment with colonization in 1584 from the permanent settlement of Jamestown in 1607, although Portugal was slightly more active in the interim in Brazil than were the English in North America.

The Portuguese, through necessity, took some rather rudimentary steps to profit from the brazilwood tree and to safeguard their discovery from foreign interlopers. In 1502, the crown awarded a contract to Fernão do Loronha, a converted Jew from Lisbon, to trade in brazilwood. In 1516, Christavão Jacques was appointed captain of the royal coast guard in an attempt to put an end to French incursions into the territory. By 1533, the Portuguese had established at least two trading stations along the northeastern coast, and it had been proven that the brazilwood trade was at least marginally profitable.[12] Nevertheless, the Por-

[10] The brazilwood tree, although no substitute for gold and other precious metals, was sufficiently valuable that the Portuguese named their new western colony after it. Other than that one commodity, however, Portugal's new colony in America seemed distinctly unpromising. The Indian economy of northeastern Brazil was confined to the cultivation of manioc, a coarse grain, and to hunting and gathering. Alexander Marchant, *From Barter to Slavery: The Economic Relations of Portuguese and Indians in the Settlement of Brazil, 1500-1580* (Baltimore, 1942), 28-33.

[11] "Anonymous Narrative," in Greenlee, ed., *Cabral's Voyage*, 60.

[12] Marchant, *Barter to Slavery*, 28-47.

6

guese colony, if indeed it deserved to be called a colony, was not a thriving enterprise. Over three decades after its discovery, Brazil was only sparsely inhabited by Europeans, and Portuguese control of the territory existed only in the legalistic phrases of the Treaty of Tordesillas. The Portuguese, at least partially because of their preoccupation with the riches of the East, were unwilling to supply the men or material necessary to eject French intruders from the area, and, as a result, no one could claim to have practical control over the territory of Brazil.

By 1530, Portugal began for the first time to think of establishing permanent settlements in Brazil. This was not a sign that she had given up the hope of a colony of commercial and military exploitation, but merely an indication that external pressures had forced the crown to look for new areas to exploit. First, the India trade was languishing; by 1530, the price of spices had dropped precipitously, a result of oversupply. The court at Lisbon, which had lived extravagantly on the revenues from the spice trade, discovered that the people of the world were disposed to consume only so much pepper. Second, both France and Spain were threatening to shut out the Portuguese from the New World. Spain, after her spectacular success in Mexico, was beginning to expand in every direction in the western hemisphere, and the French, in 1530, had succeeded in destroying one of Portugal's largest brazilwood trading posts in Pernambuco.[13]

Finally, when Cabral first happened on Brazilian shores in 1500, Spanish accomplishments in the New World were limited to three relatively unprofitable voyages by Christopher Columbus, a few exploratory voyages near the coast of Venezuela, and a relatively unstable colony on the island of Santo Domingo. By 1530, when Portugal began her plans for the permanent settlement of Brazil, reports of Cortes's success in Tenochtitlán had spread to Portugal. In 1533, the year the Portuguese actually began to colonize Brazil, Francisco Pizarro was extracting entire rooms filled with gold and silver from the captive Inca Prince Atahualpa. It was a cruel irony; Portugal had pioneered in the

[13] W. B. Greenlee, "The First Half Century of Brazilian History," Mid-America, XXV (1943), 91-120, gives a much more optimistic view of the Portuguese accomplishments in Brazil during this period, but he admits that, by 1530, there was an increasing need to strengthen Portuguese control over the area.

7

arts of navigation and exploration and had even employed Columbus at one time. Now she had to stand by and watch Spain reap the rewards. But there was still hope. Spain had invested more time and money in her western ventures than had Portugal and had not achieved substantial returns until she had penetrated into the interior. Although there was little in the Brazilian landscape that recommended it as a source of easy wealth, the Portuguese were not ready to abandon the notion that either the land or the people would eventually yield at least some of the same riches as New Spain and Peru.

The English were, if anything, even more hungry than the Portuguese for commercial and military gain in the New World, for they had entered the game of overseas expansion late. By 1555, however, they had begun to make minor inroads into markets that had long been dominated by the Venetians, Spanish, and Portuguese. Both the Muscovy Company (1555) and the Levant Company (1579) represented efforts by groups of private individuals with royal approval and occasional royal backing to challege other nations for supremacy in the eastern overseas markets.[14] But prior to the seventeenth century, the English had no overseas colonies; nor had they succeeded in gaining a strong foothold in any of the major foreign markets. Despite the "progressive," "capitalistic" spirit of the English trading companies, English overseas enterprise in the sixteenth century was a failure.[15]

And the English publicists knew it. Beginning in 1553, when Richard Eden became England's first defender of "imperialism," and culminating in the promotional tracts of the Virginia Company of London, English propagandists incessantly urged their countrymen to launch an imperialistic and exploitative enterprise before the Spanish were able to shut them off completely from the lucre to be found in the New World.[16] Most of the propagandists

[14] Andrews, I, 31-37.

[15] Charles Lucas, *The Beginnings of English Overseas Enterprise* (Oxford, 1917), 143-55 and Andrews, I, 43, claim that the joint stock company "laid the foundations of England's naval, maritime and commercial greatness," while at the same time paving the way for English democracy. Their assertion hardly seems tenable in light of the time lag of at least a century between the establishment of the joint stock companies and the bare beginnings of English success.

[16] An excellent introduction to the propaganda literature of English ex-

would have preferred, if possible, to obtain this wealth through peaceful commerce, but like the Portuguese in India and the Spanish in the New World, they were willing to use military means if necessary.

Richard Eden in his translation of Sebastian Munster's *Cosmographia* pleaded with his countrymen to take advantage of the economic and commercial possibilities of colonization and berated those who shied away from overseas expansion out of fear of the Spanish.[17] In his translation of Peter Martyr's *Decades of the Newe World* (1555), Eden became even more vocal in his advocacy of English imperialism. Although it was fashionable in England to criticize Spain for her excesses in the New World, Eden bluntly told his English readers to spend less time denouncing Spain and more time following her example. Spain, after all, was the acknowledged leader in overseas expansion; it was necessary to "stoope England stoope, and learne to knowe thy lorde and master, as horses and other brute beasts are taught to doo."[18]

Thomas Nicholas, in his translation and popularization of a section of Lopez de Gómara's biography of Hernan Cortes (1578), went even further than Eden in opening his reader's eyes to the undiscovered riches of the New World. Although Gómara's book was in effect a history of the Spanish conquest of Mexico, Nicholas in his "Epistle Dedicatory" offered it as a practical guidebook to the successful colonization of North America:

> Here shall they see the wisdome, curtesie, valour, and pollicie of worthy Captynes, yea, and the faithful hartes whiche they ought to beare unto their Princes services; here also is described how to use and correct the stubborn & mutinous persons, & in what order to exalt the good, stoute & vertuous souldiers, and chiefly, how to preserve and keepe that bewtifull Dame Lady Victorie when she is obtayned.[19]

---

pansion, and one which I have profited from enormously, is John Parker, *Books to Build an Empire: A Bibliographical History of English Overseas Interests to 1620* (Amsterdam, 1965).

[17] Richard Eden, *A Treatyse of the Newe India* . . . , in Edward Arber, ed., *The First Three English Books on America* (Westminster, 1895), 7-11.

[18] Richard Eden, *The Decades of the Newe World* . . . , in Arber, 49-60, esp. 52.

[19] Lopez de Gómara, *The Conquest of the Weast India*, trans. T. Nicholas (London, 1578; New York, 1940), aii.

9

For Nicholas, "Dame Lady Victorie" meant gold, and he was quick to assure his readers that the English, if they persevered, would find just as much gold as the Spanish. In support of this contention, he announced:

> where it was supposed that the golden metall had his beginning in the East and Weast India, neare unto the hot zoane, it is nowe approued by the venterous travellour and worthy captayne Martin Frobisher Esquire . . . that the same golden metall dothe also lie incorporate in the bowelles of the Northeaste parties.

Thus, with hopes raised by the early and erroneous reports of the Frobisher voyage, Nicholas was able to promise the English rich rewards if only they would invest in an overseas colonizing venture.[20]

These rhapsodic descriptions of the promise of the New World continued even after the English had made sustained contact with North America. Arthur Barlowe's description of the North Carolina coast, made during Sir Walter Raleigh's first voyage and later published in Richard Hakluyt's *The Principall Navigations, Voiages and Discoveries of the English Nation* is one of uncritical praise. Barlowe found the people to be "the most gentle, loving, and faithfull, void of all guile and treason, and such as lived after the manner of the golden age." The Indian women fed the English, entertained them, and even washed their feet. The men would trade fifty animal skins, worth at least fifty crowns, for one copper kettle. And, furthermore, these submissive natives lived on a land which "bringeth forth all things in abundance, as in the first creation, without toil or labor."[21]

The vision of North America as a land of wealth and effortless exploitation reached its most popular and extreme form in 1605 when George Chapman, Ben Jonson, and John Marston wrote the English comedy, *Eastward Ho!* The scene is an English tavern, the participants are perhaps a trifle loose tongued because of the wine, but their description of Virginia, even when one makes allowances for exaggeration, is revealing:

> Seagull: A whole countrie of English is there, man, bred of those that were left there in '79; they have married with the Indians, and

[20] *Ibid.*

[21] Richard Hakluyt, *The Principall Navigations, Voiages and Discoveries of the English Nation* (London, 1589), 729-33.

make 'hem bring forth as beautiful faces as we have in England; and therefore the Indians are so in love with 'hem that all the treasure they have they lay at their feete.

Scapethrift: But is there such treasure there, Captain, as I have heard?

Seagull: I tell thee, golde is more plentiful there than copper is with us. . . . Why, man, all their dripping pans and their chamberpots are pure golde; and all the chaines with which they chaine up their streets are massie golde; all the prisoners they take are fettered in golde; and for rubies and diamonds they goe forthe on holy dayes and gather 'hem by the sea shore to hang on their childrens coats. . . .[22]

Doubtless no one in the audience took at face value the description given by Seagull, but that the authors would bother even to use the dialogue is evidence that similar stories, although perhaps slightly less spectacular, were already in circulation.[23]

Even Thomas Hariot and the two Richard Hakluyts, who are generally described as having been more interested in permanent, peaceful settlement than in plunder, could not free themselves from the notion that instant wealth would be waiting for the English settlers in the New World.[24] Richard Hakluyt the Elder placed primary emphasis on the commercial-imperialist motive for colonization. After two short, perfunctory sentences indicating that he favored the spread of the Christian gospel to North America, Hakluyt spent the greater part of his essay demonstrat-

[22] Ben Jonson, George Chapman, and John Marston, *Eastward Ho!* (London, 1605; Boston, 1905), 71-72.

[23] Wesley F. Craven, *The Southern Colonies in the Seventeenth Century, 1607-1689* (Baton Rouge, 1949), 70n., maintains that the play, because it treats the wealth of Virginia in such an exaggerated manner, is actually indicative of the prevailing skepticism in England regarding the riches of the New World. Skepticism there was, but that the scene was presented at all is evidence that some people in England, however misguidedly, believed that America was a land of enormous wealth.

[24] Parker, 104-05, 109, 112; E. G. R. Taylor, *The Original Writings and Correspondence of the Two Richard Hakluyts* (London, 1935), I, 1-66, stresses the fact that the Hakluyts spent considerably more time than their contemporaries in planning for a permanent, productive European settlement in the New World. The Hakluyts also had doubts about the wisdom of relying too heavily upon Indian labor and, in fact, recommended sending a sizeable English labor force to the New World. They shared the optimism of their contemporaries, however, as to the ease with which the existing wealth of the Indians could be exploited.

11

ing the "possibility of the enlarging of the dominions of the Queen's Most Excellent Majesty, and consequently of her honour, revenues, and of her power by this enterprise." New colonies would provide markets for English woolens, "especially those of the coarsest sorts." In exchange for these reject woolen articles, England could purchase oil, wines, hops, and "most or all the commodities that we receive from the best parts of Europe." In the process of doing this, Hakluyt claimed, the English nation could also finally break the Spanish domination of the western overseas trade.[25]

The area eventually chosen by the English for their initial settlement, the James River basin, was populated by roughly 2500 members of the Powhatan Confederacy. Like the Indians of Brazil, they lived in many small, distinct, loosely supervised villages, an extremely inefficient mode of social and political organization from the standpoint of those who wished to exploit Indian wealth and labor for their own purposes.[26] While the residents of the various villages were not always hostile and warlike, their attitudes toward the English would prove to be sufficiently unfriendly to make them undependable partners in any commercial venture. And most important, the subsistence economy of the Indians of Virginia would hardly send the stock of English woolen mills soaring, nor was it capable of providing the English with the goods which they were at present purchasing in Europe. But this, after all, was not important. The dream of commercial empire, particularly the hope of making a dent in the overseas empire of the much hated and much envied Spain, was enough to make even a normally sensible man like Richard Hakluyt the Elder forget the harsh realities of the Virginia wilderness.

Even after observing at first hand the primitive state of the Indians on Roanoke Island, Thomas Hariot was able to maintain

[25] Richard Hakluyt the Elder, *Inducements to the Liking of the Voyage Towards Virginia* . . . (1585), in Taylor, II, 327-38.

[26] The total population of the Powhatan Confederacy, which spread throughout the Tidewater and Eastern Shore area, was approximately 8500. James Mooney, "The Powhatan Confederacy, Past and Present," *American Anthropologist*, IX (1907), 129-30, obtains these figures by evaluating the estimates of John Smith in Edward Arber, ed., *Travels and Works of Captain John Smith* (2d ed.; Edinburgh, 1910), I, 347-51; and William Strachey, *Historie of Travell into Virginia Britania* (London, 1612; London, 1953), 56-62.

and, indeed, bolster his optimism about America. Because the natives suffered from a "want of skill and judgment in the knowledge and use of our things," it seemed all the more "probable that they should desire our friendships and love and have the greater respect for pleasing and obeying us."[27] Richard Hakluyt, the cousin of Richard Hakluyt the Elder, even formulated contingency plans in case the natives did not turn out to be as friendly as those described by Hariot. Hakluyt suggested that the English locate their settlement at the mouth of a navigable river in order that the settlers could play off one Indian tribe against the other. They could turn to tribes located inland to defend themselves against hostile Indians on the coast, or should the inland tribes be hostile, they could ally themselves with the coastal tribes. Moreover, the Indians might even be used as allies against a more dangerous enemy, the Spanish, who had "exercised moste outrageous and more than Turkish cruelties in all the Weste Indies." The Spanish were so detested by the Indians that the English could almost surely expect Indian aid in throwing off their "most intollerable yoke."[28] Thus, if the English settlers used care in taking advantage of the existing rivalries among Indian nations and between the Indians and the Spanish and if they exploited their natural advantages over the Indians, then the natives could be made to serve the English in their quest for riches in the New World.

What we find then in the English propaganda tracts is a description of a land bountiful in exotic and valuable native produce, a land blessed with a usually docile and dependable native labor supply, and a land where precious metals might perhaps be found. Given this image of America, it is not surprising that there was much talk in seventeenth-century England of limiting Spanish expansion in the New World, of gold and precious metals, of establishing a lucrative trade with the Indians, and of persuading the Indians to do the labor necessary to build a colony for the English. Nor is it surprising that little attention was paid to the

[27] Thomas Hariot, *A Brief and True Report of the New-found Land of Virginia* (London, 1588), in David B. Quinn, *The Roanoke Voyages, 1584-1590* (London, 1955), I, 371-72.

[28] Richard Hakluyt, *Discourse on Western Planting*, in Taylor, II, 246-49, 257-65.

13

planning of an economy which might support a permanent English settlement primarily dependent upon its own labor.[29]

England's initial attitude toward colonization was thus not markedly different from that of Portugal. Each nation, because of its commercial experience in the East and because of the Spanish example in the West, geared its colonial policy toward rapid exploitation of existing wealth rather than the slower and more difficult task of planting new sources of wealth. Some envisioned simple commercial exploitation on the model of Portugal's success in India, but others had an even grander vision, a vision of gold mines and free Indian labor. Almost no one in either Portugal or England envisioned the kind of settlement that was most necessary for survival in the New World—a settlement where hard, sustained work by the European colonizers would be vital for existence.

The First Stages of Portuguese and English Colonization

The royal governments of both Portugal and England were at first content to let others bear the risks of colonization. In Brazil, the Portuguese crown, lacking the funds to launch a highly centralized, state-sponsored colonizing effort, parceled out grants of land to twelve private citizens.[30] These individuals, called *donatarios*, tended to be either military officers or members of the lesser nobility. Many of them had seen military service in India and Africa and thus were well acquainted with the ways in

[29] For additional evidence see Sir George Peckham, *A True Reporte of the Late Discoueries of the New-found Landes* (London, 1583); Augustin de Zarate, *The Discouerie and Conquest of the Provinces of Peru*, trans. T. Nicholas (London, 1581); Ralph Lane to Richard Hakluyt, 1585, in Taylor, II, 346-47; Henry Roberts, *A Most Friendly Farewell . . . to the Right Worshipfull Sir Francis Drake* (London, 1585); and Thomas Greepe, *The True and Perfecte Newes of the Woorthy and Valiaunt Exploytes, Performed and doone by . . . Syr Francis Drake* (London, 1587).

[30] The best accounts of this initial period of settlement in Brazil are Marchant, *Barter to Slavery*, 48-80; Pedro de Azevedo, "Os Primeiros Donatarios," in Carlos Malheiro Dias, ed., *Historia de Colonização Portuguesa do Brasil* (Oporto, 1923), III, 189-216; Roberto Simonsen, *Historia Economica do Brasil, 1500-1820* (Rio de Janeiro, 1937), I, 117-42; and Francisco Adolpho de Varnhagen, *Historia Geral do Brasil Antes da Sua Separação e Independencia de Portugal* (3d ed.; São Paulo, 1927), I, 180-290.

which foreign lands and peoples could be exploited.[31] Unfortunately, most of them knew nothing about the requirements of building a permanent colony based on European labor.

Although there has been much debate over whether these grants were "feudal" or "capitalistic," two of the most knowledgeable students of this period of Brazilian history, Roberto Simonsen and Alexander Marchant, have concluded that while the *donatarios* possessed political and military power which appears to be feudal in origin, the actual exercise of those powers coupled with the plainly economic motive behind the granting of them made the *donatario* system roughly similar in purpose to joint stock enterprises such as the Virginia Company. Marchant argues that feudalism implies a contract between the king and his subjects in which the king grants land in exchange for military services, while Simonsen further notes that feudalism entails a system of fixed social classes.[32] Neither of these conditions was present in Brazil. The *donatarios* themselves came from different classes and the settlers living on the *donatario* grants had ample opportunity to move up and down the social scale as their economic progress dictated. Most important, the principal duty of the *donatario* to the king and of the settlers to each individual *donatario* was to exploit the land for economic gain rather than to perform military services. To be sure, the *donatario* was to provide for the defense of his land, but only as a means of fulfilling his primary economic tasks. This is distinctly nonfeudal.[33]

The *donatarios* were granted considerable authority. They were empowered to found towns, appoint all municipal officials, levy taxes on the settlers, and even to mete out capital punishment in the case of certain stipulated crimes.[34] But the powers granted to the leaders of the Virginia Company over the settlers at Jamestown were hardly inferior. By the Charter of 1606, an appointed resident council of thirteen members was to serve as

[31] Varnhagen, I, 168-74 gives a capsule biography of each of the *donatarios*.
[32] Alexander Marchant, "Feudal and Capitalistic Elements in the Portuguese Settlement of Brazil," *Hispanic American Historical Review*, XXII (1942), 493-512; and Simonsen, I, 124-27.
[33] Marchant, "Feudal and Capitalistic Elements," 500-01. For an opposing view, see Carlos Malheiro Dias, "O Regimen Feudal das Donatarias," in Dias, ed., *Historia de Colonização*, III, 219-83.
[34] Marchant, *Barter to Slavery*, 58-60.

15

the sole governing board of the Virginia settlement. Ultimate political control over the colony was left in the hands of the king, just as it was in Brazil, but the wide range of controls necessary for the settlement, operation, and maintenance of the colony was left completely in the hands of the resident council.[35] It was authorized to settle new towns, to inflict summary punishment to anyone slandering the company or the resident council, to regulate hours of work, to ensure religious orthodoxy, and to conscript any and all settlers into military service.[36]

The initial leaders of the Jamestown experiment also had backgrounds similar to those of the group of petty nobles and military men who made up the Portuguese leadership in Brazil. The Virginia Company itself was well stocked with members of the nobility—over one-third of the total peerage had invested in the company at one time or another.[37] Those who played the most active role in the company's affairs were either wealthy merchants with considerable experience in the India trade or investors, such as the Earl of Warwick, in Elizabethan piracy ventures.[38] Their experience, like that of their Brazilian counterparts, suited them more to commercial and military exploitation than to the founding of an agrarian-based colony.

Those who participated in the first colonizing expeditions to Brazil and Virginia made it abundantly clear that they were not themselves prepared for difficult manual labor in their new environment. Most of the Portuguese *donatarios* showed a decided reluctance to exert the energy necessary to provide for the exigencies of life. This remained the case even after it became apparent that the land would not yield immediate profits in precious metals and exotic native produce. Those Portuguese settlers who achieved at least minimal success relied on Indians to provide them with

[35] Theoretically the *donatarios* had nearly unlimited powers, but the fact that the king, in 1549, was able to revoke the grants with no difficulty is proof that the crown, not the *donatarios*, possessed ultimate political authority over the lands.

[36] The Charter of April 10, 1606 and the instructions from the privy council to the leaders of the enterprise in November 1606 can be found in Alexander Brown, *The Genesis of the United States* (Boston, 1890), I, 46-75.

[37] Lawrence Stone, *The Crisis of the Aristocracy, 1588-1641* (New York, 1965), 372.

[38] Wesley F. Craven, *Dissolution of the Virginia Company: The Failure of a Colonial Experiment* (New York, 1932), 25-26.

16

food and labor to cut their brazilwood. They used a system of barter and of temporary alliances with one village against other, more hostile villages as inducements to make the Indians work for them. The system was successful at first. In return for a few relatively worthless trinkets, the Portuguese were able to obtain a significant amount of Indian labor—an amount sufficient to keep their modest colonial enterprise going. They were able not only to begin to profit from the brazilwood trade, but also to make a tentative beginning, again with the help of Indian labor, in the cultivation of sugar.[39]

Unfortunately, the system soon started to break down. The Indians quickly tired of the novelty of the Portuguese trinkets and began to demand more valuable merchandise. As competition for Indian labor increased among the settlers, the price in barter was bid up and the Portuguese found that their production costs were skyrocketing.[40] To make matters worse, the Indians of Brazil had the annoying habit of turning against their Portuguese neighbors, occasionally being so impolite as to eat them. As Francisco Adolpho de Varnhagen has pointed out in his classic multivolume *Historia Geral do Brasil*, the civilizations and life styles of the Portuguese and Indians were so different that the members of the two cultures soon developed for one another a hearty contempt, based on mutual jealousy and ignorance.[41] Moreover, the French were often in the vicinity, ready to exploit any latent hostility between the two groups.[42] Whatever the reasons for the increasing friction between the Portuguese and the Indians, it became clear after less than two decades of settlement that the Portuguese could not depend on the Indians to enter into voluntary working arrangements on a permanent and profitable basis.

The English settlers at Jamestown, as Edmund Morgan has convincingly demonstrated, were even less anxious than the Portuguese to settle down to the serious task of building a permanent settlement.[43] Instead of tending to the crucial business of gathering supplies, growing food, and building shelter, the English

[39] Marchant, *Barter to Slavery*, 63-78.
[40] *Ibid.*, 69-80.
[41] Varnhagen, I, 276-77. Unfortunately, Varnhagen shared the early Portuguese settlers' distaste for the Indians, a bias which is reflected in his history.
[42] Marchant, *Barter to Slavery*, 73, 75-78.
[43] Morgan, "Labor Problem."

17

wasted their time quarreling among themselves, looking for gold, or searching for a passage to the Pacific Ocean. When Captain John Smith left the colony in October 1609, the settlers lost what little discipline they had previously had and, neglecting even the minimal tasks necessary for survival, they ended up dying in overwhelming numbers. Discipline improved slightly with the arrival of Sir Thomas Gates and Lord De La Warr in 1610, but when Sir Thomas Dale arrived in Jamestown in 1611, he found the settlers at work at "their daily and usuall workes, bowling in the streetes."[44]

This chronic "underemployment" at Jamestown has been attributed to many factors. The surplus of derelicts and idle noblemen among the initial settlers, the lack of individual incentive in the communally oriented plan of settlement, and the low quality of work habits prevalent throughout England at the time—all offer at least a partial explanation for the early Virginians' behavior.[45] But most important, the motives behind the settlement, stated in the tracts of the English imperialist-propagandists, could not have prepared them to undertake hard, sustained work.

The English in Virginia were unwilling to abandon their hopes of finding easy wealth even after it became clear to them that Virginia was not an El Dorado. They tried continually to use Powhatan as a "front-man" for their operation—in much the same way that Cortes used Montezuma in Mexico—but the Virginia settlers soon realized that Powhatan was not so overwhelmed by the "superiority" of English civilization that he would become their servant.[46] In fact, Powhatan made a point of staying away

[44] Ibid.; Ralph Hamor, A True Discourse of the Present State of Virginia (London, 1615; Richmond, 1957), 26.
[45] Diamond, "Organization to Society," 457-75, suggests that in order to make the English settlers work, the Virginia Company continually had to increase individual incentive by loosening the corporate restraints upon them. By doing so the company did indeed increase incentive, but also experienced a corresponding reduction in the amount of discipline it could exert over the settlers. Morgan, "Labor Problem," 602-06 cites D. C. Coleman, "Labor in the English Economy of the Seventeenth Century," Economic History Review, 2d ser., VIII (1956), 280-95, to prove that the work habits that the lower-class English settlers brought with them to Virginia were not of the most rigorous nature. Stone, 331, maintains that "the rich and the well-born were idle almost by definition." This would presumably also apply to those who made the trip to Virginia.
[46] Powhatan, after grudgingly journeying to Jamestown for a "coronation"

18

from the English; thus, they lacked even the minimal advantages of the settlers of Brazil. At least in Brazil the Portuguese were able to achieve a temporary solution to their labor problem by bartering with the Indians. The Virginia colonists, because of Powhatan's determination to remain independent of all foreign "intruders," did not even succeed in developing a dependable system of trade with the Indians.[47]

A few Virginians, even after repeated failures to exploit the Indians, remained sanguine about the possibilities of eventual success. John Martin, a member of the ruling council in Virginia, was still ruminating about the advantages of Indian labor even after the dreadful massacre of 1622. Like many other Virginians, Martin no longer viewed the Indians as gentle, docile creatures, but he nevertheless thought that it would be more profitable for the English to put them to work than it would be to exterminate them. One of the ways to persuade them to work, according to Martin, was to make them much more dependent upon the English for their safety and survival. This could be achieved, he claimed, by "haueinge some 200 Souldiers on foote, contynuallie harrowinge and burneinge all their townes in wynter and spoileinge their weares."[48]

Martin was fast becoming an exception. By 1618 at the latest, most Englishmen realized that their dream of an El Dorado in Tidewater Virginia would never become a reality. To be sure, by 1614, Virginians had found that tobacco might be a potentially profitable export commodity, but many royal officials were opposed to the cultivation of a crop that was "loathsome to the eye, hateful to the nose, harmful to the brain, dangerous to the lungs, and in the black stinking fumes thereof, nearest resembling the horrible Stygian smoke of the pit that is bottomless."[49] Furthermore, the English settlers in Virginia were lacking the crucial

ceremony, told the English that he was every bit as exalted and powerful as the king of England and that he had no intention of being duped into serving the English settlers; Arber, ed., *John Smith*, I, 124.

[47] Lurie, 46-50.

[48] Susan M. Kingsbury, ed., *The Records of the Virginia Company of London* (Washington, D. C., 1933), III, 704-06.

[49] James I, *Counter-blast to Tobacco* (London, 1604), quoted in Jerome E. Brooks, *The Mighty Leaf, Tobacco Through the Centuries* (Boston, 1952), 71.

supply of labor needed to cultivate the "joviall weed"; the Indians had made it clear that they were not willing to serve the English, and those Englishmen who had settled in Virginia were too few, too specialized in their skills, and too lazy in their work habits to do it themselves.[50] The Virginia Company did everything possible to get the settlement off the ground. It offered inducements of free land to potential settlers who could pay their own passage, allowed settlers already in Virginia to increase the size of their holdings in order to increase individual incentive, instituted a more representative system of government, and encouraged the growth of food crops in order to prevent recurrence of the famines that had plagued the settlement. But nothing seemed to work.[51] In 1624, at the demise of the Virginia Company, the population of the colony stood at 1275 Englishmen, not much more than the population of the settlement in 1609.[52]

Clearly, something had to be done in both Brazil and Virginia to bolster the sagging fortunes of the two colonizing ventures. In each case private control over the colony was suspended and royal control introduced. In Brazil, in 1549, the *donatarios* were allowed to keep as much land as they had actually brought under cultivation, but much of their political power was taken over by a royal governor, a chief justice, and a treasury official.[53] In Virginia, the English crown took over the functions of the Virginia Company and became the sole proprietor of the enterprise. Although this action has frequently been interpreted in political terms, it is apparent that the considerations that moved the crown to dissolve the company were economic.[54] Neither the *donatarios* nor the

[50] At a time when the Virginia Company needed men to grow corn to keep the settlers alive it was advertising for such specialized skills as iron miners, cutlers, armorers, net makers, upholsterers of feathers, leather dressers, spinners of pack thread, mat makers, saltpeter men, tile makers, etc.; Brown, *Genesis*, I, 469-70.

[51] Craven, *Dissolution*, 47-79.

[52] W. Noel Sainsbury, ed., *Calendar of State Papers, Colonial Series. 1574-1660* (London, 1860), 43, 57.

[53] Varnhagen, I, 291-95.

[54] The debate over whether the crown acted justly when it dissolved the Virginia Company has raged continuously since 1624. Alexander Brown in his *Genesis of the United States* and later in *The First Republic in America* (Boston, 1898) attempts to prove that the king, acting out of a tyrannical desire to destroy the representative assembly that the company had instituted in Virginia, revoked the company's charter in order to stifle the bur-

officials of the Virginia Company had been successful in devising a system of labor capable of producing the kinds of profits that the Portuguese and English governments had anticipated. It was only logical that the sovereigns of the two European nations would decide on a change of management.[55]

Royal Rule in Brazil and Virginia

The introduction of royal government—after sixteen years of *donatario* rule in Brazil and seventeen years of company rule in Virginia—marks the point at which the histories of the Portuguese and English settlements in the New World begin to diverge drastically. As the royal governments of Portugal and England began to plan the future of their new, overseas responsibilities, the institutions and cultural and technological influences of the two nations made their first meaningful impact on the development of Brazil and Virginia. In some cases all that occurred was the formalization and legitimization of preexisting Portuguese and English practices in the two colonies; in other cases, Portuguese and English institutions were imposed for the first time on the frontier conditions of the colonies.

The single most important decision made by the Portuguese royal government was to continue to attempt to exploit the land and the people of the New World to the fullest extent possible. Only the emphasis had changed; the exploitation was no longer to be purely extractive, but, rather, was to be aimed at utilizing Indian and imported labor in the intensive cultivation of export crops.[56] This decision caused Tóme de Sousa, the first royal governor of Brazil, to scrap his initial plans for a humane Indian poli-

---

geoning democratic spirit of Virginia. Craven, *Dissolution*, has demonstrated that the crown's antipathy to the political forms of the settlement was decidedly secondary to its dissatisfaction with the economic inefficiency of the company.

[55] In Brazil a consolidation of government into the hands of the Portuguese monarch was made all the more necessary because of the increasing threat posed by French interlopers in the New World.

[56] This decision seems to have been a conscious one. King João III called in his most trusted advisers and specifically asked them how, given the lack of precious metals, to best exploit the land of Brazil. Celso Furtado, *Economic Growth of Brazil* (Berkeley, 1963), 5-11; Sergio Buarque de Holanda, *Raizes do Brasil* (Rio de Janeiro, 1936), 19-139.

21

cy for the colony. As the barter system broke down, the Portuguese settlers turned to outright enslavement of the Indians. Although both King João III and the royal governor disapproved of this enslavement, they were swayed considerably by the colonists' argument that with adequate labor Brazil could become one of the world's leading sugar producers. The resulting decision was a compromise. Those Indians who had demonstrated that they were hostile to the Portuguese were fair game for enslavement; those that remained at peace with the Portuguese were to be protected.[57]

Indian slavery in Brazil continued in practice, although not in law, for several centuries, but it was not in itself an adequate solution to the colony's labor shortage.[58] A number of influential people, most notably the members of the Company of Jesus, were offended by the enslavement of Indians; moreover, the Indian captives of the "just wars" were too few and often too rebellious to constitute the sole source of labor for the Brazilian colonial economy. As a result, the Portuguese turned, almost immediately after the institution of royal government in 1549, to the large-scale importation of slaves from Africa.[59]

The decision to import Negro slaves could not have been made had not conditions within Portugal itself been favorable. First, Portugal at that time possessed important commercial and mili-

[57] Marchant, Barter to Slavery, 82-84.

[58] The Portuguese crown issued cedulas prohibiting enslavement of Indians in 1570, 1605, 1609, 1648, 1655, and 1686. Nevertheless, Indians continued to be used as slaves throughout the eighteenth century. See, for example, Matias C. Kieman, The Indian Policy of Portugal in the Amazon Region, 1614-1693 (Washington, D. C., 1954).

[59] Although much has been written about Negro slavery in Brazil, a comprehensive and systematic study of the institution remains to be written. See for widely varying viewpoints, Gilberto Freyre, The Masters and the Slaves: A Study in the Development of Brazilian Civilization (2d Eng. ed.; New York, 1956); and Charles R. Boxer, Race Relations in the Portuguese Colonial Empire, 1415-1825 (Oxford, 1963). See also, Stanley Stein, Vassouras: A Brazilian Coffee Country, 1850-1900 (Cambridge, 1957); Jose Honorio Rodrigues, Brazil and Africa (New York, 1965); and Florestan Fernandes, The Negro in Brazilian Society (New York, 1969). Of lesser value are Nina Rodrigues, Os Africanos no Brasil (2d ed.; São Paulo, 1935); Donald Pierson, Negroes in Brazil: A Study of Race Contact at Bahia (Chicago, 1942); Arturo Ramos, The Negro in Brazil (Washington, D. C., 1951); and Mary M. Williams, "The Treatment of Negro Slaves in the Brazilian Empire: A Comparison with the United States," Journal of Negro History, VII (1922), 349-64.

tary advantages on the coast of Africa, and it was thus much safer and cheaper for her to import slaves than it was for other nations.[60] Second, the Portuguese could expect, with some degree of confidence, a sufficiently high rate of return on their investment in Negro slaves to warrant the expense of importing them. Again, Portuguese experience outside Brazil provided the royal government with a way to ensure this high rate of return. The Portuguese, along with the Italians, had been the leading sugar producers of the fifteenth century. Moreover, by the sixteenth century, the Portuguese had surpassed their rivals in the technological knowledge necessary to produce sugar cheaply and efficiently. All they needed to gain the major share of the world's sugar market was to expand their rather small base of operations on the island of Madeira to a larger and more productive territory.[61] Thus, the happy combination of land suitable for the cultivation of a highly profitable export crop, Portugal's superior technology in the growing and manufacturing of that product, and her ability to provide a substitute labor force guaranteed the king of Portugal a prosperous overseas colony.

As long as the Portuguese could maintain a foothold in Africa and as long as they could maintain their lead in the technology of sugar production, the Brazilian economy was able to flourish. In 1549, there were only a few hundred slaves and perhaps only a dozen sugar mills in Brazil. In 1580, there were probably 5000 slaves and 118 engenhos de açucar producing about 9,600,000 pounds of sugar each year. By the 1620s, Brazil had roughly 40,000 slaves, with an additional 15,000 being imported each year, and approximately 230 sugar mills producing 22,400,000 pounds per year.[62]

The decision, or rather the nondecision, of the English government as to the direction of the Virginia colony was strikingly different: the English crown simply let the Virginia settlers continue to grope for a way to survive. Left to themselves, Virginians gradually became dependent upon tobacco as a substitute for

[60] Furtado, 10-11.

[61] Ibid., 6-10. For a detailed history of the growth and manufacture of sugar, see Noel Deerr, The History of Sugar (London, 1949).

[62] Marchant, Barter to Slavery, 123-28; Simonsen, 168-77; Charles R. Boxer, Salvador de Sá and the Struggle for Brazil and Angola (London, 1952), 178-80.

23

the gold and silver that had eluded them. And they grew that tobacco themselves. Instead of trying to befriend the Indian or even
to capture and enslave him, the Virginians declared a policy
aimed at his total extermination. Each year after 1624, organized
expeditions fanned out from the Jamestown area bent on destroying as many Indian crops and towns as possible. The English settlers of Virginia had decided that if they could not profit from
their Indian neighbors, then the only other alternative was "perpetual enmity" with them.[63]

Nor did the Virginians turn, at least in the first century of the
colony's existence, to Africa for a labor supply. They did not make
any major investments in African slaves because they lacked precisely those advantages that the Brazilians possessed. First, England did not engage in a major way in the international slave
trade until 1672 when the Royal African Company was organized.[64] Thus, Virginians in the early seventeenth century found
it impossible to import slaves cheaply to the New World. Second,
the English crown did not believe that the economy of seventeenth-century Virginia was capable of supporting the investment
necessary for the massive importation of Negro slaves. The Spanish were far more advanced than the English in both the cultivation and the marketing of tobacco.[65] The English, because they
did not possess the necessary technology and because the royal
government initially distrusted the crop, were unwilling to risk
a major investment in order to purchase slaves for the Virginia
enterprise.[66]

To be sure, African slaves were imported into Virginia from
1619 on, and by the 1660s their presence was obvious enough

[63] Craven, *Southern Colonies*, 172-74.
[64] C. M. Macinnes, *England and Slavery* (Bristol, 1934), 20-29; Eric Williams,
Capitalism and Slavery (Chapel Hill, 1944), 30-31; Kenneth G. Davies, *The Royal
African Company* (London, 1957), 38-46.
[65] Strachey, 122-23; Lewis C. Gray, *History of Agriculture in the Southern
United States to 1860* (Washington, D. C., 1933), I, 21-22.
[66] The case of the British in the West Indies is roughly similar. As long as
the West Indian colonies' staple crop was tobacco, the number of Negroes
imported annually remained small. When in the 1640s, the British West
Indies began to produce sugar, which was more profitable than tobacco, the
volume of the slave trade increased. The supply of slaves could not equal the
demand, however, until the 1670s when the British finally participated in
a major way in the international slave trade.

24

to warrant the kind of proscriptive legislation that was to eventually strip them of nearly all human rights. But for over a century after the settling of Jamestown, white labor, indeed, free white labor, dominated the Virginia labor force. In 1624, there were only 23 blacks in a population of 1,275. By 1670, the black population had risen to 2,000, but the indentured servant population numbered 6,000, and the free white population was 20,000-25,000. By the turn of the century there were only 6,000 Negroes in a total population of over 70,000. There is no question but that the tide started to turn at that point. By 1742, Negroes constituted one-third of Virginia's population; by the Revolution they accounted for over 40 per cent of the population.[67] Yet the fact remains that during the first one hundred years of the Virginia experiment, the English were unwilling to risk an investment in Negro slaves and the labor force of seventeenth-century Virginia remained predominantly free and white.

Furthermore, the economy of Virginia during the seventeenth century was not a large-scale plantation economy, but one of middle-sized farms with landholdings averaging about 400 acres and only a few plantations over 2,000 acres.[68] Thus, while in Brazil the number of large sugar plantations rose in proportion to the rise in the Negro slave population, in Virginia the average landholding remained small as long as Negro slaves played only a subsidiary role in the economy.

This divergence in the composition of the populations of late sixteenth-century Brazil and early seventeenth-century Virginia signaled much more than a mere difference in the economic bases of the two regions. Economic considerations were paramount in shaping the initial decision regarding the nature of the labor force in each colony, but it was the consequences of that economic decision and not the considerations behind the decision that would have the most lasting effects on the cultures of the two colonies. Indeed, Virginia would eventually resort to a large-scale, single crop, commercial agricultural system much like that of Brazil,

[67] Gray, I, 351-53; Philip A. Bruce, *Economic History of Virginia in the Seventeenth Century* (New York, 1896), I, 572-73; Evarts B. Greene and Virginia D. Harrington, *American Population Before the Federal Census of 1790* (New York, 1932), 137-41, 154-55.

[68] Thomas J. Wertenbaker, *The Planters of Colonial Virginia* (Princeton, 1922), 53-59.

25

but by that time the ethnic and cultural differences in the populations of the two areas would be fixed.

Although it is unwise to accept completely Gilberto Freyre's romanticized account of Brazilian slavery and the resultant creation of a new "Luso-tropical" race from the blending of Indians, Negroes, and Europeans, it is nevertheless undeniable that the Portuguese in Brazil, for a variety of reasons, were much less averse to working, worshipping, eating, and cohabiting openly with the Indians and Negroes than were their English counterparts in North America. Both contemporary testimony—plantation records, diaries, and travelers' accounts—and subsequent developments—the influence of the Indian and Negro on eating habits, speech, religion, and, most obvious, on the complexion of the Brazilian population—attest to the evolution of Brazil into a more racially mixed society than any other colony in North America.[69]

The various explanations advanced by historians for this difference have become the subject of heated, and increasingly fruitless, debate. The "conscience" of the Catholic Church, the relative liberality of Portuguese slave codes, the paternalistic, noncapitalistic bent of the Portuguese colonizer, the dearth of Portuguese women in Brazil, and even the virility of the Portuguese

[69] Gilberto Freyre, *Masters*, and Freyre, *The Mansions and The Shanties: The Making of Modern Brazil* (New York, 1963), is responsible for changing not only the trend of historical writing on the Negro, but also, I suspect, is at least partially responsible, because of his "Luso-tropical" nationalism, for softening the attitudes of contemporary white Brazilians toward their Indian and Negro countrymen. Freyre, by boasting about his racially open society and by his considerable prestige within that society, has helped to create a self-fulfilling prophecy. He is supported in his views by, among others: Pierson, *Negroes in Brazil*; Frank Tannenbaum, *Slave and Citizen: The Negro in the Americas* (New York, 1947); Stanley Elkins, *Slavery: A Problem in American Institutional and Intellectual Life* (Chicago, 1959). On the other hand, Boxer, *Race Relations*; David B. Davis, *The Problem of Slavery in Western Culture* (Ithaca, 1966); Marvin Harris, *Patterns of Race in the Americas* (New York, 1964); and, to a lesser extent, Carl Degler, "Slavery in Brazil and the United States: An Essay in Comparative History," *American Historical Review*, LXXV (1970), 1004-28, are among the many historians who argue that slavery in Brazil and Spanish America was much harsher than the former have portrayed it. It is possible, however, to accept Boxer's, Davis's, Harris's, and Degler's less romantic view of the operation of slavery in colonial Brazil and still be persuaded that Negroes, Indians, and whites coexisted more harmoniously in Brazil than in North America.

male are among the many reasons cited for the differences between the Brazilian and North American racial situations.[70] Some of these "outside" influences from Europe were undoubtedly important in the creation of the distinctly different cultures of Brazil and Virginia, but they obscure the central and obvious fact that the Portuguese settlers of Brazil, because of their initial decision to make the Indian and Negro an indispensable part of their labor force, opened up at the very beginning the possibility of creating a genuinely multiracial society. By opting at an early stage for a system of labor that was potentially degrading and dehumanizing for the Indian and African slave, the Portuguese, paradoxically, made it impossible in their society to avoid constant contact with the Indian and the Negro and therefore impossible to avoid familiarity among races and, ultimately, impossible to avoid at least some relaxation in the white man's rigid and discriminatory social system.

Virginia, by pursuing an official policy of extermination of the Indians and an unofficial policy of nonimportation of Negro slaves, kept itself "English" in its cultural attitudes and habits. Seventeenth-century Virginians because they were not suffered to come in contact with either the Indian or the African were allowed to retain their old, Elizabethan prejudices concerning other cultures.[71] By the time Virginians had amassed enough capital and had assured themselves that the slave system would be profitable, their racial attitudes had been set. After 1700, their society would no longer be free of "foreign" cultural influences, and it would be difficult, even for the nonslaveholding yeoman farmer, to avoid

[70] See for example, Tannenbaum, 48-62, 82-90; Elkins, 52-80; and Freyre, *Masters*, 29, 185, 278, 330, 370-72, 441-52. Freyre goes so far as to say that the original settlers of Brazil were unusually oversexed:

To the wilderness, so underpopulated, with a bare sprinkling of whites, came these oversexed ones, there to give extraordinary rein to their passions. . . . Attracted by the possibilities of a free and untrammeled life, with a host of nude women around them . . . many Europeans proceeded to settle here out of predilection or of their own free will. Unbridled stallions is what they were.

[71] Winthrop Jordan, *White Over Black: The Development of American Attitudes Toward the Negro, 1550-1812* (Chapel Hill, 1968) is the one indispensable source explaining the complex process by which Englishmen in America came to reinforce and intensify their preexistent prejudices toward the Negro.

27

contact with the Negro. But by 1700, the settlers of Virginia were already committed to a society where the white European would be the dominant cultural element. The white man in Virginia, faced with the practical necessity of living in a multiracial society, would respond either by ignoring the existence of other races or, when they could not be ignored, by erecting institutional barriers between the races.

It was at this point, then, that the Brazilian and Virginian societies began to diverge most dramatically. Both the Portuguese and English desired quick and easy riches in the New World. Both found it difficult to fulfill that desire. But Brazil, because of Portugal's position in the international slave trade and her superior technology in the production of sugar, was able to keep alive the dream of a colony based on the work of others. It is one of the paradoxes of the history of colonization in the New World that the Portuguese in Brazil, unlike the English in Virginia, began the slow (and still uncompleted) task of developing relatively humane and equitable codes of behavior toward other cultures while in the very process of exploiting the people of those cultures.

9

Slavery

DAVID BRION DAVIS

Of all American institutions, Negro slavery has probably been the one most frequently compared with historical antecedents and foreign counterparts, and with the least benefit to systematic knowledge. Quite understandably, modern scholars have been so impressed by the long submission and degradation of southern Negroes, as well as by the extraordinary prevalence of racial prejudice in the United States, that they have often pictured American slavery as a system of unique and unmitigated severity that stands in marked contrast to other forms of servitude. Yet Thomas Jefferson could confidently assert that in Augustan Rome the condition of slaves was "much more deplorable than that of the blacks on the continent of America," and list barbarities and cruelties which were commonplace in Rome but presumably unknown in Virginia. Apologists for American slavery were always fond of comparing the mildness of their own institution, supposedly evidenced by a rapidly increasing Negro population, with the harshness of slavery in the West Indies or ancient Rome, where a constant supply of fresh captives made up for an appalling mortality. Yet abolitionists were always inclined to argue that the slave system of their own country or empire was the worst in history. Foreign travelers were not only subject to nationalistic prejudice but tended to rank various slave systems on the basis of fortuitous impressions or the biased

121

accounts of hospitable planters. When we recognize how often comparisons have been influenced by ulterior motives and have been directed to the fruitless question "Which nation's slavery was the worst?" we might conclude that the subject can most profitably be studied in geographical isolation.

Yet American slavery was a product of the African slave trade, which was itself an integral part of both European commercial expansion and New World colonization. Most of the components of the slave-trading and plantation systems were developed in the thirteenth and fourteenth centuries by Italian merchants who purchased Circassians, Tartars, and Georgians at commercial bases on the Black Sea and then transported them to markets in Egypt, Italy, and Spain. As early as 1300 the enterprising Italians were even working Negro slaves on sugar plantations in Cyprus. In the fifteenth century, when the Portuguese adopted similar practices in trading with West Africa, Negro slaves displaced the Moors and Russians as the lowest element in the labor force of Spain. Negroes were shipped to Hispaniola as early as 1502; and as the Spanish colonists gradually turned to the cultivation of sugar, the rising demand for labor became an enormous stimulus to the Portuguese African trade. By the seventeenth century the Atlantic slave trade had become a vast international enterprise as the Dutch, British, French, Danes, Swedes, and even Brandenburgers established forts and markets along the West African coast. On both sides of the Atlantic there was close contact between merchants, seamen, and planters of various nationalities. In addition to competing and fighting with one another, they borrowed techniques and customs, cooperated in smuggling, and gathered to buy slaves at such entrepôts as Curaçao. If the British planters of Barbados looked to Brazil as a model, Barbados itself provided the impulse for settling Carolina. There was, then, a high degree of institutional continuity which linked the European maritime powers in a common venture. A trade which involved six major nations and lasted for three centuries, which transported some 10 to 15 million Africans to the New World, and which became a central part of international rivalry and the struggle for empire, cannot be considered as a mere chapter in the history of North America.

The unpleasant truth is that there could hardly have been

successful colonization of the New World without Negro slaves, since there was no alternative source of labor to meet the needs required by the cultivation of sugar, rice, tobacco, and cotton, and since even the more diversified colonies were long dependent economically on the markets and earnings of the staple-producing regions. It must be emphasized that this common dependence on Negro slavery was never universally recognized or welcomed. From the first Spanish in Hispaniola to the British in Barbados and Virginia, colonists were slow and hesitant in committing themselves to a labor force of foreign captives. Among the frequent dreams of New World Utopias and second Edens, no one envisioned a model society of several thousand free Europeans overseeing the life and labor of several hundred thousand Negro slaves. From the beginning, racial antipathy was reinforced by the much stronger emotion of fear; and the dread of insurrection and racial war would always balance the desire for quick wealth through a reckless increase in slaves.

Nonetheless, from sixteenth-century Mexico to eighteenth-century Jamaica and South Carolina, colonial administrators were unable to maintain a reassuring ratio between white immigrants and Negro slaves. In regions where tropical or semitropical staples could be cultivated, it became clear that investment in slave labor was the key to expanded production and spectacular profit. The Negro slave played an indispensable role in the conquest and settlement of Latin America, and in the clearing and cultivation of virgin land from Trinidad to the lower Mississippi Valley and Texas. And as the possession of slaves became itself a symbol of affluence, prestige, and power, the demand for Negroes spread to urban and temperate zones. Important leaders in New England and French Canada seriously argued that only Negro slaves could meet the labor needs of their colonies. From 1732 to 1754 Negro slaves constituted more than 35 per cent of the immigrants entering New York City; by mid-century they were owned by about one-tenth of the householders of the province and accounted for 15 per cent of the total population. Meanwhile, the slave trade and American Negro slavery were sanctioned by treaties and the law of nations, by the acts and edicts of kings and parliaments, by the Spanish Council of the Indies and the great trading companies of Eng-

31

land, Holland, and France, by the Catholic Church and the major Protestant denominations. All the colonies of the New World legalized the institution, and many competed with one another for a supply of labor that was never equal to the demand. For more than three centuries the Negro slave was deeply involved in imperial wars, revolutions, and wars of independence. Insofar as the Western Hemisphere has a common history, it must center on a common experience with Negro slavery.

But did slavery mean the same thing to the various colonists of the New World? The fact that Dutch slave traders imitated the Portuguese and that a Dutch ship brought the first Negroes to Virginia did not mean that a Negro's status would be the same in Virginia as in Brazil. In England, unlike Italy and the Iberian Peninsula, true slavery disappeared by the thirteenth century. On the other hand, English jurists perpetuated the legal concept of unlimited servitude, and English judges recognized the validity of enslaving and selling infidels. We still have much to learn about the character of servitude in the sixteenth century and the later evolution of slave status in the British, Dutch, and French colonies. In making future comparative studies it would be well to keep in mind two points which should prevent hasty generalizations. First, in many societies the slave has only gradually been differentiated from other kinds of unfree workers, and his status, rights, and obligations have been defined in practice before receiving legal recognition. Second, although the actual condition of slaves has varied greatly even within a single society, there has been a remarkable persistence and uniformity in the legal concept of the slave. Since this last point has often been disregarded in comparative approaches to American slavery, we shall elaborate on it here.

The status of slavery has always been surrounded with certain ambiguities that seem related to the institution's origins. To be enslaved as a result of capture in war or punishment for crime implied total subordination to coercive authority. Yet bondage for debt or as the result of self-sale suggested merely a reciprocal exchange of labor and obedience for sustenance and protection. When a bondwoman's offspring were claimed by her owner on the same basis as the natural increase of livestock, the status was assimilated to that of movable property. In societies where slaves have largely been recruited from the native poor and have performed no specialized economic function, as in ancient China, Egypt, and the Near East, the element of reciprocal rights and obligations has taken precedence over the elements of punishment and ownership. Nevertheless, the slave was legally defined as a thing not only in the Southern United States but in ancient Egypt, Babylonia, Greece, and Rome. And the Roman conception of the slave as at once a person and a piece of movable property prevailed in medieval France, Italy, and Spain; it was extended to Latin America and was incorporated in the Code Noir for the French colonies; and it reappeared in the laws and judicial decisions of British North America. A Virginia court merely affirmed the ancient Latin concept of chattel slavery when it ruled that "Slaves are not only property, but they are rational beings, and entitled to the humanity of the Court, when it can be exercised without invading the rights of property." And when an American master claimed the offspring of his female slaves or asserted his right to move, sell, trade, bequest, or give away his chattel property, he added nothing to a legal notion of slavery that had persisted in Europe for more than two thousand years.

The definition of the slave as chattel property implied a condition of rightlessness on the part of the slave. In neither Europe nor the Americas could a slave testify in court against a free person, institute a court action in his own behalf, make a legally binding will or contract, or own property. There were, to be sure, minor exceptions and variations. Slaves were sometimes allowed to testify in certain civil cases or give evidence against a master accused of treason. In North America at various times Negro bondsmen were permitted to plead benefit of clergy and to give evidence in capital cases involving other slaves. As in Rome and Latin America, they were accorded limited rights over personal property, including horses and cattle, and might act as a master's legal agent, though never with the freedom and complex prerogatives of the Roman slave. But what stands out above the exceptions and variations is the fact that from pre-Christian laws to the slave codes of the New World the bondsman had no civil capacities and was considered only as an extension of his master's legal personality.

33

Even in Puritan Massachusetts slaves were, in the words of Cotton Mather, who was simply echoing Aristotle, "the *Animate, Separate, Active Instruments* of other men."

One of the few significant differences in the legal status of slaves was that bondsmen were denied legal marriage in ancient Rome and in Protestant America, whereas slave marriages were recognized in Carthage, Hellenistic Greece, and in Catholic Europe and America. Largely to prevent the sin of fornication, Catholic theologians even ruled that a slave might marry against his master's will. Yet according to St. Thomas Aquinas, slavery was an "impediment" to marriage, comparable to impotence, and a slave's first obligation must be to his master, not his spouse. If a master had a moral duty to try to preserve the integrity of slave families, he still had a legal claim to all slave children, and might of necessity divide husband from wife or children from parents. Since there is evidence that Latin American masters often did little to encourage or respect slave marriages, and that North American masters often recognized such marriages and tried to keep families intact, one may suspect that actual differences were more the result of individual personality and economic pressure than of legal and moral rights. The main point is that in no society have slaves had a legal claim to their wives and children.

Religious conversion has always complicated the question of a slave's status. The Muslims and ancient Hebrews drew a sharp distinction between enslaving infidels and temporarily holding servants of their own faith who had been deprived of freedom by economic necessity. Although the first Church Fathers ruled unmistakably that baptism should have no effect on the temporal status of slaves, medieval Christians showed an increasing reluctance to enslave their fellow Christians and came to think of perpetual bondage as a punishment suitable only for infidels. But the authorities who condemned the sale of Christians and yet preached slaving crusades against the infidels were ultimately faced with the problem of the baptized infidel. In 1366 the priors of Florence explained that it was valid to buy or sell slaves who had been baptized so long as they had originally come "from the land and race of the infidels." This was, in effect, the same test later applied in Virginia and other North American colonies.

Baptism was to have no effect on a slave's status unless he had been a Christian in his native country. And if the Catholic colonists felt a much greater obligation to have their slaves baptized, North American laws encouraged conversion and recognized that the Negro had a soul that might be redeemed. After a century of inaction, the Protestant churches slowly began their work of spreading religion among the slaves, and by the mid-nineteenth century the proportion of converted Negroes was probably as large in parts of the United States as in Brazil. It is doubtful, however, whether the mass of slaves in any country ever enjoyed a meaningful religious life.

There was little that was distinctive in the police regulations and penal laws restricting the lives of North American slaves. Throughout the ages, and in virtually all parts of the Western Hemisphere, slaves were prohibited from carrying arms, traveling at night or without permission, and acting with disrespect toward a freeman. Fairly typical was a law of 1785 for Spanish Santo Domingo which ordered one hundred lashes and two years in jail for any Negro who raised his hand against a white man. The penalties for such crimes as theft and assault were everywhere more severe for slaves than for others. During the eighteenth century there was a tendency in most New World colonies to abandon the most sanguinary punishments, such as mutilation, dismemberment, and burning at the stake. Harsh restrictions and terrifying punishments persisted longest in the West Indies, where the disproportion of Negroes to whites was the greatest. But even in the West Indies the long-term trend was toward more humane punishment and an extension of the slave's legal protections.

It is misleading to say that Anglo-American law never recognized the Negro slave as a human personality whose rights to life, food, and shelter were protected by law. There was ample precedent for the 1846 ruling of a Kentucky judge that "A slave is not in the condition of a horse. . . . He is made after the image of the Creator. He has mental capacities, and an immortal principle in his nature. . . . The law . . . cannot extinguish his high born nature, nor deprive him of many rights which are inherent in man." Although a master might kill his slave with impunity in the ancient Near East, the Roman Republic, Saxon England, and under certain circumstances in the Iberian Peninsula and Latin America, and although in much of British America the murder of a slave was thought to merit only a modest fine, by the early nineteenth century the slave states of North America had put the killing or maiming of a Negro bondsman on the same level of criminality as the killing or maiming of a white man. In both the British Caribbean and the Southern states, courts sometimes held that slaves were protected by common law against such crimes as manslaughter or unprovoked battery. Georgia and North Carolina both held that slaves had a right to trial by jury, and North Carolina went so far as to recognize a slave's right to resist unprovoked attack. Of course it was one thing for American states to threaten punishment for cruelty to slaves, and to make masters legally obligated to give their bondsmen adequate food and shelter and to provide for their care in sickness and old age, and it was another matter to enforce such laws when Negroes were barred from testifying against white men. Nevertheless, one can plausibly argue that in terms of legal protections and physical welfare American slaves by the 1850's were as favorably treated as any bondsmen in history.

Yet one of the paradoxes of American slavery was that the laws protecting the physical welfare of slaves were accompanied by the severest restrictions on manumission. This brings us to the most important distinction between the legal status of slaves in British and Latin America. It should be stressed that taxes and other restrictions on manumission were common in antiquity, particularly in Rome, and that freedom suffered from prejudice and legal disabilities even when the stigma of slavish origin was not associated with race. There were discriminatory freedmen's laws, for example, in medieval Spain and Italy, and in Latin America as well. But only in the Southern United States did legislators try to bar every route to emancipation and deprive masters of their traditional right to free individual slaves. It is true that thousands of American slaves were manumitted by their owners, many after buying their freedom in installments, as was far more common in Latin America. It is also true that in some areas of Latin America a slave had no more realistic chance of becoming free than did his brother in Mississippi. Nevertheless, one may conclude that slavery in North America was distinctive in its efforts to build ever higher barriers against manumission. And there is evidence that this had less to do with slavery as such than with social attitudes toward racial integration.

Although the questions are of compelling importance, we cannot begin to determine whether slavery was a source of racial prejudice or prejudice a source of slavery, nor can we explain why prejudice became more dominant in the United States than in other parts of the New World. One may briefly state the principal facts that are relevant to a comparative study of slavery. Without denying the significance of racial difference as an aggravation to American bondage, we may note that throughout history slaves have been said to be naturally inferior, lazy, cunning, thievish. lascivious, fawning, deceitful, and incapable of life's higher thoughts and emotions. When not differentiated by race, they have often been physically marked off by shaven heads, brands, tattoos, and collars. There is unmistakable evidence of racial prejudice in Italy and the Iberian Peninsula, where colored slaves generally suffered from various indignities and disabilities. In Latin America Negro bondsmen were long denied the privileges and protections of Indian workers. Nonetheless, while Latin America was by no means immune from racial prejudice, even against freemen of mixed blood, there was a gradual acceptance of racial intermixture and a willingness to accept each stage of dilution as a step toward whiteness. In the British colonies, although the first Negroes had an ill-defined status and worked side by side with white servants, there was never any tolerance of racial blending. White fathers seldom acknowledged their colored offspring, and a mulatto or quadroon was still legally classed as a Negro. These differences may have been related to religion, sexual mores, social stratification, or the proportion of white women in a colonial population. But whatever the reason, prejudice against Negroes seems to have grown in the United States with the advance of popular democracy. It can be argued that this had less to do with slavery than with the status of the free Negro in an unusually mobile and unstratified white society. In other words, differences in slave systems may not account for the fact that while the Negro in the United States today has far more economic and educational opportunities than the Negro in Latin America, he also suffers from more overt discrimination from whites who feel superior but are unsure of their own status.

By focusing thus far on the legal status of slaves, we have given an oversimplified picture of institutional homogeneity. In actuality, of course, American slavery took a great variety of forms that were largely the result of economic pressures and such derivative factors as the nature of employment, the number of slaves owned by a typical master, and the proportion of slaves in a given society. Thus we correctly categorize North American slavery as plantation and staple-crop slavery, but tend to forget that in 1820 Negro bondsmen constituted 20 per cent of the population of Southern cities and that in 1860 there were a half million slaves working in factories, on railroad construction, as stevedores, as lumberjacks, on steamboats, and in numerous other jobs unconnected with agriculture. As in ancient Athens and Rome, and as in Latin America, slaves in the Southern states were employed as valets, waiters, cooks, nurses, craftsmen, and prostitutes. In spite of these well-known facts, most comparisons of slavery in British and Latin America have assumed that the institutions were virtually monolithic. We still lack comparative studies of the domestic servant, the slave artisan, the rented worker, and the slave in manufacturing establishments.

It has been said that the latifundia of southern Italy and Sicily provided an ancient precedent for the gang labor, the rationalized system of production, and the absentee ownership of the Caribbean plantation. But one must be careful not to lump all plantation agriculture in an undifferentiated class. Since the production of sugar, for example, was a long and continuous process that could be ruined by a delay in cutting, milling, boiling, or curing, the rhythm of plantation life was probably much the same in parts of Brazil as in Jamaica and Louisiana. The cultivation of sugar and rice required heavy capital investment, and in the West Indies and South Carolina led to slave gangs of several hundred being divided for specialized tasks under constant surveillance. Slavery in colonial South Carolina, though less characterized by absentee ownership, had more in common with slavery in the West Indies than either had with the institution in Virginia and Maryland. By 1765 South Carolina's forty thousand whites were outnumbered by ninety thousand slaves;

eight years later Jamaica's sixteen thousand whites kept uneasy watch over two hundred thousand slaves. In neither society could a field slave be in close or frequent contact with white men. In Virginia, on the other hand, the proportion of Negroes and whites was roughly equal, and the typical tobacco plantation employed less than twenty slaves. Unlike any of the previously mentioned staples, cotton did not require elaborate stages of preparation and processing, and could be profitably grown on small-scale farms. It was thus not uncommon for a cotton farmer to own less than ten slaves and even to work beside them in the field. Even by 1860, after a long period of rising slave prices, nearly one-half of the Southern slaveholders owned less than five Negroes apiece; 72 per cent owned less than ten apiece and held approximately one-quarter of the entire number of American slaves.

Compared with the plantation agriculture of the West Indies and Brazil, the striking features of the American South were the wide dispersal of slave ownership and the relatively small units of production scattered over immense areas. This may have led to a greater variation and flexibility in the relationship between master and slaves, although we still lack comparative research on such vital questions as labor management, the social roles and subculture of Negroes, and the relation of plantation life to social structure. It seems plausible that if American Negroes sometimes benefited by a close relationship with white families, they were also denied the sense of massive solidarity that was probably essential for revolt. In the West Indies slaves not only had the opportunity to plan and organize revolts, but they were seldom tied by the close bonds of loyalty that led so many North American slaves to divulge plots before they were hardly formed.

This is not to suggest that North American slaves were less oppressed than those of other times and regions, but only that there were different forms of oppression. As comparative studies move ahead toward finer distinctions and a typology of slave systems, it is likely that less attention will be paid to legal status than to stages of economic development. It would be absurd to claim that all slave economies must pass through a pre-set cycle of boom and depression. Nevertheless, regardless of cultural differences and other variables, there are striking examples throughout the Americas of a pattern which began with an un-mitigated drive for quick profit, a rapid expansion in slaves and land under cultivation, and a subsequent overproduction of staples. Whenever slaves were worked under boom conditions, as in the West Indies in the mid-eighteenth century and the Brazilian coffee plantations in the nineteenth, the institution was one of grinding attrition. A more relaxed paternalism tended to appear when prices had fallen, when there was little incentive to maximize production, and when planters in longer-settled regions looked to social and cultural distinctions to differentiate them-selves from new generations of hard-driving speculators. Thus in the mid-nineteenth century there is evidence that in such states as Virginia and Maryland a more easy-going, paternalistic pattern of slavery was emerging, not unlike that of the depleted sugar plantations of Brazil. In Maryland and Delaware there was even a rapid decline in the proportion of slaves to freedmen, though this was partly a result of interstate migration. At the same time there was a heavy drain of slaves toward the expanding cotton areas of the Southwest, where the price of labor kept rising and slaves became more concentrated in the hands of a relatively few planters.

The question of stages of economic development is related to the much larger question of the place of slavery in the evolution of industrial capitalism. And here, though historians have long acknowledged the dependence of the world's cotton textile in-dustry on the slave systems of North and South America, there is an astonishing lack of systematic and comparative analysis. The whole complex relationship between capitalism and slavery is still in the realm of suggestive speculation. Scholars still debate whether slavery was profitable and whether the forms it took in America can be termed capitalistic. We do not yet fully under-stand why so many areas where slavery flourished were stultified by soil depletion and a lack of capital formation, by an absence of internal markets, of urbanization, and of technological innova-tion. And finally, if we are really to comprehend the significance of slavery and the burdens it has entailed, comparative history must explain the great challenge posed to the institution by an emerging urban, bureaucratic, and capitalistic civilization, which led to a bitter conflict between England and her Caribbean colonies, to a sharp struggle between the Brazilian coastal cities and the interior valleys, and to an epic contest between the North and South in the United States.

BIBLIOGRAPHY

The pioneering work in the comparative history of slavery is Frank Tannenbaum, *Slave and Citizen, The Negro in the Americas* (New York, 1947). Stanley M. Elkins, in *Slavery: A Problem in American Institutional and Intellectual Life* (Chicago, 1959), surveys much of the relevant literature and synthesizes the generalizations of Tannenbaum with concepts from the modern behavioral sciences. The Tannenbaum-Elkins thesis regarding the uniqueness of slavery in North America is challenged by Arnold A. Sio, "Interpretations of Slavery: The Slave Status in the Americas," in *Comparative Studies in Society and History*, VII (April 1965), 289–308; and by my own *The Problem of Slavery in Western Culture* (Ithaca, N.Y., 1966), which also analyzes attitudes toward slavery from antiquity to the early American abolitionists.

The most comprehensive study of North American slavery is still Ulrich B. Phillips, *American Negro Slavery* (New York, 1918), which needs to be supplemented by Kenneth M. Stampp, *The Peculiar Institution: Slavery in the Ante-Bellum South* (New York, 1956). John Hope Franklin, *From Slavery to Freedom* (2nd ed.; New York, 1956), offers a general survey of the Negro in America.

More specialized studies which shed light on important aspects of American slavery are Eugene D. Genovese, *The Political Economy of Slavery* (New York, 1965); Richard C. Wade, *Slavery in the Cities: The South 1820–1860* (New York, 1964); Eric Williams, *Capitalism and Slavery* (New York, 1944); and Leon F. Litwack, *North of Slavery: The Negro in the Free States* (Chicago, 1961). The debate over the profitability of slave labor is summarized by Harold D. Woodman, "The Profitability of Slavery: A Historical Perennial," *Journal of Southern History*, XXIX (August 1963), 303–325.

Elsa V. Goveia, in *Slave Society in the British Leeward Islands at the End of the Eighteenth Century* (New Haven, 1965), presents a detailed study of West Indian slavery. Negro bondage in the French colonies is described by Gaston Martin, *Histoire de l'esclavage dans les colonies françaises* (Paris, 1948) and Lucien Peytraud, *L'Esclavage aux Antilles françaises avant 1789* (Paris, 1897). For other valuable material on slavery in the New World, the student should consult J. Harry Bennett, Jr., *Bondsmen and Bishops: Slavery and Apprenticeship on the Codrington Plantation of Barbados* (Berkeley, 1958); Frank Wesley Pitman, *The Development of the British West Indies, 1700–1763* (New Haven, 1917); Lowell Joseph Ragatz, *The Fall of the Planter Class in the British Caribbean, 1763–1833* (New York, 1928); Gilberto Freyre, *The Masters and the Slaves: A Study in the Development of Brazilian Civilization* (New York, 1946); Arthur Ramos, *The Negro in Brazil* (Washington, 1951); Stanley J. Stein, *Vassouras: A Brazilian Coffee County* (Cambridge, Mass., 1957); C. R. Boxer, *Race Relations in the Portuguese Colonial Empire, 1415–1825* (Oxford, 1963), and *The Golden Age of Brazil, 1695–1750* (Berkeley, 1962).

The best survey of the slave trade is Basil Davidson, *Black Mother: The Years of the African Slave Trade* (Boston, 1961). The monumental work on slavery in medieval Europe is Charles Verlinden, *L'Esclavage dans l'Europe médiévale* (Brugge, 1955). While one cannot begin to indicate the vast literature on slavery in various societies, three titles which should not go unmentioned are William L. Westermann, *The Slave Systems of Greek and Roman Antiquity* (Philadelphia, 1955); Isaac Mendelsohn, *Slavery in the Ancient Near East* (New York, 1949); and Moses I. Finley (ed.), *Slavery in Classical Antiquity: Views and Controversies* (Cambridge, England, 1960). Finally, one should note that the volumes of the *Journal of Negro History* contain a mine of information for anyone interested in slavery in the Western Hemisphere.

Slavery in Brazil and the United States:
An Essay in Comparative History

CARL N. DEGLER

OVER twenty years ago Frank Tannenbaum made a comparison of slavery in the societies of the New World in which he argued that the differences in contemporary race relations between the United States and Latin America are to be traced to differences in the character of slavery in the two places. A decade later Stanley Elkins built a provocative book upon Tannenbaum's conclusions. More recently, Arnold Sio and David Brion Davis entered strong demurrers to the Tannenbaum-Elkins conclusions by arguing that slavery as an institution was more similar than different throughout the societies of the New World.[1]

These and a number of other writings on the comparative history of slavery in the Western Hemisphere attest to a burgeoning scholarly interest. But throughout the debate one of the prominent difficulties has been the great breadth and diversity of the areas being compared. To make convincing comparisons among some two dozen societies presents obvious problems and is open to the dangers of superficiality. It is the intention here, therefore, to draw a much more restricted comparison, not because the large problem that Tannenbaum raised will finally be resolved by such a limited approach, but simply because two countries are more manageable as variables than two continents. It is also worth noting that Brazil and the United States have the advantage of being the two most important slave societies in the New World. Both had a long history of slavery—only Cuba and Brazil retained slavery longer than the United States—and in both societies slavery occupied an important, if not actually a central, place in the economy.[2]

► Mr. Degler, professor of history at Stanford University and a specialist in the social history of the United States, received his Ph.D. in 1952 from Columbia University, where he worked under John A. Krout and Richard B. Morris. He is the author of Out of our Past: The Forces that Shaped Modern America, published first in 1959 and in a revised edition in 1970. The present article is part of a larger study of race relations and slavery in the United States and Brazil. In somewhat different form it was presented as a paper at the meeting of the Organization of American Historians in Philadelphia in April, 1969. Mr. Degler wishes to thank Eugene D. Genovese, Richard M. Morse, and Herbert S. Klein, who were commentators on that occasion, for their criticisms.

[1] The books and articles referred to are: Frank Tannenbaum, *Slave and Citizen: The Negro in the Americas* (New York, 1947); Stanley Elkins, *Slavery: A Problem in American Institutional and Intellectual Life* (2d ed., Chicago, 1969), the text of which is identical with the first edition of 1959 except for an added appendix; Arnold Sio, "Interpretations of Slavery: The Slave States in the Americas," *Comparative Studies in Society and History*, VII (Apr. 1965), 289–308; and David Brion Davis, *The Problem of Slavery in Western Culture* (Ithaca, N. Y., 1966).

[2] It has sometimes been said that the diversity of the crops and topography of Brazil resulted in a diversity of slavery that makes it difficult if not impossible to generalize about the institution in

1004

Essentially this essay seeks to answer two quite limited questions: First, in what respects were the systems of slavery in Brazil and the United States alike during their mature years—that is, during the nineteenth century—and in what ways did they differ? Second, to what extent are these differences related to the laws and practices of the state and the Church in Brazil, as both Tannenbaum and Elkins have contended? Even if these questions can be answered with some degree of certainty, it should be said that the large question that Tannenbaum raised and sought to answer in his book will not be settled. But I hope that the ground will be cleared for a new attack upon the problem.

How were the two systems of slavery alike? Tannenbaum and Elkins stress the different legal conceptions of the slave in the United States and in Latin America. Tannenbaum, for example, contrasts the definition of a slave as a chattel in the United States with the more ambiguous definition in Latin America.

In fact, *the element of human personality was not lost in the transition to slavery from Africa to the Spanish or Portuguese dominions.* He [the Negro] remained a person even while he was a slave. . . . He was never considered a mere chattel, never defined as unanimated property, and never under the law treated as such. His master never enjoyed the powers of life and death over his body, even though abuses existed and cruelties were performed.[3]

Yet an examination of Brazilian and United States law reveals striking similarities in the definition of a slave.

The law in both the United States and Brazil, for example, recognized that a slave was both a human being and a piece of property. As a Tennessee court in 1846 put it,

---

that country. It is true that slavery in the northeastern sugar regions was different in style from that practiced in Maranhão on the cotton and rice plantations. Writers on Brazilian history have noted, furthermore, that slavery was much harsher in a newly opened province like Maranhão than in the old and declining sugar areas in the northeast. (See Gilberto Freyre, *Nordeste* [Rio de Janeiro, 1937], 219; and Henry Koster, *Travels in Brazil* [2 vols., 2d ed., London, 1817], II, 292.) But the diversity of crops and terrain and the differences in "styles" of slavery that resulted are well recognized in the United States; the slavery on tobacco farms in Virginia, for example, is often contrasted with the kind of slavery on sugar or cotton plantations in Louisiana. In the United States, moreover, the threat to sell a slave "down the river" reflected a recognition that planters in the newer areas of the Deep South tended to work slaves harder than in the older regions where slavery was more firmly established. Despite their recognitions of regional diversity, however, historians of slavery in the United States have not been prevented from generalizing about the institution; hence, it would seem to be equally legitimate to ignore the regional differences in Brazilian slavery so long as an effort is made to draw evidence from most of the principal slave areas of the country. The regional differences are certainly there in both societies, but they are refinements rather than essentials. One further statement on the problems of comparison: although the literature on slavery in the United States is voluminous, there being a monograph for virtually every southern slave state, the literature on Brazilian slavery is uneven. For some important slave regions like Maranhão and Minas Gerais, for example, there are no monographic studies on slavery at all; scattered references in travel accounts and general histories must be relied upon. On the other hand, for other areas, like the coffee country to the south, two excellent, recently written monographs are available: Stanley Stein, *Vassouras: A Brazilian Coffee County, 1850–1900* (Cambridge, Mass., 1957); and Emília Viotti da Costa, *Da Senzala à Colônia* (São Paulo, 1966). Of immense importance for its historiographical impact, if nothing else, is the impressionistic, virtuoso performance of Gilberto Freyre, *The Masters and the Slaves* (New York, 1946), which deals primarily with domestic slavery in northeastern Brazil though it purports to speak of slavery in general.

[3] Tannenbaum, *Slave and Citizen*, 97–98, 103.

45

A slave is not in the condition of a horse, he is made after the image of the creator. He has mental capacities and an immortal principle in his nature, that constitute him equal to his owner but for the accidental position in which fortune has placed him . . . the laws . . . cannot extinguish his high born nature, nor deprive him of many rights which are inherent in man. . . .[4]

In 1818 a Mississippi court went so far as to observe that "Slavery is condemned by reason and the laws of nature. It exists and can only exist through municipal regulations, and in matters of doubt" the courts must lean in favor of freedom.[5] As late as 1861 an Alabama court concluded that because slaves "are rational beings, they are capable of committing crimes; and in reference to acts which are crimes, are regarded as persons. Because they are slaves, they are . . . incapable of performing civil acts, and, in reference to all such, they are things, not persons."[6]

That last statement is close, in phraseology as well as meaning, to that set forth in Brazilian slave law by its principal authority, Agostino Marques Perdigão Malheiro. "In regard to the penal code," he wrote, "the slave, as subject of the offense or agent of it, is not a *thing,* he is a *person* . . . he is a human entity." Hence he is held personally responsible for crimes. But when he is an "Object or sufferer of a crime" the matter is different. The slave is not indemnified for such injuries, though the master may be. "In the latter case the question is one of *property,* but in the other it is one of *personality.*" Perdigão Malheiro makes clear, moreover, that the position of the slave in court was not much different from that of the slave in the United States. No slave in Brazil could enter a complaint himself; it had to be done by his master or by the public authority. Nor could a slave make an accusation against his master. In fact, a slave could not give sworn testimony, only information. Perdigão Malheiro writes that in only three circumstances did a slave have standing in court: in regard to spiritual matters, such as marriage; in regard to his liberty; and in matters of obvious public concern. Only in regard to the first did the legal position of the slave in the United States differ; slave marriages had no legal basis in the United States.[7]

If there was little difference in the conception of the slave in Brazilian and United States law, there was also little difference in the law's supposed protection of the slave's humanity. Despite the general statements of some scholars,[8] both societies had laws protecting the slave against murder, mistreatment, or overwork by his master.[9] The operative question is whether the law or the

---

[4] *Judicial Cases concerning Slavery and the Negro,* ed. Helen T. Catterall (5 vols., Washington, D. C., 1926) II, 530.

[5] Charles Sackett Sydnor, *Slavery in Mississippi* (New York, 1933), 239.

[6] *Judicial Cases concerning Slavery and the Negro,* ed. Catterall, III, 247.

[7] Agostino Marques Perdigão Malheiro, *A Escravidão no Brasil: Ensaio Historico-Juridico-Social* (reprint of 1867 ed., 2 vols., São Paulo, 1944), I, 39–40, 34–45, 67.

[8] See, e.g., Tannenbaum, *Slave and Citizen,* 93.

[9] Kenneth M. Stampp, *The Peculiar Institution: Slavery in the Ante-bellum South* (New York, 1956), 192, summarizes the situation in the United States as follows: "The law required that masters be humane to their slaves, furnish them adequate food and clothing, and provide care for them during sickness and old age. In short, the state endowed masters with obligations as well as rights

church in fact interceded between the master and the slave in behalf of the latter. Certainly for the United States the evidence is not convincing. And in Brazil, too, the power of the state or the church to affect the life of the slave seems to have been limited. As Henry Koster, an English planter in Brazil, pointed out early in the nineteenth century, the Brazilian government was a weak reed on which to lean for anything, much less for control over members of the ruling slaveholding class. He tells, for example, of an instance in which one of his own slaves injured the slave of another man, but says that nothing was done about the matter. The owner of the injured slave might have pressed charges, if he so chose, "but the law of itself seldom does anything. Even in the cases of murder the prosecutor . . . has it at his option to bring the trial forward or not; if he can be bribed or otherwise persuaded to give up the accusation, the matter drops to the ground." It is not likely that the state, which was run by slaveholders, would be more energetic in protecting the slave's humanity. Koster writes that occasionally a cruel master was fined for maltreating his slaves, "but," he adds, "I never heard of punishment having been carried farther than this trifling manner of correction."[10] Later in the century another traveler, the German painter John Rugendas, put the matter even more directly. Although there were laws in Brazil limiting the use of the whip and fixing the number of lashes at one time, he wrote in 1835:

these laws have no force and probably may be unknown to the majority of the slaves and masters; on the other hand, the authorities are so removed that in actuality the punishment of the slave for a true or imaginary infraction or the bad treatment resulting from the caprice and the cruelty of the master, only encounters limits in the fear of losing the slave by death, by flight, or as a consequence of public opinion. But these considerations are never sufficient to impede the evil and it is inescapable that examples of cruelty are not lacking, which result in the mutilation and death of slaves.[11]

It is only toward the end of the era of slavery, when the abolitionists brought cases of mistreatment to court, that Brazilian laws in behalf of the slaves actually protected them.

Both Elkins and Tannenbaum emphasize the role of the Roman Catholic Church in giving the Negro slave in Latin America a higher "moral" position than in the United States.[12] If that means that the Church accepted Negro slaves as members, the churches of the United States did, too. If it means that the

---

and assumed some responsibility for the welfare of the bondsmen." For elaboration of the obligations laid down by law, see *ibid.*, 218–24.

[10] Koster, *Travels in Brazil*, I, 375–76; II, 237; Da Costa, *Da Senzala*, 295–96. Charles Expilly, a French traveler in Brazil in the 1860's, conceded that in the big cities like Rio a slave might occasionally be able to get to the police to complain of bad treatment, but, away from the cities, it was quite different. There, Expilly wrote, the power of the master was like that of "a feudal baron, who exercises in his dominion the highest and the lowest justice." There were no appeals from his sentences. "No guarantee is conceded to the slave." (Charles Expilly, *Mulheres e costumes do Brasil*, tr. Gastão Penalva [São Paulo, 1935], 361.)

[11] João Mauricio Rugendas, *Viagem pitoresca através do Brasil*, tr. Sergio Milliet (3d ed., São Paulo, 1941.) 185.

[12] Tannenbaum, *Slave and Citizen*, 62–64, 98; Elkins, *Slavery*, 73, 76–77.

Church actively intervened between master and slave in behalf of the latter, then it must be said that in Brazil the interest of the Church in and its power to protect the slave's humanity were as limited as those of the state. For one thing, few plantations had resident priests; most plantations saw a priest only once a year when he came to legalize unions and to baptize. There were not, in fact, enough priests in the country to affect the daily life of the slave, even if they had the interest to do so. As Emilia Viotti da Costa points out, not until 1885 did the archbishop of Bahia rule that no master could prevent a slave from marrying or sell him away from his spouse. Yet even at that late date, a slave could marry against his master's will only if the slave could demonstrate that he knew Christian doctrine—the Lord's Prayer, the Ave Maria, the Creed, and the commandments—understood the obligations of holy matrimony, and was clear in his intention to remain married for life. Furthermore, as in the United States, religion in Brazil was used by churchmen to buttress slavery. One priest told a group of planters: "Confession is the antidote to insurrections, because the confessor makes the slave see that his master is in the place of his father to whom he owes love, respect, and obedience. . . ."[13]

In 1887, on the eve of abolition in Brazil, the abolitionist Anselmo Fonseca wrote a long book castigating the Brazilian Catholic clergy for its lack of interest in the then highly active abolitionist movement in his country. Caustically he observed that in 1871 when Rio Branco fought for the Law of the Free Womb of slave mothers, the Church was silent, for slavery "still had much vitality. . . . It was dangerous to take it on frontally. Why did not the Bishops then show the solidarity and courage and the energy with which in 1873–74 they combated Masonry and the government?" Fonseca draws the interesting contrast between the massive indifference to the plight of the slave on the part of the Brazilian Catholic Church throughout the history of slavery and the activities of Protestant clergymen like William Ellery Channing in behalf of the slave in the United States.[14]

Slave marriages were valid in the eyes of the Brazilian Church; marriages of slaves in Protestant churches in the United States also qualified as sacramental acts, though masters, it was understood, were not bound to honor such unions. Given the weakness of the Church's control over slave masters, it is not likely that marriages of slaves in Brazil were any more enduring or protected from disruption through sale than in the United States. In any event, in Brazil only a small proportion of slaves were married by the Church. Early in the nineteenth century the reformer José Bonifacio asked for laws to compel masters to permit slaves to marry freely and to require that at least two-thirds of a master's slaves be married. Yet, forty years later, travelers still reported that few Negroes

[13] Da Costa, *Da Senzala*, 250, 271, 249.
[14] Luis Anselmo Fonseca, *A Escravidão, O clero e O abolicionismo* (Bahia, 1887), 440–41, 1–27. The references to Channing are on pages 12–15.

were married and that "rarely were [marriages] confirmed by a religious act." A traveler in 1841 found only 10 slaves married out of 2,500 on the Isle of Santa Catherina in southern Brazil. In northeastern Brazil, in Rio Grande do Norte, a local document listed only about 5 per cent of the 13,000 slaves in the province in 1874 as married or widowed, though 30 per cent of free persons were married. Of the 660,000 slaves in all of Brazil in 1875, who were 14 years or older, only about 1 out of 6 was recorded as married or widowed.[15]

In the United States the lack of protection for the informal slave family is acknowledged as a fact of slave life. Tannenbaum has summarized it well: "Under the law of most of the Southern states there was no regard for the Negro family, no question of the right of the owner to sell his slaves separately, and no limitation upon separating husband and wife, or child from its mother."[16]

Yet, for most of the nineteenth century, the same generalization is quite accurate for Brazil. Prior to 1869 there was no legal protection for the slave family, though, as was the case in the United States, a vigorous internal slave trade was a powerful cause for the breaking up of many families, whether their ties had been solemnized by the Church or not. The internal slave trade in Brazil was especially active in the middle years of the nineteenth century when the coffee areas in the South were expanding and thousands of slaves were brought down from the economically declining Northeast. One estimate in 1862 put at five thousand per year the number arriving from the North at Rio de Janeiro by coastal shipping alone. A modern authority has cited thirty thousand a year as the number that went from the North to the state of São Paulo between 1850 and 1870.[17]

There is little doubt that the disruption of the slave family was common in Brazil at least prior to 1869. Indeed, to take an extreme example, one of the great Brazilian abolitionists, Luis Gama, was sold into slavery by his own white father. Stanley Stein reports that in the 1870's it was not unknown in Vassouras for a planter to sell his mulatto offspring to a passing slave trader.[18] A law passed in 1875, prohibiting the sale of one's own children, suggests that such a practice was known even at that late date.[19] Another sign that the slave family was disintegrating throughout the nineteenth century, at least, is that antislavery reformers like Bonifacio in the early nineteenth century and others as late as 1862

[15] *Ibid.*, 268; Fernando Henrique Cardoso and Octávio Ianni, *Côr e mobilidade social em Florianapolis* (São Paulo, 1960), 128–29; Robert Edgar Conrad, "The Struggle for the Abolition of the Brazilian Slave Trade, 1808–1853," doctoral dissertation, Columbia University, 1967, 55–56.
[16] Tannenbaum, *Slave and Citizen*, 77.
[17] W. D. Christie, *Notes on Brazilian Questions* (London, 1865), 93; Pedro Calmon, *História social do Brasil* (São Paulo, 1937), 151. Roberto Simonsen, "As Consequências economica da abolição," *Revista do Arquivo Municipal de São Paulo*, XLVII (May, 1938), 261, says that in 1888 over two-thirds of the slaves in the Empire were in the provinces of Rio, Minas Gerais, São Paulo, and those to the south. I am indebted to Professor Richard Graham of the University of Utah for this reference.
[18] Stein, *Vassouras*, 159.
[19] Richard M. Morse, *From Community to Metropolis: A Biography of São Paulo, Brazil* (Gainesville, Fla., 1958), 146; Magnus Mörner, *Race Mixture in the History of Latin America* (Boston, 1967), 117.

were demanding that ways be found to protect the slave family.[20] In 1854 Baron
Cotegipe, who was later to oppose abolition, argued for limitations on the internal slave trade because it disrupted families. "It is a horror, gentlemen," he told
the Senate, "to see children ripped from their mothers, husbands separated from
wives, parents from children! Go to Law Street . . . and be outraged and
touched by the spectacle of such sufferings. . . ." In 1866 Perdigão Malheiro was
still asking that the law prevent the separation of married slave couples and
children of less than seven years of age. Without such legal protection, he contended, there was little reason to expect the slave family to exist at all.[21]

The fact is that in Brazil prior to 1869 there was no law preventing the
disruption of slave families. And even the law passed in 1869 required some
nine years of agitation before it was enacted.[22] Most slave states in the US, as
Tannenbaum has pointed out, never enacted such laws, but a few did. A law of
1829 in Louisiana prohibited the sale of children under ten; apparently it was
adhered to by slave traders. Laws in Alabama and Georgia forbade the dissolution of inherited slave families, but not others. In practice, probably most planters
in the United States tried to avoid breaking up slave families, though undoubtedly many were disrupted.[23]

Perhaps the most frequently stressed difference between slavery in Latin
America and the United States concerns manumission. Yet, even here, as Davis
has pointed out, manumission in Brazil was not unlimited, and in the US it
was not absolutely denied.[24] The purchase of freedom by the slave himself, so
much emphasized in discussions on Brazilian slavery, was, moreover, far from
rare in the United States. Sumner Matison, for example, found several hundred
examples of self-purchase. Luther Jackson, studying self-purchase in three cities
of Virginia, found twenty examples even at the height of the sectional conflict of
the 1850's and despite a law requiring removal of manumitted slaves out of the
state.[25]

On the Brazilian side of the comparison it must be said that prior to 1871,
despite tradition and the assertions of Tannenbaum and Elkins,[26] there was no
law requiring a master to permit a slave to buy his freedom. One American
historian of Brazil made a search for such a law, but found none before 1871,
when emancipationists insisted upon it; this suggests that the practice of self-

[20] Arthur Ramos, *The Negro in Brazil*, tr. Richard Pattee (Washington, D. C., 1939), 58–59.
[21] Maurilio de Gouveia, *História da escravidão* (Rio de Janeiro, 1955), 134; Perdigão Malheiro, *A Escravidão no Brasil*, II, 223.
[22] Da Costa, *Da Senzala*, 271, 385. The law prohibited selling children under fifteen away from their parents. The so-called Law of the Free Womb of 1871, however, lowered the age to twelve.
[23] Joe Gray Taylor, *Negro Slavery in Louisiana* (Baton Rouge, La., 1963), 40–41; Stampp, *Peculiar Institution*, 252, 239–41; Edward W. Phifer, "Slavery in Microcosm: Burke County, North Carolina," *Journal of Southern History*, XXVIII (May 1962), 48.
[24] Davis, *Problem of Slavery*, 262–64.
[25] Sumner E. Matison, "Manumission by Purchase," *Journal of Negro History*, XXXIII (Apr. 1948), 165; Luther P. Jackson, "Manumission in Certain Virginia Cities," *ibid.*, XV (July 1930), 306.
[26] Tannenbaum, *Slave and Citizen*, 54; Elkins, *Slavery*, 75.

purchase was not as firmly protected as has been alleged.[27] It is true that in Brazilian law there were none of the limitations that became increasingly common in the southern United States after 1830. Under Brazilian law emancipation was legal in almost any form: by letter, by will, or by explicit statement at baptism.[28] In Brazil, moreover, there were no statutes requiring the removal of emancipated slaves to other states, though such laws were characteristic of the southern United States. But Brazilian law contained a curious qualification to its otherwise liberal policy on emancipation: freedom might be revoked by the master for ingratitude on the part of the freedman, even if that ingratitude was expressed only orally and outside of the presence of the former master. Perdigão Malheiro, who reports this provision of the law, doubted that it was still valid in 1866. In 1871 the power to revoke freedom was explicitly withdrawn in an anti-slavery law, suggesting that the old provision was not such a dead letter that opponents of slavery were willing to let it remain on the statute books.[29] The provision also raises a question as to whether the law in Brazil was in fact helping to preserve the Negro's moral personality as some modern historians have argued. At the very least it encouraged masters to think of their Negroes as minors or wards rather than as persons on an equal footing. At worst, it perpetuated in the Negro that sense of subordination and inferiority derived from the degraded status of slavery, thereby counteracting whatever elevating effects might flow from the relative ease of manumission.

Some modern historians, like Tannenbaum and Elkins,[30] have emphasized the slave's right to hold property in Latin America and therefore to be in a position to buy his freedom, as contrasted with the lack of that right in the US. In Brazil, however, the law did not permit slaves to possess property, or a peculium, until near the end of the era of slavery. Perdigão Malheiro writes in his treatise on slave law that, as late as 1866, "Among us, no law guarantees to the slave his peculium; nor the disposition overall by the last will, nor the succession. . . ." However, he goes on, most masters tolerated the slave's holding property, generally permitting the slave to use it as he saw fit.[31] The same situation prevailed, by and large, in the United States, where slave property was neither recognized nor protected by law, but in practice was generally recognized by the master. Occasionally the courts would throw a protective arm around the peculium, as in a South Carolina case in 1792, when a slave was held capable of

[27] Mary Wilhelmine Williams, "The Treatment of Negro Slaves in the Brazilian Empire: A Comparison with the United States of America," *Journal of Negro History*, XV (July 1930), 331.
[28] Perdigão Malheiro, *A Escravidão no Brasil*, I, 95.
[29] *Ibid.*, 167–68; Gouveia, *História da escravidão*, 396. The Code Noir of Louisiana, which also had liberal provisions for manumission, contained the following restrictions: "We command all manumitted slaves to show the profoundest respect to their former masters, to their widows and children, and any injury or insult offered by said manumitted slaves to their former master, their widows or children, shall be punished with more severity than if it had been offered by any other person." (Quoted in Taylor, *Negro Slavery in Louisiana*, 16.)
[30] Tannenbaum, *Slave and Citizen*, 54; Elkins, *Slavery*, 246.
[31] Perdigão Malheiro, *A Escravidão no Brasil*, I, 60.

holding property separate from that of his master. On the basis of that case, a half century later, Judge J. B. O'Neall of South Carolina concluded that "by the law of this state a slave might acquire personal property."[32]

Yet, after all these qualifications have been made in the usually optimistic picture of manumission under Brazilian slavery, Brazil still appears to have been more liberal on manumission than was the US. And the principal reason for this conclusion is the higher proportion of free Negroes in Brazil than in the United States. Because of the paucity of adequate figures for both countries, a quantitative comparison can be made only for the nineteenth century. In 1817–1818 the number of slaves in Brazil was about three times that of free Negroes and mulattoes.[33] This ratio may be compared with that in the United States in 1860, when the number of free Negroes reached its maximum under slavery. At that date there were eight times as many slaves as free Negroes in the whole of the United States and sixteen times as many slaves if the comparison is made in the slave states only. As slavery came to an end in Brazil the number of free Negroes grew enormously, so that in 1872 the number of free Negroes and colored was more than double that of the slaves.[34]

Although it is not the intention of this essay to explain this difference in attitude toward manumission, if only because of the complexity of the issue, at least two suggestions are worth brief examination. One of these is that Brazilian masters were freeing the sick and the old in order to relieve themselves of responsibility and cost. Denunciations in newspapers and laws prohibiting such practices indicate that masters were indeed freeing their infirm, aged, and incurable slaves.[35] Yet it is difficult to believe that such practices, however widespread they appear to be, could have been the principal source of the relatively large free colored population. Infirm, aged, or sick slaves simply would not have been numerous enough or have been able to produce offspring in sufficient numbers to account for the great number of free colored.

Marvin Harris has advanced a more reasonable explanation, in which he emphasizes the differences in the processes of settlement and economic development in Brazil and the United States.[36] In Brazil a freed Negro or mulatto had a place in a society that was only sparsely populated and in a slave economy that was focused upon staple production. Free blacks and mulattoes were needed in the economy to produce food, to serve as slave catchers, militiamen, shopkeepers, craftsmen, artisans, and so forth. They filled the many petty jobs and performed the "interstitial" work of the economy that slave labor could not easily

---

[32] *Judicial Cases concerning Slavery and the Negro*, ed. Catterall, II, 267, 275, n.

[33] Agostinho Marques Perdigão Malheiro, *A Escravidão no Brasil: ensaio historico-juridico-social* (Rio de Janeiro, 1866), Pt. 3, 13–14.

[34] Raymond Sayers, *Negro in Brazilian Literature* (New York, 1956), 7.

[35] Da Costa, *Da Senzala*, 262–63; Stein, *Vassouras*, 79, n; see also the report of the British minister, August 1852, quoting the effort by the president of the province of Bahia to have the practice stopped by law. The report is given in Christie, *Notes on Brazilian Questions*, 218–19.

[36] Marvin Harris, *Patterns of Race in the Americas* (New York, 1964), 84–89.

perform and that white labor was insufficient to man. Octavio Ianni; writing about slavery in southern Brazil, and Nelson de Senna, describing conditions in Minas Gerais, emphasize the great variety of occupations filled by free Negroes and mulattoes.[37]

In the southern United States many plantations also allocated their labor in this fashion, that is, by importing food rather than growing it. But the food was produced by a large number of nonslaveholding whites in the South and the Northwest. Virtually from the beginning of settlement in the South there had been more than enough whites to perform all the tasks of the society except that of compulsory labor. In fact, throughout the ante bellum years, as later, the South exported whites to the rest of the nation. Hence, in the US there was no compelling economic reason for emancipation; nor, more importantly, was there any economic place for those who were manumitted. But this demographic or materialist interpretation is not the complete explanation, suggestive as it is. As we shall see later, the relative ease of manumission in Brazil was part of a larger and deeper difference in attitudes between the two societies.

Comparisons between slavery in Brazil and the United States traditionally emphasize the greater rebelliousness of slaves in Brazil. But here, too, the distinction, when examined closely, is not as sharp as has frequently been alleged. The most often mentioned measure of the greater rebelliousness of Brazilian slaves is the large slave hideaway or *quilombo* of Palmares in northeastern Brazil, which, during the seventeenth century, resisted the attacks of government and other troops for more than fifty years. Examples of other *quilombos,* less spectacular or famous than Palmares, are also well documented.[38] It is questionable, however, whether such groups of runaways, no matter how long lived or large scale, ought to be classed as slave rebellions. Generally the *quilombos* neither attempted to overthrow the slave system nor made war on it, except when whites sought to destroy them. Even Palmares would have been content to remain as an African state separate from white society if the government and the *paulistas* had left it alone.[39] Thus, if one is counting armed uprisings against slaveholders, such as took place under Nat Turner in Virginia in 1831, then the total number in Brazil is considerably smaller if one excludes the *quilombos.* For in Brazil, as in the United States, the most common expression of slave unrest was the runaway, not the insurrectionist.

[37] Octávio Ianni, *As Metamorfoses do escravo* (São Paulo, 1962), 175; Nelson de Senna, *Africanos no Brasil* (Bello Horizonte, Brazil, 1938), 62. Caio Prado Junior, *História economica do Brasil* (10th ed., n.p., n.d.), 45, asserts that cattle raising in the *sertão* of the northeast required free men rather than slaves.

[38] The fullest and most recent account of Palmares in English is R. K. Kent, "Palmares: An African State in Brazil," *Journal of African History,* VI (No. 2, 1965), 161–75. As his title suggests, Kent argues (pp. 163–64) against depicting Palmares as merely a *quilombo,* but that issue is not important in this discussion. Clovis Moura, *Rebeliões da senzala* (São Paulo, 1959), contains a number of accounts of *quilombos* aside from Palmares.

[39] See Edison Carneiro, *Ladinos e Crioulos (Estudos sôbre o negro no Brasil)* (Rio de Janeiro, 1964), 30–32, for a statement on this point by an authority on Palmares and *quilombos* in general.

Rumors of revolts were common in both countries, but, except during the last years of slavery and with the exception of a series of revolts in Bahia in the early nineteenth century, slave revolts in Brazil were scattered, and in some areas almost nonexistent. Koster, the English planter, wrote in the early nineteenth century that "Pernambuco has never experienced any serious revolt among the slaves." Modern historians of the coffee region point out that neither slave revolts nor *quilombos* were on anything but a small scale. Da Costa speaks of revolts as "rare in the coffee regions." F. H. Cardoso also found little opportunity for, or evidence of, slave revolts in Rio Grande do Sul. Girão writes that in Ceará Province in the early nineteenth century "fugitives were not common and rebellions very rare." Octavio Eduardo reports that "no series of revolts occurred in Maranhão as they did in Bahia, although the revolt of the Balaios from 1838 to 1841" attracted runaway slaves to the cause.[40]

On the other hand, general works on slave rebellions in Brazil as a whole emphasize their importance, and a recent study of the sugar areas in São Paulo Province refers to the large number of slave rebellions there.[41] In short, much work remains to be done on the extent and character of slave unrest in Brazil, and it seems safe to say that most of the writing on slave rebellions has not been careful to distinguish between military outbreaks and runaways or between those uprisings striking at the slave system directly and those simply fleeing from it, as, for example, has been done for American slave revolts by Marion Kilson.[42]

In the broadest sense, of course, both slave rebellions and runaways threatened the slave system, for they constituted avenues by which some slaves could escape from the system and raised the expectations of those who remained behind. In this regard, Brazilian slaves had somewhat greater opportunities for escape than had slaves in the United States. Actual revolts may not have been much more numerous in Brazil, but the numbers of slaves involved in those that did take place were greater, just as the size of the *quilombos* were larger than those in the United States. Stein described a revolt in Vassouras, for example, that mobilized three hundred slaves and required federal troops to suppress it. At least two revolts involving several hundred slaves were reported in 1820 in Minas Gerais. In the first half of the nineteenth century in the province of Espírito Santo, uprisings of two hundred and four hundred slaves occurred, though it is not clear whether these were revolts or collective runaways.[43]

[40] Koster, *Travels in Brazil*, II, 258; *Relações raciais entre negros e brancos em São Paulo*, ed. Roger Bastide (São Paulo, 1955), 199; Da Costa, *Da Senzala*, 300–301, 315; Fernando Henrique Cardoso, *Capitalismo e escravidão no Brasil meridional* (São Paulo, 1962), 159–60; Raimundo Girão, *A Abolição no Ceará* (Forteleza, Brazil, 1956), 42; Aderbal Jurema, *Insurreições negras no Brasil* (Recife, Brazil, 1935), 53–55; Maura, *Rebeliões da senzala*, 65–66; Octavio da Costa Eduardo, *The Negro in Northern Brazil* (New York, 1948), 18.

[41] See, e.g., Jurema, *Insurreições negras no Brasil*; Maura, *Rebeliões da senzala*; and Maria Thereza Schorer Petrone, *A Lavoura canavieira em São Paulo* (São Paulo, 1968), 121–25. Professor Graham brought the last reference to my attention.

[42] Marion D. de B. Kilson, "Towards Freedom: An Analysis of Slave Revolts in the United States," *Phylon*, XXV (2d Quar., 1964), 175–87.

[43] Da Costa, *Da Senzala*, 304; Maria Stella de Novaes, *A Escravidão e abolição no Espírito Santo* (Vitória, Brazil, 1963), 77.

The really striking examples of undoubted slave insurrections are the half dozen that erupted in and around the city of Bahia between 1807 and 1835, several of which involved pitched battles between armed slaves and government troops. It is significant that these rebellions occurred in the city, not in the plantation region. They are, moreover, among the few that can be confidently classified as violent attacks upon whites and the slave system rather than as flights to a *quilombo*.[44] But, in the history of Brazilian slavery, the Bahian revolts were unusual and, as we shall see, the consequence of special circumstances.

There were true slave revolts in the US, too, though they were fewer and generally much smaller in number of participants than in Brazil. Of the three biggest and best-known uprisings, those at Stono, South Carolina, in 1739, New Orleans in 1811, and Southampton, Virginia, in 1831, only the second involved more than one hundred slaves. The *quilombos* in the United States were considerably fewer and smaller in size than those in Brazil.[45] The climate in the US was largely responsible for the smaller number of maroons, or *quilombos*. In most of the United States the winter is simply too harsh for a *quilombo* to survive for very long, whereas the greater part of Brazil lies in the tropics. The frontier area in the United States was, moreover, too well settled and, accordingly, too well policed, especially after the seventeenth century, to provide many opportunities for colonies of runaways. The only example of a *quilombo* approaching the size and endurance of Palmares was the Second Seminole War, during which Indians and runaway blacks held out against the US Army for seven years.[46] It is significant that the struggle took place in the warmest part of the United States and in an area unsettled by whites.

Another difference between the two slave societies was the dependence of the Brazilians upon the African slave trade. Although the foreign slave trade in Brazil was supposedly ended in 1831 by treaty with Great Britain, all authorities agree that importations of slaves continued at high annual rates for another twenty years. Over 300,000 slaves entered Brazil between 1842 and 1851 alone, bringing the total number of slaves in the country to 2,500,000 in 1850, probably the highest figure ever reached.[47] There is also general agreement that the importation of large numbers of slaves into the United States ceased in 1807, with the federal prohibition of the foreign trade. Actually, every one of the slave states themselves had prohibited importation prior to 1800. Only South Carolina

---

[44] Ramos, *Negro in Brazil*, 34–37. The basic source for the revolts in Bahia is Raymundo Nina Rodrigues, *Os Africanos no Brasil* (2d ed., São Paulo, 1935), Chap. II, but Raymond Kent will soon publish a thorough examination of the revolt of 1835, a copy of which he has kindly permitted me to read in typescript.

[45] Herbert Aptheker, *American Negro Slave Revolts* (New York, 1943), *passim*, and Herbert Aptheker, "Maroons Within the Present Limits of the United States," *Journal of Negro History*, XXIV (April, 1939), 167–84.

[46] See Kenneth W. Porter, "Negroes and the Seminole War, 1835–1842," *Journal of Southern History*, XXX (Nov., 1964), 427–40.

[47] Mauricio Goulart, *Escravidão africana no Brasil* (2d ed., São Paulo, 1950), 249–63; the total figure for slaves is given in Stein, *Vassouras*, 294. Christie (*Notes on Brazilian Questions*, 69–70) insists that when he was writing, in 1865, slaves numbered three million. The lack of a census makes it impossible to arrive at anything more accurate than estimates.

reopened the trade before the federal government finally closed it. Thus even before 1807 the influx of native Africans had decreased considerably.

The larger number of recently imported Africans in Brazil all through the history of slavery probably accounts for the greater number of revolts there.[48] Revolts were hard enough to organize and carry out under any circumstances, but they were especially difficult under a slave system like that in the United States where the slaves were principally native and almost entirely shorn of their African culture or identity. In Brazil the presence of thousands of newly arrived Africans, alienated from their new masters and society while often united by their common African tribal culture, was undoubtedly a source of slave rebellion. Stein calls attention to a rash of attempted uprisings in Vassouras in the 1840's just as the number of imported Africans reached its peak. Particularly in the cities were the slaves able to retain their African languages, dances, religious rites, and other customs, even though the authorities, aware of the nucleus such African traits provided for discontent and revolt, attempted to suppress them.[49] It is certainly not accidental that the greatest revolts in Brazil were in the city of Bahia and that they were generally led by Hausa and Yoruba Negroes, who were Muslims. A common African tribal culture, language, and religion provided the necessary cement of organization and the incentives to resistance, which were almost wholly lacking among the slaves in the United States. It is significant that the documents captured from the Bahian rebels in 1835 were written in Arabic script, and, though there is some doubt as to the extent of the religious basis for the revolt, a number of the leaders were clearly Muslims.[50] In the nineteenth century, coffee planters in the southern part of Brazil were so conscious of the dangers of newly arrived slaves from the same African tribal background that they limited their purchases of such slaves to small numbers in order to minimize revolts. C. R. Boxer writes that the diversity of African nations among the slaves in eighteenth-century Minas Gerais was the chief safeguard against the outbreak of revolts.[51]

The connections between Brazil and Africa were so close in the nineteenth century that some slaves, after they earned their freedom or otherwise gained manumission, elected to return to Africa. One historian, for example, has reported on a number of leaders of nineteenth-century Nigerian society who had been slaves in Brazil, but who after manumission returned to Africa to make a living in the slave trade. So intimate was the connection between Brazil and

---

[48] Mörner (*Race Mixture in the History of Latin America*, 76) suggests that most slave revolts were led by African-born slaves.

[49] Stein, *Vassouras*, 145; Da Costa, *Da Senzala*, 232; Cardoso and Ianni, *Côr e mobilidade*, 126–27.

[50] Ramos, *Negro in Brazil*, 30–31, 36–37; Donald Pierson, *Negroes in Brazil* (Chicago, 1942), 39–40; E. Franklin Frazier, "Some Aspects of Race Relations in Brazil," *Phylon*, III (Third Quarter, 1942), 290. Kent, in the unpublished article referred to in note 44, above, strongly questions the religious basis for the 1835 revolt in Bahia, which heretofore has been the standard interpretation (See, e.g., Roger Bastide, *Les religions africaines au Brésil* [Paris, 1960], 146.)

[51] Da Costa, *Da Senzala*, 235, 252; Charles Ralph Boxer, *The Golden Age of Brazil, 1695–1750* (Berkeley, Calif., 1962), 176–77.

Africa that until 1905 at least—almost twenty years after abolition—ships plied between Bahia and Lagos, "repatriating nostalgic, emancipated Negroes and returning with West Coast products much prized by Africans and their descendants in Brazil."[52] In striking contrast is the well-known reluctance of Negroes in the United States during the ante bellum years to have anything to do with removal to Africa. That contrast emphasizes once again the overwhelmingly native character of slavery in the US and the dearth of African survivals.

The persistence, and even expansion, of the slave system of the United States without any substantial additions from importations is unique in history. Neither in antiquity nor in Latin America was a slave system sustained principally by reproduction. Even if one accepts the highest figure for smuggling into the United States—270,000 in the fifty years prior to 1860, or about 5,000 a year—the figure can hardly account for the steady and large increase in the slave population recorded by the decennial censuses. For example, in the 1790's, prior to the federal closing of the slave trade, the increase was 30 per cent; in the 1840's the increase was still 28 per cent, while the absolute average annual figures were 20,000 and 70,000, respectively. In short, it seems clear that reproduction was the principal source of slaves for the United States, at least since the first census.[53] One consequence was that the ratio between the sexes was virtually equal, a fact that was conducive to holding slaves in so-called family units as well as to breeding. (It was also conducive to greater control over the slaves.) Thus the ratio between the sexes in Mississippi counties according to the census of 1860 was about the same as among the whites. In 1860 in all of the southern slave states the numerical difference between the sexes was 3 per cent or less of the total, except in Louisiana where the surplus of males was 3.6 per cent. This ratio among the slaves was closer to an absolute balance between the sexes than obtained among the whites themselves in five southern states, where the surplus of males ran between 4 and 8 per cent of the white population. Thus in both the so-called breeding and consuming regions of the South the sexes were remarkably well balanced.

Although Gilberto Freyre writes of the Brazilian master's interest in the "generative belly" of the female slave, other writers make clear that slave breeding was not important to Brazilian slaveholders. Stein, for example, found a genuine reluctance among slaveholders to breed and rear slaves; the very hours during which male and female slaves could be together were deliberately limited.

[52] David A. Ross, "The Career of Domingo Martinez in the Bight of Benin," *Journal of African History*, VI (No. 1, 1965), 83. Freyre (*Nordeste*, 130–31) and Da Costa (*Da Senzala*, 56–57, n.) also report blacks returning to Africa and acting as slave traders. See also Donald Pierson, "The Educational Process and the Brazilian Negro," *American Journal of Sociology*, XLVIII (May 1943), 695, n.; and Gilberto Freyre, *Ordem e Progresso* (2d ed., Rio de Janeiro, 1962), 572, n. 33. The close connection between Africa and Brazil is forcefully demonstrated in José Honório Rodrigues, *Brazil and Africa* (Berkeley, Calif., 1965).

[53] The above was written before the publication of Philip D. Curtin, *The Atlantic Slave Trade. A Census* (Madison, Wis., 1969). Curtin, p. 234, estimates that after 1808 the total number of slaves entering the United States directly from Africa was fewer than 55,000.

Lynn Smith cites a number of sources to show that masters consciously restricted slave reproduction by locking up the sexes separately at night.[54]

Undoubtedly the availability of slaves from Africa accounts for some of the lack of interest in slave breeding in Brazil prior to 1851. For within five years after the closing of the slave trade, books began to appear in Brazil advising planters to follow the example of Virginians, who were alleged to be such efficient breeders of slaves that the infants were bought while still in the mother's womb.[55] These exhortations do not seem to have had much effect, however, for twenty years after the end of the African slave trade the slaveholder's customary rationale for not raising slaves was still being advanced:

"One buys a Negro for 300 milreis, who harvests in the course of the year 100 arrobas of coffee, which produces a net profit at least equal to the cost of the slave; thereafter everything is profit. It is not worth the trouble to raise children, who, only after sixteen years, will give equal service. Furthermore, the pregnant Negroes and those nursing are not available to use the hoe; heavy fatigue prevents the regular development of the fetus in some; in others the diminution of the flow of milk, and in almost all, sloppiness in the treatment of the children occurs, from which sickness and death of the children result. So why raise them?"[56]

And apparently infant mortality among slaves was amazingly high, even after the foreign slave trade had ended. One authority on the coffee region has placed it as high as 88 per cent. The census of 1870 revealed that in the city of Rio de Janeiro the mortality of slave children exceeded births by 1.8 per cent; even this shocking figure must have been a minimum since most slaves in Rio were domestic and presumably better cared for than agricultural slaves. Rio Branco, the Brazilian statesman who gave his name to an important emancipationist law, calculated that on the basis of the excess of slave deaths over births alone slavery would die out within seventy-five years. And although the British minister at Rio, W. D. Christie, was highly incensed at Brazilian complacency over the persistence of slavery, he had to admit in 1863 in a report to his home government that

the slave population is decreasing, though not considerably. . . . The mortality among the children of slaves is very great; and Brazilian proprietors do not appear to have given nearly so much attention as might have been expected, from obvious motives of self-interest, to marriages among slaves, or the care of mothers or children.[57]

One undoubted consequence of the continuance of the foreign slave trade was that Brazilian planters made no effort to balance the sexes among the slaves. Since male slaves were stronger and more serviceable, they apparently constituted the overwhelming majority of the importations throughout the history of Brazil-

---

[54] Stein, *Vassouras*, 155; T. Lynn Smith, *Brazil, People and Institutions* (Baton Rouge, La., 1963), 130.

[55] Da Costa, *Da Senzala*, 130.

[56] Quoted in Joaquim Nabuco, *O Abolicionismo*, in *Obras completas* (14 vols., São Paulo, 1944–49), VII, 89–90. The book from which Nabuco quoted was published in 1872.

[57] Da Costa, *Da Senzala*, 256; Gouveia, *História da escravidão*, 208; Christie, *Notes on Brazilian Questions*, 102, n.

ian slavery. According to one authority, on some plantations there were no female slaves. For Brazil as a whole he estimates that one Negro woman was imported for each three or four males. The statistics compiled by Stein for Vassouras support that estimate, for he found that between 1820 and 1880 70 per cent or more of the African-born slaves were males. Robert Conrad, quoting from the records of captured slave ships in the 1830's and 1840's, found ratios of one to four and one to five in favor of males.[58] The heavy imbalance between the sexes meant that once the slave trade was stopped, Brazilian slavery began to decline, for the paucity of women, not to mention the masters' lack of interest in breeding, ensured that the reduction in the foreign supply of slaves would not be easily or quickly made up.

The imbalance between the sexes in Brazil may help also to explain the somewhat greater number of rebellions and runaways in that country as compared with the United States. In the US, with slaves more or less divided into family units, for a male slave to rebel or to run away meant serious personal loss, since he probably would have to leave women and children behind. Such a consequence was much less likely in Brazil. One indication that the pairing of the sexes in the United States reduced rebelliousness is provided by a report from São Paulo toward the last years of slavery when masters were quoted as saying about a restless or rebellious slave: "It is necessary to give that Negro in marriage and give him a piece of land in order to calm him down and cultivate responsibility in him."[59]

Although it is often said or implied that slavery in Latin America in general was milder than in the United States,[60] there are several reasons for believing that in a comparison between Brazil and the US the relationship is just the reverse. Admittedly such comparisons are difficult to make since the evidence that might be mustered on either side is open to serious doubts as to its representativeness. But this problem can be circumvented in part, at least, if general classes of evidence are used. There are at least three general reasons, aside from any discrete examples of treatment of slaves, suggesting that slavery was harsher in Brazil than in the United States. First, the very fact that slavery in the US was able to endure and expand on the basis of reproduction alone is itself strong testimony to a better standard of physical care. It is true that the imbalance of the sexes in Brazil played a part in keeping down reproduction, but the high mortality of slave children and the care and expense involved probably account for the reluctance to rear slaves in the first place. Moreover, as we have seen, even after the slave trade was closed, the rearing of slave children was still resisted in Brazil. Masters said that it was easier to raise three or four white children than one black child, the difference being attributed to the "greater fragility

[58] Rodrigues, *Brazil and Africa*, 159; Stein, *Vassouras*, 155; Conrad, "Struggle for Abolition of the Brazilian Slave Trade," 55.
[59] *Relações raciais entre negros e brancos em São Paulo*, ed. Bastide, 81.
[60] See, e.g., Elkins, *Slavery*, 77–78.

of the black race." In 1862 a French visitor reported that "the most simple hygienic measures are almost always neglected by the owners of slaves, and the mortality of *'negrillons'* is very considerable, especially on the plantations of the interior."[61] Brazilians, in short, simply did not take sufficient care of their slaves for them to reproduce.

Second, there are kinds of severe and cruel treatment of slaves in Brazil that rarely occurred in the United States. A number of Brazilian sources, both during the colonial period and under the Empire in the nineteenth century, speak of the use of female slaves as prostitutes.[62] So far as I know, this source of income from slaves was unknown or very rare in the United States. Brazilian sources also contain numerous references to the use of iron or tin masks on slaves, usually to prevent them from eating dirt or drinking liquor. Indeed, the practice of using masks was sufficiently common that pictures of slaves wearing them appear in books on slavery. I have yet to see such a picture in the literature of slavery in the US, and references to the use of the mask are rare, though not unknown.[63] As already noted, Brazilian sources call attention to another practice that also suggests severe treatment: the freeing of ill, old, or crippled slaves in order to escape the obligation of caring for them. The several efforts to legislate against this practice, much less to put a stop to it, were fruitless until just before the abolition of slavery.[64] Finally, because of the imbalance of the sexes, most slaves in Brazil had no sexual outlets at all.

Though making comparisons of physical treatment may have pitfalls, the effort has value because such comparisons give some insight into the nature of the slave systems in the two countries. Some authorities, like Elkins, for example,[65] argue that a comparative analysis of treatment is not germane to a comparison of the impact of slavery on the Negro, for "in one case [Latin America] we would be dealing with cruelty of man to men, and in the other [the United States], with the care, maintenance, and indulgence of men toward creatures who were legally and morally *not* men. . . ." But this argument collapses, as Davis has pointed out,[66] when it can be shown that the law in Brazil and the United States defined the slave as both a man and a thing. Under such circumstances, treatment can no longer be confidently separated from attitudes. Instead, the way a master treats a slave, particularly *when the slave is a member of*

---

[61] Da Costa, *Da Senzala*, 257–58; Élisée Reclus, "Le Brésil et la Colonisation. II," *Revue des deux mondes*, XL (July–Aug. 1862), 391.

[62] Boxer, *Golden Age of Brazil*, 138, 165; Gilberto Freyre, *Masters and the Slaves*, 455.

[63] See the picture, e.g., in Da Costa, *Da Senzala*, facing p. 240; Gilberto Freyre, *O Escravo nos anúncios de jornais brasilieros do seculo* XIX (Recife, Brazil, 1963), 100, discusses the use of the mask; Thomas Ewbank, *Life in Brazil* (New York, 1856), 437–38, describes the masks he saw worn on the street. Stampp (*Peculiar Institution*, 304) notes that masks were sometimes used in the United States to prevent eating clay. There is at least one reference to masks in that compendium of horrors by Theodore Weld, *American Slavery as It Is* (New York, 1839), 76.

[64] References to the practice are common. See, e.g., Gouveia, *História, da escravidão*, 179; Perdigão Malheiro, *A Escravidão no Brasil*, II, 220, 348; Da Costa, *Da Senzala*, 263.

[65] Elkins, *Slavery*, 78, n.

[66] Davis, *Problem of Slavery in Western Culture*, 229, n.

a physically identifiable class, becomes a part of the historian's evidence for ascertaining the attitude of white men toward black men who are slaves, and of the way in which blacks are conditioned to think of themselves. When a master muzzles a slave, for example, he is literally treating him like a dog. The master's behavior, at the very least, is evidence for concluding that he considered his slave on the level with a dog; at the most, his behavior suggests that its source was the belief that the slave was from the beginning no better than a dog. In either case, the master's treatment of the slave is part of the evidence to be evaluated in ascertaining white men's attitudes toward black slaves. Perhaps even more important is the real possibility that a slave who is muzzled or who sees other black men muzzled may well be led to think of himself as a dog, worthy of being muzzled. In short, the treatment accorded black slaves in both societies is relevant to the question of how white men think about black men.

A second reason for making a comparison of physical treatment is to call attention to the importance of the slave trade in accounting for some of the differences between slavery in Brazil and the United States. Brazilians simply did not have to treat their slaves with care or concern when new slaves were obtainable from outside the system. That the slave trade played this role was recognized by Perdigão Malheiro in 1866, after the trade had been stopped for fifteen years. He asserted that since the closing of the traffic from abroad the treatment of slaves in Brazil had improved. No longer, he wrote, did one "meet in the streets, as in other not remote times, slaves with their faces covered by a wire mask or a great weight on the foot. . . ." Slaves were so well dressed and shod, he continued, "that no one would know who they are," that is, they could not be distinguished from free blacks. Two visiting Americans noticed the same change even earlier:

Until 1850, when the slave-trade was effectually put down, it was considered cheaper, on the country plantations to use up a slave in five or seven years, and purchase another, than to take care of him. This I had, in the interior, from intelligent native Brazilians, and my own observation has confirmed it. But, since the inhuman traffic has ceased, the price of slaves has been enhanced, and the selfish motives for taking greater care of them have been increased.[67]

But it needs to be added that the closing of the foreign slave trade in Brazil had at least one worsening effect upon the lot of the slave. It undoubtedly increased the internal slave trade, thereby enhancing the likelihood of the dissolution of slave families. Prior to 1850 the foreign slave trade probably kept to a minimum the movement of established slaves from one part of the country to another. In the United States, on the other hand, slaves prior to 1850 probably experienced more disruption of families, simply because the foreign slave trade was closed and the opening of new areas in the Southwest provided a growing

[67] Perdigão Malheiro, *A Escravidão no Brasil,* II, 114–15; D. P. Kidder and J. C. Fletcher, *Brazil and the Brazilians* (Philadelphia, 1857), 132.

market for slaves, who had to be drawn from the older regions, especially the upper South.

One of the earliest signs of discrimination against Negroes in seventeenth-century Virginia, Maryland, and even New England was the legal denial of arms to blacks, free or slave, but not to white indentured servants.[68] This discrimination constitutes perhaps the sharpest difference between the slave systems of the US and Brazil. Almost from the beginning of settlement, the Portuguese and then the Brazilians permitted not only Negroes, but slaves themselves, to be armed. Arthur Ramos has even suggested that whites encouraged the slaves to arm themselves.[69] During the wars against the French and the Dutch invaders in the sixteenth and seventeenth centuries, large numbers of slaves and free Negroes fought on the side of the Brazilians. The Dutch occupation of north-eastern Brazil, which entailed almost continuous warfare, lasted for a quarter of a century. Negroes, slave and free, also fought in the War of the Farrapos in southern Brazil against the Empire in the late 1830's. Indeed, as Roger Bastide has written, "the Negro appears in all the civil revolts, the war of the *paulistas* against the Emboabos, the wars of national independence, and one even sees them in the party struggles under the Empire, between royalists and republicans or in the rivalries of political leaders among themselves." Slaves served in the Paraguayan War of 1865-70, often being sent by masters to fight in their places or to win favor with the Emperor. Fugitive slaves also served in the Brazilian army in the nineteenth century. At the end of the Paraguayan War some twenty thousand slaves who had served in the army were given their freedom.[70]

When comparable occasions arose in the United States the results were quite different. During the American Revolution, for example, Henry and John Laurens, leading figures in South Carolina, proposed in 1779 that slaves be enlisted to help counter the military successes of the British in the southern colonies. It was understood that the survivors would be freed. Although the Laurenses were joined by a few other South Carolinians and the Continental Congress approved of the plan, the South Carolina legislature overwhelmingly rejected it. The Laurenses raised the issue again in 1781, but once more the proposal was rejected by both the South Carolina and Georgia legislatures. When the slave South was faced with a struggle for survival during the Civil War it again steadfastly refused to use slave soldiers until the very last month of the war;

---

[68] Carl N. Degler, "Slavery and the Genesis of American Race Prejudice," *Comparative Studies in Society and History*, II (Oct. 1959), 57, 64; see also Winthrop D. Jordan, *White Over Black: American Attitudes toward the Negro, 1550-1812* (Chapel Hill, N. C., 1968), 71, 125-26. Jordan notes that free Negroes served in all the wars of colonial New England, but that few slaves served in any colonial militias.

[69] Ramos, *Negro in Brazil*, 157.

[70] Charles R. Boxer, *The Dutch in Brazil, 1624-1654* (Oxford, Eng., 1957), 166-69; Cardoso, *Capitalismo e escravidão*, 153-54, n; Bastide, *Religions africaines au Brésil*, 109; Da Costa, *Da Senzala*, 401. Ianni (*Metamorfoses*, 175-76) cites an example of a slave being sent by his master to serve in place of a white man; after service, he was freed. Rodrigues (*Brazil and Africa*, 45-52) is one of several sources for the figure of twenty thousand slaves freed after the Paraguayan War.

indeed, the Confederacy rejected even free Negroes when they offered their services at the beginning of the war.[71]

That slaves in Brazil were often armed and that they rarely were in the United States is obviously a significant difference between the practices of slavery in the two places. To arm Negro slaves surely affects how one feels about Negroes, whether slave or free. As Octavio Ianni has observed, concerning the use of Negro slaves in the Paraguayan War, Brazilian whites could not help but obtain a new and larger view of Negro capabilities when blacks served as defenders of the nation.[72] How can this difference in practice be explained?

A part of the explanation is undoubtedly related to the quite dissimilar colonial histories of the two countries. Sixteenth-century Brazil was a tiny, sparsely settled colony, desperately clinging to the coast, yet attractive to foreign powers because of its wealth, actual and potential. At different times during the sixteenth and seventeenth centuries the French and Dutch attempted to wrest the colony from Portugal by actual invasion. Since the mother country was too weak to offer much help, all the resources of the colony had to be mobilized for defense, which included every scrap of manpower, including slaves. The recourse to armed slaves, it is worth noticing, was undertaken reluctantly. For as Ramos writes, Negroes were first used only as a kind of advanced guard, being denied a place in the regular army during the sixteenth and seventeenth centuries. But as the need for soldiers continued and a new generation of Brazilian-born Negroes entered the scene, the whites came to demand that they serve in the armed forces. That the acceptance of Negro troops was the result of circumstances rather than ideology is shown by the fact that the Negroes were usually segregated until the years of the Empire, and even when they were no longer set apart, "whites tended to occupy the military posts of major responsibility."[73] Use of Negroes in the colonial period was, therefore, not the result of the prior acceptance of the colored man as an equal, but of the need of him as a fighter. Throughout the eighteenth century, as before, the law *denied* Negroes and mulattoes the right to carry arms.[74]

In striking contrast is the history of the Negro in the British colonies of North America, where conditions and circumstances of settlement and development differed. In the first fifty years of settlement, when the necessities of defense might have encouraged the arming of slaves, there were very few blacks available. As is well known, in the South white indentured servants made up the great preponderance of the unfree labor supply until the end of the seventeenth cen-

---

[71] John Alden, *The First South* (Baton Rouge, La., 1961), 37–40; Benjamin Quarles, *The Negro in the American Revolution* (Chapel Hill, N. C., 1961), 60–67. Some slaves, however, were enlisted by their masters in the northern states, usually as substitutes. On the offer of blacks to support the Confederacy, see D. E. Everett, "Ben Butler and the Louisiana Native Guards, 1861–1862," *Journal of Southern History*, XXIV (May 1958), 202–204.

[72] Ianni, *Metamorfoses*, 217.

[73] Ramos, *Negro in Brazil*, 151–54.

[74] Mörner, *Race Mixture in the History of Latin America*, 52.

tury. Even at that time, in both Maryland and Virginia, Negroes constituted considerably less than one-fifth of the population. Meanwhile, the white population, servant and free, had long been more than adequate for purposes of defense. Unlike the situation in Brazil, moreover, colonial Englishmen experienced no foreign invasions and only an occasional foreign threat. In short, neither at the beginning nor at the close of the formative seventeenth century were English colonists under any pressure to use Negroes or slaves as defensive troops. As a consequence they could indulge their acute awareness of their difference in appearance, religion, and culture from Africans by permitting their social institutions to reflect this awareness. Thus in both the southern and northern colonies Negroes were resolutely kept from bearing arms. At one time, in 1652, Massachusetts had enlisted Indians and Negroes in the militia, but in 1656 this policy was reversed by the statement that "henceforth no negroes or Indians, altho servants of the English, shalbe armed or permitted to trayne." In 1660 Connecticut also excluded Indians and "negar servants" from the militia.[75]

There is one exception to the English colonists' attitudes toward the arming of slaves, but it is an exception that proves the rule. Early in the eighteenth century, when South Carolina was weak and threatened by Spanish invasion, slaves were required to be trained in the use of arms and included in an auxiliary militia.[76] The policy, however, was only temporary, since the colony was soon able to protect itself by dependence upon whites alone and the feared invasions did not materialize.

Further differences in attitudes toward Negroes and slaves in the US and in Brazil are the responses that the two societies made to the threat of slave insurrections. In both societies, it should be said, fear of slave revolts was widespread. One of the several measures that whites in the southern United States took to forestall slave insurrections was to place restrictions upon free Negroes, who were widely believed to be fomenters of slave conspiracies and revolts. Thus the uncovering in 1820 of a plot allegedly organized by the free Negro Denmark Vesey moved South Carolina and other southern states to enact new and stricter limitations on the free movement of Negroes. Fear of the free Negro as a potential instigator of slave revolts was also the principal reason for the many restrictions placed upon manumission in the southern states during the nineteenth century. The most common limitation was the requirement that all newly manumitted Negroes must leave the state. At the end of the ante bellum era several southern states so feared the influence of the free Negro that they enacted laws prohibiting manumission; at least one state passed a law requiring the enslave-

[75] *Records of the Governor and Company of the Massachusetts Bay in New England*, ed. N. F. Shurteff (5 vols., Boston, 1853–54), III, 268, 397; *Public Records of the Colony of Connecticut [1636–1776]* (15 vols., Hartford, Conn., 1850–1890), I, 349. See Jordan, *White over Black*, 122–28, for a survey of legal discrimination against free blacks in the English colonies of North America.
[76] Ulrich B. Phillips, *American Negro Slavery* (New York, 1928), 87.

ment of all free Negroes found within the state after a certain date.[77] White society obviously saw a connection between the Negro slave and the free Negro; the important thing was not that one was free and the other a slave, but that both belonged to the same race.

In one sense, of course, Brazilian slavery was also racially based. Only Negroes, and, for a while, Indians, were slaves, though in Brazil, as in the US, there was an occasional slave who was fair-skinned and with blue eyes, so that he was a white in everything but status.[78] But in Brazil the connection between the inferior status of slavery and race did not persist into freedom to the same extent that it did in the United States. If slaveholders in the US viewed the free Negro as a potential threat to the slave system, their counterparts in Brazil saw him as a veritable prop to the system of slavery. Many, if not most of the *capitães de mato* (bush captains or slave catchers), for example, were mulattoes or Negroes. One nineteenth-century Brazilian asserted that two-thirds of the overseers, slave catchers, and slave dealers in Bahia were either mulattoes or blacks. Moreover, many free blacks and mulattoes showed little if any interest in abolition, and some, evidently, actively opposed the end of slavery.[79] In Brazil, in other words, more important than race in differentiating between men was legal status. The mere fact that a man was a Negro or a mulatto offered no presumption that he would identify with slaves.

The refusal of Brazilians to lump together free Negroes and slaves is reflected also in their failure to justify slavery on grounds of race. For, contrary to the prevailing situation in the southern United States, in Brazil there was no important proslavery argument based upon the biological inferiority of the Negro. It is true that a racist conception of the black man existed in nineteenth-century Brazil,[80] but defenders of slavery on clearly racist grounds were rare among public supporters of the institution. A Brazilian historian has written that in the debates in the Brazilian legislature concerning the treaty with Britain in 1827 that closed the international slave trade, only one member of that body

[77] Stampp, *Peculiar Institution*, 232–35; John Hope Franklin, *From Slavery to Freedom* (New York, 1947), 218–19.

[78] Freyre (*O Escravo nos anúncios de jornais brasileiros do seculo* xix, 195) cites examples of light-colored slaves in the advertisements for runaways and refers to a royal order of 1773 in which it was said that, much to the shame of humanity and religion, there were slaves who were lighter than their owners, but who were called "Pretos e . . . negras." Freyre also cites an advertisement in a newspaper in 1865 in which the fugitive was described as having blond hair and blue eyes. Stampp (*Peculiar Institution*, 194) refers to blond, blue-eyed runaways in newspaper advertisements in the U. S.

[79] Williams, "Treatment of Negro Slaves in the Brazilian Empire," 327; Da Costa, *Da Senzala*, 29; Pierson, *Negroes in Brazil*, 47, n.

[80] See Stein, *Vassouras*, 133–34; Da Costa, *Da Senzala*, 354–55. Expilly provides probably the most explicit examples of racial arguments in defense of slavery. He quotes one slaveholder as saying that one could free slaves "today, and tomorrow, instead of using this freedom, they will rob and kill in order to satisfy their needs. Only by terror do they perform services. . . . I believe, gentlemen, Negroes would be baffled by freedom. God created them to be slaves." A little later, Expilly quotes the planter as saying, "The Africans represent an intermediate race between the gorilla and man. They are improved monkeys, not men." A priest is also cited as justifying slavery on the grounds that St. Thomas Aquinas claimed "that nature intended certain creatures for physical and moral reasons to be slaves." (Expilly, *Mulheres e costumes do Brasil*, 381–83.)

clearly asserted the racial inferiority of Negroes, though other kinds of defenses of slavery were made.[81] A French commentator in 1862 noted that in Brazil slaveholders "do not believe themselves obliged, like their American colleagues, to invent for the Negro a new original sin, nor to erect a system of absolute distinction between the races, nor to place an insurmountable barrier between the offspring of descendants of slaves and of those of free men."[82] The most common defenses of the system were the argument in behalf of property and the assertion that the prosperity of the country depended on slave labor. Some defenders of the institution, even late in the nineteenth century, spoke of it as a "necessary evil," as North Americans had done in the early years of the century. In 1886, as slavery in Brazil was coming under increasing attack from abolitionists, a member of the Brazilian Congress from the coffee district asserted that the planters in his area would have no objection to emancipation if they could be assured of a new, adequate supply of labor, presumably immigrants.[83] Even more dramatic is the fact that some of the principal leaders of the abolition movement who held elective office came from the slaveholding provinces of Brazil. No such willingness to contemplate the wholesale increase in the number of free blacks was thinkable in the slaveholding regions of the United States. Even defenders of slavery in nineteenth-century Brazil spoke of the absence of color prejudice in their country and noted with apparent approval the high position achieved by some Negroes and mulattoes.[84] Leaving aside the assertion that there was no prejudice in Brazil, one would find it difficult indeed to point to a slaveholder in the US in the middle of the nineteenth century who would utter publicly a similar statement of praise for free Negroes as a class.

What may be concluded from this examination of slavery in Brazil and the United States? That there were in fact differences in the practices of slavery in the two countries there can be no doubt. The explanation for those differences, however, as I have tried to show, is to be sought neither in the laws of the Crown nor in the attitude and practices of the Roman Catholic Church in Brazil. The behavior of neither state nor Church displayed any deep concern about the humanity of the slave, and, in any event, neither used its authority to affect significantly the life of the slave. Certainly demographic, economic, and geographic factors account for some of the differences between the two slave systems that have been explored in this essay. But these materialist explanations do not help us to understand the more interesting and profound difference that emerges from the comparison.

This difference becomes evident only as one contemplates the various

---

[81] Rodrigues, *Brazil and Africa*, 151.

[82] Reclus, "Brésil et la Colonisation," 386.

[83] Da Costa, *Da Senzala*, 354–56; Cardoso, *Capitalismo e escravidão*, 280; Florestan Fernandes, *A Integração do negro no Sociedade de classes* (2 vols., São Paulo, 1965), I, 200, n.

[84] Da Costa, *Da Senzala*, 358.

specific differences in conjunction with one another. In Brazil the slave was feared, but the black man was not, while in the United States the black man as well as the slave was feared. Once this difference in attitude is recognized, certain differences between the two systems are recognized as stemming from a common source. Thus the willingness of Brazilians to manumit slaves much more freely than North Americans is clearly a result of their not fearing free blacks in great numbers. (Indeed, in Brazil today, a common explanation for the obviously greater acceptance of blacks in northeastern Brazil than in the southern part of the country is that in the North there is a greater proportion of Negroes than in the South. Just the opposite explanation, of course, is current in the US, where it is said that when Negroes constitute a large proportion of the population they are more likely to be tightly controlled or restricted.) Brazilians, therefore, did not restrict manumission in anything like the degree practiced in the slave states of the United States. This same difference in attitude toward the Negro is also evident in the willingness of Brazilian slaveholders to use blacks as slave catchers and overseers, while in the US slaveholders in particular and white men in general could scarcely entertain the idea. Finally, this difference emerges when one asks why the slave trade remained open in Brazil to 1851, but was closed in most of the United States before the end of the eighteenth century. Even before the Revolution, in fact, Englishmen in North America had been seeking ways to limit the number of blacks in their midst, free or slave. In 1772, for example, the Virginia legislature asked the Crown to permit it to check the slave traffic since "The importation of slaves into the colonies from the coast of Africa hath long been considered as a trade of great inhumanity, and under its *present encouragement,* we have too much reason to fear, *will endanger the very* existence of your Majesty's American dominions. . . ." This fear that an unimpeded slave trade was dangerous ran through the history of all the English colonies, especially that of South Carolina. One of colonial South Carolina's several laws calling for limitation on the slave trade advocated encouragement to white immigration as "the best way to prevent the mischiefs that may be attended by the great importation of negroes into the province. . . ." In 1786 North Carolina placed a tax on slaves on the ground that "the importation of slaves into this state is productive of evil consequences, and highly impolitic."[85] The widespread fear of Negroes also explains why all but one of the states prohibited the importation of slaves years before the federal prohibition in 1808. Certainly there was a humanitarian motive behind the movement to stop the African slave trade, but also of great importance was the fear that if

---

[85] W. E. Burghardt Du Bois, *The Suppressions of the African Slave-Trade to the United States of America, 1638–1870* (New York, 1896), 221, 215, 229. The appendix to this work contains a number of other excerpts from colonial statutes to the same effect. Don B. Kates, Jr., "Abolition, Deportation, Integration: Attitudes toward Slavery in the Early Republic," *Journal of Negro History,* LIII (Jan. 1968), 33–47, contains a number of expressions by white Americans of their opposition to freed Negroes remaining in the United States.

the importations were not limited or stopped white men would be overwhelmed by black. For as the founding and the work of the American Colonization Society in the nineteenth century reveal, even those people in the slave states who conscientiously opposed slavery did not want the Negro as a free man in the United States.

In Brazil, on the other hand, the slave trade came to an end principally because of pressures from *outside* the society. For a quarter of a century before 1851 the British government badgered the Brazilians to put an end to the trade. It is easy to believe that without the pressure from the British and the humiliating infringements of Brazilian sovereignty by ships of the Royal Navy the Brazilians would have kept the slave trade open even longer. Apparently Brazilians rarely worried, as did the North Americans, that they would be overwhelmed by blacks.

This article opened with the observation that Tannenbaum's work began a long and continuing scholarly debate over the role that slavery in North and South America had played in bringing about a different place for the Negro in the societies of the Western Hemisphere. If the evidence and argument of this essay are sound, then the explanations of the differences offered by Tannenbaum and Elkins, at least as far as Brazil is concerned, are not supported by the evidence. But if Tannenbaum's explanation has to be abandoned, his belief that there was a strikingly different attitude toward blacks in Brazil from that in the United States has not been challenged at all. Rather it has been reinforced. For if factors like demography, geography, and the continuance of the international slave trade in Brazil help to account for some of the differences in the practices of slavery in the two societies, those same factors do not really aid us in explaining why Brazilians feared slaves but not blacks, while North Americans feared both. What is now needed is a more searching and fundamental explanation than can be derived from these factors alone or found in the practices or laws of state and church regarding the slave. Clearly that explanation will have to be sought in more subtle and elusive places, such as among the inherited cultural patterns and social structures and values of the two countries. For it is the argument of this article that the differences between Brazilian and United States slavery, rather than being the sources of the different patterns of race relations in the two countries are, in fact, merely the consequence themselves of deeper divergences in the culture and history of the two peoples.

Hispanic American Historical Review 68:3
Copyright © 1988 by Duke University Press
CCC 0018-2168/88/$1.50

Brazilian Abolition in Comparative Perspective

SEYMOUR DRESCHER*

O N the eve of the age of abolition, even intellectuals who were morally opposed to slavery were far more impressed by its power and durability than by its weaknesses. Adam Smith reminded his students that only a small portion of the earth was being worked by free labor, and that it was unlikely that slavery would ever be totally abandoned. Across the channel, the Abbé Raynal could envision the end of New World slavery only through a fortuitous conjuncture of philosopher-kings in Europe or the appearance of a heroic Spartacus in the Americas. No historical trend toward general emancipation could be assumed.[1]

Little more than a century later, the passage of the "Golden Law" through the Brazilian legislature—to the accompaniment of music, public demonstrations, and street festivities at every stage—was regarded as only a belated provincial rendezvous with progress. Until then, Brazilians had been humiliated by condescending references to their country as the last Christian nation that tolerated slavery, on a level with "backward" African and Asiatic slaveholding societies.[2] Brazilian emancipation was hailed as

*I would like to thank George Reid Andrews, Stanley L. Engerman, Frederic C. Jaher, and Rebecca J. Scott for their helpful suggestions.

1. Adam Smith, *Lectures on Jurisprudence*, R. L. Meek, D. D. Raphael, and P. G. Stein, eds. (Oxford, 1978), 181; G. T. F. Raynal, *Histoire philosophique et politique des établissements et du commerce des européens dans les deux Indes*, 7 vols. (Geneva, 1780).

2. David Brion Davis, *Slavery and Human Progress* (New York, 1984), 298; Robert E. Conrad, *The Destruction of Brazilian Slavery, 1850-1888* (Berkeley, 1972), 71. It was, of course, European-oriented members of Brazil's elite who felt most strongly that their country was humiliated by slavery and that it was a nation which played no role in building civilization or prosperity. See Joaquim Nabuco, *Abolitionism: The Brazilian Antislavery Struggle*, Conrad, trans. (Urbana, 1977), 4, 108, 117-118. On the influence of European and U.S. models on Brazilian concepts of progress and slavery, see Richard Graham, *Britain and the Onset of Modernization in Brazil, 1850-1914* (Cambridge, 1968), esp. chaps. 6 and 10, and "Causes for the Abolition of Negro Slavery in Brazil: An Interpretive Essay," *HAHR*, 46:2 (May 1966), 123-137; and E. Bradford Burns, *The Poverty of Progress: Latin America in the Nineteenth Century* (Berkeley, 1980), chap. 2.

opening a new stage in the "civilizing" of Africa and Asia. Counting from
the formation of the first abolitionist societies in the late 1780s, the Brazilian action almost precisely marked a "century of progress."

Perhaps because it occurred so late in a world dominated by a concept of libertarian progress, Brazilian abolition received relatively little
attention from those who wrote general histories of slavery.[3] The demise
of Brazilian slavery seemed to follow a path roughly prescribed by a dozen
predecessors in the Americas and Europe. This impression may have been
due in part to the fact that until recently there were few extensive analyses
of the Brazilian case,[4] a lack which was compounded by the "North Atlantic" or even national orientation of most North American and European
historians of slavery. Moreover, when Brazilian slavery has been treated
in comparative perspective, the contrast is almost invariably with the U.S.
South.[5] In this study, I shall expand the range of cases to include a number
of emancipations in areas which were subject to European polities during
the nineteenth century.

3. For good general syntheses which treat Brazilian abolition primarily as a mopping-
up operation by modernizers, see C. Duncan Rice, *The Rise and Fall of Black Slavery*
(London, 1975), 370–381; and Edward Reynolds, *Stand the Storm: A History of the Atlantic
Slave Trade* (London/New York, 1985), 90–92. The historiography of Brazilian abolition
is sometimes elaborated within a broader model of social progress in which the inherent
inefficiencies or "contradictions" of slave labor utilization converge with other causes of
technological and economic retardation. For a good example of this "convergence" thesis,
see Emília Viotti da Costa, *The Brazilian Empire: Myths and Histories* (Chicago, 1985), 148–
171 and *Da senzala à colônia* (São Paulo, 1966), chap. 5. The issue of the efficiency of slave
labor is sometimes not distinguished from the issue of technological progress in general.
See the perceptive discussion in Peter L. Eisenberg, *The Sugar Industry in Pernambuco:
Modernization Without Change, 1840–1910* (Berkeley, 1974), chap. 3 and n. 18, below.

4. But recently, see da Costa, *Brazilian Empire*, chap. 6; Robert Brent Toplin, *The
Abolition of Slavery in Brazil* (New York, 1972); and Conrad, *Destruction*. The pervasive structural foundations of Brazilian slavery are presented in greatest detail by Stuart B.
Schwartz, *Sugar Plantations in the Formation of Brazilian Society: Bahia, 1550–1835* (Cambridge, 1985), esp. chap. 16 and Robert Wayne Slenes, "The Demography and Economics
of Brazilian Slavery: 1850–1888" (Ph.D. diss., Stanford University, 1975).

5. Carl Degler, *Neither Black nor White: Slavery and Race Relations in Brazil and
the United States* (Madison, 1986); Frank Tannenbaum, *Slave and Citizen: The Negro in the
Americas* (New York, 1947); Stanley Elkins, *Slavery, a Problem in American Institutional
and Intellectual Life* (Chicago, 1959); Arnold Sio, "Interpretations of Slavery: The Slave
Status in the Americas," *Comparative Studies in Society and History*, 7:3 (Apr. 1965), 289–
308; Davis, *The Problem of Slavery in Western Culture* (Ithaca, 1966), chaps. 8 and 9.
Even Rebecca J. Scott who analyzes Cuba, the other late emancipation in Latin America,
makes only a passing reference to Brazil (*Slave Emancipation in Cuba: The Transition to
Free Labor 1860–1899* [Princeton, 1985], 284). However, Scott recognizes the comparative
opportunities afforded by the Cuban and Brazilian cases in her comments on Eric Foner,
Nothing But Freedom: Emancipation and Its Legacy (Baton Rouge, 1983), in "Comparing
Emancipations: A Review Essay," *Journal of Social History* 20:3 (Spring 1987), 565–583,
esp. 574–575. See also Davis, *Slavery and Human Progress*, 294–297. For U.S.-Brazilian
comparisons, see also Eugene D. Genovese, *The World the Slaveholders Made: Two Essays
in Interpretation* (New York, 1969), part one.

Historians of abolition usually approach causal discussions along a range of analytical categories: demographic, economic, social, ideological, and political. The historiography of abolition in Brazil, as elsewhere, is usually embedded in implicit or explicit theories about the relative weight to be assigned to each of these facets of social development and to their long- or short-term significance in the outcome. This essay will address two major elements of Brazilian abolition in comparative perspective— the demographics and economics of late Brazilian slavery, and the peculiar characteristics of Brazilian abolitionism and its opposition. I should say at the outset that I am entirely dependent on the existing historiography for the details of Brazilian development.

Demographic Dependency and Economic Viability

Slave Trade Abolition

As elsewhere in the New World, Brazilian slavery was stimulated by a shortage of labor relative to opportunities for rapid expansion in specialized commodity production. Like that of the Caribbean slave systems, the relative decline of the institution in Brazil was initially a consequence of external political pressures for the restriction of slave recruitment.[6] Exactly as in Cuba, Brazilian imports of African slaves had actually reached an all-time peak just before the enforcement of abolition in 1851.[7]

The impact of slave trade abolition on Brazil was similar to West Indian terminations in two other ways. Insofar as Brazil continued to expand its staple production, it increasingly had to rely on some combination of free and slave labor and a redistribution of its diminishing slave labor. The slave population inevitably declined, as a percentage both of the total labor force and of Brazilian capital. After 1851, that trend was inexorable and predictable.

Moreover, market pressures alone assured that, as in the British colonies and Cuba after ending slave importation from Africa, slave labor would be concentrated toward commodity production which could optimize the output from that form of labor. Certain economic sectors had to become less dependent on slavery. Without such inhibiting political

---

6. Leslie Bethell, *The Abolition of the Brazilian Slave Trade: Britain, Brazil, and the Slave Trade Question, 1807–1869* (Cambridge, 1970), 385; Conrad, *Destruction*, 65–69. On the U.S. linkage between abolition of the trade and decline of slavery, see n. 14 and 25, below. For a summary of economic models used to explain the rise and continuation of the slave trade, see Robert W. Fogel, *Without Consent or Contract: The Rise and Fall of American Slavery* (forthcoming), chap. 1.

7. David Eltis, *Economic Growth and the Ending of the Transatlantic Slave Trade* (New York, 1987), app. A.

restrictions on the flow of slave labor as occurred between islands of the British Caribbean in the decades after slave trade abolition in 1807,[8] there was a shift of Brazilian slaves from the city to the countryside in expanding frontier regions. This type of redistribution occurred even in the U.S. South, where there was a positive and high rate of postabolition natural increase.[9]

In Brazil, local expansions of the slave labor force could come only from redistribution. Shortly after African migration ended, the northeastern provinces which were losing slaves vainly attempted to follow the "British" model by prohibiting the interprovincial slave trade. As the northeasterners noted, the interprovincial flow of slaves created growing differentials of dependency on, and commitment to, slavery.[10] But, by the time political fear became more important than economic interest to the importing south-central region (in the early 1880s), it was too late. By 1884, fewer than half the provinces of Brazil had populations of more than 10 percent slaves, and more than one-fourth of the provinces (mostly northern and northeastern) were even below 5 percent, the level at which many northern U.S. states had opted for immediate emancipation.[11]

8. Eltis, "The Traffic in Slaves between the British West India Colonies, 1807-1833," *Economic History Review*, 25:1 (Feb. 1972), 55-64. For the urban decline in the British West Indies after 1807, see B. W. Higman, *Slave Populations of the British Caribbean, 1807-1834* (Baltimore, 1984), 92-99; for the urban decline in Brazilian slavery, see Mary C. Karasch, *Slave Life in Rio de Janeiro, 1808-1850* (Princeton, 1987), 61, table 3.1.

9. Compare the percentage reductions in numbers of slaves in Ceará, Pernambuco, Bahia, and Sergipe in Brazil's Northeast from 1864 to 1884 with those in the northern tier of U.S. slave states—Maryland, Virginia, Kentucky, and Missouri—from 1840 to 1860. Also compare Conrad, *Destruction*, app. 3 with Bureau of the Census, *Negro Population in the United States, 1790-1915* (New York, 1968), 57, table 6. On the general shift of slave labor toward the South-Center, see also da Costa, *Da senzala*, 132-137. For the impact of slave trade constriction and concentration of ownership in Cuba, see Jordi Maluquer de Motes, "Abolicionismo y resistencia a la abolición en la España del siglo XIX," *Anuario de Estudios Americanos*, 43 (1986), 311-331, esp. 323-324.

10. Conrad, *Destruction*, 65-69. According to Conrad, the nonimporting areas of the Northeast might have begun to consider the potential increase of prices for their slaves even before abolition of the trade in 1850-51. The antiabolitionist "Barbacena Project" of 1848 was opposed by some representatives of the northern provinces. See Conrad, "The Struggle for the Abolition of the Brazilian Slave Trade: 1808-1853" (Ph.D. diss., Columbia University, 1967), 289-303. Some indication of the impact of slave trade abolition on the northeastern planters is the fact that, circa 1850, slaves normally outnumbered free laborers on Pernambuco sugar plantations by more than 3:1. But "by 1872 free workers outnumbered slaves in all occupational categories, from 14:1 in unskilled labor and 5:1 in agricultural labor, to 3:1 in domestic labor." See Eisenberg, *Sugar Industry*, 180.

11. Conrad, *Destruction*. Just ten years earlier, in 1874, 14 of the 21 provinces of Brazil had slave populations of more than 10 percent, and only 2 had levels of under 5 percent. In the declining regional economy of the Northeast slavery became a relatively more urban phenomenon. See Thomas W. Merrick and Douglas H. Graham, *Population and Economic Development in Brazil, 1800 to the Present* (Baltimore, 1979), 69-71.

By the last quarter of the nineteenth century, the free population of the Northeast had grown sufficiently to facilitate the transition to free labor in that less dynamic region. Within southern Brazil itself, a new regional differentiation developed in the mid-1880s. As foreign immigration to São Paulo increased rapidly, the Paulista planters joined the ranks of the abolitionists, leaving the slaveowners of Rio de Janeiro and Minas Gerais in isolation.[12]

Two comparative demographic points can be emphasized. The regional divisions in Brazil developed over a much shorter period than in the southern United States, because of the different reproduction rates in the two slave societies. Also, free immigrants were few compared to those of the antebellum United States. As an alternative agricultural labor force they seem to have played a last-minute role, relieving the labor crisis of the Paulista planters, and helping to convert them to abolition in 1887–88. It would thus appear that highly organized foreign labor recruitment was more a response to the prospect of imminent abolition in the mid-1880s than a long-term causal variable.[13] For the generation after abolition of the slave trade, free mass immigration was an uncertain potential rather than an actuality.

Brazil's situation resembled the Caribbean model more than that of the United States in that abolition of the African slave trade condemned slavery to a speedy relative decline. The political significance of redistribution seems to have been dramatically borne out in only one generation. It reduced urban interest in the system and it stimulated higher slave prices and concentration of ownership. The frequently remarked Brazilian planters' acceptance of the "inevitability" of slavery's decline (even when used as a political argument against the need for further abolitionist legislation) was based on a logical assessment of the data and an accurate reading of Caribbean history.[14]

12. Slenes, "Demography," chaps. 6–8. See also Merrick and Graham, *Population*, 82–83.

13. Toplin, *Abolition*, 162.

14. The relative demographic decline of U.S. slavery was different from that of Brazil and the Caribbean area primarily in that it was drawn out over a longer period because of a high rate of natural reproduction. Without African imports to match free European migration in the half century before 1860, that decline became progressively more apparent. Peter Kolchin's recent comparison of U.S. and Russian masters interestingly concludes that the U.S. slaveowners were both more entrepreneurial and more paternalistic than their absentee and rentier-minded counterparts among the Russian nobility. The decisive division of slaveowner "mentalities" therefore occurs between the capitalist-paternalist masters of the U.S. South, on the one hand, and the capitalist-rentier lords of Russia, on the other. In Brazil, too, entrepreneurial and paternalistic characteristics are arguably combined. Kolchin, *Unfree Labor: American Slavery and Russian Serfdom* (Cambridge, MA, 1987), 126–156, 357–361; Slenes, "Demography," chap. 11.

A glance at the Cuban example reinforces both the general causal weight assigned to the ending of the slave trade and the political significance of regional differentiation resulting from its termination. The constriction of the African slave supply was a more drawn out and fluctuating process in Cuba than it was in Brazil. Cuban import flows were generally more volatile.[15] Cuban slave prices rose about as rapidly as Brazil's between the 1830s and 1860, but Cuban prices were always higher, and the total value of its staple exports grew faster. This indicates that market pressures for finding alternative sources of labor were felt more keenly in Cuba than in Brazil, and may explain Cuba's earlier recourse to non-African labor. In regional terms, Cuba's poorer eastern provinces were less able to afford either slave or Asiatic labor, and as in Brazil's Northeast, those Cuban provinces produced movements more willing to add elements of abolitionism to their political agenda in the 1860s and 1870s.[16]

Everywhere in the Euro-American bound labor systems except the southern United States, recruitment from without played a crucial role. For centuries, expansion had been effected via the transoceanic slave trade, as in the case of Afro-Caribbean slavery; by binding the native population, as with Russian peasants; or by combining both methods, as in the Brazilian recruitment of both Indians and Africans. During the nineteenth century, Brazil followed the circum-Caribbean pattern which required transoceanic transfers of Africans for expansion.[17] Without such recruitment, all the systems (with the one exception noted) faced deteriorating active population ratios, as well as a variety of other difficulties. If, as David Eltis cogently argues, the "natural limits" of slavery (in

15. One can measure the comparative volatility of these two most important slave-importing areas of the Americas during the last generation of the transatlantic slave trade. During the period 1826–50, Brazil's average quinquennial importation of slaves was 192,500. The widest deviations from this mean were a low of 93,700 (or 49 percent of the average) in 1831–35, and a high of 257,500 (or 139 percent) in 1846–50. By contrast, Cuba's quinquennial average importation in the period 1836–60 was 53,500 slaves. The widest deviations from this mean were a low of 15,400 (or 29 percent) in 1846–50 and a high of 95,700 (or 179 percent) in 1836–40. Three of Cuba's five quinquennia fell outside the Brazilian extremes. The same general conclusion holds if the time span is doubled. During the 50 years between 1801 and 1850, Brazil's highest quinquennial average importation (1846–50) was 2.75 times greater than its lowest (1831–35). During the 50 years between 1811 and 1860, Cuba's highest quinquennial average (1816–20) was 8.3 times greater than its lowest (1846–50). My calculations are derived from figures in Eltis, *Economic Growth*, 243–244, tables A.1 and A.2.

16. Between 1862 and 1877, the slave populations of Cuba's eastern provinces declined by 77 percent, while in the great sugar provinces of the West the decline was only 31 percent. The differential impact of the Ten Years War had much to do with this contrast. As in Brazil, however, where the staple prospered, slavery persisted. See Scott, *Slave Emancipation*, 87.

17. Eltis, *Economic Growth*, part two. As late as 1830, Brazilians turned toward interior recruitment of Indian labor when British pressure seemed to threaten importations from Africa. See Conrad, "The Struggle for the Abolition of the Brazilian Slave Trade," 216–217.

terms of changing technology, decreasing land-labor ratios, management techniques, lower profits from slave labor, or potential slave supply) were nowhere in sight at any point in the nineteenth century, many of the supposed contradictions and stresses observed within slave economies are primarily consequences of slave trade abolition, rather than contradictions between slavery and economic growth.[18]

Economic Growth

The degree of dependence of New World slave societies on external recruitment probably constitutes their most important socioeconomic characteristic from start to finish. As agricultural and extractive frontiers, they also tended to be more dependent for technological innovation and even for much of their cultural self-definition on the increasingly "free" metropolises. Only rarely was one or another of these slave societies able to imagine itself as an autonomous economic and political actor,[19] and Brazil alone developed a domestically based slave trade with Africa well before the beginning of interventionist British abolitionist diplomacy. This stood Brazil's slaveowners in good stead during the semiclandestine stage of the slave trade after Waterloo. However, before restriction of the African labor supply, almost all slave economies were probably expanding faster in population and wealth than the metropolitan societies which dominated them politically. Even the roughest statistical approximations would have led one to conclude that Brazil in particular was more than

18. Eltis, *Economic Growth*, 14. In the cases of the British West Indies, the U.S. South, and Cuba the claims of a contradiction between slavery and technology, or slavery and productivity, are challenged by recent economic analysis. For Cuba, see Scott, *Slave Emancipation*, 26–28; for the British West Indies, see R. Keith Aufhauser, "Slavery and Technological Change," *The Journal of Economic History*, 34:1 (Mar. 1974), 34–50; for the United States, see Stanley L. Engerman, *Time on the Cross: The Economics of American Negro Slavery*, 2 vols. (Boston, 1974), I, chap. 6 and Fogel, *Without Consent or Contract: The Rise and Fall of American Slavery* (forthcoming), chap. 3. The discussion of Brazilian slavery within a historiographical framework of rise, prosperity, and decline is well illustrated in Stanley J. Stein's excellent *Vassouras: A Brazilian Coffee County, 1850–1900: The Roles of Planter and Slave in a Plantation Society*, reprint ed. (Princeton, 1985), part 4. This approach was recently challenged by Slenes, "Grandeza ou decadência? O mercado de escravos e a economia cafeeira da Província do Rio de Janeiro, 1850–1888," in *Brasil: História econômica e demográfica*, Iraci del Nero da Costa, ed. (São Paulo, 1986), 103–155. Free labor, however, constricted, was a second best alternative among the most entrepreneurial Paulistas. See Verena Stolcke and Michael M. Hall, "The Introduction of Free Labour on São Paulo Coffee Plantations," *Journal of Peasant Studies*, 10:2 (Jan. 1983), 170–200. The Paulista planters of Rio Claro continued to buy slaves until the eve of abolition. See Warren Dean, *Rio Claro: A Brazilian Plantation System, 1820–1920* (Stanford, 1976), 52.

19. Perhaps those who came closest to independence were the U.S. southern elites in 1776 and 1860, and the Brazilian planters at the time of national independence. Only the 1860 southerners, however, explicitly claimed that their peculiar institution might operate indefinitely against the free labor trend in the Western world.

matching Portugal in total population growth, growth of the value of exports, and with regard to other similar indicators during the period before independence.

By most of the usual criteria of economic development, Brazilians were unlikely to have been impressed by the "progress" of Portugal at the beginning of the nineteenth century. With a population of only 2,000,000 in 1700, between 300,000 and 500,000 Portuguese departed for Brazil over the course of the eighteenth century. On the eve of its own movement for independence, Brazilian agricultural growth contrasted markedly with relative Portuguese industrial and agricultural stagnation, and Brazilian reexports largely accounted for Portugal's trade surplus with England.[20]

In the second half of the nineteenth century, Brazilians, especially those who traveled abroad, increasingly measured themselves against a broader West, in which the long-term weaknesses of their society became more manifest with each passing decade. In this respect, the significant comparisons were not those of the marketplace such as crop output, productivity, profits, the net worth of slaveholders, or the aggregate wealth of the nation. What was important was Brazil's relative dearth of railroads, canals, towns, factories, schools, and books. The echoes of Alexis de Tocqueville's contrast between the bustle of free societies and the stagnation of slave societies in the United States resonated among the Brazilian elite.[21]

Long before 1850, it was clear that Brazil's demographic dependency on

---

20. See the essays by Maria Luiza Marcílio and Dauril Alden, in *The Cambridge History of Latin America*, Bethell, ed. (Cambridge, 1984–), II, 37–63 and 602–660, esp. 602–612 and 649–653. The abolition of slavery in Portugal in 1773 had no visible impact on its economic growth. Even at the end of the age of Brazilian slavery, Portugal remained "backward by any contemporary standard," and "only the eye of faith could detect much in the way of economic development there." Eric J. Hobsbawm, *The Age of Empire 1875–1914* (New York, 1987), 18.

21. See Alexis de Tocqueville, *Democracy in America*, 2 vols., J. P. Mayer, ed. (Garden City, NY, 1969), 345–348. It should be noted that in per capita terms the railroad milage of the U.S. South was almost equal to that of the North just before secession. See Fogel and Engerman, *Time on the Cross*, I, 254–255. Graham argues that, compared with Brazil, the slave South of the United States was far from being economically underdeveloped. See "Slavery and Economic Development: Brazil and the United States South in the Nineteenth Century," *Comparative Studies in Society and History*, 23:4 (Oct. 1981), 620–655. On the development of railway building in the south-central provinces of Brazil, see C. F. van Delden Laerne, *Brazil and Java: Report on Coffee-Culture* (London/The Hague, 1885), chap. 8. In 1889, the provinces of Rio de Janeiro, São Paulo, and Minas Gerais had 65 percent of Brazil's total railroad milage. See Mircea Buescu, "Regional Inequalities in Brazil During the Second Half of the Nineteenth Century," *Disparities in Economic Development Since the Industrial Revolution*, Paul Bairoch and Maurice Levy-Leboyer, eds. (London, 1981/1985), 349–358. For an interpretation of Brazilian slave trade abolition tied closely to the political economy of transportation development, see Luiz-Felipe de Alencastro, "Répercussions de la suppression de la traite des noirs au Brésil," delivered at the Colloque International sur la Traite des Noirs, Nantes, 1985 (forthcoming).

Africa was the most critical ingredient in slavery's viability as an economic system.

Brazil also contributes to the labor "flexibility" debate in slavery historiography. The argument has often been made that slaves were "immobilized" labor compared with wage laborers.[22] Whether or not slaveowners in the South proved to be more market responsive than entrepreneurs using free labor in the North in the antebellum United States, Brazilian slavery seems to have been as flexible and fluid as that of the U.S. South in the redistribution of labor in the generation after slave trade abolition. Comparing the interregional slave migrations within the U.S. South and Brazil, Robert Slenes concludes that, in proportion to the populations of the respective exporting regions, "the two migration currents were about the same size."[23] In regional terms, it would appear that the "exporting" Brazilian slave areas were divesting at a faster rate than those in the upper South of the United States during the generation before their respective emancipations.

As can be seen in the cases of the British West Indies, the United States, Cuba, and Brazil, all of the dynamic plantation economies produced a variety of crops so long as the traffic with Africa remained unimpeded. In the British Caribbean and the U.S. South, that situation ended in 1808. Thereafter, the former moved toward a concentration on sugar and the latter toward cotton. In Cuba, the trend was toward expansion of all produce into the 1830s. With increasing constriction in the 1840s the slave labor force began to concentrate on sugar production and to increase its productivity. After full prohibition of the African labor supply and the beginning of gradual emancipation in 1870, the convergence of slavery and sugar became even more pronounced. In 1862, the major sugar zones of Cuba (Matanzas and Santa Clara) had 46 percent of Cuba's slave population; by 1877 they had 57 percent. A "ruralization" of slavery, similar to that of the U.S. cotton zone and the Brazilian coffee zone, occurred in Cuba.[24]

Of course, this demographic/economic flexibility came at the cost of regional political divergence. Contrary to convergence models of abolition, we confront the paradox that Brazilian economic and political variables operated against each other in some respects. Economic winners hastened their institution's political decline, while the economic losers for

22. See Genovese, *The Political Economy of Slavery: Studies in the Economy and Society of the Slave South* (New York, 1965), 227.
23. Slenes, "Demography," 145, ff. See also Anyda Marchant, *Viscount Maúa and the Empire of Brazil* (Berkeley, 1965), 269.
24. On Cuban slave concentration, consult Eltis, *Economic Growth,* 190–193 and Scott, *Slave Emancipation in Cuba,* 86–90.

TABLE I: Distribution of Foreigners, United States and Brazil

United States 1860	% of all foreigners	% of total population	Brazil 1872	% of all foreigners	% of total population
Free states and western territories	86.5	17.5	Provinces with the lowest proportion of slaves [a]	13.2	1.2
Slave states	13.5	3.5	Provinces with the greatest proportion of slaves [b]	86.8	2.9

Sources: *The Statistical History of the United States, From Colonial Times to the Present* (Stanford, 1965), 11–12; *Population of the United States in 1860* (Washington, 1864), 300; *Recenseamento da População do Imperio do Brasil . . . agosto de 1872*, Quadros geraès.

Notes: On the eve of secession in 1860, there were four million foreigners in the United States. Indeed, there were more foreigners in the southern slave states in 1860 than in all of Brazil at the time of the Rio Branco law. However, insofar as attracting free European immigration was concerned, the northern United States already contained more than four times as many foreigners in 1860 as the South of 1860 and Brazil of 1872 combined. Whether measured by total migrations or in per capita terms, the flow of European free migration was clearly toward the free labor zone of North America.

a. Includes 11 provinces at, or below, the median proportion of slaves.

b. Includes 9 provinces and the Município Neutro (Rio de Janeiro) above the median.

a time futilely attempted to retard slave labor flexibility by warning of political divergence.[25] Eventually Ceará, the most distressed province in preemancipation Brazil (where the only transferable capital left by 1880 was in slaves), became the pioneer province in emancipation. Moreover, the trend toward free labor in the Brazilian Northeast after 1850 was not associated with industrialization as in the U.S. Northeast: industry did not come first to Ceará or to Amazonas as it did to Massachusetts. After 1850, urbanization proceeded more swiftly in the cities located adjacent to the principal slave holding and slave-importing provinces of the South-Center than those in the slave-exporting Northeast. European immigration also flowed primarily to just those areas that were among the last to be converted to abolition in 1887–88. Many of the indicators of "progress" rhetorically used to demonstrate the greater dynamism of the northern United States in the analysis of antebellum slavery (industrialization, transporta-

25. Conrad, *Destruction*, 65–69. In the case of the United States, the movement of slaves toward the frontier initially strengthened the institution by providing for the entrance of new slave states to match the free labor settlement to the north. Later, the movement of slaves out of some border states aroused anxiety about a declining political commitment to slavery in those areas. I designate as convergence theories of abolition those which assume that all or most of the major economic variables (labor, credit, technology, productivity, profitability) combined with each other to induce the abolition process. For a recent elaboration of the general case against such a role for economic growth in slave zones of the nineteenth-century Americas, see Eltis, *Economic Growth*, passim.

tion, urbanization, immigration) seemed to favor the more dynamic slave regions of Brazil.[26]

The Brazilian case therefore suggests that the enterprises, urban areas, and provinces least involved in economic growth and modernization were the first to turn against slavery. This is consistent with Eltis's conclusion that the burgeoning of nineteenth-century European and North American capitalism fueled the general expansion of slavery in terms of investment, consumer demand, and technological innovation.[27] However, there was no area of Brazil, before the mid-1800s, which could assume the role of a "free labor" abolitionist zone, as in the Anglo-American (i.e., British and United States) case. Until late in the emancipation process, "pressure from without" came predominantly from beyond the Brazilian polity.

Political Abolition

Comparative analysis of the politics of Brazilian emancipation might begin with any one of a number of salient criteria. One can distinguish between violence and nonviolence in the process;[28] between abolitions which came from "above" (Russia, the Netherlands, etc.) and those which came from "below" (Haiti);[29] between gradual and partial abolitions (Pennsylvania, Argentina, Venezuela) and simultaneous and total abolitions (France,

26. See Temperley, "Capitalism, Slavery, and Ideology," *Past and Present*, 75 (May 1977), 94–118. See Davis, *Slavery and Human Progress*, 110, for the classic Emersonian comparison of freedom and slavery. It should be noted that even the antebellum South compared favorably with Europe on a number of indexes of "progress." See Fogel and Engerman, *Time on the Cross*, I, 256 and II, 163–164.

Regional comparisons indicate that immigrant flows could hardly have played the same role in Brazil as they did in the United States after 1850. At the time that Brazil passed its gradual emancipation law, the overwhelming proportion of its foreigners resided in those provinces with the highest percentage of slaves—exactly the inverse of the situation in the United States on the eve of its Civil War (see Table I).

Regarding urban areas, a relatively high level of slave labor (either within urban areas or in the adjacent province) does not appear to have been a major deterrent to those foreigners who located themselves in Brazil. Four major cities with substantial foreign populations had substantial slave populations. They were also located in provinces with above median slave populations (see Table II).

27. Regarding manufacturing, slaves in Rio de Janeiro were beginning to be incorporated into nineteenth-century factory employment when the abolition of the slave trade and the coffee boom drained slaves from the cities to the plantation areas. See Eulália M. Lachmeyer Lobo, "A história do Rio de Janeiro" (Rio de Janeiro, 1975), mimeograph, as summarized in Merrick and Graham, *Population*, 51; see also Karasch, "From Porterage to Proprietorship: African Occupations in Rio de Janeiro 1808–1850," in *Race and Slavery in the Western Hemisphere: Quantitative Studies*, Engerman and Genovese, eds. (Princeton, 1975), 369–393. This is consistent with Claudia Dale Goldin's conclusion that slaves in the U.S. South were drawn out of urban areas by strong agricultural demand (*Urban Slavery in the American South, 1820–1860: A Quantitative History* [Chicago, 1976], conclusion).

28. Genovese, *World*, part one.

29. Kolchin, *Unfree Labor*, 49–51.

TABLE II: Percentage of the Labor Force in Selected Urban Areas

Area	Slaves	Foreigners	Slaves in province
Rio de Janeiro	21.1	34.7	45.2 (Rio de Janeiro)
Pôrto Alegre	23.4	13.9	18.7 (Rio Grande do Sul)
São Paulo	15.0	9.9	21.6 (São Paulo)
Recife	16.7	10.1	14.3 (Pernambuco)
Brazil			11.9 (provincial median)

Sources: For the percentage of the labor force in the four largest cities, Merrick and Graham, *Population and Economic Development*, 73; for the median provincial percentages, Table I, above.

Massachusetts); or between compensated emancipations (Britain, France, Denmark) and uncompensated emancipations (the United States, Brazil). Some of these taxonomies seem designed to engender terminological disputes. For example, if we include all legislative acts, from minor restrictions on further recruitment to complete and immediate freedom of contract for all labor, all abolitions, including even the Haitian revolutionary case, were gradual. Similarly, there is simply no case in the plantation Americas in which slaveholders prostrated themselves before economic forces and consensually agreed to initiate abolition.[30] From the historical point of view, all emancipations in the plantation Americas were initiated by exogenous pressures on the planter class.[31]

In formal terms, Brazilian slavery was gradually brought to an end by parliamentary legislation. Abolition occurred in three major political stages: the effective prohibition of the African slave trade in 1851; the passage of the "free birth" (Rio Branco) law in 1871; and the passage of the "Golden Law" of emancipation in 1888. The first stage virtually terminated transatlantic recruitment of slaves. The second deprived the slave system of its means of endogenous reproduction. The third registered the accelerating impact of the extraparliamentary demolition of chattel slavery.

Considering all three stages as part of a single historical development, how can one best view this process in comparative terms? In a study of British and French antislavery in the period between 1780 and the end of the U.S. Civil War, I suggested a contrast between an Anglo-American

30. Genovese, *World*, 14.
31. For the first wave of abolition see Davis, *The Problem of Slavery in the Age of Revolution, 1770–1823* (Ithaca, 1975), chaps. 1 and 2. For Haiti, see C. L. R. James, *The Black Jacobins: Toussaint L'Ouverture and the San Domingo Revolution* (London, 1938). For the Spanish Caribbean, see, inter alia, Arthur F. Corwin, *Spain and the Abolition of Slavery in Cuba, 1817–1886* (Austin, 1967).

and a continental European model of abolitionism.[32] The distinguishing characteristics of the Anglo-American variants were their relatively broad appeal and long duration. Citizens in Great Britain and the United States attempted to bring public pressure to bear on reluctant or hostile economic interests and hesitant agencies of the state. They used mass propaganda, petitions, newspapers, public meetings, lawsuits, and boycotts, presenting ever more radical antislavery action as a moral and political imperative. They achieved, at least occasionally, a reputation for fanaticism. Organizationally, this form of abolitionism tended to be decentralized in structure, and rooted in widely dispersed local communities. Anglo-Americans usually aimed at inclusiveness, welcoming participants who were otherwise excluded from the ordinary political process by reason of gender, religion, race, or class.

The "continental" variants usually had different tendencies. Their leaders were reluctant or unable to seek mass recruitment. They concentrated on plans of abolition (submitted to, or commissioned by, the central government) containing elaborate provisions for postemancipation labor control and planter compensation. They often attempted to act as brokers between external pressure groups (including British abolitionists) and their own slaveowners. Public discussion was restricted to the capital or the chief commercial center. Continental abolitionists, in other words, preferred to work quietly from within and from above. They almost never were considered as fanatics, even by their adversaries. Continental variants also tended to be limited in duration. A small movement would typically form in response to an external (usually British) stimulus. It would last only until the abolition of its nation's own slave trade or slave system. Continental abolitionist societies remained satellites of their British counterpart, and failed to capture any mass following on their own soil.

French abolition was a partly anomalous case. During the Great French Revolution, the source of collective mobilization for emancipation was the slaves in the French Caribbean. Even so, during most of France's age of abolition (1788–1848), the movement was a continental variant—a discontinuous series of elite groupings, unable and usually unwilling to stimulate mass appeals. French slave emancipation occurred in two surges (1793–94 and 1848), with an intervening restoration of slav-

32. Seymour Drescher, "Two Variants of Antislavery: Religious Organization and Social Mobilization in Britain and France, 1780–1870," in Anti-Slavery, Religion, and Reform: Essays in Memory of Roger Anstey, Christine Bolt and Drescher, eds. (Folkestone, UK/ Hamden, CT, 1980), 43–63.

ery under Napoleon wherever his military forces prevailed. Every major French abolitionist thrust (1794, 1815, 1831, and 1848) came in the wake of a revolution, with little abolitionist mobilization in the metropolis; France was a case of abolition without mass abolitionism.[33]

In the Spanish empire, abolition was generally contingent on the fate of colonial mobilizations for national independence. The process on the American continent extended over half a century until the 1860s. Some areas with relatively small slave systems enacted total emancipation in one legal step, in the immediate aftermath of political independence. Others, like Venezuela, Peru, and Argentina, began the process during the independence struggle but moved through slow stages with frequent retrenchments. Cuba, however, was Spain's most important New World slave colony, and its nineteenth-century path to abolition clearly reveals the significance of the absence of strong metropolitan antislavery mobilization. Cuba's dependency on Spain imposed few ideological or political constraints on its slave system for the first two-thirds of the century. On the contrary, Spain was the most extreme example of the "continental" variant of abolitionism; not even a nominal movement existed before the U.S. Civil War. Until southern secession, the United States also provided a formidable counterweight to British abolitionist diplomacy, and was undoubtedly decisive in permitting Africans to reach Cuba for more than a decade after the Brazilian slave trade crisis of 1850. Even after the northern victory in 1865 and the emergence of political abolitionism in Spain, much of the initiative for abolition within the Spanish empire came from foreign countries and the colonial periphery (Cuba and Puerto Rico).[34]

Brazil appears to have shared some characteristics of both major variants of abolitionism. Before the late 1860s, Brazil conformed pretty closely to the continental European model. During the final phase, in the 1880s,

33. Drescher, *Capitalism and Antislavery: British Mobilization in Comparative Perspective* (London/New York, 1987), chap. 3; Davis, *The Problem of Slavery in the Age of Revolution*, 137–148.

34. On Spanish American abolition in general see Leslie B. Rout, *The African Experience in Spanish America, 1502 to the Present Day* (New York, 1976); Herbert S. Klein, *African Slavery in Latin America and the Caribbean* (New York, 1986), chap. 11. For Venezuela, see John V. Lombardi, *The Decline and Abolition of Negro Slavery in Venezuela, 1820–1854* (Westport, 1971). For Argentina, see George Reid Andrews, *The Afro-Argentines of Buenos Aires, 1800–1900* (Madison, 1980). For Cuba and Puerto Rico, see Corwin, *Spain*, esp. chaps. 6–15 and David R. Murray, *Odious Commerce: Britain, Spain and the Abolition of the Cuban Slave Trade* (Cambridge, 1980). Maluquer characterizes Spanish policy toward Cuban slavery and the slave trade before 1860 as a politics of silence and inaction. See "Abolicionismo," 312–322. A shadowy abolitionist society appears to have been formed in Madrid in 1835 (ibid., 315–316). As with its more public Parisian counterpart, the probable stimulus was the implementation of British slave emancipation in the West Indies in 1834. See Drescher, *Dilemmas of Democracy: Tocqueville and Modernization* (Pittsburgh, 1968), 155–166.

it came to more closely resemble the Anglo-American variant, and developed its own original characteristics of popular mobilization.

For almost 60 years, from the Anglo-Portuguese treaty of 1810 to the end of the U.S. Civil War, Brazil conformed to the European pattern in the sense that exogenous forces played a far greater role than endogenous ones in the timing of moves toward abolition. Great Britain's role was preponderant in linking the achievement of independence with formal abolition treaties. Britain also intervened in Brazilian domestic slavery over *emancipado* issues, i.e., over the treatment of ostensibly free Africans who had been rescued from illegal slaving ships. Even more blatantly than in the European context, moreover, the British government "colonized" abolitionism in Brazil through secret subsidies and covert agents.[35]

If slave trade abolition was the first and most important step in the destruction process, it is instructive to consider the Brazilian case in comparative political perspective. Throughout the tropical Americas, the abolition of the slave trade was opposed by expanding plantation areas before such legislation was passed, and was massively evaded afterward for as long as the enforcing polity was willing to connive at large-scale smuggling. A huge proportion of Brazil's slave labor force in the second third of the nineteenth century entered the country after the first prohibition in 1831.[36] Given the economic incentive for expansion, however, it is noteworthy that nowhere in the Americas did slaveowners attempt to resist slave trade abolition with military force. The U.S. South was clearly the most acquiescent, with a majority of southern legislators willing to abolish imports at the first constitutional opportunity, in 1807. (Indeed, even those states that originally made constitutional postponement of the abolition question a prerequisite of entry into the union did not make perpetuation a sine qua non of union). Even in secession, the Confederacy did not move to reopen the slave trade. Elsewhere (as in the British case) the majority of slaveowners engaged in protracted lobbying efforts against prohibition.[37] Yet a minority of planters readily acquiesced, and in no case did ending of the trade cause a major internal upheaval in slave societies.

The Brazilian case is especially interesting in political terms. Brazil—along with Cuba—was one of the last two slave societies in the Americas to effectively prohibit African recruitment. Despite other similarities to the U.S. South, there had been relatively little endogenous political activity in Brazil against the illegal traffic during the generation before 1850,

35. Bethell, *Abolition*, 313; Eltis, *Economic Growth*, 114–119, 140–141, 214–216.
36. Eltis, *Economic Growth*, 243–244, table A.1.
37. See Drescher, *Econocide: British Slavery in the Era of Abolition* (Pittsburgh, 1977), 181.

certainly nothing comparable in scale to British agitation in favor of abolition. The major push for Brazilian abolition of the trade thus came from outside the nation—in a virtual *casus belli*, in June of 1850. When the British navy mounted an attack on slave ships within Brazilian territorial waters, a number of remarkable results ensued. Unlike the localized impact of naval interventions on the coast of Africa, the entire slave trade to Brazil was brought to a precipitous end.[38] The only nominally independent slave society in the Americas acquiesced in the total elimination of what had been its major source of plantation labor recruitment for centuries. Since the Brazilian elite's commitment to slavery was a primary source of common loyalty,[39] such rapid enforcement and the inaction of the traders, slaveowners, and potential slaveowners are indeed striking, although not out of line with developments elsewhere.

From the perspective of established slaveowners, a general restriction on their long-run powers of expansion was an obvious setback, but its acceptance both spared them the short-term trade losses entailed in a British naval blockade and, as in the U.S. South, offered the medium-term gains of a rise in slave prices flowing from abolition. The immediate losers were outsiders on the verge of becoming slaveholders. The acquiescing planters were mortgaging their political future.

A second important observation concerns the absence of attempts to use public opinion or mass demonstrations, either against the British violators by proslavers or against the Portuguese slavers by supporters of the British demands. The political decision was made behind closed doors, in secret session. Popular opinion might have been welcome after the Chamber had acted, but it was not incorporated into the decision-making process itself either for resistance or for acquiescence.[40]

Sectoral Divisions

Comparative analysis also seems to support those interpretations of Brazilian abolition which emphasize the significance of regional and sectoral differentiation without the need for recourse to sociopsychological divisions of the planter class along progressive-bourgeois and traditionalist-paternalist lines.[41] The demographic decline of slaves produced by ter-

38. Bethell, *Abolition*, 380–383.
39. A. J. R. Russell-Wood, ed., "Preconditions and Precipitants of the Independence Movement in Portuguese America," *From Colony to Nation: Essays on the Independence of Brazil* (Baltimore, 1975), 38.
40. Bethell, *Abolition*, 335–341. Eisenberg, *Sugar Industry*, 152, speaks of the British action as an "unreturnable insult." On the other hand, there was agitation in the late antebellum South to reopen the slave trade, in order to diffuse ownership and support for slavery.
41. See Toplin, *Abolition*, chap. 1; Genovese, *World*, 75–93; Elizabeth Fox-Genovese

mination of the slave trade, combined with the differential expansion of the slave-based economy, produced an accelerated emptying of certain economic sectors which had still been tied into slavery under the lower labor costs of the African slave trade. The same regional erosion occurred in the United States, but over a much longer period. Some of the southern calculations about the need for secession in 1860 were based on perceived trends of slavery's decline in the border states.[42]

The British West Indian case offers an interesting exception to regional erosion that supports the general model. Despite the slave price gap which opened up between the developed and the frontier colonies between British slave trade abolition in 1807 and emancipation in 1833, none of the British slave colonies broke ranks before 1833 in the manner of Amazonas and Ceará in Brazil. The ability of British slaveowners to transfer slaves to high-price areas was legally curtailed. Consequently, the process of regional divestment could not occur.[43] Redistribution of labor occurred only between crops or within separate island labor markets. One of the principal advantages of the use of slave labor over free workers was thus reversed in the British case during the interregnum between slave trade abolition and emancipation.[44]

As already mentioned, by the time the political consequences of the free market in slaves clearly outweighed the economic advantages to slaveowners in Brazil, it was far too late. The social consensus in favor of slavery at the time of independence had dissolved. The relationship between abolition and the increasing economic concentration of slavery seems as clear as in the case of geographical redistribution. It has been shown that for the U.S. South there was "a striking increase in the percentage of farm operations with no slaves," from less than 40 percent in 1850 to approximately 50 percent in 1860. Not only was the percentage of southerners in the total U.S. population falling, but the percentage of southern families who owned slaves was also steadily dropping in the generation before

and Eugene D. Genovese, in *Fruits of Merchant Capital: Slavery and Bourgeois Property in the Rise and Expansion of Capitalism* (New York, 1983), 47–48, reiterate their emphasis on the basically seigneurial labor relationships of northeastern Brazil, but their conclusion (pp. 394–395) places all slaveholders within the same antimodern category. For a discussion of alternative models of planter behavior, see Slenes, "Demography," chap. 1.

42. Compare Slenes, "Demography," chap. 11 and Gavin Wright, *The Political Economy of the Cotton South: Households, Markets, and Wealth in the Nineteenth Century* (New York, 1978), 37, and n. 9, above.

43. Peter F. Dixon, "The Politics of Emancipation: The Movement for the Abolition of Slavery in the British West Indies, 1807–1833" (D. Phil. thesis, Oxford University, 1971); Eltis, *Economic Growth*, 8–9.

44. Higman, *Slave Populations of the British Caribbean 1870–1834* (Baltimore, 1984), 67–69.

1860. The rising proportion of slaveless white families was probably more significant politically than any distinction between large and small slaveholders, because a southerner who owned just two slaves and *nothing else* was as rich as the average antebellum northerner. The need to maintain the loyalty of the nonslaveholding backbone of the electorate was the major task of the dominant party in the South.[45]

In addition to the effects of regional redistribution, rising Brazilian slave prices after 1850 must have prevented more and more Brazilians from entering into slaveowning altogether. Aspirations to ownership and a stake in the future of the system receded, as the free population increased more rapidly than the slave. I have found no figures on the percentage growth of slavelessness in Brazil after 1850, but the available analyses of slave redistribution, price trends, and slave/free population ratios after 1850 all point in the direction of a parallel to the antebellum South. The short-term benefits to existing owners of capital may conceivably have weakened their resolve to oppose abolition of the slave trade in 1850, but thereafter the same factors weakened the potential appeal of slavery to nonowners, eroding the consensual base of slavery.

The Politics of the Planters

The early historiographical focus on planters in Brazilian abolition appears to be quite reasonable, in view of their general dominance and cohesiveness in imperial Brazilian society. Since the abolitionist process was, from the slaveowners' perspective, first initiated from without, the Brazilian case can perhaps be most fruitfully examined within the comparative context of responses to abolitionist threats.

There were certain similarities between the slaveowners' situations in Brazil and the U.S. South on the eve of the external threats to their respective slaveries. Plantation profits were generally increasing in both economies during the first half of the nineteenth century, which should have encouraged counterabolitionist action. The same upward trend was true of long-term demand for their staples.[46]

---

45. Wright, *Political Economy*, 34–35. On southern fears of a class division between slaveholders and "no-property men," see Michael F. Holt, *The Political Crisis of the 1850s* (New York, 1978), 225–226, 246–247. See also Paul D. Escott, *Many Excellent People: Power and Privilege in North Carolina, 1850–1900* (Chapel Hill, 1985), chap. 2.
46. For the United States, see Fogel and Engerman, *Time on the Cross*, 92–94; for Brazil, see Eltis, *Economic Growth*, 186. Slave prices in Pernambuco almost doubled during the 1850s, and reached an all-time peak in 1879 (Eisenberg, *Sugar Industry*, 153). "In coffee-producing Rio de Janeiro, moreover, nominal slave prices rose even higher, and reached a peak in the late 1870s at a level nearly four times that of the early 1850s. The coffee sector's greater prosperity allowed the coffee planters to outbid the sugar planters for slaves, and after 1850 Pernambuco began shipping slaves south" (ibid., 156).

But there were divergences between the two economies which made for very different outlooks in contemplating courses of action. The coffee planters of the Brazilian South-Center would have been less buoyed by the nature of their market in 1850 or in 1871 than were their U.S. counterparts. The latter might rationally have anticipated that secession would succeed without violence. Their major premise was that the South, "safely entrenched behind her cotton bags . . . can defy the civilized world—for the civilized world depends on the cotton of the South." Their optimism was supported by northern disarray and by the fears voiced in England about a cotton famine.[47]

The situation of the Brazilian planters in 1850 was quite different. They were presented at the outset with a military fait accompli which offered only the choice between preparation for war and acquiescence in the ending of the slave trade. No one was under the illusion that a British blockade of Brazilian coffee or sugar exports would quickly bring a major component of the English economy to its knees. The British public and government could always be tougher toward coffee- and sugar-producing areas than toward cotton-producing ones. Only a political regime able to dismiss short-term economic considerations could seriously have considered challenging the British navy. There is no indication that Brazilian society was remotely organized for a scorched trade policy in the mid-nineteenth century, and the Brazilian government seems to have played a continental-style mediating role between Britain and Brazil's slaveowners.

After 1865, the timing of the initial movement toward gradual emancipation in Brazil also seems to have been dominated by external events, including emancipation in the United States and the Spanish Caribbean and the Paraguayan War. Early explorations of popular channels of abolitionism (extraparliamentary organization and newspaper appeals) were confined to a very small section of the elite until the national legislation was actually presented in the form of a "free womb" emancipation bill in 1871.[48]

By 1871, the model of emancipation by birth, as Robert Conrad notes, had been among the tested formulas for emancipation for almost a century. It had most recently been employed in the Spanish colonies the year before.[49] One might, of course, emphasize the limitations of the Rio Branco Law in order to enhance the significance of the mass mobilization phase of the 1880s. It should be noted, however, that the law certainly cut down the projected duration of slavery from a multigenerational perspective to the lifespan of a slave. It definitively set the clock running on termination.

47. Wright, *Political Economy*, 146–147.
48. Conrad, *Destruction*, chap. 5.
49. Ibid., 87–90; Corwin, *Spain*, chap. 13.

Subsequent popular mobilization made a difference of perhaps 10 to 15 years in the duration of Brazilian slavery. Although abolitionists in the 1880s were quick to note that slaves born in 1870 could live for another 60 to 70 years,[50] the active slave population would have been so small and so aging a proportion of the labor force by 1900 that it is difficult to imagine further resistance to accelerated, and even compensated, immediate emancipation. Compensation based on the European model would have become far more palatable as the pool of prime, able-bodied slaves evaporated. In some other areas where gradual legislation was passed (e.g., New York State, 1799) the tendency was for acceleration of the emancipation clock as the slave labor pool shrank and aged.[51]

Brazil's was the only plantation society to peacefully enact free womb emancipation entirely from within. In 1870, Brazil was operating under far less serious direct external and internal threats than Cuba.[52] Why then did Brazil adopt a law which was so definitive about the outer time limit of its slave system, and one which did not offer a guarantee of compensation to planters against the eventuality of further accelerated emancipation?

Conrad's study indicates that during the gradual emancipation debate an area *within* Brazil—the Northeast—began to play the role of mediating the transition to a free labor system. However, the social dynamics of realignment within the Northeast are still insufficiently clear.[53] Were the northeastern deputies of still substantial slave areas responsive to slaveholders who already felt secure in their ability to make the transition to free labor over another generation? The willingness of slaveowners from Pernambuco or Bahia to support the law, when between 12 and 20 percent of their populations were still slaves, stands in stark contrast to Delaware's refusal to consider a compensated emancipation proposal by Abraham Lincoln in 1861, when that state had fewer than 2,000 remaining slaves.

The opposition to the Rio Branco Law raises equally interesting questions. It was located primarily in the dynamic South and South-Center (although São Paulo divided evenly).[54] Given the region's expanding need for interprovincial labor recruitment, why was the resistance not far greater when the Rio Branco bill was introduced? Faced with the histori-

50. See Toplin, *Abolition*, chap. 2, pp. 92–96.
51. Arthur Zilversmit, *The First Emancipation: The Abolition of Slavery in the North* (Chicago, 1967), 212–213.
52. See Corwin, *Spain*, 144–171, 294–299; Scott, *Slave Emancipation*, chaps. 2 and 3; and Murray, *Odious Commerce*, chap. 14.
53. Conrad, *Destruction*, 91–93. Even as late as 1884–85 in northeastern Brazil it was possible for small elite electorates of less than a thousand voters to nearly defeat Nabuco's candidacy for the Chamber of Deputies. Nabuco was defeated in his bid for reelection in Recife in 1886. See Carolina Nabuco, *The Life of Joaquim Nabuco* (Stanford, 1950), chaps. 11 and 13.
54. Conrad, *Destruction*, 301, table 21.

cal record, the planters could hardly have been in doubt that abolitionists, like Oliver Twist, always came back for more. Where was the cry of "no emancipation without compensation," which had unified British, French, Dutch, and Danish colonial planters before their respective emancipations, often postponing abolition for decades? The Rio Branco Law was obviously no more than a stop-gap measure for those Brazilians who wished to "catch up" with their century.

The behavior of the Brazilian slaveholders can be contrasted most dramatically with that of the southern United States after Lincoln's election climaxed a decade of escalating sectional crisis. In Brazil, there was some sectional revitalization of federalism in response to the developing emancipationism of the late 1860s and a resurgence of republicanism in reaction to gradual emancipation demands in 1870–71. But there seems to have been no serious move in the Brazilian South to either overthrow the regime or withdraw from it. For the period 1865–71, the limits of political mobilization on both sides are again evident, but those on the part of Brazil's dynamic southern slaveowners are more intriguing because it was their future which was being most compromised.

The historian of North Atlantic abolitions is therefore struck by the absence of a united front of the major slaveholding provinces against the gradual termination of the institution. Supporters of reform could argue their case before thousands in the theaters of Rio de Janeiro, a city whose hinterland was one of the three most "hard core" slave provinces, with a delegation in the Chamber of Deputies that voted by a ratio of three to one against the law.[55] (The fact that the Município Neutro deputies also voted 3 to 0 against the law indicates that as late as 1870 neither economic modernization, nor urbanization, nor slave disinvestment had yet converted the enfranchised notables of Rio.[56]) The proslavery forces did not even attempt to match the preemptive censorship against abolitionism which was so characteristic of the antebellum U.S. South. Could New Orleans have been, like Rio, the venue for the largest antislavery debates in the entire country during the Kansas-Nebraska controversy or the 1860 election?

The disunity of slaveowners at the national level circa 1870 and the weakness of civil threats at the regional level stand in contrast not only to the southern states of the United States in the late 1850s but even to Jamaica. In 1830–31, the first mass petition for immediate emancipation in Great Britain, combined with new ministerial restrictions on the planters' disciplinary powers, triggered the most vigorous proslavery

55. Ibid., 93.
56. Ibid., 301, table 21. As late as 1870, more than one-fifth of Rio's population was still slave. Karasch, *Slave Life*, 61, table 3.1.

countermobilization in Jamaican history. Public assemblies throughout the island threatened secession. As a result, the last round of imperial restrictions was virtually suspended. (On the other hand, planter mobilization also helped to stimulate the most widespread slave revolt in British Caribbean history a few months later.[57]) By contrast, Brazilian elite suspicion of popular mobilization, revealed in the crisis of 1850, may again have kept planter action to a low level of nonviolent opposition in 1870. A detailed consideration of the slaveowners' perceptions and actions in 1870–72 would make an important addition to the historiography of Brazilian abolition and of the demise of New World slavery.

Popular Abolitionism

In the final phase of emancipation (1880–88), Brazil became the only non-English-speaking country to develop a full-blown, Anglo-American-style variant of antislavery. Brazilian mass abolitionism was largely confined to the years just before the Golden Law of 1888.[58] As in the British case, Brazilian emancipation was enacted by the regular legislative process, and, as in the British case, the legislature lagged behind popular action.

The early phase of the Brazilian popular movement drew on Anglo-American recipes for mobilization: newspaper publicity, mass rallies, autonomous abolitionist local organizations, and the underground railroad.[59] In the final phase, however, Brazilian abolitionism was distinctive and inventive. The first public rallies in Brazil were held in theaters and concert halls rather than in the town halls, courts, churches, and chapels which formed the centers of British and U.S. abolitionist rallies. Anglo-American antislavery mobilized in the image of familiar political structures: through town meetings, formal petitions, and deputations to the legislature. Abolitionist meetings followed the rules and discourse of parliamentary procedures. At critical moments, Anglo-American electoral campaigns had to address slavery as a central national issue. Candidates were forced to take explicit positions on slavery-related questions before aroused, and ultimately decision-making, audiences.[60] Brazilian popular mobilization apparently flowed more easily from the familiar modes of public entertainment than political organization. The proportion of programs devoted

---

57. See Dixon, "Politics," 203; Drescher, *Capitalism*, 106–108; Mary Turner, *Slaves and Missionaries: The Disintegration of Jamaican Slave Society, 1787–1834* (Urbana, 1982), 163.

58. Conrad, *Destruction*, chap. 9; Toplin, *Abolition*, chap. 3.

59. Conrad, *Destruction*, 193 ff.; Toplin, *Abolition*, 86 ff.

60. Drescher, *Capitalism*, chap. 4.

to music and poetry at rallies would probably have surprised a veteran of the British antislavery lecture campaigns. Petitioning in particular seems to have played less of a role in Brazil than in Anglo-American abolitionism. Although petitioning was permissible in both imperial Brazil and monarchical France, in neither country was it central to the antislavery movement.[61]

Yet the inventiveness of Brazilian popular abolitionism extended far beyond the public concert and the victory carnival. Perhaps because of the inertia of its political system, Brazilian abolitionism's distinguishing characteristic was to be seen in decentralized direct action. Brazil created two new patterns of direct and nonviolent action which enabled much of the nation to dismantle its slave system without any special enabling legislation, province by province, municipality by municipality, and even city block by city block.

There are few more dramatic stories in the history of abolition than the collective liberations of Ceará, Goiás, and Paraná in the mid-1880s. For the first time in Brazilian history, "free" labor zones, analogous to the European metropolis or the U.S. North, were established in whole provinces, as well as in urban areas of all major regions in Brazil. Popular liberations were enacted entirely outside the formal political and bureaucratic channels of the central government. When local ordinances were involved, they were likely to be ratifying what had already taken place.[62] Never before in the history of Brazil had mass political agitation simultaneously extended over the whole territory of the nation or involved so many Brazilians. As with Anglo-American abolitionism, Brazilian mobilization afforded an entrée for large numbers of people who had not previously participated in the national political process. From accounts of participation in the victory celebrations, it would also appear that far more people identified with abolition in 1888 than with the establishment of the republic in 1889.[63]

A second Brazilian form of direct action was equally original in style, scale, and effectiveness. Once de facto zones of freedom were established in provincial and urban areas, the Brazilian "underground railroad" came into its own. By any measure it was the largest such network in the history

61. Ibid. For recourse to the theaters see, inter alia, Carolina Nabuco, *The Life of Joaquim Nabuco*, 74. The Spanish abolitionist society, like that of Brazil, initially tended to favor artistic appeals rather than conventional political rallies (Maluquer, "Abolicionismo," 324). Spanish and Cuban abolitionism also adopted petitioning as a tactic in the early 1880s. See Corwin, *Spain*, 309.

62. Conrad, *Destruction*, chap. 11.

63. Toplin, *Abolition*, 256; June E. Hahner, *Poverty and Politics: The Urban Poor in Brazil, 1870–1920* (Albuquerque, 1986), 72.

of New World slavery. The very term "underground railroad" is something of a misnomer. It defers too much to its U.S. predecessor. Fleeing slaves often used the Brazilian *overground* railway itself. More often than in the United States, flight was undertaken collectively, with whole plantations being simultaneously abandoned. Abolitionist initiatives were indeed so open and so numerous that the policing system simply broke down in entire provinces.[64] In contrast to most emancipations, Brazilian planters seem to have had to conduct their counterattacks without access to either the full panoply of official coercion or the active cooperation of the free masses.[65] At critical moments in the spread of collective flight, the cities and the armed forces proved unreliable and indeed hostile to enforcers of the law.

Although a nonviolent termination of slavery by the refusal of slaves to continue working without wages had been unsuccessfully attempted at a late stage in the British emancipation process, the inability of Brazilian officials to mobilize the coercive forces of the state was decisive in the accelerating success of the Brazilian movement. Therefore, in the late nineteenth century, Brazil came as close to demonstrating a "withering away of the estate," despite planter opposition, as any slave system in the Americas except Haiti's.

Violence was not absent from Brazilian abolition. However, given the size of its slave population and the scale of its movement, Brazilian emancipation lies at the nonviolent end of the spectrum. In recounting the bloodiest incidents, historians indicate implicitly that violence and brutality were regarded as exceptional, not normative. Bloodshed shocked the public, rather than polarizing it. The fact that one of the worst incidents of vigilante violence involved two U.S. veterans of the Confederate Army, who taunted Brazilian slaveowners for their lack of manhood and honor, is certainly illustrative. In this instance the government of one of the major slave provinces of Brazil was forced, by public opinion, to indict the participants, although the charges were not pursued to a conclusion.[66]

64. Toplin, *Abolition*, chap. 8; Conrad, *Destruction*, chap. 16.
65. Toplin, *Abolition*, 213. Planter organization against abolitionism in the northeastern provinces seems to have come very late, in reaction to the Ceará abolition of 1883–84, and the planters themselves were deeply divided over the question of gradualism vs. immediatism (Eisenberg, *Sugar Industry*, 166–170). The Cuban path to abolition followed the earlier Spanish American pattern. Until after the U.S. Civil War the Spanish military presence and political repression made open proslavery and nonviolent antislavery mobilization impossible. See Robert L. Paquette, *The Conspiracy of La Escalera* (forthcoming). The Ten Years War for national independence in 1868–78 opened the door to selective manumissions for military purposes and partial abolition in areas under rebel control. But if insurrection accelerated gradual abolition in the 1870s, the settlement of the conflict inhibited popular agitation in favor of the final emancipation legislation of the 1880s.
66. Toplin, *Abolition*, 212–213; Conrad, *Destruction*, 256–257. The most violent series

When the slaves engaged in violence, they seem to have directed their attacks toward overseers, and only occasionally toward masters. The fact that many surrendered themselves to the authorities immediately after such incidents indicates a substantial level of trust, at least in the non-brutality of the authorities. Virtually absent are accounts reminiscent of the horrors of St. Domingue, with slaves burning their plantations and eventually extending the repertoire of vengeance to the women and children of their owners. (Also entirely absent are the scenes of calculated terrorism as carried out by planters and public authorities both before and after the St. Domingue uprising, including all the refinements of torture.) Even the British West Indies had experienced the largest slave uprising in their history less than two years before emancipation. The Brazilian slaves, by contrast, appear to have concluded that neither bloody insurrections nor guerrilla warfare were necessary or productive.[67]

Most significant, in comparative terms, was a fourth class of participants in the abolition process, the free masses, who seem to have played their major role in Brazilian abolition less as laborers than as political actors. It is not elite attitudes toward the laboring masses but attitudes of the nonslave masses toward slavery and abolition that most need further articulation by historians.[68] Slavery as an institution was ultimately dependent on those who were neither masters nor slaves. Masters required more than just passive acquiescence to support their system of domination. During the eighteenth century, British West Indians began to lose control over the slaves they brought to England when the London populace failed to cooperate in returning runaways.[69]

But the free population in Brazil did more than refuse to condone planter violence and to tolerate the formation of free towns at the edges of the cities. Nonslaveholders participated as emissaries to the countryside, encouraging large-scale flight. They made it impossible for slave-owners and their employees to deal with resistance by ordinary policing and patrol methods. The phenomenon of abolitionists fanning out into the

---

of confrontations apparently occurred in the plantation areas of Campos in Rio de Janeiro, where fazendeiro-led gangs resorted to "lynch law." Even in Campos, however, the power of the slaveowners was openly challenged by abolitionist leaders and armed defenders. See Toplin, *Abolition*, 220–222.

67. Compare James, *Black Jacobins*, with the accounts in da Costa, Toplin, and Conrad. On the Jamaica uprising in 1831–32, see Michael Craton, *Testing the Chains: Resistance to Slavery in the British West Indies* (Ithaca, 1982), chap. 22.

68. Relations between the elite and the free poor in the countryside are analyzed for one locality in Hebe Maria Mattos de Castro, *Ao sul da história* (São Paulo, 1987), but the link between those relationships and the national political process of abolition has not yet been systematically investigated.

69. Drescher, *Capitalism*, chap. 2.

countryside with relative impunity was novel in plantation slave societies: elsewhere, abolitionists and slaves were usually separated by thousands of miles of water or (as in the United States) by the solidarity of a very hostile free local population. How to account both for Brazilian permeability to abolitionism and for the failure of the slaveowners to sufficiently mobilize against the British ultimatum in 1850, gradual abolition in 1871, or popular abolition in the mid-1880s remains the most intriguing political question about Brazil in comparative perspective.

Racial Ideology and Abolition

The ideological mobilization of Brazilian masters was in one respect more analogous to that found in the British, French, and Russian empires than to that of the United States. The pro-slavery "positive good" argument of the U.S. South, so highly articulated in both religious and racial terms, played a relatively minor role in Brazilian political discourse. As in the Caribbean and in Russia, Brazilian planters invoked arguments based more on economic necessity, social order, and the advantages of gradual change than on slavery as a superior form of economic, racial, and social organization.[70] This occurred despite the fact that theories of innate racial superiority and social Darwinism were attaining ever-increasing respectability in Europe and the United States during the decades just before Brazilian emancipation.

In his comparative study of U.S. and Russian slavery, Peter Kolchin concludes that the extent to which bondsmen were considered to be outsiders affected the nature and vigor of the defense of servitude. Slaves in the U.S. South were regarded as alien in origin and nature. They belonged to a racial minority of "outsiders," and most members of that minority were slaves. Hence, the equation of slaves as both black and alien could be more existentially sustained. In Russia, the peasants, perceived as "natives," were the overwhelming majority of the population.[71] The formulation of a racially based mobilization of proslavery ideology was thus dependent on the degree of overlap between racial and juridical divisions. In this respect, Brazil conceived of itself as intrinsically multiracial long after whites in the United States were determined to think of theirs as a country of white people. There was no major movement in Brazil to re-

---

70. Toplin, *Abolition*, 131; Conrad, *Destruction*, 167. Spanish defenders of the status quo, like their Brazilian counterparts, stressed economic necessity or political constraints, not the intrinsic superiority of slavery. See Maluquer, "Abolicionismo," 321. Compare with the Anglo-American positive good argument in Marcus Cunliffe, *Chattel Slavery and Wage Slavery: The Anglo-American Context 1830–1960* (Athens, GA, 1979), chap. 1.

71. Kolchin, *Unfree Labor*, 170–191.

export free blacks to Africa, although some abolitionists called for racial removal in the 1830s.[72] At the very time that a movement to deport free blacks was being launched in the United States, serious proposals were still being made in Brazil to replace the threatened supply of slaves by recruiting free Africans. In Brazil, the importation of Chinese workers also continued to be seriously debated when the United States was moving to prohibit their immigration. (The unresponsiveness to Chinese immigration projects seems to have come as much from the Chinese as from the Brazilian side.[73])

In terms of race, the crucial difference between Brazil and the U.S. South as it affected the political process was not potential sources of labor recruitment but the relative proportions of slaves and free blacks. For the politics of abolition, the "degrees of freedom" were more important than the degrees of constriction. At the time of independence, the Brazilian free colored population was already almost a third as great as the slave population. A communally based mobilization in defense of unfree labor would presumably have required (among other things) a free majority racially distinguished from the slave population. In the Brazilian situation, slaveholders could not, at any point during the crisis of their system, mobilize either a credible political-military defense against external pressure or a sectional defense against internal pressures. In this they resembled Caribbean slave societies rather than the U.S. South. Caribbean planters did not have the option of mobilizing free masses in the colonial areas. The Russian situation was analogous. There were no nonserf "masses" to mobilize in defense of the existing social structure, only peasants who identified more closely with the serfs than with the lords.[74]

In Brazil and Cuba, a mass mobilization of all free people in defense of slavery would have required risking a social revolution, appealing to a racially mixed, disenfranchised rural population. The Iberian slave polities were distinctive in having developed a free sector which was racially more mixed and socially more hierarchical than that of the United States. Politically speaking, the "free" masses of Brazil and Cuba were the functional equivalents of the free masses of continental Europe, useless or worse to the planters in a long-term struggle against external abolitionism.[75] On the

---

72. Repatriationist ideologies based on racism were not absent in Brazil. Early abolitionists in particular argued for the removal of former slaves from Brazilian society. See Manuela Carneiro da Cunha, *Negros, estrangeiros: Os escravos libertos e sua volta à África* (São Paulo, 1985), 84–86. Once again, it is the lower level of collective action for these ends in Brazil compared with the United States that is striking.

73. Conrad, *Destruction*, 33–36, 133.

74. Kolchin, *Unfree Labor*, 177–183.

75. The role of the Spanish "Volunteers" as defenders of the imperial connection and

other hand, the free colored urban masses of Brazil, equally uninvolved in the national political process, were also not generally accessible to the abolitionists. Emília Viotti da Costa and June Hahner note the failure of abolitionism to attract large numbers of former slaves and free colored workers. Brazilian abolitionists were aware of this problem as late as the very eve of emancipation.[76]

Comparative analysis therefore seems to highlight the significance of political organization and demography in accounting for Brazil's path toward abolition. The planters of the U.S. South, accustomed for two generations to sharing decision making with the vast number of individuals owning few or no slaves, had forged a regional identity resting on economic and racial solidarity which Brazilian planters had never, and probably could never have, replicated in their hierarchical regime of "notables."[77] Lacking both the political and racial building blocks for a slaveowner *herrenvolk* democracy, the planters tacked cautiously within the narrow boundaries of their political system against the combined pressures of a shrinking demographic base, an expanding national economy, and a contemptuous free world. In 1830, Brazil was still one of many unenfranchised, illiterate, unindustrialized nations with a large, permanently bound labor force. Two generations later, it stood virtually alone.

---

the traditional political economy during Cuba's Ten Years War may demonstrate how ethno-cultural interests could be linked to a defense of slavery. Communal or cultural loyalties could even cause slaves to reject outsiders with abolitionist agendas as they did in some British islands during the Anglo-French conflict of the 1790s. On the British Caribbean, see David Geggus, "The Enigma of Jamaica in the 1790s: New Light on the Causes of Slave Rebellions," *William and Mary Quarterly*, 44:2 (Apr. 1987), 274–299, esp. 292 and Craton, *Testing the Chains*, 180–210. In both cases, however, the planters were auxiliaries to imperial military forces.

76. Da Costa, *Da senzala*, 438. Hahner emphasizes that color-class divisions within Brazil's cities contributed to the fact that "most dark-skinned Brazilians did not participate in the formal abolitionist movement," and class divisions were evident within the movement as well (*Poverty and Politics*, 67–68).

77. A majority of Brazil's population in the early nineteenth century was deemed "marginal," both to the economy and to the polity. See Caio Prado, Jr., *The Colonial Background of Modern Brazil*, Suzette Macedo, trans. (Berkeley, 1967), 328–332; and Michael C. McBeth, "The Brazilian Recruit during the First Empire: Slave or Soldier?" in *Essays Concerning the Socioeconomic History of Brazil and Portuguese India*, Alden and Dean, eds. (Gainesville, 1977), 71–86. There appears to have been considerable ideological, as well as social, continuity of attitudes toward the *desclassificados* in the colonial period. See, e.g., Laura de Mello C. Souza, *Desclassificados do ouro: A pobreza mineira no século XVIII* (Rio de Janeiro, 1982) and Andrews, "Race and the State in Colonial Brazil," *Latin American Research Review*, 19:3 (1984), 203–216. Compare this configuration of class relations with Fletcher M. Green, *Democracy in the Old South, and Other Essays* (Nashville, 1969), chap. 3; Steven Hahn, *The Roots of Southern Populism: Yeoman Farmers and the Transformation of the Georgia Upcountry, 1850–1890* (New York, 1983), 99; Fox-Genovese and Genovese, *Fruits*, chap. 9; and John McCardell, *The Idea of a Southern Nation: Southern Nationalists and Southern Nationalism, 1830–1860* (New York, 1979), 319–335.

Regional divestment, urban-rural and crop redistributions, concentration of slave ownership, and above all Brazil's increasing divergence from the Western model of civil liberty weighed against the status quo. As conflicts of interest and outlook grew wider the consensus of slaveholders eroded. As their numbers dwindled, demoralized slaveowners faced an increasingly popular abolitionism without the potential for a racially grounded antiabolitionism.[78]

It is important to note that not all Brazilian planters subscribed to the European model of civil progress implied in the antislavery ideology. Moreover, the high price of slaves until the final wave of abolitionist mobilization indicates that Brazilian slaveowners, like their counterparts in Cuba, conducted their slave enterprises within relatively short-term time horizons, even after the implementation of gradual emancipation legislation. But three final observations about Brazilian ideology and self-identification are worth making. First, as in much of Latin America, a Europeanized social future, including the demise of slave labor, remained the dominant forecast of Brazil's destiny. Second, some of those who most vigorously rejected the model of Europeanization in other respects (for example, Sílvio Romero's *História da literatura brasileira* in 1888), emphatically supported an egalitarian and fusionistic racial destiny for Brazil.[79] And third, the "patriarchal" vision of Brazil did not fade away without many nostalgic literary evocations. However, no school arose in Brazil during the nineteenth century which successfully crystallized that diffuse counteregalitarian mentality into a cultural identification with the perpetuation of slavery. Brazilian planters remained closer to the ideological norm of the Americas than to that of the antebellum U.S. South.

Conclusion

Brazilian abolition seems to offer some intriguing contrasts with abolition in other slave societies. There was no profound revolutionary crisis in Brazil before 1888 to stimulate the extension of abolitionist appeals to broader social sectors, and not until the Paraguayan War of the 1860s did Brazil experience military problems even slightly analogous to those which accelerated moves toward abolition in much of Spanish America. At the same time, a distinctive political characteristic of the process in Brazil was the inability of planters to rally the country around the principle of slavery, and to use exogenous threats as a catalyst for effective countermobilization. The midnineteenth century was a moment when nationalism

78. On late divisions among the planters, see Toplin, *Abolition*, chap. 9 and Conrad, *Destruction*, chap. 16.
79. Burns, *The Poverty of Progress*, 62–63, 79.

was emerging throughout the West as a rallying point for intensive state-building. The U.S. South linked its bid for national independence to its "peculiar" institution. The southerners failed to achieve nationhood, but only after a massive military and political mobilization of resources. Brazil, however, never developed an interregional nationalism against the British in 1830–50, or a regional nationalism against gradual abolition in 1865–72 and immediate abolition in 1880–88. Brazilian slaveowners lacked the tradition of, or the means for, orderly popular mobilization, and they clearly hesitated to construct such mechanisms before 1850, when slavery was still a consensual institution. Even a planter-led popular mobilization entailed the risk of losing control over the political process at a time when abolitionist attacks were as yet cautious and sporadic. Much like the French *pays légal* of the 1830s and 1840s, Brazilian planters clung to a regime of notables.

Concentrating on the planters and the cities, students of Brazilian abolition have paid less attention to the rural free population. Only recently has there been a historiographical focus on small-scale cultivators which would allow historians to speculate why the free poor were never asked to defend their traditional community on a scale or intensity equal to what occurred in the southern United States. Did planters never even imagine appealing to the rural free masses in favor of slavery because of their distrust of their neighbors? Was the relationship between slaves and free people in the rural areas different in Brazil because of the cumulative effect of manumissions and the consequent existence of bonds which did not exist in the racially more polarized U.S. South? Or did southern U.S. planters play a role that had no parallel in Brazil—shielding nonslaveholders from low wages and the risks of the world market, and guaranteeing the free masses considerable comfort by contemporary world standards?[80] Although historians duly note tensions which existed between yeomen and slaveowners of the antebellum United States, the relative strength of the southern commitment to slavery remains a critical benchmark for comparisons with Brazil. The South had become politically democratic for the white male population in the half-century before the secession crisis, and the abolition of slavery was not on the southern political agenda because no substantial group of southern nonslaveholders elected men to state office who fundamentally challenged that institution. To secessionist leaders, nonslaveholders may still have posed political

---

80. Hahn, *The Roots of Southern Populism*, 88; Fox-Genovese and Genovese, *Fruits*, 250; Holt, *The Political Crisis of the 1850s*, chap. 8. For the relatively high wages of free laborers in the South, see Fogel, "Without Consent," 155.

problems, but in the struggle that followed far more was asked of them and given by them than the planters of Brazil requested even of themselves.

Equally significant in Brazil was the dearth of nonelectoral alternatives through which to popularize antislavery. The Catholic church, like established churches everywhere, proved very reluctant to mount any challenge to the status quo in general, and to Brazilian slavery in particular. There was no counterpart in Brazil to the dissenting denominations of early nineteenth-century Anglo-American society that facilitated local and regional abolitionist organization. As the French case also showed, a highly centralized religious authority was not easily accessible to abolitionist penetration.

Newspapers and other means of mass communication were alternative sources of mobilization. Here one could note the limitations of Brazilian literacy and a weaker national communications network compared with Anglo-America. In general, Brazil lacked the national network of voluntary associations which so impressed de Tocqueville in the nineteenth-century United States. Brazilian abolitionists therefore had to improvise along different lines. The result was to add some startling pages to the history of slavery. In the last phase, it was an extraparliamentary abolitionism, forcing a reluctant legislature and a demoralized planter elite to verify a fait accompli.

In the end, two major characteristics force themselves on our attention. Brazil presents us with an example of a planter class which, though it successfully resisted termination of the slave trade for two generations, could not after that successfully mobilize against abolitionism, even with a constitution made to order for its domination of society. Secondly, Brazil offers us the case of an urban abolitionist movement which had to effect emancipation primarily through ingenious ad hoc agitation and temporary coalitions of diverse groups largely outside the political framework. Abolitionists could dismantle slavery but could not dictate any of the terms of social change beyond that. The Golden Law, like the first French emancipation decree in 1794, was a tersely worded death warrant for a collapsing structure. The very brevity of the law revealed the limits of Brazilian abolitionism—no compensation for the slaveholders, no welfare for the slaves, no planned transition to a new order.

In this respect, it is noteworthy that the major monographs on Brazilian abolition discuss postabolition Brazil almost exclusively in terms of the fate of former masters and former slaves, and are virtually silent on the continuity and impact of antislavery. The abolitionist movement appears to have dissolved even more quickly than it had formed. There was no concerted movement to aid the freed slaves, and neither was Brazilian abolitionism an ideological and organizational exemplar for a multitude of other reform mobilizations as in Anglo-America, although it did have echoes in the *jacobinos'* agitation of the 1890s.[81] Brazil offered its slave-holders little leverage to resist external pressures for liberation, but it provided the abolitionists with little leverage to follow through after slave emancipation. Brazilian abolition seems to have lacked the means of political reproduction.

81. Brian Harrison, "A Genealogy of Reform in Modern Britain," in *Anti-Slavery*, 119–148 and *Peaceable Kingdom: Stability and Change in Modern Britain* (Oxford, 1982), chap. 8. In isolated instances, the Brazilian abolitionist mobilization did have an organizational and ideological spillover effect analogous to that of the English mass mobilizations a half century earlier. Rio typographers sought to transfer the abolitionist momentum into "a new abolition for the *free slaves*," and their intensive participation in the abolitionist victory celebration played a role in stimulating a more militant labor organization. See Hahner, *Poverty and Politics*, 86–87. Indeed, the rarity of successful social movements in Brazil may have contributed to the psychological impact of abolition among skilled workers (ibid., 87).

A Tale of Two Plantations:
Slave Life at Mesopotamia in Jamaica
and Mount Airy in Virginia, 1799 to 1828

Richard S. Dunn

ON January 1, 1809, John Tayloe, one of Virginia's leading planters, took a detailed census of the 384 slaves on his Mount Airy estate, listing each man, woman, and child by name, age, occupation, and monetary value. On the same day the overseer for a big Jamaican absentee planter, Joseph Foster Barham, was taking a similar census of the 322 slaves on Barham's Mesopotamia estate in which he listed each person by name, age, occupation, and physical condition. Thousands of other North American and West Indian slave inventories survive, especially in probate records, but what gives the Mount Airy and Mesopotamia lists special value is that the owners of these estates made a systematic practice of cataloguing their slave gangs annually over a long time span. The Barhams at Mesopotamia kept annual inventories from 1751 to 1832; seventy-five of these lists survive.[1] The Tayloes at Mount Airy kept annual inventories from 1808 to 1855, and forty-five of these lists survive.[2] Setting the two lists of 1809 against each other, we

Mr. Dunn is a member of the Department of History, University of Pennsylvania. He wishes to thank the American Philosophical Society for supporting his research at Oxford and London, and the National Endowment for the Humanities for supporting his research in Virginia. He drafted the article while a visiting member of the Institute for Advanced Study in Princeton, and benefited greatly from comments offered by colleagues at an Institute seminar and at a University of Pennsylvania history workshop.

[1] The Mesopotamia slave lists are filed in the Clarendon Manuscript Deposit, Barham Papers, Boxes b. 34, 35, and 36, Bodleian Library, Oxford University. The lists run in a broken series covering the years 1736, 1743-1744, 1751-1752, 1754-1769, 1771-1776, 1778, 1780-1781, 1784-1785, 1790-1806, 1808-1819, 1822-1832. From 1762 onward the lists are especially valuable because they give the age as well as the name, occupation, and condition of each slave. I wish to thank the earl of Clarendon for permitting me to use the Barham Papers, and Stanley L. Engerman both for pointing out data in this collection which I otherwise would have overlooked and for making helpful criticisms.

[2] The Mount Airy slave lists are found in four inventory books in the Tayloe Papers, Virginia Historical Society, Richmond. The earliest of these books, kept by John Tayloe III, contains slave lists for 1808-1823 and 1825-1828 (MSS 1 T2118d538). The other three, kept by his son William Henry Tayloe, contain slave lists for 1829-

can compare the structure of a Virginia plantation with a Jamaica plantation at a particular moment—just as the slave trade was closing in the United States and the British West Indies. Setting the two series of inventories against each other, we can make a running comparison between the two estates over a considerable stretch of years, and get a sense of two distinctly different slave communities in action.

Two bricks do not make a house, and it cannot be claimed that Mount Airy was representative of all Chesapeake plantations or Mesopotamia of all Caribbean estates. Still, microcosmic case studies have their utility, especially for studying such a topic as slave life, where the macrocosmic work of the cliometricians has stirred such controversy. Quantification itself is surely not at issue; the historian who wishes to interpret slave records cannot get very far without employing techniques of aggregative analysis. What is at issue is the cliometricians' habit of counterfactual hypothesis, their manipulation of synthetic figures extrapolated from mathematical models, and their certitude that by such tactics they can "correct" the "errors" of previous interpreters.[3] Quite apart from the question of the historical accuracy of the cliometricians' findings, their abstract mode of computation tends to rob men and women of individual personality, strips communities of local variety, and turns both people and places into digits in a data bank. The present essay attempts a more intimate picture of slave life. The Mesopotamia and Mount Airy inventories are so richly detailed that one can tease from them a sense of time and motion. The inventories generate statistical information about a considerable number of people—1,400 slaves owned by the Barhams and 1,100 slaves owned by the Tayloes—but the strength of the documentation lies more in its quality than in its quantity. Close examination of conditions on

---

1836 (MSS 1 T2118d13410); for 1837-1838 (MSS 1 T2118d13424); and for 1840-1847 and 1849-1855 (MSS 1 T2118a13). Probably the series began well before 1808 and continued after 1855, but other inventory books seem not to have survived. I wish to thank the Virginia Historical Society for permitting me to use the Tayloe Papers.

[3] This is not the place to detail the bulky polemical literature concerning the cliometric approach to the history of slavery A good way to enter the debate is to compare Robert William Fogel and Stanley L. Engerman, *Time on the Cross: The Economics of American Negro Slavery*, 2 vols. (Boston, 1974), with Herbert G. Gutman's sharply critical review essay, "The World Two Cliometricians Made," *Journal of Negro History*, LX (1975), 54–227. For examples of cliometric work based more on hypothesis than on historical evidence see the essays by Richard Sutch, Jack Ericson Eblen, and Claudia Dale Goldin in Stanley L. Engerman and Eugene D. Genovese, eds., *Race and Slavery in the Western Hemisphere* (Princeton, N.J., 1975). It should be added that both the quantitative and the nonquantitative students of U.S. slavery have concentrated overwhelmingly on the years 1830-1860 because documentation for this period is much richer than for the colonial and early national periods. The Tayloe slave lists have extra value because they permit close investigation of slave life before 1830.

these two estates suggests that slave life—like any other variety of human experience—defies precise statistical formulation. Three-dimensional people emerge with variegated life histories and complex communal roles.[4]

In 1809 the slave gangs at Mesopotamia and Mount Airy were about equal in size. The 322 slaves at Mesopotamia constituted a fairly typical Jamaican plantation labor force, for the island was completely dominated by the estates of a few hundred sugar planters, and Mesopotamia was only slightly above average in strength for a Jamaican sugar estate. By Virginia standards, on the other hand, the 384 slaves at Mount Airy constituted a production force of exceptional size, for in Virginia only a few planters owned large gangs, and the great majority of slaves were distributed among middling and small farmers. Furthermore, while Mesopotamia was situated in Jamaica's richest sugar-growing district, Mount Airy lay in a tidewater region of declining agricultural importance, where the planters had switched from tobacco to wheat and corn in search of a viable product. The slaves at Mesopotamia were engaged in a labor-intensive enterprise, partly agricultural and partly industrial, that required a large, coordinated work force. The slaves at Mount Airy were doing much the same work as small free farmers elsewhere in the United States. Sugar production was the sole concern at Mesopotamia and the sole rationale for the organization of the slave force there. At Mount Airy commercial agriculture was less vitally important, and the slaves on this estate spent considerably less than half their labor in the production of cash crops.

The owners of the two estates, the Barhams and the Tayloes, had been large landholders and slaveholders in Jamaica and Virginia respectively for four generations. As big planters, they reflected in their contrasting life styles some of the basic differences between the two societies. The Tayloes lived in

[4] The Mesopotamia and Mount Airy slave lists form two of the longest series presently known. Amother long series of 27 lists from Worthy Park estate in Jamaica, spanning the years 1784-1838, is analyzed by Michael Craton and Garry Greenland, *Searching for the Invisible Man*, forthcoming. I am much indebted to Mr. Craton for letting me read his manuscript and for fruitful discussion comparing Worthy Park with Mesopotamia. For background information on Jamaica in the early 19th century see Edward Braithwaite, *The Development of Creole Society in Jamaica, 1770-1820* (Oxford, 1971), and Orlando Patterson, *The Sociology of Slavery: An Analysis of the Origins, Development and Structure of Negro Slave Society in Jamaica* (Rutherford, N.J., 1969). The closest equivalent studies for Virginia are Robert McColley, *Slavery and Jeffersonian Virginia*, 2d ed. (Urbana, Ill., 1973), and Gerald W. Mullin, *Flight and Rebellion: Slave Resistance in Eighteenth-Century Virginia* (New York, 1972). For full discussion of a Jamaican estate comparable to Mesopotamia see Michael Craton and James Walvin, *A Jamaican Plantation: A History of Worthy Park, 1670-1970* (Toronto, 1970); and for discussion of a Northern Neck Virginia slaveholder comparable to Tayloe see Louis Morton, *Robert Carter of Nomini Hall: A Virginia Planter of the Eighteenth Century* (Williamsburg, Va., 1941).

the Northern Neck, tracing their property back to Col. William Tayloe (d. 1710), who laid out a tobacco farm on the Rappahannock River, manned at the time of his death by twenty-one slaves. His son John Tayloe I (1687-1747), the chief architect of the family fortune, established an ironworks on the upper Rappahannock, opened up new farms in four Virginia counties and in Maryland, obtained a seat on the Virginia Council, and left his heirs a force of 328 Negroes, one of the grandest mid-eighteenth-century slave gangs in the Chesapeake region. In the next generation John Tayloe II (1721-1779) played the role of leisured gentleman. At Mount Airy, overlooking the Rappahannock, he built an imposing mansion and laid out a mile-long race course. Though he sat on the council, John II was better at horse breeding than at politics, and though he accumulated further property, much of it was lost during the Revolutionary War. His son John Tayloe III (1771-1828)— the owner of Mount Airy in our period—spent his youth in England at Eton and Cambridge as though no Revolution had taken place. The 1787 tax lists credit him with 11,200 acres and 290 slaves in four counties—less property than his grandfather had possessed. Still, John III remained one of the chief slaveholders in the state and by far the largest property holder in Richmond County. As his family grew (he had seven sons and five daughters to provide for), he picked up additional property in Virginia, Maryland, the District of Columbia, and Kentucky. He built the elegant Octagon House as his town residence in Washington, and founded the Tappahannock Jockey Club to promote horse breeding and racing. On his death, he left the fifth generation of Tayloes a rich legacy of twenty-three farms, three ironworks, city houses in Washington, and some 700 slaves.[5]

By contrast, the Barhams, like most big Jamaica planters, had become absentees. They traced their island holdings back to Col. Thomas Foster, who started a sugar estate in the western parish of St. Elizabeth in the 1670s, and to his son Col. John Foster (1681-1731), who opened additional sugar estates. John Foster's widow married a Jamaica physician, Dr. Henry Barham (1692-1746), and in 1736 they retired to England, well able to afford the luxury of absenteeism, since their six Jamaican properties produced a gross income of around £20,000 per year. John Foster's youngest son, Joseph Foster (1729-1789), took the name Joseph Foster Barham and inherited from

[5] For a biographical sketch of the Tayloe family see *Virginia Magazine of History and Biography*, XVII (1909), 369n-375n. Col. William Tayloe's estate was inventoried at his death in Richmond County Wills and Inventories, 1709-1717; John Tayloe I's will and inventory are *ibid.*, 1725-1753; John Tayloe II's will is in the Richmond County Will Book, 1767-1787—all in the Virginia State Library, Richmond. John Tayloe III's will, dated Dec. 1827, is in the Tayloe Papers, MSS 1 T2118d539-545. His property holdings for 1787-1788 have been calculated by Jackson T. Main, "The One Hundred," *William and Mary Quarterly*, 3d Ser., XI (1954), 383-384.

his stepfather the Mesopotamia estate in the fertile Westmoreland plain on the southwestern tip of the island. Though he lived as an absentee proprietor in Shropshire, Barham took unusual interest in the spiritual welfare of his slaves. He urged Moravian missionaries to come to Jamaica, where they established a station at Mesopotamia. In 1768, during the early days of this mission, eighty-four of Barham's slaves were baptized, and in 1816, when the Gothic novelist "Monk" Lewis visited Mesopotamia, he found the Moravians still at work, though only fifty slaves now belonged to their church. The owner of Mesopotamia in our period was Joseph Foster Barham II (1759-1832), of Stratford Place, Middlesex. This gentleman lived on an even handsomer scale than his Virginian counterpart John Tayloe III, was rich enough to marry an earl's daughter, and sat in Parliament. During his twenty-seven years in the House of Commons Barham worked actively for the sugar lobby, but he also voted in the 1790s to abolish the slave trade, and he published a pamphlet in 1823 favoring gradual emancipation of the slaves—on condition that the West Indian proprietors be handsomely compensated for their loss.[6]

In 1809 the Tayloes' Mount Airy estate and the Barhams' Mesopotamia estate, roughly equal in scale, were quite different in arrangement. The Tayloes' Mount Airy Department, or Rappahannock Farms, consisted of nine separate but interdependent units, each managed by its own overseer, strung a distance of thirty miles along both sides of the river. Six of these units were in Richmond County on the north bank, one was in Essex County on the south bank, and two were in King George County farther up the north bank. Perhaps forty whites lived on the whole estate; Tayloe himself had a family of eleven in this year, and most of his overseers seem to have had wives and children. The central unit, Mount Airy proper, was the home plantation where Tayloe resided for half of each year, from April to October; he took his family to Washington for the winter months. No farming was done at Mount Airy. The 106 slaves who lived there in 1809 were employed as domestic servants or craft workers. The other eight units—Old House (where the first Tayloe mansion had stood), Doctors Hall, Forkland, Mask-

[6] For information on Joseph Foster Barham see *Gentlemen's Magazine: and Historical Chronicle* (London, 1832), Pt. I, 102, Pt. II, 573, and Joseph Foster Barham, *Considerations on the Abolition of Negro Slavery* (London, 1823). The Barham holdings in Jamaica in 1739 can be traced via Edward Long's list of 428 sugar plantations for that year, Additional Manuscripts, 12, 434, 1-12, British Museum. Their holdings in 1754 can be traced via the quitrent list of Jamaican landholders, C.O. 142/31, Public Record Office. For the Moravians see M. G. Lewis, *Journal of a West India Proprietor, 1815-1817*, ed. Mona Wilson (Boston, 1929 [orig. publ. London, 1834]), 152-153. I am much indebted to Althea Silvera, West India Reference Library, Institute of Jamaica, Kingston, for additional information on the Barhams.

field, Menokin, Gwinfield, Hopyard, and Oakenbrow—were all farms, with a total of 8,000 acres. The 278 slaves who lived on these eight quarters in 1809 produced about 7,000 bushels of wheat and 14,000 bushels of corn for Tayloe to sell.[7] In the eighteenth century the Tayloes had grown tobacco on the Rappahannock, but no tobacco was cultivated in 1809.

Mesopotamia was differently organized, with all 322 slaves grouped into a single sugar production unit of 2,448 acres. Four hundred acres were planted in cane, and the rest of the land was used for cattle pens, pasture, and slave provision grounds, or was left uncultivated. Like all the big Jamaican sugar estates, Mesopotamia had its own mill for grinding the cane, a boiling house and a curing house for converting the cane juice into sugar, and a distillery for converting the sugar by-products into rum. The Mesopotamia workers produced about 250 hogsheads of sugar and 120 puncheons of rum for sale in 1809.[8] As at Mount Airy, they were divided into agricultural laborers, craft workers, and domestics, but they all lived together in a single village. To manage this work force Joseph Foster Barham II employed a small and highly transitory staff of whites. The overseer and five or six bookkeepers and artisans lived on the estate, and another two or three whites lived six miles away at the Barham storehouse in the port town of Savanna la Mar. Occasionally this staff included married men with wives and children, but most were single males, and few stayed on the Barham payroll for more than a year or two.[9] Thus the blacks at Mesopotamia outnumbered the whites by a ratio of 50:1, whereas at Mount Airy the ratio was closer to 10:1.

Today the Virginia Tayloes still live at Mount Airy in their sandstone mansion of Italianate design built in 1755. From this house, standing on a hill above the river, one can easily recapture the scene in 1809: the terraces, gardens, orangery, bowling green, and deer park, and down below the site of the old race course and the farmland where the Tayloe slaves once grew wheat and corn. But at Mesopotamia there are few tangible reminders of the Barhams' presence. Sugarcane is now cultivated at this estate by the Barham Sugar Workers Co-operative, a new experiment in which the cane workers own and operate their farm communally. The Barham Farm cane is processed at a giant modern factory several miles away. The old Mesopotamia

---

[7] No Mount Airy production figures survive for 1809, but in 1811 Tayloe's Rappahannock farms produced 8,664 bu. of wheat, of which 7,003 were sold, and the corn crop totaled 14,119 bu., with another 2,906 bu. in rent from Tayloe's tenants. See John Tayloe's Minute Book, 1811-1812, Tayloe Papers, MSS 1 T2118a10.

[8] No Mesopotamia production figures survive for 1809, but in 1817 the estate produced 254 hogsheads of sugar, of which 248 were sold, and 120 puncheons of rum, of which 113 were sold. Expense accounts, 1816-1817, Barham Papers, Box b. 33.

[9] There are lists of the white staff at Mesopotamia for the years 1789-1798 and 1816-1817, *ibid.*, Boxes b. 33, 36.

sugar works are in ruins, the old plantation house has been torn down, and only a pair of stone gate pillars and a few Barham and Moravian missionary gravestones recall the bygone activities of the slave-owning sugar magnates.[10]

What can be learned about slave life on these two estates from the Mount Airy and Mesopotamia inventories? Since space does not permit analysis of all 2,500 slaves owned by the Tayloes and Barhams during the 104 years covered by the two sets of inventories, we shall focus on the 668 slaves who lived at Mount Airy during a twenty-year span, 1809-1828, and the 548 slaves who lived at Mesopotamia during an equivalent and overlapping period, 1799-1818.[11] Tracing the individual histories of these 1,216 people, we can compare demographic trends, family structure, and labor patterns in the two slave gangs, as well as the managerial policies of the two owners.

Unfortunately, it is impossible to convey in brief compass the richly detailed biographical information in these inventories about hundreds of Mount Airy and Mesopotamia slaves. To illustrate, let us follow the careers of two people, chosen at random from the top of the alphabet—a woman named Agga at Mount Airy and a man named Augustus at Mesopotamia. In 1808 Agga was a thirty-one-year-old spinner valued at £70, which was slightly above the standard adult female price at Mount Airy. Her father had been a gardener; both parents were dead or gone by 1808. Her husband, Carpenter Harry, was forty-two in that year. Agga and Harry had four young children: ten-year-old John, who was put in a field gang for the first time in 1808 and sold in 1819; eight-year-old Michael, who entered the work force as a carpenter in 1812; three-year-old Kitty, who was sent to the Tayloes' house in Washington as a domestic in 1815; and one-year-old Caroline, who was sold in 1818. Agga had four more children in 1808, 1810, 1813, and 1818. Her two younger boys, Tom and George, became carpenters like their father and brother, and her two younger girls, Georgina and Ibby, became field hands.

[10] I wish to thank H. Gwynne Tayloe for generously showing me his family house at Mount Airy. The house is described by Thomas Tileston Waterman and John A. Barrows, *Domestic Colonial Architecture of Tidewater Virginia* (New York, 1968), 126-137. Mesopotamia is described by Paul F. White and Philip Wright, *Exploring Jamaica* (New York, 1969), 166-167; and the *Jamaica Daily News*, Feb. 19, 1975, has an article on the Barham Sugar Workers Co-operative.

[11] The dates chosen for Mesopotamia are a decade earlier than for Mount Airy because of an awkward three-year gap (1819-1821) in the Mesopotamia records, during which time Barham imported about 110 slaves from Springfield estate. This short gap may seem trifling, but the missing birth and death lists obscure the demographic data, and the 110 new Springfield slaves who first appear in 1822 are not identified as family groups, hence making more difficult the already formidable task of analyzing family structure. Since Mesopotamia's records are complete for the years 1799-1818, this equivalent span has been substituted.

Agga was forty-one years old when her last baby was born, and fifty-two when her husband died. In 1844, when the most detailed of the Mount Airy lists was taken, she was sixty-seven and in failing health, but still employed as a spinner. One son lived with her in 1844; two daughters and seven grandchildren lived on neighboring Rappahannock farms; the other five children and five traceable grandchildren had moved away or died.

In the Mesopotamia list Augustus is recorded as an invalid in 1809, having retired from the work force at age sixty-seven. One can trace Augustus through almost his entire long career via fifty-seven Mesopotamia inventories. He first appears on a crude list dated April 18, 1743, before the Mesopotamia managers began keeping annual records or listing the slaves by age. At this time Augustus was about three years old; his name appears toward the bottom of the boys' group with half a dozen other children who in later lists turn out to be the same age. Eight lists later, in 1756, he is promoted from the boys' to the men's group; he was then about sixteen years old and valued at £75, the price of an able adult working man at that date. In 1762, when the Mesopotamia lists become much more detailed, Augustus is described as twenty-two years old, in good health, and employed as a distiller, a post he held for the next forty years. In 1768 he was baptized into the Moravian church with the name of Peter (though he remains Augustus on the slave lists) and recovered from the smallpox without ill effect. He began to decline in health in his early forties, being characterized as "sickly" for the first time in 1781. By 1785 he was spitting blood. Nevertheless, he kept working in the still house until 1802, when he was transferred to the easier job of head watchman. In 1809, when he was retired to invalid status, he was probably two years older than his then stated age of sixty-seven, and he died at seventy-two on February 16, 1812.

As is evident from these two examples, the Mount Airy and Mesopotamia inventories are more precise and systematic documents than most population counts or census returns, including modern ones, because they were reworked annually over a long period, and because they report at least four variables per year for each slave. Thus they surmount the problem of record linkage, which is so bothersome in attempting to compare any two census lists compiled at ten-year intervals. In the Mesopotamia list for 1809 there are nine males with the name of John, and on the corresponding Mount Airy list there are twelve Johns; but each of these individuals can be distinguished from the others by maternal lineage, occupation, state of health, and especially by age. Reporting of age is seriously defective in most forms of census taking. Demographers put little credence in the stated ages of elderly people, and develop compensatory techniques to combat obvious tendencies toward age heaping—overreporting of age in even digits and in multiples of five and ten—or such more subtle problems as the under-reporting of females aged ten to nineteen and the overreporting of females aged twenty-five to thirty-four.[12]

If such defects are built into current census taking, it is obvious that age statements for slaves on most eighteenth- and nineteenth-century documents are mere guesswork. But the ages of the Mesopotamia and Mount Airy slaves can usually be accurately established. Neither set of lists shows significant age heaping or other signs of gross distortion. At Mesopotamia the Barhams kept birth registers after 1773, so that the exact ages of most slaves born on the estate during our period are recorded. The Tayloes did not keep birth registers, but the birth years for nearly half the Mount Airy slaves can be established. In compiling their lists, the census takers sometimes carelessly repeated last year's age or capriciously added ten years when a person looked old or sick. The stated ages of some elderly slaves cannot be verified and are doubtless inflated, but most other errors can be corrected. Since a great many of the slaves who were brought into the two estates arrived as children, the initial age estimates for these people are probably not wildly wrong, and the census takers endeavored to correct errors. For instance, an African girl named Matura, who arrived at Mesopotamia in 1792, was classified at first as eleven years old, but the next year her age was advanced to fourteen. Four years later, at the (corrected) age of eighteen, Matura had her first child— and as we shall see, this was early for motherhood in Mesopotamia. Thus the two series stand up under close inspection as consistent and reliable; their greatest shortcoming is that they generally identify only the mothers, not the fathers, of slave children, and thus preclude full analysis of family structure.

Table I compares demographic trends on the two estates. As is well known, over a span of two centuries the Virginia slave population experienced marked natural increase while the Jamaican slave population experienced marked natural decrease. Virginia planters imported fewer than 150,000 slaves between 1609 and 1808, and the black population of the state in 1809 was about 415,000. Jamaican planters imported something like 750,000 slaves between 1655 and 1808, yet the black population on the island in 1809 was only about 350,000.[13] As Table I demonstrates, Mount Airy and Mesopotamia reflected these demographic conditions. The most basic contrast between the two slave communities was that Tayloe's slaves increased and multiplied, whereas Barham had to keep restocking Mesopotamia with fresh purchases. The Mount Airy totals in Table I are partly conjectural,

[12] Ansley J. Coale and Paul Demeny, *Methods of Estimating Basic Demographic Measures from Incomplete Data* (New York, 1967), 19-21.

[13] For slave import and black population estimates see Philip D. Curtin, *The Atlantic Slave Trade: A Census* (Madison, Wis., 1969), 52-59, 71-74, 136-145; U.S. Bureau of the Census, *Negro Population, 1790-1915* (Washington, D.C., 1918), 45-57; George W. Roberts, *The Population of Jamaica* (Cambridge, 1957), 35-43, 65; and Braithwaite, *Development of Creole Society*, 152, 168, 207.

TABLE I
SLAVE POPULATION CHANGES OVER TWENTY YEARS

	Mount Airy, Virginia, 1809-1828			Mesopotamia, Jamaica, 1799-1818		
	Male	Female	Total	Male	Female	Total
Population at outset	219	165	384	190	174	364
Increase:						
Born	131	116	247	61	63	124
Purchased	3	0	3	28	32	60
Moved in[a]	17	17	34	0	0	0
	151	133	284	89	95	184
Decrease:						
Died	45	43 ⎫		132	101	233
Est. died	27	13 ⎬ 128				
Sold	8	29 ⎫		0	0	0
Est. sold	5	10 ⎬ 52				
Moved out[b]	53	31 ⎫		0	0	0
Est. moved out	32	9 ⎬ 125				
Freed	1	0	1	2	4	6
	171	135	306	134	105	239
Population at close	199	163	362	145	164	309
Recorded Birth rate	39.83 per 1000			18.89 per 1000		
Recorded Death rate	20.64 per 1000			35.49 per 1000		

Notes: [a] From other outlying Tayloe estates.
         [b] To other outlying Tayloe estates.

because John Tayloe III was constantly switching slaves from one quarter to another, or handing over farms (with slaves attached) to his sons, or opening new farms, or selling surplus slaves, without leaving adequate record. It is thus impossible to tell which of the thirty-four slaves who moved into the Rappahannock farms during this period were bought, and which were

111

transferred from outlying Tayloe estates. Likewise, it is impossible to tell what happened to ninety-six of the 306 slaves who dropped off the Tayloe lists. But inspection of the 209 known deaths, sales, and transfers during this period reveals a persistent pattern: those Mount Airy slaves who were sold or transferred were generally in their 'teens or twenties, whereas Mount Airy slaves who died were almost always younger or older than this—under ten or over thirty.[14] The Mount Airy estimates in Table I assume that the ninety-six unidentifiable deaths, sales, and transfers follow exactly the same pattern as the 209 that are known.

The vital rates in Table I pose an interpretive problem. The demographers Ansley Coale and Paul Demeny have published 192 model life tables and nearly 5,000 stable population tables, derived mainly from twentieth-century European vital statistics and census returns, so as to estimate the full range of population parameters in various regions of the world. Historians interested in slave demography have employed these tables to project birth rates for eighteenth- and nineteenth-century slave populations at around 50 per 1,000 with death rates in the low to mid-thirties.[15] But this assumes that past slave populations experienced the same range of fertility and mortality levels as current nonenslaved populations. The demographic patterns for Mount Airy slaves do indeed seem compatible with Coale and Demeny's schedules. Tayloe kept no vital registers; hence his inventories clearly under-report infant births and deaths. Furthermore, he moved many slaves off the estate, thus depressing the fertility and obscuring the mortality of his population. But Mesopotamia's vital rates appear to be more accurate. Barham's bookkeepers kept birth and death registers that report the deaths of newborn infants. Quite possibly they failed to note many other infant births and deaths; but even if the reported vital rates are far too low, the Mesopotamia data on age composition, longevity, and rate of natural decrease make a very poor fit with all of Coale and Demeny's tables. Clearly, the demographic pattern at Mesopotamia differed radically from Mount Airy's; I believe that it also differed from all observed modern populations.

[14] Of the 88 Mount Airy slaves whose deaths are recorded between 1809 and 1828, 48% were children under 10, only 9% were in their 'teens or 20s, and 43% were adults over 30. Of the 121 slaves recorded as sold or transferred, 25% were children under 10, 55% were in their 'teens or 20s, and only 20% were over 30.

[15] The model tables are published in Ansley J. Coale and Paul Demeny, *Regional Model Life Tables and Stable Populations* (Princeton, N.J., 1966); their "West" family of tables—the only set to encompass non-European demographic experience—draws no data from slave populations. Jack Eblen uses these tables to postulate natural increase and high birth rates among the Cuban and Jamaican slaves. Eblen, "On the Natural Increase of Slave Populations," in Engerman and Genovese, eds., *Race and Slavery*, 244-247. However, Michael Craton's analysis of demographic evidence at Worthy Park estate, Jamaica, supports my findings.

The striking feature of the Mesopotamia vital records is the feeble birth rate. In an average year seventy-five women of child-bearing age lived on the estate, yet they produced only six recorded live births. Whether or not these figures are correct, 109 more slaves died than were born, 1799-1818, and Barham sustained his work force only by importing sixty new slaves. These new slaves came mainly in a single transaction from Cairncurran estate in Jamaica, rather than from Africa. No Mesopotamia slaves had been bought from African traders since 1792, with the result that by 1809 only 19 percent of the slave force had come straight from Africa, another 19 percent had been bought from other Jamaican plantations, and 60 percent were born at Mesopotamia.[16] Those coming from Africa had arrived at Mesopotamia in small lots of ten or a dozen; most commonly they had been teenage boys. The "seasoned" slaves acquired from neighboring plantations came in much larger groups—40 from Three Mile River estate in 1786, 61 from Southfield in 1791, 56 from Cairncurran in 1814, and about 110 from Springfield around 1820. Obviously, these people knew each other already, and they came in family groups, parents with children, the very old and the very young, and almost as many females as males. Thus while in the mid-eighteenth-century Mesopotamian slave life had been marked by ethnic diversity, with Negroes coming from various regions of West and Central Africa, speaking different languages and holding conflicting values, with the passage of time the estate became far more homogeneous, not to say inbred. Table I suggests the extremely immobile character of slave life on this estate. Negroes born at Mesopotamia almost invariably spent their entire lives there. Negroes bought from an African trader or from another planter were almost never sold again. Between 1751 and 1818 only four Mesopotamia slaves were sold, ten were manumitted, and five ran away. None were transferred to Joseph Foster Barham's other sugar estate, the Island, in neighboring St. Elizabeth parish.

Everything was different at Mount Airy. There were twice as many recorded births as deaths on this estate, few new slaves were imported, and the slight population decline between 1809 and 1828 is explained by a massive exodus of slaves—approximately 177 in twenty years. At least thirty-nine Rappahannock slaves—predominantly young males—were sent 180 miles west to the Tayloes' Cloverdale ironworks in Botetourt County beyond the Blue Ridge in 1811-1814. Another twenty-two went to Windsor Farm in King George County in 1820-1821. When John Tayloe III bought Deogg Farm in King George County in 1824, he staffed it entirely with slaves drawn from his neighboring Rappahannock farms. John III stated in his will that he disliked separating slave families, and the inventories show that he generally did sell mothers with their young children. But not always. In 1816 Forkland

---

[16] The origins of the remaining 2%—mainly old people who had been living on the estate since the 1740s—cannot be traced.

Cate was sold without her four-year-old son Alfred, and Gwinfield Rachel was sold without her six-year-old son Billy. A number of girls were separated from their mothers and sold at about age nine, and by the time they reached their early 'teens boys and girls were at the prime age for transfer to a new quarter or for sale off the estate. For example, a boy named John, after spending the first decade of his life with his mother at Doctors Hall, was put in the field gang at Forkland at age eleven, was then switched to Old House at age fifteen, and was sold at age eighteen. Almost all of these Negroes must have been native Virginians. Back in the early eighteenth century the Tayloes had established their slave force with Africans, but John III had no need for the slave trade and small need for slave purchases. Only three of the 668 slaves on the Mount Airy lists for 1809-1828 are identified as "newly purchased." Starting as he did in the late 1770s with about 200 Negroes, Tayloe could, through the process of natural increase alone, come close to building up his force to the point where, fifty years later, he had 700 slaves to distribute among his seven sons.[17]

Examination of the shifting population on one Rappahannock farm, the Hopyard quarter, shows how Tayloe's system worked. This farm had a slave force of forty-six in 1809, of whom twenty-six were classified as working field hands. During the next twenty years thirty slaves were born at Hopyard, three grown slaves moved in, and thirty-nine dropped off the lists. Five of these thirty-nine were moved to other Rappahannock farms, four were moved to Cloverdale, nine died, and eleven were sold—ten of them in a single year, 1816, when two women, Kesiah and Patty, were sold together with eight of their young children. Ten of those who disappeared from the Hopyard lists cannot be traced, but judging by their ages, five of them probably died and five were probably transferred out of the Rappahannock district. Thus Hopyard—a comparatively small population unit—produced some twenty-five slaves for sale or transfer in twenty years. By 1828 the Hopyard gang had dropped to forty, but since twenty-seven of these were classified as working hands, the farm was as strongly staffed as in 1809. Only

[17] My figures on the total size of John Tayloe's slave force are only approximate. I have tried to trace his holdings from 1787 onward through the annual county personal property tax lists in the Va. State Lib., but this is hard to do, since he and his sons held slaves in many counties and the tax assessors frequently confused their slaves with slaves held by planters named Taylor. The process followed by John Tayloe III is easier to trace in the records of a contemporary South Carolina cotton planter, Peter Gaillard, who inherited his property in 1784 and retired from business in 1825. Gaillard started with 134 slaves, bought 125 more (mainly in the 1800s in order to set up his three elder sons), and sold 35. During his 40 years of plantership his slave force doubled through natural increase: 456 births as against 237 deaths. Thus by 1825 he was able to give 433 slaves to his eight children and still have 10 left to attend him in his old age. See Peter Gaillard's Account and Memorandum Book, Gaillard Papers, South Carolina Historical Society, Charleston.

nineteen of the forty-six slaves who were there in 1809 were still there twenty years later. But some families remained largely intact. Four men and four women, very probably married couples, and nineteen of the four women's children and grandchildren accounted for most of the Hopyard population in 1828.

At Mount Airy, as at Mesopotamia, the age profile of the slave population fluctuated considerably from year to year. In Table II age distribution within the two slave gangs has been averaged out over a twenty-year period to show basic differences between the proportions of males and females, young and old, on the two estates. Several obvious and important differences emerge. Mount Airy had a much higher proportion of children—naturally enough, since the recorded birth rate was greater. Mount Airy had a much younger population, with the median age at twenty, as against twenty-seven in Mesopotamia. Mount Airy had a higher proportion of males, including young adult males of prime working age (20-34). Mesopotamia had a higher proportion of females in every age group above fourteen, most particularly young women of prime child-bearing age (20-29). This makes the low Mesopotamia birth rate especially puzzling. Mesopotamia also had a higher proportion of relatively old people, with nearly 20 percent of the population beyond the age of forty-five, and a higher percentage than at Mount Airy beyond the age of sixty.

At Mesopotamia, as was generally the case on West Indian sugar estates, the females proved tougher than the males and better able to survive the trauma of slavery. In the eighteenth century, when the Barhams kept restocking from African slave traders, they maintained a pronounced male

TABLE II
AGE DISTRIBUTION OVER TWENTY YEARS

| | Mount Airy 1809-1828 | | Mesopotamia 1799-1818 | |
| | Percent of Total Pop. | | Percent of Total Pop. | |
Age	Males	Females	Males	Females
0-14	22.1	17.9	14.7	14.4
15-19	6.1	4.0	4.6	5.0
20-24	5.5	3.8	3.8	4.0
25-29	3.9	3.4	4.5	4.1
30-34	4.1	2.8	3.1	3.4
35-39	3.2	2.9	5.7	4.3
40-44	3.3	2.5	5.0	3.7
45-	7.5	7.0	8.9	10.8
Totals	55.7	44.3	50.3	49.7

115

majority—as high as 148 males for every 100 females in 1772, for example. But between 1799 and 1818 this male preponderance disappeared, and by 1818 the females were in a decided majority (88/100). The significance of this shift in the sex ratio becomes clearer if we focus attention on those Mesopotamia slaves of prime working age, between seventeen and forty years old, who were categorized as "able bodied" rather than sickly, weak, or diseased. The number of healthy slaves of prime age at Mesopotamia was always strikingly small—ranging from one-fourth to one-third of the total slave force. During the 1799-1818 span 52 percent of the healthy prime-aged slaves at Mesopotamia were women. Thus much of the heavy labor at Mesopotamia had to be performed by females who—especially since they produced few children—occupied a role radically different from that taken by women in most western societies.

At Mount Airy the women remained a minority. Part of the explanation is demographic, for, as Table I shows, there was a surplus of male births between 1809 and 1828. But the sex ratio was also powerfully affected by the Tayloes' transfer of slaves from Mount Airy. Clearly, the Tayloes valued women well below men, as shown by the inventory of 1809, where the females are priced at an average of £53 6s. 2d. apiece as against £64 2s. 2d. for the males.[18] About two-thirds of the slaves transferred from the Rappahannock district to other family farms were males—thus helping to build a solid majority of men on the Tayloe work gangs. Enough females stayed at Mount Airy to perform domestic tasks and to assure a healthy rate of natural increase. The rest were sold.

About three-quarters of the Mount Airy slaves sold between 1809 and 1828 were female. Of the twenty-nine female sales for which we have definite record, four were small children, all sold with their mothers. Sixteen were girls aged nine to seventeen; of these, eleven were sold separately from their kin and none had babies of their own. The remaining nine were mature women, of whom seven were mothers, sold in combination with thirteen of their young children. From a practical standpoint it was doubtless sensible to sell slave girls at the preadolescent/adolescent stage of life, when they commanded a price that amply repaid the cost of their upbringing and when they were old enough to work for a new owner, yet still too young for motherhood. There is no evidence whatsoever that the Tayloes practiced slave breeding in the sense that they mated Negroes forcibly, frequently, or promiscuously in order to sell the surplus progeny. But plainly the Tayloes did prefer male to female workers, and they maintained an artificially unbalanced sex ratio in their Mount Airy slave gang.

[18] Likewise at Mesopotamia the female slaves in scattered lists from 1786 to 1814 were priced at an average of £71.17.9 apiece as against £84.0.3 for the males.

The conditions described thus far did nothing to bolster family life among the slaves. The character of household and family structure at Mesopotamia and Mount Airy is difficult to discover, since the white men who compiled the slave inventories took small interest in such matters and seldom even identified husbands or wives. But it is certain that many slaves on both estates maintained conjugal family units. For family structure at Mesopotamia the best evidence comes in 1814, when the fifty-six newly purchased slaves from the Cairncurran estate are listed in family groups rather than by the usual division into males and females.[19] The first sixteen entries from this list are reproduced below to show the character of record keeping at Mesopotamia:

Name	Age	Occupation	Condition	Value (£)
Smart	37	Head Driver	Prime	200
Lettice	35	Field	Prime	145
Peggie	12	Field	Healthy	100
Job	5	Small Gang	Healthy	50
Camilla	33	Field	Able	160
Bob	3		Yaws	30
Leicester	5		Yaws	40
John Savey	9		Healthy	60
Exeter	55	Head Mason	Aged	140
Sally	37	House Cook	Prime	160
Bessie	13	House Wench	Healthy	130
Richard	11	Small Gang	Healthy	85
Joe	7	Small Gang	Healthy	70
Mary	5		Healthy	55
Jean	3		Healthy	40
Ann	1½		Healthy	30

These sixteen persons evidently belonged to three families: Smart and Lettice with two children; Camilla with three children and no mate; Exeter and Sally with six children. To be sure, Smart and Exeter are not specifically identified as husbands or fathers, but unless we are to suppose that the record keeper put down names at random—which is highly implausible—the list indicates that these men headed their respective families. A conspicuous feature of the list is that very young children worked in the field in the Small Gang, also known as the hogmeat or grass gang.

Camilla, without a mate on arrival at Mesopotamia, gave birth to her

[19] The list of Cairncurran slaves, dated Jan. 29, 1814, is in the Barham Papers, Box b. 34.

next child fourteen months later. Her small boys, Bob and Leicester, suffered from a common West Indian infectious disease, the yaws, characterized by skin eruptions and bone lesions. John Savey may have been a mulatto, named after his white father, which would explain why he was unemployed although a healthy nine year old. However, he was priced low for a mulatto, was never recorded as mulatto in the Mesopotamia lists, and soon went into the field gang in which mulattoes almost never worked. Exeter appears rather old for his wife and brood of young children, but he was evidently a robust person, still alive at age seventy-three when the last Mesopotamia list was made in 1832. Sally, a prolific breeder by Jamaican standards, had two more children after arrival at Mesopotamia. Viewed collectively, forty-five of the fifty-six Cairncurran slaves arrived in family groups.

How many of these Cairncurran families lived in nucleated households at Mesopotamia is unknown. Evidence from other contemporaneous Jamaican estates argues that rather few did so. Mating was often casual, parents frequently lived in separate establishments, and households containing children were more often headed by women than by men. In the Jamaican slave kinship network, the maternal bond was the key element, for a grown son tended to live with his mother until her death or stayed as close as possible in the house next door.[20] Demographic conditions also powerfully affected family life. In the case of the Cairncurran slaves, by 1832 when the last Mesopotamia inventory was taken, eighteen years after their arrival, twenty-two people from this group of fifty-six had died, and nineteen of the survivors were weak, diseased, or invalided. Of the twelve family groups in 1814, eight had lost one or both parents by 1832, and four had lost one or several children. The one stalwart exception was Exeter's and Sally's family of eight, all still alive, the father nearly blind and the mother caring for him, while their six grown children labored in the cane fields.

The other great impediment to family life among the Mesopotamia slaves was the white overseers' and bookkeepers' sexual exploitation of the black women. Fourteen of the 124 babies born at Mesopotamia between 1799 and 1818 were mulattoes or quadroons—11 percent of the total births. This ratio may not seem high, but it must be remembered that only about six white men lived on the estate at any one time as against some ninety black men between the ages of seventeen and fifty. A white man living at Mesopotamia was twice as likely as a black man to sire a slave baby, a

<hr>

[20] See B. W. Higman, "Household Structure and Fertility on Jamaican Slave Plantations: A Nineteenth-century Example," *Population Studies*, XXVII (1973), 527-550. Compare Charles B. Dew's analysis of slave family life at a Virginia ironworks, 1811-1813, in "David Ross and the Oxford Iron Works: A Study of Industrial Slavery in the Early Nineteenth-Century South," *WMQ*, 3d Ser., XXXI (1974), 189-224.

finding which provides some idea of the frequency of interracial sexual intercourse. The whites preferred their slave mistresses to be young: of the nine women who bore mulatto or quadroon infants during this twenty-year span, one was only fifteen years old and four others were under twenty. The whites also preferred light-complexioned women, such as Mulatto Ann, who worked in the overseer's house from age ten on, and bore two quadroon children when she was sixteen and eighteen. Neither Ann nor any of the other women used by the whites at Mesopotamia was manumitted. A twenty-three-year-old field slave named Judy, the mother of two Negro children, bore a mulatto boy named Archibald; sl.e remained in the field gang and bore six more Negro children. Her son Archibald, being a mulatto, was placed in the overseer's house at age six and trained as a carpenter at age sixteen, but he must have been an unhappy person for he became a chronic runaway and died of the yaws when he was twenty-seven. Another sad story is the case of Batty, a field slave who caught the eye of the overseer, Patrick Knight, when she was a young mother in her twenties. Batty had two daughters by Knight, and in 1803, when she was twenty-nine, he manumitted both girls, took Batty out of the field gang, and installed her in his house. For the next thirteen years Batty lived with Knight and bore him two more children. Her sixth baby was a Negro child, and at about the age of forty she contracted the Coco Bays, a disease akin to leprosy. So Batty was sent back to the Mesopotamia work force, though she was sick, to toil her declining years as a washerwoman and grass cutter.

In Virginia mulattoes and quadroons were not identified as such in the records; thus there is no direct evidence of miscegenation at Mount Airy. But the evidence of disrupted family life is abundant. In 1816, when the Tayloes sold Hopyard Kesiah and Hopyard Patty with eight of their children, two of Patty's teenage children stayed at Hopyard and no male mates went with Kesiah and Patty. Similarly, in 1820, when Bob and his wife Betty were sent from Oakenbrow quarter to Windsor farm with their three youngest children, their older three teenage children stayed at Oakenbrow. A fuller sense of the disjointed nature of family life at Mount Airy comes from inspection of the inventory for 1835, a few years beyond our period. This is an exceptionally interesting list because it identifies both parents of all the small children on the estate and thereby records many of the slave marriages.[21] The following extract shows the character of this 1835 list:

[21] The inventory for 1835 is in the first inventory book kept by William Henry Tayloe, John III's third son, who inherited Mount Airy and four adjoining farms in 1828 (Tayloe Papers, MSS 1 T2118d13410, 43-46). William Henry Tayloe's inventories for 1844 and 1845 are likewise useful, since they identify the parents of almost all the adult slaves living at Mount Airy in those years. Ibid., MSS 1 T2118a13.

Car[penter]. Bill and his wife Esthers .... wife Winney Jr.

Children		Urias 7
Winney 8		Paul 5
Anne 7		China 3
Juliet 5		Prince .... Inf[ant]
James 3		
Charlotte .... Inf[ant]		Marilla's—Husband Decd.

Rose 8

Tom and his wife Winneys   Jacob and his wife Mary
    William .... out in field   Kate .... 10 in Ala[bama]
    Grace 7
    Chapman 4

Altogether, thirty-five Mount Airy slave families can be reconstructed by combining this inventory of 1835 with the earlier lists.

The five Mount Airy families shown in the illustration above are not listed completely. Esther had a ten-year-old daughter working at the Tayloe house in Washington; Mary had a fourteen-year-old son working in a field gang; and Marilla had five grown children, three of whom lived on the same quarter with her in 1835. Except for Winney's twelve-year-old son William, this list excludes working children, but when Mount Airy boys and girls did enter the work force they sometimes were sent far away—like ten-year-old Kate in the example above, who went to Alabama in 1836. When this list was drawn up, the Tayloes were in the process of moving Negroes from several of their Virginia estates to Alabama in order to open new cotton plantations there. By 1836 William Henry Tayloe had transferred forty-seven of his Mount Airy slaves—mainly young unmarried men and women—to Alabama, and by 1855 he had more slaves there than in Virginia.

The Mount Airy kinship network was pervasive in 1835; almost every slave had several blood relatives living on the estate. Yet of the thirty-five identifiable slave families, fifteen were lacking one or both parents, and in most families the children were widely dispersed. Furthermore, in the twenty families where husband and wife were both still living, only five couples regularly lived together. The others worked at separate quarters, often many miles apart, which doubtless helped to depress the Mount Airy fertility rate. Carpenter Bill in the illustration above was a polygamist who lived at Mount Airy while his two wives, Esther and Winney, lived at Landsdown with parallel sets of young children. Another polygamist in 1835 was a man named Oliver who was owned by a neighboring planter. Oliver had two wives and eight children at Doctors Hall quarter. Three other outside males were married to Mount Airy women; one of them was a free black named David, by whom Forkland Criss bore a family of ten slave children. As at Mesopo-

tamia, most young Mount Airy children seem to have lived with their
mothers but not with their fathers. And since the Tayloes kept more male
than female slaves, a great many Mount Airy men had no marriage partners
unless they mated with women from neighboring estates. According to the
1835 list, almost all the eligible Mount Airy women had husbands, while only
a third of the men in their twenties and thirties had local wives—a fact that
must have contributed powerfully to masculine feelings of inadequacy and
frustration.[22]

We turn now to the employment pattern on the two estates. Table III
compares the distribution of jobs at Mount Airy and Mesopotamia in 1809.
According to these figures, Barham employed his slave force much more fully
than did Tayloe. At Mesopotamia four-fifths of the Negroes were allotted
tasks, and many more women and children worked than at Mount Airy.

Tayloe designated as working hands only those slaves mature and strong
enough to do a full "share" or a half "share" of labor apiece—in practice, all
able-bodied Negroes over the age of ten[23]—but the younger children also
must have had light tasks to keep them occupied, if not productive. At
Mesopotamia boys and girls were put to work at age six, generally in the
hogmeat or grass gang, to gather grass and straw from the fields to feed the
livestock. At age ten they usually graduated to harder assignments, such as
hoeing the young cane and carrying dung in the third field gang. At fifteen or
sixteen they might move up to the second field gang and spend the next few
years weeding the cane and cleaning the pastures. At about twenty they
would be ready for the Great Gang and its backbreaking toil of digging the
cane holes and cutting the ripe cane. Slaves who started out as field laborers
were rarely switched to craft or domestic jobs. Only workers in their prime
did the heavy field labor. At Mesopotamia men who were past forty and
sickly became jobbers or watchmen; old or ailing women became field cooks,
nurses, or washerwomen. Very likely some of the older Mount Airy slaves
listed as nonworkers performed similar marginal tasks.

On both plantations a majority of the laborers in 1809 were field hands,
but there were a good many skilled and favored job holders. At Mesopotamia
a small managerial elite—the drivers of the field gangs, the chief craftsmen,
and Quasheba the African female doctor—received special rations of rum
each week. The Mesopotamia craft workers were all male; almost all of them

[22] For a considerably more positive picture of the slave family in 18th-century
Maryland see Allan Kulikoff, "The Beginnings of the Afro-American Family in
Maryland," in Aubrey C. Land *et al.*, eds., *Law, Society, and Politics in Early
Maryland: Essays in Honor of Morris Leon Radoff* (Baltimore, 1976).
[23] The overseer on each Rappahannock farm got one or more "shares" of the
crop, encouraging him to extract maximum output from the workers, who in 1809
produced an average about 50 bu. of wheat and 100 bu. of corn apiece.

TABLE III
LABOR PATTERNS AT MOUNT AIRY AND MESOPOTAMIA IN 1809

	Mount Airy			Mesopotamia		
	Males	Females	%	Males	Females	%
A. Workers						
Drivers	0	0	0.00	4	1	1.55
Craftworkers	33	14	12.24	25	0	7.76
Domestics	18	17	9.11	8	15	7.14
Field Cooks	0	0	0.00	0	6	1.86
Fieldworkers	86	58	37.50	45	92	42.55
Jobbers	7	0	1.82	7	0	2.17
Transport	5	0	1.30	6	0	1.86
Stockkeepers	0	0	0.00	14	2	4.97
Watchmen	0	0	0.00	19	0	5.90
Nurses	0	0	0.00	0	11	3.42
Total	149	89	61.98	128	127	79.19
B. Nonworkers						
Too young	61	63	32.29	20	16	11.18
Too old	2	5	1.82	4	6	3.11
Too sick	7	8	3.91	11	10	6.52
Total	70	76	38.02	35	32	20.81
C. Totals	219	165	100.00	163	159	100.00

had learned their jobs as boy apprentices and pursued the same routine for years. The fact that nearly half of them were over the age of forty in 1809 indicates—as one might guess—that craft workers survived longer than field laborers. No fewer than ten houseboys, maid servants, and cooks waited on the overseer and the bookkeepers, and four slaves assisted the Moravian missionaries at their chapel. At Mount Airy the proportion of skilled and semi-skilled workers was considerably higher—34 percent of those employed, as compared with 21 percent at Mesopotamia.[24] Because the Tayloes lived at Mount Airy, they had twenty-six domestics, and the overseers at the outlying farms had one or two house servants each. As at Mesopotamia, the Mount Airy artisans and domestics entered their jobs as children and, once established, were far less likely to be transferred or sold than were the field laborers.

[24] This figure at Mount Airy is unusually high. Fogel and Engerman, in their analysis of southern U.S. slave occupations around 1850, claim that 26.3% were in skilled or semi-skilled jobs (*Time on the Cross*, I, 38-40), but Gutman argues that the true figure was 15% or lower ("The World Two Cliometricians Made," *Jour. of Negro Hist.*, LX [1975], 111-128).

The labor pattern at Mount Airy was designed to achieve almost total self-sufficiency. The field workers raised corn and pork—the staple slave foods in Virginia—and tended their vegetable gardens in off hours. Using cotton grown and ginned on the estate, and wool sheared from local sheep, the seventeen spinners and weavers made coarse cloth for slave apparel and fine cloth for household linen. The four shoemakers tanned and dressed leather from Mount Airy cattle to make coarse shoes for the slaves and custom shoes for the Tayloes, as well as harness for the horses, mules, and oxen.[25] The nine smiths and joiners built and repaired wagons, ploughs, and hoes, and shod horses, while the twenty-two carpenters, masons, and jobbers moved about the estate erecting and repairing buildings. Tayloe's wagoner carted goods from one unit to another, and his schooner, *The Federalist*, manned by four slave sailors, carried his cash crop of Rappahannock wheat, flour, corn, and oats to Baltimore or Alexandria.

By contrast, the Mesopotamia labor pattern was by no means designed for self-sufficiency. In order to keep his slaves alive and working, Barham shipped food, tools, and clothing from Britain. On the mountain land bordering the estate the slaves cultivated crops of cocco roots and plantains— an equivalent to Mount Airy's cornmeal—but quite often these provision crops were ruined by tropical storms or drought. In 1815 and again in 1816 the Mesopotamia overseer bought a ton of cocco roots as emergency rations to prevent starvation. For protein the slaves depended largely on meager allotments of salt herring shipped from England—150 barrels in 1817, or half a barrel per slave per year.[26] Livestock were plentiful on this estate—448 cattle in 1809, for example—but they were used to produce manure for fertilizer or as draft animals, and only three steers were slaughtered annually for the slaves as a special Christmas treat. No cloth was made at Mesopotamia; instead, Barham bought about two thousand yards of coarse oznaburgh linen annually, or seven yards per slave, together with thread, scissors, and needles, so that his Negroes could make their own clothes. There were no shoemakers—unneeded since slaves wore no shoes—and no local ironworks to supply ironmongery and nails. The three Mesopotamia blacksmiths did not manufacture farm implements as at Mount Airy, so that every tool and piece of machinery had to be imported. Not even the labor force was self-sufficient. Whenever major repairs were needed at the sugar factory, managers hired white masons and coppersmiths rather than trust the work to their slave craftsmen. And during the two years 1816-1817 they paid £930— the cost of a dozen new slaves—in order to hire extra Negro laborers to hole

[25] The Mount Airy artisans also did custom work for the Tayloes' white neighbors. See Tayloe Account Book, 1789-1828, Tayloe Papers. MSS 1 T2118d357.

[26] The Mesopotamia expense accounts for 1816-1817 are in the Barham Papers. Box b. 33.

the cane fields, clean the pastures, and plant provisions, since the regular work gangs could not handle all the necessary field tasks.

Another big difference between the employment patterns of the two estates is that the female slaves did much more of the basic labor at Mesopotamia. Table III shows that two-thirds of the agricultural laborers on that estate were women and girls. Even on the Mesopotamia Great Gang, where the hardest work was done, there were thirty-one women and twenty-two men in 1809. Females did much of the heavy labor at Mount Airy also, but more of them worked in craft or domestic jobs, and nearly half were excused from employment. Motherhood was no excuse, however. Thirty-eight Mount Airy women had one or more living children under the age of six in 1809, and all but two of them had full-time jobs. Sally, a twenty-nine-year-old field hand at Doctors Hall, had five young children in 1809 and gave birth to eight more by 1826, while continuing to do her "share" of farm labor. Motherhood was more honored at Mesopotamia, because the birth rate was so alarmingly low. Here the overseer made a practice of moving pregnant members of the Great Gang to the second field gang, where the work was lighter. Matura, the mother of five children, was taken off the Great Gang permanently in 1809 so that she could look after her youngsters. At Mesopotamia all mothers of newborn infants were paid a bonus of £1 in cash "for raising their children," and nursing mothers received a quart of oatmeal and a pint of sugar each week.[27]

Not surprisingly, the Mesopotamia management favored those mulatto and quadroon slaves who had been sired by the white staff. Of the seventeen mulattoes and one quadroon living on the estate in 1809, six were house servants, two were carpenters, one attended the Moravian missionaries, and the rest were too young for employment. Mulattoes at Mesopotamia generally began work when they were nine years old, three years later than the Negroes, and they never labored in the fields. At the opposite end of the spectrum, the management discriminated particularly against native Africans. Of the sixty-two persons at Mesopotamia in 1809 who had come via the slave trade, only Quasheba the doctor was recognized as an important figure. Over 80 percent were relegated to gang labor in the fields.[28]

But how meaningful were these occupational titles? Did the field hands really spend all their time in the fields or the blacksmiths at the forge? Fortunately, the Tayloe plantation records include three work logs dated just before and after 1809, showing the actual tasks performed each day of the

[27] Mesopotamia food allotments, June 1802, *ibid.*, Box b. 36; expense accounts, 1816-1817, *ibid.*, Box b. 33.
[28] Of these Africans, 43% were field workers in 1809, and another 39% were jobbers, watchmen, nurses, or invalids who had formerly worked in the field gangs. Craton and Walvin find much the same pattern for mulattoes and Africans at Worthy Park (*A Jamaican Plantation*, 138-140).

year by the Mount Airy craft workers, and each week of the year by the Rappahannock farm gangs.[29] From these logs it is evident that the Tayloe slaves did indeed have distinct occupations. The 144 field workers labored almost exclusively on agricultural tasks, spending more time on the corn crop than on any other job—some twenty weeks during the course of the year. They spent ten weeks on the wheat crop and three weeks on the oats crop. The artisans joined in the grain harvest for two weeks in June and July but otherwise worked exclusively at their crafts. Work assignments were variegated, with new tasks assigned every two or three days. Throughout the year the slaves were kept busy six days a week. Apart from Sundays, they had nine days of vacation: Easter Monday, Whit Monday, two free Saturdays in May and July, and a five-day Christmas break from December 25 to 29.

Though the Mount Airy artisans and field hands had separate and specialized functions, their work rhythms were closely synchronized. During the coldest six weeks from mid-December to the end of January, when the previous season's crops had all been harvested and the winter wheat was in the ground, the field workers and jobbers shucked and beat corn, cut and hauled timber to the saw mill for fence rails and posts, and cut ice from the Rappahannock creek. The carpenters meanwhile operated the saw mill, while the smiths and joiners repaired ploughs, wagons, and harnesses for spring ploughing. In February the field hands worked with the carpenters and joiners in putting up fencing, with the jobbers in clearing and manuring the fields for ploughing, and with the sailors in loading the previous year's corn on *The Federalist* for shipment to Alexandria. In March the field gangs planted oats, in April corn, and in May cotton and peas, while the smiths and joiners repaired their tools. In mid-April, just before the Tayloe family arrived for the summer from Washington, eighty-five laborers from five of the Rappahannock farms came to Mount Airy to dress up the mansion lawn. In late May the field workers began to weed the corn, while the smiths, joiners, and carpenters were making and mending rakes, cradles, and scythes for the coming harvest. In mid-June the wagoner went to Kinsale, a nearby town, to fetch five barrels of whiskey for the harvest. The wheat crop at Old House, Doctors Hall, and Forkland was harvested in one frenzied week during mid- or late June; forty-five extra hands were pressed into service— the smiths, masons, joiners, carpenters, and jobbers cut and cradled the grain, while the spinners, shoemakers, and weavers raked and bound it into sheaves. John Tayloe III personally supervised operations; in June 18, 1801, he com-

---

[29] John Tayloe III's Minute Book for Jan. 1-Dec. 7, 1805, Tayloe Papers, MSS 1 T2118a8, records craft work daily and field work weekly. His Minute Book for 1811-1812 does the same for Jan. 9-Sept. 4, 1811, and Feb. 10-Dec. 31, 1812, *ibid.*, MSS 1 T2118a10. His Spinning Minute Book itemizes the amount of cotton and wool spun at Mount Airy every week for Jan. 1806-Dec. 1807, *ibid.*, MSS 1 T2118a9.

plained to a correspondent of being "just from my harvest field and fatigued to death."[30]

In July the seasonal pressure continued, as all hands joined for a week to cut and rake the oats crop at Old House. During the next weeks the field gangs worked mainly in the corn fields, hilling and hoeing the plants. In August they cut the hay and threshed the wheat. The jobbers helped with the hay, the carpenters made grain barrels, and the smiths and joiners worked as usual on ploughs and wagons. In September the wagoner and sailors helped the field hands to load Tayloe's schooner with wheat for the Baltimore market. Now it was time to gather the corn leaves as fodder, and to start the long process of seeding the winter wheat. With the fall racing season approaching, the smiths set to work to shoe Tayloe's racehorses. Shortly after the races, the Tayloes departed for Washington, and the craft workers could now make necessary repairs on the mansion house—as in 1805, when the carpenters, joiners, masons, and jobbers worked for a month reshingling the mansion roof under the supervision of a hired white builder. In October the spinners joined the field hands at picking cotton, and from mid-November to mid-December, with the wheat fields finally seeded, the field hands harvested the corn and hauled the stalks to the saw mill. Just before and after Christmas, the slackest work period of the year, Tayloe's masons, carpenters, and jobbers were sent to repair the Richmond County courthouse.

For the Mesopotamia labor force no equivalent work logs have survived. But a field labor book, dated 1796-1797, for Newton plantation in Barbados—a sugar estate of about the same strength as Mesopotamia—records the daily tasks of field and craft workers throughout the year.[31] The work pattern recorded at Newton did not necessarily hold true for Mesopotamia, since Barbadian and Jamaican planting practices differed significantly. Nonetheless, these Barbados work logs are certainly of some help. For one thing, they suggest that craft workers on a Caribbean sugar estate were less clearly differentiated from field workers than they were on a big Virginian estate like Mount Airy. The coopers and masons at Newton estate spent a full two months each year working with the field hands on the sugar harvest, and once the cane was processed, the specialists in the sugar factory labored in the fields for the next six months. Field laborers were ranked by ability in both systems, categorized in Virginia as full "shares" or half "shares," and were sorted in the Caribbean into three gangs, with the first gang (Great Gang) always assigned the hardest jobs. As at Mount Airy, work assignments were

[30] John Tayloe III to John Rose, John Tayloe Letter Book, 1801, *ibid.*, MSS 1 T2118d170.

[31] Newton Plantation Field Labor Book, May 5, 1796-Apr. 26, 1797, Newton Papers, MS 523/110, University of London Library. A second field labor book for the adjoining Barbados plantation of Seawalls, running from Jan. 1 to Sept. 4, 1798, is *ibid.*, MS 523/122.

changed every few days, and it would be a mistake to suppose that slaves on a sugar estate spent all their time planting and cutting cane. The Newton logs show that the first and second gangs spent the equivalent of six months per year in sugar production, three months raising guinea corn for cattle and slave food, two months repairing the cattle pens, and another month at such miscellaneous tasks as cultivating yams, potatoes, and peas.[32] On one day each year all plantation work was stopped, and every man, woman, and capable child was given cloth, a needle, and thread, and set to work stitching together his or her set of clothes for the following year.

At Mount Airy the Tayloes stretched seasonal employment into year-round employment by letting their slaves work at a leisurely pace. Three masons took fifteen working days to build a cottage chimney; thirty working hands at Old House took eight weeks to sow 258 bushels of wheat. Only at harvest time did people work under extreme pressure for several weeks. But in the Caribbean the sugar harvest lasted for four months or more, from January or February to May or June. And while at Mount Airy the heaviest labor was done by horses, mules, and oxen, at Newton—or Mesopotamia—the slaves did the work of draft animals. The Newton first-gang slaves spent nearly one week in every month at the brutal task of cane holing by hand. Crop time was the period of prime pressure, since the various stages in the sugar-making process were so closely synchronized. At Newton the fifty strongest members of the first gang cut the cane and ten members of the second gang loaded it into carts and took it to the mill where another ten workers from the first and second gangs ground it, while fourteen workers processed the cane juice at the boiling house, and three still-house workers converted molasses from the boiling house into rum. This was not a continuous four-month process; every few days the cutting gang was shifted to lighter tasks in order to recruit strength. But the work clearly took its toll. At Newton, in relatively slack periods, only 3 or 4 percent of the field workers reported sick, but after a week of holing or cutting cane the number rose to 9 or 10 percent. Even the holidays were fewer at Newton than at Mount Airy—only four days off per year: Good Friday, a free day in mid-October, and two days at Christmas.

We are now in a better position to examine the demographic contrast between Mesopotamia and Mount Airy, which is the most mysterious and also the most crucial aspect of our inquiry. Why did the Mesopotamia slave population suffer such pronounced natural decrease while the Mount Airy slave population enjoyed pronounced natural increase? Why in particular did the Mesopotamia women produce so few children, only half as many as the

[32] There were 155 workers on average in the three Newton plantation field gangs in 1796-1797, compared with Mesopotamia's 137 field workers in 1809.

TABLE IV
MOTHERHOOD AT MOUNT AIRY AND MESOPOTAMIA

| | Mount Airy, 1809-1828 | | Mesopotamia, 1799-1818 | |
	Number	%	Number	%
A. Childless Women	50	32.67	100	50.00
Mothers	103	67.32	100	50.00
	153		200	
B. Size of Completed Families:				
1 child		4.55		36.84
2-3 children		9.09		26.32
4-6 children		40.91		26.32
7-9 children		36.36		8.77
10-13 children		9.09		1.75
		100.00		100.00
Average no. live births per mother	6.36		3.07	
Average age of mother at first live birth	19.32		20.47	
C. Infant and Childhood Mortality:				
Percent died during first year		6.94		10.09
Percent died aged 1-10		15.28		16.06
Percent surviving past 10th birthday		77.78		73.85

Mount Airy women? Table IV compares the females aged seventeen and over who lived on these two estates during our twenty-year span. There are 200 potential mothers at Mesopotamia and 153 at Mount Airy. The smaller number at Mount Airy reflects the fact that many females on that estate were sold or transferred before they reached child-bearing age. Of the 200 Mesopotamia women, exactly half appear to have borne no live children. The other 100 are identified in the estate records as mothers—including seventeen women who bore some or all of their children on other Jamaican plantations before coming to Mesopotamia. At Mount Airy two-thirds of the women can be identified as mothers. This percentage is undoubtedly too low, for the Mount Airy records fail to pick up either the mothers of children who were grown by 1809 or the young future mothers who had children after they were transferred off the estate in their late 'teens or twenties. Of the 153 Mount Airy women in Table IV, only seven can definitely be categorized as sterile. In my opinion, close to 90 percent of the Mount Airy women bore children, compared with about 55 percent at Mesopotamia.

128

The other striking difference is that the Mesopotamia women who did bear children had much smaller families. As Table IV shows, only 37 percent of the Mesopotamia mothers had four or more children, whereas 86 percent of the Mount Airy mothers had families this large. The average Mesopotamia mother had less than half as many children as her Virginia counterpart. She entered into her first successful pregnancy a year later. If she bore more than one child, the births were spaced five months farther apart than at Mount Airy, and she had her last baby three years earlier. These averages conceal much significant variation. If we focus for a moment on those women who lived through the entire thirty-year period of possible reproduction (ages fifteen to forty-four), we find enormous range in age at first birth, child spacing, and age at last birth. The youngest mothers on both estates were only fourteen years old, while two Mesopotamia women had their first babies at age thirty-two. About 20 percent of the Mount Airy mothers gave birth before they were seventeen, twice the percentage at Mesopotamia, which suggests a possible difference in the age of menarche. At the other end of the cycle, nearly half of the Mount Airy mothers bore children into their forties—again twice the percentage at Mesopotamia. The presence of the white managerial staff was clearly a factor in the Mesopotamia fertility schedule, since more than half of the babies produced by mothers under the age of seventeen on this estate were mulattoes. Minny, a seamstress at the overseer's house, was the most prolific Mesopotamia mother; she bore eight sons and two daughters in twenty-five years, and three of these children were mulatto. Minny was forty-five when her last boy (a Negro) was born in December 1815, and to honor the occasion the baby was named Joseph Foster Barham. But Minny was a rarity in a community of small families.

According to Table IV, relatively few infants died on either estate, reflecting the incompleteness of infant birth and death records, especially at Mount Airy. The figures for children over age one are more reliable, especially for Mesopotamia with its immobile population. Unless the Mesopotamia infant records are completely misleading, newborn babies and young children died at about the same rate on the two estates, thus ruling out infant mortality as a factor in explaining the demographic difference between the two plantations. The key issue is clearly fertility—the low fertility of the Mesopotamia slave women.

There is no simple explanation for the low fertility at Mesopotamia. At least half a dozen separate factors contributed to the problem. In the first place, women lived less long than at Mount Airy, and experienced fewer years at risk of pregnancy. Half of the childless Mesopotamia women and a third of the mothers died in their twenties or thirties, during the prime childbearing years. At Mount Airy only about a tenth of the women died at this age. Yet longevity is certainly not the only factor in our equation, nor probably the most important one, for the chief point to be made here is that the Mount Airy slaves had quite long life expectancy, and even the Mesopotamia slaves had longer life expectancy than many populations with stronger birth rates. At age seventeen a Mount Airy female could expect to live thirty-nine more years, a Mesopotamia female thirty-one years. Over 80 percent of the Mount Airy women lived long enough to reach menopause. Even at Mesopotamia the childless women averaged twenty-one years at risk of pregnancy without producing a live birth, and 40 percent of them lived on the estate throughout the years of possible reproduction. Likewise, most Mesopotamia mothers of one or two children lived on for many years after their babies were born. Nearly 60 percent reached the age of menopause, and the average mother bore her children within a space of seven years while experiencing twenty-three years at risk of pregnancy. While the longevity of the Mount Airy women thus helps to explain their large families, life expectancy at Mesopotamia was not sufficiently restricted to account by itself for the low birth rate in this community.

A second factor is the sex and age ratio, which in Caribbean slave populations is frequently seen as the chief reason for low fertility. As Table II has shown, however, neither the sex nor the age structure at Mesopotamia was unfavorable. The sexes were always much better balanced on this estate than at Mount Airy, where the young men consistently outnumbered the young women by nearly two to one. There was always a larger number of women of child-bearing age at Mesopotamia than at Mount Airy. Indeed, the age structure of the Mesopotamia population was seemingly very favorable to high fertility. Between 1799 and 1818 the proportion of females aged fifteen to forty-four averaged 24.5 percent of the total Barham slave force. At Mount Airy, because so many girls were sold or transferred, the proportion of potentially fertile females was significantly smaller: between 1809 and 1828 it averaged 19.4 percent. Thus if imbalance between the sexes and a low proportion of young women depress the birth rate, one should look for problems at the Tayloe estate rather than at Mesopotamia.

A third factor is the presence at Mesopotamia of African-born women with African child-rearing habits. It has been argued that Caribbean slave populations had low birth rates because so many of the women were Africans. Fertility rates in West Africa are thought to have been generally low; and when African women were shipped to America they reproduced less actively than creole slave women, being habituated to a long nursing period with a resultant wide spacing between births.[33] At Mesopotamia, however,

[33] This line of argument is advanced by Michael Craton, "Jamaican Slave Mortality: Fresh Light from Worthy Park, Longville and the Tharp Estates," *Journal of Caribbean History*, III (1971), 1-27, and by Russell R. Menard, "The Maryland Slave Population, 1658-1730: A Demographic Profile of Blacks in Four Counties," *WMQ*, 3d Ser., XXXII (1975), 29-54.

the differences between African-born and creole women were not pronounced. Of forty-two African women during the 1799-1818 span, twenty-three (55 percent) were childless, and the nineteen African mothers averaged 2.42 children each. They bore their children at no wider intervals than the creole women, so the probability is that all the mothers followed the same nursing practices. The Mesopotamia women collectively did space their children more widely than at Mount Airy, with an average interval between live births of three years and three months, compared with two years and ten months at Mount Airy.[34] But there is little evidence that this was because they nursed their infants longer. If we compare the most fecund mothers on both estates—those who bore seven or more children—we find no difference whatsoever in child spacing. The Mesopotamia and Mount Airy mothers in this category both averaged two years and six months between births. In fact, these women generally gave birth every two years, with an occasional shorter gap when the nursing period was broken off by the death of the last-born infant, and an occasional longer gap perhaps caused by a miscarriage or stillbirth. Mothers of small families, especially at Mesopotamia, had extremely irregular birth intervals, ranging up to ten years, and such eccentric spacing is better explained by sexual abstinence, intermittent fecundity, miscarriages, and abortions than by nursing habits.

A fourth factor is the debilitating work regimen imposed upon the Caribbean slaves, which presumably robbed them of vitality and dulled their sexual instincts. As we have seen, the labor pattern was more punishing at Mesopotamia, and women of child-bearing years performed much more heavy work than at Mount Airy. Unfortunately, there is no way of demonstrating a correlation between this debilitating labor and slave infertility. Analysis of job distribution at Mesopotamia during the 1799-1818 span shows that mothers and childless women held the same range of jobs in almost exactly the same proportions. The heaviest labor was done by the Great Gang, and on an average 34 percent of the Mesopotamia women over seventeen were assigned to this gang. Of the childless women in Table IV, 36 percent worked in the Great Gang; of the mothers with one to three children, 32 percent worked in the Great Gang; of the mothers with four or more children, 35 percent worked in the Great Gang. Similarly, at the other end of the spectrum, the lightest work was done by the domestic servants who attended the white staff; 6 percent of the Mesopotamia women were assigned to these jobs—5 percent of the childless women, 7 percent of the mothers with one to three children, and 6 percent of the mothers with four or more

[34] Herbert S. Klein and Stanley L. Engerman, who stress the difference between U.S. and British West Indian nursing practices in an unpublished paper, "The Demographic Study of the American Slave Population," find a U.S. child-spacing interval of only 2.5 years and a British West Indian rate of 3.5-4.0 years.

children. These figures seem to show that work assignments had no effect whatsoever on the birth rate. Yet it remains difficult to believe that years of rugged labor in the cane fields did not reduce slave procreation, increase the chance of miscarriage, and lower slave fertility.[35]

A fifth factor, possibly the most important one, is inadequate nutrition, which can depress fertility by impairing female reproductive development. Biologists have established that the timing of the adolescent growth spurt and menarche, the maintenance of regular menstrual function, the recovery of reproductive ability after childbirth, and the timing of menopause are all directly affected by the female's state of nourishment. A severely under-nourished woman, with inadequate fat storage in her body, will achieve menarche belatedly, will experience irregular menstrual cycles or none at all, and will enter menopause early. If she manages to conceive and bear a child, pregnancy and lactation will draw thousands of calories from her meager energy stores, so that she will be slow to recover reproductive ability for another pregnancy.[36] Certainly the Mesopotamia women betray symptoms of impaired reproductive development: delayed first births, long and irregular birth intervals, and early final births.

The estate death records contain some evidence of dietary deficiency, as well as bad sanitation, which further undermined the health of the Barham slaves. By the manager's own reckoning, 11 percent of the slaves died "bloated" or from "dropsy." These vague terms covered a wide range of bodily swellings, undoubtedly caused in many cases by protein and vitamin deficiencies. Another 9 percent died of "flux" or various forms of dysentery, promoted by unsanitary living conditions. This was a larger number than the 8 percent who died from malaria and other tropical fevers. Another 11 percent of the deaths were attributed to such African diseases as hookworm, guinea worm, yaws, leprosy, and elephantiasis, which were much more common in Jamaica than in Virginia. Among the remaining chief causes of death were—in rank order—tuberculosis, pleurisy, smallpox, epilepsy, and venereal disease. Nearly 3 percent of the slaves were said to have died in plantation accidents, but only two men in eighty years committed suicide, and

[35] It is perhaps significant that 40% of the Mesopotamian live births were concentrated in the four months October-January and only 25% in the four months April-July. A number of the pregnancies that should have come to term in April-July may have resulted in fetal deaths because of the mothers' field labor during the sugar harvest season.

[36] Rose E. Frisch, "Demographic Implications of the Biological Determinants of Female Fecundity," *Social Biology*, XXII (1975), 17-22.

[37] A comparable set of death records for Worthy Park estate in Jamaica has been analyzed by Michael Craton, with findings very similar to mine. I am indebted to Mr. Craton for the use of his unpublished essay, "Death, Disease and Medicine on Jamaican Slave Plantations: The Example of Worthy Park, 1792-1838."

only five women died during childbirth. Obviously, these mortality statistics cannot be taken too seriously, especially since 17 percent died of "old age" and another 9 percent died as "invalids." In any case, the correlation between ill health and infertility is inexact. A woman named Esther suffered continuously from "weakness" and yaws during her life at Mesopotamia, but she bore six children. Luna was incapable of employment because of her bad sores, but she gave birth to seven children. Ophelia contracted venereal disease when she was thirty and was retired from the field gang, but she had two more children and lived another twenty years. And Sabina began to experience epileptic seizures at twenty-eight but bore three more children and died at sixty-three.

Still another factor that could have contributed to low fertility at Mesopotamia is the aggressive role of the white overseers and bookkeepers, who requisitioned the sexual services of a good many young slaves. These women, if they wished to prolong their status as concubines, may have aborted their mulatto offspring in order to keep physically attractive. The large number of mulatto births at Mesopotamia, however, makes this proposition unlikely. Other Mesopotamia women may have practiced sexual abstinence or committed abortion because they could not stand the prospect of bringing babies into a world of enslavement. Several of the Mesopotamia children who died during infancy were "overlaid" by their mothers. Were such events accidental or intentional?

Finally, we should not forget the Mesopotamia men. It is surely a mistake to focus exclusively on the female slaves, for the males must have had much to do with the low birth rate. If longevity was a factor, the men had shorter life expectancy than the women, and many Mesopotamia females must have stopped bearing children when their mates died. If the work regimen was a factor, it was the men who were forced into the most exhausting jobs. If nutrition was a factor, the men suffered more than the women from chronic debility. Frequently weak or sick, flogged and maimed far more often than the females when they resisted or malingered or ran away, humiliated by an arrogant cadre of white masters who took their women, the Mesopotamia men had lost all powers of leadership and independence—and this loss in psychic power may well have drained their sexual potency.

Thus, despite the wealth of statistical information about slave life at Mesopotamia and Mount Airy, many questions cannot be answered and many issues cannot be settled. Ultimately the observer who wonders why Jamaican slaves behaved differently from Virginian slaves is reduced to armchair psychology. But at least we can document telling differences— some of them rather surprising—between the two communities. At Mesopotamia the slave population was cooped up; at Mount Airy it was in constant movement. Mesopotamia families were more inbred than Mount Airy families, and less disrupted by sales and transfers. Mesopotamia women were tougher than their men and dominated the work force, whereas Mount Airy women were reckoned to be more marginal than their men and were frequently sold. Vocational opportunities were narrower at Mesopotamia than at Mount Airy, the work load was harder, the food and clothing were less adequate, the disease environment was more threatening. In consequence, Mesopotamia slaves died earlier than at Mount Airy and produced fewer children.

The owner of Mesopotamia, Joseph Foster Barham, was a conscientious master by the Jamaican standards of the day. Few other sugar magnates paid missionaries £70 per year to instruct their slaves in the Christian religion, or published arguments for the abolition of West Indian slavery,[38] or required their agents to keep meticulous track of the blacks who inhabited their estates. During the eighty years of record keeping the Mesopotamia slaves never rebelled; very few of them ran away permanently; and during a smallpox epidemic the white managers showed their humanity by inoculating even the aged invalids in order to keep them alive. Nonetheless, the Mesopotamia records give us a deeply depressing picture of slave life on this estate, a picture reaffirming the universal opinion of modern scholars that Caribbean slavery was one of the most brutally dehumanizing systems ever devised.

John Tayloe III likewise emerges from his letter books and account books as a thoroughly benevolent and well-intentioned master. Working and living conditions on his Rappahannock estate must have been exceptionally relaxed, for Tayloe was no profit-maximizing entrepreneur. His well-worn fields produced modest yields, his work force was far larger than necessary, and the rhythm of the place evoked leisured gentility rather than business efficiency. And yet this paternalistic planter manipulated and exploited his slaves to a high degree. Thus my portrait of slave life at Mount Airy is ambiguous, and just how it fits into the general debate about the character of slavery in the United States is rather hard to say. As Stanley Elkins has recently pointed out, a long scholarly tradition that stressed white brutality and white damage has been superseded by a new emphasis on black achieve-

[38] While Barham was Wilberforce's ally in the British abolition movement, his tract, *Considerations on the Abolition of Negro Slavery*, was studded with pejorative remarks about the Negro as a person and a worker. In 1806 he offered Wilberforce a solution to the West Indian labor problem: substitute Chinese coolies for Negro slaves. Robert Isaac Wilberforce, *The Life of William Wilberforce*, III (London, 1839), 272.

ment and black resistance.[39] The Mount Airy evidence can be used to buttress either side of this debate, but on the whole I believe that it better supports the older tradition. While Tayloe was not a brutal master, his slave regimen was, it seems to me, designed to thwart black achievement and to defuse black resistance. His system offered extremely little scope for the dynamic economic, cultural, and social slave achievements currently celebrated by Robert Fogel, Stanley Engerman, Eugene Genovese, and Herbert Gutman.[40] But however noxious Tayloe's system, if one had to be a slave, Mount Airy was a better place to live than Mesopotamia.

[39] Stanley M. Elkins, "The Slavery Debate," *Commentary*, LX (Dec. 1975), 40-54.
[40] I am thinking here of Fogel and Engerman's *Time on the Cross*, Eugene D. Genovese's *Roll, Jordan, Roll: The World the Slaves Made* (New York, 1974), and Herbert G. Gutman's *The Black Family in Slavery and Freedom, 1750-1925* (New York, 1976).

CULTURE CONTACTS AND NEGRO SLAVERY

STANLEY M. ELKINS

Associate Professor of History, Smith College

(*Read November 9, 1962, in the Symposium on Our Contacts with American Indians, Polynesians, and Africans*)

IN THE long course of history, European and African peoples have come into contact under a great variety of circumstances. In the Western Hemisphere, however, Africans and Europeans met each other in such unprecedented numbers, and under conditions so extraordinary, during the period of discovery and settlement that the consequences persisted for centuries. For practical purposes all such contacts were first made, in both North and South America, through the single medium of Negro slavery.

It would be logical to imagine, therefore (slavery being what it is), that the resulting relationships between whites and blacks should show a uniformity of pattern everywhere in the New World. And yet nothing could be farther from the case.

For one thing, "slavery" never was, in any age, the simple and self-evident relationship that the name seems to imply. The term "slavery" is not a very precise one; it has had to be defined and given its particular content by the particular societies that have practiced it. The term can be, and has been, used to cover the widest variety of relationships, ranging all the way from a relatively limited claim on a man's labor to absolute control over his life. We know that just such a variety characterized slavery in the Old World in classic times, and there is reason to think that something of the sort existed in the New World in later times.

A number of historians in recent years have considered the possibility that slavery in the Latin countries of South America meant something very different from what it meant in the British colonies of North America. The evidence is not as full as we should like; much remains to be done; and the question is far from settled as to details. But something of a pattern *is* visible—enough so, at any rate, to present the problem that concerns us today.

At first glance, the slave systems that developed under the Spanish and Portuguese in Latin America had a great deal in common with the one established by the English in the West Indies and North America. So far as sheer physical cruelty was concerned, there does not seem to have been much to choose between them. Both insisted on the essentially paternal character of the master-slave relationship, yet in practice neither offered the Negro slave any absolute protections against a brutal master. On the other hand, both claimed a real concern for the slave's welfare, and there is evidence in both areas to confirm this. There is other evidence, also in both, that denies it. On a simple physical basis, therefore, it is very hard to make meaningful distinctions that will hold up in any broad general way.

And yet this is not the only basis on which the two slave systems can be compared. There were other sorts of differences—differences in the very character and structure of the institution itself—that seem to have been quite significant in their consequences. Slavery as it was developed by the English was a rigid, highly formalized institution within which every aspect of a slave's life, including all those things which we think of as the minimum rights and privileges of a human being, were systematically subordinated to the one controlling fact: that he was the property of his master. Aside from the "right" to life and maintenance, he could make no claim on society that would in any way diminish his value as property. The examples are so familiar, from our own national past, that I need do no more than mention them. The separation of husbands from wives, of mothers from children, and any degree of coercion short of outright murder that was needed to make a slave work, were condoned by the law. The slave's status as property made it logically impossible for him to have property of his own, or to make contracts, or to give testimony in courts of law. Such was the rigidity of the English system that even manumission was a legal and logical difficulty. It was possible in law but discouraged in practice. And a former slave, a man who *had* been manumitted, found it very hard to fit himself into a society where the idea of property had so dominated all the basic relationships between black men and white.

The slave systems of the Spanish and Portuguese, on the other hand, whatever else may be said of them, were legally far less rigid than that of the English. The slave may have been the property of his master, yet he could own property himself. It was illegal and immoral to separate a husband and wife. In some areas a slave was guaranteed a fixed number of holidays during which he might work for himself; in others, the law allowed him the right to have his price declared so that he might, if he could accumulate the necessary money, buy himself from his master. The precise arrangements of Latin American slavery varied widely from place to place—yet by the same token it is quite apparent that they lacked the consistency and remorseless logic that governed slavery in North America.

It was far easier to become a free man in Brazil or Spanish America than it ever was in Virginia or the British West Indies. Emancipation was socially approved in most places; nowhere was it systematically discouraged. Once a man had become free, moreover, his position in the community was by no means a hopeless one. A wide range of occupations was open to the former slave in almost every Latin American country, and there are examples of exceptional careers achieved by men of color. It may not have been the rule, but it was certainly possible. It was even possible to do something that would have been incomprehensible in English America; a man might acquire—through bribery, special favor, or in some cases outright purchase—an official certificate of "whiteness" which entitled him to all the rights and privileges of high society. When slavery was finally abolished altogether, it was seldom accompanied by the upheaval and disruptions that followed emancipation in North America. And it is not irrelevant to add that the Negroes and mulattoes of Latin America today—all descendants of slaves—occupy a position that is socially very different from that of their counterparts in the United States.

What is the explanation for all this? How does one account for what appears to have been the surprising flexibility of Latin American slave institutions and the uniform rigidity of those established by the English? There seems to be almost as many answers to this question as there are historians who have thought about it. The evidence for any single hunch is subject to much dispute, and for this very reason none of us is willing to close any debate on any of them. In that spirit I should like to share some of the more interesting speculations with you.

One very plausible explanation for the differences between Latin American and North American slavery rests on legal history alone. Whereas the English common law had no categories and no body of precedent for dealing with slavery such was hardly the case with the Spanish and Portuguese—both of whom had had long experience with slavery. The slave codes that the Spanish and Portuguese instituted in their New World colonies were based on practices whose roots went all the way back to the Roman Law of classical times. These laws, revised in the Middle Ages and made increasingly more humane, were less concerned with the property rights of the master—as Anglo-Saxons think of "property"—than with the human rights of the slave. How generally they were enforced in the New World is a matter we need to know more about. But where they were, the Negro slave was guaranteed a range of rights and protection that were not to be found in the slave codes developed in British North America.

A second theory as to why the Iberian colonist should have been willing to be more flexible than the English—both in evolving their slave institutions and in accepting emancipated slaves into free society—is based on differences of attitude about color. The first dark-skinned people that the English met in any substantial numbers, and on anything like intimate terms, were Negroes from Africa. To the English, a black skin and an uncivilized savage meant much the same thing, and to imagine such people on terms of equality or even as full human beings, lay quite outside their experience. The Spanish and Portuguese on the other hand, had experienced centuries of domination by the Moors. Dark-skinned people, in their eyes, were neither strange nor necessarily inferior. Even their standards of physical beauty (which, when you think of it, is a very basic matter indeed) were subtly influenced by the Mediterranean setting of their history, their experience, and their culture. Although the Spanish were, in their own way, just as conscious of race as other European peoples have been, the fact of race does not seem to have dominated every other relationship in anything like the degree that it has with the Anglo-Saxons. The Iberians always somehow found it easier to make exceptions in cases of individual talent.

Still another explanation for the differences

ween slavery in the English and in the Iberian colonies might be found in the fundamental relationships between the men and the women. These matters were handled very differently in the two cultures. The English, unlike either the Portuguese or the Spanish, sent substantial numbers of unmarried girls to the New World—which meant that the young bachelor in Virginia, even if he had very little property, might eventually expect to find an English wife. The social consequences of such a policy can readily be appreciated. Although there is much evidence of miscegenation in colonial Virginia, the offspring of such unions between white and black were condemned from the moment of their birth. They were invariably illegitimate and were seldom recognized by their fathers. In Brazil, on the other hand, where the Negro population was large and white women relatively scarce, relationships between white masters and slave women would exist on a basis that went considerably beyond the merely casual. The children might not be accepted as the fully legitimate heirs of their father—though in some cases they were—but their status in the community was very different from what it would have been in Virginia the Carolinas. Once a generation of such children had come of age in a community, it would become very difficult to draw a sharp line between the races or to insist that a dark skin automatically implied personal inferiority.

A situation in some ways similar to this actually developed in early nineteenth-century New Orleans, though I should add that its origins on the white side were to a large extent non-Anglo-Saxon. Yet Southern mores were already so firmly fixed, even then, that a generation of intelligent and well-educated quadroons had relatively little impact on Southern racial attitudes. A fourth and final explanation for these contrasts between North and South American slavery one to which I myself have strong leanings. is based on the differences between the Roman law and the common law (which I have already referred to), plus the presence of a powerful church and crown in Latin America and the absence of anything comparable in English America. not only did the Spanish and Portuguese inherit tradition of Roman law that defined a slave as something more than property, but the Spanish church had a vested interest in all the souls under

its charge, white or black, and the crown considered all men within its dominion—slave or free —as its subjects. The Church insisted that the marriage ties of the slave be respected, and that the master never forget the slave's status as a human being with an immortal soul. The concern of the Church was paralleled by that of the crown and by the active interference of royal officials in matters of slave welfare.

How regularly or consistently this surveillance was actually exercised is a matter of question. But the important thing is that it was possible, and that this was the way in which the official conscience defined the relation of master and slave. In short, the slave institutions of Latin America did represent something of an adjustment to different sets of interests—an adjustment between the European colonists on the one side. and the Church, the crown, and a tradition of law and morality that protected the slave on the other.

The key fact of North American slavery was that it was developed in one direction only—to suit the economic needs of the planter-colonists— and with no countervailing pressures from church, crown, or law. Virginia in the early eighteenth century gives us the very epitome of all this. There, we find no Roman law, no official "conscience" in matters of slave welfare, no traditions and no precedents for the governance of slaves, no prior experience with people of color, no royal interference in any matter that would make a difference to a slave, and no church with power enough to impose itself on slave policy in any way at all. Instead, we have a community with all the blessings of local self-rule—political, social, economic, religious, and moral—and where the local rulers were the local planting gentry. We have here a setting peculiarly appropriate to the common law. In it, the absence of prior codes and prior experience means that the immediate requirements of the society and economy will be absorbed directly into the law. And when large numbers of alien black men and women are introduced into this society as slaves, no prior accumulations of experience or law need stand in the way of there being defined in the most direct and logical manner possible. The ultimate controlling factor, that is, in every relationship between white man and black will be the black man's status as property.

by STANLEY ELKINS &
ERIC McKITRICK

*both of the University of Chicago, who are
collaborating on a volume of essays in
American history.*

Institutions and the Law of Slavery: The Dynamics of Unopposed Capitalism

IT WAS inherent in the state of sensibility which Western civilization had attained by the nineteenth century, that slavery, perforce involving the most basic values of humanity, should at that time become morally absorbing to both Europeans and Americans. Englishmen, Frenchmen, Spaniards, and Portuguese each responded to the oppressive subject at various levels of intensity in thought and action; out of their complex experience each could focus upon slavery a variety of resources, that they might judge its evils, mitigate its abuses, and finally abolish it altogether.[1] There is a certain sense in which the same might be said of the Americans. Yet the simple and harsh moral purity of our own antislavery movement, from the 1830's on, gave it a quality which set it apart from the others. Every phase of that movement—the theory of society which was its backdrop, the intellectual expressions upon which it drew, the slogans which it sent to the marketplace, the schemes for practical action which it evolved—all combined to produce in our abolitionists that peculiar quality of abstraction which was, and has remained, uniquely American. For them, the question was *all* moral; it must be contemplated in terms untouched by expediency, untarnished by society's organic compromises, uncorrupted even by society

[1]The nineteenth century saw the steady collapse of slavery as an institution. The determined efforts of Wilberforce and Clarkson to end the slave trade were internationally successful by 1823 when Portugal joined Spain, France, and England in outlawing it. In the Spanish-speaking countries of Central and South America slavery itself was gradually eliminated during the first half of the century. It had already been abolished in the British West Indies by 1834 and in the colonies of France by 1848. When in 1858 Portugal proclaimed a status of peonage with eventual freedom for all its slaves, the future of slavery had become very dim indeed.

3

itself. It involved a moral urgency which by mid-century would seize the entire North.

But while our thinkers and reformers considered the issue in such abstract purity, in such simple grandeur, there was, in principle if not in fact, an alternative philosophical mode. Slavery might have been approached not as a problem in pure morality but as a question of institutional arrangements—a question of those institutions which make the crucial difference in men's relationships with each other—of those arrangements whereby even so theoretically simple a connection as that between master and slave might take any of a dozen forms, forms among which the sharpest and finest of moral distinctions might be made. This approach was of course never taken, and to expect it of nineteenth-century Americans would be to make impossible demands upon their experience. It is, however, still of interest to ask why this should be so. Why should the American of, say, 1830 have been so insensitive to institutions and their function?

Consider the seeming paradox of how by that time, in the very bright morning of American success, the power of so many American institutions had one by one melted away. The church had fallen into a thousand parts. The shadow of an Anglican church, disestablished in the wake of the Revolution and its doom forever sealed by the yearly anarchy of the camp-meeting, was all that remained in the South of vested ecclesiastical authority; and in New England the Congregational church, which had once functioned as a powerful state establishment, was deprived of its last secular supports early in the century. It was not that religion itself was challenged—quite the contrary—but as a source both of organized social power and internal discipline the church had undergone a relentless process of fragmentation. Religious vitality everywhere was overwhelming, but that vitality lay primarily in the demands for individual satisfaction— which took inevitable and repeated priority over institutional needs. The very ease with which the great evangelical sects could divide, by a sort of cellular fission, into myriads of tiny independent units, showed that the institutional balance between official coercion and individual self-expression had completely broken down.[2]

---

[2] A positive distinction must be made between religious enthusiasm and organized ecclesiastical power. The great religious revival that followed the War of 1812 did not renew the strength and vitality of the older religious establishments in their *institutional* character. What actually tended to happen was that with new churches springing up everywhere, both the ideal of a learned ministry and the role of the individual minister as a powerful leader in the community could hardly avoid being drastically undermined. See Richard Hildreth, *The History of the United States of America* (New York, 1858), VI, 597. Moreover, the new democratic sects—by their very nature—could have only the most limited kind of success in creating national organizations of their own, capable of wielding centralized power and discipline. William W. Sweet, *The Story of Religion in America* (New York: Harper & Brothers, 1930), p. 258.

4

As for the bar, it was the sheer profusion of lawyers on the American scene, their numbers daily increasing, that made a central focus of traditional and vested power among them out of the question; no such continuing structure as the English bar, with its institutional self-awareness, its standards of competence and discipline, its stabilized recruitment, its Temples and Inns of Court, could exist in America. There was a brief period, in the later eighteenth century, when organizations of the bar in our Eastern cities did appear capable of providing such a nucleus of stability. But here too, as with the church and ministry, the great expansion getting under way after the War of 1812, bringing so widespread a demand for services of whatever quality, soon made it clear that individual drives rather than institutional needs would prevail. With the democratization of the bar and its inevitable decline in standards, came a deterioration of whatever institutional bulwarks the bar might have developed.[3]

In our politics, as elsewhere, the old organizational balance was dissolving; something new and unprecedented was emerging in the shape of mass parties. In a way, of course, the sheer formlessness of the new system would cloak an inscrutable logic; its very innocence of principle would foster a special conservatism, its apparent lack of focus would be its own protection, enabling it to act as a kind of super-institution absorbing the functions of a dozen institutions which no longer existed. Yet in its very birth it was necessary that an older, a more stable and traditional conception of political responsibility should disappear. The Federalist party, even in New England, was by 1830 utterly dead. The Federalists, though in actual policy hardly different from their successors, had assumed and embodied certain traditional attributes of political life which later establishments did not and could not provide. Taking their impulse and *esprit* from the Fathers themselves, their very aura of exclusiveness made possible a certain sharpness of focus. They took for granted the tradition that politics was an occupation for men of affairs, property, and learning. The

[3]By the eve of the Revolution the power of the bar, especially in New York and Massachusetts, had come to be such that it could not only maintain rigid controls over its own standards of admission and professional conduct, but also function as a potent force in society at large—"the judges and principal lawyers," according to Lieutenant-Governor Cadwallader Colden in 1764, being "proprietors of extravagant grants of land or strongly connected with them in interest or family alliances. . . ." Quoted in Charles Warren, *A History of the American Bar* (Boston: Little, Brown & Co., 1911), p. 99. However, by 1830 all this had changed: "the tide of early nineteenth-century democracy carried before it almost all previously existing standards of admission to the profession: Every man was as good as every other, and everyone should find open the gate to self-advancement in any field." The bar ceased to have any meaning as a conservative institution, and in 1851 Indiana recognized this fact by providing in its constitution that "Every person of good moral character, being a voter, shall be entitled to admission to practice law in all courts of justice." James Willard Hurst, *The Growth of American Law: The Law Makers* (Boston: Little, Brown & Co., 1950), p. 250. See also pp. 278, 285.

5

Federalist party, by its very air of vested interest, came closer than any of its successors to providing a clear institutional nucleus for the loyalty and commitment of other vested interests in society—the intelligentsia, the ministry, the bar, the propertied classes.[4] But the wide democratization of politics in the 1820's ordained that political life in the United States should assume a completely new tone, one quite different from that imagined by the Fathers. Even the Jeffersonians, following the Federalists, had moved more or less instinctively to establish institutional safeguards for political leadership, discipline, and power; yet they too, in the 1820's, saw their special creation, the Congressional caucus, swept away and damned as an engine of aristocracy and privilege.[5]

Even in the country's economic activity this breakdown of structural equilibrium was quite as evident as it was in other sectors of public life. The reasonably stable economic organizations maintained by the great trading families of the East were being challenged by a rising class of petty industrialists everywhere. It need not be supposed that these mercantile and banking structures were in a state of decline, yet in a relative sense their power and leadership, amid the sheer proliferation of small enterprise, no longer carried the decisive weight of former times.[6] The very

[4] By 1820, writes Ostrogorski, the "alliance between the magistracy, the clergy, property, and culture, was collapsing. The eclipse of the Federalists, who were the living image of government by leaders, robbed it of one of its strongest supports. The influence of the clergy, which had been one of the main props of the Federalists, was being thrust out of lay society." M. Ostrogorski, *Democracy and the Organization of Political Parties,* trans. Frederick Clarke (New York: Macmillan Co., 1908), II, 26-27.

[5] Ostrogorski, *Democracy* . . ., II, 28-29, 39.

[6] In the Revolutionary and post-Revolutionary period there was little question but that an overwhelming share of the social and economic leadership rested with the Eastern mercantile upper crust—a group which, far from being "destroyed" by the Revolution, was actually reconstituted by infusions of new blood. Robert A. East, *Business Enterprise in the American Revolutionary Era* (New York: Columbia University Press, 1938), pp. 13-14, 237-38, 261-62. In New York, according to Dixon Ryan Fox, "There was still a merchants' party just as there had been before the Revolutionary War," and this class—flanked by the bar, the Episcopal church, and the trustees of Columbia College—formed the strength and support of the Federalist party well into the nineteenth century. D. R. Fox, *The Decline of Aristocracy in the Politics of New York* (New York: Longmans, Green & Co., 1919), pp. v, 11-12, 17-18, 28-29, & *passim*. Yet by 1830 this too had changed: "in a country such as ours, where the touch of energy could turn resources into wealth, prescriptive rights could not long remain unchanged. In no colony had the lines of old caste been more clearly drawn than in New York; in no state were they more completely rubbed away." *Ibid.,* p. v. Economically the key to this fact was to be found in the sheer diffusion of power implicit in the growth of petty manufactures—which, due to "economies peculiar to small enterprises, the impossibility of engrossing either the redundant natural resources of the country or its rapidly expanding markets, and the manufacturing opportunities offered in the West"—could not possibly be dominated by the older establishments, no matter how large. See Victor S. Clark, *History of Manufactures in the United States* (1929 ed., reprinted New York: Peter Smith, 1949), I, 457. In no decade did such enterprises grow more rapidly in numbers than in that of the 1830's. Ernest L. Bogart, *Economic History of the American People* (New York: Longmans, Green & Co., 1936), p. 385.

6

tone of business life assumed a character peculiarly indicative of what was happening. Its keynote was the individual, confronted with boundless opportunity, a veritable new culture-hero, one might have thought, was being fashioned on the frontier of the Old Northwest: the young man on the make, in whose folklore the Eastern banker, bulwarked in privilege and monopoly, would forever remain a tarnished symbol.[7] Capitalism was burgeoning indeed, but in anything but a conservative way; its very dynamism was breaking old molds. Whatever institutional stability American capitalism could conceivably develop was at its lowest possible ebb in 1830.

And yet it was a society whose very energy and resources had themselves become a kind of stability. Traditional guarantees of order, for such a society, had become superfluous. Its religion was so dynamic that it needed no church; its wealth and opportunity were so boundless that a center of financial power could lose its meaning; and in its need for politicians and lawyers by the thousands it could do without a governing class and ignore many an ancient tradition of bench and bar. Thus for the American of that day it was the very success of his society—of capitalism, of religious liberalism and political democracy—that made it unnecessary for him to be concerned with institutions. Had he a "past"? Yes; it was already two hundred years old—but he could afford to forget it. Had he once known "institutions"? Yes, of a sort, but he could now ignore their meaning: *his* style of life did not depend upon them.[8] His new system of values could now impeach "society" itself, that very society which had made success possible and which offered him his future: he no longer seemed to need it—it became an abstraction which even bore certain allusions to the sinister. He was able to imagine that "stability" resided not in social organization but in "human nature." He no longer appeared to draw from society his traditions, his culture, and all his aspirations; indeed he, the transcendent individual—the new symbol of virtue—now "confronted" society; he challenged it as something of a conspiracy to rob him of his birthright. Miraculously, all society then sprang to his aid in the celebration of that conceit.

We may suppose that such was not merely the general sense, but one shared by those men who in other societies would be called "intellectuals" —those men whose preoccupation it traditionally is to reflect and express

[7]"Originally a fight against political privilege, the Jacksonian movement [of the 1830's] had broadened into a fight against economic privilege, rallying to its support a host of 'rural capitalists and village entrepreneurs.'" Richard Hofstadter, *The American Political Tradition* (New York: Alfred A. Knopf, 1949), p. 66.
[8]One or two contrasts with European society make this significant: take, for example, the life of the British aristocracy, with its close relationship to the church, army, and government, or that of the Prussian Junker, who depended on a strong state and an army for the very meaning of his personality.

7

in various ways the state of society at large, its tensions, its ills, its well-being. So we should also ask about the consequences which such a happy state of things might have had for *intellectual* activity. Might there not have been (in spite of everything) a price? Where, for instance, were art and learning, in such a setting, to find their occupation? "No author, without a trial," wrote the lonely Hawthorne in his preface to *The Marble Faun*, "can conceive the difficulty of writing a romance about a country where there is no shadow, no antiquity, no mystery, no picturesque and gloomy wrong, nor anything but a commonplace prosperity, in broad and simple daylight, as is happily the case with my dear native land." It was a society with few problems and few visible institutions that set the American intellectual, such as he was, peculiarly on his own, and made him as susceptible as anyone else to the philosophy of self-help. In the America of the 1830's and '40s there was no other symbol of vitality to be found than the individual, and it was to the individual, with all his promise, that the thinker, like everyone else, would inexorably orient himself. Every reward which the age offered seemed pointed out by the way of self-reliance. But the thinker, thus oriented, left himself without a specific and concrete sense of society as such, and without even a strong sense of himself as belonging to a community of other men of intellect. He was involuntarily cut off from the sources of power (the political, ecclesiastical, and financial power had become more and more diffuse), so that he could no longer operate, as it were, in the midst of things. For this generation the very concept of power—its meaning, its responsibilities, its uses—was something quite outside its experience. We may guess that it was in this generation and in these circumstances that our "alienated intellectual" was born, and we may picture a connection between this "alienation" and the peculiar abstractness of our thought on the subject of slavery.

I

We have delayed introducing our primary subject long enough to draw some attention to that state of mind in which Americans faced the gravest social problem—slavery—that had yet confronted them as an established nation. Theirs had been, considering the bulk of their achievement, a mild existence in which the stimulus of chronic and complex institutional tensions had been absent; it was in such a setting that their habits of thought had been shaped; such was the experience with which they might approach the ills of society and deal with questions of deep morality.

Slavery, by the 1830's, freely offended the sensibilities of all Christendom. It was a problem partaking of the Christian conception of sin. Mortal

8

sin lay in the path of all who dealt in slaves, and it was defined and given meaning by the Christian church in countries where the church had power. Slavery, by its very age, had even assumed the character of *original* sin, entailed as it was upon living generations by their predecessors. In America, slavery was unique among the other institutions of society. In one section of the country it had existed for over two centuries, having become interwoven with the means of production, the basic social arrangements, and the very tone of Southern culture. Slavery in the South, rather than diminishing, had spread. Though it had been a source of discomfort there a generation before, men could now see it, under pressure, as the keystone of a style of life in a sense that was not true of any other institution in American society. Conversely, it was at this very time that Americans of the North found themselves suddenly confronted, as it were, with slavery's full enormity.[9]

"No picturesque and gloomy wrong"—Hawthorne here referred to a society which, distinguished from the civilizations of Europe, was not concretely acquainted with sin. The innocence of America and the wickedness of Europe would form one of the great themes of nineteenth-century literature, but of all the writers who used it, perhaps it was Hawthorne's most distinguished biographer, Henry James, who best understood how even "sin," in European culture, had been institutionalized. There, an actual place had been made for it in life's crucial experience. It had been classified from time out of mind and given specific names; the reality of "lust," "avarice," and "oppression" had given rise to the most intricate of social arrangements, not for eliminating them, but for softening their impact and limiting their scope—for protecting the weak and defining the responsibilities of the strong. One powerful social agency in particular had made of iniquity its special province, and had dealt with it in a thousand forms for centuries. All this may well have been in James's mind when he exclaimed of America: *"no church."*

What, then, might be expected to happen if sin *should* suddenly become apparent, in a nation whose every individual was, at least symbolically, expected to stand on his own two feet? The reaction was altogether destructive. The sense of outrage was personal; the sense of *personal* guilt was crushing. The gentle American of mild vices was transformed into the

[9] By Jefferson's time, slavery in the older planting states—especially in Virginia—had become considerably less profitable than had been the case earlier in the eighteenth century, and Virginians of the post-revolutionary era had begun to examine slavery from the point of view of their consciences, as well as economically. Yet the opening of the Southwest frontier in the late 1790's, followed by the Louisiana Purchase, together with the spread of cotton culture to those regions and the perfecting of mechanical aids to large-scale production, had given slavery a new lease on life. By the 1830's the full implications of this resurgence were becoming visible.

9

bloody avenger. It would seem that the reaction of a society to sin (as well as to any other problem) depends on the prior experience of that society: whether the wrong shall be torn out root and branch, or whether terms are to be made with it, depends on how intimate that society is with evil in all its forms. The outraged innocent can be a thousand times more terrible than the worldly temporizer. By 1830 the spread of slavery had begun to force upon Americans a catalogue of unsuspected revelations. And accordingly, their guilt and outrage was harrassed and quickened from the days of Garrison's first blasts in 1831—"harsh as truth, uncompromising as justice"—until the upheaval of 1861 in which slavery was destroyed with fire and sword.

The Northerner and the Southerner, more and more inclining, in the thirty years before the Civil War, to stand at polar opposites on all questions touching slavery, had at least a feature of style in common: each expressed himself with a simple moral severity. Each in his way thought of slavery as though it were a gross fact with certain universal, immutable, abstract features unalloyed by considerations of time and place. To the Northern reformer, every other concrete fact concerning slavery was dwarfed by its character as a moral evil—as an obscenity condemned of God and universally offensive to humanity. The Southerner replied in kind; slavery was a positive moral good—a necessary arrangement sanctioned in Scripture, and thus by God Himself, in which an inferior race must live under the domination of a superior. "Slavery, authorized by God, permitted by Jesus Christ, sanctioned by the apostles, maintained by good men of all ages, is still existing in a portion of our beloved country."[10] "As a man, a Christian, and a citizen, we believe that slavery is right; that the condition of the slave, as it now exists in slaveholding states, is the best existing organization of civil society."[11] These were characteristic replies to sentiments such as those of the abolitionist George Bourne, who in 1934 had written, "The Mosaic law declares every slaveholder a THIEF; Paul the Apostle classes them among the vilest criminals. . . . To tolerate slavery, or to join in its practice is an insufferable crime, which tarnishes every other good quality. *For whosoever shall keep the law and yet offend in one point, he is guilty of all.*"[12] Neither antagonist, in short— burning with guilt or moral righteousness, as the case may have been— could quite conceive of slavery as a social institution, functioning, for bet-

[10]Mary H. Eastman, *Aunt Phillis's Cabin; or, Southern Life as it is* (Philadelphia, 1862), p. 24.

[11]From the Washington *Telegraph,* quoted in LaRoy Sunderland, *Anti-Slavery Manual* (New York, 1837), p. 52.

[12]George Bourne, *Picture of Slavery in the United States of America* (Middletown, Conn., 1834), pp. 11-12. Italics in original.

10

ter or worse, by laws and logic like other institutions, mutable like others, a product of human custom, fashioned by the culture in which it flourished, and capable of infinite variation from one culture to another.

There is, in justice, little reason to expect that the question should have been argued otherwise then it was, in view of the intellectual setting available to the pre-Civil War generation. Yet we ourselves might see how slavery could in fact assume greatly differing institutional forms, were we to make a series of comparisons having to do with slavery as it existed in two very different types of culture. The two most obvious ones available for such a purpose are the liberal, Protestant, secularized, capitalist culture of America, and the conservative, paternalistic, Catholic, quasi-medieval culture of Spain and Portugal and their New World colonies. Let us proceed to an examination of the former.

II

How had Negro slavery in the United States come into being? There was nothing "natural" about it; it had no necessary connection with either tropical climate or tropical crops: in Virginia and Maryland, where the institution first appeared and flourished, the climate was hardly tropical, and the staple crop—tobacco—might have been grown as far North as Canada. It had nothing to do with characteristics which might have made the Negro peculiarly suited either to slavery or to the labor of tobacco culture: slavery in past ages had been limited to no particular race, and the earliest planters of colonial Virginia appear to have preferred a laboring force of white servants from England, Scotland, and Ireland, rather than of blacks from Africa. Nor was it a matter of common-law precedent, for the British colonists who settled the areas eventually to be included in the United States brought with them no legal categories comparable to that of "slave," as the term would be understood by the end of the seventeenth century. "Slavery," considered in the abstract as servile bondage, had existed elsewhere for centuries; indeed, the natives of Africa had known it intimately. Yet nothing was inherent, even in the fact of *Negro* slavery, which should compel it to take the form that it took in North America. Negro slavery flourished in Latin America at that same period, but there the system was strikingly different. In certain altogether crucial respects slavery, as we know it, was not imported from elsewhere but was created *here*—fashioned on the spot by Englishmen in whose traditions such an institution had no part. American slavery was unique, in the sense that for symmetry and precision of outline nothing like it had ever previously been seen.

11

An important essay by Oscar and Mary Handlin[13] has compelled our attention to these facts. Although the first shipload of twenty Negroes had arrived in Virginia in 1619, it was not until the 1660's that the key item in the definition of their status—term of servitude—was clearly fixed in law. The earliest Negroes tended at first to fall into the various servant categories long familiar to the common law of England, none of which in a practical sense included perpetual and inherited chattel bondage.[14] The bulk of agricultural laborers coming into the colonies at this period were white servants whose terms, as time went on, were to become more and more definitely fixed by indenture, and the Negroes, so far as the law was concerned, were regarded as "servants" like the rest; there was no articulated legal structure in the colonies to impede their becoming free after a term of service and entering society as artisans and holders of property without stigma of color. Indeed, color at that time was less of a determinant than was the profession of Christianity; it was still assumed that baptism should make a difference in status.[15] Manumission, moreover, for whatever reason, was a practice common enough to be taken for granted, and was attended by no special legal restrictions.

Yet all this began changing drastically with the 1660's. The very need for new colonists to people the country, and the very preference of planters for English-speaking whites rather than African savages as laborers, had already set into motion a trend to define in law the rights of white servants. To encourage the immigration of such servants and to counteract homeward-drifting rumors of indefinite servitude under desperate conditions, it was becoming more and more the practice to fix definite and limited terms of indenture—five or six years—as a guarantee that a clear future awaited the white man who would cast his lot with the colonies. The Negro, as the Handlins put it, "never profited from these enactments. Farthest removed from the English, least desired, he communicated with no friends who might be deterred from following. Since his coming was involuntary, nothing that happened to him would increase or decrease his numbers."[16]

[13]See Oscar and Mary F. Handlin, "Origins of the Southern Labor System," *William and MMary Quarterly*, VII, 3rd series (April, 1950), 199-222.
[14]The state of villeinage, which had once flourished in England during the middle ages, had many of the attributes which later characterized plantation slavery. Yet one aspect of slavery which, as we shall presently see, was crucial—the legal suppression of the personality—was never present in villeinage. The status of villein, moreover, had by the seventeenth century become virtually extinct in England.
[15]This assumption, having its roots in tradition, was still persistent enough throughout most of the seventeenth century that as late as the 1690's colonial assemblies felt the necessity to declare, in legal enactments, that baptism did not confer on the slave the right to be manumitted. See John Codman Hurd, *The Law of Freedom and Bondage in the United States* (Boston, 1858), I, 232, 250, 297, 300-1.
[16]Handlin, "Origins of Southern Labor System," *William and Mary Quarterly*, p. 211.

12

In short, every improvement in the status of the white servant, in widening the gulf between his condition and that of the Negro, served to dramatize the deepening significance of color and in effect to depress the black ever closer to a state of perpetual slavery. This tendency was ultimately recognized by the legislatures of Maryland and Virginia, and they were led to embody in law what had already become fact.

All negroes or other slaves within the province [according to a Maryland law of 1663], and all negroes and other slaves to be hereafter imported into the province, shall serve *durante vita;* and all children born of any negro or other slave, shall be slaves as their fathers were for the term of their lives.[17]

Such was the first legal step whereby a black skin would itself ultimately be equatable with "slave."

Now the Negro had probably, as a matter of actual practice, become a slave long before this time. In all likelihood the delay in *defining* his status may be ascribed to the fact that the number of Negroes in the colonies up to the 1660's had never been more than a handful,[18] and thus hardly warranted special legislation. But the important thing to note is that for some forty years there existed no ready-made structure of law to receive the incoming Negro and to guarantee automatically that he would become a slave serving for life. Legally the question was still open. However, once the initial step had been taken, and once Negroes began arriving in appreciable numbers—as they did in the years following the Restoration—there was, as it turned out, little to impede the relentless inclination of the law to remove ambiguities. A further course of legislation in the colonies —to which by then had been added the Carolinas—was inaugurated in the period roughly centering about the turn of the seventeenth century, and began suppressing, with a certain methodical insistence, whatever rights of personality still remained to the Negro slave. It was thus that most of the features marking the system of American slavery, as the nineteenth century knew it, had been stamped upon it by about the middle of the eighteenth.

Yet before reviewing in greater detail the legal aspects of this servitude, we should note that the most vital facts about its inception remain quite

[17]Quoted in Hurd, *Law of Freedom and Bondage,* I, 249. A Virginia act of the year before had assumed and implied lifetime slavery. It provided special punishments for servants who ran away in the company of "negroes who are incapable of making satisfaction by addition of a time." Helen T. Catterall, *Judicial Cases Concerning American Slavery and the Negro* (Washington: Carnegie Institution, 1926 ff.), I, 59. The matter was made explicit when in 1670 it was enacted that "all servants not being Christians, imported into this colony by shipping, shall be slaves for their lives. . . ." Hurd, *Law of Freedom and Bondage,* I, 233.

[18]See footnote 22.

13

unaccounted for. The reasons for its delay have been satisfactorily explained —but why did it occur at all? Why should the drive to establish such a status have gotten under way when it did? What was the force behind it, especially in view of the prior absence of any sort of laws defining slavery? We may on the one hand point out the lack of any legal structure automatically *compelling* the Negro to become a slave, but it is only fair, on the other, to note that there was equally little in the form of such a structure to *prevent* him from becoming one. It is not enough to indicate the simple process whereby the interests of white servants and black were systematically driven apart: what was its dynamic? Why should the status of "slave" have been elaborated, in little more than two generations following its initial definition, with such utter logic and completeness as to make *American* slavery unique among all such systems known to civilization?

Was it the "motive of gain"? Yes—but with a difference. The motive of gain, as a psychic "fact," can tell us little about what makes men behave as they do; the medieval peasant himself, with his virtually marketless economy, was hardly free from it. But in the emergent agricultural capitalism of colonial Virginia we may already make out a mode of economic organization which was taking on a purity of form never yet seen, and the difference lay in the fact that here a growing system of large-scale staple production for profit was free to develop in a society where no prior traditional institutions, with competing claims of their own, might interpose at any of a dozen points with sufficient power to retard or modify its progress. What happens, we might well ask, when such energy meets no limits?[19]

Here, even in its embryonic stages, it is possible to see the process whereby capitalism would emerge as the principal dynamic force in American society. The New World had been discovered and exploited by a European civilization which had always, in contrast with other world cultures, placed a particularly high premium on *personal* achievement, and it was to be the special genius of Englishmen, from Elizabeth's time onward, which

[19]Ever since the time of Marx and Engels (and indeed, before), the idea of "Capitalism" has been a standard tool in the analysis of behavior on a social level. Up to a point this tool is useful; it can throw light on changes in behavior patterns at the point where capitalistic methods and habits in a society begin to supersede feudal ones. In Europe it made some sense. Here is how Engels argued: "According to this conception," he wrote in *Anti-Dühring*, "the ultimate causes of all social changes and political revolutions are to be sought, not in the minds of men, in their increasing insight into eternal truth and justice, but in changes in the mode of production and exchange; they are to be sought not in the *philosophy* but in the *economics* of the epoch concerned." But then what does this idea have to tell us about the *differences* between two societies, *both* capitalist, but in one of which the "means of production" have *changed* into capitalistic ones, and in the other of which the means of production were never anything *but* capitalistic—and in which no other forces were present to resist their development?

14

would transform this career concept from its earlier chivalric form into one of economic fulfillment—from "glory," in short, to "success." Virginia was settled during the very key period in which the English middle class, by revolution, forcibly reduced the power of those standing institutions which most directly symbolized society's traditional limitations upon personal success and mobility—the church and the crown. What the return of the crown betokened in 1660 was not so much "reaction" as the fact that all society had by then somehow made terms with the Puritan Revolution. Virginia had proven a uniquely appropriate theater for the acting out of this narrower, essentially modern ideal of personal—of *economic* success. Land in the early days was cheap and plentiful; a ready market for tobacco existed; even the yeoman farmer could rise rapidly if he could make the transition to staple production; and above all there was a quick recognition of accomplishment, by a standard which was not available in England but which was the *only* one available in Virginia: success in creating a plantation.[20]

The decade of the 1660's—inaugurated by the restoration of the Stuart monarchy—marked something of a turning point in the fortunes of the colony, not unrelated to the movement there and in Maryland to fix irrevocably upon the Negro a lifetime of slavery. It was during this decade that certain factors bearing upon the colony's economic future were precipitated. One such factor was a serious drop in tobacco prices, brought on not only by overproduction but also by the Navigation Acts of 1660 and 1661,[21] and the market was not to be fully restored for another twenty years. This meant, with rising costs and a disappearing margin of profit,

[20]Despite the relative mobility of English society since Tudor times, personal achievement and status still inhered in any number of preferable *alternatives* to trade and production. But the openness of Virginia lay in the fact that *purely* capitalistic incentives were being used to get people to come there. No nobles, with their retinues of peasants, migrated to the colony; indeed, there was little reason why the ideal of "making good" should in itself hold many attractions for an aristocracy already established. But for others there were rewards for risk-taking which were simply not available in England. True, Virginia did develop its own aristocracy, but it had to be a created one, based on terms peculiar to the new country, and—at least as a basis for aspirations—theoretically open to everyone. At any rate the standards for joining it were not primarily chivalric: to be a "gentleman" one must first have been a successful planter.

[21]These Acts embodied the Puritan mercantilist policy which Cromwell had never been able to enforce but which had been taken over by the Restoration government. Their general purpose was that of redirecting colonial trade (much of which had been engrossed by the Dutch during the Civil War) through the hands of English merchants. Their immediate effects on tobacco, before the market could readjust itself, was, from the viewpoint of colonial planters, most unfavorable. By limiting the sale of Virginia tobacco to England and requiring that it be transported in English ships, the Navigation Acts cut off Virginia's profitable trade with the Dutch and temporarily crippled its profitable foreign markets. This, according to Thomas J. Wertenbaker, was the basic cause for the serious drop in tobacco prices. See *Planters of Colonial Virginia* (Princeton: Princeton University Press, 1922), pp. 85-87, 90.

15

that commercial production on a small-scale basis was placed under the most serious of disabilities. Another factor was the rise in the slave population. Whereas there had been only about 300 of them in 1650, by 1670 there were, according to Governor Berkeley, 2000 slaves in a servant population of 8000. This was already 25 per cent, and the figure was even more significant for the future, since the total white servant population could never be counted on to exceed their average annual immigration over any given period, multiplied by five or six (the usual term, in years, of their indenture), while the increase of slaves over the same period would be cumulative.[22] Such a development would by now be quite enough to stimulate the leaders of the colony—virtually all planters—to clarify in law once and for all the status of lifetime Negro servitude. The formation in 1662 of a Royal Company of Adventurers for the importation of Negroes symbolized the crown's expectation that a labor force of slaves would be the coming thing in the colonies.[23]

It was thus in a period of relatively hard times that it became clear, if the colony of Virginia were to prosper, that capitalism would be the dynamic force in its economic life. "Success" could no longer be visualized as a rise from small beginnings, as it once could, but must now be conceived as a matter of substantial initial investments in land, equipment, and labor, plus the ability to undertake large annual commitments on credit. With the fall in tobacco prices and the tiny margin of profit the yeoman farmer found it difficult enough to eke out a bare living, let alone think of competing with

[22]"40,000 persons, men, women, and children, of which 2,000 are black slaves, 6,000 Christian servants for a short time. Gov. Berkeley." Evarts B. Greene and Virginia D. Harrington, *American Population Before the Federal Census of 1790* (New York: Columbia University Press, 1932), p. 36. This figure may be looked at two ways. From the standpoint of *later* populations, one may call attention to its smallness. But consider how it must have appeared to the man looking back to a time only two decades before, when the number of Negroes was negligible. Now, in 1670, with Negroes constituting a full quarter of the servant population (a proportion which gave every promise of increasing), they become a force to be dealt with. By now, men would take them into account as a basis for future calculations in a way which previously they had never needed to do. The very laws demonstrate this. Moreover, Negroes had accumulated in large enough parcels in the hands of the colony's *most powerful* men as to develop in these men deep vested interests in the Negroes' presence and a strong concern with the legal aspects of their future. Among the land patents of the sixties, for example, may already be seen Richard Lee with eighty Negroes, Carter of Corotoman with twenty, the Scarboroughs with thirty-nine, and numerous patents listing fifteen or more. Philip Alexander Bruce, *Economic History of Virginia in the Seventeenth Century* (New York: Macmillan Co., 1907), II, 78.

[23]The subsequent increase of slaves in Virginia was not largely the work of this company. But its formation under royal protection, coming at the time it did, appears to form part of a general pattern of expectations regarding the future state of labor in the plantation colonies. This, taken together with the drop in tobacco prices, coincident with the Navigation Acts and the first general laws on perpetual servitude, all coming at once, seem to add up to something: that profitable enterprise, when possible at all, would henceforth as never before have to be conceived in terms of heavily capitalized investment, and that more and more men were recognizing this.

16

the large planter or of purchasing slaves or servants' indentures.[24] Success was still possible, but now its terms were clearer, and those who achieved it would be fewer in numbers. The man who managed it would be the man with the large holdings—the man who could command a substantial force of laborers, white or black—who could afford a sizable yearly investment in the handling of his crop: in short, the capitalist planter.

The period beginning in the 1680's and ending about 1710 marked still a new phase. It saw, now under conditions of comparative prosperity, the full emergence of the plantation as the basic unit of capitalist agriculture. By about 1680 the market for Virginia and Maryland tobacco had been restored, though it is important to note that this was accompanied by no great rise in prices. It was rather a matter of having recaptured the European market by the process of flooding it with cheap tobacco and underselling competitors. Returning prosperity, therefore, meant something far more concrete to the man with resources, who could produce tobacco in large enough amounts to make a slim profit margin worthwhile, than to the one whose productivity was limited by the acreage which he and his family could work. These years also witnessed the initial exploitation of the Carolinas, a process which moved much more directly toward large agricultural units than had been the case in Virginia.[25] The acceleration of this development toward clarifying the terms of commercial production—large plantations and

[24]This had not always been so; the aspirations of a farmer in, say, 1649, with prices at 3 pence a pound, could include a wide range of possibilities. But now, with the price at one-fourth of that figure and costs proportionately much greater than formerly, he could hardly think of the future realistically in terms of becoming a planter. See Lewis Cecil Gray, *History of Agriculture in the Southern States to 1860* (Washington: Carnegie Institution, 1933), I, 263. Now this does not mean that after 1660 the yeoman farmer invariably faced destitution. A great deal depended on how such a farmer conceived his future. The man who made his living from diversified subsistence and who planted tobacco as an extra-money crop would undoubtedly suffer less from a drop in prices than the heavily-capitalized planter. However if this same farmer hoped to emulate "his predecessors of the earlier period in saving money, purchasing land . . . and becoming a substantial citizen, the task was well nigh impossible of accomplishment." Wertenbaker, *Planters of Colonial Virginia*, p. 97. See also pp. 96-100, for an extended discussion of the effects of this depression on the yeomanry as a class.

[25]The Carolina proprietors had a far clearer notion of the terms on which money was to be made from their colony than had been true of the London Company of sixty years before with regard to Virginia. They appear at the very outset to have fostered the establishment of large estates, and a number of such estates set up in the 1670's and 80's were organized by Barbados men with first-hand plantation experience. See Gray, *History of Agriculture*, I, 324-25; see also J. P. Thomas, "Barbadians in Early South Carolina," *South Carolina Historical Magazine*, XXXI (April, 1930), 89. Although a dominant staple was not to emerge until some time later, with rice and indigo, it seems to have been conceived in terms of large units to a degree never envisaged at a comparable stage in the development of Virginia. One index of this is quickly seen in the composition of the laboring population there; a little over a generation after the first settlements the ratio of Negro slaves to whites in the total population could be safely estimated at about one to one, whereas the same ratio would not be attained in Virginia until late in the eighteenth century. Greene and Harrington, *American Population*, pp. 124, 137.

17

substantial investments—had a direct connection with the widening of the market for slaves during this same period. Hand in hand with large holdings went slaves—an assumption which was now being taken more or less for granted. "A rational man," wrote a South Carolina colonist in 1682, "will certainly inquire, 'when I have Land, what shall I doe with it? What commoditys shall I be able to produce, that will yield me money in other countrys, that I may be inabled to buy Negro-slaves, (without which a planter can never doe any great matter)?' "[26] The point had clearly passed when white servants could realistically, on any long-term appraisal, be considered as preferable to Negro slaves. Such appraisals were now being made in terms of capitalized earning power, a concept appropriate to large operations rather than small, to long-term rather than short-term planning.

It was, of course, only the man of means who could afford to think in this way. But then *he* is the one who most concerns us—the man responsible for Negro slavery. Determined in the 60's and 70's to make money despite hard times and low prices, and willing to undertake the investments which that required, he could now in the 80's reap the fruits of his foresight. His slaves were more valuable than ever—a monument to his patience and planning. What had made them so? For one thing he, unlike the yeoman farmer, had a large establishment for training them and was not pressed by the need—as he would have been with white servants on limited indenture—to exploit their *immediate* labor. That labor was his permanently. And for another thing, the system was by now just old enough to make clear for the first time the full meaning of a second generation of native-born American Negroes. These were the dividends: slaves born to the work, and using English as their native tongue.[27] By the .1690's the demand for slaves in the British colonies had become so great, and the Royal African Company so inefficient in supplying them, that in 1698 Parliament revoked the Company's monopoly on the African coast and threw open the traffic to independent merchants and traders. The stream of incoming slaves, already of some consequence, now became enormous, and at the same time the annual flow of white servants to Virginia and the Carolinas dropped sharply. By 1710 it had become virtually negligible.[28]

[26]Quoted in Gray, *History of Agriculture,* I, 352.
[27]This is another point of view from which to consider the 1671 figure (cited in footnote 22) on the Virginia slave population. The difference between the 300 Negroes of 1650 and the 2000 of 1670 is substantial—nearly a sevenfold increase. According to Berkeley's testimony the importations over the previous seven years had not been more than two or three cargoes. If this were true it would be safe to estimate that a significant number of that 2000 must already have been native-born American Negroes. As for the period to which the above paragraph has reference—fifteen or twenty years later—the number of native-born must by then have increased considerably.
[28]Greene and Harrington, *American Population,* pp. 136-37, 173; Gray, *History of Agriculture,* I, 349-50.

18

What meaning might all this have had for the legal status of the Negro? The connection was intimate and direct: with the full development of the plantation there was nothing, so far as *his* interests were concerned, to prevent unmitigated capitalism from becoming unmitigated slavery. The planter was now engaged in capitalistic agriculture with a labor force entirely under his control. The personal relationship between master and slave—in any case less likely to exist on large agricultural units than on smaller ones—now became far less important than the economic necessities which had forced the slave into this "unnatural" organization in the first place. For the plantation to operate efficiently and profitably, and with a force of laborers, not all of whom may have been fully broken to plantation discipline, the necessity of training them to work long hours, giving unquestioning obedience to their masters and overseers, superseded every other consideration. The master must have absolute power over the slave's body—and the law was developing in such a way as to give it to him at every crucial point. Physical discipline was made virtually unlimited[29] and the slave's chattel status unalterably fixed.[30] It was in such a setting that those rights of personality traditionally regarded between men as private and inherent—quite apart from the matter of lifetime servitude—were left virtually without defense. The integrity of the family was ignored, and slave marriage was deprived of any legal or moral standing.[31] The condition of a bondsman's soul—a matter of much concern to church and civil authority in the Spanish colonies—was here very quickly dropped from consideration. A series of laws enacted between 1667 and 1671 had systematically removed any linger-

[29]As early as 1669 a Virginia law had declared it no felony if a master or overseer killed a slave who resisted punishment. According to the South Carolina code of 1712, the punishment for offering "any violence to any christian or white person, by striking, or the like" was a severe whipping for the first offense, branding for the second, and death for the third. Should the white man attacked be injured or maimed, the punishment was automatically death. The same act provided that a runaway slave be serverely whipped for his first offense, branded for his second, his ears cut off for the third, and castrated for the fourth. It is doubtful that such punishments were often used but their very existence served to symbolize the relationship of absolute power over the slave's body. Hurd, *Law of Freedom and Bondage,* I, 232; Thomas Cooper and D. J. McCord, (eds.), *Statutes at Large of South Carolina* (Columbia, S. C., 1836-41), VII, 357-59.

[30]Slaves in seventeenth-century Virginia had become, as a matter of actual practice, classed on the same footing as household goods and other personal property. The code of 1705 made them a qualified form of real estate, but that law was in 1726 amended by another which declared that slaves were "to pass as chattels." Bruce, *Economic History,* II, 99; Hurd, *Law of Freedom and Bondage,* I, 242. The South Carolina code of 1740 made them "chattels personal, in the hands of their owners and possessors and their executors, administrators and assigns, to all intents, constructions and purposes whatsoever. . . ." *Hurd,* I, 303.

[31]Bruce (*Economic History,* II, 108) describes a will, written about 1680, in which a woman "bequeathed to one daughter, . . . a negress and the third child to be born of her; to a second daughter, . . . the first and second child to be born of the same woman." See also footnote 33.

19

ing doubts as to whether or not conversion to Christianity should make a difference in status: henceforth it made none.[32] The balance, therefore, involved on the one side the constant pressure of costs, prices, and the problems of management, and on the other the personal interests of the slave. Here, there were no counterweights: those interests were unsupported by any social pressures from the outside; they were cherished by no customary feudal immunities; they were no concern of the government (the king's main interest was in tobacco revenue); they could not be sustained by the church, for the church had little enough power and influence among its own white constituencies, to say nothing of the suspicion its ministers aroused at every proposal to enlarge the church's work among the blacks. The emergent institution of slavery, in short, was unchallenged by any other institutions.[33]

The result was that the slave, utterly powerless, would at every critical

[32]Handlin, "Origins of Southern Labor System," *William and Mary Quarterly*, p. 212. The Maryland law of 1671 could leave no possible doubt in this matter, declaring that any Christianized slaves "Is, are and be and shall att all tymes hereafter be adjudged Reputed deemed and taken to be and Remayne in Servitude and Bondage and subject to the same Servitude and Bondage to all intents and purposes as if hee shee they every or any of them was or were in and Subject vnto before such his her or their Becomeing Christian or Christians or Receiving of the Sacrament of Baptizme any opinion or other matter or thing to the Contrary in any wise Notwithstanding." William Hand Browne, (ed.), *Archives of Maryland* (Baltimore, 1884), II, 272. See also footnote 15.

[33]What this meant to the Negro is admirably reflected in a book by Morgan Godwyn, an Anglican minister who served in the 1670's both in Barbados and in Virginia. Godwyn's book, *The Negro's and Indian's Advocate*, was a plea for the care of the Negro's soul. He attacked the planters for keeping religion from the slaves, for "Not allowing their children *Baptism;* nor suffering them upon better terms than direct *Fornication*, to live with their Women, (for Wives, I may not call them, being never married). And accounting it Foppish, when Dead, to think of giving them *Christian,* or even decent Burial; that so their pretence for Brutifying them, might find no Contradiction." (p. 37) In Godwyn's eyes the planters were men "who for the most part do know no other God but money, nor Religion but Profit." (Preface) He quotes one Barbadian who "openly maintained . . . that Negroes were beasts, and had no more souls than beasts, and that religion did not concern them. Adding that they [his fellow Barbadians] went *not* to those parts to save souls, or propagate religion, but to get Money." (p. 39) Even the care of white souls in the colonies appears to have occupied a rather low order of concern. The Attorney-General of England in 1693 objected strenuously to the erection of a college in Virginia, though he was reminded of the need to educate young men for the ministry and was begged to consider the souls of the colonists. "Souls! Damn your souls," he replied, "make tobacco." (Quoted in Wertenbaker, *Planters of Colonial Virginia*, p. 138.) It is doubtful if the planters of Virginia were quite so brutal as the Barbadians in their attitude toward the Negro or in the management of their plantations, but even in Virginia Godwyn found that the idea of teaching religion to the Negro slave was thought "so idle and ridiculous, so utterly needless and unnecessary, that no Man can forfeit his Judgement more, than by any proposal looking or tending that way." (p. 172) That such an attitude had not changed by the eighteenth century is suggested by a piece in the *Athenian Oracle* of Boston in 1707, in which the writer declared, "Talk to a *Planter* of the *Soul* of a *Negro,* and he'll be apt to tell ye (or at least his actions speak it loudly) that the Body of one of them may be worth twenty pounds; but the Souls of an Hundred of them would not yield him one Farthing." Quoted in Marcus W. Jernegan, "Slavery and Conversion in the American Colonies," *American Historical Review*, XXI (April, 1916), p. 516.

20

point see his interests further depressed. At those very points the drive of the law was to clarify beyond all question, unembarrassed by the perplexities of competing interests—to rationalize, simplify, to make more logical and symmetrical—the slave's status in society. So little impeded was this pressure to define and clarify that all the major categories in law which bore upon such status were very early established with great thoroughness and completeness. The unthinking aggressions upon the slave's personality which such a situation made possible becomes apparent upon an examination, in greater detail, of these legal categories. They may be roughly classified— in addition to "term of servitude," which we have already considered—as "marriage and the family," "police and disciplinary powers over the slave," and "property and other civil rights."*

*A continuation of this study, dealing with slavery in capitalist and non-capitalist cultures, will be published in a subsequent issue of this journal.

21

by STANLEY ELKINS &
ERIC McKITRICK

*continue their study of the legal aspects
of slavery.*

Institutions and the Law of Slavery:
Slavery in Capitalist and
Non-Capitalist Cultures

THE four major legal categories which defined the status of the American slave were "term of servitude," "marriage and the family," "police and disciplinary powers over the slave" and "property and other civil rights." The first of these, from which somehow all the others flowed, had in effect been established during the latter half of the seventeenth century; a slave was a slave for the duration of his life, and slavery was a status which he transmitted by inheritance to his children and his children's children.[1]

It would be fairest, for several reasons, to view the remaining three categories in terms of the jurisprudence of the nineteenth century. By that time the most savage aspects of slavery from the standpoint of Southern practice (and thus, to a certain extent, of law) had become greatly softened. We may accordingly see it in its most humane light, and at the same time note the clarity with which its basic outlines remained fixed and embodied in law, much as they had been laid down before the middle of the eighteenth century.[2]

[1] The process whereby this came about is discussed in Part I of the present essay, "The Dynamics of Unopposed Capitalism," *AMERICAN QUARTERLY*, Spring, 1957.

[2] We have a further advantage in regarding the law of slavery in the light of the nineteenth century. Two general developments of that period inspired a great wealth of writing on the subject in the form of commentaries by jurists and *obiter dicta* by judges, as well as a fresh course of marginal legislation bearing on some of slavery's social implications. These developments were the expansion of slavery into the Gulf states and—much more important—the moral pressures being exerted on Southerners both from the North and from abroad. The bulk of the Southern response to this latter fact took the form of various kinds of defenses of slavery, but for Southern jurists it naturally stimulated a re-examination of the legal aspects of their "peculiar institution."

159

161

That most ancient and intimate of institutional arrangements, marriage and the family, had long since been destroyed by the law, and the law never showed any inclination to rehabilitate it. Here was the area in which considerations of humanity might be expected most widely to prevail, and indeed, there is every reason to suppose that on an informal daily basis they did: the contempt in which respectable society held the slave-trader, who separated mother from child and husband from wife, is proverbial in Southern lore.[3] On the face of things, it ought to have been simple enough to translate this strong social sentiment into the appropriate legal enactments, which might systematically have guaranteed the inviolability of the family and the sanctity of the marriage bond, such as governed Christian polity everywhere. Yet the very nature of the plantation economy and the way in which the basic arrangements of Southern life radiated from it, made it inconceivable that the law should tolerate any ambiguity, should the painful clash between humanity and property interest ever occur. Any restrictions on the separate sale of slaves would have been reflected immediately in the market; their price would have dropped considerably.[4] Thus the law could permit no aspect of the slave's conjugal state to have an independent legal existence outside the power of the man who owned him: "the relation of master and slave is wholly incompatible with even the qualified relation of husband and wife, as it is supposed to exist among slaves. . . ."[5] Marriage, for them, was denied any standing in law. Accordingly, as T. R. R. Cobb of Georgia admitted, "The contract of marriage not being recognized among slaves, none of its consequences follow. . . ."[6] "The relation between slaves," wrote a North Carolina judge in 1858, "is essentially different from that of man and wife joined in lawful wedlock . . . with slaves it may be dissolved at the pleasure of either party, or by the sale of one or both, depending on the caprice or necessity of the owners."[7]

[3] "In all the category of disreputable callings, there were none só despised as the slave-trader. The odium descended upon his children and his children's children. Against the legal right to buy and sell slaves for profit, this public sentiment lifted a strong arm, and rendered forever odious the name of 'Negro-trader.' " Beverly B. Munford, *Virginia's Attitude Toward Slavery and Secession* (New York: Longmans, Green & Co., 1909), pp. 101-2.

[4] This may be tested against what did typically happen in cases where restrictions were placed by the seller himself upon the separation of slaves with whom he was obliged, for whatever reason, to part. "In proportion as these restrictions put important limitations on the purchaser's rights and were safeguarded, they lessened the slave's salability." Frederic Bancroft, *Slave-Trading in the Old South* (Baltimore: J. H. Furst Co., 1931), p. 214.

[5] *Howard v. Howard*, 6 Jones N.C. 235 (Dec., 1858), quoted in Helen T. Catterall, *Judicial Cases Concerning American Slavery and the Negro* (Washington: Carnegie Institution, 1926 ff.), II, 221.

[6] Thomas R. R. Cobb, *An Inquiry into the Law of Slavery in the United States of America* (Philadelphia, 1858), p. 246.

[7] Quoted in Catterall, *Judicial Cases*, II, 221.

160

It would thus go without saying that the offspring of such "contubernial relationships," as they were called, had next to no guarantees against indiscriminate separation from their parents.[8] Of additional interest is the fact that children derived their condition from that of their mother. This was not unique to American slavery, but it should be noted that especially in a system conceived and evolved exclusively on grounds of property there could be little doubt as to how such a question would be resolved. Had status been defined according to the father's condition—as was briefly the case in seventeenth-century Maryland, following the ancient common law—there would instantly have arisen the irksome question of what to do with the numerous mulatto children born every year of white planter-fathers and slave mothers. It would have meant the creation of a free mulatto class, automatically relieving the master of so many slaves on the one hand, while burdening him on the other with that many colored children whom he could not *own*. Such equivocal relationships were never permitted to vex the law. That "the father of a slave is unknown to our law" was the universal understanding of Southern jurists.[9] It was thus that a father, among slaves, was legally "unknown," a husband without the rights of his bed,[10] the state of marriage defined as "only that concubinage . . . with which alone, perhaps, their condition is compatible,"[11] and motherhood clothed in the scant dignity of the breeding function.[12]

As regards matters of police and discipline, it is hardly necessary to view

[8]The few exceptions—none of which meant very much in practice, except perhaps the law of Louisiana—are discussed in Bancroft, *Slave-Trading*, pp. 197-221. "Louisiana, least American of the Southern States," writes Mr. Bancroft, "was least inhuman. In becoming Americanized it lost many a liberal feature of the old French *code noir*, but it forbade sale of mothers from their children less than ten years of age (and *vice versa*) and bringing into the State any slave child under ten years of age without its mother, if living. The penalty for violating either prohibition was from $1,000 to $2,000 and the forfeiture of the slave. That would have meant much if it had been strictly enforced." (p. 197.) This raises a very interesting question. Why, if any American state should turn out to be less "inhuman" in its slave code than others, would it be Louisiana? It is our assumption that the discussion in the present essay on the law of slavery in Latin America offers significant clues which go beyond the mere fact that Louisiana was "different."

[9]*Frazier* v. *Spear*, 2 Bibb (Ken.), 385 (Fall, 1811), quoted in Catterall, *Judicial Cases*, I, 287.

[10]"A slave has never maintained an action against the violator of his bed. A slave is not admonished for incontinence, or punished for fornication or adultery; never prosecuted for bigamy, or petty treason for killing a husband being a slave, any more than admitted to an appeal for murder." Opinion of Daniel Dulany, Esq., Attorney-General of Maryland, quoted in William Goodell, *The American Slave Code in Theory and Practice* (New York, 1853), pp. 106-7.

[11]*State* v. *Samuel* (*a slave*), 2 Dev. and Bat. (N.C.), 177 (Dec., 1836), quoted in Catterall, *Judicial Cases*, II, 77.

[12]"The thing to do was to breed the Negro girls young. 'A girl of seventeen that had borne two children was called a "rattlin' good breeder" and commanded an extraordinary price.' " Frank Tannenbaum, *Slave and Citizen* (New York: Alfred A. Knopf, 1947), p. 82. The quotation is from Bancroft, *Slave-Trading*, p. 79.

161

the typical slave's lot in the nineteenth century as one of stripes and torture. Indeed, the truth would doubtless not be greatly stretched were we to concede Ulrich Phillips' sympathetic picture of a just regime tempered with paternal indulgence on the majority of well-run plantations. Among decent Southerners the remark, "I have been told that he does not use his people well," was a pronouncement of deep social censure.[13] Yet here again what impresses us is not the laxity with which much of the daily discipline was undoubtedly handled, but rather the completeness with which such questions, even extending to life and limb, were in fact under the master's dominion. "On our estates," wrote the Southern publicist J. D. B. DeBow in 1853, "we dispense with the whole machinery of public police and public courts of justice. Thus we try, decide, and execute the sentences in thousands of cases, which in other countries would go into the courts."[14] The law deplored "cruel and unusual punishment." But wherever protection was on the one hand theoretically extended,[15] it was practically canceled on the other by the universal prohibition in Southern law against permitting slaves to testify in court, except against each other, and in any case the courts generally accepted the principle that the line between correction and cruelty was impossible to determine. Thus a Virginia judge in 1827, faced with an indictment against a master "for cruelly beating his own slave," felt bound to decline jurisdiction with the rhetoric demand: "without any proofs that the common law did ever protect the slave against minor injuries from the hand of the master, . . . where are we to look for the power which is now claimed for us?"[16] To the jurist Cobb, it seemed

[13]"There is a public sentiment to which they are amenable; a cruel, neglectful master is marked and despised; and if cruel and neglectful by proxy, he does not escape reprobation." Nehemiah Adams, *A South-Side View of Slavery* (1855), p. 97. Such a man, according to Frederick Law Olmsted, was known as a "nigger-killer." *Journey in the Seaboard Slave States* (New York: G. P. Putnam's Sons, 1904), I, 120-21.

[14]DeBow, *Industrial Resources* (1852-53), II, 249, quoted in A. B. Hart, *Slavery and Abolition* (New York: Harper & Bros., Publishers, 1906), p. 112.

[15]There was, for example, a South Carolina law of 1740 which provided that "In case any person shall wilfully cut out the tongue, put out the eye, castrate, or cruelly scald, burn, or deprive any slave of any limb or member, or shall inflict any other cruel punishment, other than whipping, or beating with a horsewhip, cowskin, switch, or small stick, or by putting irons on, or confining or imprisoning such slave, every such person shall, for every such offense, forfeit the sum of one hundred pounds current money." Goodell, *American Slave Code*, pp. 159-60.

[16]*Commonwealth* v. *Turner*, 5 Randolph 678 (Nov., 1827), quoted in Catterall, *Judicial Cases*, I, 150. It was in the same spirit that Judge Ruffin of North Carolina expressed himself in the case of *State* v. *Mann* in 1829. "But upon the general question whether the owner is answerable, *criminalter*, for a battery upon his own slave . . . the Court entertains but little doubt. That he is so liable has never been decided, nor, as far as is known, been hitherto contended. There has been no prosecutions of the sort. The established and uniform practice of the country in this respect is the best evidence of the portion of the power deemed by the whole community requisite to the preservation of the master's dominion. . . . The power

162

clear on principle "that the battery of a slave, without special enactment, could not be prosecuted criminally."[17] Public opinion itself should, it was generally held, deter wanton brutalities. But the final argument was that of self-interest. "Where the battery was committed by the master himself, there would be no redress whatever, for the reason given in Exodus 21:21, 'for he is his money.' The powerful protection of the master's private interest would of itself go far to remedy this evil."[18]

Even the murder of a slave found the law straining all its resources to avoid jurisdiction.[19] Murder was indeed punishable, but under circumstances peculiar to the state of slavery, not in ways applying to white society, and always under the disabilities which barred the testimony of Negroes in the courts. An act of North Carolina in 1798 provided that the punishment for "maliciously killing a slave" should be the same as for the murder of a free person—but it did not apply to an outlawed slave, nor to a slave "in the act of resistance to his lawful owner," nor to a slave "dying under moderate correction."[20] The law in South Carolina allowed that in the absence of competent witnesses to the homicide of a slave, the affidavit of the accused was admissible in his favor before a jury.[21] The criminal jurisprudence of Virginia had never known, before 1851, a case of "more atrocious and wicked cruelty" than that of one Souther, who had killed his slave, Sam, under the most lurid circumstances.[22] Yet the conviction

of the master must be absolution, to render the submission of the slave perfect. I most freely confess my sense of the harshness of the proposition. I feel it as deeply as any man can. . . . But it is inherent in the relation of master and slave. . . . We cannot allow the right of the master to be brought into discussion in the Courts of justice. The slave, to remain a slave, must be made sensible that there is no appeal from his master. . . ." Quoted in Goodell, *American Slave Code,* pp. 171-73.

[17]Cobb, *Inquiry,* p. 90. "This [the Negro's helplessness] is one of the most vulnerable points in the system of negro slavery," Cobb admitted, "and should be further guarded by legislation." *Ibid.,* p. 98.

[18]Cobb, *Inquiry,* p. 98.

[19]"It would seem that from the very nature of slavery, and the necessarily degraded social position of the slave, many acts would extenuate the homicide of a slave, and reduce the offence to a lower grade, which would not constitute a legal provocation if done by a white person." Cobb, *Inquiry,* p. 92.

[20]Goodell, *American Slave Code,* p. 180. There was a law in Tennessee to the same effect and in virtually the same words. See John Codman Hurd, *The Law of Freedom and Bondage in the United States* (Boston, 1858), II, 90.

[21]Cobb, *Inquiry,* p. 96.

[22]"The negro was tied to a tree and whipped with switches. When Souther became fatigued with the labour of whipping, he called upon a negro man of his, and made him cob Sam with a shingle. He also made a negro woman of his help to cob him. And after cobbing and whipping, he applied fire to the body of the slave; about his back, belly and private parts. He then caused him to be washed down with hot water, in which pods of red pepper had been steeped. The negro was also tied to a log and to the bed post with ropes, which choked him, and he was kicked and stamped by Souther. This sort of punishment was continued and repeated until the negro died under its infliction." *Souther v. Commonwealth,* 7 Grattan 673 (June, 1851), quoted in Catterall, *Judicial Cases,* I, 224.

163

was for murder in the second degree, and Souther escaped with five years in the penitentiary. In general, the court's primary care—not only in the killing of slaves by persons *other* than the master, but also in cases where the slave himself had committed murder and was executed by the state— was for the pecuniary interest of the owner. Numerous enactments provided for compensation in either event.[23] It was precisely this pecuniary interest, indeed, which was at the very heart of legal logic on all such questions. Just as it was presumed to operate against "cruel and unusual punishment," so it became virtually a *non sequitur* that a man should kill his own slave. The principle had been enunciated very early: "it cannot be presumed that prepensed malice (which alone makes murder felony) should induce any man to destroy his own estate."[24]

The rights of property, and all other civil and legal "rights," were everywhere denied the slave with a clarity that left no doubt of his utter dependency upon his master. "A slave is in absolute bondage; he has no civil right, and can hold no property, except at the will and pleasure of his master."[25] He could neither give nor receive gifts; he could make no will, nor could he, by will, inherit anything. He could not hire himself out or make contracts for any purpose—even including, as we have seen, that of matrimony—and thus neither his word nor his bond had any standing in law. He could buy or sell nothing at all, except as his master's agent, could keep no cattle, horses, hogs or sheep, and—in Mississippi at least—could raise no cotton. Even masters who permitted such transactions, except under express arrangement, were uniformly liable to fines.[26] It was obvious, then, that the case of a slave who should presume to buy his own freedom—he being unable to possess money—would involve a legal absurdity. "Slaves have no legal rights in things, real or personal; but whatever they may acquire, belongs, in point of law, to their masters."[27]

Such proscriptions were extended not only over all civil rights, but even to the civic privileges of education and worship. Every Southern state except Maryland and Kentucky had stringent laws forbidding anyone to teach slaves reading and writing, and in some states the penalties applied to the educating of free Negroes and mulattoes as well. It was thought that "teaching slaves to read and write tends to dissatisfaction in their minds,

[23]See Hurd, *Law of Freedom and Bondage*, I, 253, 296-97, 300.

[24]"An act about the casuall killing of slaves" (Virginia, 1669), Hurd, *Law of Freedom and Bondage*, I, 232.

[25]Opinion of Judge Crenshaw in *Brandon et al. v. Planters' and Merchants' Bank of Huntsville*, 1 Stewart's Ala. Report, 320 (Jan., 1838), quoted in Goddell, *American Slave Code*, p. 92.

[26]*Ibid.*, pp. 89-104.

[27]*Ibid.*, p. 88.

164

and to produce insurrection and rebellion";[28] in North Carolina it was a crime to distribute among them any pamphlet or book, not excluding the Bible. The same apprehensions applied to instruction in religion. Southern society was not disposed to withhold the consolations of divine worship from its slaves, but the conditions would have to be laid down not by the church as institution, not even by the planters as laity, but by planters *as planters*. The conscientious master no doubt welcomed having the gospel preached to his slaves, provided that they should hear it, as J. W. Fowler of Coahama County, Mississippi, specified, "in its original purity and simplicity." Fowler wrote to his overseer that "in view of the fanaticism of the age it behooves the Master or Overseer to be present on all such occasions."[29] Alexander Telfair, of Savannah, instructed his overseer that there should be "No night-meeting or preaching . . . allowed on the place, except on Saturday night & Sunday morn."[30] Similar restrictions found their way into the law itself. Typical were the acts of South Carolina forbidding religious meetings of slaves or free Negroes "either before the rising of the sun or after the setting of the same," and of Mississippi permitting slaves, if authorized by their masters, to attend the preaching of a *white* minister. It was a state of things deplored by the Southern churches, for the law had been none of their doing. "There are˥over TWO MILLIONS of human beings in the condition of heathen," lamented the Presbyterian Synod of South Carolina and Georgia in 1833, "and some of them in worse condition."

In the present state of feeling in the South, a ministry of their own color could neither be obtained NOR TOLERATED. But do not the negroes have access to the gospel through the stated ministry of the whites? We answer, No. The negroes have no regular and efficient ministry: as a matter of course, no churches; neither is there sufficient room in the white churches for their accommodation.[31]

But the church could do nothing. Its rural congregations were full of humane and decent Christians, but as an institution of authority and power, it had no real existence.

It is true that one of the most attractive features of the plantation legend as it has come down to us, and which is dear to every Southerner with a sense of his past, was the paternal affection of the good master for his blacks, and the warm sentiments entertained in Southern society at large for the faithful slave. The other side of the coin, then, might appear as

[28]Goodell, *American Slave Code*, p. 321.
[29]Ulrich B. Phillips (ed.), *A Documentary History of American Industrial Society* (Cleveland: Arthur H. Clark Co., 1910), I, 115.
[30]*Ibid.*, I, 127.
[31]Quoted in Goodell, *American Slave Code*, p. 334.

165

something of a paradox: the most implacable racial antagonism yet observed in virtually any society. It was evolved in the Southern mind, one might say, as a simple syllogism, the precision of whose terms paralleled the precision of the system itself. All slaves are black; slaves are degraded and contemptible; therefore all blacks are degraded and contemptible and should be kept in a state of slavery. How had the simple syllogism come into being? That very strength and bulwark of American society, capitalism, unimpeded by prior arrangements and institutions, had stamped the status of slave upon the black with a clarity which elsewhere—as we shall shortly see—could never have been so profound, and had ,further defined the institution of slavery with such nicety that the slave *was*, in fact, degraded. That the black, as a species, was thus contemptible seemed to follow by observation. This assumption took on a life of its own in the attitudes of the people, and the very thought of such a creature existing outside the pale of their so aptly devised system filled the most reasonable of Southerners with fear and loathing. This—in a certain sense quite apart from the demands of the system itself—may account for many of the subsidiary social taboos—the increasing severity of the laws against manumission, the horror of miscegenation, the depressed condition of the free Negro and his peculiar place in Southern society: all signs of how impossible it was to conceive a non-slave colored class. Nothing in their experience had prepared them for it; such a class was unnatural, logically awry, a blemish on the body politic, an anomaly for which there was no intellectual category.

There should be no such unresolved terms, no such unfactorable equations, in a society whose production economy had had such dynamic and unencumbered origins. Both reason and instinct had defined the Negro as a slave, and the slave as

that condition of a natural person, in which, by the operation of law, the application of his physical and mental powers depends . . . upon the will of another . . . and in which he is incapable . . . of . . . holding property [or any other rights] . . . except as the agent or instrument of another. In slavery, . . . the state, in ignoring the personality of the slave, . . . commits the control of his conduct . . . to the master, together with the power of transferring his authority to another.[32]

The basic fact was, of course, that the slave himself was property. He and his fellow-bondsmen had long since become "chattels personal . . . to all intents, constructions and purposes whatsoever."[33]

[32]Quoted in Handlin, "Origins of Southern Labor System," *William and Mary Quarterly*, p. 200.
[33]See Footnote 30.

II

In the slave system of the United States—so finely circumscribed, so cleanly self-contained—virtually all avenues of recourse for the slave, all lines of communication to society at large, originated and ended with the master. The system was, we say, unique, *sui generis*. The closest parallel to it at that time was to be found in the Latin American colonies of Spain and Portugal. But the differences between the two systems are so much more striking than the similarities that we may, with profit, use them not as parallels but as contrasts. In the Spanish and Portuguese colonies, we are immediately impressed by the comparative lack of precision and logic governing the institution of slavery there: we find an exasperating dimness of line between the slave and free portions of society, a multiplicity of points of contact between the two, a confusing promiscuity of color, such as would never have been thinkable in our own country.[34] But before attempting to establish legal and customary classifications on the slave's condition in these places, in some manner corresponding to those we used for the United States, something should be said about the social and institutional setting in which slavery, in Spain and Portugal themselves, was both considered and practised.

Although the Spanish and Portuguese trade in Negro slaves would not become of primary importance until about the same period as did that of England, the civilization of the Iberian peninsula was one in which slavery had long been familiar: laws, customs and attitudes concerning it had been fixed for centuries. Indeed, the culture and traditions were rich in continuities with classical times—with the Romans themselves, who had known all about slavery. Slavery had been considered by Roman statesmen and publicists, and in succeeding centuries by the Latin church fathers. The church of Rome, in its Holy Scripture, preserved and perpetuated traditions in which the Jews of antiquity had not only held slaves but had also made endless rules for their treatment and governance. Many parts of the Justinian Code dealt with slavery. Moors, Jews and even Spaniards had been held in slavery, a fact implicitly recognized in the codification of Spanish law undertaken in the thirteenth century by King

[34]Here we should like to acknowledge our great debt to the work of Frank Tannenbaum, whose book, *Slave and Citizen* (New York: Alfred A. Knopf, 1947), has done so much to influence both the state of mind and the conceptual structure which we bring to this question. Two earlier works upon which we have also drawn heavily are Father Dieudonné Rinchon's *La Traite et l'Esclavage des Congolais par les Européens* (Wetteren, Belgium, 1929), and Sir Harry Johnston's *The Negro in the New World* (London: Methuen & Co., Ltd., 1910).

167

Alfonso the Wise.[35] Thus the situation of the first *Negro* slaves, who probably came to the Iberian peninsula about the middle of the fifteenth century, was at the very outset quite different from that of the first slaves to arrive in Virginia early in the seventeenth. For here they found already waiting a legal and social setting incredibly complex, thick with the experience of centuries, and peculiarly fitted to receive and absorb them.

The "logic" of this tradition, Biblical and classical in its origins, would have been incomprehensible to publicists of nineteenth-century America, both North and South—even though each drew upon it for their arguments. In it, there was a clear recognition and implicit sanction of slavery; nowhere was it denied (and thus the Southerner was right); at the same time, held as it were in suspension, was the universal presumption that such servitude, violating the divine and natural equality of man, was "against both reason and nature"[36]—and here, of course, the Northerner was right. But the fact that these two contrary principles could be supported in such illogical equilibrium within the same body of law and custom, made it possible for the system of slavery to exist, both in Spain and in the New World colonies, in a form which differed immensely from that of the United States. That this *was* indeed possible requires further explanation, for even after a wide-scale plantation order—based on Negro slave labor—had been established in Latin America, the ancient assumptions and legal sanctions governing slavery carried over into it with great tenacity and persistence.

Of all the national states of Western Europe, Spain, though dynastically united to a substantial degree late in the fifteenth century (and having even absorbed Portugal in the sixteenth),[37] remained, long into modern times, much the most "medieval." Its agriculture retained many of the subsistence features characteristic of manorial economy. Its social stability was guaranteed by that standing alliance of church and state upon which every feudal community rested: there, on a national scale, the Inquisition maintained at extravagant cost the dual secular-spiritual concept of society so characteristic of the Middle Ages and so repugnant to every modern notion. Moreover, having to deal with the Moslems on Spanish soil, the Spaniards had built crusades and the crusading temperament into their basic experience, where it actively remained long after the collapse of

[35]This was a codification (*Las Sieste Partidas del Rey Don Alfonso el Sabio*) which dealt extensively with slavery and "which in itself," according to Mr. Tannenbaum, "summarizes the Mediterranean legal *mores* of many centuries. . . ." *Slave and Citizen*, p. 45.

[36]"Slavery is a condition and institution which people made in antiquity through which men, who were naturally free, enslave themselves and submit to the dominion of others against reason and nature." *Las Sieste Partidas*, quoted in *ibid.*, p. 45, n.

[37]A union which lasted from 1580 to 1640.

168

the other crusaders' states in Asia Minor. This fact was directly responsible for the failure to develop a banking and commercial class comparable to those existing elsewhere, for the chronic persecutions of the Moors and Jews deprived the kingdom of its most energetic and experienced business-men. Banking services tended to be performed in very large part by foreigners, and Spanish wealth quickly found its way to places outside the realm. The monarchy's role in all such matters was conceived in a highly paternal and "illiberal" way, and laissez faire was just as unaccept-able in economic life as was free-thinking in religion. Such ventures as explorations and the founding of colonies required the crown's financial support to an extent unnecessary in England and Holland—which in turn made possible a degree of royal control over them not to be found in those countries. The royal houses of Spain and Portugal had been the first in the race for overseas colonies—the crown and grandees being overwhelm-ingly oriented to "glory" rather than "success"—but they in time found themselves outstripped by the English and Dutch, and saw the fruits of their glory dribble away to London, Antwerp and other successful centers of banking. Enterprise under the Spanish crown, in short, did not have the favorable setting enjoyed by the adventurers of England. Thus the establishment of great plantations in Cuba, Santo Domingo, Brazil and elsewhere in the sixteenth and seventeenth centuries did not mean un-mitigated capitalism, as would be the case under the free skies of Virginia, Maryland and the Carolinas. Other institutional concerns were present besides those involved with production, and we may say that it was pre-cisely here that the great difference lay.

No such dramatic transvaluation of social norms as occurred in seven-teenth-century England, to accommodate the new standards of the bour-geoisie, would ever take place in Spain. There, the concept of private property—peculiarly appropriate to the demands of an entrepreneurial class—would not develop with nearly the elaborateness that characterized it elsewhere. In at least one respect this fact had very interesting conse-quences. In the master-slave relationship, the balance between property rights and human rights stood in a vastly different ratio—much to the ad-vantage of human rights—from that seen in the American South, all the cruelty and bigotry of this quasi-medieval society to the contrary not-withstanding.

In the colonies of Latin America we are thus able to think of the church, the civil authority and the property concerns of the planter-adventurer as constituting distinct and not always harmonious interests in society. The introduction of slaves in the colonies brought much discomfort to the royal conscience; when the trade in Negroes became of consequence

169

171

the monarchs gave it their growing concern and it never occurred to them not to retain over it a heavy measure of royal control. Charles V, persuaded by Las Casas in 1517 to sanction Negro slavery, turned against the principle late in his reign and ordered the freeing of all African slaves in Spanish America.[38] In 1570 King Sebastian of Portugal issued an order to the colonists of Brazil which forbade the taking of slaves except by "licit means," specifying that in any case they must be registered within two months or all authority over them be forfeited.[39] A century later it had become clear to the monarchs of Spain that both the demands of their colonists for labor and the revenue needs of the royal treasury required that the trade in African Negroes be accorded full legitimacy. But the king in 1679 still had to be assured "whether meetings of theologians and jurists have been held to determine whether it is licit to buy them as slaves and make asientos for them and whether there are any authors who have written on this particular question. . . ."[40] Again we find the king of Spain, in a *Real Cedula* of 1693, commanding the Captain-General of Cuba to call upon all masters of slaves, and to "say to them in my name that they must not, for whatever motive, rigorously tighten the wage they receive from their slaves, for having been tried in other places, it has proved inconvenient harming the souls of these people. . . ." Since slavery was "a sufficient sorrow without at the same time suffering the distempered rigor of their master," any excesses were to be punished by applying "the necessary remedy."[41] The monarchy, met with the full force of this new enterprise—new at least with respect to its proportions—made terms. But the energy with which it imposed its own terms was drawn both from the ancient sanctions regarding servitude and from the traditional force of the crown's institutional prerogatives.

The other item in this equation was the presence of a powerful church with needs of its own. A considerable measure of its power as an institution naturally depended upon its position of leadership in matters touching the morals of society. The maintenance of that leadership required the church as a matter of course to insist on a dominant role in the formulation of all policy which might bear on the morality of the slave system and have consequences for the Faith. The terms it made with slavery

[38]Johnston, *Negro in the New World*, p. 39. It has to be added that one year after Charles' retirement to the monastery of Saint-Just in 1558, slavery and the slave trade was resumed.

[39]Rinchon, *La Traite et l'Esclavage*, pp. 140-41. This order applied to native Indians.

[40]"Resumé of the Origin of the Introduction of Slaves into Spanish America" (1685), quoted in Elizabeth Donnan, *Documents Illustrative of the History of the Slave Trade to America* (Washington: Carnegie Institution, 1930 ff.), I, 346.

[41]Quoted in Tannenbaum, *Slave and Citizen*, p. 89.

170

paralleled those made by the crown, and exhibited the same ambiguities. In effect, the church with one hand condemned slavery, and with the other came to an understanding with it as a labor system. Its doctrine asserted in general that the practice of slavery and the slave trade was fraught with perils for those of the faithful who engaged in it, and that they stood, at innumerable points, in danger of mortal sin. The immoralities connected with the trade compelled again and again the attention of church writers, and it was in this sense that the Franciscan Father Thomas Mercado had denounced it in 1587 as fostering "two thousand false-hoods, a thousand robberies, and a thousand deceptions."[42] More temperately summarizing the most learned opinion of his age, Germain Fromageau, a doctor of the Sorbonne, declared in 1698 that "one can neither, in surety of conscience, buy nor sell Negroes, because in such commerce there is injustice."[43] In any case, as an eighteenth-century prelate, Cardinal Gerdil, categorically stated, "Slavery is not to be understood as conferring on one man the same power over another that men have over cattle. . . . For slavery does not abolish the natural equality of man. . . ."[44]

At the same time the church, in its character as an institution, functioning in the society of men, could not afford to proscribe slavery as unconditionally immoral, if for no other reason than that the majority of Christendom's overseas dominions would thus have been stained in depravity—a position which, for almost any procedural purposes, would have been absurdly untenable. Its casuists, therefore, readily found sanctions in tradition whereby slavery might exist under the church's official favor. Thus the Council of the Indies, after meetings with theologians, jurists and prelates of the church, assured the king of Spain

that there cannot be any doubt as to the necessity of those slaves for the support of the kingdom of the Indies . . .; and [that] with regard to the point of conscience, [the trade may continue] because of the reasons expressed, the authorities cited, and its longlived and general custom in the kingdoms of Castile, America, and Portugal, without any objection on the part of his Holiness or ecclesiastical state, but rather with the tolerance of all of them.[45]

The Jesuits would labor excessively in places such as Brazil to mitigate the evils of slavery; the papacy itself would denounce it in various ways in

[42]Tannenbaum, *Slave and Citizen*, p. 62.
[43]From *La Dictionnaire des Cas de Conscience*, quoted in Rinchon, *La Traite et l'Esclavage*, p. 148.
[44]James J. Fox, "Ethical Aspect of Slavery," in Charles G. Hebermann and others (eds.), *The Catholic Encyclopedia* (New York: Encyclopedia Press, Inc., 1913), XIV, 40.
[45]"Minutes of the Council of the Indies" (1685), quoted in Donnan, *Documents*, I, 351.

171

1462, 1537, 1639, 1741, 1815 and 1839; at the same time the church "could no more have proclaimed the abolition of slavery," as Father Rinchon remarks, "than it could have imposed the eight-hour day or the rate of family incomes."[46]

Yet in the very act of certifying the practice of slavery, in admitting its economic necessity, and even in holding slaves of its own, the church had, as it were, bargained with the system so that its own institutional needs and its perogatives in matters of morality might still be maintained at the visible maximum and protected against infringement. The effects of this determination are overwhelmingly evident in the actual workings of slavery in Latin America. They are evident, indeed, at nearly every point in the traffic itself, for the potent hand of the church fell upon the sequence of events long before it terminated in America. It had missionaries on the soil of Africa, proselytizing among the natives and operating great establishments there. It was highly sensitive to the possibility that the Faith, in the course of the trade, might be corrupted. The Inquisition in 1685, faced with an impending transaction which would turn over a portion of the trade to the Dutch, sternly urged the king that,

in case any contract is made with the Dutch, you will please to ordain that all necessary orders be provided and issued for the utmost care of the conservation and purity of our Holy Catholic Faith, because one can very justly fear that if the negroes come by way of the Dutch, they may be greatly imbued with doctrines and errors . . . and . . . this council should advise the inquisitors to exercise special vigilance.[47]

The contract was eventually made, but the Dutchman who received it was forced to take ten Capuchin monks to his African factories for the religious instruction of the Negroes, to support them and to allow them to preach in public.[48] The Inquisition had a tribunal in the Indies which would punish any "heretic" (meaning Dutch or Flemish) who tried to introduce his creed there during the course of business.[49] Every slave bound for Brazil was to receive baptism and religious instruction before being put on board,[50] and upon reaching port every ship was boarded by a friar who examined the conscience, faith and religion of the new arrivals. The friar was there

[46]*La Traite et l'Esclavage*, p. 158.

[47]"Report of the Council of the Inquisition to the King" (1685), quoted in Donnan, *Documents*, I, 339.

[48]"Minutes of the Council of the Indies" (1685), *ibid.*, pp. 348-49.

[49]*Ibid.*, p. 348. No one, according to the report, had hitherto been rash enough to attempt this.

[50]"[They] are catechised and receive baptism, a rite which has been found to console their minds under their unhappy circumstances." Carl Berns Wadström, *An Essay on Colonisation . . .* (London, 1794), p. 125.

"to investigate the individual's orthodoxy just as today the immigrant's health and race are investigated."[51]

It would be misleading—and indeed, quite subversive to our argument—to imply that slavery in the colonies drew its total character from the powerful influence of the church. But we may assert that the church, functioning in its capacity as guardian of morals, *was* responsible for whatever human rights were conserved for the slave within the grim system. What it came to was that three formidable interests—the crown, the planter and the church—were deeply concerned with the system, that these concerns were in certain ways competing, and that the product of this balance of power left its profound impress on the actual legal and customary sanctions governing the status and treatment of slaves. These sanctions were by no means what they would have been had it been left to the planting class alone to develop them systematically with reference only to the requirements of a labor system. And now as we take note of them, let us have recourse to the same rough categories used with respect to the American South: term of servitude, marriage and the family, police and discipline and property and other civil rights.

III

Neither in Brazil nor in Spanish America did slavery carry with it such precise and irrevocable categories of perpetual servitude, "durante vita" and "for all generations," as in the United States. The presumption in these countries, should the status of a colored person be in doubt, was that he was free rather than a slave.[52] There were in fact innumerable ways whereby a slave's servitude could be brought to an end. The chief of these was the very considerable fact that he might buy his own freedom. The Negro in Cuba or Mexico had the right to have his price declared and could, if he wished, purchase himself in installment. Slaves escaping to Cuba to embrace Catholicism were protected by a special royal order of 1733 which was twice reissued. A slave unduly punished might be set at liberty by the magistrate. In Brazil the slave who was the parent of ten children might legally demand his or her freedom.[53] The medieval Spanish code had made a slave's service terminable under any number of contingencies—if he denounced cases of treason, murder, counterfeiting or the

[51]Gilberto Freyre, *The Masters and the Slaves* (New York: Alfred A. Knopf, 1946), p. 41.

[52]"In the Cuban market freedom was the only commodity which could be bought untaxed; every negro against whom no one had proved a claim of servitude was deemed free. . . ." William Law Mathieson, *British Slavery and its Abolition*, quoted in Tannenbaum, *Slave and Citizen*, p. 53n.

[53]Johnston, *Negro in the New World*, p. 89.

173

rape of a virgin, or if he performed various other kinds of meritorious acts
—and although by no means all such practices found their way into the
seventeenth and eighteenth century legal arrangements of Latin America,
much of their spirit was perpetuated in the values, customs and social
expectations of that later period. It is important to appreciate the high
social approval connected with the freeing of slaves. A great variety of
happy family events—the birth of a son, the marriage of a daughter, anni-
versaries, national holidays—provided the occasion, and their ceremonial
was frequently marked by the manumission of one or more virtuous servitors.
It was considered a pious act to accept the responsibility of becoming god-
father to a slave child, implying the moral obligation to arrange eventually
for its freedom. Indeed, such freedom, in Cuba and Brazil, might be purchased for a nominal sum at the baptismal front.[54] All such manumissions
had the strong approval of both church and state, and were registered gratis
by the government.[55]

In extending its moral authority over men of every condition, the church
naturally insisted on bringing slave unions under the holy sacraments.
Slaves were married in church and the banns published; marriage was a
sacred rite and its sanctity protected in law. In the otherwise circumspect
United States, the only category which the law could apply to conjugal
relations between slaves—or to unions between master and slave—was
concubinage. But concubinage, in Latin America, was condemned as licentious, adulterous and immoral; safeguards against promiscuity were provided in the law,[56] and in Brazil the Jesuits labored mightily to regularize
the libertinage of the master class by the sacrament of Christian marriage.[57]
Moreover, slaves owned by different masters were not to be hindered from
marrying, nor could they be kept separated after marriage. If the estates
were distant, the wife was to go with her husband, and a fair price was
to be fixed by impartial persons for her sale to the husband's master.[58] A
slave might, without legal interference, marry a free person. The children
of such a marriage, if the mother were free, were themselves free, inasmuch
as children followed the condition of their mother.[59]

[54]"What we have said in this paragraph is virtually a paraphrase of the information which Mr. Tannenbaum has collected and so skillfully summarized on pp. 50,
53-54, 57-58 of *Slave and Citizen.*
[55]Johnston, *Negro in the New World*, p. 42.
[56]"The master of slaves must not allow the unlawful intercourse of the two sexes,
but must encourage matrimony." Spanish slave code of 1789, quoted in *ibid.*, p. 44.
Although slaves were allowed "to divert themselves innocently" on holy days, the
males were to be kept apart from the females. *Ibid.*, p. 44.
[57]Freyre, *The Masters and the Slaves*, p. 85.
[58]Johnston, *Negro in the New World*, pp. 44-45.
[59]Tannenbaum, *Slave and Citizen*, p. 56.

174

The master's disciplinary authority never had the completeness which it had in the United States, and nowhere did he enjoy powers of life and death over the slave's body. Under the Spanish code of 1789 slaves might be punished, for failure to perform their duties, with prison, chains or lashes, "which last must not exceed the number of twenty-five, and those must be given them in such manner as not to cause any contusion or effusion of blood: which punishments cannot be imposed on slaves but by their masters or the stewards."[60] For actual crimes a slave was to be tried in an ordinary court of justice like any free person,[61] and conversely, the murder of a slave was to be prosecuted just as that of a free man would be.[62] Excessive punishments of slaves—causing "contusion, effusion of blood, or mutilation of members"—by plantation stewards were themselves punishable. Although gross violations of the law occurred, the law here was anything but the dead letter it proved to be in our own Southern states. In the important administrative centers both of Brazil and the Spanish colonies there was an official Protector of slaves, known variously as the syndic, procurador, or Attorney-General, under whose jurisdiction came all matters relating to the treatment of slaves. His functions were nurtured by a well-articulated system of communications. The priests who made the regular rounds of the estates giving Christian instruction were required to obtain and render to him information from the slaves regarding their treatment, and investigation and the necessary steps would be taken accordingly. These priests were answerable to no one else for their activities. In addition, the magistrates were to appoint "persons of good character" to visit the estates thrice yearly and conduct similar inquiries on similar matters. A further ingenious provision in the Spanish code caused all fines levied, for mistreatment and other excesses against slaves, to be divided up three ways: one-third went to the judge, one-third to the informer and one-third to the "Fines Chest." Finally, the justices and Attorney-General themselves were made accountable to the crown for failure to carry out these ordinances. An implicit royal threat underlay all this: should the fines not have the desired effect and should the ordinances continue to be broken, "I," His Majesty promised, "will take my measures accordingly."[63]

As was implied in his right to purchase his own freedom, the slave in the Spanish and Portuguese colonies had the right to acquire and hold property. This meant something specific; in Brazil a master was obliged

---

[60] Johnston, *Negro in the New World*, p. 45.

[61] The sentence, however, was apparently to be executed by the master. *Ibid.*, p. 45.

[62] *Ibid.*, pp. 45-46. The code does not make it clear whether the penalty would be the same against the slave's master as against another person. But in any case the murderer, master or other, was liable to prosecution.

[63] *Ibid.*, pp. 45-46.

175

by law to give liberty to his slaves on all Sundays and holidays—which totaled eighty-five in the year—during which a slave might work for himself and accumulate money for his purchase price,[64] and the Spanish code of 1789 provided that slaves must be allowed two hours each day in which to be employed in "occupations for their own advantage."[65] In many places slaves were encouraged to hire themselves out regularly (there were skilled artisans among them as well as ordinary laborers), an arrangement which was to the advantage both of the master and the slave himself, since the latter was allowed to keep a percentage of the wage. Slaves even in rural areas might sell the produce of their gardens and retain the proceeds.[66] For all practical purposes slavery here had become, according to Mr. Tannenbaum, a contractual arrangement: it could be wiped out by a fixed purchase price and left no taint. "There may have been no written contract between the two parties, but the state behaved, in effect, as if such a contract did exist, and used its powers to enforce it."[67] It was a contract in which the master owned a man's labor but not the man.

As for the privileges of religion, it was here not a question of the planting class "permitting" the slave, under rigidly specified conditions, to take part in divine worship. It was rather a matter of the church's insisting—under its own conditions—that masters bring their slaves to church and teach them religion. Such a man as the Mississippi planter who directed that the gospel preached to his slaves should be "in its original purity and simplicity" would have courted the full wrath of the Latin church. Here the power of the Faith was such that master and slave stood equally humbled before it. The master had an obligation, not self-assumed but imposed by church and state, to concern himself with the spiritual life of his slaves— to protect their morals and see that they led a good life. "Every one who has slaves is obliged to instruct them in the principles of the Roman Catholic religion and in the necessary truths in order that the slaves may be baptized within the (first) year of their residence in the Spanish dominions." Such was the very first item taken up in the Spanish slave code.[68]

There were certain assumptions implied herein which made it impossible that the slave in this culture should ever quite be considered as mere property, either in law or in society's customary habits of mind. These assumptions, perpetuated and fostered by the church, made all the difference as to how he would be treated by society and its institutions, not only

[64] It was not even uncommon for ex-slaves who had thus acquired their freedom to become actual slaveholders on their own account. *Ibid.*, p. 90.
[65] *Ibid.*, p. 44.
[66] Tannenbaum, *Slave and Citizen*, pp. 58-61.
[67] *Ibid.*, p. 55.
[68] Johnston, *Negro in the New World*, p. 43.

176

while a slave but also if and when he should cease to be one. They were, in effect, that he was a man, that he had a soul as precious as any other man's, that he had a moral nature, that he was not only as susceptible to sin but also as eligible for grace as his master—that master and slave, in short, were brothers in Christ.

The Spaniards and Portuguese had the widespread reputation by the eighteenth century—whatever may have been the reasons—for being among all nations the best masters of slaves.[69] The standards for such a judgment cannot, of course, be made too simple. Were slaves "physically maltreated" in those countries? They could, conceivably, have been treated worse than in our own nineteenth-century South, without altering the comparison— for even in cruelty, the relationship was that of man and man.[70] Was there "race prejudice"? No one could be more arrogantly proud of his racial purity than the Spaniard of Castile, and theoretically there were rigid caste

[69]"The Spaniards, Portuguese and Danes are undoubtedly the best masters of slaves," wrote Carl Berns Wadström in 1794. The English and Dutch were in his opinion the worst. *Essay on Colonization*, p. 151, n. The Portuguese and Brazillians "rival the Spaniards for first place in the list of humane slave-holding nations," writes Sir Harry Johnston. "Slavery under the flag of Portugal (or Brazil) or of Spain was not a condition without hope, a life in hell, as it was for the most part in the British West Indies and, above all, Dutch Guiana and the Southern United States." *Negro in the New World*, p. 89. "The Spaniards themselves maltreated their slaves less than did the planters of the Antilles or of North America at a later period." P. Chemin-Dupontès, *Les Petites Antilles* (Paris, 1909), quoted in *ibid.*, p. 42, n. Moreau de Saint-Méry, writing of the slaves of Spanish Santo Domingo, remarks, "To their masters they are more like companions than slaves." *Topographical and Political Description of the Spanish Part of Saint-Domingo* (Philadelphia, 1796), quoted in *ibid.*, p. 42, n. The French planters of Haiti and the Americans of Georgia both complained that the Spanish code of 1789 would (and did) induce their slaves to escape to the Spanish dominions. *Ibid.*, p. 46.

[70]Most writers and students do seem to think that the system was "milder" in the Spanish colonies and in Brazil—but nobody has ever claimed that it was a life of ease and comfort. An interesting summary of observers' opinions on this and other points is Margaret V. Nelson, "The Negro in Brazil as Seen Through the Chronicles of Travellers, 1800-1868," *Journal of Negro History*, XXX (April, 1945), 203-18. See also James Ferguson King, "Negro History in Continental Spanish America," *Jour. of Negro H.*, XXIX (Jan., 1944), 7-23. "The fact is," as Donald Pierson remarks, "that slavery in Brazil [and, one might add, in Spanish America as well] was both mild *and* severe." The severe side of it, indeed, is discussed with very disagreeable particulars by Arthur Ramos in his *Negro in Brazil* (Washington: Associated Publishers, Inc., 1939), pp. 20-22. It could further be pointed out that comparisons, when made, were made most frequently with the British colonies of the eighteenth century, especially the British West Indies. In the United States, on the other hand, by (say) 1850, slavery in a "physical" sense was in general, probably, quite mild. However, even if it had been milder here than anywhere else in the Western hemisphere, it would still be missing the point to make the comparison in terms of physical comfort. In one case we would be dealing with the cruelty of man to man—and in the other, with the care, maintenance and indulgence of men toward creatures who were legally and morally *not* men—not in the sense that Christendom had traditionally defined man's nature. It is, in short, the *primary* relationship that matters. Masters and slaves in Brazil, according to João Ribeiro, "were united into families, if not by law, at least by religion." Quoted in Donald Pierson, *Negroes in Brazil* (Chicago: University of Chicago Press, 1942), p. 81.

177

179

lines—but the finest creole families, the clergy, the army, the professions, were hopelessly "defiled" by Negro blood:[71] the taboos were that vague in practice. Was there squalor, filth, widespread depression of the masses? Much more so than with us—but there it was the class system and "economic underdevelopment," rather than the color barrier, that made the difference. In these countries the concept of "beyond the pale" applied primarily to beings outside the Christian fold, rather than to those beyond the color line.[72]

We are not, then, dealing with a society steeped, like our own, in traditions of political and economic democracy. We are concerned only with a special and peculiar kind of fluidity—that of their slave system—but upon this alone hinged a world of difference. It was a fluidity that permitted a transition from slavery to freedom that was smooth, organic and continuing. Manumitting slaves, carrying as it did such high social approval, was done often, and the spectacle of large numbers of freedmen was familiar to the social scene. Such opportunities as were open to any member of the depressed classes who had talent and diligence were open as well to the ex-slave and his descendants. Thus color itself was no grave disability against taking one's place in free society; indeed, Anglo-Saxon travelers in nineteenth-century Brazil were amazed at the thoroughgoing mixture of races there. "I have passed black ladies in silks and jewelry," wrote Thomas Ewbank in the 1850's, "with male slaves in livery behind them. . . . Several have white husbands. The first doctor of the city is a colored man; so is the President of the Province."[73] Free Negroes had the same rights before the law as whites, and it was possible for the most energetic of their numbers

[71] Even the legendary corruption of the Spanish upper classes was apparently bi-racial in the New World. Beye Cisneros of Mexico City, during the course of the debates on the Spanish constitution of 1811, declared, "I have known mulattoes who have become counts, marquises, *oidores*, canons, colonels, and knights of the military orders through intrigue, bribery, perjury, and falsification of public books and registers; and I have observed that those who have reached these positions and distinctions by reprehensible means, have been granted the corresponding honors without repugnance, despite their mixed blood. . . ." James F. King, "The Colored Castes and American Representation in the Cortes of Cádiz," *Hispanic American Historical Review*, XXXIII (Feb., 1953), 56. The looseness of practice which permitted such frequent "passings over" was actually commended by the acting Captain-General of Venezuela in a despatch to the Secretary of State for the Indies in 1815; "The State greatly gains," he wrote, "for the increase of the upper class, even though it be artificial, is to its interest." J. F. King, "A Royalist View of the Colored Castes in the Venezuelan War of Independence," *Hisp. Am. Hist. R.*, XXXIII (Nov., 1953), 528. See also Richard M. Morse, "The Negro in São Paulo, Brazil," *Jour. of Negro H.*, XXXVIII (July, 1953), 290-306.

[72] "The thing that barred an immigrant in those days was heterodoxy: the blot of heresy upon the soul and not any racial brand upon the body." Freyre, *Masters and the Slaves*, pp. 40-41.

[73] *Life in Brazil, or the Land of the Cocoa and the Palm* (London, 1856), quoted in Tannenbaum, *Slave and Citizen*, p. 4.

178

to take immediate part in public and professional life. Among the Negroes and mulattoes of Brazil and the Spanish colonies—aside from the swarming numbers of skilled craftsmen—were soldiers, officers, musicians, poets, priests and judges. "I am accustomed," said a delegate to the Cortes of Cádiz in 1811, "to seeing many engaged in all manner of careers."[74]

All such rights and opportunities existed *before* the abolition of slavery—and thus we may note it as no paradox that emancipation, when it finally did take place, was brought about in all these Latin American countries "without violence, without bloodshed, and without civil war."[75]

IV

In contrasting the two slave systems—those of the United States and of the Spanish and Portuguese colonies—we have drawn upon material which is historically familiar. Yet we have wished to arrange it in such a way that its theoretical usefulness might be most fully exploited. Several lines of inquiry have been held in mind, and one of them is embodied in the discussion just concluded. This has involved the conservative role of institutions in any social structure. We have observed the principle in a setting where two or more powerful interests were present to limit each other; we have tested it negatively in a setting where a single interest was free to develop without such limits. The latter case was productive of consequences which could hardly be called, in the classical sense of the term, "conservative."[76]

[74]J. F. King, "The Colored Castes and American Representation in the Cortes of Cádiz," *Hisp. Am. Hist. R.*, XXXIII (Feb., 1953), 59. See also Irene Diggs, "Color in Colonial Spanish America," *Jour. of Negro H.*, XXXVIII (Oct., 1953), 403-26.

[75]Tannebaum, *Slave and Citizen*, p. 106.

[76]The reader should be told that the argument of the present essay has been so arranged as to establish the framework for two other, quite distinct arguments. One has to do with the ways in which a social structure lays down, for the individuals who compose it, institutional conditions for the actual formation of character and personality. Here the key terms are "closed" systems and "open" systems: the American South (for purposes of contrast) representing the former, and Brazil and Spanish America the latter. The other argument also involves institutions—the question of what difference the presence or absence of institutions may have made in the way slavery, *as an intellectual subject*, was handled in this country. We are elaborating these ideas in two other essays: "Slavery and Personality," and "Slavery and the Intellectual," shortly to be published elsewhere.

179

BETWEEN SLAVERY AND FREEDOM *

I

I have taken my title from the *Onomastikon* or *Word-Book* of an Alexandrian Greek of the second century of our era named Julius Pollux. At the end of a longish section (3.73-83) listing, and sometimes exemplifying, the Greek words which meant "slave" or "enslave", in certain contexts at least, Pollux noted that there were also men like the helots in Sparta or the *penestae* in Thessaly who stood "between the free men and the slaves". It is no use pretending that this work is very penetrating or systematic, at least in the abridged form in which it has come down to us, but the foundation was laid in a much earlier work by a very learned scholar, Aristophanes of Byzantium, who flourished in the first half of the third century B.C. The interest in the brief passage I have cited is that it suggests in so pointed a way that social status could be viewed as a continuum or spectrum; that there were statuses which could only be defined, even if very crudely, as "between slavery and freedom". Customarily Greek and Roman writers were not concerned with such nuances. To be sure, the Romans had a special word for a freedman, *libertus,* as distinguished from *liber,* a free man. When it came to political status, furthermore, distinctions of all kinds were made, necessarily so. But for social status (which I trust I may be permitted, at this stage, to distinguish from political status), and often for purposes of private law, they were satisfied with the simple antinomy, slave or free, even though they could hardly have been unaware of certain gradations.

There is a Greek myth which neatly exemplifies the lexical point, a myth certainly much older than its first surviving literary reference in the *Aga-*

* This is the text, slightly modified, of a lecture I gave to the Royal Anthropological Institute in London on May 30, 1963. I have kept annotation to a bare minimum. For Graeco-Roman slavery, see the bibliographical essay in the volume of articles I edited, *Slavery in Classical Antiquity* (Cambridge, Eng., 1960). My colleague, Mr. E. R. Leach of King's College, kindly read and criticized the manuscript. I have also benefited from the opportunity to discuss the *servi Caesaris* with Mr. P. R. C. Weaver of the University of Western Australia, and problems of American slavery with Professor A. A. Sio of Colgate University.

183

memnon of Aeschylus produced at Athens in 458 B.C. Hercules was afflicted with a disease which persisted until he went to Delphi to consult Apollo about it. There the oracle informed him that his ailment was a punishment for his having killed Iphitus by treachery, and that he could be cured only by having himself sold into slavery for a limited number of years and handing over the purchase price to his victim's kinsmen. Accordingly he was sold to Omphale, queen of the Lydians (but originally a purely Greek figure), and he worked off his guilt in her service. The texts — which are fairly numerous and scattered over a period of many centuries — disagree on several points: for example, whether Hercules was sold to Omphale by the god Hermes or by friends who accompanied him to Asia for the purpose; whether his term of servitude was one year or three, and so on.[1]

One has no right to expect neatness in a myth, of course, nor, for that matter, in the legal institutions of the archaic society in which this particular myth arose. The ancient texts all speak of Hercules being "sold", and to describe his status while in Omphale's service they employ either *doulos*, the most common Greek word for "chattel slave", or *latris*, a curious word that meant "hired man" and "servant" as well as "slave". The word *latris* upsets modern lexicographers and legal historians, but the historical situation behind the lexical "confusion" is surely that in earlier Greece, as in other societies, "service" and "servitude" did in fact merge into each other. The Biblical code was explicit (*Deuteronomy* 15.12-17): "If thy brother . . . be sold unto thee and serve thee six years; then in the seventh year thou shalt let him go free from thee . . . And it shall be, if he say unto thee, I will not go out from thee; because he loveth thee and thy house, because he is well with thee; then thou shalt take an awl, and thrust it into his ear unto the door, and he shall be thy servant for ever."

Cynical remarks are tempting. Quite apart from the very real possibility that the six-year limitation was, as one distinguished authority has phrased it, "a social programme rather than actually functioning law",[2] there is an odd ring about "if he say unto thee, I will not go out from thee; because he loveth thee and thy house". One suspects that the transition from a more limited bondage to outright slavery was neither so gentle nor so voluntary; that, unlike Hercules, the victims in real life, once caught up in bondage, had little hope of release; that, as in peonage, their masters could find devices enough by which to hold them in perpetuity. The sixth-century Athenian statesman Solon, referring to debt-bondsmen, used these words: "I set free those here [in Athens] who were in unworthy enslavement,

---

[1] The most important sources are Sophocles, *Trach.* 68-72. 248-54. 274-76 (with scholia); Apollodorus, *Bibl.* 2.6.2-3; Diodorus 4.31.5-8.

[2] D. Daube, *Studies in Biblical Law* (Cambridge, Eng., 1947), p. 45; cf. the important recent article of E. E. Urbach, "The Laws regarding Slavery . . . of the Period of the Second Temple, the Mishnah and Talmud". *Annual of Jewish Studies*, 1 (London. 1963). pp. 1-54.

trembling at the whim of their masters."[3] And the Greek words he employed were precisely those which became the classical terminology of chattel slavery: *douleia* - slavery; *despotes* - master; *eleutheros* - a free man. Modern scholars, too, regularly speak of enslavement for debt. Why not? Why play with words? Why draw elaborate, abstract distinctions?

The men Solon liberated belonged to a restricted though numerous class: they were Athenians who had fallen into bondage to other Athenians in Athens. His programme did not extend to non-Athenians, outsiders, who were slaves in Athens, just as the Biblical six-year limitation was restricted to "thy brother", a fellow-Hebrew, and did not extend to the Gentile. Nor was this merely a sentimental distinction, empty rhetoric holding up vain hopes to the in-group, pretending that they were different from the outsiders when in fact they shared the latter's fate. The whole story of Solon (like the closely analogous struggles in early Roman history) proves that the distinction was meaningful, though it may have been in abeyance in any individual case or in any given span of time. For Solon was able to abolish debt-bondage — indeed, he had been brought to power for that express purpose — following a political struggle that bordered on civil war. Athenian bondsmen had remained Athenians; now they re-asserted their rights as Athenians, and they forced an end to the institution — servitude for debt — which had deprived them *de facto* of all or most of those rights. They were not opposed to slavery as such, only to the subjection of Athenians by other Athenians. Hence, whatever the superficial similarity, this was not a slave revolt; nor did ancient commentators ever make such a connection, despite their resort to slave terminology.

I am not now concerned with the history of debt-bondage and its abolition or of clientage in Athens or Rome, nor for the moment with giving precise content to the notion of "rights". I am merely trying, as a preliminary, to establish the need to distinguish among kinds of servitude, even though contemporaries were themselves not concerned to do so, at least not in their vocabulary. The matter of revolts is worth pursuing a little further in this connection. The debt-revolt syndrome was one of the most significant factors in the early history of both Greece and Rome, and it even survived into classical history. Helot revolts were equally important and very persistent in the history of Sparta. Chattel slaves, on the other hand, showed no such tendency at any time in Greek history and only for a brief period, between about 135 and 70 B.C., were there massive slave revolts in Roman history.[4] Towards the end of antiquity, finally, there was more or less continual revolt

[3]   Quoted in Aristotle, *Const. of Athens* 12.4.
[4]   The basic, though brief, study is now Joseph Vogt, *Struktur der antiken Sklaven-kriege* (Akad. d. Wiss. u. d. Lit., Mainz, *Abhandlungen*, 1957, no. 1). See also Peter Green, "The First Sicilian Slave War", *Past & Present*, 20 (1961), pp. 10–29, with discussion in no. 22 (1962), pp. 87–92; Claude Mossé, "Le rôle des esclaves dans les troubles politiques du monde grec...", *Cahiers d'histoire*, 6 (Lyon, 1961), pp. 353–60.

in Gaul and Spain by depressed and semi-servile peasants and slaves acting in concert.[5]

To explain the differences in the revolt pattern, and particularly in the propensity to revolt, by the differences in treatment, by the relative harshness or mildness of the masters, will not do. The one distinction which stands out most clearly is this, that the chattels, who were both the most rightless of all the servile types and the most complete outsiders in every sense, were precisely those who showed the weakest tendency to cohesive action, the weakest drive to secure freedom. Under certain conditions individual slaves were permitted considerable latitude and eventual emancipation was often held out as an incentive to them. That is another matter, however. Slaves as slaves showed no interest in slavery as an institution. Even when they did revolt, their objective was either to return to their native lands or to reverse the situation where they were, to become masters themselves and to reduce to slavery their previous masters or anyone else who came to hand. Insofar as they thought about freedom, in other words, they accepted the prevailing notion completely: freedom for them, as individuals, included the right to possess other individuals as slaves. Debt-bondsmen and helots, in contrast, fought — when they fought — not only to transfer themselves, as individuals, from one status to the other, but to abolish that particular type of servitude altogether (though not, significantly, to abolish all forms, and particularly not chattel slavery).

II

To a Greek in the age of Pericles or a Roman in Cicero's day, "freedom" had become a definable concept, and the antinomy, slave-free, a sharp, meaningful distinction. We are their heirs, and also their victims. Sometimes the results are amusing, as in the first efforts in the Far East in the nineteenth century to cope with the word "freedom" for which they had no synonym and which till then was "scarcely possible" in, say, Chinese.[6] And sometimes the results are very unfunny, as when western colonial administrators and well-meaning international organizations decree the immediate abolition of such practices as the payment of bride-wealth or the "adoption" of debtors on the ground that they are devices for enslavement.[7] My subject, however, is not current social or political policy but history; the simple slave-free antinomy, I propose to argue, has been equally harmful as a tool of analysis when applied to some of the most interesting

[5] See E. A. Thompson, "Peasant Revolts in Late Roman Gaul and Spain", *Past & Present*, 2 (1952), pp. 11–23.
[6] E. G. Pulleyblank, "The Origins and Nature of Chattel Slavery in China", *J. Econ. Soc. Hist. Orient*, 1 (1958), pp. 185-220, at pp. 204–205.
[7] See, e.g., H. N. C. Stevenson, *The Economics of the Central Chin Tribes* (Bombay, 1943), pp. 175–80.

and seminal periods of our history. "Freedom" is no less complex a concept than "servitude" or "bondage"; it is a concept which had no meaning and no existence for most of human history; it had to be invented finally, and that invention was possible only under very special conditions. Even after it had been invented, furthermore, there remained large numbers of men who could not be socially located as either slave or free, who were "between slavery and freedom", in the loose language of Aristophanes of Byzantium and Julius Pollux.

Let us look at one particular case which came before the royal court of Babylonia in the middle of the sixth century B.C., in the so-called neo-Babylonian or Chaldaean period.[8] A man borrowed a sum of money from a woman who was head of a religious order, and gave her his son as a debt-bondsman. After four years the woman died and both the debt and the debt-bondsman were transferred to her successor. The debtor also died and his son, now his heir, found himself in the position of being simultaneously the debtor and the debt-bondsman (an oddity in the ancient Near East, I may add parenthetically, where the transfer of wives and children for debt was common, but the transfer of the debtor himself was rare, unlike the Graeco-Roman practice). After ten years the bondsman paid over a quantity of barley from his own resources and went to court. The judges made a calculation, according to the conventional ratios, translating each day's service into barley and then translating the barley (both the real barley and the fictitious barley) into money; this arithmetic produced a sum which was equal to the original loan plus 20% interest per annum for ten years; the court ruled, accordingly, that the debt was now paid up and the bondsman was liberated.

During his ten years of service was the bondsman who was working off his father's debt (which became his debt) a free man or a slave? Were the Israelites in Egypt slaves because they were called upon, as were most native Egyptians, to perform compulsory labor for the Pharaoh? The answer seems clearly to be "Neither"; or better still, "Yes and no". In analogous situations the Greeks and Romans defined such service obligations as "slave-like", and that catches the correct nuance. There were in Babylonia and Egypt chattel slaves in the strict property sense, whose services were not calculated at so much barley or so much anything per day, who could not inherit, own property or take a matter to court. But there was no word in the languages of these regions to encompass all the others, those who were not chattel slaves. To call them all "free" makes no sense because it wipes out the significant variations in status, including the presence of elements of unfreedom, among the bulk of the population.

[8] V. Scheil, "La libération juridique d'un fils donné en gage ... en 558 av. J.-C.", *Rev. d'Assyriologie*, 12 (1915), pp. 1–13; cf. H. Petschow, *Neubabylonisches Pfandrecht* (*Abh.* Akad. Leipzig, Phil.-hist. Kl., 48, no. 1, 1956), pp. 63–65.

187

If one examines the various law codes of the ancient Near East, stretching back into the third millennium B.C., whether Babylonian or Assyrian or Hittite, the central fact is the existence of a hierarchy of statuses from the king at the top to the chattel slaves at the bottom, with rules — in the penal law, for example — differentiated among them. Translators often enough employ the term "a free man", but I believe this to be invariably a mistranslation in the strict sense, the imposition of an anachronistic concept on texts in which that concept is not present. It is enough to read the commentaries appended to the translations to appreciate the error: each such rendition requires the most complex contortions in the commentary if the various clauses of the codes are not to founder in crass inner contradictions once "free man" has been inserted. What the codes actually employ are technical status-terms, which we are unable to render precisely because in our tradition the hierarchy and differentiation of statuses had been different. Hence, for example, careful Hittitologists resort to such conventional renditions as "man of the tool", which may not be very lucid but has the great advantage of not being downright misleading. The English word "slave" is a reasonable translation of one such status-term, but it is then necessary to emphasize the fact that slaves were never very significant and never indispensable in the ancient Near East, unlike Greece or Rome.

The neo-Babylonian case I have discussed took place 60 or 70 years before the Persian Wars, by which time the Greek city-state had achieved its classical form, in Asia Minor and the Aegean islands as well as on the mainland of Greece, in southern Italy and Sicily. Proper analysis of classical Greece would require far more space than I have at my disposal, for the society was not nearly so homogeneous throughout the many scattered and independent Greek communities as we often pretend.[9] I shall confine myself to two cities, Athens and Sparta, in the fifth and fourth centuries B.C., the two cities which the Greeks themselves considered the best exemplars of two sharply contrasting social systems and ideologies.

Athens is, of course, the Greek city that comes first to mind in association with the word "freedom". And Athens was the Greek city which possessed the largest number of chattel slaves. The actual number is a matter of dispute — as are nearly all ancient statistics or, better, statistical guesses — but much of the debate is largely irrelevant since no one can seriously deny that they constituted a critical sector of the labour force (in a way which slaves never did in the ancient Near East). My own guess is of the order of 60-80,000, which would give a ratio to the free population about the same

---

[9] On this point see Finley, "The Servile Statuses of Ancient Greece", *Rev. int. des droits de l'antiq.*, 3rd ser., 7 (1960), pp. 165–89; D. Lotze, *Metaxy eleutheron kai doulon. Studien zur Rechtsstellung unfreier Landbevölkerungen in Griechenland ...* (Berlin, 1959).

as in the southern states of the United States in the first half of the nineteenth century, but with a different distribution pattern. Proportionally more Athenians than Southerners owned slaves, but there were few if any great concentrations in single hands because there were no plantations, no Roman *latifundia*.

For our present concern there are a number of points to be made about slavery in Athens, which I shall run through briefly.

1) There were no activities in which slaves were not engaged other than political and military, and even those two categories must be understood very narrowly, for slaves predominated in the police and in what we should call the lower civil service. Contrariwise, there were no activities in which free men were not engaged, which slaves monopolized: they came nearest to achieving that in mining and domestic service. In other words, it was not the nature of the work which distinguished the slave from the free man but the status of the man performing the work.

2) Slaves were outsiders in a double sense. After Solon's abolition of debt bondage, no Athenian could be a slave in Athens. Hence all slaves to be found there had either been imported from outside the state or had been born within to a slave mother. "Outside the state" could mean a neighboring Greek state as well as Syria or southern Russia — the law never forbade Greeks to enslave other Greeks, as distinct from Athenians and Athenians — but the evidence seems to show that the great majority were in fact non-Greeks, "barbarians" as they called them, and that is why I say "outsiders in a double sense".

3) Slaveowners had the right, essentially without restriction, to free their slaves, a right which seems to have been exercised with some frequency, especially among domestic servants and skilled craftsmen, though, as usual, we are unable to express the pattern numerically.

4) The contemporary attitude was summed up by Aristotle when he wrote (*Rhetoric* 1367a32): "The condition of the free man is that he does not live under the restraint of another." In that sense, manumitted slaves were free men, if we ignore, as we legitimately may in this outline analysis, conditional manumissions and minor obligations towards the ex-master. But in another sense "free man" is an excessively loose category. The distinction between citizens and free non-citizens was not merely political — the right to vote or hold office — but went much deeper: a non-citizen could not own real property, for example, except by special grant of that privilege by the popular assembly, a grant which was rarely made. Nor, for much of the period under consideration, could a non-citizen marry a citizen; their children were by definition bastards, subject to various legal disabilities and excluded from the citizen-body. Manumitted slaves were not citizens, though free in the loose sense, and hence they suffered all the limitations on freedom I have just mentioned. In addition, it should be noted that in-

sofar as slaves were often freed relatively late in life, and insofar as any children born to them were not freed along with them – practices which existed though we do not know in what proportion of the cases — to that extent freed women were effectively denied the right to procreate free children.

Now let us look at Sparta in the same period, the fifth and fourth centuries B.C., and in the same schematic way.

1) The Spartiates proper were a relatively small group, perhaps never more than 10,000 adult males and declining from that figure more or less steadily during our period.

2) Such chattel slaves as existed were wholly insignificant. In their place there existed a relatively numerous servile population known as helots (a word with a disputed etymology) who were scattered over extensive territories in the southern and western Peloponnese, in the districts of Laconia and Messenia. Again we lack figures, but it is certain that the helots outnumbered the Spartiates, perhaps several times over (in contrast to Athens where the proportion of slaves to free was probably of the order of 1:4, of slaves to citizens less than 1:1).

3) Who the helots were in origin is disputed. They may even have been Greeks to begin with, but whether so or not, they were the people of Laconia and Messenia, respectively, whom the Spartans subjugated and then kept in subjection in their own home territories. That immediately distinguished them — and distinguished them sharply — from the chattel slave "outsiders", not only genetically but also in later history, for they were bound together by something far more than just the weak negative factor of sharing a common fate, by ties of kinship, nationhood (if I may use the term) and tradition, all perpetually reinforced through their survival on their native soil.

4) Insofar as it makes any sense to use the terminology of property, the helots belonged to the state and not to the individual Spartiates to whom they were assigned. (Parenthetically I should say that the word "belonged", which explains the willingness of the Greeks to call the helots "slaves", is justified by the existence of a further Peloponnesian population who were politically subject to Sparta but were at the same time free and citizens of their own communities, the *perioeci*, whom I am ignoring in this discussion.)

5) It follows from the previous point that only the state could manumit helots. They did so only in one type of situation: when military service by helots was unavoidable, those selected were freed, either beforehand or as a subsequent reward. Once freed they did not become Spartiates but acquired a curious and distinct status, as did Spartiates who lost their standing for one reason or another, so that, as in Athens, the category of "free men" was a conglomeration, not a homogeneous single group.

These points do not exhaust the picture, nor do they by any means exhaust the range of differences between Athens and Sparta, but I trust I have said enough to make it clear not only that the differences were very sharp but also that the number of status possibilities was very considerable. It remains to add that whereas for our subject Athens was typical of the more highly urbanized Greek communities on the mainland of Greece and in the Aegean islands, Sparta was, taken whole, unique. However, if we narrow our focus solely to the helots, then parallels were far from uncommon, less so in Greece proper than in the areas of Greek dispersion east and west, such as Sicily or the regions bordering on the Black Sea, where native populations were reduced to a status sufficiently like that of the helots to warrant their being bracketed with them, as Pollux did, under the rubric "between the free men and the slaves".[10]

Now, merely to illustrate the variety which actually existed, I want to look briefly at the institution we know from the so-called law code of Gortyn in Crete.[11] The text we have was inscribed on stone in the fifth century B.C. but the provisions may be much older. The code is far from complete, and there are some devilishly difficult problems in interpretation. It is clear, however, that there was a servile population which in some sense "belonged" to individual Gortynians who could buy and sell them (apparently with restrictions hinted at, but not clarified, in the code), unlike the situation in Sparta with which too easy comparisons are often made. Yet this same servile population had rights which slaves in Athens lacked. For example, the rules regarding adultery and divorce and the provisions regulating relations between bondsmen and free women leave no doubt that it is proper to speak of marriage, of a relationship which was more than the Roman contubernium between slaves, because it created enforceable rights, but which was at the same time far less than a marriage between free persons. For one thing, an unfree husband was not his wife's tutor; that role was fulfilled by her master. For another, such a marriage did not lead to the creation of a kinship group, although it created the elementary family for certain purposes. Hence a composition payment for adultery could be arranged with the kinsmen of a free woman, but only with the master of a servile woman. (Parenthetically, I should also note that debt-bondsmen are clearly differentiated in the code from the bondsmen I have been discussing.)

After the conquests of Alexander the Great, finally, when Greeks and Macedonians became the ruling class in Egypt, Syria and other lands of the ancient Near East, they found no difficulty in adapting themselves to the social structure which had been in existence there for millennia, modifying

---

[10] In addition to Lotze, op. cit., see D. M. Pippidi, "Die Agrarverhältnisse in den griechischen Städten der Dobrudscha in vorrömischer Zeit", in Griechische Städte und einheimische Völker des Schwarzmeergebietes (Berlin, 1961), pp. 89–105.
[11] See the works cited in n. 9 and D. Lotze, "Zu den woikees von Gortyn". Klio, 40 (1962). pp. 32–43.

the top of the pyramid more than the bottom. A city in the Greek style like Alexandria had its chattel slaves just as in Athens; in the Egyptian countryside, however, the peasantry remained in its traditional status, neither free nor unfree. Royal grants of land to favorite ministers included whole villages along with their inhabitants. Compulsory labor services of various kinds were imposed on them, precisely as on the Israelites a thousand years earlier. Our greatest historian of this era, Rostovtzeff, has written of this peasantry that "They possessed a good deal of social and economic freedom in general and of freedom of movement in particular, . . . And yet they were not entirely free. They were bound to the government and could not escape from this bondage, because on it depended their means of subsistence. This bondage was real, not nominal." [12] Which both makes my point and illustrates, in the vagueness and inadequacy of its formulations, how far we still are from a proper analysis of the social pattern.

The Romans, who eventually replaced the Greeks as rulers of this whole area, had a history of servitude more like that of Athens than of Sparta or the Near East, but with features of their own worth our notice. They, too, had an internal crisis in the archaic period brought about by massive debt-bondage. They, too, then turned to chattel slaves on a large scale, the form of dependent labor which was characteristic of Rome in what I shall arbitrarily define as its classical period, roughly speaking, the three centuries between 150 B.C. and 150 A.D. "Rome" is here ambiguous: we normally use it to refer both to the city on the Tiber and to the whole of the Roman Empire, which by the end of the classical age extended from the Euphrates to the Atlantic. I want to focus on neither, however, but on Italy, the Latin heartland of the Empire, which had become sufficiently uniform socially and culturally to warrant our treating it as a unit. And I want to single out a few characteristics of slavery in Italy which contribute new dimensions to the picture I have drawn so far.

1) The great landed estates of Italy, the *latifundia*, which specialized in ranching, olive- and wine-production, remained, at least until the American South replaced them, the western model of slave agriculture *par excellence*. Slave numbers there, and in the rich urban households, reached proportions far exceeding anything in Greece. In the final struggle between Pompey and Caesar, for example, Pompey's son enlisted 800 slaves from his shepherds and personal attendants to add to his father's army.[13] In a law of 2 B.C., Augustus restricted to 100 the number of slaves a man could manumit in his will, and only an owner of 500 or more was permitted to free that many.[14] A certain Pedanius Secundus, who was prefect of the city in A.D.

[12]   *The Social & Economic History of the Hellenistic World* (3 vols., Oxford, corr. ed., 1953), I 320.
[13]   Caesar, *Bell civ.* 3.4.4.
[14]   Gaius, *Inst.* 1.43.

61, maintained 400 slaves.[15] These are examples at the upper end of the scale, to be sure, but they help fix the whole level.

2) Upon manumission a freedman acquired the status of his ex-master, so that the freed slave of a Roman citizen became a citizen himself, distinguished by certain minor disabilities (chiefly with respect to his former master) but none the less a citizen with the right to vote and to marry in the citizen class. This last had interesting and amusing implications. Within the Roman imperial territory there was a complicated variety of free statuses in the sense that there were numerous non-Romans, free and citizens of their communities, who lacked both the political rights of Roman citizenship and the *ius conubii*, the right to contract a marriage with a Roman citizen. But an ex-slave, by the mere private act of manumission, which required no approval from the government, automatically jumped the queue, in law at any rate, provided his master was a Roman citizen.

3) A significant proportion of the industrial and business activity in Rome and other cities was carried on by slaves acting independently, controlling and managing property known as a *peculium*. This was a legal device invented in the first instance to permit adults to function independently while still technically in *patria potestas*, the tenacity of which in Rome is one of the most remarkable features of the social history of that civilization. The extension of *peculium* to slaves created legal problems of great complexity — in the event of a lawsuit, to give the most obvious example — but they do not concern me now, apart from one notable anomaly. It was possible, and by no means rare, that a *peculium* included one or more slaves, leaving the slave in charge of the *peculium* in the position of owning other slaves *de facto*, though not *de jure*. The reason I have singled out *peculium* can perhaps best be clarified by some rhetorical questions. In what sense were a slave loaded with chains in one of the notorious agricultural *ergastula* and a slave managing a sizeable tannery which was his *peculium* both members of the same class we (and the Romans) call "slaves"? Who was more free, or more unfree, a slave with a *peculium* or a "free" debt-bondsman? Can the concept of freedom be usefully employed at all in such comparisons?

4) In order to insure their administrative control, the early emperors, beginning with Augustus and reaching a crescendo under Claudius and Nero, made extensive use of their own *familiae* in running the Empire. The *servi* and *liberti Caesaris*, the emperor's own slaves and freedmen, took charge of the bureaus and even headed them for a time. Careful investigation has shown that even among these imperial slaves their children were not as a rule freed along with them if they were also slaves — there are complications here, arising from the status of the mothers, which I need not go into — but stayed on as *servi Caesaris*, advancing in the service if they were

[15] Tacitus, *Ann.* 14.43.4.

capable and earning their own freedom in time. Hence the interesting situation was created in which important civil servants not only came out of the slave class but left their children behind in that class. And more interesting still, the generalization may be made that in Rome of the first century of our era, much the greatest opportunity for social mobility lay among the imperial slaves. No one among the free poor could have risen to a status like that of head of the bureau of accounts, or, for that matter, to anything like the many lower posts in the administration. I doubt if I need make further comment.

III

All the societies I have been discussing, from those of the Near East in the third millennium B.C. to the end of the Roman Empire, shared without exception, and throughout their history, a need for dependent, involuntary labor. Structurally and ideologically, dependent labor was integral, indispensable. In the first book of the Pseudo-Aristotelian *Oeconomica* we read: "Of property, the first and most necessary kind, the best and most manageable. is man. Therefore the first step is to procure good slaves. Of slaves there are two kinds, the overseer and the worker." Just like that, without justification or embellishment. There is no need to pile on the quotations; it is simpler to note that not even the ancient believers in the brotherhood of man were opponents of slavery: the best that Seneca the Stoic and St Paul the Christian could offer was some variation on the theme, "status doesn't matter". Diogenes the Cynic, it is said, was once seized by pirates and taken to Corinth to be sold. Standing on the auction block he pointed to a certain Corinthian among the buyers and said: "Sell me to him; he needs a master." [16]

Most revealing of all is the firm implication in many ancient texts, and often the explicit statement, that one element of freedom was the freedom to enslave others. Aristotle wrote the following in the *Politics* (1333b38ff., translated by Barker): "Training for war should not be pursued with a view to enslaving men who do not deserve such a fate. Its objects should be these — first, to prevent men from ever becoming enslaved themselves; secondly, to put men in a position to exercise leadership . . .; and thirdly, to enable men to make themselves masters of those who naturally deserve to be slaves." It may be objected that I am unfair to select a text from Aristotle, the most forthright exponent of the doctrine of natural slavery, a doctrine which was combatted in his own day and generally rejected by philosophers in later generations. Let us then try another text. About the year 400 B.C. an Athenian cripple who had been taken off the dole on the ground that the amount of property he owned made him ineligible,

[16]   Diogenes Laertius 6.74.

appealed formally to the Council for reconsideration of his case. One of his arguments was that he could not yet afford to buy a slave who would support him, though he hoped eventually to do so.[17] Here was no theorist but a humble Athenian addressing a body of his fellow-citizens in the hope of gaining a pittance from them. The implications — and the whole psychology — could scarcely be brought out more sharply.

I do not propose to revive the old question of the origin of the inequality of classes, to ask why dependent labor was indispensable. My starting-point is the fact that everywhere in the civilizations under consideration, as far back as our documentation goes (including the new documentation provided by the Linear B tablets), there was well established reliance on dependent labor. All these societies, as far back as we can trace them, were already complex, articulated, hierarchical, with considerable differentiation of functions and division of labor, with extensive foreign trade and with well-defined political and religious institutions.

It is rather what happened thereafter which interests me now: the essentially different development as between the Near East and the Graeco-Roman world, and, in the latter, the sharp differences in different periods as well as the unevenness of development in different sectors. I have already indicated the most fundamental difference, namely, the shift among Greeks and Romans from reliance on the half-free within to reliance on chattel slaves from outside, and as a corollary, the emergence of the idea of freedom. A wholly new social situation emerged, in which not only some of the components were different from anything known before but also the relationships and spread among them, and the thinking. We may not be able to trace the process but we can mark its first literary statement beyond any doubt, in the long poem, the *Works and Days*, in which Hesiod, an independent Boeotian landowner of the seventh century B.C., presumed freely to criticize his betters, the "bribe-devouring princes" with their "crooked judgments".

In another poem, the *Theogony*, also attributed to Hesiod — and it does not matter whether the attribution is right or not, for the *Theogony* and the *Works and Days* were approximately contemporary, which is enough for this discussion — the same new social situation found expression in another area of human behavior, in man's relations with his gods. As Frankfort phrased it, the author of the *Theogony* "is without oriental precedent in one respect: the gods and the universe were described by him as a matter of private interest. Such freedom was unheard of in the Near East..."[18] It was a firm doctrine in the ancient Near East that man was created for the sole and specific purpose of serving the gods: that was the obvious extension by one further step of the hierarchical structure of society. Neither Greek nor Roman religion shared that idea. Man was created by the gods,

[17] Lysias 24.6.
[18] H. Frankfort, ed., *Before Philosophy* (Penguin ed., 1949), p. 250.

of course, and he was expected to serve them in a number of ways, as well as to fear them, but his purpose, his function, was not that, and surely not that alone. Institutionally the distinction may be expressed this way: whereas in the Near East government and politics were a function of the religious organization, Greek and Roman religion was a function of the political organization.

Hesiod is often called a peasant-poet, which is inexact, for Hesiod was not only himself an owner of slaves but he assumes slavery as an essential condition of life for his class. From the first, therefore, the slave-outsider was as necessary a condition of freedom as the emancipation of clients and debt-bondsmen within. The methods by which outsiders were introduced into the society need not concern us. But it is worth a moment to consider one aspect of the outsider situation, the "racial" one, which is being much discussed today, both by historians and sociologists, chiefly with reference to the American South. It is important to fix in mind that "outsiders" were often neighbors of similar stock and culture; that though the Greeks tried to denigrate the majority of their slaves with the "barbarian" label and though Roman writers (and their modern followers) are full of contemptuous references to "Orientals" among their slaves and freedmen, the weaknesses of this simple classification and its implications were apparent enough even to them. The decisive fact is that widespread manumission and the absence of strict endogamy together destroy all grounds for useful comparison with the American South on this score. I need not go into the variations in antiquity with respect to rights of marriage — I have already indicated the significance of the Roman practice which granted freedmen full rights of *conubium*, for example, and that should be enough to show that the "racial" element in the concept of the outsider, though not zero, was essentially irrelevant, both in fact and in the ideology. When the Roman lawyers agreed on the formulation, "Slavery is an institution of the *ius gentium* whereby someone is subject to the *dominium* of another, contrary to nature," [19] they were saying in effect that slavery was indispensable, that it was defensible only on that ground, and that one was liable to be enslaved just because one was an outsider. An outsider, in short, was an outsider. That tautological definition is the best we can offer. Hence the expansion of the Roman Empire, for example, automatically converted blocks of outsiders to free insiders.

Why, we must then ask, was the historical trend in some Greek communities, such as Athens, and in Rome towards the polarity of the free insider and the slave outsider, while elsewhere no comparable development occurred (or where incipient signs appeared, they soon proved abortive)? Max Weber suggested that the answer lay in the loosening of the royal grip on trade and the consequent emergence of a free trading class who acted as social

[19]   *Digest* 1.5.4.1.

catalysts.[20] I have no great confidence in this hypothesis, which can neither be verified nor falsified from Greek or Roman evidence. The decisive changes occurred precisely in the centuries for which we lack documentation, and for which there is no realistic prospect of new documentation being discovered. I must confess immediately that I have no alternative explanation to offer. Reexamination of the body of Greek and Roman myth may help, but the hope lies, in my opinion, in the very extensive documentation of the ancient Near East.

I say "hope", and no more, because it is no use pretending that study of Near Eastern servitude has taken us very far. One reason is the primitive classification into slave and free which has been my theme, and I now want to return to this and suggest an approach. Merely to say, as I have thus far, that there were statuses between slavery and freedom is obviously not enough. How does one proceed to formulate the differences between a Biblical bondsman who hoped for release and the man who chose to remain a slave in perpetuity and had his ear bored to mark his new status? Or between a helot in Sparta and a chattel in Athens?

The Sicilian Greek historian Diodorus, writing as a contemporary of Julius Caesar, gives us the following variation on the Hercules-Omphale myth. Hercules, he says, produced two children during the period of his stay with the Lydian queen, the first by a slave-woman while he was in servitude, the second by Omphale herself after he had been restored to freedom. Unwittingly Diodorus has pointed the way. All men, unless they are Robinson Crusoes, are bundles of claims, privileges, immunities, liabilities and obligations with respect to others. A man's status is defined by the total of these elements which he possesses or which he has (or has not) the potential of acquiring. Actual and potential must both be considered: the potential of the *servi Caesaris*, for example, was always a factor in the psychology of status in the early Roman Empire, and sometimes it became an actuality, when one of them climbed high enough on the civil service ladder and was freed. Obviously none of this can be expressed in numerical, quantitative terms: it is not a matter of one man having one more privilege or one more liability than another. Rather it is a matter of location on a spectrum or continuum of status; the *servi Caesaris* as a class, in this language, stood nearer the freedom end than did the *servi* of any private owner in Rome.

It is possible, furthermore, to work out a typology of rights and duties. By way of illustration, I suggest the following rough scheme:[21]

1) Claims to property, or power over things — a category which is itself complex and requires further analysis: for example, the difference between the power of a slave over his *peculium* and the power of an owner in the

[20] "Agrarverhältnisse im Altertum", in his *Gesammelte Aufsätze zur Sozial- und Wirtschaftsgeschichte* (Tübingen, 1924), pp. 1–288, at pp. 99–107.
[21] This is substantially the scheme I first formulated in the article cited in n. 9.

strict sense; or differences according to the different categories of things, land, cattle, money, personal possessions, and so forth.

2) Power over human labor and movements, whether one's own or another's — including, of course, the privilege of enslaving others.

3) Power to punish, and, conversely, immunity from punishment.

4) Privileges and liabilities in judical process, such as immunity from arbitrary seizure or the capacity to sue and be sued.

5) Privileges in the area of the family: marriage, succession and so on — involving not only property rights and rights of *conubium*, but, at one step removed, the possibility of protection or redemption in case of debt, ransom or blood-feud.

6) Privileges of social mobility, such as manumission or enfranchisement, and their converse: immunity from, or liability to, bondage, penal servitude and the like.

7) Privileges and duties in the sacral, political and military spheres.

I have said enough, I trust, to forestall any suggestion that I am proposing a mechanical procedure. In Athens chattel slaves and wealthy free noncitizens (Aristotle, for example) were equally barred from marriage with a citizen; in terms of my typology, they both lacked the privilege of *conubium*. It would be absurd, however, to equate them in a serious sense just on that score. Or to take a more meaningful instance of quite another kind: Athenian slaves and Spartan helots both belonged to someone, but the fact that the someone was a private individual in the one case, the Spartan state in another, introduced a very important distinction. These various combinations must be weighed and judged in terms of the whole structure of the individual society under examination.

If I am then asked, What has become of the traditional property definition of a slave? Where on your continuum do you draw the line between free and slave, free and unfree? — my answer has to be rather complicated. To begin with, the idea of a continuum or spectrum is metaphorical: it is too smooth. Nevertheless, it is not a bad metaphor when applied to the ancient Near East or to the earliest periods of Greek and Roman history. There one status did shade into another. There, although some men were the property of others and though the gap between the slave and the king was as great as social distance can be, neither the property-definition nor any other single test is really meaningful. There, in short, freedom is not a useful category and therefore it is pointless to ask where one draws the line between the free and the unfree.

In classical Athens and Rome, on the other hand, the traditional dividing line, the traditional distinction according to whether a man is or is not the property of another, remains a convenient rule of thumb for most purposes. For them the metaphor of a continuum breaks down. But the problem has not been to understand those two, relatively atypical, societies, but the others, societies which we have not understood very well just because, in my view, we have not emancipated ourselves from the slave-free antinomy. And if my approach proves useful, I suggest it will lead to a better understanding of Athens and Rome, too, where the category of "free man" needs precise subdivision.

I might close with a highly schematic model of the history of ancient society. It moved from a society in which status ran along a continuum towards one in which statuses were bunched at the two ends, the slave and the free — a movement which was most nearly completed in the societies which most attract our attention for obvious reasons. And then, under the Roman Empire, the movement was reversed; ancient society gradually returned to a continuum of statuses and was transformed into what we call the medieval world.

M. I. FINLEY
Jesus College, Cambridge

The Idea of Slavery

The Problem of Slavery in
Western Culture
by David Brion Davis.
Cornell, 505 pp., $10.00

M. I. Finley

In the year AD 61 the prefect of the city of Rome, Pedanius Secundus, was murdered by one of the slaves in his town house. Under the law, not only the culprit but all the other slaves in the household had to be executed, in this instance numbering four hundred. There was a popular outcry and the Senate debated the question. Some senators rose to plead clemency, but the day was carried by the distinguished jurist, Gaius Cassius Longinus, who argued that all change from ancestral laws and customs is always for the worse. When a mob tried to prevent the sentence from being carried out, the emperor personally intervened on the side of the law, though he rejected another proposal that Pedanius's ex-slaves should also be punished by banishment. That, he said, would be unnecessary cruelty.

The emperor was Nero and it has been suggested that one of the unsuccessful advocates of mercy may have been his closest adviser, the Stoic philosopher Seneca, in whose writings there are some powerful passages calling for the treatment of slaves as fellow-humans. Not once, however, did Seneca suggest that the institution itself was so immoral that it ought to be abolished. For that radical idea the western world still had to wait more than 1500 years, while philosophers, moralists, theologians, and jurists—save for an isolated voice here and there to whom no one listened—discovered and propagated a variety of formulas which satisfied them and society at large that a man could be both a thing and a man at the same time. This ambiguity or "dualism" is the "problem of slavery" to which Professor Davis has devoted a large, immensely learned, readable, exciting, disturbing, and sometimes frustrating volume, one of the most important to have been published on the subject of slavery in modern times.

THE GENESIS OF THE BOOK was a modest one. Professor Davis set out to make a comparative study of British and American antislavery movements. Gradually he began to appreciate that "the problem of slavery transcended national boundaries" in ways he "had not suspected." Slavery was brought to the New World at a time when it had disappeared from most of Europe; yet there were no hesitations, no gropings, because the heritage of the Bible, classical philosophy, and Roman law provided a ready-made set of regulations and a ready-made ideology. Differences within the New World, between the Anglo-Saxons in the north and the Latins in the south, between Protestant and Catholic colonies, appeared, on closer examination, to be tangential and far less significant than "their underlying patterns of unity." On this particular topic Professor Davis has now come forward with powerful support for a recent trend in scholarship running counter to the romantic idealized image of Latin American slavery, and in particular of race relations in the southern hemisphere, which had long prevailed, a view perhaps best known from the works of the Brazilian Gilberto Freyre and from Frank Tannenbaum's seminal little book *Slave and Citizen*. In

The New York Review

short, Professor Davis came to the conclusion that "there was more institutional continuity between ancient and modern slavery than has generally been supposed" and that "slavery has always raised certain fundamental problems that originated in the simple fact that the slave is a man."

From this conclusion a new and fundamental question followed. If the "legal and moral validity of slavery was a troublesome question in European thought from the time of Aristotle to the time of Locke," why was it that not until the 1770s were there "forces in motion that would lead to organized movements to abolish . . . the entire institutional framework which permitted human beings to be treated as things"? This development, he rightly says, "was something new to the world." Slavery had declined markedly in the later Roman Empire, not as a result of an abolitionist movement but in consequence of complex social and economic changes which replaced the chattel slave by a different kind of bondsman, the *colonus*, the *adscriptus glebi*, the serf. Modern slavery, in contrast, did not become slowly transformed. It was abolished by force and violence. Attempts to picture "antislavery and efforts to Christianize and ameliorate the condition of slaves as parts of a single swelling current of humanitarianism" falsify the historical record. "All such dreams and hopes ran aground on the simple and solid fact, which for centuries had been obscured by philosophy and law, that a slave was not a piece of property, nor a half-human instrument, but a man held down by force."

THE BOOK Professor Davis started to write was thus converted into a large project of which this is the first volume (though a self-contained one) carrying the story from antiquity to the early 1770s. The story, it must be stressed, is essentially one in the history of ideas. "A problem of moral perception" is how he himself phrases it.

This book . . . makes no pretense of being a history of slavery as such, or even of opinion concerning slavery . . . I have been concerned with the different ways in which men have responded to slavery, on the assumption that this will help us to distinguish what was unique in the response of the abolitionist. I have also been concerned with traditions in thought and value from which both opponents and defenders of slavery could draw. I hope to demonstrate that slavery has always been a source of social and psychological tension, but that in Western culture it was associated with certain religious and philosophical doctrines that gave it the highest sanction.

As an essay in the history of ideas—more precisely, of ideology, a word which Professor Davis curiously shies away from—the book is brilliant, filled with detail yet never losing control of the main threads, subtle and sophisticated and penetrating. Even the relatively brief

and derivative first part, on ancient and medieval thinking, has some fine insights. Then, with the discovery of America, Professor Davis comes into his own. No man, surely, has read so much or so deeply on the subject; the footnotes provide the most complete bibliography we have; too complete indeed, and one wishes he had been more discriminating in his selection of titles. It is impossible in a review to survey the ground covered or the multiplicity of fresh ideas and suggestions. But an example or two will indicate how complicated is the counterpoint that is woven throughout around the "dualism" concept. Early on the *leitmotif* emerges. The question is posed as to why in the later Roman Empire and the early Middle Ages, when "slavery all but disappeared from most parts of Europe," we do not find "the Church turning away from its compromises with the Roman world and using its great moral power to hasten a seemingly beneficial change." Professor Davis answers:

The most plausible explanation would seem to lie in the complex network of mental associations, derived from antiquity, which connected slavery with ideas of sin, subordination, and the divine order of the world. To question the ethical basis of slavery, even when the institution was disappearing from

exist in nearly every nation? If slavery violated the natural law of equality and the divine law of human brotherhood, could not the same be said of the family, private property, social orders, and government?

The heretical sects were a threat all the time, for they seized on those ideas implicit in Christianity "that were potentially explosive when torn from their protective casings and ignited in the charged atmosphere of class rivalry and discontent." They had to be contained, and they were. Not until the middle of of the eighteenth century did an English sect finally take a firm official stand against slavery (while the Church of England remained indifferent). The Quakers came to that after a long period of inner conflict on the subject, but by then society had been so transformed that the moral issues acquired new practical implications.

In a period of intense soul-searching, of desire for self-purification and of concern over their image in the eyes of others, a decision to refrain from dealing in slaves was a means of reasserting the perfectionist content of their faith. It was a way of prescribing a form of selfish economic activity without repudiating the search for wealth; . . . a way of affirming the individual's

LIBERTY.

view, would be to question fundamental conceptions of God's purpose and man's history and destiny. If slavery were an evil and performed no divinely appointed function, then why had God authorized it in Scripture and permitted it to

moral will, and the historic mission of the church, without challenging the basic structure of the social order.

So BALD A SUMMARY invites the charge of mere cynicism, but nothing would be more unjust. Behind the summaries lie meticulous accounts of the intense intellectual and moral struggles that went on in the search for a moral position. In all societies which are characterized by class or national conflicts and divergence of interests, ideology is necessarily ambivalent. No account is adequate which fails to reveal how ideology serves both to criticize and to preserve the social order at the same time, and the careless or blinkered observer automatically dismisses as cynicism any analysis which gives due weight to the second function. On the subject of slavery, the crowning paradox is that the rationalist attack on Christian theology in the eighteenth century brought the slave no nearer to freedom. Locke had already shown how a defense of slavery could be reconciled with natural rights. Now, "insofar as the Enlightment divorced anthropology and comparative anatomy from theological assumptions, it opened the way for theories of racial inferiority."

And yet, at the point where this book ends, anti-slavery *had* become a program and eventually it was to become a successful major political issue. Slavery *was* finally abolished in the West. Why? It is on that decisive question that I find Professor Davis's account frustrating. "For some two thousand years men thought of sin as a kind of slavery. One day they would come to think of slavery as sin." Who are "they"? "By the early 1770s a large number of moralists, poets, intellectuals, and reformers had come to regard American slavery as an unmitigated evil." It is only a little unfair to remind Professor Davis of Jim Farley's remark, towards the close of Adlai Stevenson's first presidential campaign. Someone at a party was being jubilant over the fact that nearly all intellectuals were for Stevenson. "All sixty thousand of them," retorted Farley. Moralists, poets, intellectuals, and reformers did not destroy slavery. The Civil War did that, and Professor Davis himself has, as a by-product, delivered a crushing blow against the "unnecessary conflict" school of historians. I do not, of course, wish to deny the essential role of several generations of abolitionists. But nothing did or could happen until their moral fervor became translated into political and military action, and how that came about cannot be answered by the history of ideas. Nothing is more difficult perhaps than to explain how and why, or why not, a new moral perception becomes effective in action. Yet nothing is more urgent if

an academic historical exercise is to become a significant investigation of human behavior with direct relevance to the world we now live in.

It would be gross injustice to call this book an academic historical exercise or to suggest that Professor Davis is unaware of the central question. Throughout the volume there are sharp comments very much to the point. In a brief note on the rather mechanical economic explanations in Eric Williams's *Capitalism and Slavery*, Davis joins the opposition but then adds that one cannot "get around the simple fact that no country thought of abolishing the slave trade until its economic value had considerably declined." He knows and uses the most recent discussions (down to Eugene Genovese's *Political Economy of Slavery*, published in 1965) of the profitability of slavery and its effects on economic growth. He agrees that it is "theoretically possible" that such divergences with respect to freed slaves as existed between North and South America "had less to do with the character of slavery in the two countries than with economic and social structures which defined the relations between colored freedmen and the dominant white society." He mentions the wars of the eighteenth century and the changes in the balance of power, which "brought a growing awareness of the instability and inefficiency of the old colonial system." And it may be that what I am looking for will find its proper place in the next volumes.

YET THE FACT REMAINS that the comments I have just quoted are really asides, often relegated to footnotes, and I do not think it is a sufficient defense that a man has a right to choose his own subject, in this case the history of ideas. Slavery is not an autonomous system: it is an institution embedded in a social structure. It is no longer the same institution when the structure is significantly altered, and ideas about slavery have to be examined structurally too. Only by remaining in the realm of abstractions can Professor Davis lay so much emphasis on the "institutional continuity" between ancient and modern slavery. He is in consequence led astray on several important aspects. His account of slavery among the Hebrews and other ancient Near Eastern societies suffers from precisely the weakness he has

The New York Review

so effectively exposed in the case of Latin American slavery. He has allowed his authorities to mislead him into taking at face value pious hopes which he penetrates easily when they appear in Seneca or modern writers. And he has misjudged the social ambience by failing to appreciate sufficiently that for most of human history labor for others has been involuntary (quite apart from compulsions exercised by either family or wage-earning, which are of a different order from the kind of force that is the final sanction against slaves, serfs, peons, debt bondsmen, coolies, or untouchables). Slavery in that context must have different overtones from slavery in a context of free labor. The way slavery declined in the Roman Empire, to repeat an example I have already given, illustrates that. Neither moral values nor economic interests nor the social order were threatened by the transformation of slaves and free peasants together into tied serfs. They were—or at least many powerful elements in society thought they were—by proposals to convert slaves into free men.

What sets the slave apart from all other forms of involuntary labor is that, in the strictest sense, he is an outsider. He is brought into a new society violently and traumatically; he is cut off from all traditional human ties of kin and nation and even his own religion; he is prevented, insofar as that is possible, from creating new ties, except to his masters, and in consequence his descendants are as much outsiders, as unrooted, as he was. The final proof of non-status is the free sexual access to slaves which is a fundamental condition of all slavery (with complex exceptions in the rules regarding access of free females to slave males). When Professor Davis writes, "Bondwomen have always been the victims of sexual exploitation, which was perhaps the clearest recognition of their humanity," he has stood the situation on its head. Sexual *exploitation* is a denial, not a recognition, of a woman's humanity, whether she is slave or free.

I HAVE STATED the slave-outsider formula schematically and therefore too rigidly. Structural differences emerge clearly when one considers how much societies have differed with respect to the freed slave. At one extreme stood Rome, which not only allowed almost unlimited rights to individual masters to free their slaves but which also automatically enrolled the freedmen as citizens if their owners were citizens. At the other extreme was the American South. Professor Davis produces evidence that by 1860 there were more free Negroes, even in the South, than is often realized. Nevertheless, the emancipation process was hemmed in by very stringent regulations. And the fate of the freed slave in the United States hardly needs spelling out. What does need a careful look is the question of color, which is too central to be evaded out of sentimentality and on which Professor Davis has an important chapter (as usual, in the realm of ideas). Dr. Williams holds that "slavery was not born of racism, rather, racism was the consequence of slavery." One wishes profoundly that one could believe that. However, the slave-outsider formula argues the other way, as does the fact that as early as the 1660s southern colonies decreed that henceforth all Negroes who were imported should be slaves, but whites should be indentured servants and not slaves. The connection between slavery and racism has been a dialectical one, in which each element reinforced the other.

Racism has already outlived slavery by a century. Why, we are entitled to ask, did the "revolutionary shift in attitudes towards sin, human nature, and progress," which we may concede to have been a necessary condition of anti-slavery, not extend to racism? Is slavery any more a sin than the denial of civil rights, concentration camps, Hiroshima, napalm, torture in Algeria, or apartheid in South Africa or Rhodesia? Why did the new moral perception succeed in wiping out one sin and not the others? It is that question which makes this book a profoundly disturbing one. There is cold comfort here for anyone who trusts to the slow ameliorative process of a growing humanitarianism, of the "progressive development of man's moral sense" which Thomas Jefferson found in history. In Professor Davis's lapidary phrase, "faith in progress smothered [Jefferson's] sense of urgency" when it came to slavery. □

The Slave Economies in
Political Perspective

Eugene D. Genovese and Elizabeth Fox-Genovese

The economic interpretations of the slave economies of the New World, as well as those social interpretations which adopt the neoclassical economic model but leave the economics out, assume everything they must prove. By retreating from the political economy from which their own methods derive, they ignore the extent to which the economic process permeates the society. They ignore, that is, the interaction between economics, narrowly defined, and the social relations of production on the one hand and state power on the other. For any economic system remains not merely a method of allocating scarce resources, but a system that, at least on the margin and frequently more pervasively, commands those scarce resources. Even an international market such as that which prevailed in the Atlantic world during the eighteenth and early nineteenth centuries depends heavily on the state formations that guarantee the ultimate command of economic goods. Neoclassical economists achieve their theoretical sophistication by falling silent on the social relations of production that ultimately determine the prices of commodities in the market. In other words, these economists mystify reality by abstracting prices from the social relations of production and then blithely assuming that their abstraction provides an effective analytic substitute for those social relations.

Even in a society such as our own where most facets of human life pass through the market, there remain pockets of nonpriced labor—for example, the household work of many women and the early reproduction of human capital. In the eighteenth-century Atlantic world, commercial capital organized the market and fed off it, but it did not evenly penetrate all productive sectors. Typically, commercial capital organized the surplus production of larger or smaller domestic units of labor before the trans-formation of labor-power into a commodity. In this respect, the slave plan-

This essay is the presidential address delivered to the Organization of American Historians at New Orleans, April 12, 1979. Eugene D. Genovese and Elizabeth Fox-Genovese are members of the history department at the University of Rochester.

tations of the Old South and elsewhere had much in common with the households and farms of the northern North American colonies and states.

The southern slaveholders' recourse to a domestic metaphor to explain their relationship with their labor force thus simultaneously evoked the declining seigneurialism of their remote historical origins and certain neo-Aristotelian features of the domestic bases of commercial capital in what would prove to be more progressive sectors. But the political basis of their command of labor no longer required notions of the social household. Repudiating patriarchy and hierarchy in the public sphere, the government of the new United States turned more directly to the language of the market to justify its exercise of political power. The political systems rested upon the equal participation of propertied males and left the transmission of sovereignty within the various domestic units to the discretion of members of the political community. Political power thus remained impregnated with the duality that characterized commercial capital as well. It left unresolved the discontinuity between the public and the private spheres, just as commercial capital left unresolved the discontinuity between relations of exchange and relations of production; it tolerated—and may even have depended upon—pockets of authoritarian command that contradicted its most cherished principles of equality.

Historically, commercial capital proved a proverbial Janus, at once looking forward and backward. It bound within the market system both archaic and revolutionary forces. It even generated rationalized and relatively efficient variants of archaic relations of production—most notably, the slave economies. Within the economic sector, the decisive threshold lay at the transformation of labor-power into a commodity. But commercial capital could not itself cause this transformation, as some scholars—most recently Immanuel Wallerstein—suggest.[1] Rather, commercial capital contributed to organizing economic space and exchange in a way that permitted the eventual emergence of a fully developed capitalist system. An understanding of this process requires full attention to the role of politics, and especially of state power, in assuring the ruling class an adequate command over its resources, including labor, and an adequate share of the international market. From this perspective, it should come as no surprise that the abolition of slavery in the United States occurred not as a simple economic transfer of resources, nor as internal social reform, but as a bloody civil war.

The export-oriented colonial economies spawned by West European expansion produced some of the greatest anomalies in the history of capitalism, among the most arresting of which was the coexistence of high profits and high growth rates with manifest retardation of economic development. Critics of Robert William Fogel's and Stanley L. Engerman's *Time on the Cross* have called into question their claims for the relative efficiency of southern agriculture, based as they are on the application of a factor-productivity index

[1] Immanuel Wallerstein, *The Modern World-System: Capitalist Agriculture and the Origins of the European World-Economy in the Sixteenth Century* (New York and London, 1974). Wallerstein's book has reopened a debate over the historical role of merchant capital that dates at least from Marx's attack on the very concept of "merchant capitalism." See Karl Marx, *Capital: A Critical Analysis of Capitalist Production* (3 vols., Moscow, 1961), I, chaps. 23–33.

method few economists think appropriate and fewer historians think tenable at all.[2] But the South undoubtedly did enjoy an impressive growth in total and per capita wealth from colonial times to secession.

No one, not even those classical political economists who led the attack on slavery as an inefficient system, could reasonably deny that it could generate high profits and attendant growth rates under three conditions: fresh land; a steady supply of cheap labor; and a high level of demand on the world market. The economic indictment of slavery has focused on structural consequences. The origins of the prosperity of the slave economies lay primarily in the force of the world demand for certain staples under narrow conditions of production; and the high levels of profit and growth disguised deep structural weaknesses that condemned slave societies to underdevelopment, eventual stagnation, and political disaster.

In the bold alternative view offered by *Time on the Cross*, the slave states not only achieved a growth rate and levels of profitability comparable to the best, but achieved something economists mysteriously call "viability." If by viability they mean that, at the secular level, more money was being earned than spent, then we must answer that that much may be taken for granted in a competitive market world. If, more seriously, they mean that the rate of return equaled the interest rate, the problem has been fudged.

At issue is the flexibility of the slave system—its ability to reallocate resources when faced with the secular decline of decisive sectors. In this sense, economists could judge the slave economy viable only if they could demonstrate that the planters could and would shift capital to the free-labor sector whenever it proved profitable to do so. But they could not provide any empirical justification for such long periods of depression as that of the late 1830s and 1840s, and they would have to ignore the structural characteristics of the slave economy, as well as the social and psychological characteristics of slave society. It is difficult to believe that a regional ruling class of resident planters, whose lives had been formed by a relationship of theoretically absolute power over other human beings and by pretensions to community lordship, could blithely dispense with the very foundations of their social and psychological existence, merely in response to a balance sheet of profit and loss.

The standard economic interpretations err in assuming that the slaveholders can be understood as ordinary capitalists who functioned as units in the marketplace. When they are perceived as a social class, with discrete material interests, moral sensibility, ideological commitment, and social psychology, then the question of the economic viability of their system takes on an entirely different meaning. Since their interests, material and ideological, clashed with those of the larger capitalist world, the question of viability reduces to one of

[2] Robert William Fogel and Stanley L. Engerman, *Time on the Cross* (2 vols., Boston, 1974), I, 192; Robert William Fogel and Stanley L. Engerman, "The Relative Efficiency of Slavery: A Comparison of Northern and Southern Agriculture in 1860," *Explorations in Economic History*, VIII (Spring 1971), 353–67; Thomas L. Haskell, "Were Slaves More Efficient? Some Doubts about *Time on the Cross*," *New York Review of Books*, XXI (Sept. 19, 1974), 38–42; Paul A. David, Herbert G. Gutman, Richard Sutch, Peter Temin, and Gavin Wright, *Reckoning with Slavery: A Critical Study in the Quantitative History of American Negro Slavery* (New York, 1976), 208–23, 313–19, and *passim*.

military and political power: Was their economy strong enough and flexible enough to support their pretensions and guarantee their safety as a ruling class? From this point of view, a long economic slump or a growing fear of isolation and incipient decline could be expected to generate, not a shift of resources to a free-labor economy inside or outside the South, but mounting pressure for war, conquest, or some alternative political solution.

Thus, those economic interpretations that assume that the slaveholders lived, thought, and acted as ordinary bourgeois assume everything they must prove; cannot begin to illuminate the titanic struggle for power that rent the American union; and reduce the impressive complexity of slavery as a social system to the behavior pattern of a single industry, if indeed not a single firm. Yet, even most of those who criticize Fogel and Engerman for these assumptions do no more than introduce minor qualifications. With the exception of such Marxists as Harold Woodman, Raimondo Luraghi, Jay Mandle, and Michael Greenberg, the critics of Fogel and Engerman—Paul David, Peter Temin, Kenneth Stampp, Gavin Wright, Herbert Gutman, Richard Sutch, and others—merely object to the extreme formulation of assumptions and derivative theses that they themselves share.[3]

Once these misplaced assumptions from neoclassical economics are dropped, the anomalies become less puzzling and the apparent contradictions disappear. Consider, for example, the very different results of soil exhaustion and wasteful agricultural methods in the North and South. The waste and destruction resulted primarily from an enormous abundance of land, rather than from slavery *per se*, for it simply did not pay to conserve resources. But as soil exhaustion and agricultural depression struck the eastern areas of the free states, capital shifted, not only to the West but into commercial, industrial, and even agricultural diversification within the East itself. In the South, however, the older areas, locked into a slave economy, found it difficult to adjust and fell back toward subsistence. In the end, slave sales sustained the older regions and allowed the slaveholders to keep going. Even when the region showed a modest economic recovery, the bases of which remain debatable, it remained at an economic level that undermined the slaveholders' political power.

The history of the sugar colonies of the Caribbean and of the Brazilian Northeast and, later, the gold mining districts of Minas Gerais, followed a similar economic course. The significant differences among the cases flowed much less from variations in economic process than from variations in the class nature and political power of the slaveholders in each region.

The impressive performance of the Old South in scoring high profits and growth had parallels in other New World slave economies. And for that reason, among others, the explanations of Fogel and Engerman appear suspect. They stress the high rate of slave reproduction and attribute the slaves' economic

---

[3] For an attempt to clarify the differences between Marxist and non-Marxist criticism of *Time on the Cross*, see Eugene D. Genovese, "The Debate over *Time on the Cross*: A Critique of Bourgeois Criticism" (forthcoming). But see also Harold D. Woodman, "Economic History and Economic Theory: The New Economic History in America," *Journal of Interdisciplinary History*, III (Autumn 1972), 323–50.

performance to an internalization of bourgeois norms within a remarkable incentive system. But what are we to do with Barbados during the seventeenth century, Jamaica and Saint-Domingue during the eighteenth, or different regions of Brazil during the seventeenth, eighteenth, and nineteenth? None of these slaveholding countries boasted a self-reproducing labor force, and the attribution of a bourgeois work ethic to the slaves would inspire laughter on all sides. Saint-Domingue, the richest slaveholding colony of its day, stood convicted of harboring one of the bloodiest, most vicious planter classes and social systems in the New World. And if the Luso-Brazilian planters of Bahia—whose waterfront is known formally as the Bay of All Saints and informally as the Bay of Almost All Sins—qualified as puritanical capitalists, then words have lost all meaning.

An interpretation of the performance of the slave economies must account for the recurrence of a common pattern throughout the hemisphere. First, the slaveholding countries—those in which slavery dominated the economies—exhibited stunning levels of profitability and prolonged periods of economic growth. Second, in every case the boom rested on the export sector and approximated reliance on a single crop. And third, in each case, the end of the boom left in its wake an economic wreck. No slaveholding country or region crossed the threshold to industrialization. None adjusted to emancipation so as to launch a new cycle of growth that passed into structural development. All became marked by what is euphemistically called underdevelopment, which left a legacy of poverty, misery, and colonial dependency. The abolition of slavery in most countries was disorderly: a great revolution in Saint-Domingue; a civil war in the United States; a general strike of slaves in the Danish West Indies; protracted wars of national liberation in much of Spanish America; a crisis of the national state in Brazil; and disruptive political struggles even in the British Caribbean. The depth and destructiveness of these political crises would not have existed if the slave economies had not extruded retrogressive ruling classes, the removal of which demanded radical surgery. In any event, the special features of the North American case cannot be accounted for by an interpretation that fails to account for similarities and differences within the slaveholding sector of the hemispheric economy.

The Western Hemisphere as a whole, not merely the United States and Brazil, had a moving frontier. For example, the decline of Barbados resulted in a shift of labor and capital to Jamaica and elsewhere—a process not much impeded by imperial boundaries. All Caribbean colonies had mixed populations, and economic resources crossed political lines. The expulsion of the Dutch from Brazil, where they had contributed much to the growth of the sugar industry, shifted capital, labor, and managerial talent not only to other Dutch colonies but to British and French as well. The great slave revolt in Saint-Domingue, as it passed into an epoch-making national revolution, sent French planters and their slaves scurrying not only to Cayenne and other French colonies but to Louisiana, Cuba, Venezuela, and other countries. The sugar countries rose and fell—with capital and labor in geographical movement analogous to the movement along the North American and Brazilian frontiers. So long as land remained available at prices unthinkably low by

European standards—so long as colonial settlers faced empty spaces or spaces that could be emptied by a controlled dose of genocide—resources would be shifted, and the grim wastefulness of the system as a whole would be disguised.

Labor presents a startling complication. Everywhere, except in the Old South, labor costs were kept at acceptable levels by resort to the transatlantic slave trade. The slave reproduction rates oscillated between negative and inadequately positive, and only the reinforcement of fresh African cargoes could fuel the system. The great exception, the southern states of North America, alone operated during the great periods of boom and expansion with a slave force internally generated. The social, economic, and political origins and consequences of this unique circumstance deserve the most elaborate analysis. For the moment, let it suffice that the United States solved the problem in its own way. But that way meant not low slave prices, but steadily rising prices that may be called low only in relation to the returns earned by the capitalization of labor under specific market conditions. In the end, therefore, it was the third element of the conjuncture—the world demand for certain staples—that exercised the most important influence over the economy in the Old South, as it did in other slave economies.

At first glance, the force of the world demand for staples hardly seems worth dwelling upon. After all, what is unusual about an industry's requiring a market? But the slave economies, despite their typical reliance on monoculture, cannot be treated as analogues of particular industries, as a brief review of the relationship between the slave economies and the world market should demonstrate.

The early sugar economy prefigured that of the modern New World colonial economies in general and the plantation-slave economies in particular. During the early sixteenth century, sugar had remained a luxury good used primarily for treating wine. By the second quarter of the century, however, increased supply from the Atlantic islands led to a collapse in prices, which stimulated a more general use in the making of preserves and confectionary. Prices again rose. That is, supply from the colonial periphery outran world demand and thereby induced a precipitous decline in prices. Falling prices stimulated experimentation with new uses; rising demand led to rising prices, which encouraged a new burst on the supply side and a consequent outstripping of demand.

Thus, as early as the period 1670–1690, overproduction plunged the sugar economies of Brazil and the Caribbean into crises that ruined both planters and their creditors. This pattern recurred many times. Yet, during the 140 years following 1570, sugar production in Brazil rose by 450 percent. Heavy capital investment, which sugar in contradistinction to tobacco and then cotton required, proceeded apace with the securing of a relatively cheap labor force of slaves to stimulate production. For technical as well as political reasons, the refining process was shifted to Europe: The Portuguese, in a misguided attempt to strengthen their Brazilian colony, forbade refining in Lisbon, only to suffer the direct competition of Amsterdam and Hamburg. Later, economic forces produced similar results in the cotton industry, political interventions or no.

When Caribbean sugar production ran afoul of market gluts the ensuing crises led to a shift of resources to fresher land in newly developed colonies. Thus, one factor—land—alone accounted for the regional economy's ability to survive the periodic purges of the market generated by the tendency toward overproduction.

Brazil fared better. When its sugar economy declined, slave-based gold mining opened up in Minas Gerais. When that lucrative industry began to decline, coffee-growing plantations spread in the South in response to a new mass demand in Europe. By the beginning of the last quarter of the nineteenth century, however, this final plantation boom had begun to run its course, and the slave regime sailed into a political crisis conditioned by the defeat of the North American Confederacy and propelled especially by the political and military debacle in the Paraguayan War and the disintegration of the monarchy. In Brazil, as elsewhere, slavery had long been able to generate impressive spurts of quantitative growth and high profits without generating the structural and institutional conditions for the development and consolidation of national economic power. Technologically, the sugar industry of Brazil remained remarkably backward; that of Louisiana developed only within narrow geographic limits and under tariff protection; and that of Cuba underwent revolutionary transformation under the impact of foreign capital, at a time when the planters regarded the fate of slavery as sealed by the defeat of the Confederacy and were desperately looking for a new system of production.[4]

The entire economic history of the Old South, from the rise of King Cotton at the beginning of the nineteenth century to World War II, reflected the force of international demand. When the world market was good, as during the 1830s and 1850s, profits soared and growth proceeded apace; when the market slumped, depression and retrogression set in. So long as slavery existed, no foundation for industrialization or economic diversification was laid. Those who insist that the South had developmental possibilities, the realization of which only the periodic return of high cotton prices prevented, have many hard questions to answer. To begin with, they have not been able to point to a single slave society in world history that realized such possibilities, nor to any country that carried through an industrial revolution without first severing the laboring classes from the means of production.

Since the South had no effective substitute for cotton as a staple, the comparative disadvantage to the older regions did not generate a significant internal shift of resources. Maryland constituted a nightmare model for the planters of the Lower South, especially those in such depressed cotton states as South Carolina. The pronounced sale of slaves to the Cotton Belt and the inability of the planters to find an adequate substitute for tobacco was steadily transforming Maryland into a free state. Virginia was undergoing a similar transformation, albeit slowly. Delaware was a slave state in name only. The

[4] The indispensable introduction to the literature remains Noel Deerr, *The History of Sugar* (2 vols., London, 1949-1950). For an evaluation of the political and economic process as a whole, see Eugene D. Genovese, *The World the Slaveholders Made: Two Essays in Interpretation* (New York, 1969), esp. 21-102.

slave sector in Missouri was declining relative to the free, and Kentucky was no longer secure. The fears of the cotton planters of the Lower South were realized during the secession crisis, when Maryland, Missouri, Kentucky, and Delaware, as well as the western counties of Virginia, remained loyal to the Union.

In other words, although the derived demand for slaves demonstrated considerable flexibility within southern labor markets, the emerging political consequences were ominous. This very mechanism was gravely weakening the social regime in the slave-selling states and thereby the political power of the slaveholders in the slave-importing states as well. To make matters worse, the renewed cotton prosperity of the 1850s threatened to speed up the process of dissolution in the Upper South. With cotton prices once again at ten cents per pound, the southeastern planters shifted land previously withdrawn back into cotton production. Thus, South Carolina, which had been exporting slaves since about 1820, found itself facing a labor shortage that promised to bid even more slaves away from Virginia and Maryland and that, for good measure, stimulated renewed interest in the reopening of the African slave trade—a measure that could only provoke the most bitter political quarrels within the South as well as between South and North.

Something similar occurred in Brazil, where the decline of sugar profits led to a shift of labor and capital from the Northeast to the gold-mining districts of Minas Gerais and later to Rio de Janeiro and the coffee-growing South. The decline also facilitated the growth of basically seigneurial labor relationships on the northeastern countryside. The social and political context differed fundamentally from that of the Old South, but in both cases the resultant decline in the political power of the slaveholders in a region once at the center of a slave society undermined the regime from within and contributed to the gathering momentum of abolitionist attack.

Consideration of some special features of the growth of the cotton economy may help clarify the argument. The spread of short-staple cotton dramatically raised the supply during the 1830s—the period known as the "flush times" of Alabama and Mississippi. Speculative slave buying ran high, fed by a politically induced expansion of bank notes. Regional growth reached eye-catching proportions, and the boldest and ablest of the planters accumulated huge fortunes. Typically, however, the supply outstripped the demand, and by the early 1840s the British textile manufacturers had stocked hundreds of thousands of bales. The panic of 1837 and the ensuing depression therefore hit the South doubly hard, for even when the worst should have been over, years of low prices continued while inventories were slowly worked off. Not until the end of the 1840s did prices recover, if we except 1838 and 1846 when good prices accompanied short crops occasioned by droughts.

During this long depression the southern press sparkled with calls for diversification, manufacturing, reallocation of resources, and elimination of middlemen's profits by promotion of direct trade with Europe. Conventions of planters and of merchants solemnly resolved upon reform and self-reliance. In the end, nothing much changed. Economists and historians continue to argue about the "causes," but the difficulties inherent in the system as a system cannot be explained away. When a shift of capital to industry, difficult enough under slavery, could be effected, the labor force, to produce adequately in manufacturing, had to be given incentives that drove the planters to protest against the subversion of discipline in the countryside.

When that problem could be kept within safe limits, the weakness of the home market, with its huge population of slaves and white subsistence farmers, took its toll. Since the system depended on export crops, the pressure to switch to manufactures came precisely at the worst time, when purchasing power was low and northern firms, facing gluts of their own, were ready to undersell newcomers. Direct trade with Europe remained a will-o'-the-wisp since imports could not keep pace with exports, and ships would have to return in ballast. A shortage of capital and entrepreneurship plagued all such attempts. Those who remain fixated on growth rates have yet to explain this dearth. And they have yet to deny that much of the accumulated wealth that was not sunk back into slaves and quantitative expansion was raked off by northern and European factors, shippers, commission merchants, insurance agents, and bankers, so that much of the multiplier effect of southern investment benefited others.

We confess to finding it absurd that Marxists should have to fight so hard to convince neoclassicists that the liberation of entrepreneurship historically accompanied the free market, especially the market in labor-power, and that entrepreneurship, like science, technology, education, and investment in "human capital" in general, arose as a function of freedom and everywhere suffered in the absence of freedom.

A few statistics on investment in human capital will suggest both the historical problem and the basis for so many diverse historical interpretations. The problem concerns only the Old South, for the slaveholding societies in the rest of the hemisphere remained entirely backward in this respect. In the South, the ratio of pupils to the white population was less than 6 percent, whereas it was more than 18 percent in the North. Since the blacks lived overwhelmingly in the South and formed the backbone of the labor force, their inclusion would cut the southern ratio by almost a half. Illiteracy statistics showed 7.5 percent for southern whites, as against only 2 percent for northern. The South had a white population less than half that of the North—roughly six to thirteen million—but it had less than one-third the schools, one-fourth the libraries, and one-half the library books. In each case, and in others that could be cited, the southern investment in "human capital" was concentrated heavily in the Upper South, with the cotton states—the heart of the slave economy—backward.

Still, the South's record did compare favorably with that of many other countries, and it has even been argued that the South deserved to rank as a major industrial power. Here again, the abstraction of statistics from the social and political context obscures the actual historical problems. The intrinsic strength of investment in human capital—its contribution to "viability"—like the economic performance in general, ultimately emerged as a political question. The southern slaveholders, beyond doubt, felt themselves gravely threatened by the outside world during the last three decades or so of their regime. Thus, only one kind of comparison makes sense: How well were they doing relative to those northern elements whose rising power threatened them so? That is, to what extent could their regime take advantage of the astonishing development of the national economy, with its ability to attract immigrant labor, advanced technology, and foreign capital without foreign control, and its ability to launch a broad-based industrial revolution capable of raising it to world power? The question answers itself. However much growth the slave economy displayed in an abstract sense, every passing year weakened the political and military power of its ruling class relative to those it had to confront.

The transportation system, too, took its toll. Of what use are the statistics that show the South with more miles of railroad than this or that country, if the structure of the system is left out of account? Those who set out to exploit colonies, and who in so many cases impoverished them, often built roads and railroads as the first order of business. The southern leaders built their own transportation system colonial-style: It bound the staple-producing plantation districts to the ports and largely bypassed the upcountry. The system did not facilitate commodity exchange within a national or regional market; it facilitated exports. Here too, it resembled other export-oriented colonies based on some form of dependent labor.

Those who wish to construct abstract models of growth and development could doubtless show that a concerted attack on these and related problems remained a theoretical possibility. Historically, however, the slaveholders had no such option. They had a common stake in slave labor as an investment, as a fountainhead of material interest, as the basis of their social system, ideology, and social psychology; and they could solve none of these problems without falling upon each other in a war of conflicting particular interests. But their class roots in slave labor set them off from the outside world and threw them collectively on the defensive. Disunity had to be avoided and divisive internal political issues kept within limits. When the degree of political unity necessary for a common policy arrived, it was based on secession, territorial expansion, and if necessary, war—on the militant defense of slave property.

During the long depression of the 1840s the South did try, with some success, to raise more foodstuffs and to retreat to subsistence in order to cushion the disaster. Even so, the rising number of bankruptcies did not lead to a diminution of output. Property changed hands, but many slaveholders were saved by massive debt repudiations, including the simple device of flight to the virgin soils of Texas and Arkansas. The individual planters, as one might expect, sought a solution to low prices in greater volume. Thus, the retreat toward subsistence in the older regions was overwhelmed by a steadily expanding slave population that represented invaluable capital gains to financially harrassed planters. Cotton production during the depressed decade rose by 88 percent, and it probably would have risen higher had more attention not been paid to the food supply.

The participants in the recent debate over the role of the demand for cotton in the economic growth of the Old South have curiously ignored the earlier history of tobacco. Yet Jacob Price, among the many valuable contributions in his excellent work, *France and the Chesapeake*,[5] suggestively analyzes the relationship between a tendency toward overproduction and a peculiar demand structure during the second and third quarters of the eighteenth century. A brief inquiry into the history of the tobacco colonies will demonstrate how, with some instructive variations, the tobacco economy during this period foreshadowed the fate of the cotton economy during the second half of the nineteenth century.

The early history of the tobacco colonies contains few surprises. Once again, an increase in world demand stimulated an expansion that quickly passed into overproduction, with attendant gluts awaiting a new surge of demand. The earliest prosperity occurred during the first half of the seventeenth century as a result of a fortuitous time lag between the burgeoning of European demand and the recognition that tobacco could easily be grown in most of Europe. Thus, the sharp rise in demand, which accompanied urban expansion and reflected the masses' first shift of income to what commentators drolly considered a luxury good, arose when the colonists had a moment of grace. Subsequently, measures by the crown, both in England and France, to restrict production at home enormously strengthened the bases of colonial production.

This expanding demand was European, not merely British. As early as the beginning of the eighteenth century, the British were exporting more than 60 percent of the tobacco shipped from America—a percentage that rose to 90 by the eve of the American Revolution. In any case, the earliest cycle based on indentured-servant labor and small freeholds passed into a new cycle based on slave labor. Between 1670 and 1690 prices fell sharply, and the structure of the Chesapeake tobacco industry began to totter. The development of North Carolina was stunted for a long time to come—a striking illustration of the extent to which the colonial economies lay at the mercy of a fickle international market for single commodities—and South Carolina turned to rice production, which tided it over until the rise of King Cotton. Rice production had the advantage of a ready market in the West Indies, which could not feed its swelling slave population. The depression made a particular impact on the Virginia-Maryland tidewater, which provides a clue to the ability of the slave economy to weather a good many such storms during the subsequent 150 years. The stronger planters, as well as the smallholders, shifted to the production of wheat and other foodstuffs. They thereby demonstrated that if they could meet interest payments on their debts, or simply avoid payment, they could retreat into subsistence and ride out the storm.

Prices rebounded by 1700, although increased competition from Holland and Germany hindered the recovery. Prices collapsed again by 1710, revived slowly during the next twenty years and more vigorously between 1730 and 1750. Thereafter, during the third quarter of the eighteenth century intermittent recession plagued the industry. The tidewater, facing rising costs and wasteful

[5] Jacob Price, *France and the Chesapeake: A History of the French Tobacco Monopoly, 1674-1791, and of Its Relationship to the British and American Tobacco Trades* (2 vols., Ann Arbor, 1973). For an evaluation of this remarkable work and a comment on the larger problems it raises, see Elizabeth Fox-Genovese's review article, *Journal of Modern History*, 46 (Dec. 1974), 691-701.

labor practices, began a shift away from tobacco and stepped up wheat production to take advantage of free-state urban markets and, much later, the Brazilian market, and the beginning of a secular reliance on the export of surplus slaves. The collapse of tobacco production at tidewater proceeded along with, and in a sense in response to, the westward expansion of tobacco production. Thus, colonial production surged forward, and with it the renewed tendency for supply to outstrip demand.

The decline of tobacco production in the West Indies accompanied the rise of sugar—a much more profitable crop—and presents no special problem. The decline at Chesapeake tidewater is another matter, for unlike the agricultural decline in the older free-labor colonies and states of British North America, the decline of the staple crop did not usher in agricultural and industrial diversification, a more balanced economy, and a renewed growth. Notwithstanding spurts of wheat production as a substitute staple, it encouraged a retreat toward subsistence, with the planters forced to shift both labor and capital out of the region altogether. This process continued in the western tobacco regions of Virginia and Kentucky down to the Civil War. True, prices periodically revived—early in the nineteenth century, for example, a booming market for cheap chewing tobacco and snuff had a salutary effect; the collapse of cotton prices between 1837 and 1849 lowered costs in the tobacco region at a time when prices were at profitable levels; and tobacco, like other southern staples, profited from the balmy conditions of the late 1850s. But as a region, the Tobacco Kingdom found itself exporting slaves, shifting toward free labor, and in danger of having the slave-labor basis of its society fatally undermined.

The market conditions of the second and third quarters of the eighteenth century shed much light on the structural weaknesses of the slave economies over time. During the seventeenth century British imperial policy had contributed significantly to the prosperity of the tobacco colonies by curtailing production at home—a policy greatly reinforced by similar action in France, which persisted throughout the *ancien régime*. The French policy of curtailing production and thereby compelling reliance on British colonial tobacco made sense, however startling at first glance. It stemmed from a heightened desire for revenues, which could not have effectively been extracted from local tobacco producers but could be extracted at high levels from the international trade. The French established a tobacco monopoly as a monopsonistic buyer. The crown thereby sacrificed the interests of French consumers and national economic prosperity to its own dynastic fiscal requirements. As a result, it raised about 7 percent of its total revenue—no small matter for a regime sliding into a protracted fiscal crisis destined to cost it its life.

The French took a large share of the tobacco that the British reexported in 1775. Indeed, the wars of 1702-1713, by severely curbing the reexport trade, undoubtedly contributed much to the earlier depression. But the significance of French demand transcended the obvious support it gave to the prosperity of Britain's North American tobacco colonies. As Price has shown, the pressures of soil exhaustion and the speculative westward movement would have produced a severe depression during the third quarter of the eighteenth century, if the monopolistic practices of the French crown had not kept international demand at an artificially high level. We are confronted, therefore, with an inversion of the situation observed for the cotton economy of the 1860s. Whereas the collapse of the cotton supply, occasioned by the Civil War in America, obscured a secular decline in world demand, in the earlier period the artificial and increasingly precarious propping-up of tobacco demand obscured an unfolding secular crisis in supply. The prosperity of the tobacco plantations revealed itself as a hostage to a world market itself subject to violent political interventions and, in any event, unlikely to facilitate, much less promote, secular economic development.

Notwithstanding the parallels and similarities between the earlier and later cycles of slave-based production in all parts of the hemisphere, a marked dissimilarity occurred in the slave reproduction rates, and the unique performance in the Old South had important economic implications. The political and economic history of the Atlantic slave trade set the stage for that unique performance. One after another, the southern states closed the trade after the Revolution in response to the moral pressure of the time and, probably much more important, to the panic engendered by the great revolution in Saint-Domingue and the renewed awareness of the explosive potential of heavy ratios of blacks to whites and African-born to American-born slaves.

This fear was nothing new. Periodically, the southern colonies had reduced the trade or shut it down completely in response to slave insurrections and conspiracies. In this way, black militancy had a profound effect on the early course of southern economic as well as political and social development. But the attitude of the southern states reflected more directly economic factors. Specifically, the deepening depression in the tobacco colonies simultaneously caused a loss of interest in slave imports and a rising interest in slave exports to the Deep South. Naturally, the closing of the African trade drove slave prices upward, with attendant capital gains for the planters of the slave-selling states. Conversely, South Carolina, alone among the slave states, reopened the African trade in an effort to replenish losses from the American Revolution and to stock slaves before the expected closure of 1808, for a promising new staple, upland cotton, was offering new opportunities.

The most dramatic part of this story came in the nineteenth century, during which the Negro population increased three-fold after the closing of the African slave trade. This period, 1800–1860, with its extraordinary demographic expansion, was precisely the period of the rise of the Cotton Kingdom and the territorial expansion of the slave system. Thus, the slave regime matured in the United States under special conditions.

The positive demographic performance predated the abolition of the African slave trade, although undoubtedly strengthened by it. Intermittent tobacco depression and periodic taxation of imports in response to fear of slave revolt provided a functional equivalent for the economic effects of abolition, but only because they proceeded within a specific social structure. In Virginia and Maryland and to a lesser extent in the Lower South, the planters, from an early date, were residents not absentees. Their exceptionally close relationship to their slaves provided some protection against the tendency of the absentee-overseer system to concentrate on quick returns at the expense of long-term investment. The South Carolina coast, however, resembled nothing so much as Barbados and was dominated by a ruling class whose "callous disregard for human life and suffering," in the words of Forrest McDonald, "was probably unmatched anywhere west of the Dnieper."[6] As might be expected, the natural increase of slaves lagged badly and matched Virginia levels only at a much later date, when conditions had changed.

The living conditions of the slaves, which proved so conducive to reproduction, undoubtedly reflected considerable initiative by the slaves themselves. The calculations by Fogel and Engerman of the nutritional value of the slaves' basic diet has come under heavy attack, but the participants on both sides of the debate have slighted the most interesting question. The slaves did not rely on the basic diet of fat pork and corn meal provided by their masters. Rather, they supplemented it by fishing, hunting, raising fowl, and keeping gardens.

The total economic performance reflected the specially favored circumstances of the North American economic system. While indebtedness remained a pressing problem, as in all the slaveholding countries and colonies, the southern planters during the nineteenth century did not have to mortgage themselves to the African slave traders. If many southern planters, in speculative bursts, bought slaves unwisely in the domestic slave trade, their misfortune was balanced by the capital gains that accrued to those in less productive areas who were selling. The large tracts of cheap land made possible a shift to food production and a retreat toward autarky during periods of low tobacco or cotton prices. In the smaller islands of the West Indies, planters had to import food for their slaves, and a collapse of sugar prices or the wartime interruption of trade, or such natural disasters as hurricanes threatened starvation. Famine did not trouble the United States during the nineteenth century, and severe underfeeding occurred only exceptionally.

These circumstances hardly justify sweeping generalizations about the entrepreneurial rationality of the master class. Indeed, they suggest a very different kind of economic flexibility, appropriate to a regime that had managed to cushion itself against the vicissitudes of the market by retaining, if not creating, a significant nonmarket sector within the heart of its export-oriented economy. And this flexibility—this particular form of adjustment to the world market—suggests nothing so much as the historical experience of merchant capital in its mobilization of precapitalist labor systems within an expanding international capitalist mode of production.

Periods of prosperity in other slave societies also invariably reflected booms in the export sector and, in every case, generated hard driving, even by local standards, and a marked tendency toward negative reproduction rates. Some highlights of Brazilian history may illustrate. Gilberto Freyre's rose-colored view of slave life in the Brazilian Northeast during the colonial period has been sharply attacked by virtually all recent scholars. The persistent dependence of the sugar plantations on the African slave trade—the inability to secure

[6] Forrest McDonald, *The Formation of the American Republic. 1776–1790* (Baltimore. 1965), 65.

anything close to an adequate rate of reproduction—has provided only one kind of evidence to support the contrary view that Brazil was indeed a hell for blacks. Freyre has been charged, among other things, with having read nineteenth-century evidence back into the seventeenth and eighteenth centuries— that is, with confusing conditions of economic decline and stagnation, reminiscent of Maryland and Virginia, with conditions of economic boom reminiscent of Alabama and Mississippi during their flush times.[7]

The evidence from the early nineteenth century also supports Freyre's critics. With the collapse of Saint-Domingue, the value of Brazil's sugar exports rose by 1,000 percent, and the emphasis on maximum exploitation of labor was temporarily reintroduced. The great slave revolts that shook Bahia between 1807 and 1835, the last of which came within an ace of success, may in part be attributed to these economic conditions.

The nineteenth-century experience in Cuba paralleled that of the sugar-growing Brazilian Northeast. The collapse of the sugar industry in Saint-Domingue spurred the transformation of Cuba. A small-farm, tobacco-growing economy gave way to a plantation economy that frenetically produced sugar and consumed slaves. Cuba, which had enjoyed a reputation during the eighteenth century for being one of the New World's gentler and more humane slave countries became, during the nineteenth, one of the harshest and most brutal. Simultaneously, southern Brazil arose on the strength of a coffee boom, fed by a vigorous if illicit African slave trade. The coffee planters drove their slaves mercilessly, not only in response to the lure of an expanding world market, but also in the knowledge that the fall of the Confederacy placed slavery everywhere on borrowed time. In the Old South, the slave regime, however brutal and exploitative, developed under social conditions that substantially cushioned the worst effects of financial speculation and world market pressures.

At the root of the interpretation sketched here lies a particular evaluation of the historical role of merchant capital, which Marx first advanced and Maurice Dobb developed.[8] It insists that merchant capital has exerted a conservative influence in all except the most extraordinary circumstances and that under seigneurial and other precapitalist modes of production it has generally retarded industrial development while stimulating economic growth. Modern

[7] Gilberto Freyre, *The Masters and the Slaves: A Study in the Development of Brazilian Civilization*, trans. Samuel Putnam (New York, 1964). The rejection of Freyre's interpretation appears to be complete, but controversy continues to rage over the alternatives. For our viewpoint and citations to those of others, see Eugene D. Genovese, "Materialism and Idealism in the History of Negro Slavery in the Americas," *In Red and Black: Marxian Explorations in Southern and Afro-American History* (New York, 1971), 23–52. Important work has appeared since then, but we know of no attempt to resurrect Freyre's interpretation.

[8] Maurice Dobb, *Studies in the Development of Capitalism* (New York, 1947). See also R. H. Hilton, ed., *The Transition from Feudalism to Capitalism* (London, 1976). Our views on this problem are elaborated in Eugene D. Genovese, *World the Slaveholders Made*, 3–113; and Elizabeth Fox-Genovese, *The Origins of Physiocracy: Economic Revolution and Social Order in Eighteenth-Century France* (Ithaca, 1976); Elizabeth Fox-Genovese, "The Physiocratic Model and the Transition from Feudalism to Capitalism," *Journal of European Economic History*, IV (Winter 1975), 725–37; and Elizabeth Fox-Genovese, "Poor Richard at Work in the Cotton Fields: A Critique of the Psychological and Ideological Presuppositions of *Time on the Cross*," *Review of Radical Political Economics*, VII (Fall 1975), 67–83.

colonial and plantation economies, based on monoculture and subjected to the sway of commercial capital, have embodied features of two different economic systems. They have arisen from the world capitalist mode of production and have, from the beginning and virtually by definition, functioned within a world market. But they have simultaneously rested on slave or other dependent labor systems that have deprived them of the best social and ideological as well as economic advantages of a market in labor-power, in contradistinction to that market in labor itself which slavery's capitalization of labor made possible.

Thus, among other ramifications, the macroeconomic structure of the plantation sector of the world economy had only an indirect relationship to the microeconomic structure of individual plantations, considered as firms. Both structures exhibited economies of scale in the production of crops that can command a viable, if sometimes speculative, price on a market external to the system of commodity exchange and labor control within the individual firms.

Whatever the contribution of economies of scale, the slaveholders' most powerful advantage over the yeomen was, as Gavin Wright has pointed out, financial.[9] So long as the economy depended upon monoculture and the export market, with little chance to shift resources internally, those with the capital to command land and slaves had disproportionately large opportunities. In other words, the very dependence of the slave system on commercial capital created massive, if temporary, opportunities for the ruling class to amass great wealth.

The colonial expansion of capitalism not only absorbed precapitalist economic systems; it created them. The enserfment of the Russian peasants during and after the sixteenth century, the second serfdom in eastern Europe, the economic exploitation of the highland Indian communities of Mexico and Peru, and the rise of plantation-based slave regimes in the American lowlands may, from this point of view, be seen as varying expressions of colonial capitalist expansion. They represent nothing so much as the power of commercial capital to adjust unfree labor systems to the rising demand of West European mass markets, which themselves, however paradoxically, arose on free labor—on the emergence of labor-power into a commodity. Within this process, slavery represented a major advance over quasi-seigneurial alternatives, for it permitted greater economic rationalization and a more flexible labor market.

What slavery could not do, despite its economies of scale and its financial advantages, was to lay the foundations for sustained growth and qualitative development. Nowhere did it advance science and technology; generate self-expanding home markets adequate to encourage industrial diversification; accumulate capital within its own sphere for industrial development; or encourage the kind of entrepreneurship without which modern industry would have been unthinkable. In these economic terms, therefore, it produced spectacular growth in response to the demand of an outside society but

[9] Gavin Wright, "Prosperity, Progress, and American Slavery," in David, Gutman, Sutch, Temin, Wright, *Reckoning with Slavery*, 302–38. See also Gavin Wright, *The Political Economy of the Cotton South: Households, Markets, and Wealth in the Nineteenth Century* (New York, 1978).

simultaneously guaranteed stagnation and decline once that support was withdrawn.

Fogel and Engerman have reasonably stressed the long periods of prosperity for the slaveholders and economic growth for the slave economies as *prima facie* evidence of viability. Their argument, while reasonable in terms of the bourgeois economics they share with most of their critics, reopens the question of what bourgeois economists and historians, whether for or against Fogel and Engerman, mean by viability. From our point of view, viability can only refer to the political security of the human beings who commanded the regimes—to the slaveholders. And at that, there remains the theoretical possibility, noted by Fogel and Engerman themselves, that a socially retrogressive regime might achieve such viability by inflicting unspeakable horrors on its people. But that trifle aside, nothing in the interesting and discretely valuable new work in economic history undermines the thesis that slavery condemned the slaveholders to a political fate which makes all appeals to the prosperity of a *longue durée* beside the point. For the specific kind of economic stagnation that their economies suffered closed the road to an industrial revolution—to that economic development without which the slaveholders remained at the mercy of their enemies. That the confrontation with those enemies took half a century or more to unfold poses interesting secondary questions but does not weaken the primary argument.

All slave societies in the New World met the same economic fate and left wrecks in their wake. That of the Old South, however, had a special quality. In striking contrast to the West Indies and in partial contrast to Brazil, the Old South produced a slaveholding class capable of seizing regional political power and of deeply influencing national politics for more than half a century. Thus, the structural economic deficiencies of the regime did much more than create painful problems of readjustment once the world demand schedule for staples slackened. Rather, they confronted, even in anticipation, a powerful retrograde social class with the prospect of defeat and disaster.

Only in this political context do discussions of the economic viability of slavery take on meaning. And in the end, the historical verdict sustains the older view against all revisionist caveats: Northern freedom, not southern slavery, generated the political, economic, and military wherewithal for the nation's survival, development, and rise to world power.

EUGENE D. GENOVESE

MATERIALISM AND IDEALISM IN THE HISTORY OF NEGRO SLAVERY IN THE AMERICAS

The study of Negro slavery in the United States is verging on a new and welcome development as historians begin to appreciate the need for a hemispheric perspective. In 1950 Allan Nevins entitled the appropriate chapter of his *Emergence of Lincoln* "Slavery in a World Setting," and in 1959 Stanley M. Elkins rescued the work of Frank Tannenbaum from an undeserved obscurity. It was Tannenbaum's remarkable essay, *Slave & Citizen* (1947) that first demonstrated the sterility of treating Southern slavery in national isolation, although the point had been made previously. Oliveira Lima, as early as 1914, had discussed the profound differences between Brazilian and North American race relations and historical experiences with slavery, and Gilberto Freyre has been offering suggestive comparisons since the 1920's.[1] Without making unreasonable claims for Tannenbaum's originality, we may credit him with having been the first to show that only a hemispheric treatment could enable us to understand the relationship between slavery and race relations and the social and political dynamics of the transition from slavery to freedom. Simultaneously, the questions Tannenbaum posed and the method he suggested wiped out the line between history and the social sciences. Elkins' controversial book illustrates how quickly the discussion must pass into considerations of psychology and anthropology. The improved prospects for comparative analysis derive in part from the advances being made by Spanish American and especially Brazilian historians, sociologists, and anthropologists and in part, as Magnus

---

EUGENE D. GENOVESE is professor of history at Sir George Williams University.
[1] Allan Nevins, *The Emergence of Lincoln*, 2 vols. (New York, 1950); Frank Tannenbaum, *Slave & Citizen: The Negro in the Americas* (New York, 1947); Manoel de Oliveira Lima, *The Evolution of Brazil Compared with that of Spanish and Anglo-Saxon America* (Stanford, 1914); Roy Nash, *The Conquest of Brazil* (New York, 1926); Gilberto Freyre, "Social Life in Brazil in the Middle of the Nineteenth Century," *Hispanic American Historical Review*, V (Nov. 1922), 597-628.

Mörner suggests, from the excellent work done recently on slavery in the Iberian peninsula itself.[2]

Under the circumstances it is appropriate that the first sweeping assault on Tannenbaum's thesis should come from Marvin Harris, an anthropologist, and equally appropriate that the assault implicitly should accept Tannenbaum's main point—that slavery and race relations must be studied hemispherically.[3] The argument has been joined on two levels: on such specific questions as the significance of different slave codes, the degree of paternalism in the social system, and the daily treatment of slaves; and on such general questions of method and philosophy as reflect the age-old struggle between idealist and materialist viewpoints. The specific questions will hopefully be settled in due time by empirical research; the second are likely to stay with us. Since empirical research will necessarily be conditioned by contending viewpoints, we must make every effort to clarify the methodological and philosophical issues or risk wasting a great deal of time and effort talking past each other and chasing solutions to spurious problems. The value of Harris's book, apart from specific contributions to our knowledge, is that it extends the discussion in a fruitful way. Presumably, its deficiencies of style will not deny it a hearing. Unlike Harris's *The Nature of Cultural Things*, which comes close to being unreadable, *Patterns of Race in the Americas*, despite lapses into unnecessary jargon and some regrettable rhetoric, is straightforward and vigorous. Unfortunately, it is marred by savage polemical excursions. Harris appears to be a man of strong and, to me, admirable social views, but I fear that he is among those who confuse ideological zeal with bad manners. As a result, his harsh attacks on opposing scholars, some of whom are deservedly respected for their fairness and generosity to others, often result in unjust and arbitrary appraisals of their work and, in any case, leave the reader with a bad taste.

I propose to discuss Harris's demand for a materialist alternative to the idealist framework of Tannenbaum, Freyre, and Elkins and

[2] Magnus Mörner, "The History of Race Relations in Latin America: Comments on the State of Research," *Latin American Research Review*, I (1966), 17-44. Pages 35-44 contain an excellent bibliography.

[3] Marvin Harris, *Patterns of Race in the Americas* (New York, 1964). Since Harris published, David Brion Davis has brought out his splendid *The Problem of Slavery in Western Culture* (New York, 1966), which takes up a critical stance toward Tannenbaum. His criticisms, which will be noted briefly below, are tangential to the main task of his book. Harris's book is, so far, the only attempt to replace the full burden of Tannenbaum's argument.

to avoid, so far as possible, discussions of specific differences about data. Those differences may be left to specialists and will not be resolved without much more work by scholars in several disciplines. I propose, too, to ignore Harris's illuminating work on the highland Indian societies. Since the book has much to offer on these and other themes it should be understood that no balanced review is intended here. Even if the book suffers from as grave weaknesses of method and assumption as I believe, it would retain considerable value on other levels and may properly be evaluated more fully elsewhere.

Tannenbaum divides the slave systems of the western hemisphere into three groups—Anglo-Saxon, Iberian, and French. The Anglo-Saxon group lacked an "effective slave tradition," a slave law, and religious institutions concerned with the Negro; the Iberian had a slave tradition and law and a religious institution imbued with the "belief that the spiritual personality of the slave transcended his slave status"; the French shared the religious principles of the Iberian but lacked a slave tradition and law.[4] Tannenbaum, to his cost, ignores the French case and does not, for example, discuss the *Code Noir.* Were he to do so, he might reflect further on the significance of the Iberian codes, for the *Code Noir* was notoriously a dead letter in Saint-Dominigue.

The burden of Tannenbaum's argument rests on his estimate of the strength of the Catholic Church in relation to the landowners and of the extent to which the law could be or was enforced. He undoubtedly takes too sanguine a view of Brazilian slavery and simultaneously greatly underestimates the force of community pressure and paternalism in reducing the harshness of the Southern slave codes. He risks broad generalizations and necessarily sacrifices much in the process; many of his generalizations, with qualifications, nonetheless obtain. The essential point is not that Brazilian slaves received kinder treatment, but that they had greater access to freedom and once free could find a secure place in the developing national culture. Tannenbaum, accepting the authority of Gilberto Freyre, does suggest a correlation between class mobility, the absence or weakness of racism, and kind treatment, but he does so tentatively, and it forms no essential part of his argument.

Tannenbaum demonstrates that the current status of the Negro in the several societies of the New World has roots in the attitude

---

[4] Tannenbaum, p. 65, n. 153.

toward the Negro as a slave, which reflected the total religious, legal, and moral history of the enslaving whites. From this assertion he proceeds to a number of theses of varying value. When, for example, he relates the acceptance of the "moral personality" of the Negro to the peaceful quality of abolition, we may well wonder about Haiti, or about Brazil, where the peaceful abolition followed decades of bloody slave insurrections and social disorders,[5] or about the British islands, where peaceful abolition followed a denial of that moral personality. We may, accordingly, take the book apart; it was intended to open, not close, the discussion of an enormously complicated subject. The essentials of the viewpoint remain in force: (1) Slavery was a moral as well as a legal relationship; (2) where tradition, law, and religion combined to recognize the moral personality of the slave, the road to freedom remained open, and the absorption of the freedmen into the national culture was provided for; (3) the recognition of moral personality flowed from the emergent slaveholders' legal and religious past, the extent and nature of their contact with darker peoples, and their traditional view of man and God—of their total historical experience and its attendant world view. Tannenbaum draws the lines much too tightly. As David Brion Davis shows, the duality of the slave as man and thing always created problems for enslavers, who rarely if ever were able to deny the slave a moral personality.[6] We may nonetheless note a wide range of behavior and attitude within such recognition, and Tannenbaum's problem therefore remains with us.

The great weakness in Tannenbaum's presentation is that it ignores the material foundations of each particular slave society, especially the class relations, for an almost exclusive concern with tradition and cultural continuity. Tannenbaum thereby avoids essential questions. How, for example, did the material conditions of life in the slave countries affect their cultural inheritance? Tannenbaum implies the necessary victory of the inheritance over contrary tendencies arising from immediate material conditions. Thus, Harris can label his viewpoint idealist and insist, as a materialist, that material conditions determine social relations and necessarily prevail over counter-tendencies in the historical tradition. The special usefulness of Harris's book lies in the presentation

---

[5] Richard Graham, "Causes of the Abolition of Slavery in Brazil: An Interpretive Essay," *Hispanic American Historical Review*, XLVI (May 1966), 123-137.

[6] Davis, *passim*. This point is one of the leading theses of Davis's book.

of an alternative, materialist interpretation and the concomitant attention paid to many problems that Tannenbaum avoids or obscures. Unfortunately, his materialism, like that of such earlier writers as Eric Williams, is generally mechanical and soon reveals itself as a sophisticated variant of economic determinism. It is, in short, ahistorical.

Harris vigorously attacks Freyre for asserting that Brazil has been a virtual "racial paradise," but his discussion actually reinforces Freyre's argument. Harris, like Charles Wagley,[7] insists on a close relationship between class and race and insists that Brazilian Negroes have always faced intense discrimination because of their lower-class status. Brazil's racial paradise, he argues, is occupied only by "fictional creatures"; the real Negroes of Bahia and elsewhere suffer immensely as members of the lower classes in a country in which the rule of thumb alleges a correlation between class and race.[8]

Harris slips into a position that Wagley largely avoids. Wagley, too, attacks Freyre by drawing attention to the class dimension of race relations. He denies the absence of racism and refers to the "widely documented color prejudice in almost every part of the nation."[9] Yet, Wagley properly adds that despite prejudice and discrimination Brazilian racial democracy is no myth. Brazilians happily do not usually put their racial chatter into practice: Continuing miscegenation undermines racial lines, and the doctrine that "money whitens the skin" prevails. In these terms, so different from those which might be applied to the United States, we may look at Brazilian racial democracy as a reality relative to other societies, or as myth relative to national standards and pretensions and fully appreciate the force of Octavio Ianni's reference to "the intolerable contradiction between the myth of racial democracy and the actual discrimination against Negroes and mulattoes."[10]

The admirable work of C. R. Boxer at first glance supports Harris against Freyre, but that glance proves deceptive. Boxer dismisses as "twaddle" the notion that no color bar exists in the Portuguese-speaking world and brings us back to earth from Freyre's flights of romantic fancy, but he does not overthrow the

---

[7] Charles Wagley, *An Introduction to Brazil* (New York, 1963), p. 132.
[8] Harris, p. 64.
[9] Wagley, p. 238; *cf.* pp. 140-142.
[10] Octavio Ianni, *Raças e classes socialis no Brasil* (Rio de Janiero, 1966), p. 15.

essentials of Freyre's argument.[11] What Boxer does show is how painful a struggle has had to be waged and how much racism has persisted. The strides toward racial democracy that he describes in *Race Relations in the Portuguese Colonial Empire, Portuguese Society in the Tropics, The Golden Age of Brazil,* and elsewhere remain impressive when considered against Anglo-Saxon models. The question is what accounts for the greater "plasticity" (to use Freyre's word) of the Portuguese. The economic and demographic features of colonization, stressed almost exclusively by Harris, played a great role, but the careful research of so skeptical and cautious a historian as Boxer shows the force of legal, moral, religious, and national traditions. Viewed polemically, Boxer's work destroys the propagandistic nonsense of Dr. Salazar's court historians but only qualifies the main lines of argument in Freyre and Tannenbaum.

In asserting a racial paradise all Freyre could possibly mean is that considerable racial mobility exists and that discrimination is held within tolerable bounds. The criticisms of Wagley, Harris, Boxer, and others demonstrate the existence of an acute class question with a racial dimension; they do not refute Freyre's main claim that society is not, by the standards of the Anglo-Saxon countries, racially rent. Freyre is undoubtedly open to criticism, for he slides impermissably from race to class. He insists that miscegenation "never permitted the endurance in absolute antagonisms of that separation of men into masters and slaves imposed by the system of production. Nor the exaggerated development of a mystique of white supremacy nor of nobility."[12] When he writes that miscegenation negated the class antagonism of master and slave, he talks nonsense; but when he writes that it inhibited—he does not say prevented—a mystique of white supremacy, he is surely correct.

Freyre, possibly in response to criticism of his earlier exaggerations, tries to qualify his lyrical praise of Luso-Brazilian racial attitudes and practices. Sometimes, although by no means consistently even in his most recent work, his evaluations are so well balanced as virtually to accept the criticisms and qualifications offered on all sides:

---

[11] C. R. Boxer, *Salvador de Sá and the Struggle for Brazil and Angola, 1602-1686* (London, 1952), p. 235.
[12] Gilberto Freyre, *O Mundo que o portugues criou & Uma Cultura ameaçada: A Luso-Brasileira* (Lisbon, 1940), p. 41.

Not that there is no race or color prejudice mixed with class prejudice in Brazil. There is. . . . But no one in Brazil would think of laws against interracial marriage. No one would think of barring colored people from theatres or residential sections of a town.[13]

The main point for Freyre is not that race prejudice has been absent but that "few Brazilian aristocrats were as strict about racial impurity as the majority of the Anglo-Saxon aristocrats of the Old South were"[14] and that the Brazilian Negro "has been able to express himself as a Brazilian and has not been forced to behave as an ethnic and cultural intruder."[15] Harris writes: "Races do not exist for Brazilians. But classes do exist both for the observer and *for* the Brazilians."[16] With these words he surrenders the argument.

Law, Church, and cultural tradition are not viewed by Tannenbaum, or even Freyre, as unambiguous forces for racial equality. Both men appreciate the internal conflicts and are concerned with the different outcomes of these conflicts in different cultures. "The colonial governments, the Spaniards, and the *criollos* treated the mestizo as an inferior human being."[17] Much race prejudice, Tannenbaum adds, existed and exists against Indians and Negroes throughout Latin America. He notes too, in a striking comment on class and race, that United States Negroes can and do advance themselves personally in the economic, social, and political arenas with greater ease than do Latin American Negroes, for whom class rigidities and the economic backwardness of society present severe. limitations.[18] The distance between rich and poor, cultured and uncultured in Latin America "is obviously not racial, not biological, nor based on color of skin or place of origin, but it is perhaps even more effective as a dividing line, and perhaps more permanent. It is an ingrained part of the total scheme of things."[19]

---

[13] Gilberto Freyre, *New World in the Tropics: The Culture of Modern Brazil* (New York, 1963), p. 8. At that, he underestimates the extent of prejudice and discrimination. See *e.g.,* the important sociological studies of Fernando Henrique Cardoso and Octavio Ianni, *Côr e mobilidade social em Florianópolis* (São Paulo, 1960); and Roger Bastide and Florestan Fernandes, *Brancos e negros em São Paulo,* 2ª ed. (São Paulo, 1959).
[14] Freyre, *New World,* p. 82.
[15] Freyre, *New World,* p. 144.
[16] Harris, p. 64. Original emphasis.
[17] Frank Tannenbaum, *Ten Keys to Latin America* (New York, 1965), p. 43.
[18] Tannenbaum, *Ten Keys,* pp. 49-51.
[19] Tannenbaum, *Ten Keys,* p. 52. Similarly Elkins draws attention to Hispanic race prejudice and discrimination against Negroes. "Was there squalor, filth, widespread depression of the masses? Much more so than with us—but there it was the class system and economic 'underdevelopment,' rather than the color

Harris rejects, on principle, the idea that Portuguese tradition, law, and religion could overcome the counter-pressures inherent in Brazilian slavery. He makes some strange assumptions in his often admirable discussion of political relations of Church, state, and landowner in highland and lowland America. He properly portrays each as a separate entity, struggling for control of material resources, but he portrays them as only that. Apart from a grudging phrase here and there (and we find a touch of sarcasm even there), he leaves no room for landowners who on many matters would follow the advice and teaching of the Church simply out of religious commitment, nor for a state apparatus deeply infused with Catholic ethics, nor for a Church with a genuine sense of responsibility for the salvation of souls. Instead, he offers us three collective forms of economic man. Harris repeatedly dismisses as romantic nonsense and the like arguments appealing to Catholic sensibility or inherited values. He misses much of Tannenbaum's implicit schema of a society resting on a balance of power between state, church, and family-based economic interests, and he misses Elkins' acute restatement of Tannenbaum's schema as descriptive of a precapitalist society in which minimal room is provided for unrestricted economic impulse.

The burden of Harris's criticism lies in his badly named chapter, "The Myth of the Friendly Master." He begins by asserting that "Differences in race relations within Latin America are at root a matter of the labor systems in which the respective subordinate and superordinate groups become enmeshed. . . . A number of cultural traits and institutions which were permitted to survive or were deliberately encouraged under one system were discouraged or suppressed in the other. . . ."[20] He contrasts his view with those of Tannenbaum and Freyre: "It is their contention that the laws, values, religious precepts, and personalities of the English colonists differed from those of the Iberian colonists. These initial psychological and ideological differences were sufficient to overcome whatever tendency the plantation system may have exerted toward parallel rather than divergent evolution."[21] Tannenbaum and Freyre may be read this way but need not be. Harris has reduced their

---

barrier, that made the difference" (*Slavery: A Problem in American Institutional and Intellectual Life* [Chicago, 1959], p. 79).

[20] Harris, p. 65.
[21] Harris, pp. 65-66.

position to its most idealistic and superficial expression. Harris is not alone among social scientists of deserved reputation in caricaturing their ideas. K. Oberg, for example, hails *Patterns of Race in the Americas* for having demolished the supposedly prevalent notion that these patterns could be traced to "the Iberian soul or the inherent racism of the Anglo-Saxon."[22] For polemical purposes this reading scores points, but it does not get us very far. Tannenbaum and Freyre may be—and in my opinion ought to be—read another way, for each in effect describes the historical formation of slaveholding classes.

It is easy but unenlightening to dismiss discussions of psychology and ideology as if they were mere prejudices of romantics when laid against material interests. Harris, like every sensible man, rejects "simplistic economic determinism" and single-factor explanations,[23] but on close inspection he rejects the simplistic rather than the economic determinism. "From the standpoint of an evolutionary science of culture," he writes, "it matters not at all if one starts first with changes in the techno-environmental complex or first with changes in the institutional matrix; what matters is whether or not there is a correlation."[24] For him, however, the correlation reduces itself to an ideological reflection of the material reality. What Harris's materialism, in contradistinction to Marxian materialism, fails to realize is that once an ideology arises it alters profoundly the material reality and in fact becomes a partially autonomous feature of that reality. As Antonio Gramsci says about Marx's more sophisticated and useful comments on the role of ideas in history:

The analysis of these statements, I believe, reinforces the notion of "historical bloc," in which the material forces are the content and ideologies the form—merely an analytical distinction since material forces would be historically inconceivable without form and since ideologies would have to be considered individual dabbling without material forces.[25]

This understanding of ideology and economics as reciprocally in-

[22] K. Oberg, Comment on Harris's article, "The Cultural Ecology of India's Sacred Cattle," *Current Anthropology*, VII (Feb. 1966), 62.
[23] *Cf.*, Marvin Harris, "The Economy Has No Surplus?" *American Anthropologist*, LXI (April 1959), 188.
[24] Harris, "The Economy Has No Surplus?" p. 194.
[25] Antonio Gramsci, *Il Materialismo storico e la filosofia di Benedetto Croce* (Turin, 1949), p. 49.

fluential manifestations of particular forms of class rule may be contrasted with Harris's mechanistic and economistic view. He replies to a friendly critic who seeks to defend him against the charge of economic determinism by embracing it proudly: "I share with all economic determinists the conviction that in the long run and in most cases ideology is swung into line by material conditions—by the evolution of techno-environmental and production relationships."[26] Psychology and ideology are, however, as much a part of class formation as economic interest. Harris implies that ideology simply reflects material interests, which fluctuate sharply, but the ideology of a ruling class ought to be understood as its world view—the sum of its interests and sensibilities, past and present. An essential function of the ideology of a ruling class is to present to itself and to those it rules a coherent world view that is sufficiently flexible, comprehensive, and mediatory to convince the subordinate classes of the justice of its hegemony. If this ideology were no more than a reflection of immediate economic interests, it would be worse than useless, for the hypocrisy of the class, as well as its greed, would quickly become apparent to the most abject of its subjects.[27]

Harris admits that the Portuguese in Portugal exhibited little race prejudice but adds that "This datum can only be significant to those who believe that discrimination is caused by prejudice, when the true relationship is quite the opposite."[28] He argues, especially for Brazil, along the lines that the Marxists, Eric Williams and C. L. R. James, have argued for the Caribbean and that American Marxists and non-Marxists like Herbert Aptheker and the Handlins have argued for the United States.[29] Unhappily, Harris asserts what needs to be proven, and the assertion exposes the fundamental weakness in his ideological armor: He insists, on principle, that the relation-

---

[26] Marvin Harris, Reply to Criticism, appended to his article, "The Cultural Ecology of India's Sacred Cattle," *Current Anthropology*, VII (Feb. 1966), 64.

[27] The most suggestive discussions of the problem from a Marxian point of view are to be found in Gramsci's *Opere*, but see also John M. Cammett's excellent introduction to Gramsci's life and thought, *Antonio Gramsci and the Origins of Italian Communism* (Stanford, 1967).

[28] Harris, *Patterns of Race*, p. 67.

[29] *Cf.*, Eric Williams, *Capitalism & Slavery* (New York, 1961) and *The Negro in the Caribbean* (Manchester, England, 1942); Herbert Aptheker, *American Negro Slave Revolts* (New York, 1943); Oscar and Mary F. Handlin, "Origins of the Southern Labor System," *William and Mary Quarterly*, 3rd Series, VII (April 1950), 199-222; C. L. R. James, *The Black Jacobins: Toussaint L'Ouverture and the San Domingo Revolution*, 2nd ed. (1963).

ship must be one way and makes the case for materialism rest on this dogma. "If, as asserted, the Iberians initially lacked any color prejudice, what light does this shed upon the Brazilian and other lowland interracial systems?"[30] According to this view, the past plays no vital role in the present except for transmitted technology. If the case for materialism rests on a denial of the totality of human history and on the resurrection of an economic determinism brought to a higher level of sophistication, materialism has poor prospects.

It is easy to dismiss as idealism or subjectivity the view that prejudice existed prior to discrimination, but the tenacious defense of this position by such sober and diverse scholars as Carl Degler, Juan Comas, Arnold A. Sio, and David Brion Davis ought to give us pause. Davis recounts the various origins of anti-Negro prejudice in Europe. "The fact that Africans had traditionally been associated with Noah's curse of Canaan," he notes for example, "may have disposed some Europeans to regard them as suitable for bondage."[31] Winthrop D. Jordan has made a simple point to present us with a complex reality. He has convincingly traced the origins of anti-Negro prejudice in New England to the prior existence of slavery, discrimination, and racism in Barbados.[32] Thus, we may obediently agree on the materialist formula—exploitation→discrimination→prejudice—and find ourselves nowhere except with the further ahistorical assumption that ideas, once called into being, have no life of their own.[33] As M. I. Finley observes:

For most of human history labor for others has been involuntary. . . . Slavery in that context must have different overtones from slavery in a context of free labor. The way slavery declined in the Roman Empire . . . illustrates that. Neither moral values nor economic interests nor the social order were threatened by the transformation of slaves and

[30] Harris, *Patterns of Race*, p. 68.
[31] Davis, p. 281.
[32] Carl Degler, "Slavery and the Genesis of American Race Prejudice," *Comparative Studies in Society and History*, II (Oct. 1959), 49-66; Juan Comas, "Recent Research on Racial Relations—Latin America," *International Social Science Journal*, XIII, No. 2 (1961), 271-299, esp. p. 291; Arnold A. Sio, "Interpretations of Slavery: The Slave Status in the Americas," *Comparative Studies in Society and History*, VII (April 1965), 289-308; Winthrop D. Jordan, "The Influence of the West Indies on the Origins of New England Slavery," *William and Mary Quarterly*, 3rd Series, XVIII (April 1961), 243-250.
[33] In another essay Jordan gropes for a formulation that would subsume both prejudice and discrimination instead of relating them to each other causally. His answer is neither clear nor convincing, but he has presented the problem in a sensitive and illuminating way. See "Modern Tensions and the Origins of American Slavery," *Journal of Southern History*, XXVIII (Feb. 1962), 18-30.

free peasants together into tied serfs. They were—or at least many powerful elements in society thought they were—by proposals to convert slaves into free men.

What sets the slave apart from all other forms of involuntary labor is that in the strictest sense, he is an outsider. He is brought into a new society violently and traumatically; he is cut off from all traditional human ties of kin and nation and even his own religion; he is prevented from creating new ties, except to his masters, and in consequence his descendants are as much outsiders, as unrooted, as he was. . . .

Dr. [Eric] Williams holds that "slavery was not born of racism, rather racism was the consequence of slavery." One wishes profoundly that one could believe that. However, the slave-outsider formula argues the other way, as does the fact that as early as the 1660s southern colonies decreed that henceforth all Negroes who were imported should be slaves, but whites should be indentured servants and not slaves. The connection between slavery and racism has been a dialectical one, in which each element reinforced the other.[34]

The most balanced and suggestive statement on the Portuguese remains Boxer's:

One race cannot systematically enslave members of another on a large scale for over three centuries without acquiring a conscious or unconscious feeling of racial superiority.[35]

The good sense of this observation enables us to grasp the necessarily racist influence of Negro slavery on European cultures without destroying our ability to distinguish between levels of influence and without compelling us to turn our backs on either historical-traditional or ecological processes.[36] The work of the distinguished Brazilian Marxian scholar, Caio Prado, Jr., may be cited as an illustration of the way in which the force of the historical inheritance can be taken into account in a materialist analysis. For Prado the historical conditioning stressed by Freyre and Tannenbaum played its part precisely because the material basis of life and espe-

[34] M. I. Finley, review of Davis, *The Problem of Slavery* in *New York Review of Books*, VIII (Jan. 26, 1967), 10.

[35] C. R. Boxer, *Race Relations in the Portuguese Colonial Empire, 1415-1825* (Oxford, 1963), p. 56.

[36] Regrettably, even Boxer slights the historical dimension. It is noteworthy that he begins his survey, *Race Relations*, with the conquest of Ceuta in 1415 and leaves aside the racial conditioning of Portuguese life that preceded it. For an excellent statement of the intersection of tradition and economic milieu in the formation of Brazilian attitudes see Roger Bastide, "Race Relations in Brazil," *International Social Science Bulletin*, IX, No. 4 (1957), 495-512, esp. 495-496.

cially the class relationships provided room for it to breathe, but, given this room, it seriously affected that basis and those relationships.[37]

Harris's failure to grasp the historical and class nature of Tannenbaum's argument appears most strikingly in his reference to English law. Tannenbaum notes that slavery and a slave code had long disappeared in England, which therefore had no legal tradition to humanize the practice of colonial slavery. "Why this legal lacuna should have been significant for the course run by slavery in the United States is quite obscure."[38] There is nothing obscure about it, and Harris could find the answer in Elkins' discussion of a slave system's rise amidst an "uncontrolled capitalism." Here again, idealists or no, Tannenbaum and Elkins have greatly deepened our understanding of the processes by which specific slaveholding classes were formed, and those processes are, or ought to be, the central concern of a materialist interpretation of history.

"At one point, and one point only," Harris writes, "is there a demonstrable correlation between the laws and behavior, the ideal and the actual, in Tannenbaum's theory: the Spanish and Portuguese codes ideally drew no distinction between the ex-slave and the citizen, and the actual behavior followed suit."[39] This one point kills Harris's argument since Tannenbaum set out to explain the absorption of former slaves into the national culture in Brazil and the extreme difficulties in the United States. Harris has much to offer to complement the work of Freyre and Tannenbaum. In particular, he is strong on the economic and material exigencies of colonial Brazil and their influence in promoting race patterns. Instead of seeing a two-fold process within which colonial conditions reinforced tradition and allowed it to expand and within which tradition altered, however secondarily, material conditions, he insists dogmatically on either/or. "One can be certain that if it had been materially disadvantageous to the Latin colonists, it would never have been tolerated—Romans, *Siete Partidas* and the Catholic Church notwithstanding."[40] Harris may be certain; others may be permitted some doubt. Had such a divergence occurred, the out-

---

[37] Caio Prado Junior, *Formação do Brasil contemporaneo: Colonia,* 7ª ed. (São Paulo, n.d.), pp. 103-104; *Evolução política do Brasil e outros estudos,* 4ª ed. (São Paulo, n.d.), pp. 46-47.

[38] Harris, *Patterns of Race,* p. 70.

[39] Harris, *Patterns of Race,* p. 79.

[40] Harris, *Patterns of Race,* p. 81.

come would have been determined by the strength of the contending forces, with Church and state opposing slaveholders and with the conscience and consciousness of the slaveholders split among various commitments. Harris's crystal ball-gazing constitutes not materialism but fatalism, not history but a secular equivalent of theology.

Harris misunderstands and misrepresents Tannenbaum as arguing that Negro slaves were better treated in Brazil than in the United States. Tannenbaum does express such an opinion, but he merely accepts Freyre's probably erroneous judgment; it forms no essential part of his thesis. Tannenbaum could live comfortably with evidence that Brazilian slaves were treated more harshly than American, for his case rests on the degree of class and race mobility. Harris, by identifying Tannenbaum with Freyre here and by merging two separate theses in Freyre, confuses the issues. Elkins argues quite sensibly that Hispanic slaves could have been more severely mistreated than American "without altering the comparison." Harris replies, in one of his most inexcusable polemical outbursts, with sarcasm and personal abuse, but he does not reply to the argument.[41]

Harris's discussion of demographic and economic forces in the formation of a mulatto population and a class of free blacks is a solid contribution, notwithstanding some statistical juggling, but the methodological difficulties reappear. He insists that Brazilian slaveholders "had no choice but to create a class of half-castes" to function as soldiers, cattlemen, food-growers, and intermediaries of various kinds.[42] Unlike the United States, he notes, Brazil lacked a white population large enough to serve as a middle class and to provide a political and military establishment. Brazilian slaveholders consequently smiled on the elevation of the mulattoes. Winthrop D. Jordan also questions the emphasis on national characteristics by pointing out that in the British West Indies, where conditions similar to those in Brazil existed, Anglo-Saxon hostility toward miscegenation was much softened and a much greater respect for the mulatto emerged.[43] Yet, the juxtaposition of the British West Indies, the United States, and Brazil favors a qualified version of Tannenbaum's argument, for what emerged in the islands

---

[41] Elkins, p. 77; Harris, *Patterns of Race*, p. 75.

[42] Harris, *Patterns of Race*, p. 86.

[43] Winthrop D. Jordan, "American Chiaroscuro: The Status and Definition of Mulattoes in the British Colonies," *William and Mary Quarterly*, 3rd Series, XIX (April 1962), 183-200.

was not the Brazilian pattern but a compromise: a three-caste system in which "coloreds" were set apart from both whites and blacks. The material conditions of life had indeed prevailed over the purely ideological-institutional inheritance, as materialists would expect, but that inheritance significantly shaped and limited the force of those conditions.

Harris cites the work of Fernando Ortiz to show that law and tradition fared badly in Cuba against economic pressure. Here again, however, he assumes a fatalistic stance. Sidney W. Mintz also cites the Cuban case as especially instructive, but he does so with greater perception and caution: Cuba, he writes, shows what happens to "those rosy institutional arrangements which protected the slave, once slavery became part of the industrial plantation system. . . . Institutional restrictions may have hampered the maturation of slave-based agricultural capitalism in Cuba; but . . . could not prevent it. In the mid-nineteenth century, Cuban slavery dehumanized the slaves as viciously as had Jamaican or North American slavery." Mintz notes that Tannenbaum and Elkins "circumvent critical evidence on the interplay of economic and ideological forces." Elsewhere he writes that the way men were treated in colonial Caribbean societies was "determined much more by the level of economic development than by the ideologies of the different metropolitan powers."[44] The words "much more than" leave considerable room for the autonomous force of ideology. If Harris were to restrict himself within the limits of Mintz's critique, he might help develop the work of Freyre, Tannenbaum, and Elkins along materialist lines, but instead he declares ideological war. Mintz's remarks on the intersection of ideology and economics constitute the beginning of a new departure, although I should prefer to subsume both within a synthetic analysis of social classes that avoids compartmentalizing their constituent human beings. Social classes have historically formed traditions, values, and sentiments, as well as particular and general economic interests. Harris, like Mintz, Eric Williams, and others, refers to the components of the slaveholders' world view and the possible divergence between economic interests and traditional commitments. The solution of these problems awaits empirical research. A materialist interpreta-

---

[44] Sidney W. Mintz, review of Elkins' *Slavery* in *American Anthropologist,* LXIII (June 1961), 579-587; "Labor and Sugar in Puerto Rico and in Jamaica, 1800-1850," *Comparative Studies in Society and History,* I (March 1959), 273-283, quote from p. 283. On the effects of commercialization see Sio, *Comparative Studies in Society and History,* VII (April 1965), 298-308.

tion must account for the full range of possibilities, but it can do so
only if it eschews economic determinism and a narrow ecology for
a concern with the historical formation of class interests and antagonisms under specific geographic and technological conditions.[45]

Harris makes much of the philosophical idealism of Freyre,
Tannenbaum, and Elkins but does not analyze it. Since Freyre has
written at some length on his method and viewpoint Harris ought
to examine them specifically instead of contenting himself with the
application of labels. That Freyre, Tannenbaum, and Elkins may
be safely classed as idealists I do not deny, but their superb work
ought to warn their philosophical opponents that the subject matter
resists simplistic materialist schemata. A review of Freyre's methodological comments will lay bare the weakness of idealist interpretations and also the elusiveness of the reality which makes such
interpretations possible and even enormously helpful.

Freyre's critique of historical materialism is especially suggestive,
for he rejects it without hostility and indeed with considerable ap-
preciation. "However little inclined we may be to historical materialism," he writes, "which is so often exaggerated in its generalizations
—chiefly in the works by sectarians and fanatics—we must admit
the considerable influence, even though not always a preponderant
one, exerted by the technique of economic production upon the
structure of societies and upon the features of their moral physiog-
nomies. It is an influence subject to the reaction of other influences,
yet powerful as no other. . . ."[46] Freyre's words strike sharply at

---

[45] The limits of the ecological viewpoint are brought out with great skill by
Clifford Geertz. Several passages from his book, *Agricultural Involution: The
Processes of Ecological Change in Indonesia* (Berkeley, 1963) are especially
useful:
How much of the past growth and the present state of Indonesian culture and
society is attributable to ecological processes is something to be determined, if at
all, at the end of inquiry, not at the beginning of it. And as political, stratificatory,
commercial, and intellectual developments, at least, seem to have acted as
important ordering processes in Indonesian history, the final awarding of pre-
potency to ecological developments seems no more likely than that they will
turn out to have been inconsequential (p. 11).
On the contrast between Japanese and Javanese society:
Given, then, all the admittedly background differences, one can hardly forbear
to ask when one looks at these two societies: "What has happened in the one
which did not happen in the other?" A satisfactory answer to such a question
would involve the whole economic, political and cultural history of the two
civilizations . . . (p. 131).
A search for the true diagnosis of the Indonesian malaise takes one, thus, far
beyond the analysis of ecological and economic processes to an investigation
into the nation's political, social, and cultural dynamics (p. 154: the last sentence
in the book).
[46] Gilberto Freyre, *The Masters and the Slaves: A Study in the Development
of Brazilian Civilization*, 2nd English-language ed. (New York, 1956), p. xxvii.

economic determinism, which has roots in Marxism where it clutters up rich fields, and at certain schools of ecology, but they are generally consistent with a properly understood dialectical materialism. What is primarily missing in Freyre's organic view of society is a suitable concern for class antagonisms as the historical motor force, but that is precisely what is missing from Harris's materialism.

Freyre's objections to historical materialism rest largely on his narrow economic reading of Marxian theory. In *The Mansions and the Shanties* he refers to an essay by Lefebvre des Noëttes in which it is asserted that moral suasion proved helpless against slavery until technological developments gave it room to expand. Freyre asks if this means "the absolute dependence of moral progress on material progress, as narrowly sectarian 'historical materialists' claim. . . ?"[47] He answers negatively, citing the United States as proof that slavery and technological progress could coexist. I doubt that the United States would offer him much evidence to refute even vulgar Marxism on this point, but we need not discuss the specific questions now. The main point is that he sees Marxism as an economic and technological determinism; in effect, he describes it in terms much more appropriate to certain schools of ecology. If it is Marxism, then certainly it is the kind that once drove Marx to protest, *"Je ne suis pas un marxiste."* The class element has somehow disappeared, but without it historical materialism is a senseless abstraction.

If historical materialism is not a theory of class determinism, it is nothing, but to be a theory of class determinism it must accept two limitations. Certain social classes can only rise to political power and social hegemony under specific technological conditions. The relationship of these classes, from this point of view, determines the contours of the historical epoch. It follows, then, that changes in the political relationship of classes constitute the essence of social transformations; but this notion comes close to tautology, for social transformations are defined precisely by changes in class relationships. What rescues the notion from tautology is the expectation that these changes in class relationships determine—at least in outline—the major psychological, ideological, and political patterns, as well as economic and technological possibilities, that changes in class structure constitute the most meaningful of all social changes. To argue that they constitute the only meaningful

---

[47] Gilberto Freyre, *The Mansions and the Shanties: The Making of Modern Brazil* (New York, 1963), p. 305.

changes is to reduce historical materialism to nonsense and to surrender its dialectical essence.

Freyre's idealism appears most crudely in his discussion of Portuguese colonization. He refers to the "task" of colonization as being "disproportionate to the normal resources of the population, thereby obliging the people to maintain themselves in a constant state of superexcitation, in the interests of large-scale procreation."[48] Lapses into teleology and mysticism abound in his writings, and one could, if one wished, put them side by side to prove him quaint or foolish. He who wastes time doing so will be the loser, for Freyre's thought is too rich for us to focus on its weak side. To see where Freyre is going we need to analyze his notion of the "creative image."

In writing of Brazilian patriarchal society and of the intersection of Indian, Negro, and European cultures Freyre "was trying to accomplish a pale equivalent of what Picasso has masterfully accomplished in plastic art: the merging of the analytic and the organic approaches to man: what one of his critics has called 'a creative image.' "[49] Freyre seeks to use methods and data of the physical, biological, and social sciences to assist in what is essentially an artistic project, for only through artistic image can the wholeness of man and his world be glimpsed. He admits the large role assigned to intuition in his work.[50] In a passage, which seems to me to reflect a strong Sombartian influence, he writes, "The truth really seems to be that only 'within' the living whole of human development can the relations between what is arbitrarily considered rationality and irrationality in human behavior, or between different human cultures, be fully understood."[51] Properly disciplined, this concern with getting "within" a society should mean a concern with its spirit—its dominant ideology, system of values, and psychological patterns. Freyre's effort can and should be assimilated into a historical view of social classes, for it is essentially an attempt to grasp the wholeness of a society's world view, including its self-image. Only two steps are required to place Freyre's viewpoint on materialist ground. The first takes us to the realization that society's world view must necessarily be essentially the view of its ruling class; the second to the realization that, in order to rule, a ruling

[48] Freyre, *Masters and Slaves*, p. 262.
[49] Freyre, *Masters and Slaves*, p. xxi.
[50] Freyre, *Masters and Slaves*, p. xxi.
[51] Freyre, *Masters and Slaves*, p. xxii.

class must be sufficiently wise and flexible to incorporate much from the manners and sentiments of the classes being ruled.

Freyre is therefore not toying with us when he writes that he endeavors to be "almost entirely objective" but that at certain points he introduces an "objective-introspective" method. His purpose is to be able to feel life as lived by his long-dead subjects in all its "sensual fullness of outline."[52] This attempt at psychological reconstruction, he wisely observes, depends less on "the strictly psychological approach of academic psychologists than that of novelists who have found it necessary to add a psychological time to the conventional chronological one, in novels otherwise historical in their substance. . . ."[53] In this spirit he constructs, for example, a historical-psychological model of Indian and African personality traits, as absorbed into Brazilian culture.[54] So far as possible, he strives to discover the roots of these divergent patterns in social and technical modes of life. The problem lies in the elusiveness of a full explanation. The mechanisms and the extent of the inheritance of acquired group characteristics continue to elude us and may to some degree always do so. Recognition of this elusiveness and of how few definite, scientifically demonstrated conclusions we can borrow from psychologists or from other social and biological scientists throws Freyre and the rest of us back on our own fragile ability as social historians to reach for everything at once. Poetry, for us as well as for the ancient Greeks, remains truer than history. As Freyre reminds us:

The human being can only be understood—in so far as he can be understood—in his total human aspect; and understanding involves the sacrifice of a greater or lesser degree of objectivity. For in dealing with the human past, room must be allowed for doubt, and even for mystery. The history of an institution, when undertaken or attempted in keeping with a sociological criterion which includes the psychological, inevitably carries us into zones of mystery where it would be ridiculous for us to feel satisfied with Marxist interpretations or Behaviorist or Paretist

---

[52] Freyre, *Masters and Slaves*, p. lviii.

[53] Freyre, *Masters and Slaves*, p. lxix. Perhaps the most straightforward illustration of Freyre's method is, appropriately, *Mother and Son: A Brazilian Tale* (New York, 1967), which he describes as a semi-novel and in which fictional situations are meant to represent historical and social reality, apparently on the principle of *se non e vero, e ben' trovato*. As the narrator writes of a character about whom he planned to write and who suddenly appears before him in real life (p. 4): "I must be aware that she had existed before I had imagined her; if she had not, I would not have tried to conjure her up."

[54] Freyre, *Masters and Slaves*, pp. 284-285.

explanations, or with mere description similar to those of natural history.[55]

Freyre's willingness to speak approvingly of intuition, "mystery," and the sacrifice of objectivity opens him to attack and even ridicule from those who are content to ignore the challenge. Yet Freyre's intuition, like the passionate opposition to racial and social injustice that informs all of Harris's work, has its place. As Gramsci observes, "Only passion sharpens the intellect and cooperates to render intuition clearer."[56] Freyre, sensing the elusiveness of historical truth and the dangers of strict rationalism, has raised serious objections to materialist theory, and only superficial mechanists could fail to realize as much. Since a full reply would entail an effort beyond the editor's and reader's patience, I should like to restrict myself to a few observations.

The strength of Marxian materialism, relative to other materialisms, is its dialectic, which gives it, or ought to give it, the flexibility and wholeness Freyre demands. The principle of interrelatedness is fundamental to Hegelian and Marxian dialectics and cannot be sacrificed to convenient notions of simple causation. If dialectical materialism is taken seriously, it must assert historical continuity as well as discontinuity. Every historical event necessarily embraces the totality of its components, each of which brings to that event the product of its total historical development. For this reason alone, a failure to respect the force of a people's tradition and historically developed sensibility will always prove fatal to materialist thought and betray it into mechanism. The task of those who would confront Freyre's idealism with a convincing materialism is to account for the complexity of societies in their historical uniqueness and for the special manifestations of the human spirit embodied in each such society.

Freyre's recourse to an idealist stance results from an irresponsible attitude toward the complex reality he seeks to explain. In his methodological preface to his study of post-monarchical Brazil, he identifies his subject as a society entering the modern world with a persistent tradition of patriarchalism; and he identifies his method as less the historical than the anthropological and psychological.[57]

[55] Freyre, *Mansions and Shanties*, p. xxix.
[56] Quoted by Cammett, *Antonio Gramsci*, p. 197.
[57] Gilberto Freyre, *Ordem e progresso: Processo de disintegração das sociedades patriarcal e semipatriarcal no Brasil sob o regime do trabalho livre . . .*, 2 Vols.

Life, he insists, is a process of development of values and lends itself only partially to scientific analysis.[58] Perhaps so, but as Marx, Freud, and Weber, among others, have argued, it is both necessary and possible to deal rationally with the irrational and to develop, at least in approximation, a disciplined approach to a reality so rich that we shall certainly never fully grasp it. The most attractive inheritance of Marxism from the Hegelian dialectic is the simultaneous assertion of progress toward essential knowledge and yet the ultimate elusiveness of the whole. It is this inheritance that makes Marxian philosophy, when it is not trampled on by political imbeciles, enthusiastically embrace the experimental sciences without fear of losing its dogmatic virginity. Freyre's weakness lies in his unwillingness to try to discipline his many-sided viewpoint. I do not suggest that he ought to tell us which "factor" in the social organism he analyzes is "primary"—I cannot imagine what a "historical factor" is, and the assignment of primacy would do violence to the spirit of his work. I do suggest that we need some clue to the motor force of social change. Freyre fails us here; hence the sharpness of Harris's critique.[59]

Freyre's failure—like Harris's—emerges most clearly from his friendly reply to an author who "would place responsibility for the principal defects in our social, economic, and moral development

---

(Rio de Janeiro, 1962), pp. xxiv. I deliberately pass over Freyre's extension of his psychological method in his theory of Luso-Tropicalism. This extension raises a different set of problems, beyond the scope of this paper. See Freyre, *The Portuguese and the Tropics* (Lisbon, 1961), esp. p. 9.

[58] Freyre, *Ordem e progresso*, pp. xxxii-xxxiii. It is only a short step from this attitude to a romanticization of the Brazilian past. Stanley J. Stein is harsh but not unjust when he rebukes Freyre for transforming hypotheses advanced in the *Masters and Slaves* into "facts" simply by restating them in later books. See Stein, "Freyre's Brazil Revisited: A review of *New World in the Tropics: The Culture of Modern Brazil*," *Hispanic American Historical Review*, XLI (Feb. 1961), 113.

[59] There is also, apparently, a political and ideological component to this sharpness. Freyre's writings on Angola and Moçambique have come close to apologetics for Dr. Salazar's imperialist policies. Harris sees a direct line between Freyre's point of view on Brazilian colonization and his recent political pronouncements. As one who has seen the ravages of Portuguese imperialism first hand and who has done good work in exposing them, Harris is incensed. I agree that there is a direct line between the two sets of views, but I also think that Freyre's polite criticisms of Portuguese racial policies as "un-Portuguese" ought to be given due weight. His views of past and present can be related to a general ideological commitment that looks to me—he would probably deny it—as a sophisticated greater-Brazilian nationalism. In any case, we dare not permit criticisms of Freyre's politics to blind us to the value of his contributions to history and sociology. His formulations on Brazilian history and culture must be examined strictly on their merits.

upon slavery . . . where I am inclined to put the blame upon
monoculture and the latifundia. . . ."[60] The difference, Freyre
argues, is one of emphasis, and each emphasis does fall on the
material conditions of life. Ironically, Harris's position is close to
Freyre's, although more rigid, for Freyre himself often slides into a
narrow mechanism when he discusses specific historical problems
rather than theoretical and methodological ones. He does not, for
example, pay nearly enough attention to the feudal-Catholic tradition in his discussions of morality, sexual relations, sadism in
pedagogy, and some other matters.[61] The advantage of emphasizing slavery rather than monoculture lies not in the superior virtue
of one "factor" over the other, but in the focus on human relationships. The special quality of master-slave relationships in Brazilian
slavery lies in their being a special case in a broad pattern of quasi-
feudal, paternalistic relationships brought from Portugal and re-
invigorated on the virgin soil of Bahia and Penambuco. Freyre
himself contributes much toward such an analysis in at least two
ways: (1) by treating the slave plantation as an integrated community and (2) by seeing that community as a projection of the
traditional family unit. Tannenbaum's early formulation of the
problem remains one of the best:

It is better to speak of a slave society rather than of slavery, for the
effects of the labor system—slave or free—permeate the entire social
structure and influence all of its ways. If we are to speak of slavery,
we must do it in its larger setting, as a way of life for both master and
slave, for both the economy and the culture, for both the family and
the community.[62]

What needs to be explored is the relationship between this peculiar
class structure and the prevalent psychological and ideological
patterns in society.

A parallel weakness in Freyre's attempt at synthetic analysis may
be found in his discussion of the economic ills of monoculture.
These surely were not absolute. If they crippled society at a certain
point, they did so because they badly compromised the ruling class
and hampered its ability to rule with that even-handedness without

---

[60] Freyre, *Masters and Slaves,* pp. 64-65, n. 176; *cf., O Mundo que o portugues criou,* p. 108.
   [61] *Cf., Masters and Slaves,* pp. 368, 401, 416-417, n. 34.
   [62] Frank Tannenbaum, "A Note on the Economic Interpretation of History,"
Political Science Quarterly, LXI (June 1946), 248.

which the successful exercise of social hegemony would be impossible. Whether slavery or monoculture caused soil exhaustion is not an especially useful question, for they were functionally related. More to the point, they represented social and economic aspects of a specific form of class rule. In economic experience, as in the psychology of the leading strata, the relationship of master to slave proved decisive: it set limits to labor productivity, the flexibility of organization, the growth of the home market, and the accumulation of capital. It determined, in essential respects, the sensibilities of those who could and did place their imprint on society.[63]

Of the planters Freyre writes that they "represented, in the formation of Brazilian society, the most typical of Portuguese tendencies: namely, settledness, in the sense of patriarchal stability. A stability based upon sugar (the plantation) and the Negro (the slave hut). . . . I would merely set alongside the purely material or Marxist aspect of things or, better, tendencies the psychologic aspect. Or the psycho-physiologic."[64] Harris has not yet answered this challenge satisfactorily. We need not choose between Freyre's eclecticism and Harris's version of materialism. The historical task, to which a properly understood materialism seems to me to offer the best solution, is two-fold: to relate satisfactorily the psychological, "material," and other aspects of a society to each other in such a way as to present reality as integrated social process; and to avoid a sterile functionalism by uncovering the fundamental pattern of human relationships conditioning both material and spiritual life. To fulfill this task we need to examine historical continuity, with its cumulative traditions and ways of thought, as well as ecology, more narrowly understood. Freyre's idealism may, as Harris alleges, weaken his work, but neither Freyre nor any of us could be expected to do better by rejecting a concern for the whole man in a social setting that links past to present. At his best Freyre is marvellously dialectical, as in his pregnant remarks on the Brazilian adaptation of the Portuguese language,[65] or in his discussion of the psychology of the Portuguese colonizer, which he

---

[63] The most suggestive starting point for a psychology of slaveholding may be found in G. W. F. Hegel, *The Phenomenology of Mind*, 2 Vols. (London, 1910), I, 183 ff. I have tried to sketch, in a preliminary way, the slaveholding experience in the United States: *The Political Economy of Slavery* (New York, 1965), pp. 31-34.

[64] Freyre, *Masters and Slaves*, p. xl.

[65] Freyre, *Masters and Slaves*, p. 348.

relates to the "intimate unity" of Portuguese culture as "a consequence of the processes and of the conditions of Portuguese colonization."[66]

The sad part of Harris's book, which is so impressive in many of
its particular analyses, is the implicit conflict between his denigra-
tion of ideas, ideals, and values and his passionate plea for racial
and social justice. How ironical that he should end his book with an
exhortation—to whom and to do what is not clear:

The backwardness of vast multitudes of the New World peasantry, illiterate, unskilled, cut off from the twentieth century and its brilliant
technological advances did not simply happen by itself. These millions,
about whose welfare we have suddenly been obliged to concern ourselves, were trained to their role in world history by four centuries of
physical and mental conditioning. They were deliberately bottled up.
Now we must either pull the cork or watch the bottle explode.[67]

In the context of his book these words are puzzling and might
easily be dismissed, were it not for the obvious personal sincerity
and social urgency they suggest. One is tempted to reply to Harris
in the words Tannenbaum used many years ago to reply to Eric
Williams:

It is hard to be a child of the Renaissance and a high priest of economic
interpretation. If slavery was merely economic, and if economic forces
are the only conditioning factor in shaping human institutions, then why
all the indignation and the sarcasm? Why the appeal to moral forces, to
justice, and to humanity?[68]

Harris, by attempting to construct a materialism that bypasses the
ideological and psychological elements in the formation of social
classes, passes over into a variant of vulgar Marxism. In so doing,
he ranges himself much further away from a consistent and useful
materialism than do the idealists themselves, for he turns from
everything living in modern materialism—its dialectics and sense of
historical process—and offers us the dead bones of a soulless
mechanism.

[66] Freyre, *O Mundo que o portugues criou*, p. 39; *New World in the Tropics*,
p. 54.
[67] Harris, *Patterns of Race*, p. 99.
[68] Tannenbaum, *Political Science Quarterly*, LXI (June 1946), 252.

Slavery and Economic Development: Brazil and the United States South in the Nineteenth Century

RICHARD GRAHAM
University of Texas at Austin

All history is comparative. The judgments historians make are derived from some explicit or implicit standard of comparison. Thus, when historians describe the antebellum South in the United States as technically backward, rural, nonindustrial, socially retrograde, and paternalistic, they mean to say that it was so in comparison with the North.[1] When historians of nineteenth-century Brazil describe it in the same terms, they compare it either to the hegemonic capitalist areas of that period, including the United States North, or to Brazil itself at later periods in its history.[2] Rarely do they compare it with the United States South. The explanations for economic development or its absence so far offered by both these groups of historians—and especially the

I gratefully acknowledge the contributions to this article of my students at the Universidade de São Paulo and the Universidade Federal Fluminense where I conducted seminars on this topic. I have also profited from comments made by Mariano Diaz Miranda, Albert Fishlow, Sandra Lauderdale Graham, Barnes Lathrop, Nathaniel Leff, John Lombardi, Fernando Novais, Julius Rubin, Stuart Schwartz, and Joseph E. Sweigart. Financial support was provided by the Institute of Latin American Studies, University of Texas at Austin. I presented an earlier version of this study before the Latin American Studies Association in April 1979.

[1] Even when some scholars deny the validity of the adjectives, they still compare the South with the North, as do Robert William Fogel and Stanley L. Engerman, "The Economics of Slavery," in *The Reinterpretation of American Economic History*, Robert William Fogel and Stanley L. Engerman, eds. (New York: Harper and Row, 1971), 333–38, an argument subsequently reproduced in their *Time on the Cross: The Economics of American Negro Slavery* (Boston: Little, Brown, 1974).

[2] Celso Furtado, *The Economic Growth of Brazil: A Survey from Colonial to Modern Times,* Ricardo W. de Aguiar and Eric Charles Drysdale, trans. (Berkeley: University of California Press, 1963), 107–14. Within Brazil it has become common practice to compare the Paraíba Valley and its port city of Rio de Janeiro with the allegedly more progressive, industrializing west-central part of the state of São Paulo and the city by that name: e.g., Wilson Cano, *Raízes da concentração industrial em São Paulo* (São Paulo: Difel, 1977), esp. 20–42, 244–51; Warren Dean, "The Planter as Entrepreneur: The Case of São Paulo," *Hispanic American Historical Review,* 46 (May 1966), 143–45. Comparisons have also been made between the coffee-exporting southeast and the sugar and tobacco regions of the northeast: e.g., Nathaniel H. Leff, "Economic Development and Regional Inequality: Origins of the Brazilian Case," *Quarterly Journal of Economics,* 86 (May 1972), 243–62.

0010-4175/81/4523-2371 $2.00 © 1981 Society for Comparative Study of Society and History

interpretations of the impact of slavery—await examination within such a comparative framework.[3]

The arguments of this article are several. I begin by pointing out that, when the United States is compared to Brazil, it is clear that, far from being a backward and underdeveloped area, the South surged far ahead.[4] Brazil's developmental sluggishness in comparison with the South cannot be attributed to the presence of slavery, since even with slavery the South experienced a much greater degree of development than did Brazil.[5] Next, I suggest that the contrasting importance of coffee and cotton to the progress of industrial capitalism is a central consideration in understanding the different courses of economic growth in these two areas. Finally, the social structure among the free population in the two places differed radically and set contrasting economic and ideological limits within which development could occur; to some degree these structures were inherited from the respective mother countries before and without reference to slavery. My general purpose, however, is to set out problems for further investigation within a comparative framework and to isolate those factors that require particular attention from scholars specializing in each area.[6]

[3] Comparative work on slavery and race relations has yielded rich dividends as shown by Carl Degler, *Neither Black nor White: Slavery and Race Relations in Brazil and the United States* (New York: Macmillan, 1971) and other authors he cites; although a few historians have acknowledged the need to compare the economic performance of the American South to other plantation economies, no one has yet done so systematically: see, e.g., Morton Rothstein, "The Cotton Frontier of the Antebellum United States: A Methodological Battleground," *Agricultural History*, 44 (January 1970), 150, 154, 156, 161, 162; and his "The Antebellum South as a Dual Economy: A Tentative Hypothesis," *Agricultural History*, 41 (October 1967), 373-82. On the comparative study of plantation systems, see Seminar on Plantation Systems of the New World, *Plantation Systems of the New World: Papers and Discussion Summaries*, Social Science Monographs, no. 7 (Washington, D.C.: Pan American Union, 1959); Leo Waibel, "A forma economica de 'plantage' tropical," Walter Alberto Egler, trans., in Waibel, *Capítulos de geografia tropical e do Brasil* (Rio de Janeiro: Instituto Brasileiro de Geografia e Estatística, 1958), 31-50; and Edgar T. Thompson, *The Plantation: A Bibliography*, Social Science Monographs, no. 4 (Washington, D.C.: Pan American Union, 1959).

[4] Stanley L. Engerman has suggested that comparison of the American South with England or France would lead to similar conclusions. "A Reconsideration of Southern Economic Growth, 1770-1860," *Agricultural History*, 49 (April 1975), 345, 351, 353-54.

[5] I do not intend to trivialize the argument as to the impact of slavery on development; it surely helped slow development in both areas and, in any event, no one has argued that slavery alone was responsible for underdevelopment in either area. But it has been an implicit if not explicit tenet of many studies that slavery was *principally* to blame: e.g., Eugene D. Genovese, "The Significance of the Slave Plantation for Southern Economic Development," *Journal of Southern History*, 28 (November 1962), 422-37; Harold D. Woodman, "Economic History and Economic Theory: The New Economic History in America," *Journal of Interdisciplinary History*, 3 (Autumn, 1972), 343; João Manuel Cardoso de Mello, "O capitalismo tardio (contribuição à revisão crítica da formação e desenvolvimento da economia brasileira)" (Ph.D. diss., Universidade Estadual de Campinas, 1975). In this article I wish to draw attention to other aspects in the history of economic development that need to be examined.

[6] In the notes I have tried to indicate beginning points in the literature: Specialists in either United States or Brazilian history will find many lacunae in their own field but it is hoped that they may discover useful suggestions for reading in the other.

Those qualities that Douglass North once identified as "salient features of the South's economic structure"[7] could better have been applied to Brazil: the production for an international market of a single major staple, a tropical or semitropical crop; the plantation system based on the labor of slaves on large estates; the geographical shift of the crop associated with allegedly worn-out soils and impelled by surging prices; the presence of a large and relatively forgotten segment of the population that was neither slave nor planter; low investment in human capital; few large cities; a small local market for industrial goods; a lack of industrialization; and the location outside its borders of both the principal sources of capital and the controlling centers of its commercial life, insurance business, and carrying trade. The presence of slavery in both areas may seem, I think erroneously, to explain the other features they had in common.

Despite similarities between Brazil and the South, comparisons have not been drawn systematically or at length. Perhaps other historians—wiser than I—have been deterred by the well-known difficulties of writing comparative history: First, comparative studies of causation, here as elsewhere, lead to a bewildering array of differing factors that could explain variation. (Comparisons emphasize most of all that only cautious conclusions can be drawn about cause and effect in history.) Second, it is difficult to find two major processes occurring exactly at the same time.[8] Cotton began to increase rapidly as a southern product in the last decade of the eighteenth century; its planters hit their full stride when they moved into the lower South in the 1820s from which time cotton accounted for half of all United States exports; and planters faced the need to reorganize totally their labor relations in the 1860s. In Brazil the first real growth of coffee production did not occur until the 1820s, and it did not account for half of Brazil's exports until the 1850s. Coffee planters did not have to deal with the end of slavery until the 1880s. Meanwhile, conditions in the world market changed, ideologies changed, the Civil War in the United States itself affected Brazilians; in short, so many factors varied that identification of particularly significant points of difference becomes problematic. Similarly, since both societies changed continuously, comparisons are not to be made as between two photographs but as between two movies.

Finally, we must specify exactly what geographical areas are being compared. Both Brazilians and North Americans had used slaves to produce export products since colonial times, most notably sugar in Pernambuco and Bahia, tobacco in Virginia and Maryland. Cotton first gained importance in South Carolina and Georgia, while later its production centered in Alabama, Mississippi, and Louisiana. Coffee became initially prominent in the valley of

[7] Douglass C. North, *The Economic Growth of the United States, 1790–1860* (Englewood Cliffs, N.J.: Prentice-Hall, 1961), 128.

[8] Furtado, *Economic Growth,* 164–65, argued that the difference in timing in export strength is the major factor to be considered in the differing records of development in the two countries.

the Paraíba River in the area feeding the port of Rio de Janeiro. Its cultivation gradually spread southwestward up the river and, finally, in the 1880s, into new regions of west-central São Paulo province, moving further west and south later on. A good part of this movement occurred only after the abolition of slavery in 1888. Geographical and chronological boundaries to the study thus define one and the same problem.[9] Historians, alert to the dangers of aggregating data for the American South, have begun carefully to distinguish not only among states but also among counties and regions within states. So far, such fine distinctions have not been drawn in Brazil, although the next generation of historians will surely grapple with the problem of doing so.[10] In this article I compare two neocolonial economies focused on the export of cotton and coffee grown in particular regions with slave labor. Because of the nature of the data gathered so far, I am forced to leave the outer boundaries somewhat vague. Nevertheless, there is enough central ground for comparability to suggest some general points on the mesh of slavery with economic growth.

The prevailing view of the antebellum South as a poor region has obscured its true position on a world-wide scale showing the distribution of wealth by region. Evidence of its level of development relative to that of Brazil can be seen, for instance, in transportation, agricultural technology, and industrialization, three areas then considered preeminent measures of economic progress. The South, aided by its geography, possessed a far superior transportation system. The coastal escarpment in Brazil, which borders the coffee region, runs much closer to the sea than in North America and cuts off the kind of rivers that penetrate the tidewater regions of South Carolina and Georgia. Brazil's extensive and navigable river system drains a region—the Amazon Valley—that has to this day defied man's effort to bring it into commercial production, whereas the Mississippi and its tributaries, besides linking today's Midwest to the South, also carried southern cotton to the port of New Orleans. To be sure, the major early coffee region occupied a river valley, the Paraíba, but rapids break this river along most of its course and waterfalls separate it from the sea, so that planters could use it to ship coffee

---

[9] The geographical spread of coffee within the province of São Paulo is graphically presented in Sérgio Milliet, *Roteiro do café: análise histórico-demográfica da expansão cafeeira no estado de São Paulo*, Estudos Paulistas, no. 1 (São Paulo: n.p., 1938), 23–28; similar maps have not been prepared for the province of Rio de Janeiro, but for the distribution of slaves in 1883, see Orlando Valverde, *La fazenda de café esclavista en el Brasil*, Cuadernos Geograficos, no. 3 (Merida, Venezuela: Universidad de los Andes, 1965), 41. Maps showing similar movement of slaves and cotton can be found in Fogel and Engerman, *Time on the Cross*, 45; and Lewis Cecil Gray, *History of Agriculture in the Southern United States to 1860* (New York: Peter Smith, 1941), 684, 890–91. Cotton was planted in new areas of the South after slavery, but not with the same impact as in Brazil.

[10] On distinctions within the cotton South, see especially Gavin Wright, *The Political Economy of the Cotton South: Households, Markets, and Wealth in the Nineteenth Century* (New York: Norton, 1978), 20–22.

for, at most, only a few miles from plantation to local commercial center. In the coffee area of west-central São Paulo also, rapids interrupt the rivers that flow westward away from the nearby ports and toward the Río de la Plata, over a thousand miles away.[11]

The road system of the American South easily surpassed that of Brazil, partly because of the more favorable topography, partly because of greater capital resources, and partly because of institutions more suited to the mobilization of energies toward road building. Although travellers in the South complained bitterly about the muddy tracks that passed for roads, these nevertheless did form a network which spanned the cotton South and upon which wheeled vehicles—wagons and stagecoaches—traversed regularly. Even if many roads led only as far as the nearest point on a navigable river—and later to a railhead—even so they carried the cotton to gins and to market. Community effort, frequently impelled by a local tax, built these roads and elected local officials to oversee them; landowners supplied the labor, that is, either their own or that of their slaves.[12]

In Brazil's coffee region, hairpinning trails plunged precipitously from the upland valley to the coast. Mule trains or slave caravans traversed them, but not, generally speaking, wheeled vehicles. Roughly laid flat stones on the steepest curves provided an occasional firm footing, but elsewhere roads remained quagmires when it rained—and rainfall along the escarpment averages 147 inches per year. Central or provincial (i.e., state) governments financed the construction and maintenance of these roads; planters and county governments on the one side and higher authorities on the other constantly clashed over assignment of responsibility for their poor state. Individual local planters, without cooperative effort, sometimes built private roads that led from plantation to river or (later) to railroad, but county governments re-

[11] On shipments on the Paraíba River, see Louis Agassiz and Elizabeth Cabot Gary Agassiz, *A Journey to Brazil*, 2d ed. (Boston: Ticknor and Fields, 1868), 121. On the difficulty of using the São Paulo rivers for transportation, see Sérgio Buarque de Holanda, *Monções*, 2d ed., Biblioteca Alfa-Omega, História, no. 8 (São Paulo: Alfa-Omega, 1976), 40-46, 77-107. For lack of financial resources governments did little then or later to construct locks and canals to make these rivers navigable; *cf.* Carter Goodrich, ed., *Canals and American Economic Development* (New York: Columbia University Press, 1961).

[12] Frederick Law Olmstead, *The Cotton Kingdom: A Traveller's Observations on Cotton and Slavery in the American Slave States*, Arthur M. Schlessinger, ed. (New York: Knopf, 1953), 128-29, 343-44; George Rogers Taylor, *The Transportation Revolution, 1815-1860*, Economic History of the United States, no. 4 (New York: Harper and Row, 1951), 15-16; U. B. Phillips, *A History of Transportation in the Eastern Cotton Belt to 1860* (New York: Columbia University Press, 1908), 12, 59-61, 69, 127, 129; William Eleijus Martin, *Internal Improvements in Alabama*, Johns Hopkins University Studies in Historical and Political Science, ser. 20, no. 4 (Baltimore: Johns Hopkins Press, 1902), 27-32; Alfred Glaze Smith, *Economic Readjustment of an Old Cotton State: South Carolina, 1820-1860* (Columbia: University of South Carolina Press, 1958), 137-38, 143, 153-54; Milton S. Heath, *Constructive Liberalism: The Role of the State in Economic Development in Georgia to 1860* (Cambridge: Harvard University Press, 1954), 233-34, 239, 249-52.

mained helpless to command the efforts of the planters for community needs. A private toll-collecting company built the first macadamized road in Brazil in the 1840s, and not until 1861 did it complete an extension into the coffee region.[13]

Yet Brazilians still relied entirely on roads, such as they were, long after American southerners had turned to railroads. Here again, most of what has been written about southern railways compares them to those of the North, behind which the South sadly lagged.[14] But when contrasted with Brazil, that picture radically alters and becomes even more startling when we consider that the South also enjoyed excellent river transportation through the new cotton areas.[15] Table 1 compares the extent of rail lines in the two regions at

[13] José Alípio Goulart, *Tropas e tropeiros na formação do Brasil*, Coleção Temas Brasileiros (Rio de Janeiro: n.p., 1961); Luis C. Almeida, *Vida e morte do tropeiro* (São Paulo: Martins, 1971); Carlos Borges Schmidt, *Tropas e tropeiros* (São Paulo: n.p., 1932); Jean Baptiste Debret, *Voyage pittoresque et historique au Brésil; ou séjour d'un artiste français au Brésil, depuis 1816 jusqu'en 1831 inclusivement*, facism. ed., 3 vols. (Rio de Janeiro: Record; New York: Continental News, 1965), II, 117, and plate 37; Richard M. Morse, "Some Themes of Brazilian History," *South Atlantic Quarterly*, 51 (Spring 1962), 169; Richard P. Momsen, Jr. *Routes Over the Serra do Mar: The Evolution of Transportation in the Highlands of Rio de Janeiro and São Paulo* (Rio de Janeiro: privately printed? 1964); Alberto Ribeiro Lamego, *O homem e a serra*, 2d ed. (Rio de Janeiro: Instituto Brasileiro de Geografia e Estatística, 1963); Caio Prado Júnior, *The Colonial Background of Modern Brazil*, Suzette Macedo, trans. (Berkeley: University of California Press, 1967), 298-307, 481 n. 42; Emília Viotti da Costa, *Da senzala à colônia*, Corpo e Alma do Brasil, no. 19 (São Paulo: Difusão Européia do Livro, 1966), 154-73; Maria Thereza Schorer Petrone, *A lavoura canavieira em São Paulo. Expansão e declínio (1765-1851)*, Corpo e Alma do Brasil, no. 21 (São Paulo: Difusão Européia do Livro, 1968), 186-222; Stanley J. Stein, *Vassouras, a Brazilian Coffee County, 1850-1900*, Harvard Historical Studies, no. 69 (Cambridge: Harvard University Press, 1957), 91-101; Vânia Fróes Bragança, "Contribuição para o estudo da crise e extinção do Município de Estrela," in *Ensaios sobre a política e economia da província fluminense no século xix*, Richard Graham, ed. (Rio de Janeiro: Arquivo Nacional for the Universidade Federal Fluminense, 1974), 104-28; Robert H. Mattoon, Jr., "Railroads, Coffee, and the Growth of Big Business in São Paulo, Brazil," *Hispanic American Historical Review*, 57 (May 1977), 276-77; A. R. Neto, *A Estrada da Graciosa* (Rio de Janeiro: Revista Rodovia, 1945); Fulvio C. Rodrigues, *A União e Indústria, pioneira das estradas de rodagem brasileiras (ensaio)* (Rio de Janeiro: Gráfica do "Jornal do Brasil," 1934). The oxcart had long been used in Brazil but, having a fixed axle, was not suitable for the steep inclines of the coffee region. José B. Sousa, *O ciclo do carro de boi no Brasil* (São Paulo: Editora Nacional, 1958). Some wagon roads traversed the flat sugar regions of northern Rio de Janeiro province. Cleveland Donald, "Slave Society and Abolitionism in Campos County, Brazil, 1750-1888" (manuscript in preparation), 88, 93.

[14] E.g., Harold D. Woodman, *King Cotton and His Retainers: Financing and Marketing the Cotton Crop of the South, 1800-1925* (Lexington: University of Kentucky Press, 1968), 152, 188. On southern railroads, see Phillips, *History of Transportation*, 132-396; Robert C. Black, III, *The Railroads of the Confederacy* (Chapel Hill: University of North Carolina Press, 1952); Robert S. Cotterill, "Southern Railroads, 1850-1860," *Mississippi Valley Historical Review*, 10 (March 1924), 396-405; Smith, *Economic Readjustment*, 148, 156-60, 170-76, 191-92; Heath, *Constructive Liberalism*, 254-92.

[15] On Brazilian railroads, see Richard Graham, *Britain and the Onset of Modernization in Brazil, 1850-1914*, Cambridge Latin American Studies, no. 4 (Cambridge: Cambridge University Press, 1968), 51-72 and the sources cited therein; Mattoon, "Railroads"; Odilon Nogueira de Matos, *Café e ferrovias: a evolução ferroviária de São Paulo e o desenvolvimento da cultura cafeeira*, 2d ed., Biblioteca Alfa-Omega, História, no. 2 (São Paulo: Alfa-Omega, 1974).

TABLE 1

Railroads in Brazil and the United States South, 1850-90

	1850	1860	1880	1890
All Brazil				
Kilometers	0	176	3,412	9,648
Kms/1,000 people	0	0.020	0.290	0.673
Coffee area[a]				
Kilometers	0	112	2,655	5,962
Kms/1,000 people	0	0.043	0.055	0.999
All the South				
Kilometers	3,347	14,750	23,779	47,084
Kms/1,000 people	0.372	1.325	1.440	2.351
Cotton area[b]				
Kilometers	1,958	5,857	12,081	23,384
Kms/1,000 people	0.564	1.387	2.057	3.384

[a] Rio de Janeiro province, Município Neutro, São Paulo, and Minas Gerais.
[b] Alabama, Georgia, Louisiana, Mississippi, and South Carolina.
SOURCES: On U.S. population: U.S. Bureau of the Census, *Historical Statistics of the United States, Colonial Times to 1970* (Washington, D.C.: U.S. Government Printing Office, 1975), I, 24-37. On U.S. railroads: John F. Stover, *The Railroads of the South, 1865-1900: A Study of Finance and Control* (Chapel Hill: University of North Carolina Press, 1955), 5, 193. On Brazilian population as a whole: Giorgio Mortara, "Desenvolvimento, composição e distribuição da população do Brasil," in Brazil, Instituto Brasileiro de Geografia e Estatística, Laboratório de Estatística, *Contribuições para o estudo da demografia do Brasil*, 2d ed. (Rio de Janeiro: Fundação IBGE, 1970), 439. On population of the coffee provinces: Brazil, Conselho Nacional de Estatística, Instituto Brasileiro de Geografia e Estatística, *Anuario estatístico do Brasil—1964* (Rio de Janeiro: Imp. Nacional, 1964), 30, with interpolations for missing dates. On Brazilian railroads: J. P. Wileman, comp., *The Brazilian Year Book, Second Issue—1909* (London: McCorquodale, 1909), 612.

various periods. Brazil as a whole in 1890 enjoyed only half as many kilometers per person as had the South thirty years earlier. (Also see maps.)

Few aspects of the history of the South surprise the Brazilian specialist as much as the high level of southern agricultural technology. Those who debate the backwardness or efficiency of southern agriculture always compare it with the North.[16] But in Brazil, even the common plow was rarely seen. Granted that in the older coffee areas, the exceedingly steep hills could not be plowed even "up and down on slopes" as was done in Georgia,[17] and that coffee cultivation had special requirements. Granted also that Brazilians used some plows, and that more investigation of the history of Brazilian agricultural technology must be done before we can speak confidently about the differences. However, Brazilians made virtually no use of scrapers, cultivators,

[16] E.g., Fogel and Engerman, *Time on the Cross*, 191-209.
[17] Paul W. Gates, *The Farmer's Age: Agriculture, 1815-1860*, The Economic History of the United States, no. 3 (New York: Harper and Row, 1960), 142-44.

RAILROADS OF THE SOUTH
IN 1865

0   50 100 150 200 miles
0   80 160 240 320 km.

BAHIA

GOIÁS

MINAS GERAIS

ESPÍRITO
SANTO

Uberaba

Conselheiro
Lafaiete

Tres Corações

SÃO PAULO

Juiz de Fora

Campos

RIO DE JANEIRO

Campinas

Sorocaba

Rio de Janeiro

São Paulo

PARANA

RAILROADS OF BRAZIL IN 1890

0   50 100 150 200 miles
0   80 160 240 320 km.

627

harrows, or mechanical seeders until the twentieth century. The hoe remained the principal instrument of farm labor in Brazil and, in general, oxen never gave way to mules, remaining in use in coffee regions until the tractor began to take their place after 1950. Rare even today on family farms are mechanical corn shellers.[18] Even a hasty reading of the agricultural history of the South makes ludicrous the claim by some Brazilian historians that planters in the Paraíba Valley did not use modern agricultural equipment because of the incompatibility between mechanization and "slave relations of production" or that slaves were "incapable of productively managing techniques which require the use of machines." In the United States South slaves managed sophisticated tools and machines.[19]

In Brazil as in the South, planters cleared the forest with slash-and-burn techniques and ensured the fertility of the soil they used principally by moving onto new lands.[20] Historians must more critically examine the alleged exhaustion of the soil in both areas: Certainly the comparative advantage of new areas and the profitability of extensive rather than intensive land use proved a major obstacle to the use of modern agricultural technology. It may also be questioned whether older areas actually declined or simply failed to keep up with increased productivity in new ones.[21] In any case, planters in both regions tended to put newly cleared lands into production whenever possible.

[18] Franklee Gilbert Whartenby, *Land and Labor Productivity in United States Cotton Production, 1800-1840* (New York: Arno, 1977), 109-12; Gates, *Farmer's Age,* 135, 136, 144; John Hebron Moore, *Agriculture in Ante-Bellum Mississippi* (New York: Bookman Associates, 1958), 114, 121, 165, 167, 169-73, 182-83, 187-89; Gray, *History of Agriculture,* 792-800; T. Lynn Smith, *Brazil: People and Institutions,* 3d ed. (Baton Rouge: Louisiana State University Press, 1963), 372-90; Carlos Borges Schmidt, *Técnicas agrícolas primitivas e tradicionais* (Rio de Janeiro: Conselho Federal de Cultura, 1976), 91-117; *idem, O milho e o monjolo; aspectos da civilização do milho. Técnicas, utensílios, e maquinaria tradicionais,* Documentário da Vida Rural, no. 20 (Rio de Janeiro: Ministério da Agricultura, Serviço de Informação Agrícola, 1967), 39-40 and illus. facing p. 32.

[19] The quotations are, respectively, from Cano, *Raízes da concentração,* 28; Mello, "O capitalismo tardio," 54. It is well known that slaves worked cotton gins and compresses as well as coffee hulling and drying equipment much of which, in both cases, meant working with complicated steam-driven equipment. Robert S. Starobin, *Industrial Slavery in the Old South* (New York: Oxford University Press, 1970), 22; Stuart Bruchey, *The Roots of American Economic Growth, 1607-1861; An Essay in Social Causation* (New York: Harper and Row, 1968), 173; Graham, *Britain,* 45-46; C. F. van Delden Laerne, *Brazil and Java: Report on Coffee-Culture in America, Asia, and Africa to H. E. the Minister of the Colonies* (London: W. H. Allen, 1885), 310-21; Herbert H. Smith, *Brazil—the Amazons and the Coast* (New York: Scribner's, 1879), 512-27; and Affonso de Escragnolle Taunay, *História do café no Brasil,* 15 vols. (Rio de Janeiro: Departamento Nacional do Café, 1939-1943), VII, 225-82. Brazilian authors have argued that the use of slaves slowed the introduction of such machinery or that the use of the machinery underminded the slave system. Costa, *Da senzala à colônia,* 177-88; Jacob Gorender, *O Escravismo colonial,* Ensaios, no. 29 (São Paulo: Atica, 1978), 563. A comparative study of processing machinery has yet to be made. It is probably true that technical improvements were not as essential to the growth of a slave system as they were to a capitalist one based on salaried labor.

[20] Gray, *History of Agriculture,* p. 197; T. L. Smith, *Brazil: People and Institutions,* 364-72.

[21] Avery O. Craven, *Soil Exhaustion as a Factor in the Agricultural History of Virginia and Maryland, 1606-1860,* University of Illinois Studies in Social Sciences, vol. 13, no. 1 (Urbana:

Despite these similarities, planters in the United States also made some effort to maintain soil quality of existing fields. They sometimes applied cow manure, no doubt less difficult to do on open cotton fields than under semipermanent rows of coffee bushes. Chemical fertilizer, guano, potash, and lime—all used to some degree in the South—remained virtually unknown in Brazil. Similar contrasts can be noted regarding the practices of contour plowing, crop rotation, terracing, and draining. Although Brazilian planters used labor profligately, I am unaware of their undertaking such backbreaking tasks as digging swamp mud to spread on fields. Coffee planters did some mulching of the bushes with dead leaves or the sweepings after the harvest, and slaves cultivated around the bushes twice a year. Lewis Cecil Gray described the much more systematic practice in the South by the 1820s and 1830s of cutting up the cotton stalks and plowing them under.[22]

True, Brazilians did try out new seeds, but relatively few planters read agricultural journals as many of them were totally illiterate. Within the few Brazilian publications, agricultural improvements received some attention to

University of Illinois, 1926), 11-12, 19, 163; A. G. Smith, *Economic Readjustment*, 58, 68, 84, 90, 95, 97, 106; Fogel and Engerman, *Time on the Cross*, 196-99; Maxine Margolis, "Historical Perspectives on Frontier Agriculture as an Adaptive Strategy," *American Ethnologist*, 4 (February 1977), 42-64. The introduction of similar considerations into Brazilian historiography is long overdue for it is still commonplace to speak of the Paraíba Valley as being in decline much earlier than was really the case; and historians of Brazil, as was once the case for those of the South, still ascribe this alleged decline to the "routine" spirit of the planters in the older area and to their supposed irrationality in holding onto outdated practices, but in doing so, these scholars ignore the relative costs of land, capital, and labor that may have made such decisions highly rational. Stein, *Vassouras*, 214; Mello, "O capitalismo tardio," 80.

[22] Gray, *History of Agriculture*, 199, 700-701, 801-807; Gates, *Farmer's Age*, 134, 135-37, 140, 144; Moore, *Agriculture*, 112-21, 145, 164-205, 239 n. 35; Rosser H. Taylor, "The Sale and Application of Commercial Fertilizers in the South Atlantic States to 1900," *Agricultural History*, 21 (January 1947), 46-48; *idem*, "Commercial Fertilizers in South Carolina," *South Atlantic Quarterly*, 29 (April 1930), 179-89; Weymouth T. Jordan, "The Peruvian Guano Gospel in the Old South," *Agricultural History*, 24 (October 1950), 211-21; William K. Scarborough, *The Overseer: Plantation Management in the Old South* (Baton Rouge: Louisiana State University Press, 1966), 175; Stein, *Vassouras*, 33-34, 50; Schmidt, *Técnicas*, 159-63. The precise extent to which scientific practices were used in the South is the subject of some debate among North American historians, partly because they have not firmly decided what the comparative standard will be, that is, how much is a lot? Eugene Genovese, *The Political Economy of Slavery: Studies in the Economy and Society of the Slave South* (New York: Pantheon, 1965), 85-99, has convincingly denied that there was widespread use of fertilizer in the South, but my point here relates to a comparison with Brazil. See also A. G. Smith, *Economic Readjustment*, 88-100. Gorender, *Escravismo colonial*, 222, relying too heavily on Genovese, also fails to consider the difference in degree between Brazil and the American South. Julius Rubin, "The Limits of Agricultural Progress in the Nineteenth-Century South," *Agricultural History*, 49 (April 1975), 362-72, has argued that not slavery but climate inhibited the spread of many of these practices in the South. More research in Brazil may uncover a use of fertilizer there greater than my estimate. Manure was used systematically on tobacco fields in the colonial South and in colonial Brazil. Gray, *History of Agriculture*, 198-99, 801-2; and Catherine Lugar, "The Portuguese Tobacco Trade and Tobacco Growers of Bahia in the Late Colonial Period," in *Essays Concerning the Socioeconomic History of Brazil and Portuguese India*, Dauril Alden and Warren Dean, eds. (Gainesville: University Presses of Florida, 1977), 33, 55, 67-68. There is also some evidence that sugar planters in nineteenth-century Campos used manure. Donald, "Slave Society," 96.

be sure, and reformers sometimes published tracts on agricultural techniques, but planters and journalists carried on no extended debates regarding agricultural methods nor did they express widespread concern with these matters. Brazilians hardly ever formed specifically agricultural societies, except to withstand the onslaught of abolitionists in the 1880s; not until the end of the century did they hold fairs to stimulate adoption of better agricultural methods.[23] Brazil lagged far behind the South in every aspect of agricultural technology.

The South was also far more industrialized than Brazil. So far I have noted differences in the agricultural sector and in transportation facilities; contemporaries, however, despite some hesitations, usually saw industrialization as the final measure of progress.[24] Textile factories, shoe manufactures, flour mills, and iron foundries thickly peppered the South by comparison with Brazil.[25] Much more systematic examination of industrial progress is required before the exact dimensions of the gap can be stated, but its overall nature is clear. Table 2 points to the differences in the manufacturing of textiles.

[23] Gates, *Farmer's Age*, 138, 143-44; Fogel and Engerman, *Time on the Cross*, 198; Scarborough, *Overseer*, 136; *O Auxiliador da Industria Nacional* (Rio de Janeiro, 1835-1888); Rio de Janeiro, Instituto Fluminense de Agricultura, *Revista Agricola* (1869-1891); Francisco Peixoto de Lacerda Werneck, *Memoria sobre a fundação e costeio de uma fazenda na provincia do Rio de Janeiro* (Rio de Janeiro: Laemmert, 1847); Stein, *Vassouras*, 121-24; John D. Wirth, *Minas Gerais in the Brazilian Federation, 1889-1937* (Stanford: Stanford University Press, 1977), 192-201. The "efficient" management of large numbers of workers was a practice common to both coffee and cotton plantations. See Fogel and Engerman, *Time on the Cross*, 200-209; Stein, *Vassouras*, 163; Laerne, *Brazil and Java*, 253-382.

[24] On the hesitations see Genovese, *Political Economy of Slavery*, 221-39. My own view of "development" would focus more on human needs and a just social order; but that was not the general nineteenth-century attitude either in Brazil or in the South.

[25] Starobin, *Industrial Slavery*, 13-25; Victor Clark, "Manufactures during the Antebellum and War Periods," in *The South in the Building of the Nation*, Vol. V of *Economic History*, James C. Ballagh, ed. (Richmond: Southern Historical Publications Society, 1909), 313-35, esp. 331; Robert Royal Russel, *Economic Aspects of Southern Sectionalism, 1840-1861*, University of Illinois Studies in the Social Sciences, vol. 9, nos. 1-2 (Urbana: University of Illinois, 1924), 225-30; Fred Bateman and Thomas Weiss, "Manufacturing in the Antebellum South," in *Research in Economic History: An Annual Compilation of Research*, Paul Uselding, ed. (Greenwich, Conn.: JAI Press, 1976), I:3; idem, *A Deplorable Scarcity: The Failure of Industrialization in the Slave Economy* (Chapel Hill: University of North Carolina Press, 1981); Charles B. Dew, *Ironmaker to the Confederacy* (New Haven: Yale University Press, 1966); J. F. Normano, *Brazil, a Study of Economic Types* (Chapel Hill: University of North Carolina Press, 1935), 97-103; Stanley J. Stein, *The Brazilian Cotton Manufacture. Textile Enterprise in an Underdeveloped Area, 1850-1950* (Cambridge: Harvard University Press, 1957), 1-77; Warren Dean, *The Industrialization of São Paulo, 1880-1945*, Latin American Monographs, no. 17 (Austin: University of Texas Press for the Institute of Latin American Studies, 1969), 3-80; Graham, *Britain*, 125-59.

William N. Parker, in his article "Slavery and Southern Economic Development: An Hypothesis and Some Evidence," *Agricultural History*, 44 (January 1970), 115-26, makes the point that it is important to distinguish among small, medium, and large-scale industries and that medium-size factories may be most conducive to economic development; he then presents an exhaustive list of manufacturing enterprises in the South. Were the sources available in Brazil, I am sure no list equivalent in size could be compiled.

TABLE 2

*Cotton Textile Manufacturing
in the United States South and in Brazil*

	South, 1860	Brazil, 1885
Number of textile mills	159[a]	48[b]
Number of spindles	290,359	66,466
Number of workers	9,906	3,172

[a] Seventy of which were in Alabama, Georgia, Louisiana, Mississippi, and South Carolina; and fifty-six of which were in North Carolina and Virginia.
[b] Thirty-three of which were in Minas Gerais, São Paulo, Rio de Janeiro, and the city of Rio de Janeiro.
SOURCE: Ernest M. Lander, *The Textile Industry in Antebellum South Carolina* (Baton Rouge: Louisiana State University Press, 1969), 79; Stanley J. Stein, *The Brazilian Cotton Manufacture: Textile Enterprise in an Underdeveloped Area, 1850-1950* (Cambridge: Harvard University Press, 1957), 21, 191; U.S. Census Office, *Manufactures of the United States in 1860* (Washington, D.C.: U.S. Government Printing Office, 1865), 14, 82, 203, 299, 437, 559, 578, 638.

Although Brazil can claim superb iron ore resources, the few iron foundries of Brazil worked principally with imported pig.[26]

Brazil's industrial backwardness has heretofore most often been explained by the presence of slavery, and a consideration of this argument is appropriate at this point. In Brazilian historiography it has become almost a truism that industrialization and slavery were mutually antagonistic. Indeed, the ending of the slave system there is generally explained by citing internal contradictions that became more intense as slave labor itself produced the wealth that undid the foundations of slavery: Increased exports finally stimulated the rise of a few cities and earned foreign exchange, which paid for more and more capital goods. Larger cities meant a larger consuming market. Eventually, Brazilians or foreigners set up some textile plants, flour mills, shoe factories, and other industries. Rails laid to carry away the product of slave-worked plantations also made industrial goods accessible to formerly isolated plantations. On the plantations themselves increased prosperity enabled planters to invest in coffee processing machinery.

All these developments, it is argued, lessened the attractiveness of slave labor, which could best be used at rough and repetitive agricultural tasks, rather than at skilled industrial ones. The complete alienation of the slave from his labor dampened his initiative and reduced his interest in caring for equipment. He responded weakly to incentives. Furthermore, the high capital

[26] *Cf.* Kathleen Bruce, *Virginia Iron Manufacture in the Slave Era* (1940; rpt. New York: Augustus M. Kelley, 1968), esp. p. 452, map showing location of iron furnaces, with William S. Callaghan, "Obstacles to Industrialization: The Iron and Steel Industry in Brazil during the Old Republic" (Ph.D. diss., University of Texas at Austin, in progress).

investment in the slave himself slowed the turnover of profit from his labor; encouraged the owner to maintain him constantly at work and thus weakened the impetus toward investment in labor-saving machinery; and hampered the fledgling industrialist in times of retrenchment, since he could not dismiss workers in order to cut costs. In addition, the attitudes of slave-owning planters remained "premodern" and patriarchal, status-conscious and inclined to costly display of wealth and position rather than to entrepreneurship and investment. Drawing both on Weber and on Marx, several authors have elaborated on these themes.[27]

The North American experience casts doubt on most of these generalizations and suggests a more ambiguous historical reality. Industrialists there did not hesitate to use slave workers. Five percent of the entire slave population—around 200,000 persons—worked in industry. Skills were systematically taught the industrial slaves, and many of them performed highly technical jobs, as well as exercising managerial functions. Railroads relied on slave labor extensively, not only for construction but in such responsible positions as that of brakeman.[28]

The hiring-out system obviated some of the obstacles to industrialization alleged to be inherent in the slave system. Owners rented their slaves to others, in the United States often industrialists, who, if financial conditions worsened, could return them to their masters. These would then put the slaves to other employment. About one fifth of all slaves working in industry in the South were hired from someone else. In Brazil also it was a common practice to own slaves in order to rent them out. Such industries as there were may have relied on hired slaves; more could have. Instead, most of the hired slaves

---

[27] Costa, *Da senzala à colônia*, 154-220; Fernando Henrique Cardoso, *Capitalismo e escravidão no Brasil meridional. O negro na sociedade escravocrata do Rio Grande do Sul*, Corpo e Alma do Brasil, no. 8 (São Paulo: Difusão Européia do Livro, 1962), 133-62, 186-204; Florestan Fernandes, *A Revolução burguesa no Brasil: ensaio de interpretação sociológica* (Rio de Janeiro: Zahar, 1975), 86-146; Cano, *Raízes da concentração*, 31-42. See references to these same themes among the United States historians cited by Stanley L. Engerman, "Marxist Economic Studies of the Slave South," *Marxist Perspectives*, 1:1 (Spring, 1970), 150, 154-56, 163 n. 26.

[28] Starobin, *Industrial Slavery*, esp. 11, 15, 126, 168-73, 182-86. Unfortunately, Starobin did not make the essential distinction on size of factories, but see p. 50 on their rural locations and *cf*. p. 59; on the profitability of using slaves in industry, see pp. 146ff., although some of his calculations and argument may be subject to question, as on pp. 156 and 186. Other sources on the use of slaves in industries include A. G. Smith, *Economic Readjustment*, 126-27; Bruce, *Virginia Iron Manufacture*, 231-58; Charles B. Dew, "Disciplining Slave Ironworkers in the Ante-bellum South: Coercion, Conciliation, and Accommodation," *American Historical Review*, 79 (April 1974), 393-418; Ernest M. Lander, *The Textile Industry in Antebellum South Carolina* (Baton Rouge: Louisiana State University Press, 1969), 43-44, 49, 88-93; Tom E. Terrill, "Eager Hands: Labor for Southern Textiles, 1850-1860," *Journal of Economic History*, 36 (March 1976), esp. 86; and Gavin Wright, "Cheap Labor and Southern Textiles before 1880," *Journal of Economic History*, 39 (September 1979), 655-80. On one point evidence from the South supports the views advanced for Brazil: Sabotage and other forms of resistance were a distinct possibility. See Starobin, *Industrial Slavery*, 42, 77-91, and Lander, *Textile Industry*, 35.

performed domestic duties or worked as porters and stevedores carrying and loading coffee. It will be important to learn whether the practice of hiring out was more or less widespread in Brazil than in the South. But the flexibility it engendered in the United States was presumably as possible in Brazil.[29]

If the prosperity and industrial strength of the antislavery North rested, to some degree, on the profits derived from the commerce in slave-grown cotton,[30] did such a contradiction appear within the South itself, as Brazilain historians argue happened in Brazil? Did the very prosperity built on slavery lead to the erosion of the slave system? Richard Wade lends support to the Brazilian's point of view and argues that slaves were systematically driven from Southern cities by those whose values found encouragement in the growth of urban centers and industrial prosperity.[31] Yet here, ironically, he could have profited by considering the Brazilian case, since a similar decline in the number of urban slaves in Brazil has long been understood to spring from the increasing demand for their labor in the countryside and to have preceded the

[29]Starobin, *Industrial Slavery*, 12, 128ff.; Dew, "Disciplining Slave Ironworkers." The comparative costs of renting as against buying a slave are calculated for the United States by Robert Evans, Jr., "The Economics of American Negro Slavery, 1830-1860," in Universities-National Bureau Committee for Economic Research, *Aspects of Labor Economics* (Princeton: Princeton University Press, 1962), 185-243, and for Brazil by Pedro Carvalho de Mello, "The Economics of Labor in Brazilian Coffee Plantations, 1850-1888," University of Chicago, Department of Economics, Report no. 7475-8 (Chicago: 1974); but see Robert Wayne Slenes, "The Demography and Economics of Brazilian Slavery, 1850-1888" (Ph.D. diss., Stanford University, 1975), 249-54. On the use of slaves in industry in Brazil, see Stein, *Brazilian Cotton Manufacture*, 51; and on hiring out slaves in Brazil for domestic duties, see Sandra Lauderdale Graham, "Female Domestic Servants in Rio de Janeiro, 1860-1910" (Ph.D. diss., University of Texas at Austin, in progress).

In nineteenth-century Brazil, perhaps even more than in the South, slaves often hired themselves out, finding their own work to do for a wage and returning a fixed sum to their masters. These slaves, like those of southern cities, acted virtually as free men, arranged their own work and wages, often secured their own housing, and sometimes acted as contractors, hiring free laborers or employing other slaves. Although the practice was widespread in both southern and Brazilian cities, it was eventually outlawed in the South, whereas it was licensed in Brazil. Gilberto Freyre, *Sobrados e mucambos* 3d ed., 2 vols. (Rio de Janeiro: José Olympio, 1961), 500; Frank Tannenbaum, *Slave and Citizen, the Negro in the Americas* (New York: Knopf, 1947), 58-61; Mary C. Karash, "Slave Life in Rio de Janeiro, 1808-1850" (Ph.D. diss., University of Wisconsin, 1972), 166, 462-81; Richard C. Wade, *Slavery in the Cities: The South, 1820-1860* (New York: Oxford University Press, 1964), 38-54; Starobin, *Industrial Slavery*, 135-37; Peter H. Wood, *Black Majority: Negroes in Colonial South Carolina from 1670 through the Stono Rebellion* (New York: Norton, 1975), 207-11, 214-15, 229. I have found no evidence that skilled whites in Brazil objected to the self-hire system, as they did in the United States South. Clement Eaton, *The Growth of Southern Civilization, 1790-1860* (New York: Harper, 1961), 167; Starobin, *Industrial Slavery*, 128, and 128n. Surely the relationship between employer and employee is qualitatively different from that between owner and owned; in the hiring-out system, both relationships existed simultaneously, with wide implications for the growth of capitalism which also need to be explored comparatively.

[30]North, *Economic Growth*, 101-21; but cf. criticisms of his model in Rothstein, "Cotton Frontier," 153-54.

[31]Wade, *Slavery in the Cities*, 243-81. Claudia Goldin, *Urban Slavery in the American South, 1820-1860: A Quantitative History* (Chicago: University of Chicago Press, 1976), corrects Wade on this score; also see Fogel and Engerman, *Time on the Cross*, 102.

rise of urban abolitionism. Some planters of the South actively opposed industrialization because it would lead, they feared, to immigration of white workers who might threaten continuation of slavery. Although Brazilian planters
opposed protective tariffs and may have been cool to industrial impulses, they
did not consider immigration a threat; some eventually even joined the
abolitionists and decreed the end of slavery in order, as they saw it, to be able
to get more immigrants for their fields—not their factories.[32] Insofar as slavery produced or encouraged those forces opposed to industry, the results were
certainly very different in these two slave regions. Therefore, although historians may have correctly described some aspects which accompanied the
Brazilian lack of industrial progress, they need to question the alleged direct
causative link to slavery.

The South possessed more slaves than Brazil and, as shown in Table 3,
slaves in America formed a significantly larger proportion of the population
than in Brazil; yet the South surged ahead in industrialization, in transportation, and in agricultural technology. The higher number of slaves evidently
cannot explain the difference, since the North, without slaves, developed even
further. Nor can it be argued that even though the South had more slaves, the
institution itself was not as strong as in Brazil; on the contrary, the strength of
the slave system in the United States was so great that it may be said to have
required a civil war to end it.[33] What other factors, then, could explain the
difference?

Some historians have insisted that Brazil's dependence on international
trade and capital explains its failure to industrialize. It allegedly relied too
heavily on the export of one crop; the profits from merchandising the crop
went into the hands of foreign merchant houses, foreign shipping firms,
foreign insurance companies; and these profits were therefore not available for
domestic investment.[34] Yet Table 4 shows that cotton made up a major part of
North American exports as well. The United States, furthermore, exported
over two thirds of its cotton production in every year except two from 1820 to

[32] Genovese, *Political Economy*, 221-35; Richard Graham, "Causes for the Abolition of
Negro Slavery in Brazil: An Interpretive Essay," *Hispanic American Historical Review*, 46 (May
1966), 123-27. Whether immigrants in Brazil joined abolitionist ranks in large numbers and
whether they did so for fear of competition from slave labor is not yet known, but seems doubtful.
Rebecca Baird Bergstresser, "The Movement for the Abolition of Slavery in Rio de Janeiro,
Brazil, 1880-1889" (Ph.D. diss., Stanford University, 1973); Black Brazilian freedmen com-
plained about immigrants competing with them for jobs rather than vice-versa. Karasch, "Slave
Life," 398, 555.

[33] Barrington Moore, Jr., *Social Origins of Dictatorship and Democracy: Lord and Peasant in
the Making of the Modern World* (Boston: Beacon, 1966), 111-55.

[34] Nelson Werneck Sodré, *História de burguesia brasileira*, Retratos do Brasil, no. 22 (Rio de
Janeiro: Civilização Brasileira, 1965), 77-88, 142-57; Fernandes, *Revolução burguesa*, 179-97;
Ciro F. S. Cardoso, "Sobre os modos de produção coloniais da América," in *América colonial*,
Theo Santiago, ed. (Rio de Janeiro: Pallas, 1975), 110-111, makes the point that international
dependence and slavery together explain underdevelopment, and criticizes those, especially
North American historians, who stress only one half of the formula.

TABLE 3

Slaves as Percentage of Total Population,
Brazil (1872) and United States South (1860)

Region	Percentage slave
U.S. South (15 states plus District of Columbia)	32.1%
South Carolina	57.2
Mississippi	55.2
Louisiana	46.9
Alabama	45.1
Georgia	43.7
Average of 5 principal cotton states	49.6
All Brazil	15.2
Rio de Janeiro province	37.4
São Paulo province	18.7
Minas Gerais	18.1
Município Neutro (city of Rio de Janeiro)	17.8
Average of 3 principal coffee states	24.7
Average of 3 principal coffee states plus city	23.0

SOURCES: United States, Bureau of the Census, *Population of the United States in 1860. Compiled from the Original Returns of the Eighth Census* (Washington, D.C.: U.S. Government Printing Office, 1864); Brazil, Directoria Geral de Estatistica, *Recenseamento da população do Imperio do Brazil* [sic] *a que se procedeu no dia 1° de agosto de 1872* (Rio de Janeiro: Leuzinger, 1873–1876).

1860, and at least 80 percent in all but three years from 1825 to 1845.[35] Cotton not destined for Britain was mainly exported to the North. British firms financed most of the merchandising of cotton; insofar as they did not, the profits of cotton commerce fell primarily into the hands of northern merchants.[36] The interest of Great Britain in the United States South has long been recognized and proved an important diplomatic consideration during the American Civil War.[37] Certainly the southerners, like the Brazilians, produced an export crop and depended on others for its commercialization. The fact that Brazil was thus dependent does not explain the lag in economic development.

[35] Stuart W. Bruchey, *Cotton and the Growth of the American Economy, 1700-1860: Sources and Readings* (New York: Harcourt, Brace, 1967), Table 3-A. The country as a whole did not focus as much on the production of exports as did Brazil, but the South did.

[36] Rothstein, "Cotton Frontier," 153, 163-64; Woodman, *King Cotton,* 150n.; Ralph W. Hidy, *The House of Baring in American Trade and Finance: English Merchant Bankers at Work, 1763-1861,* Harvard Studies in Business History, no. 14 (Cambridge: Harvard University Press, 1949), 74-75, 105-7, 173-76, 184-89, 254-59, 298-301, 359-64; A. G. Smith, *Economic Readjustment,* 162.

[37] Ephraim Douglass Adams, *Great Britain and the American Civil War,* 2 vols. (London: Longmans, Green, 1925); Brian Jenkins, *Britain and the War for the Union,* (Montreal: McGill-Queen's University Press, 1974), I, esp. 281-305: "Bibliographical Essay."

263

TABLE 4
Cotton and Coffee Exports
as Percentage of Total Exports of the
United States and Brazil, Respectively

	United States	Brazil
1816–20	39%	
1821–25	48	18%
1826–30	49	20
1831–35	56	41
1836–40	63	46
1841–45	55	42
1846–50	46	41
1851–55	53	49
1856–60	54	49
1861–65		49
1866–70		43
1871–75		52
1876–80		61
1881–85		59
1886–90		63

SOURCES: George Rogers Taylor. *The Transportation Revolution, 1815–1860*. Economic History of the United States. no. 4 (New York: Harper & Row, 1968), 451; Brazil, Conselho Nacional de Estatística. Instituto Brasileiro de Geografia e Estatística. *Anuario estatístico do Brasil*, Ano V: *1939/1940* (Rio de Janeiro: Imp. Nacional, 1941), 1379.

The greater ease with which industrial capitalism spread into the South may have sprung from the very lack of national boundaries between it and the North. Geographical proximity, together with other affinities, surely encouraged northern investors to place some of their funds in southern enterprises rather than, say, in France. At any rate, despite the draining of southern financial resources to northern cities, at least some of these resources eventually returned to the South to a degree far greater than in Brazil, where the industrial and commercial center was in an entirely different country. And possibly there was some transfer southward of the values of the northern bourgeoisie.

In other ways also the extremely close ties between the South and the world capitalist system partly explain the higher levels of agricultural, transportational, and industrial technology it enjoyed. For to say technology is to say capital, and the South attracted more capital than Brazil.

The South may not have attracted enough capital or as much as southerners wished. Like Brazil, for instance, it encountered difficulty in raising capital for railroad building. Although planters and local merchants in both areas often took the initiative in creating railroad companies, sometimes investing their own resources, they also needed outside investors and found they had to attract them with special stimuli. In both places, government authorities played an important role in this process. In Brazil, the national and provincial governments, acting together, guaranteed a return of 7 percent on capital invested in approved rail lines. In addition, the Brazilian central government bought a substantial share of stock in one major railroad that served the coffee region and, when the company failed, took over direct ownership and operation of the entire venture; later in the century provincial governments also owned and operated railroads directly. In the South, government support of railroad building consisted of indirect assistance through provision of free land surveys by state employees, tax exemptions, monopoly franchises, and grants of public land, as well as much direct aid such as cash subsidies and loans, guarantees of railroad bonds and, frequently, outright ownership. Southern counties and cities employed public funds further to aid railroad building. Both Brazilian and American southern governments borrowed money to finance this aid, frequently from England; governments in both regions felt the need to apply the resources of the state because capitalists in England and in the North had other, more profitable or less risky investments to make.[38] From the figures shown in Table 1, however, it is clear that despite similar obstacles, more capital found its way into Southern railways than into Brazilian ones.

I noted earlier that the South employed a higher level of agricultural technology than Brazil; and the higher level, by definition, represented greater capital investment. Where did it come from? Two means existed to pay for capital goods—whether industrial or agricultural—purchased outside the region: exports or loans and investments. Contemporaries easily saw that a developing region, as we might call it today, could pay for capital goods with its exports. Whether export earnings would be used for such a purpose or spent on consumer goods instead depends on issues to be explored below, but the potential for purchase of capital goods lay in exports.[39] Measuring the relative potentials of cotton and coffee exports to pay for such imports is more

[38] Stein, *Vassouras*, 101-2; Graham, *Britain*, 51-72, 99-105; Julian S. Duncan, *Public and Private Operation of Railways in Brazil*, Studies in History, Economics, and Public Law, no. 367 (New York: Columbia University Press, 1932); Black, *Railroads*, 40, 42, 44-45; John F. Stover, *The Railroads of the South, 1865-1900: A Study of Finance and Control* (Chapel Hill: University of North Carolina Press, 1955), 7-8; A. G. Smith, *Economic Readjustment*, 167-70, 176-90; Merl E. Reed, "Government Investment and Economic Growth: Louisiana's Ante-Bellum Railroads," *Journal of Southern History*, 28 (May 1962), 183-201; Milton S. Heath, "Public Railroad Construction and the Development of Private Enterprise in the South before 1861," *Journal of Economic History*, 10 (supplement, 1950), 40-53; Heath, *Constructive Liberalism*, 254-92, esp. 287-88; Carter Goodrich, *Government Promotion of American Canals and Railroads, 1800-1890* (New York: Columbia University Press, 1959), 87-120, 152-62, 270; Cotterill, "Southern Railroads," 404-5.

[39] I have shown in another study that the proportion of capital goods among Brazil's imports from Great Britain rose steadily from 14 percent in the early 1850s to 37 percent by the 1890s. Graham, *Britain*, 330-32. More attention needs to be paid in both areas to where agricultural equipment and industrial machinery were manufactured.

difficult than recognizing the importance of doing so. For instance, United States imports from abroad—paid for with cotton—went to both North and South. In Brazil, the coffee region probably received even more than it paid for.[40] Table 5 shows that cotton provided a much greater potential for capital-goods purchases by the United States as a whole than coffee did for Brazil, even if the comparison is made for the last years of slavery in both areas. Moreover, the difference is cumulative. Further research on regional economies of the two countries will be required to specify their shares of the resulting earnings, and Table 5 does not show exports from the South to the North. We can nevertheless conclude that cotton planters had substantially more wealth for investment in railroads, industry, and agricultural tools and machinery than did coffee planters. Curiously, the terms of trade (the ratio of export prices to import prices) may have been more favorable to Brazil than to the United States during the era of slavery. Douglass North has argued that favorable terms of trade impelled North American economic growth and development, but export-led growth could certainly be questioned if the same results were shown to be absent in Brazil even with more favorable terms of trade.[41]

Besides using its current exports to pay for capital goods, a region may be able to count on foreign investments and loans. Which of these two areas—the American South or Brazil—most attracted international investors? The flow of capital between nations is extremely difficult to calculate and it is even harder (perhaps impossible) to specify the exact region that received the funds. Certainly a much larger share of British investment went to the United States as a whole than to Brazil, but we cannot readily determine how much of that share went to the South.[42]

[40] Leff, in his article "Economic Development and Regional Inequality," 258-59, in effect argues that Brazil's lagging northeast could have brought the result of its export earnings closer home had the area not been part of the Brazilian polity; could the same argument not be made for the American South? Perhaps the secessionists were right. Cf. Thomas F. Huertas, "Damnifying Growth in the Antebellum South," *Journal of Economic History*, 39 (March 1979), 98-100.

[41] Cf. North, *Economic Growth*, 244, with Nathaniel H. Leff, "Tropical Trade and Development in the Nineteenth Century: The Brazilian Experience," *Journal of Political Economy*, 81 (May–June 1973), 682. North chooses a base year (1830) in the midst of the cotton boom, while Leff uses a period (1826-30) which lies closer to the beginning of the surge in coffee exports; thus comparisons between these two indices are precarious. On regional terms of trade, see Huertas, "Damnifying Growth," 97.

[42] The difficulties of investigating both the balance of payments and transfers of capital for the nineteenth century are suggested by Albert H. Imlah, "British Balance of Payments and Export of Capital, 1816-1913," *Economic History Review*, 2d ser., 5:2 (1952), 208-39; also see S. E. Saul, *Studies in British Overseas Trade, 1870-1914* (Liverpool: Liverpool University Press, 1960), esp. 67; Leland H. Jenks, *The Migration of British Capital to 1875* (1927; rpt. New York: Barnes & Noble, 1973); Bruchey, *Roots*, 133; J. Fred Rippy, *British Investments in Latin America, 1822-1949. A Case Study in the operations of Private Enterprise in Retarded Regions* (Minneapolis: University of Minnesota Press, 1959), 150-58.

TABLE 5
Value of Coffee and Cotton Exports from Brazil and the United States,
Respectively, before the End of Slavery (in thousands of pounds sterling)

(1)	(2)	(3)	(4)	(5)	(6)
					Ratio:
Year	Cotton	Coffee	Year	Coffee	Col. (2)/(5)
1826	5,636	690			
1827	6,613	774			
1828	5,065	659			
1829	5,985	705			
1830	6,684	663			
1831	5,696	964			
1832	7,145	1,832			
1833	8,151	2,770	1861	7,410	1.1
1834	10,154	2,604	1862	6,229	1.6
1835	13,339	2,495	1863	6,172	2.2
1836	14,638	2,396	1864	6,647	2.2
1837	12,986	2,217	1865	6,764	1.9
1838	12,640	2,346	1866	6,711	1.9
1839	12,575	2,575	1867	7,431	1.7
1840	13,115	2,479	1868	7,113	1.8
1841	11,156	2,305	1869	6,224	1.8
1842	9,773	2,110	1870	6,903	1.4
1843	10,086	1,921	1871	7,469	1.4
1844	11,101	1,886	1872	9,592	1.2
1845	10,624	2,048	1873	11,995	0.9
1846	8,782	2,362	1874	12,744	0.7
1847	10,968	2,701	1875	13,463	0.8
1848	12,731	2,589	1876	12,583	1.0
1849	13,634	2,352	1877	11,525	1.2
1850	14,781	3,184	1878	12,056	1.2
1851	23,063	3,951	1879	12,025	1.9
1852	18,063	3,936	1880	11,421	1.6
1853	22,476	4,040	1881	10,578	2.1
1854	19,219	4,894	1882	10,185	1.9
1855	18,099	5,547	1883	11,249	1.6
1856	26,362	5,861	1884	12,411	2.1
1857	27,018	5,518	1885	11,405	2.4
1858	26,979	5,082	1886	12,107	2.2
1859	33,149	5,904	1887	14,230	2.3
1860	39,385	7,426	1888	10,857	3.6

Note: The columns have been arranged to facilitate comparison of the exports during the last years of slavery in both countries.
SOURCES: Stuart Bruchey, *Cotton and the Growth of the American Economy: 1790-1860, Sources and Readings* (New York: Harcourt, Brace & World, 1967), Table 3-K (conversion is to pounds at the official exchange rate of $4.44 to the pound until 1834, and $4.87 after that date); Brazil, Conselho Nacional de Estatística, Instituto Brasileiro de Geografia e Estatística, *Anuario estatístico do Brasil*, Ano V: *1939/1940* (Rio de Janeiro: Imp. Nacional, 1941), pp. 1374-75 (figures adjusted from fiscal to calendar year throughout).

Planters wishing to mechanize or apply new fertilizing techniques (or buy land and slaves) could borrow from factors, their commission agents in the cities. In both Brazil and the South, the factor provided the bulk of the credit extended to planters, but most of the money so lent financed the marketing operation itself or paid for regular operating expenses before the crop was sold. The factors, in turn, borrowed from other institutions: Baring Brothers, the commercial bankers, sometimes opened credits of up to £20,000 to creditworthy southern factors, but in Brazil, British banks sometimes preferred to lend to import-export houses, frequently also British, who then lent to factors.[43] Comparing the amount of credit offered by factors in Brazil and in the United States will probably be impossible because of their large number and varied interests.

Somewhat more solid ground, but still only symptomatic, is the much greater prevalence of banking institutions in the South than in Brazil. The dividing lines between merchants who sold on credit, merchant-bankers, and full-fledged banking institutions, of course, is not always clear. But the number of formally constituted banks in Brazil certainly lagged far behind that of their counterparts in the American South even if the South trailed the North. Each state wrote its own bank laws in the United States and, especially before 1835, banking legislation imposed few restrictions on banks' rights to issue currency, lend a high proportion of their deposits, or virtually abandon liquidity.[44] So they proliferated in the South whereas banks did not operate significantly in Brazil at all until after 1850. But the legislation itself supplies

[43] Woodman, King Cotton, 162 and passim; Joseph E. Sweigart, "Financing and Marketing Brazilian Export Agriculture: The Coffee Factors of Rio de Janeiro, 1850-1888" (Ph.D. diss., University of Texas at Austin, 1980); David Joslin, A Century of Banking in Latin America; To Commemorate the Centenary in 1962 of the Bank of London and South America, Limited (London: Oxford University Press, 1963), 163; Charles Jones, "Commercial Banks and Mortgage Companies," Business Imperialism, 1840-1930: An Inquiry Based on British Experience in Latin America, D. C. M. Platt, ed. (Oxford: Clarendon, 1977), 17-52; Reports on Business Houses, Rio de Janeiro, 1852, Baring Brothers Papers (London), House Correspondence, HC 16.

[44] Pinto de Aguiar, Bancos no Brasil colonial: tentativas de organização bancária em Portugal e no Brasil até 1808, Coleção de Estudos Brasileiros Série Marajoara, no. 31 (Salvador: Progresso, 1960); Barbara Levy, História dos bancos comerciais no Brasil (Rio de Janeiro: IBMEC, 1972); Anyda Marchant, "A New Portrait of Mauá, the Banker: A Man of Business in Nineteenth-Century Brazil," Hispanic American Historical Review, 30 (November 1950), 411-31; idem, "A sorte não o permitiu," Revista do Instituto Histórico e Geográfico Brasileiro, vol. 192 (1946), 46-59; Jones, "Commercial Banks," 31-32; Sweigart, "Financing and Marketing"; A. G. Smith, Economic Readjustment, 193-217; George D. Green, Finance and Economic Development in the Old South: Louisiana Banking, 1804-1861 (Stanford: Stanford University Press, 1972), 202; J. van Fenstermaker, The Development of American Commercial Banking, 1782-1837, Printed Series, no. 5 (Kent, Ohio: Kent State University Bureau of Economic and Business Research, 1965), 77-95; Earl Sylvester Sparks, History and Theory of Agricultural Credit in the United States (New York: Crowell, 1932), 83-111; Bruchey, Roots, 148; Heath, Constructive Liberqlism, 159-230.

only one and a very small part of the explanation for the contrasting number of banks.

In both areas, not surprisingly, banks built links to the money markets of Britain. During the 1830s especially, British investors bought the bonds of southern banks, which in growing numbers lent to southern importers, wholesalers, storekeepers, factors, and planters. Although in the 1850s the direction of this generosity shifted somewhat to the North, it remained significant. One prominent Brazilian banker at midcentury—Viscount Mauá—also established intimate links to British financial houses. I have no information on British holdings of Brazilian bank bonds, but several banks owned outright by the British opened their doors in Brazilian cities from 1862. They operated primarily with funds supplied by local depositors so that no significant transfer of investment capital resulted from their operations.[45] On the other hand, in Brazil as in the United States, shorter-term commercial credit depended heavily on international linkages. The local banker in both regions was tied into a vast chain of credit relationships that did not respect national boundaries. And capital resources were always greater in London, and later in New York, than they were in New Orleans or Rio de Janeiro.

The prevailing interest rates provide another test for the relative availability of capital. Unfortunately, no one has compiled regular series on interest rates for the South or for Brazil. Rates in the South appear, on the whole, to have been substantially lower, and loans there more easily raised, than in Brazil. Alfred Smith reports rates in the South between 4 and 7 percent, but Harold Woodman speaks of a range from 5 to 18 percent, settling finally on 8 percent as the most prevalent. Historians similarly disagree about Brazil, but tend toward higher figures. A contemporary observer reported 10 to 12 percent "at least" as the cost of borrowing in the coffee districts of São Paulo in the early 1880s. Whereas Robert Greenhill refers to rates in the coffee zones as being "up to 24 percent," Pedro Carvalho de Mello estimates that the rate ranged from 8 to 12 percent.[46] Specifying the exact amount of

[45] Woodman, *King Cotton,* 162-63; Graham, *Britain,* 65-99, 189-90; Anyda Marchant, *Viscount Mauá and the Empire of Brazil: A Biography of Irineu Evangelista de Sousa (1813-1889).* Berkeley: University of California Press, 1965); Joslin, *Century of Banking,* 60-84; Jones, "Commercial Banks," 18.

[46] A. G. Smith, *Economic Readjustment,* 76, 105, 107, 108; Woodman, *King Cotton,* 52-53; Laerne, *Brazil and Java,* 225; Robert Greenhill, "Brazilian Coffee Trade," in *Business Imperialism, 1840-1930: An Inquiry Based on British Experience in Latin America,* D. C. M. Platt, ed. (Oxford: Clarendon, 1977), 205; Pedro Carvalho de Mello, "The Economics of Labor in Brazilian Coffee Plantations, 1850-1888" (Ph.D. diss., University of Chicago, 1977), 147; Helio Oliveira Portocarrero de Castro, however, in his article on "Viabilidade econômica da escravidão no Brasil: 1880-1888," *Revista Brasileira de Economia,* 27 (January-March 1973), 49, puts the range at 7 to 10 percent, going on to acknowledge that it was "common" to find coffee planters borrowing at 12 percent in the 1880s; finally, see Nathaniel H. Leff, "Long-term Viability of Slavery in a Backward, Closed Economy," *Journal of Interdisciplinary History,* 5

financial resources available in the two areas remains, therefore, a task for further research, and a difficult one, but the general proportion looms clearly. Planters (and industrialists) in Brazil faced more serious difficulties in raising funds than their counterparts in the United States South.[47]

Given that the direction followed by investment capital derived from decisions made outside of Brazil or the South, the ultimate explanation for a relative paucity of agricultural credit in Brazil springs from the greater willingness of lenders to finance the production and merchandising of cotton than of coffee. They must have considered cotton a surer bet. And that conclusion is not surprising when one considers the place of each crop within the rising industrial system of Europe or the North. Cotton was central as a raw material. Whereas coffee exports went to importer-roasters in the consuming areas and then directly to the wholesalers, cotton went to manufacturers with extensive investments in machinery designed to transform raw cotton into cloth. The textile manufacturer's investment was much greater than the roaster's; so was his need to minimize risk. The cotton manufacturer counted heavily on continuous supplies. Furthermore, the number of workers employed in the transformation of cotton dwarfed the equivalent employment in roasting coffee. If coffee supplies had been cut off, the progress of industrial capitalism would not have been affected, but the threat to cotton production posed by the American Civil War sent ripples through the entire world economy.[48] Although financing cotton production ran the short-run risks of oversupply and falling prices, in the end cotton easily secured its place as an essential raw material while coffee remained primarily a dessert, albeit also a slightly addictive stimulant.

(Summer 1974), 106, who compares rates of 6 to 8 percent for American cotton planters with 12 to 18 percent for Brazilian coffee growers. See also Sidney Homer, *A History of Interest Rates*, 2d ed. (New Brunswick, N.J.: Rutgers University Press, 1977).

The impact of higher interest rates in Brazil on the elevated rate of manumission of slaves and the lower level of care for their health and reproduction have only recently been noted; in addition to works cited above, see Jaime Reis, "Abolition and the Economics of Slave-holding in North East Brazil," Occasional Papers no. 11 (Glasgow: Glasgow Institute of Latin American Studies, n.d.), mimeographed, 11, 16; David Denslow, "The High Importation-to-Stock Ratio for Slaves in Northeastern Brazil: An Interpretation" (Paper delivered at the Southwestern Social Sciences Conference, San Antonio, Texas, March 1975), 9n., in which he cites his "Sugar Production in Northeastern Brazil and Cuba" (Ph.D. diss., Yale University, 1974), ch. 2; and Pedro Carvalho de Mello, "Estimating Slave Longevity in Nineteenth-Century Brazil," University of Chicago, Department of Economics, Report no. 7475-21 (Chicago, n.d.); *idem*, "Economics of Labor," Report no. 7475-8.

[47] The very fact that coffee and cotton offered export potential led these planters into international debt as it led them into using slaves. Engerman, "Marxist Economic Studies," 160; Robert E. Baldwin, "Patterns of Development in Newly Settled Regions," *Manchester School of Economic and Social Studies*, 24 (May 1956), 161–79; Robert R. Russel, "The General Effects of Slavery upon Southern Economic Progress," *Journal of Southern History*, 4 (February 1938), 34–54.

[48] William Otto Henderson, *The Lancashire Cotton Famine, 1861–1865*, Economic History Series, no. 9 (Manchester, England: Manchester University Press, 1934).

But capital was not invested only in the production, transport, or marketing of cotton. Planters and merchants in both areas shifted some of their accumulated capital into industrial enterprise, often borrowing the funds to pay for equipment. Southerners, as we have seen, however, did so to a much greater degree than did Brazilians. Contrasting social structures may suggest that even with equivalent export earnings, Brazil would not have invested as much in industry as did the American South. For the size of the market crucially affects industrial development, and the better distribution of the South's wealth meant a larger demand for industrial goods.[49] The South enjoyed the benefits of a more equitable social system and profited as well from the greater social mobility which fostered entrepreneurship. A significant amount of its export earnings were invested in production rather than consumed. These differences need to be explored and explained.

Land tenure is one measure of the distribution of wealth in an agricultural society. The image of the large estate with the plantation house dominating a vast acreage of cotton or endless fields of coffee typifies the traditional view of both areas. Frank Owsley launched a vigorous debate when he argued that men of middling wealth, with few or no slaves and moderate landholdings, predominated in much of the South. Although romanticizing them as the "plain folk of the Old South," he convincingly showed that the social categories of the South were more numerous and complex than the three groups—planters, poor whites, and slaves—portrayed earlier. Most heads of agricultural families (with the important exception of the slaves) owned their land; landowners comprised 80 to 85 percent of the rural population. Owsley compiled statistical tables for sample counties in various agricultural regions of the South and showed that, even in the richest black belt areas, half the slaveowners owned fewer than twenty slaves. And of the farmers who owned no slaves, only about a fifth were landless.[50]

Owsley failed to consider, however, what proportion of the land fell into the hands of that small percentage who owned, say, more than 5,000 acres. So when he said that he was determining with "reasonable accuracy the social structure of the rural South," one can only question his definition of "social structure."[51] In a devastating critique, Fabian Linden showed that in the black belt, for instance, the wealthiest 5 percent of the farm population owned 33

[49] The relationship between income distribution, market size, and industrial growth is admittedly still subject to much dispute; see, for instance, Stanley L. Engerman, "Discussion," in "Slavery as an Obstacle to Economic Growth in the United States: A Panel Discussion," Alfred H. Conrad et al., eds., Journal of Economic History, 27 (December 1967), 543; Bateman and Weiss, "Manufacturing in the Antebellum South," I, 1–44.

[50] Frank L. Owsley, Plain Folk of the Old South (Baton Rouge: Louisiana State University Press, 1949), 7, 16, 200–201; also see Herbert Weaver (one of Owsley's many students), Mississippi Farmers, 1850–1860 (Nashville: Vanderbilt University Press, 1945).

[51] Owsley, Plain Folk, 17; according to data on pp. 174 and 200, 0.88 percent of slaveholders in Lowndes County, Mississippi, and 0.24 percent of those in the Georgia black belt as a whole owned more than 5,000 acres each in 1850.

percent of the land.[52] Furthermore, Owsley paid insufficient attention to the quality of the land held by different classes of landowners and the possible tendency to concentrate land eventually. Even more important, he did not compute the distribution of slaves.[53] There is no doubt that wealth concentrated in the hands of the few in the South.

Whether the concentration was "extreme" or "normal" depends entirely on the basis of comparison, whether agricultural regions of the American Midwest, industrial cities of the northeastern United States, or Brazilian coffee regions. Since by implication, at least, historians have always linked this concentration with the owning of slaves, it makes sense to compare the South with another slaveowning society.

But the debate on the concentration of wealth cannot yet be transferred to Brazil for lack of concrete and specific information there on land tenure and the distribution of slaves. Allegedly, Brazilian planters tended to engross the better land as it increased in value during the spread of coffee cultivation. Since, as I will note below, land titles remained chronically and deliberately unclear and the political power of the wealthy unquestioned, it makes sense to believe that the original small owners would have sold out. Some historians have argued, however, that the owners of small tracts with marginal soils were needed by the planters as suppliers of foodstuffs to workers on plantations.[54] But the true nature of land distribution in Brazil still remains unknown.[55]

[52] Fabian Linden, "Economic Democracy in the Slave South: An Appraisal of Some Recent Views," *Journal of Negro History*, 31 (1946), 163; he shows (p. 159) that, in the Delta region of Mississippi, estates larger than 2,000 acres held by 8.8 percent of the landholders accounted for 34.2 percent of the land. Linden agrees (p. 187), however, that the two-class stereotype is invalid.

[53] A. G. Smith, *Economic Readjustment*, 80; Randolph B. Campbell, "Planters and Plain Folk: Harrison County, Texas, as a Test Case, 1850-1860," *Journal of Southern History*, 40 (August 1974), 369-98; Wright, *Political Economy*, 24-42; idem, " 'Economic Democracy' and the Concentration of Agricultural Wealth in the Cotton South, 1850-1860," *Agricultural History*, 44 (January 1970), 63-93. Lee Soltow, *Men and Wealth in the United States, 1850-1870* (New Haven: Yale University Press, 1975), 136, has concluded that 80 percent of freemen in the South in 1860 owned no slaves; but Otto H. Olsen, "Historians and the Extent of Slave Ownership in the Southern United States," *Civil War History*, 18 (June 1972), 111, focusing on white families in the cotton South, shows that this number declines to 52 percent in South Carolina and Mississippi.

[54] Maria Sylvia de Carvalho Franco, *Homens livres na ordem escravocrata* (São Paulo: Instituto de Estudos Brasileiros, 1969), 94-95; Warren Dean, *Rio Claro: A Brazilian Plantation System, 1820-1929* (Stanford: Stanford University Press, 1976), 19; Stein, *Vassouras*, 47-48; Alcir Lenharo, *As Tropas da moderação (o abastecimento da Corte na formaçao política do Brasil, 1808-1842)*, Coleção Ensaio e Memória, no. 21 (São Paulo: Símbolo, 1979). But Robert E. Gallman, "Self-Sufficiency in the Cotton Economy of the Antebellum South," *Agricultural History*, 44 (January 1970), 5-23, shows that in the United States large planters sold foodstuffs to small farmers rather than vice versa; see also Moore, *Agriculture*, 179, 182. If for coffee, as for cotton, harvesting took more workers than any other operation on the plantation, then there would have been excess labor available to grow food during the remainder of the year. Harold D. Woodman, "New Perspectives on Southern Economic Development: A Comment," *Agricultural History* 49:2 (April 1975), 379; Gorender, *Escravismo colonial*, 241.

[55] Some studies on the history of land tenure in Brazil include José da Costa Porto, *Estudos*

Historians have so far presented only isolated data which defy generalization. A standard measure that allows for comparisons of inequality is the Gini Index (where zero represents perfect equality and 1.0 perfect inequality). Alice Cannabrava, in the most comprehensive study done in Brazil, has shown that in 1818—when production of subsistence crops was still widespread in the province of São Paulo and coffee was far from predominant—the Gini Index there for land distribution *among landowners* reached 0.86.[56] But if very few agricultural workers owned land, even this figure would fall short of representing the extent of the inequality. For instance, using the 1890 figures from two parishes in a coffee-rich county presented in Table 6, I calculated the Gini Index number for the distribution of land among landowners as 0.65; but if all men over age twenty are considered as potential landowners, the number rises to 0.98.[57] That is why Owsley's study remains so important: in the South there were far more small landowners than in Brazil. Without considering the landless, Gavin Wright has calculated the Gini Index figure for acreage among landowners in the South in 1860 at 0.60.[58] Until historians devise inventive ways of using the Brazilian data and work systematically on this problem, no firm conclusions can be drawn as to the distribution of landed wealth there. Probably, however, access to the ownership of land was steeply more difficult in Brazil than in the American South. One bit of information that suggests this is that in colonial days the size of the land grants in Brazil dwarfed those of the South.[59]

Information on slaveholdings in Brazil is even sketchier than the land

---

sobre o sistema sesmarial (Recife: Imp. Universitaria, 1965); Rui Cirne Lima, *Pequena história territorial do Brasil. Sesmarias e terras devolutas,* 2d ed. (Porto Alegre: Livraria Sulina, 1954); idem, *Terras Devolutas* (Porto Alegre: Globo, 1936); Alberto Passos Guimarães, *Quatro séculos de latifúndio* (Rio de Janeiro: Paz e Terra, 1968); Felisbello Freire, *História territorial do Brasil* (Rio de Janeiro: Typ. "Jornal do Commercio," 1906); Louis Couty, *Pequena propriedade e immigração européia* (Rio de Janeiro: Imprensa Nacional, 1887). A comparison between the North American homestead law and the Brazilian land law of 1850 is made by Emília Viotti da Costa, *Da monarquia à república: momentos decisivos* (São Paulo: Grijalbo, 1977), 127–47.

[56] Alice P. Cannabrava, "A repartição da terra na Capitania de São Paulo, 1818," *Estudos Economicos,* 2 (December 1972), 113.

[57] I computed the index figures by using the method indicated by Charles M. Dollar and Richard J. Jensen, *Historian's Guide to Statistics: Quantitative Analysis and Historical Research* (New York: Holt, Rinehart, 1971), 122–24.

[58] Wright, *Political Economy,* 23; he also uses (p. 26) the value of real estate and ends up with a Gini Index number of 0.73. There is much debate on this issue among United States historians: Soltow, *Men and Wealth,* 130, calculated a Gini Index among all landowners in the entire United States in 1860 at 0.62 and showed that if all farmers were included—not just landowners—the figure would rise to 0.78. For the South, he presented data only for landowners (p. 133) and—working with value, not acreage—pushed the figure up to Brazilian levels at 0.88. Meanwhile, rural townships in the United States North yielded Gini Index figures hovering around 0.50. Gloria L. Main, "Inequality in Early America: The Evidence from Probate Records of Massachusetts and Maryland," *Journal of Interdisciplinary History,* 7 (Spring 1977), 560.

[59] In Portuguese America, the king had granted huge tracts of land called *sesmarias* to his favorites; sometimes these grants were measured in many square leagues. See Guimarães, *Quatro séculos,* 39-55. Subsequently, these *sesmarias* were broken up by sale and inheritance to a

TABLE 6

Land Distribution in Two Parishes of Vassouras County, Brazil, 1890

	Proprietors and potential proprietors			Landholdings	
Size of holdings in alqueires[a]	Number	Percentage of proprietors	Percentage of potential proprietors[b]	Alqueires	Percentage
Over 100	26	13	0.54	3,765	57
51–100	15	7	0.31	950	13
26–50	28	14	0.58	945	14
16–25	22	11	0.46	390	6
11–15	17	8	0.35	179	3
6–10	41	20	0.86	264	4
1–5	56	27	1.17	138	2
0	4585	—	95.72	0	0

[a] An *alqueire* in this region was equivalent to approximately 12 acres.
[b] Potential proprietors are all men over 20 years of age. Since the census tables for age do not indicate sex, I applied the same ratio of male to female as was true for the entire population of each parish. The tables for age did not indicate race. The 1890 census did not list occupation.
SOURCES: Stanley J. Stein, *Vassouras, a Brazilian Coffee County, 1850–1900*, Harvard Historical Studies, no. 69 (Cambridge: Harvard University Press, 1957), 225; Brazil, Directoria Geral de Estatistica, *Synopse do recenseamento de 31 de dezembro de 1890* (Rio de Janeiro: Officina da Estatistica, 1898), 115; Brazil, Directoria Geral de Estatistica, *Idades da população recenseada em 31 de dezembro de 1890* (Rio de Janeiro: Officina da Estatistica, 1901), 353–57.

tenure data. Government officials destroyed the bulk of slave registers—begun in 1871—soon after slavery was abolished, in order to rob planters of any basis on which to claim compensation. No manuscript census data have yet turned up for the coffee districts at the height of the boom. Historians will want to sample probate records, although the poor will be thus underrepresented. We cannot now say whether slaveholdings were more or less concentrated in Brazil than in the South, although the lower cost of slaves in Brazil may have made them easier to acquire.[60]

degree not usually considered by Brazilian historians. *Cf.* Fernandes, *Revolução burguesa*, 16–26, with Rae J. D. Flory, "Bahian Society in the Mid-Colonial Period: The Sugar Planters, Tobacco Growers, Merchants, and Artisans of Salvador, 1680–1725" (Ph.D. diss., University of Texas, 1978), 24. In colonial times in the United States South, it became a common practice to grant fifty acres for every person a settler brought with him. Although huge tracts were subsequently engrossed by a few individuals, the general southern pattern seems to have been one of much smaller holdings than in Brazil; see Gray, *History of Agriculture*, 325, 381–403; Samuel G. McLendon, *History of the Public Domain of Georgia* (Atlanta: Foote and Davies, 1924); Robert S. Cotterhill, "The National Land System in the South," *Mississippi Valley Historical Review*, 16 (March 1930), 495–506; Richard R. Beeman, "Labor Forces and Race Relations: A Comparative View of Colonization of Brazil and Virginia," *Political Science Quarterly*, 86 (December 1971), 633. All this is not to deny that in Brazil also there were many more social strata than the very rich and the very poor.
[60] Soltow, *Men and Wealth*, 136, concluded that the Gini Index figure for the distribution of slaves among slaveowners in the South in 1860 was 0.62; but if all freemen were considered the

What we can conclude with unquestionable certainty is that better records regarding land tenure and slave ownership exist for the United States than for Brazil. No national census at all was taken in Brazil until 1872, it did not include land ownership, and its manuscript schedules (which would show slave ownership) have since been lost, perhaps deliberately destroyed. The few extant local manuscript censuses, mainly for the period before the coffee boom, generally omitted land holdings. In 1850 the Brazilian congress issued a land law which established a land registry (dependent on landowners' sworn statements), but the law was fitfully enforced and the records it produced have been scattered. Tax records, so useful to Owsley, presume a land tax, a bureaucracy prepared to collect it, and a population prepared to pay it, at least most of the time.[61] The absence of so many of these records in Brazil indicates the sharp differences between the two areas, differences with deep roots in the social history, political economy, and cultural heritage of each area.

The financial condition of that great number of persons who were neither slaves nor wealthy planters impinges directly on any consideration of the size of the market for manufactures.[62] Were free agricultural workers better off in the South than in Brazil? Most of those in the South, as noted above, owned some land, a condition probably absent in Brazil. The tradition of the yeoman farmer had no equivalent in Luso-Brazilian experience. Assuredly, the truly poor whites lived similarly: outside the market economy, in abject poverty, barefoot, sick, and malnourished.[63] Still, the average free person in the South probably had a much bigger share of the area's buying power than did his Brazilian counterpart. When combined with the greater wealth of the region as

---

figure would be 0.93. Furthermore, if slaves were included as potential property holders, the number would rise still further. See Lee Soltow, "Comment," in *Six Papers on the Size Distribution of Wealth and Income*, Lee Soltow, ed. (New York: Columbia University Press for the National Bureau of Economic Research, 1969), 26. Also see Wright, *Political Economy*, 27, where the Gini Index for slaveholding among slaveowners is calculated at 0.79, rising in some places to 0.85. For the placer mining region of Brazil, long after its decline, Gorender (*Escravismo colonial*, 435) shows a rather even distribution of slaves. Stuart Schwartz suggests this was the trend in all of Brazil. "Patterns of Slaveholding in the Americas: New Evidence from Brazil," *American Historical Review* (in press).

[61] Warren Dean, "Latifundia and Land Policy in Nineteenth-Century Brazil," *Hispanic American Historical Review*, 51 (November 1971), 606-25. A group of researchers working under the direction of Professor Ismênia de Lima Martins of the Universidade Federal Fluminense in Niterói has been organizing the land registry records for the state of Rio de Janeiro; in the United States land taxes antedate even independence. Gray, *History of Agriculture*, 618.

[62] On the failure of this group to provide an adequate market for industrial goods, see Genovese, "The Significance of the Slave Plantation," 422-37; but see the qualifying remarks on this matter made by Parker, "Slavery and Southern Economic Development," 117. Also see Bruchey, *Roots*, 162-72, esp. 171.

[63] Cf. Eaton, *Growth of Southern Civilization*, 169-70, with Monteiro Lobato, *Urupês*, 2d ed. (São Paulo: Brasiliense, 1947), 235-36. Historians of Brazil need to differentiate among the *caipiras* more carefully, as Eaton does, and as Emilio Willems begins to do in "Social Differentiation in Colonial Brazil," *Comparative Studies in Society and History*, 12:1 (January 1970), 31-49.

a whole, the purchasing power of Southern consumers far outstripped that of the Brazilians.

Immigration did not help Brazil redress that imbalance. Even before the end of slavery, thousands of European immigrants moved onto the Brazilian plantations to work alongside slaves. This phenomenon contrasts with the experience in North America where immigrants avoided the rural slave areas. The fact can be explained by the changing circumstances of Europe, the diminished opportunities for acquiring land in the United States, and the widespread and justified belief that Brazilian slavery was about to end, as well as the recruitment efforts of Brazilian planters. By working under conditions that approached those of slavery, however, the immigrants did not by their presence immediately increase the number of consumers in Brazil. On the contrary, their availability probably slowed the growth of real wages.[64] So the relative poverty of the nonslaveowning, nonslave rural class in Brazil continued despite immigration and doubtless limited the market for industrial goods both in the countryside and in the towns.

The towns and cities of the American South probably offered a larger market for industrial goods than did Brazil's nonrural areas. Estimating the extent of urbanization in Brazil is difficult because the Brazilian census of 1872 (and subsequent ones) presented population figures by parishes within counties, usually without differentiating between urban and rural areas. Since the territory of parishes varied greatly and no one has yet calculated the area of each one, even the density of population cannot be known at this time. Outside visitors to both Brazil and the South describe sleepy, small towns, and the absence of bustling commercial centers, but my own reading of traveller's accounts and secondary sources leads me to believe that the South enjoyed a more active town life, with more local merchants and more exchanging of goods, than did Brazil.[65] Joaquim Nabuco, the Brazilian abolitionist, described the effect of slavery upon Brazilian towns in this way:

[64] Michael M. Hall, "The Origins of Mass Immigration in Brazil, 1871-1914" (Ph.D. diss., Columbia University, 1969); Thomas H. Holloway, "Migration and Mobility: Immigrants as Laborers and Landowners in the Coffee Zone of São Paulo, Brazil, 1886-1934" (Ph.D. diss., University of Wisconsin, 1974); idem, "The Coffee Colono of São Paulo: Migration and Mobility, 1880-1930," Land and Labour in Latin America, Kenneth Duncan and Ian Rutledge, eds. (Cambridge: Cambridge University Press, 1977), 301-32; idem, "Creating the Reserve Army? The Immigration Program of São Paulo, 1886-1930." International Migration Review, 12 (Summer 1978), 187-209; Alfredo Ellis Júnior, Populações paulistas, Biblioteca Pedagógica Brasileira, ser. 5, no. 27 (São Paulo: Editora Nacional, 1934), 57-79; Leff, "Tropical Trade," 688, 690-91; Ana Maria dos Santos, "Immigration and the Ideology of Modernization: The Brazilian Meanings of North American Immigration" (typescript).

[65] Cf., e.g., Olmstead, Cotton Kingdom, 212-21, with Richard F. Burton, Explorations of the Highlands of the Brazil; with a Full Account of the Gold and Diamond Mines; Also, Canoeing down 1500 Miles of the Great River São Francisco from Sabará to the Sea, 2 vols. (London: Tinsley, 1869), I, 34-115. Also see Woodman, King Cotton, 189-91; Goldin, Urban Slavery, 11-27; Thomas W. Merrick and Douglas H. Graham, Population and Economic Development in Brazil, 1800 to the Present (Baltimore: The Johns Hopkins University Press, 1979), 186-89. The

With the exceptions of Santos and Campinas in São Paulo province, Petrópolis and Campos in Rio de Janeiro, Pelotas in Rio Grande do Sul, and a scattering of other towns, there are not commercial houses outside the [provincial] capital cities where anything can be found beyond a small stock of items essential to life, and even these are crude or adulterated. . . . For this reason, whatever is not ordered directly from the capital reaches the consumer through the peddler alone.[66]

If indeed the towns of Brazil were less numerous, smaller, with a slower pace of commercial activity, the explanation may be sought both in the smaller value of the principal commodity of trade and in the more skewed distribution of wealth. A few Brazilian planters, who preferred to transact business at the capital, could not provide employment for the storekeepers, smithies, liverymen, lawyers, doctors, bankers, clerks, and others about whom one reads in the descriptions of southern American towns.

Towns in the South bustled especially on election day. By 1860 it was not just the men of means who could vote, but almost every free white adult male.[67] True, some historians argue convincingly that the political, social, and cultural predominance of the rich planter gave the South its distinct quality as compared to the North; everyone aspired to be such a planter, and as a seigneur he continued to exercise patronage and influence.[68] When contrasted with Brazil, however, a different view of the South emerges. The strength of landowners—or of any group—eludes precise measurement, but it would certainly be hard to believe that in the coffee regions of Brazil any real political power rested among small landowners or poor whites.[69] Even in the

---

fact that the Brazilian census did not distinguish town and country derives, of course, not just from the nature of political units, but from the very concept of the *urbs*, another subject for comparative study; see Richard W. Morse, "Prolegomenon to Latin American Urban History," *Hispanic American Historical Review*, 52 (August 1972), 359-94.

[66] Joaquim Nabuco, *Abolitionism: The Brazilian Antislavery Struggle*, Robert Conrad, trans. and ed. (Urbana: University of Illinois Press, 1977), 125. A similar description appears in Olmstead, *Cotton Kingdom*, 528-29.

[67] Fletcher M. Green, "Democracy in the Old South," *Journal of Southern History*, 12 (February 1946), 14-15.

[68] Genovese, *Political Economy*, 28-31; the property held by legislators has been studied by Ralph A. Wooster, *The People in Power: Courthouse and Statehouse in the Lower South, 1850-1860* (Knoxville: University of Tennessee Press, 1969); but Eugene D. Genovese has retorted that studies of the social origins of politicians reveal "what every fool always knew," namely, that politicians were usually lawyers, "Yeomen Farmers in a Slaveholders' Democracy," *Agricultural History*, 49 (April 1975), 339. Also see Douglas F. Dowd, "Discussion," in "Slavery as an Obstacle," Conrad *et al.*, eds., 537; and Roger W. Shugg, *Origins of Class Struggle in Louisiana: A Social History of White Farmers and Laborers during Slavery and After, 1840-1875* (1939; rpt. Baton Rouge: Louisiana State University Press, 1972), 121-56.

[69] On measuring the political power of landowners, see Richard Graham, "Political Power and Landownership in Nineteenth-Century Latin America," in *New Approaches to Latin American History*, Richard Graham and Peter H. Smith, eds. (Austin: University of Texas Press, 1974), 112-36. Note, however, that Raymundo Faoro, *Os donos do poder: formação do patronato político brasileiro*, 2d ed. (Porto Alegre and São Paulo: Globo and Editora da Universidade de São Paulo, 1975), has argued that the Brazilian state was totally independent of the influence of the landowners and was even antagonistic to them. Roderick J. Barman maintains that even poor

twentieth century the political weight of the *matuto* (backwoodsman) is negligible and Brazilian politicians have appealed to a rural lower class only to their sorrow. In contrast, Michael Johnson argues that fear among large planters that the rising democratic pressures from less wealthy southerners threatened their political dominance impelled—at least in part—the secession movement in Georgia. Poor southerners could vote even when illiterate, while in Brazil the legally instituted property tests for voters, although ignored when it suited local potentates, became ever more restrictive just as the end of slavery approached.[70]

Now it would be going too far to say that the political power of the average southener *explains* the greater distribution of wealth; the explanation may work in the opposite direction. But the two phenomena are closely linked, especially when considered over a long period of time. And it is remarkable to note, for instance, the amount of public money invested in human development in the South. On this score it far outdistanced Brazil no matter how much it may have lagged behind the North. Only 21 percent of the free persons in Brazil in 1872 could read (22.7 percent in the coffee provinces), while the equivalent figure in the South in 1850 was already 79.7 percent.[71] Whereas in 1860 there were 512 persons in the South for every physician or surgeon (572 in the 5 leading cotton states), there were 5,048 potential patients for each doctor in Brazil in 1872 (and 9,026 within the coffee provinces).[72] The greater amount of attention paid to such human needs in North America surely led to a better-fed, healthier, more energetic work force and entrepreneurial cadre among the free. It reflects, furthermore, a belief, shared even by the Southern planters, regarding the over-all benefits to be derived from such investments. Both the general ethos and the particular practices stem from changes in

---

whites had considerable power, "The Brazilian Peasantry Reexamined: The Implications of the Quebra-Quilos Revolt, 1874-1875," *Hispanic American Historical Review*, 57 (August 1977), 401-24; but Linda Lewin presents strong evidence to the contrary in "Some Historical Implications of Kinship Organization for Family-based Politics in the Brazilian Northeast," *Comparative Studies in Society and History*, 21:2 (April 1979), 266-67, 277-78, 289-90, and also in her "The Oligarchical Limitations of Social Banditry in Brazil: The Case of the 'Good' Thief Antonio Silvino," *Past and Present*, no. 82 (February 1979), 116-46.

[70] Michael P. Johnson, *Toward a Patriarchal Republic: The Secession of Georgia* (Baton Rouge: Louisiana State University Press, 1977); Eaton, *Growth of Southern Civilization*, 173, 175-76; José Honório Rodrigues, *Conciliação e reforma no Brasil, Um desafio histórico político*, Retratos do Brasil, no. 32 (Rio de Janeiro: Civilização Brasileira, 1965), 135-62; but see Mircea Buescu, *Brasil, Disparidades de renda no passado: subsidios para o estudo dos problemas brasileiros* (Rio de Janeiro: Apec, 1979), 78-108.

[71] The Brazilian figures are derived from the 1872 census and refer to the percentage of total literates among the total free over six years of age. Brazil, Directoria Geral de Estatistica, *Recenseamento ... 1872* (Rio de Janeiro: Leuzinger, 1873-76); the data on the United States are from Eaton, *Growth of Southern Civilization*, 160; also see Engerman, "Reconsideration," 353n., who reports the literacy rate among whites in the South at 84 percent.

[72] U.S. Census Office, *Population of the United States in 1860* (Washington, D.C.: U.S. Government Printing Office, 1864); Brazil, *Recenseamento ... 1872*.

political structures that predate the age of cotton, alterations Brazilians had not experienced. Before turning to those antecedents, however, we also need to consider contrasting degrees of social mobility and divergent cultural qualities.

Accelerated social mobility both sprang from increased entrepreneurial reward and led to it. Thus, the opportunities offered by a relatively even distribution of wealth in an economy attracting sizeable overseas investments and able to pay for abundant imported capital goods encouraged entrepreneurs, who then expected social elevation. In return, the permeability of higher social strata to entrants from below who had acquired wealth through saving, hard work, and risk-taking contributed further to attracting entrepreneurial effort. Now, the degree of social mobility, like the power of large landowners, becomes a matter of emphasis. We need not exaggerate the ease of upward or downward movement among North Americans, whether in the seventeenth, the nineteenth, or the twentieth centuries, and Brazil never had a totally rigid social system that excluded all mobility. But when the two societies are considered side-by-side, the comparison suggests greater fluidity in the United States South.[73] If southerners invested proportionately more of their personal incomes and more of the export earnings of the region in further growth and development than was the case in Brazil, the explanation may lie in the contrasting patterns of social mobility. A systematic study of such mobility in the two areas is very much needed.

Brazil outdistanced the South in one kind of social mobility. I refer to the frequency of manumission. As shown in Table 7, free blacks and mulattos in Brazil far outnumbered either the slaves or the whites. Carl Degler has noted this difference and, by particularly focusing on the subsequent fate of the mulatto, has considered the middling position of this racial group as central to explaining the absence of a sharp color line in Brazil today.[74] I extend Degler's argument about the mulatto to the free blacks as well: The liberal, egalitarian ideology of North Americans made it almost impossible to find space for free men whom whites nevertheless considered inferior. Only two categories existed: free-and-equal or slave. The many-layered Brazilian social structure placed every individual either above or below someone else. There is no equivalent word in English for the Brazilian concept of *condição* (literally, "condition"), a term used to indicate precise social place. Because Brazil had such an elaborate stratification, no threat to the established order was posed by a large number of freed blacks and mulattos. So, whereas there the freeing of a slave was viewed as a properly paternalistic act, in the American South such

---

[73] Soltow, *Men and Wealth*, 176, shows that property holdings in the South tended to increase with age, that 80 percent of those who were sixty years old owned some property, and concludes that young men could reasonably aspire to acquire it.

[74] Degler, *Neither Black nor White*, 213-64.

TABLE 7

Population of Brazil and United States South, by Race

	Brazil, 1872	South, 1860
Black and mulatto slaves	1,510,810	3,953,696
Free blacks and mulattos	4,245,428	261,918
Total blacks and mulattos	5,756,238	4,215,614
Whites	3,787,289	8,097,463
Total population	9,543,527	12,313,077
Free blacks and mulattos as percentage of all blacks and mulattos	74%	6%
Free blacks and mulattos as percentage of total population	44%	2%

SOURCE: David W. Cohen and Jack P. Greene, eds., *Neither Slave nor Free: The Freedman of African Descent in the Slave Societies of the New World* (Baltimore: The Johns Hopkins University Press, 1972), 314, 339.

action threatened the very structure of society, and freed slaves often had to leave or face reenslavement.[75] Thus the greater social control extant in Brazil made this limited form of mobility (from slave to freed black) more possible than in the United States.[76] It was not a difference that contributed to economic development.

Differences in the degree of social mobility and in political structures lead to questions about culture. The effect of culture upon economic development has long been debated and it is not my purpose to lay the question to rest. The Protestant ethic has proven an inadequate explanatory tool elsewhere, and Brazil's Catholicism can probably account for little in this regard, although some may argue that it fit into and strengthened a corporate society.[77] The

[75] David W. Cohen and Jack P. Greene, eds., *Neither Slave nor Free: The Freedman of African Descent in the Slave Societies of the New World* (Baltimore: Johns Hopkins University Press, 1972), 86-92, 267-68, 318-21; John Hope Franklin, *The Free Negro in North Carolina, 1790-1860* (1943; rpt. New York: Norton, 1971).

[76] The reduced amount of control exercised by Southern elites over the free population may explain why the practice of self-hire among slaves, referred to earlier, posed a threat not felt in Brazil. Similarly, one should note the successful unionization of white workers in Southern cities, long before any similar movement in Brazil. Genovese, *Political Economy*, 232-33; Eaton, *Growth of Southern Civilization*, 165-67; Starobin, *Industrial Slavery*, 118-19, 127; Boris Fausto, *Trabalho urbano e conflito social (1890-1920)*, Corpo e Alma do Brasil, no. 46 (São Paulo: Difel, 1977), 41-44.

[77] H. M. Robertson, *Aspects of the Rise of Economic Individualism: A Criticism of Max Weber and His School* (Cambridge: Cambridge University Press, 1933); James Broderick, S. J., *The Economic Morals of the Jesuits: An Answer to Dr. H. M. Robertson* (London: Oxford University Press & Humphrey Milford, 1934); Kurt Samuelson, *Religion and Economic Action*, E. Geoffrey French, trans., D. C. Coleman, ed. (New York: Basic Books, 1961); Rosalie Wax and Murray Wax, "The Vikings and the Rise of Capitalism," *American Journal of Sociology*, 61 (July 1955), 1-10; V. A. Demant, *Religion and the Decline of Capitalism. The Holland Lectures for 1949* (London: Faber and Faber, 1952).

presence or absence of the "spirit of capitalism" begs the question, and the psychology of disadvantaged groups does not seem particulalry applicable to the American South as a contrast to Brazil.[78]

One can probably agree, however, with those authors who allege that wherever the bourgeoisie ruled, the cultural qualities that lead to entrepreneurship were emphasized and rewarded, almost by definition; and that, in contrast, a landed aristocracy more highly valued status, deference, and leisure.[79] The problem here is to account for the difference between two areas both of which, at first glance, seem to have been ruled by a seigneurial class. I believe Robert Fogel and Stanley Engerman are mistaken when they insist the South was as "capitalistic" as the North, even if we accept their definition of the word; but the South was surely much more dominated by the values of the bourgeoisie than was Brazil. Although some Brazilian planters invested in railways, the majority refused to contribute even to community road-building programs, unmoved by the possibility of greater profits through improved transportation. They knew that fuzziness in land titles strengthened their authority, for the law can be the recourse of the weak even if originally drawn up by the strong. So they did not insist on clear property boundaries or work to clear their titles from conflicting claims, measures that could have facilitated the use of their land as security on loans. Many of them long resisted efforts to reform the mortgage laws—even though this would have increased the flow of credit to agriculture—I think because, more than the southerners, they saw land as a source of power as well as profit.[80] A study of comparative ideology among planters appears long overdue and will point not to black-and-white

[78] Werner Sombart, *The Quintessence of Capitalism: A Study of the History and Psychology of the Modern Business Man,* M. Epstein, trans. and ed. (London: Fisher Unwin, 1915); Alexander Gerschenkron, "Social Attitudes, Entrepreneurship and Economic Development," *International Social Science Bulletin,* 6:3 (1954), 252-58; Everett E. Hagen, *On the Theory of Social Change: How Economic Growth Begins* (Homewood, Illinois: Dorsey, 1962); David C. McClelland, *The Achieving Society* (Princeton: Van Nostrand, 1961); Alec P. Alexander, "The Supply of Industrial Entrepreneurship," *Explorations in Entrepreneurial History,* 2d ser., 4 (Winter 1967), 136-49.

[79] Fernandes, *Revolução burguesa;* Genovese, *Political Economy.*

[80] The two positions on the South are most clearly expressed in Genovese, *Political Economy,* 13-36, and Fogel and Engerman, *Time on the Cross.* Also see Carl N. Degler, "Plantation Society: Old and New Perspectives on Hemispheric History," *Plantation Society in the Americas,* 1 (February 1979), 13-14. For critiques of Fogel and Engerman's positions on this matter, see Paul A. David and Peter Temin, "Capitalist Masters, Bourgeois Slaves," *Journal of Interdisciplinary History,* 5 (Winter 1975), 445-57; idem, "Slavery: The Progressive Institution," *Journal of Economic History,* 34 (September 1974), 739-83; and Elizabeth Fox-Genovese, "Poor Richard at Work in the Cotton Fields: A Critique of the Psychological and Ideological Presuppositions of *Time on the Cross,*" *Review of Radical Political Economics,* 7 (Fall 1975), 67-83. I believe the hegemony of the Northern bourgeoisie in this one nation-state may have forced southern planters, in self defense, to articulate a more seigneurial position than their behavior belied. On mortgage law and clarity of land titles, see Sweigart, "Financing and Marketing," 109-217. On the relationship of culture to economic growth, see William H. Nicholls, *Southern Tradition and Regional Progress* (Chapel Hill: University of North Carolina Press, 1960).

contrasts, but to varying shades of gray; we will thus need to articulate precise criteria by which to measure seigneurialism.

To explain why the South was less seigneurial than Brazil the historian cannot point only to slave relations of production. He must look much further into the past. The independence movements of the two areas had sharply divergent social meanings. Whereas students of North American history debate whether or not the American Revolution enhanced the country's social democracy and eased the rise of new social groups to political power,[81] historians of Brazil today agree that the slow process of independence, which ended there in 1840, signified the unquestioned preeminence of the wealthy in the halls of power. Although landowners in the frontier region clashed with those in older settled areas, and merchants and bureaucrats vied for position too, the small landowners and urban petit bourgeoisie profited little if at all.[82]

The colonial structures of Brazil and of the South were as dissimilar as were their societies later on. There has been less research so far on Brazil than on the South, and the simplistic views of rigid social "estates" preventing all movement in Brazil will surely be discarded; but even a cursory reading of the history of the two regions leads the observer to believe that Brazil must have had a lesser degree of social equality and mobility than the southern colonies, little as the latter may have had of either.[83] Such differences left their mark and helped shape the life of succeeding generations. The larger consuming market and the greater propensity to invest among mid-nineteenth-century Southerners, as compared to Brazilians, owe much to that heritage.

The social structures of the mother countries from which these two areas emerged as colonies also seem significantly different. Nothing symbolizes that difference more clearly than the contrasting nature of the English and Portugese revolutions of 1640. Although there is much controversy over the meaning of the Puritan Revolution, one need only consider the social groups of contemporaneous Portugal and the conservative nature there of the anti-Spanish revolt of 1640 to realize how different were the structures from which the two colonies originated.[84] Social changes taking place in England long

[81] The highlights of the debate are noted succinctly in Thomas C. Barrow, "The American Revolution as a Colonial War for Independence," *William and Mary Quarterly,* 25 (July 1968), 452n.-453n.

[82] José Honório Rodrigues, *Independência: revolução e contra-revolução,* 5 vols. (Rio de Janeiro: Francisco Alves, 1975); Carlos Guilherme Mota, ed., *1822: Dimensões* (São Paulo: Perspectiva, 1972); Thomas H. Flory, "Judge and Jury in Imperial Brazil: The Social and Political Dimensions of Judicial Reform, 1822-1848" (Ph.D. diss., University of Texas at Austin, 1975); F. W. O. Morton, "The Conservative Revolution of Independence: Economy, Society, and Politics in Bahia, 1790-1840" (Ph.D. diss., University of Oxford, 1974); and Fernandes, *Revolução burguesa,* 31-85; but *cf.* Faoro, *Os donos do poder,* I, 241-312.

[83] Fernandes, *Revolução burguesa,* 15-30; R. J. D. Flory, "Bahian Society," 96-157; Gary B. Nash, *Class and Society in Early America* (Englewood Cliffs, N.J.: Prentice-Hall, 1970), and especially the readings he suggests.

[84] Lawrence Stone, *The Causes of the English Revolution, 1529-1642* (New York: Harper and

before 1700 will require as much attention from the historian who attempts to understand the South's economic history as does slavery. Put more boldly, part of the explanation for contrasting situations in Brazil and the South will be found in the seigneurial values and hierarchically structured society more firmly present in Portugal than in England and imported to Brazil with less erosion; differences, in other words, that run deeper and endured longer than the institution of slavery.

From these differences in respective pasts of Brazil and the American South sprang the concentration of wealth in fewer hands in the case of Brazil and the smaller investment there in human development. The more limited market in Brazil was not so much due to slavery as derived from an inequality in the distribution of wealth among the free, a condition that dates back to the very settlement of Brazil. The South, like the American North, emerged out of a society where a bourgeois revolution had already begun before colonization. This fact helps explain the relative clarity of land titles, the prevalence of yeomen farmers, and the threat felt by Southern planters in face of rising middle groups. Slavery may have slowed economic development somewhat in both the South and Brazil, but to use it as the major explanatory device for the persistently slow pace of development in Brazil is to ignore even larger forces.

The contrasts in social structure and in the role within industrial capitalism of each area's export crop—cotton as an essential raw material, coffee as a dessert—when combined with the greater value of the South's exports, can explain the other differences examined here: The South drew on richer capital resources, applied a higher level of agricultural technology, lived with better transportation services, and witnessed more industrial growth. The comparison of Brazil with the South furthermore suggests that, in order to understand the relationships between slavery and economic development, we must consider parameters set by historical developments over a very long course of time.

Row, 1972); Eduardo d'Oliveira França," Portugal na época da Restauração" (doctoral thesis, Universidade de São Paulo, 1951). The debate on the situation in England is reflected in Lawrence Stone, "Social Mobility in England, 1500-1700," *Past and Present*, no. 33 (April 1966), 16-55; Alan Everitt, "Social Mobility in Early Modern England," *Past and Present*, no. 33 (April 1966), 56-73; W. A. Speck, "Social Status in Late Stuart England," *Past and Present*, no. 34 (July 1966), 127-29; and Lawrence Stone, "Social Mobility," *Past and Present*, no. 35 (December 1966), 156-57.

ANGLICANISM, CATHOLICISM AND THE NEGRO SLAVE *

I

In recent years, American scholars have begun to search for the uniqueness of the American institution of Negro slavery, by contrasting it with the experience of the other colonizing nations of Europe in the New World. Even as far back as the 17th century, a sharp difference in slave institutions was noted between English, French and Spanish possessions, yet few historians until recently have attempted to analyze the causes and consequences of these distinctions.

Beginning with the work by Frank Tannenbaum,[1] which was expanded by Stanley Elkins,[2] such a preliminary comparative study has been undertaken. Concentrating on the vast structure of the law, these two scholars have relied essentially on a comparative legal analysis. Critics have challenged their generalizations on the grounds that there exists a great distinction between the model of the law and the reality of practice, while recently the very distinctness of the legal structure has been questioned.[3]

But while subjecting these pioneer attempts to internal textual criticism, few have attempted to challenge their conclusions and generalizations by empirical investigation. The aim of this paper is to take such an approach, by subjecting to detailed analysis the slave systems of two colonial powers in the New World. It studies the operation of one crucial aspect of the slave system, the relationship between infidel Negro and Christian Church, in two highly representative colonies, those of Cuba and Virginia.

The problem of dealing with non-Christian African Negro slaves was one of the most difficult tasks faced by the churches of the New World in the colonial period. Whether of the Roman Catholic or Protestant denomination,

* Research for this article was made possible by a grant from the Social Science Research Council.
[1] Frank Tannenbaum, *Slave and Citizen, the Negro in the Americas* (New York, A. A. Knopf, 1947).
[2] Stanley M. Elkins, *Slavery, A Problem in American Institutional and Intellectual Life* (Chicago, University of Chicago Press, 1959).
[3] Arnold A. Sio, "Interpretations of Slavery: The Slave Status in the Americas", *CSSH*, VII, No. 3 (April, 1965), 289-308.

each metropolitan church suddenly found its colonial parishes flooded with human beings held in bondage and ignorant of the doctrines of Christianity. For each church the question of the validity of that bondage had to be dealt with, and for each the human and Christian nature of the African Negro had to be determined. While the problem might be ignored in the first hours of establishing a functioning church among the white colonists, and dealing with the problem of the evangelization of the American Indians, these questions had to be eventually resolved before a Christian kingdom could be established on the shores of the New World.

How the two metropolitan churches dealt with the African Negro slaves would be determined by a host of considerations, from the question of organizational differences, to the problem of religious climate. Whatever the cause, however, the patterns of dealing with these slaves, which they both evolved, would have a profound impact on the life of the bondsmen. For especially in the Pre-Enlightenment world, when religious thought and action completely pervaded the life of Colonial America, the attitudes and actions of the church did much to create and define the moral, legal, social and even economic position of the Negro, slave and free, within colonial society.

II

Within colonial Latin American society the Spanish Catholic Church was the prime arbiter in the social and to a considerable extent in the intellectual life of all men. Not only did it define the moral basis of society and determine the limits of its intellectual world view, but it also sanctified and legalized the most basic human relationships. While this was the traditional role of the Church in Catholic Europe, and especially within Spain, the Church in the New World also faced the unique task of dealing with non-European peoples and defining their place within traditional social patterns.

Acutely aware of this problem from the first days of the conquest, the Church conceived of its primary function in the New World as an evangelical one. Putting aside its harsh and negative role as defender of the faith, which dominated its European attitudes against the other "peoples of the book", it adopted a positive role of sympathetic conversion of virgin peoples to the true faith.[4]

---

[4] The evangelizing mission of the Catholic Church in the New World was in fact a truly novel and powerful departure from previous experience. While the wars of *reconquista* against the Moors had brought the expansion of the faith, this had been through means of the fire and sword. Only in rare instances were attempts made to convert Mohammedans and Jews to Christianity peacefully, and thus despite the religious overtones of the centuries-long *reconquista*, the whole concept of evangelization was practically non-existent. Even when the opening up of virgin territories suddenly brought this great movement to life within Spanish Catholic circles, it was an entirely unique

While the thrust of this missionary activity was directed toward the American Indians,[5] the evangelical Catholic Church of the New World also intimately concerned itself with the other great religiously primitive peoples, the African Negro slaves. From the beginning of slave importation, in fact, the Church took up the position that the African Negroes were to be considered part of the New World Church, on much the same level as the untutored Amerindians. And while the Church was often forced to concede colonists prior claims for the labor of these black and brown races, it never relinquished its position as the guardian of the moral, religious and even social life of the untutored Indian and Negro races within its New World domain.

This dominant role of the Church in the life of the Negro slaves is well illustrated in the history of the Cuban Church. Because of the virtual extinction of the pre-contact Indians on the island and the subsequent dominance of the slave population, the Cuban Church was forced to give its undivided attention to its Negro communicants, almost from the first years of colonization. Eventually becoming the most heavily populated Negro colony in Spanish America, Cuba, more than any other area, tended to set the pattern of Church-slave relations.

In defining its attitude toward the African slave, the Cuban clergy were of course governed by the ideas which had evolved on the institution of slavery and on African Negroes both in the contemporary mores of Iberians and in the decrees of the Metropolitan Church. In both sets of standards there had been built up in the Iberian peninsula an historic pattern which preceded the creation of the modern Spanish state. The sub-Saharan Negro as well as the North African peoples had had intimate contact with the population of Spain from recorded times to the 16th century. Especially important in the armies and slave populations of the Spanish Moslem states, the Iberian peoples had long accepted the individuality, personality and co-equality of the Negro. In fact, large numbers of Negroes mixed freely in slavery under the Moslem and Christian states, with Iberian Christians, Eastern European Slavs and other Mediterranean peoples.[6]

---

phenomenon, with no parallel in Europe. Thus while the New World church was pacifically preaching a gentle Christ to the Indians, the peninsular church during these same three centuries of colonial rule, waged an unrelenting war against Jews, Moors, *mudejares, moriscos, conversos,* judaizers, Lutherans and Calvinists. Intolerant defender of the faith at home, it proved to be unusually tolerant, patient and intelligently assimilationist in its encounters with the New World pagans. As one scholar concluded, "Militant Spain guarded its religious purity in the metropolitan territory with the sword, and turned itself into a missionary at the service of the same faith in the New World." Antonio Ybot León, *La iglesia y los eclesiasticos españoles en la empresa de indias,* 2 vols. (Barcelona, Salvat Editores, 1954-1963), I, 347-50.
[5] See e.g., Robert Ricard, *La "conquête spirituelle" du Mexique* (Paris, Institut d'ethnologie, 1933).
[6] On the role of the African Negro in medieval Spain, see E. Lévi-Provençal, *Histoire*

Since North African Berbers blended into mulatto and black sub-Saharan Negroes, there was no reason for the white Iberians to conceive of these Africans as anything but normal human beings. As for their position under the slave systems developed by the Christian kingdoms of the North, they were treated as co-equal to all other non-Christian peoples, with the same obligations, duties and even rights. For those in the Castilian region, this meant that they were under the modified Roman slave laws elaborated in *Las Siete Partidas* of Alfonso X, a 13th-century codification of existing Castilian law and custom, which was the fountainhead for the slave code later to be applied to the New World.

The most fundamental aspect of the slave sections of *Las Siete Partidas* was the initial proposition that the institution of slavery was against natural reason.[7] It declared that "slavery is the most evil and the most despicable thing which can be found among men, because man, who is the most noble, and free creature, among all the creatures that God made, is placed in the power of another ...".[8] While recognizing it as an institution of long standing and custom which had to be continued, the code considered it a necessary evil rather than a positive good; thus the slave was to be guaranteed every possible right which he held as a member of the human community, with modification of these rights only where absolutely necessary.

From this position, it followed that the basic legal personality of the slave was to be preserved as much as possible. While the slave was forced to relinquish his natural primary right to liberty, he was guaranteed his other rights to personal security and even the right to property. From the point of view of the Church, his secondary or social rights were even more important. Thus the slave was guaranteed the right of full Christian communion, and through the sanctity of the Church, the right to marriage and parenthood.

To guarantee the sanctity of these sacraments, the Catholic Church, according to these 13th century codes, was made responsible for their fulfillment even in the face of opposition from masters. Thus the Church itself had to pay compensation to masters if slaves married outside their own master's

---

de l'espagne musulmane, 3 vols. (Paris, G.-P. Maisonneuve, 1950-1953), III, 72, 74-75, 177-78; 208ff.; Charles Verlinden, *L'esclavage dans l'europe médiévale, péninsule ibérique – France* (Bruges, "De Tempel", 1955), pp. 225-26, 358-62; José Antonio Saco, *Historia de la esclavitud desde los tiempos mas remotos hasta nuestra dias*, 3 vols. (Barcelona, Jaime Jepus, 1875-77), II, 140-41. – African Negro slaves were still a known and recognized element within Iberia's small slave population right up to the opening up of the modern slave trade with West Africa by Portugal in the 15th century. *Ibid.*, III, 36; Elizabeth Donnan, *Documents Illustrative of the History of the Slave Trade to America*, 4 vols. (Washington, Carnegie Institution of Washington, 1930-1935), I, 1.
[7] *Las siete partidas del rey Alfonso el sabio, cotejadas con varios codices antiguos, por la Real Academia de Historia*, 3 vols. (Madrid, Imprenta Real, 1807), III, 117, Partida IV, titulo xxi, ley 1.
[8] *Ibid.*, 30, Partida IV, titulo v, introdución.

household, so that the couples could be united.[9] It also had to guarantee that no families that were legally bound together could be separated, especially through sale overseas.[10] Finally, the Church was used by the state to encourage the process of manumission as much as possible.[11]

With the opening up of the New World to African slavery, the Castilians transferred these historic codes to the overseas "kingdoms" with little change, adding to them only as local conditions warranted. In the first years, this meant dealing with the background of the African immigrants. When raw blacks (*bozales*) were heavily imported directly from Africa after the granting of the *asientos*, it was suddenly discovered that many of these religiously "primitive" peoples were in fact practicing Moslems. Having as its major aim the religious purity of the Indies, especially in regard to its old enemy, the Crown quickly suppressed all such importations, and thenceforth only "primitive" *bozales* were allowed to enter, and they, like the Indians, fell into the same tutorial status as regards the Church.[12] While this meant exclusion of Indians and Negroes from the priesthood for this period, it also meant that they were exempt from the jurisdiction of the Inquisition.

Although the majority of the Catholic Church both in Spain and the New World had early and successfully attacked the legality and practice of enslaving the Indians,[13] only a few exceptional clerics contested the right to Negro slavery.[14] For the Negro was not originally a subject of the Crown of

[9] *Ibid.*, 31-32, Partida IV, titulo v, ley 2.
[10] *Ibid.*, ley 1.
[11] Among the numerous laws on manumission see *ibid.*, 121-22, Partida IV, titulo xxii, ley 1.
[12] Fernando Ortiz, *Hampa afro-cubana: los negros esclavos, estudio sociologico y de derecho público* (La Habana, Revista Bimestre Cubana, 1916), p. 343 n; also José Antonio Saco, *Historia de la esclavitud de la raza africana en el nuevo mundo y en especial en los paises americo-hispanos*, 2 vols. (Barcelona, Jaime Jepus, 1879), I, 69.
[13] Silvio Zavala, *La filosofía política en la conquista de América* (Mexico, Fondo de Cultura Economica, 1947), chap. iv. For the ending of Indian slavery in Cuba, see Irene Aloha Wright, *The Early History of Cuba, 1492-1586* (New York, Macmillan Co., 1916), pp. 229, 232.
[14] Las Casas, who had stood at first for the introduction of Negro slaves, later held that the Negroes were unjustly enslaved, "for the same reasoning," he claimed, "applies to them as to the Indians." Alonso de Montufar, archbishop of Mexico, in 1560 questioned the enslavement of the Negroes, while Fray Tomas de Mercado in his work *Tratos y contractos de mercaderes* (1569) attacked the right of procuring and enslaving Negroes in Africa itself. Bartolome de Albornoz in his *Arte de contratos* (1573) approved of the slave trade in Moors from Berber, Tripoli and Cyrenaica, but rejected entirely the trade in Negroes from Ethiopia and the Portuguese traffic in it. Perhaps the most outstanding figures in the evangelical mission to the African Negro slave in the New World were two 17th-century friars: Pedro Claver, who worked among the Negro slaves arriving at Cartagena, for which he was later canonized, and the American Jesuit, Alonso de Sandoval who wrote the famous evangelical tract, *De instaurada aethiopum salute* (1627). Silvio Zavala, *New Viewpoints on the Spanish Colonization of America* (Philadelphia, University of Pennsylvania Press, 1943), p. 65; Zavala, "Relaciones historicas entre indios y negros en Iberoamerica", *Revista de las Indias*, Vol. XXVIII, No. 88 (1946), pp. 55-65; Saco, *Historia de la esclavitud de la raza africana,*

Castile and his enslavement had occurred prior to his entrance into the Spanish realms. This left the clerics no legal grounds and less moral will for denying the practice, since it was initiated, according to the thinking of the day, by the heathens themselves. But while the Church never officially opposed the institution of Negro slavery, it deliberately interfered in the direct relationship between master and slave on the grounds that both were communicants in the Church and that nothing must challenge this primary Christian right to salvation and the sacraments.

This responsibility of the Church to care for its Negro communicants, as well as to guarantee that no subject of the Crown was not a practicing Christian, was specifically laid on the New World clergy by the Crown itself. In the very opening book of the *Leyes de Indias*, the famous compilation of colonial legislation, the Crown demanded that the Church take especial care in dealing with Negro slaves. It stated that:

> We order and command to all those persons who have Slaves, Negroes and Mulattoes, that they send them to the Church or Monastery at the hour which the Prelate has designated,[15] and there the Christian Doctrine be taught to them; and the Archbishops and Bishops of our Indies have very particular care for their conversion and endoctrination, in order that they live Christianly, and they give to it the same order and care that is prepared and entrusted by the laws of this Book for the Conversion and Endoctrination of the Indians; so that they be instructed in our Holy Roman Catholic Faith, living in the service of God our Master.[16]

Nor was the Church itself slow in meeting these demands, and in its earliest colonial synods it dealt long and extensively with the problems of its Negro members. Given the close tie which existed between civil and canonical law, the legislation issuing from these synods became an essential part of the Cuban slave legislation.[17]

The first of these colonial Church synods to meet in the Caribbean was the Dominican provincial synod which met early in the 17th century on the island of Española. Held under the auspices of the Archbishopric of Española, which included all of the West Indies, Cuba, Florida, and Venezuela,[18] this first Caribbean Church synod spent a good part of its time considering

---

I, 252-55; Rafael Altamira, *Historia de España y de la civilización española*, 5 vols. (Barcelona, Juan Gili, 1900-1930), III, 242.

[15] "We order that in each one of the towns of Christians a determined hour each day, be designated by the prelate in which all the Indians, Negroes and Mulattoes, free as well as slave, that there are within the towns, are brought together to hear the Christian Doctrine." This same law also provided a similar arrangement for those who worked and lived in the countryside. *Recopilación de leyes de los reynos de las Indias*, 3 vols. (Madrid, D. Joaquin Ibara, 1791), I, 4-5, Libro I, titulo i, ley 12.

[16] *Ibid.*, 5, Libro I, titulo i, ley 13.

[17] Ortiz, *op. cit.*, p. 348.

[18] Ybot León, *op. cit.*, II, 55.

the problem of its Negro communicants. With strong royal representation, in the person of the Governor and President of the Audiencia of Santo Domingo,[19] the leading bishops and clerics prepared, after much discussion, a series of laws and ordinances known as *sanctiones*.[20] Because of royal representation and support, these Latin codes were later translated into Spanish and became the official civil code within the *audiencia*, as well as being canonical law for the ecclesiastical province.[21]

One of the very earliest of these *sanctiones* of the Provincial Dominican Council and the first dealing with the Negro concerned the very basic task of determining if the Negro had been properly admitted into the church:

Since we learn from a certain experienced leader that Negroes have been transported from Africa and brought from other parts to these Indies without benefit of baptism, so if at some time it is claimed that these were besprinkled with holy water by traders when they are put ashore by us it is recommended that they be questioned concerning their baptism: that is, if they have received the water of baptism before they left from Africa, or on the sea, or in any other place or whether they did not receive it at all? ... Also one may question them whether at the time they received the baptism they had obtained any knowledge, however imperfect, concerning the performance of this sacrament which was conferred upon them, ... and also whether they willingly received this holy water at the time it was offered to them. If however, any of these conditions are found to be lacking in their baptism, they must be baptized anew.[22]

In the next section it was stated that redoing the baptism was essential if there were any doubts, because to the Negro "it is thus shown that the privilege of the sacrament is given to them, and the Negroes know themselves to be baptized equal to the others".[23] It followed that no cleric of the province could "confer baptism upon Negro adults unless they have been imbued first with the Christian doctrine",[24] which education was to be undertaken as soon as they entered the province, by a priest specifically designated for this task.[25] If Negroes refused to be baptized, they were given two to three months "during which the fear of the doctrine must be found". At the end of this time the cleric "may administer baptism to them, provided they are, one and all, sorry for their transgressions, they display the sign of this sorrow, and they realize the power of the sacrament of baptism".[26]

As for the sacrament of confirmation, it was demanded that the "priest

[19] Fr. Cipriano de Utrera, "El Concilio Dominicano de 1622, con una introdución historica", *Boletín eclesiastico de la arquidiócesis de Santo Domingo* (1938-1939), pp. 8-9.
[20] The original Latin ordinances, or *Sanctiones Concilii Dominicani*, are reprinted in *ibid.*, pp. 23-81.
[21] *Ibid.*, pp. 10-11.
[22] *Sanctiones Concilii Dominicani*, Sessio Secunda, Caput I, Sectio vii.
[23] Sessio Secunda, Caput I, Sectio vii.
[24] Sessio Secunda, Caput I, Sectio ix.
[25] Sessio Secunda, Caput I, Sectio x.
[26] Sessio Secunda, Caput I, Sectio ix.

even warns the master of Negroes to place before these same ones the means
and the place to receive this divine sacrament, but if they do otherwise they
may be punished with a judgement".[27] In the sacrament of marriage, it was
required that at Negro weddings (as in the case of Indian ones) two special
benedictions be given instead of the usual one, to impress them with the
importance of this sacrament.[28] In the case of an unbaptized Negro contract-
ing marriage with someone already baptized, it was required that a new
agreement be made and the marriage ceremony be repeated. And this was
ʾɔ be done as soon as possible, "so that the benefits of marriage may be
rightfully enjoyed".[29]

Negroes were not to be granted absolution until they had overcome their
ignorance and inexperience and had finally accepted the faith.[30] It was also
provided that every qualified confessor could hear the confessions of Negroes.[31]
Again, with the administration of extreme unction as with all other sacraments, it was demanded that the Negro be taught its meaning and accept its
significance before it could be administered to him.[32]

It was required by these *sanctiones* that Negroes who lived at great dis-
tances from the churches and worked in the country should hear mass at least
at six festive holy days per year. If the master was not willing to allow his
slaves to hear mass at least these six times, then the prelate was to see to his
legal chastisement.[33] The Church council also demanded that "no master of
Negroes may put slaves to any servile work on the festive days, nor may he
hire others; under the penalty of ten silver pounds for the first transgression,
for the second he will truly be implicated with excommunication".[34] For the
Negroes on these days were to be taught by the priest "so that they may learn
the articles of faith and reap the harvest of sacraments".[35]

Largely supporting the declarations and ordinances of the Dominican
Provincial Synod of 1622, and also providing further clarifications of the
rights of Christian Negroes, were the *Constituciones* published by the Church
synod which met for the Cuban diocese in June of 1680. Constitución IV
repeated a proviso that had become an essential part of the imperial slave
code, that is, that all slaves be instructed in the Roman Catholic faith and be
baptized within a year of their admittance into the Indies.[36]

[27] Sessio Secunda, Caput II, Sectio iii.
[28] Sessio Secunda, Caput IV, Sectio iii.
[29] Sessio Secunda, Caput IV, Sectio vii.
[30] Sessio Secunda, Caput V, Sectio i.
[31] Sessio Secunda, Caput V, Sectio vi.
[32] Sessio Secunda, Caput VII, Sectio iv.
[33] Sessio Tertia, Caput I, Sectio iv.
[34] Sessio Tertia, Caput I, Sectio v.
[35] Sessio Quarta, Caput VII, Sectio ii.
[36] Fernando Ortiz, *Hampa afro-cubana: los negros brujos* (Madrid, Librería de Fernando Fe, 1906), p. 304. This same command was also contained in the very first
chapter of the 1789 Slave Code, see "Real Cedula de Su Magestad sobre la educación,

It also provided that *bozales* could not be married by a priest until both parties were baptized.[37] In attempting to deal with this problem, the Diocesan Synod was forced to take into account the African background of the slave and to adjust the Catholic atmosphere to the matrimonial situation brought by the slave from his native land. "Because there come many Indians ... and Negro *bozales*, married in their infidelity: we order that wanting to live together in this bishopric, after being baptized, their marriage be ratified *in facie ecclesiae* [in the sight of the Church]." If either partner refused the faith, he or she was given up to seven months and six warnings to be baptized. If after this time elapsed they still refused baptism they could not continue their marital relations. And "if any of the said infidels come married with many wives" he was required to be baptized and married to the first one with whom "according to their custom and rites" he had contracted marriage. If the first one could not be so ascertained, then the male could marry the one he desired. And it was also required that if he was married within the direct parental line (mother, sister, etc.), his marriage was declared invalid and the couple had to separate before baptism was administered.[38]

The Diocesan Synod also attempted to eradicate a continuing problem, that of unscrupulous masters who, for either personal reasons or those of economic expediency, tried to prevent their slaves from marrying or refused to honor these marriages. Thus Constitución V established that "marriage should be free" and ordered that:

no master prohibit his slaves against marriage, nor impede those who cohibit in it, because we have experienced that many masters with little fear of God and with serious damage to their consciences, proscribe that their slaves not marry or impede their cohibition with their married partners, with feigned pretexts; ...

In this same law, masters were prohibited from taking their slaves outside of Havana to sell them unless they took husband and wife together. Constitución VI added that masters could not sell their slaves overseas or in remote parts, in order to impede marital cohibition. If this was done, then the slaves sold in this manner should be brought back with the master paying the expense.[39]

The local Church did all in its power to carry out the intent of the metropolitan slave codes, and to guarantee to their Negro communicants their full rights. They met in powerful synods to deal with local conditions and the unique backgrounds of their particular colored congregants, and always legislated in favor of the fullest freedom and rights that were permissible. While the upper clergy dealt with these problems in law, the lower clergy, especially at the parish level, effectively carried this law into practice.

---

trato y ocupaciones de los esclavos en todos sus dominios de Indias ...", reprinted in *Revista de Historia de America*, No. 3 (September, 1938), pp. 50-51.
[37] Constitución III, quoted in F. Ortiz, *Los Negros Esclavos* ..., p. 348.
[38] *Ibid.*, pp. 349-50.
[39] *Ibid.*, p. 349.

This correlation between law and practice is abundantly supported by the local parish statistics available on the administration of the sacraments. What these materials indicate is that the slave and free colored population had the same percentage and absolute figures of baptism as the white population. According to the census of 1827, for example, when whites represented 44% and the slaves 41% of the total population,[40] each group respectively had 12,938 and 12,729 baptisms performed on the island in that year.[41]

Not only were slaves and free colored fully admitted into the Church, but they also heavily participated in all the sacraments, and most importantly in that of marriage as well. Thus, for example, in the four years from 1752 to 1755, the Rector of the Cathedral Church at Santiago de Cuba reported 55 slave marriages to 75 free white marriages in his parish.[42] At this time the entire urban population of Santiago de Cuba consisted of 6,525 whites, and 5,765 slaves,[43] which means that the slave marriages in that period represented one out of 105 slaves in the city, and the free whites one out of 96.3. In short, despite the sharp differences in education, social status, and wealth, the slave marriage rate was very close to that of the free white rate. This is all the more extraordinary a figure, given the fact that a large portion of the adult population, of all colors and social conditions, lived in free unions because of the high cost of clerical ceremonies.

This same pattern is repeated in the local parish of Santo Tomas, also in the jurisdiction of the Santiago de Cuba Church. In the parish census for 1824 there were listed 794 married whites, 855 free colored married persons, and 855 married slaves. This breaks down into a percentage of 44% for the whites, 42% for the free colored and 29% for the slaves of the adult population, that is, of persons seventeen or older.[44] On the one hand these figures reveal the great extent of illegal unions among adults of all races, but they also seriously under-rate the slave marriages. For the general statistics of the entire island consistently reveal that the free colored marriage rate was considerably below that of the colored slaves.

Thus, in 1827 there were listed a total of 1,868 white marriages, 1,381 slave marriages and only 385 free colored marriages. The ratios in the total population figures for that year come to one marriage performed for 166 white persons, for 207 colored slaves and 236 free mulattoes, the worst being one out of 347 free Negroes.[45] The reason for the high slave marriage rate

[40] Ramón de la Sagra, *Historia economico-política y estadística de la isla de Cuba* (Habana, Imprenta de las viudas de Arazoza y Soler, 1831), pp. 7-8.
[41] *Ibid.*, p. 20. The free colored, who made up 15% of the total population in 1827, had 4,826 baptisms.
[42] Archivo General de Indias [hereafter cited as AGI], Sevilla, Audiencia de Santo Domingo, legajo 516, no. 30, June 14, 1758.
[43] Sagra, *op. cit.*, p. 3.
[44] AGI, Santo Domingo, leg. 223, February 15, 1824.
[45] Sagra, *op. cit.*, pp. 20, 24. In France at this time, the figure was one married couple for each 134 persons. *Ibid.*, p. 24 n.

as contrasted to the free colored population appears to be the fact that the slave population was accountable to a master, and through him to the local church, and was therefore far more under the influence of the local parish priest.

Another remarkable factor is the large number of legal marriages between free and slave persons. Of the 702 colored marriages on record in six selected parishes of Havana between 1825 and 1829, 278 were between slaves, 293 between free persons and 131 involved a slave and a free person.[46]

All of these baptismal and marriage statistics re-enforce the fact that civil and canonical law was the very essence of actual practice, and that the Negro slave enjoyed co-equal status with his masters before the sacraments of the Church. That the Church was so effective in carrying law into practice and constantly guaranteeing these rights, is also due to the extraordinarily large number of priests on the island. In the census of 1778, exclusive of nuns, there were listed 1,063 practicing clergy in Cuba. This meant that for the island's total population of 179,484, there was one priest for every 168 persons, a figure not even approached in any country in the Americas today.[47]

Aside from its direct role in the sacraments and the carrying out of Catholic education, the Church also encouraged manumission by impressing on masters that it was a meritorious act in the eyes of God. On his special Saint's day, or in honor of a marriage, a birth, or a recovery from a severe illness, a master would give thanks to God by freeing some of his slaves. The Crown greatly encouraged these procedures by making it possible to manumit a slave by simple declaration of the master in a church before the local priest.[48]

That the work of the clergy in providing a moral climate conducive to manumission was successful can also be seen in the statistics. From the early days of slave importation, a large free colored class began to appear in Cuba, largely as a result of voluntary manumission by their masters. By the 1560's the free colored population on the island was numerous enough to elect its own *aguacil*, or constable, in Havana,[49] and by the end of this century they had already fielded one full company of free colored militia of around 100 men.[50] By the end of the next century the free Negro community was able to

[46] *Ibid.*, p. 65.
[47] For the 1778 census breakdown, see AGI, Indiferente General, leg. 1527, December 31, 1778. For a clerical census of the Americas in 1959, see Donald S. Castro, *et al.*, *Statistical Abstract of Latin America, 1963* (U.C.L.A., Center of Latin American Studies, 1964), p. 22. The lowest figure for any contemporary Latin American country was Chile, with one priest for every 2,750 Catholics. The United States figure in 1965, is 1 priest to 778 practicing Catholics. *The Official Catholic Directory, 1965*, General Summary, pp. 1-2.
[48] Tannenbaum, *op. cit.*, pp. 53ff.
[49] Saco, *Historia de la esclavitud de la raza africana*, I, 221.
[50] For the history of the first company of *pardos libres* (free mulattoes) of Havana see, AGI, Santo Domingo, leg. 418, no. 7, 1714.

sponsor a full battalion of some 800 men,[51] and by the census of 1774 the island listed 30,847 free colored, as opposed to 43,333 Negro slaves, making the free colored some 41% of the total black population on the island.[52] In fact, from this first census, until the era of mass illegal importations of African slaves after 1820, the percentage of freedmen to slaves never fell below 36%. Even at its lowest ebb, in 1841, the free colored class still numbered 152,838, 26% of the total colored population. When this mass illegal trade was finally halted in the late 1850's, the temporary disequilibrium was overcome; by 1861 the free colored accounted for 39% of the total colored or 213,167 free persons as against 339,872 slaves.[53]

The Church was not only the most important factor in encouraging and maintaining the impetus to voluntary manumission, which accounts for the majority of freedmen, it also encouraged *coartación*. Most fully developed in Cuba, *coartación* was the system whereby a slave had the right to purchase his freedom from his master. The slave was granted the right to appear in court at any time to have his price fixed and to begin to pay his purchase price in agreed installments after the initial down payment, usually a minimum sum of 50 pesos, or something like 1/4 of his value. Once a slave became *coartado* he had a whole range of rights including the right to change masters if he could find a purchaser for his remaining price, and to buy his freedom as soon as he was able. Because of the expense and labor involved, it was only the exceptionally able artisan and urban slave who most benefitted from the system, though it was open to rural plantation slaves as well, and it has been estimated that about 4,000 per year took advantage of it.[54]

Throughout the whole practice of *coartación* the Church played a vital role, for it was the prime guarantor of the free time and labor of the Negro outside his master's jurisdiction. To obtain funds, the Negro slave was permitted by custom and the Church to work for himself in his own private truck garden, or *conuco*, on all holy days and Sundays. Income from these *conucos* was also exempted from tithe payments. This was a very unusual privilege in colonial society, where the *diezmos*, or tithes, were the most universal form of production and property taxes.[55] Finally in seeking a reliable third party to hold his savings toward the initial down payment, and also to help him present his legal case, the Negro slave often relied on the local parish priest.[56]

---

[51] AGI, Santo Domingo, leg. 419, no. 8, 1715.
[52] Sagra, *op. cit.*, p. 3.
[53] The figures for the census from 1774-1827 can be found in *ibid.*, pp. 3-6; and for those for the census from 1841-1861 are calculated by Julio J. Le Riverend Brusone, in Ramiro Guerra y Sanchez, *et al.*, *Historia de la nación cubana*, 10 vols. (La Habana, Editorial Historia de la Nacion Cubana, 1950), IV, 170.
[54] For a complete discussion of this system, see Herbert H. S. Aimes, "Coartacion: A Spanish Institution for the Advancement of Slaves into Freedmen", *Yale Review*, XVII (February, 1909), 412-31; and Ortiz, *Los negros esclavos*, pp. 313ff.
[55] AGI, Santo Domingo, leg. 152, ramo 2, no. 39, September 24, 1680.

Although the clergy did not interfere with the actual functioning of the slave regime, they could be critical of it. The Bishop of Santiago de Cuba in the late 17th century bitterly complained that the masters were not properly clothing their slaves, so that the latter were often embarrassed to come to Church. He warned the masters that they were under obligation to provide the slaves with decent clothing, and not force them to provide for themselves.

The clergy also criticized the Negroes, especially on matters of laxity in church attendance and disinterest in learning their doctrine. This same Bishop who concerned himself over the poor dress of his Negro communicants, also was rather shocked at the indifference of some of the slaves to Church service. He charged that many were not attending mass on holidays and Sundays, before they began to work on their own properties, and that others were not seriously learning their lessons. In both situations he wanted the civil authorities to intervene, and in the latter case even proposed that instead of the present gentle method of instruction, the local clergy should adopt "the method by which the clerical teachers of New Spain and Peru teach their Indians", that is by using the whip on them in front of their fellow communicants if they forgot their lessons.[57]

This stern attitude was the exception rather than the rule, most clergy dealing gently with their Negro church-goers. One who attempted to mold custom to the Church, and who largely succeeded, was Bishop Pedro Agustin Morel de Santa Cruz, in the middle of the 18th century. When he took up residence he found that there were 21 Negro clubs, or *cabildos*, in Havana where Negroes of both sexes gathered on holidays and Sundays to drink, dance "in extremely torrid and provocative dances" and commit other excesses too sinful to mention. Many told the Bishop that it was better to leave these *cabildos* alone, for they provided a reasonable outlet for the slaves and freedmen without causing undue harm. But, he declared, "not being satisfied with similar scruples, I attempted the gentle method of going by turns to each of the *cabildos*, to administer the sacrament of confirmation, and praying the Holy Rosary with those of that organization (*gremio*), before an Image of Our Lady which I carried with me. Concluding this act, I left the image in their houses, charging them to continue with their worship and devotion. . . ." He then named a specific clergymen to each of the *cabildos* to go to them on Sundays and holidays to teach them Christian doctrine. He also placed each *cabildo* in charge of a particular Virgin that it was to venerate under the direction of a clergyman. This unusual and enthusiastic bishop went so

---

[56] Such for example was the experience of the parish priest of the copper mining town of Santiago del Cobre in the 17th century with his 500 free and slave Negro communicants. AGI, Santo Domingo, leg. 417, no. 15, December, 1709.
[57] AGI, Santo Domingo, leg. 151, ramo 2, no. 22, February 22, 1682.

far as to propose that his clergymen should learn the various African languages spoken by the slaves so that they might teach them better.[58]

Although this step was never taken, there is no question of the successful syncretization of Catholicism with the African folk religions brought to Cuba by the Negro slaves. Bishop Morel de Santa Cruz's action was only one link in a long chain of effort to construct a *cofradía* (or religious brotherhood) system by the Church. This was so successful that the African *cofradías* came to play a vital role in the social life of both slaves and freedmen, with their own saints and special functions in various holy marches and carnivals. Usually organized along lines of regional African origins, their members coming from the same *nación*, or geographic location, these were both religious and benevolent associations. They were not only normal *cofradías* tied to the local church and carrying saintly images in religious processions, but cooperated with the *cabildos* in other activities. Throughout the year the *cabildo* acted as a mutual relief association, the chief of the *cabildo* aiding his subordinates if they were sick; their general funds were also used to pay burial expenses and sometimes to free old and invalided slaves. They also maintained *cabildo* houses as general meeting-places for the members of the *cofradía*, available to them at all times. Finally, the *cabildos* were recognized as legitimate political agents for the slaves and freedmen in dealing with the local authorities, thus providing outlets for political organization and leadership.

The African *cabildo* was not peculiar to Cuba, but existed throughout the Spanish and Portuguese Indies wherever Negroes were congregated. It had its origins in medieval Seville, whose Negro *cofradías* and *cabildos* were active and fully recognized from as far back as the fourteenth century. As early as 1573, the Havana municipal government ordered that all the Negroes of the city turn out for the Corpus Christi processions, "the same as they assisted in the famous one of Seville". In the great religious processions, the Negro *cabildos* in fact played an increasingly important part. Though outright African fetishes were quickly prohibited from display, the local saints and virgins were so entwined with African mythology and even costume that these displays often tended to perpetuate pre-New World patterns and beliefs.[59]

The most important religious processional for these organizations was the famous Christmas festival of the Day of the Kings. This day was recognized throughout the island as a special day for the Negro *cabildos* and *cofradías* and almost unlimited license was permitted by the white authorities in the great dances, drinkings and ceremonies. For the Negroes, both slave and free, it was the crowning event in their year, and provided an unparalleled opportunity for individual and community expression for the entire Negro

[58] AGI, Santo Domingo, leg. 515, no. 51, 1755.
[59] An excellent study of these cabildos is Fernando Ortiz, "Los cabildos afro-cubanos", *Revista Bimestre Cubana*, XVI (1921), 5-39.

population. Thus, between religious processions, annual *dia de reyes* celebrations and the daily conduct of their *cofradías* and *cabildos* the Negro masses were provided by the Church with a vast and crucial outlet for social expression and community development.[60]

While providing a rich fabric of social existence for the masses under the canopy of the Church, the Cuban clergy also aided the exceptionally able Negro to break through the rigid class-caste barriers of the white community through their control over the educational processes. Since, at the pre-university level, education was exclusively in the hands of the church, primary and secondary education was available to the exceptional and upwardly-mobile free Negro. Education was the only means by which a colored person could break through from the lower economic classes, at least to the learned professions, and possibly higher. For sons of prosperous colored artisans and successful colored militia officers, both mulattoes and Negroes, the open opportunity of the schools run by the secular and regular clergy was their avenue for mobility of their children.

For example, the mulatto, or *pardo*, Antonio Flores, a militia officer in Havana in the mid-18th century, had a son who had graduated with highest distinctions from the courses of Theology and Grammar offered by the local Jesuit college of Havana. When his son's right to enter the University was challenged on the grounds of his color, Flores, in bitter though unsuccessful opposition, pointed out to the Council of the Indies the innumerable examples of free Negro and mulatto children who had attended local church and primary schools in pre-university training courses.[61] And while the University consistently fought the entrance of colored persons into its ranks, the large number of petitions of colored persons to the Crown demanding the right to practice a profession to which they had already been trained, indicates that many succeeded in "passing" with little trouble, through the combination of light skins and the pre-collegiate training they had received from the clerical schools.[62] And even given denial of University admission to the majority of free colored, the very possession of a secondary *colegio* education in the days of mass illiteracy and non-professional university programs, was more than enough to break into the professional classes and the upper social levels. To read and write, at least, according to the Church, if not the colonial universities, was a right open to all, and a right which held out almost unlimited opportunities for the few who could achieve it.

Concerned for his social existence, his freedom, his family, and his soul, and even in a minority of cases for the training of his mind, the Church

---

[60] Fernando Ortiz, "La fiesta afro-cubana del 'dia de reyes' ", *Revista Bimestre Cubana*, XV (1920), 5-26.
[61] AGI, Santo Domingo, leg. 1455, no. 5, 1760.
[62] For example, see the petition of the mulatto Auditor of War of Cuba, who was a law graduate of the University, in AGI, Santo Domingo, leg. 2236, October 1, 1791.

deeply and vitally committed itself to its guardian role with its Negro slave communicant. Because it effectively controlled an important part of their lives, the Church was unquestionably the primary intermediary agent between master and slave, and the only institution which daily claimed its rights, as opposed to the property rights of the masters.

Although the Church could not abolish the rigors of harsh plantation servitude, it could modify that life to the extent of guaranteeing minimal periods of rest and independence for the blacks. The Church could also guarantee a degree of self-expression for all slaves, which enabled them to escape the close confines of bondage in many ways and thus to validate their human personality and potential. Finally it could create the panoply of mores and attitudes which permitted the Negro to be treated as a co-equal human being, and allowed him to fully merge into Cuban society when the harsh regime of slavery was destroyed.

III

Like Cuba, Virginia was settled by a dominant established church, in this case the Church of England. Both Spain and England at the times of colonization had a hierarchical metropolitan church which was closely tied to the royal government and was considered one of the major governing institutions of the realm. But while the counter-reformation Church of Spain was able to suppress all opposition to its religious authority, the Anglican Church found itself constantly struggling against Protestant dissenter groups who attempted to challenge its established authority. However, at the time of the initial planting of Virginia, the Crown and the Church were fully united and the Anglican Church was declared the established church of the colony. As early as 1606, the Crown decreed that the Virginia Company "... should provide that the true word and service of God should be preached, planted and used, *according to the Rites and Doctrine of the Church of England*".[43] In the first organization of the Company, there was even a bishop of the realm, John King of the London diocese, who was a leading member.[44] Through these actions, Anglicanism was guaranteed as the religion of the colonists, and from then until the end of the colonial period, the Church of England was overwhelmingly the state Church of Virginia, and its membership encompassed the majority of the population.

But while there was never any challenge to the religion of the metropolitan

[43] Quoted in Arthur Lyon Cross, *The Anglican Episcopate and the American Colonies* (Cambridge, Harvard University Press, 1924), p. 10.
[44] George Maclaren Brydon, *Virginia's Mother Church and the Political Conditions Under Which it Grew*, 2 vols. (Richmond, Virginia Historical Society, 1947-1952), I, 40-42.

Church in Virginia, the Crown never established the leadership and organization whereby the established church could function in its accustomed manner in the colony. In sharp contrast to Cuba, where this problem was never raised, the Crown and the hierarchy made no attempt to fit the colony into the normal functioning of the Church. Whereas Cuba had its first bishop appointed in 1516 just five years after the conquest, neither the Archbishop of Canterbury nor the Crown saw fit to appoint a native bishop, nor even to place the colony within the jurisdiction of an insular diocese.

The Bishop of London, because of his connection with the Company, originally assisted in providing clergymen and some financial assistance to establishing the Virginia church, but this tenuous connection was destroyed when the Company was dissolved by the Crown in 1624. While the Company provided land for church income, divided the colony up into parishes and encouraged the migration of clergymen,[65] it made no effort to obtain the establishment of a native bishop, primarily because of the cost; nor was the Church or the Crown at this time the least bit interested in subsidizing such a venture, or even in considering it.

Because of this amazing and gross neglect, the colonists within a few short years had completely usurped hierarchical authority and had transformed the centuries-old organization of English church government. In traditional English ecclesiastical organization, the local landowner, or other outside body or institution, had the power to nominate ministers for the local parish within their jurisdiction. This meant that the landowner or institution could present his own candidate for the local parish office to the Bishop for investiture. The Bishop then had the power to certify or reject the nominee, but once invested with his office, the clergyman served for life. The local parishioners had no say either in the nomination or investiture process, and had no recourse but to accept their minister on a life basis. The minister, in fact, was accountable only to the church, and only the Bishop could control him. What duties the local parishioners' vestry and churchwarden performed were all determined by law and were subservient to the local clergymen.[66]

The Church hierarchy also had the task of guaranteeing religious uniformity, and had extensive civil-ecclesiastical functions. Thus the Bishops could appoint special courts to try and condemn heretics; they had full jurisdiction over marriages, the probating of wills, the collation to benefices, the appointment of notaries; and extensive rights over tithes and other ecclesiastical taxes.[67]

Without the hierarchic structure, however, most of these functions could not be maintained; and, in fact, rapid erosion soon wiped out the complete edifice of the church as it was known in England. Although the Company at first appeared to claim the right of nomination of clergymen to Virginia parishes,

[65] *Ibid.*, pp. 10-11.
[66] *Ibid.*, pp. 42-44.
[67] *Ibid.*, p. 67; Cross, *op. cit.*, p. 2.

it seems not to have exercised that right, but simply sent out pre-ordained clergymen, which left open the question of their initiation into their parishes. With the dissolution of the Company, and the failure of English authorities to claim their rights, the local colonists absorbed all power. First the General Court of Virginia, consisting of the members of the upper house of the General Assembly, claimed that the right of nomination, or presentation, devolved on them from the Company. They also proceeded to absorb a host of other juridical, administrative and even ecclesiastical matters which by tradition belonged to the Bishop. This meant that control over vital statistics, notaries, wills, etc., the establishment of parishes, the naming and defining of all ecclesiastical offices, the collection of tithes; the regulation of church conduct and even the maintenance of purity of faith and dogma, was determined, not by the Bishop, canonical law courts and ecclesiastical officials as in England, but by the local General Assembly of Virginia.[68]

While central authority now came to rest in a popular civil assembly, the local church came increasingly under the power of the parishioners themselves, rather than the ministry. Developing new institutions and adopting old practices to local conditions, the colonists began to establish their own distinctly unique form of Church government, at whose center stood the all-powerful locally elected board of governing parishioners known as the Vestry.

With the devolution to the General Assembly of all matters pertaining to the Church, the Assembly in turn gave to each local parish vestry a multitude of civil and ecclesiastical rights and obligations, and made it the prime institution of a new type of established church. As early as the 1620's the Assembly was providing that local churchwardens and leading members of the parish should concern themselves with the maintenance of the church. From this simple maintenance task the evolving vestry organization quickly began to assume ever greater powers. A reflection of this occurred in 1643, when, in a formal legal enactment, the Assembly provided that each parish should have a vestry, and "that the most sufficient and selected men be chosen and joyned to the minister and churchwardens to be of that Vestrie". Among the tasks enumerated for the Vestry, was the crucial absorption of the right of nomination. The 1643 Act declared "that the vestrie of evrie parish . . . shall henceforward have power, to elect and make choyce of their ministers. . . ."[69] The vestry was to present the minister candidate for their parish appointment to the governor, not to a bishop, as in England, and the governor then made the formal induction and confirmation of that minister to hold the given office for life.[70]

While creation of the first vestries seems to have been by appointment of the General Court,[71] by the 1640's the Assembly provided that the vestry was

[68] Brydon, op. cit., I, 67-68; 86ff.
[69] William Waller Hening, The Statutes at Large, being a Collection of the Laws of Virginia, 13 vols. (New York, R and W and G. Bartlow, 1823), I, 241-42.
[70] Brydon, op. cit., I, 92.

to be organized on the basis of election from among the parishioners. By the time of the codification of the laws on the Church by the General Assembly in 1662, it was provided:

That for the makeing and proportioning the levyes and assessments for building and repayring the churches, and chappells, provision for the poore, maintenance of the minister, and such other necessary *duties* for the more orderly manageing all parociall affaires, *Be it enacted* that twelve of the most able men of each parish be by the major part of the *said* parish, *chosen* to be vestry-men out of which number the minister and vestry to make choice of two churchwardens yearly, as *alsoe* in the case of death of any vestry man, or his departure out of the parish, that the said minister and vestry make choice of another to supply his roome . . .[72]

By this act, which abolished the electoral system, the vestries in fact became autocratic local bodies of the leading planters, who exercised enormous control over social and economic conditions within the parish. After their initial establishment, elections never took place, and members usually held their office till death or resignation. When vacancies occurred, the vestrymen themselves proceeded to choose leading planters as members. So oligarchic and powerful did these vestries become, that one of the constant themes of colonial Virginian history was the popular, and continually unsatisfied, demand for periodic elections and the breakup of this autocratic control.[73]

Given this entrenched self-perpetuating planter leadership in control of the Church, the role of the transitory minister could be only a subordinate one at best. In complete contradiction to the entire organization of the Church of England, the Vestry refused to present their ministers for induction. Since induction by the Governor would guarantee the minister his parish for life, barring ill conduct, the Vestries simply refused to present their ministers, and by this means made the minister's position completely dependent on the goodwill of his leading parishioners. Though the royal governors had full power to force induction on the Vestries, not one governor in the entire history of the colony saw fit to exercise this right, out of fear of vestry power.[74]

This entire system was bitterly attacked by regular Church of England clergymen. The mid-17th century clergymen, Morgan Godwyn, who served in Virginia and the British West Indies, scornfully called this arrangement a "probational tenure" system,[75] while the Bishops' representative in the colony, Commissary James Blair, at the end of the century, was badly disturbed by

---

[71] *Ibid.,* p. 93.
[72] Hening, *Statutes,* II, 44-45.
[73] One of the major reforms of Bacon's rebellion was the call for vestry elections every three years. Brydon, *op. cit.,* I, 97.
[74] Philip Alexander Bruce, *Institutional History of Virginia in the Seventeenth Century,* 2 vols. (New York, G. P. Putnam's Sons, 1910), I, 136-39.
[75] Morgan Godwyn, *The Negro's and Indians Advocate, Suing for their Admission into the Church* (London, J. D., 1680), p. 168.

what he described as this "Custom of making annual Agreements with the Ministers, which they [i.e., the vestries] call by a Name coarse enough, *viz.* Hiring of the Ministers; so that they seldom present any ministers, that they may by that Means keep them in more Subjection and Dependence."[76] In short, stated the commissary, "they are only in the nature of Chaplains", whose tenure of office was dependent on an annual agreement renewable at the option of a small body of men.[77] Thus any independence on the part of the clergymen was quickly suppressed by the planters, who by the very nature of their positions would naturally be the strongest representatives of the status quo in the community. As Godwyn noted, they "obstruct all designs for the good of those Churches, and to report all things already so well settled as not needing the least amendment or alteration".[78]

Because of these developments, the regular clergy of England by and large refused to come to Virginia. For as Blair lamented, "no good Ministers that were inform'd of it would come into the Country, and if they came ignorant of any such Custom, they quickly felt the Effects of it in the high Hand wherewith most Vestries manag'd their Power, and got out of the Country again as soon as they could".[79] A goodly portion of the practicing clergymen in Virginia, until well into the 18th century, were in fact deacons, or as Morgan Godwyn called them, "*Lay-Priests* of the *Vestries ordination*".[80]

Even in his very vocation, the minister was challenged by the vestry. Thus the Reverend Hugh Jones in 1724 warned that ". . . in several places the clerks [of the parish] are so ingenious or malicious, that they contrive to be liked as well or better than the minister, which created ill-will and disturbance, besides other harm".[81] Given the chance, he charged, they will usurp almost all of the clergymen's functions, even to the giving of sermons, and warned that they should have their functions carefully defined by law to prevent these abuses.

So all-embracing was parishioner influence and control, that the clergyman had to win popular endorsement, and constantly keep his congregation happy, which of course excluded all possibilities of independent thought or challenge to the given moral and social situation, for this was the sure road to ruin. This dependence was so pervasive, in fact, that often parishioners even went so far, in this era of non-conformity, as to question and modify standard

---

[76] Henry Hartwell, James Blair and Edward Chilton, *The Present State of Virginia,* 2d ed. (Williamsburg, Colonial Williamsburg, Inc., 1940), p. 66.

[77] *Ibid.,* p. 67.

[78] Godwyn, *op. cit.,* Preface, p. i. According to Godwyn the Virginia colonists chafed at the cost of Church tithes, and quickly lost their interest in the Anglican creed, because, he charged, Virginians "for the most part do know no other *God* but *Money,* nor *Religion* but *Profit*".

[79] Hartwell, Blair and Chilton, *loc. cit.*

[80] Godwyn, *op. cit.,* p. 170.

[81] Hugh Jones, *The Present State of Virginia,* 2d ed. (Chapel Hill, University of North Carolina Press, 1956), p. 96.

Church dogma. Reverend Jones noted in his analysis of contemporary Virginia: "In several respects the clergy are obliged to omit or alter some minute parts of the liturgy, and deviate from the strict discipline and ceremonies of the Church; to avoid giving offence. . . ."[82]

While the mother church soon became deeply aware of the heterodoxy and complete breakdown of the established church in Virginia, it could do little to change the situation. Deeply involved in religious civil wars at home, it was not until after the Restoration that the Church of England could even begin to deal with the situation. It was only with the investiture of Henry Compton as Bishop of London, in 1675, that the Church finally forced the crown to place the colony within a diocese. For a number of historical reasons, the Bishopric of London was chosen; however, traditions were so entrenched that this brought little real change. The Bishop made no attempt to oppose vestry control, or to retake possession of his normal ecclesiastical or civil functions, or even his right of investiture. His only concern was to maintain some kind of purity of dogma by guaranteeing minimal standards for clergymen. This he did by forcing the colonists to accept only accredited clergymen licensed by himself. Thus in the instruction to Governor Culpeper of Virginia, the Bishop had the Crown declare that "no Minister be prefrr'd by you to any Ecclesiastical Benefice in that our Colony *without a Certificate from the Lord Bp. of London, of his being conformable to the Doctrine of the Church of England*".[83]

While the Bishop eventually succeeded in sending a representative to the colony, with the title of commissary, or vicar general, this clergyman could only exercise moderating influence, and had to persuade rather than enjoin acceptance of church rules.[84] The first commissar, James Blair (1689-1743) created much heat, but little concrete change,[85] and despite all attempts of several energetic London Bishops, the Vestries could not be forced to induct their ministers, leaving the majority of them to the arbitrary will of their congregations. Through the commissary rule of Blair and his successors, some positive results were attained with the problem of providing a regular ordained clergy for all the parishes, but in the end, the commissaries had little or no effect at reforming the general structure of the Virginia Church. When the metropolitan hierarchy realized this failure, it attempted to establish a resident Bishop for the American colonies. But this was a potentially powerful challenge to local authority, and colonial opposition was so constant and vehement against this idea that the matter was never carried to fruition, despite all the strenuous efforts made by the mother church.[86]

[82] *Ibid.*, p. 98.
[83] Quoted in Cross, *op. cit.*, p. 26.
[84] *Ibid.*, pp. 3-4, 44.
[85] *Ibid.*, pp. 78-80.
[86] For the history of this struggle, see Cross, *loc. cit.*, and Carl Bridenbaugh, *Mitre*

Not only was the Church after the Restoration terribly concerned about the religion of the white colonists, but it also began to take an increasingly involved position on the status of the Negro and Indian heathens within England's American Empire. This concern with the plight of the Negro slave, especially, is heavily attested to by the growing movement for conversion, education and even emancipation among the lower and upper clergy. This movement began as early as the end of the 17th century, and one of its first advocates was Morgan Godwyn, the angry clergyman, who served both in the British West Indies and the colony of Virginia, and whose *The Negro's and Indians Advocate* (1680) created a good deal of sentiment. This growing awareness of the complete lack of impact of the Church on the Negro slaves, in sharp contrast to the Catholic Church in the Spanish and French islands, as many Church of England men noted,[87] caused the Bishop of London to put pressure on the Crown.

In the royal instructions to Governor Culpeper of Virginia in 1681-1682, the Crown proposed that:

Ye shall endeavour to get a Law passed for the restraining of any inhuman severity which by ill masters or overseers may be used towards their Christian Servants or Slaves. And you are alsoe with the assistance of the Council and Assembly, to find out the best means to facilitate and encourage the conversion of Negroes to the Christian Religion, *wherein you are to leave a due* caution and regards to ye property of the Inhabitants and safety of the Colonies.[88]

The unusual restraint of this request indicates the royal government's recognition of the primacy of local law and custom over the humanitarian demands of the clergymen.

Nevertheless, the English hierarchy was becoming deeply concerned over the failure of the colonials to Christianize the Negro slaves. Finding that little could be accomplished directly through regular Church and governmental channels, despite the establishment relationship of the Church, the Bishops 'decided that the only alternative was a missionary society, completely

---

and *Sceptre, Transatlantic Faiths, Ideas, Personalities and Politics, 1689-1775* (New York, Oxford University Press, 1962).

[87] In his famous denunciation of West Indian Slavery, for example, the Reverend James Ramsay constantly contrasted the British to the French treatment of slaves. "In the French colonies," he declared, "the public pays an immediate attention to the treatment and instruction of slaves. The intendants [gov't administrative officers] are charged with their protection, proper missionaries are appointed for the purpose of training them up to a certain degree of religious knowledge; and ample estates and funds are allotted for their maintenance of these ecclesiastics." "The respect in which marriage is held, brings a farther advantage to French slaves. The ceremony is solemnized by the priest, and the tie continues for life. This gives them an attachment to their families, ... that is seldom seen among English slaves; where the connection between the sexes is arbitrary, and too frequently casual." Rev. James Ramsay, *An Essay on the Treatment of African Slaves in the British Sugar Colonies* (London, James Philipps, 1784), pp. 52, 54.

[88] *The Virginia Magazine of History and Biography*, XXVIII (1920), 43-44.

financed from England. Thus in 1701, the hierarchy in England founded the famous Society for the Propagation of the Gospel in Foreign Parts.[89]

That one of the primary aims of the Society was conversion of the slaves was understood by the Bishops from the very beginning. Thus in the annual sermon given to the society in 1710, Bishop William Fleetwood bitterly attacked the refusal of the masters of slaves to permit their conversion to Christianity. He claimed the refusal to permit baptism and Christian education was:

A thing so common in all our *Plantations* abroad, that I have reason to doubt, whether there be any Exception of any People *of ours*, who cause their slaves to be Baptized. What do these people think of Christ? ... That He who came from Heaven, to purchase to Himself a Church, with his own precious Blood, should sit contented, and behold with unconcern, those who profess themselves his Servants, excluding from its Gates those who would gladly enter if they might, and excercising no less Cruelty to their Souls (as far as they are able) than to their Bodies?

These People were made to be as Happy as themselves, and are as capable of being so; and however hard their Condition be in this World, with respect to their Captivity and Subjugation. ... They were bought with the same Price, purchased with the same Blood of Christ, their common Saviour and Redeemer; and on order to all this, they were to have the Means of Salvation put into their Hands, they were to be instructed in the Faith of *Christ*, to have the Terms and Conditions fairly offered to them.

Not only did Bishop Fleetwood attack the very Christianity of the masters, but also considered that this was probably their greatest sin, for he declared, "no Man living can assign a better and more justifiable Cause, for God's withholding Mercy from a *Christian*, than that *Christian's* with-holding the Mercy of *Christianity* from an Unbeliever".[90] The radical Bishop even went so far as to attack slavery itself, holding, as Adam Smith was later to proclaim, that hired labor was a far superior system and that slavery should be abolished. He attacked the ideas of colonists, which held that Christianity challenged the slave status, but instead of proclaiming the docility of slaves under Christian doctrine as some clerics did, he properly attacked the Christianity of the colonists who would refuse to treat fellow human beings with Christian brotherly love. Finally, he proposed that the Society take up the crucial task of Christianizing the infidels, Negroes and slaves, and that this example would have a powerful impact on the masters, who apparently are unimpressed by "the Example both of *French* and *Spaniards* ... , who all along have brought their Slaves to Baptism".[91]

[89] H. P. Thompson, *Into All Lands, The History of the Society for the Propagation of the Gospel in Foreign Parts, 1701-1950* (London, S. P. C. K., 1951), chap. 1.
[90] This sermon is reprinted in its entirety in Frank J. Klingberg, *Anglican Humanitarianism in Colonial New York* (Philadelphia, Church Historical Society, 1940), pp. 203-204.
[91] *Ibid.*, p. 211.

This call appears to have been heeded, for in the annual sermon of 1740, Bishop Secker pointed to the work of the Society in this special area. But the Bishop noted the vast difficulty still faced by the Church in this work as only a few had been converted and thousands yet remained outside the fold.

For it is not to be expected, that Masters, too commonly negligent of Christianity themselves, will take much Pains to teach it to their Slaves: whom even the better Part of them are in a great measure habituated to consider, as they do their Cattle, merely with a View to the Profit arising from them. Not a few therefore have openly opposed their Instruction, from an Imagination, now indeed proved and acknowledged to be groundless, that Baptism would entitle them to Freedom. ... And some, it may be feared, have been averse to their becoming Christians, because, after that, no Pretence will remain for not treating them like Men.[92]

Both within and without the society, the upper clergy were beginning, by the middle of the 18th century, to put pressure on the colonies to change their local customs and laws on these subjects, and to create a new panoply of beliefs that would permit the Church to carry on the work of conversion in a positive atmosphere.

The Bishop of London in 1742 put great pressure on Commissary Blair to get the local government to support a school for Negroes, and to indicate to them his great zeal in converting Negroes to the Christian faith.[93] But incapable of even fully protecting standard dogma and church practice, Blair and his successors could accomplish little. As for the SPG, the demands on its resources were so great, that it concentrated its efforts on the British West Indies, where the bulk of the New World slaves resided, and on the colonies in which the Church was unestablished.[94]

This meant, in essence, that whatever the feelings of the hierarchy in England as to the desirability of conversion of the slaves to Christianity and their participation in the sacraments, this desire had little if any impact on New World conditions. The religious life of the slave remained wholly dependent upon the will of his master, and this was determined almost exclusively by local custom. With no clergymen capable of opposing these assumptions and customs, the planters felt under no obligation to change their ways.

Unfortunately, custom was indifferent, if not openly hostile, to the conversion of Negro slaves. In the early years of the 17th century, there had existed the almost universal belief that conversion for the slave required his freedom, since Christians could not hold Christians in bondage. While the General Assembly eventually declared that this was not so,[95] the idea was

---

[92] *Ibid.*, p. 217.
[93] *William and Mary Quarterly*, 1st Series, IX (1901), 225.
[94] Thompson, *op. cit.*, chap. 3.
[95] The Virginia legislature itself seriously accepted the thesis that Christianity was

hard to uproot, and persisted throughout the colonial period. Even when this factor was resolved or admitted by the reluctant master, there was still the key fear of education making the slaves intractable. As the Reverend Hugh Jones reported, he constantly tried to disprove this latter assumption among colonials. "As for baptizing Indians and Negroes," he said, "several of the people disapprove of it, because they say it often makes them proud, and not so good servants: But these, and such objections, are easily refuted, for Christianity encourages and orders them to become more humble and better servants, and not worse, then when they were heathens." He did agree with general opinion, however, which held that Negro slaves should not be taught to read and write, since this "has been found to be dangerous upon several political accounts, especially self-preservation".[96]

While masters could be found who sponsored the baptism of their slaves, encouraged them to learn the catechism, and some who even read to them from the Bible, these were the exception rather than the rule. The pattern, in fact, was quite haphazard, and in the majority of cases conversion was never properly undertaken. This is well revealed in a survey of the colonial church of Virginia carried out in the early 18th century. In 1724 Commissary Blair sent out an extraordinarily revealing and exhaustive questionnaire to all the parishes of Virginia. Among the questions asked was: "Are there any Infidels, bond or free, within your Parish; and what means are used for their conversion?" The 29 clergymen who answered the inquiry give the overwhelming impression of only moderate clerical interest in the problem, and general planter indifference, if not hostility. As the Reverend George Robertson of Bristol Parish reported, "I have several times exhorted their Masters to send such of them as could speak English to Church to be catechised but they would not. Some masters instruct their Slaves at home and so bring them to baptism, but not many such".[97] The Reverend Henry Collings of St. Peter's Parish reported that of the Negro slaves in his parish "Some . . . are suffered by their respective masters to be baptized and to attend on divine service but others not."[98] The Reverend John Warden reported that in his parish "some masters will have their slaves baptised and others will not, by reason that

incompatible with slavery, and in its early definitions actually defined slaves as those who were not Christians. Thus in 1670 it enacted a statute which declared that "all servants not being christians imported into this country by shipping shalbe slaves for life." Henings, *Statutes*, II, 283. This was finally rectified in 1682 when the Assembly decreed that: "all servants except Turks and Moores . . . which shall be brought or imported into this country, either by sea or land, whether Negroes, . . . Mulattoes or Indians, who and whose parentage and native country are not christian, although afterwards, and before such their importation . . . they shall be converted to the christian faith; . . . shall be judged, deemed and taken to be slaves. . . ." *Ibid.*, 490-91.
[96] Jones, *op. cit.*, p. 99.
[97] William Stevens Perry (ed.), *Historical Collections Relating to the American Colonial Church*, 5 vols. (Hartford, Church Press Company, 1870-1878), I, 267.
[98] *Ibid.*, p. 269.

they will not be surities for them in Baptism",[99] while Alexander Forbes reported that in his parish the local Negro slaves "as soon as they are capable they are taught and baptised by the care of some Masters, but this too much neglected by many".[100] The clergymen of Henrico and Southwark parishes respectively replied of the slaves in their parishes that "their Masters, do no more than let some of them now and then go to Church for their Conversion", and that "there are some of their Masters on whom I do prevail to have them baptised and taught, but not many".[101] The Reverend John Brunskill of Willmington Parish probably best summed up the problem when he concluded that:

The Negroes who are slaves to the whites cannot, I think, be said to be of any Religion for as there is no law of the Colony obliding their Masters or Owners to instruct them in the principles of Christianity and so they are hardly to be persuaded by the Minister to take so much pains with them, by which means the poor creatures generally live and die without it.[102]

Even for the minority that were baptized, converted and taught the Christian religion, there were no positive rewards. No matter how Christian, no master allowed his slaves to be married. For if the sacrament of marriage was not to be made totally ridiculous, Negro slaves could not be admitted: it deprived human agencies of the right to separate the couple, and this was never accepted. Even when the best of masters died, the constant fluidity of fortunes meant that no slave community could remain intact beyond a few generations. Families were not sold together; to do so was uneconomic and therefore impractical. As the Virginia Baptist chronicler John Leland noted in 1790, "the marriage of slaves, is a subject not known in our code of laws.

[99] *Ibid.*, p. 289.
[100] *Ibid.*, p. 295.
[101] *Ibid.*, pp. 304, 306.
[102] *Ibid.*, pp. 277-278. Interestingly, the few records which survive of slave education and conversion carried out by masters, come not from Church of England slave owners, but from Presbyterians and Quakers. Thus Roberts Pleasants, one of the wealthiest planters of Virginia in the 18th century, and a Quaker, not only converted his slaves, but even educated and eventually freed them. Adair P. Archer, "The Quakers' Attitude towards the Revolution", *William and Mary Quarterly*, 2d Series, I (1921), 168. For his part, the Presbyterian planter Colonel James Gordon, in his journal in 1761 noted that "Several strange negroes come to Mr. Criswell [the local presbyterian teacher] to be instructed, in which he takes great pains." *William and Mary Quarterly*, 1st Series, XI (1903), 223. Nevertheless, despite these and other efforts, the consensus of historical opinion is best summed up by Marcus W. Jernegan who declared that throughout the colonial period, "most of the slaves lived and died strangers to christianity" and that "with comparatively few exceptions the conversion of negro slaves was not seriously undertaken by their masters. On the contrary many of them strenuously and persistently opposed the Church of England, and the Society for the Propagation of the Gospel in Foreign Parts...." Marcus W. Jernegan, "Slavery and Conversion in the American Colonies", *American Historical Review*, XXI, no. 3 (April, 1916), 504; also see Jerome W. Jones, "The Established Virginia Church and the Conversion of Negroes and Indians, 1620-1760", *Journal of Negro History*, XLVI, no. 1 (January, 1961), 12-31.

What promeses soever they make, their masters may and do part at pleasure".[103]

As for the complex web of social organizations to which the Cuban slave had recourse this simply did not exist under the established church of Virginia. There were no fraternal brotherhoods, no great processionals and special holidays, and absolutely no syncretization of Christian belief with folk religion of African origin. For the Negro slaves on the frontier of Virginia after 1740 there did exist the possibility of admission into the evangelical movement known as the "Great Awakening". From 1740 and especially after 1760 numbers of Methodist, Baptist, Presbyterian, and a host of other sect preachers began invading the frontier counties of Virginia above the tidewater.[104] For these preachers, most of whom like Wesley himself were bitter opponents of slavery, welcomed the Negroes into the Church. Thus John Leland in his Virginia Chronicle of 1790 reported:

The poor slaves, under all their hardships, discover as great inclination for religion as the free-born do, when they engage in the service of God, they spare no pains. It is nothing strange for them to walk 20 miles on Sunday morning to meeting, and back again at night. They are remarkable for learning a toon soon, and have very melodious voices.

They cannot read, and therefore are more exposed to delusion than the whites are; but many of them give clear, rational accounts of a work of grace in their harts, and evidence of the same by their lives. When religion is lively they are remarkable fond of meeting together, to sing, pray and exhort, and sometimes preach, and seem to be unwearied in the procession. They seem in general to put more confidence in their own colour, then they do in whites; when they attempt to preach, they seldom fail of being very zealous; their language is broken, but they understand each other, and the whites may gain their ideas. A few of them have undertaken to administer baptism, but it generally ends in confusion; they commonly are more noisy in time of preaching than the whites, and are more subject to bodily exercise, and if they meet with any encouragement in these things, they grow extravagent.[105]

But these camp meetings and non-hierarchical churches were not open to the majority of Virginia Negroes, who lived in the predominantly Church of England areas. Nor were the masters too ready to permit them to go to revivalist gatherings. As Leland himself notes: "... many masters and over-seers will whip and torture the poor creatures for going to meeting, even at night, when the labor of the day is done".[106] As fear of insurrection developed in the period after independence, such meetings became less and less common, public gatherings of more than a few slaves being prohibited.[107]

[103] John Leland, The Virginia Chronicle (Norfolk, Prentis and Baxter, 190), p. 8.
[104] Ibid., pp. 21ff; also see Wesley M. Gewehr, The Great Awakening in Virginia, 1740-1790 (Durham, Duke University Press, 1930).
[105] Leland, op. cit., p. 13.
[106] Ibid., p. 9.
[107] C. G. Woodson, The Education of the Negro Prior to 1861 (New York, G. P. Putnam's Sons, 1915), chaps. vii, viii.

HERBERT S. KLEIN

Not only was the Church incapable of undertaking a general conversion of the slaves, but it was also unable to promote manumission. Thus the common pattern of church-inspired individual planter manumission, which was accepted custom and practice in Cuba, was unknown in Protestant Virginia. Though the Methodists and Quakers early demanded that their members give up slave trading and emancipate their slaves, and though several revolutionary leaders followed their enlightenment thought to its logical conclusion and freed their Negroes, no powerful undercurrent of emancipation ever occurred. Quaker emancipations were few and of little consequence, and the Methodist leadership was soon forced to condone the existence of slaveholding even among its traveling clergy, and to give up its proposals for emancipation.[108] As for the Anglican hierarchy, while it too developed a powerful commitment to emancipation at the end of the 18th century, it took forceful Parliamentary legislation to carry out emancipation even in the West Indies. As for Virginia this emancipation movement never found echo in the local episcopal hierarchy, when the latter was finally established in 1790.[109]

The clergy of Virginia were unable to convince the planters that emancipation was a good act in the sight of God, and was to be considered a common and accepted form of pious action, as in Cuba. Nor could the morally aroused and committed clergy, of whatever denomination, convince the masters that slavery was essentially a moral evil and that on these grounds the slaves should be emancipated as soon as possible. Neither forcing emancipation on moral grounds from above, nor having it become a part of routine common practice from below, the whole emancipation movement in Virginia was at best a haphazard and distinctly minor affair. In fact, from the late 17th to the late 18th century it was to all intents and purposes outlawed by the State. By 1691 the reaction had become so intense, that the General Assembly of Virginia declared that "great inconveniences may happen to this countrey by setting of negroes and mulattoes free", and provided under heavy penalty, that owners who emancipated their slaves had to pay for their transportation out of the country within six months.[110] Not satisfied with this restriction on the growth of the free Negro class, the legislature next made it impossible for

[108] On the failure of the Methodists, see Gewehr, *op. cit.*, pp. 242-49; and for the Quakers see Thomas E. Drake, *Quakers and Slavery in America* (New Haven, Yale University Press, 1950).
[109] Though the Anglican church consecrated native candidates between 1784 and 1790, which enabled the Americans to establish the Protestant Episcopal Church in the United States, the new bishops were subservient to local interests and Vestry government was in no way changed. See Cross, *op. cit.*, pp. 263ff; Clara O. Loveland, *The Critical Years, The Reconstruction of the Anglican Church in the United States of America: 1780-1789* (Greenwich, Seabury Press, 1956); Edward Lewis Goodwin, *The Colonial Church in Virginia* (Milwaukee, Morehouse Pub. Co., 1927), pp. 127ff. for the early bishops of the Diocese of Virginia.
[110] Hening, *Statutes*, III, 87-88.

a master to free his slaves even on his own initiative. By a law of 1721 all emancipation was prohibited "except for some meritorious services, to be adjudged and allowed by the governor and council".[111]

By these extreme measures, the free Negro population, which probably numbered around 350 in 1691, was kept for the next century to its natural increase alone; by 1782 there were only some 2,800 freedmen in the state.[112] In this year, however, under the impact of the revolution and the growth of clerical opposition, a new law permitted open emancipation at the discretion of the owner.[113] By the first federal census of 1790, the number of freedmen had increased to 12,866. Even with this increase, the free colored population represented only 4% of the total colored population. Nor did the half-century between the first federal census and the Civil War see any major change. The percentage slowly rose from decade to decade, but with almost the identical number of colored, just over 550,000 in Cuba and Virginia in 1860/1861, Virginia had only 58,042 freedmen (or 11%) to Cuba's 213,167 (or 39%).[114]

As for the development of education for the free Negroes, this was informal and haphazard in the extreme, except for one short-lived experiment. In the late 1720's, Dr. Thomas Bray, who had been commissary in the State of Maryland for the Bishop of London, helped found a group of missionaries known as "Bray's Associates" who directed considerable attention to founding schools for Negroes in the American Colonies. A leading founder of the SPG, Dr. Bray received a private donation of £900 for this purpose.[115] After setting up a successful school with the aid of Benjamin Franklin in Phila-delphia in 1759, Dr. Bray helped establish a Negro school in Williamsburg in 1764. Under the direction of Commissary Dawson, local clerics and Mrs. Ann Wager, the school soon opened its doors to 24 Negro students, and made major progress in the area.[116] It appears to have won some local support, for a local printer, Mr. William Hunter, left in his will in 1761, some £7 for the support of Mrs. Wager.[117] But despite the initial success and support granted to the school, with the death of Mrs. Wager in 1774, the school ceased to operate. In fact, in the agitation of those years all the Negro and Indian

---

[111]   *Ibid.*, IV, 132.
[112]   John H. Russell, *The Free Negro in Virginia, 1619-1865* (Baltimore, Johns Hopkins Press, 1913), pp. 10-11.
[113]   Hening, *op. cit.*, XI, 39-40.
[114]   U.S. Bureau of the Census, *Negro Population 1790-1915* (Washington, Government Printing Office, 1918), p. 57, table 6. It should be noted that Virginia had the largest number and percentage of freedmen in its colored population in 1860 of any slave state in the Union except Maryland, which was a unique border state.
[115]   Thompson, *op. cit.*, pp. 9-19, 42-43.
[116]   Mary F. Goodwin, "Christianizing and Educating the Negro in Colonial Virginia", *Historical Magazine of the Protestant Episcopal Church*, I, no. 3 (September, 1932), 148-51.
[117]   *William and Mary Quarterly*, 1st Series, VII (1899), 13.

schools on the North American continent founded by Dr. Bray and his associates, as well as by the SPG, collapsed. The Williamsburg school seems to have been the model for another which lasted five years in the 1770's in Fredericksburg, but with the American Revolution, the source of English enthusiasm and funds for these schools was destroyed and local planter interest seems to have become exhausted.[118] Apparently neither free nor slave Negroes were permitted regular education by the local county schools.

There was some attempt by the Vestries, however, to provide for the free Negroes, orphans and poor, some type of apprenticeship in which they were also taught to read and write by the person to whom they were indentured. The Vestry of Petsworth Parish in 1716 required that for his indenture, Mr. Ralph Bevis was to:

give George Petsworth, a mulattoe boy of the age of 2 years, 3 years' schooling, and carefully to Instruct him afterwards that he may read well in any part of the Bible, also to instruct and Learn him ye sd mulattoe boy such Lawful way and ways that he may be able after his Indented time expired to gitt his own Liveing, and to allow him sufficient meat, Drink, washing, and apparill, until the expiration of ye sd time &c. . . .[119]

But these indentured and apprenticeship programs were for only a few free Negroes, and aside from the temporary Negro school experiment on the eve of the American Revolution, the Church seems to have made almost no serious or successful effort to educate the Virginia Negro. No Negro was admitted to William and Mary College, and none appears to have been trained by the Church in local parish schools for the liberal professions, as was the case in Cuba, while in the harsh reaction which took place by the early 19th century, even basic literacy was denied the freedmen.[120]

Thus the Virginia Church, dominated by the planter elite, offered no educational escape opportunities either for free or slave Negroes. It totally denied the right to slave marriages, and by and large in the colonial period did not even Christianize the majority of African Negroes. Finally, the established Church in Virginia did nothing to enrich the community life of the Negroes. The religious brotherhoods, the pageantry and processions, the folk religious syncretization, which were such an important part of the fabric of Catholic Cuba, were alien to Anglicanism. Although the dissenter groups in the "Great Awakening" after 1740 provided some compensation in the evangelical and

---

[118] Thompson, op. cit., chap. 4.
[119] William and Mary Quarterly, 1st Series, V (1897), 219; also see the case of Robert, son of the free Negro woman Cuba, who was bound out in Lancaster County in 1719 till his twenty-first birthday. William and Mary Quarterly, 1st Series, VIII (1899), 82.
[120] In 1800 the General Assembly specifically prohibited the local parishes from requiring the masters to teach the indentured free colored children to read or write, and by the 1830's the state legislature was prohibiting all types of schooling and education for even free Negroes who were willing to pay the costs. Russell, op. cit., pp. 140, 144-45.

revivalist meetings (which were to give birth to the future Negro church movement) these were confined to the frontier in the colonial period and involved only a few thousand Negro slaves. For the "Great Awakening" in Virginia was the work of only a handful of ministers and never penetrated into the Tidewater parishes where the overwhelming majority of slaves lived under Anglican masters.

Within the great plantation areas, despite all the efforts of the Bishop of London and his commissaries, the few local clergy were hardpressed to maintain even the established Church among the white colonists. As late as 1774, Virginia had only 104 Church of England clergymen,[121] in a total population of roughly 447,000 persons,[122] just one to over 4,000 colonists. Nor was this ratio unusual, for the Reverend James Ramsay in his famous attack on slavery in the British West Indies, asked for an ideal of one clergymen per 3,000 inhabitants to carry out the needed Christianization of the Negroes.[123]

Few in number, operating on provisional contracts based on the consent of the congregation, and completely subservient to the planter-dominated Vestry, and working against ingrained opposition to conversion, it is surprising that the Church of England accomplished as much as it did. Unfortunately, when moral pressure within the Church finally brought the metropolitan hierarchy to put pressure on the Crown and Parliament to over-ride local slave legislation, it was already too late for Virginia. The anti-slavery crusade did not fully get under way, despite the sentiments of such early leaders as Bishop Fleetwood, until after 1783, when the colonies were no longer a part of the British Empire. Although it was to have a profound influence on the British West Indies and on the abolition of the Slave Trade, the severance of political ties and the establishment of an independent Episcopalian Church in Virginia rendered the North American colonies impervious to this great moral crusade. How differently events might otherwise have turned out is shown by the impact of the aroused church on the eventual education, Christianization and emancipation of the British West Indian Negro slave.[124]

Too involved with defense of its very position at home in the 17th century, the Church of England had allowed the colonists to usurp its power and authority, and to create for themselves a congregational church organization. While this allowed more religious liberty for the white colonists, and greater individual expression in this age of religious non-conformity and dissent, it

[121] Brydon, op. cit., II, 608-614.
[122] Evarts B. Greene and Virginia D. Harrington, American Population before the Federal Census of 1790 (New York, Columbia University Press, 1932), p. 141.
[123] Ramsay, op. cit., pp. 265-66.
[124] For the history of this struggle see Reginald Coupland, The British Anti-Slavery Movement, 2d ed. (London, Frank Cass and Co., 1964), along with Frank Klingberg, The Anti-Slavery Movement in England, A Study in English Humanitarianism (New Haven, Yale University Press, 1926).

was fatal to the rights of the Negroes and Mulattoes, slave and free. When the Church finally turned its attention to the issue, it was too late, and the emancipation of the colonies of the North American continent destroyed the hope of the colored peoples that the Church would protect their rights and liberties as human beings.

IV

Having compared the impact of the Church on the lives of the Negro slaves within two distinct New World colonies, we have a clearer conception of the uniqueness and the consequent differences between the two institutions of Negro slavery. As Elkins and Tannenbaum have properly pointed out, the Church was one of the most crucial institutions which had the power to intervene in the relations between master and slave and to help mold that relationship.

In Cuba, the Church took an immediate daily concern and involvement, and succeeded in molding custom and patterns, as well as commanding obedience to higher authorities. From the beginning the Church viewed its own role toward the slaves as distinct from that of the masters and succeeded in establishing its claim on the mind, soul and time of the Negroes, free or slave. Not troubled by the belief that Christianity was incompatible with the slave status and working with established Iberian attitudes toward the Negro and his place within the Catholic society, the Cuban clergy were able to mold and modify the conditions of human bondage for the African Negro. Capable of carrying imperial and synodal edicts into immediate effect, the Cuban clergy effectively Christianized the imported slaves and freely admitted them into the Church. For the slaves this admittance provided inestimable social advantages and rights, as well as duties, and a host of concrete immediate advantages, from rest days on Sunday to the full sanctity of the family through the sacrament of marriage. In the syncretization of African religions in folk catholicism, and in the organization of *cofradías*, *cabildos*, and religious processionals, the Africans were provided with a rich cultural and community existence, which paradoxically eased their assimilation into society. Finally, the Church stood as the great potential benefactor to the exceptionally able, who, through church education, could achieve a new upper class status within society.

None of these things occurred for the Virginia Negro. Beginning with the planters' open hostility even to the admittance of Negroes into the Church, and faced by usurpation of authority by the parishioners, the fight even for minimal conversion was an uphill struggle for the Church of England. Involved with defense of the Church at home, the Anglican hierarchy allowed the Church abroad to be converted into a democratic congregational organization. It therefore had as much as it could do to guarantee church conformity among the white colonists, and had little energy to spare for the Negro, and even less for the Indian. Fully aware of the progress of the Catholic Church in these two areas, and morally sensitive to the issues, the metropolitan Anglican hierarchy could not develop enough power and unity prior to 1776 to break down the American congregational control and overcome planter hostility toward its conversion and incipient emancipation efforts.

Unlike the Cuban Church, the Church of England could not rely on the Crown for unquestioned support on these matters, for in the organization of the Empire, control over slavery and the Negro was left exclusively to the local government. Thus the Anglican Church could not build up a panoply either of canonical or civil law to guarantee free entry of the Negroes into the Church, and even more importantly to provide them with the full rights to the sacraments. As for the local legislature, the glaring silence of Virginia law as to the religious rights and condition of the Negro slave reflects the totally marginal character of slave Christianity, where it even existed. With such hostility built up in the colonial period against conversion, it was impossible for the Church even to suggest that slaves be legally married before God, or that the family had to be protected against the economic needs of the planter.

Even in the revivalist churches of the upland parishes, the "Great Awakening" and the participation of the Negro slaves was a short-lived affair, and within a few decades of Independence, the Virginia branches of the Baptist, Methodist and Presbyterian churches had conformed to planter opinion and had, by and large, contained slave conversion and participation to a minimum. As for the Virginia Episcopal Church, the successor after 1790 to the Church of England, its own decay and even greater dependence on planter support, made it take even less of an interest in Negroes, slave or free, than its colonial originator.

Denied the full rights of the Christian, with his family unrecognized by the Church or the state, with his previous religious experience rendered totally useless and destroyed, and his chances for self and community expression severely curtailed if not openly discouraged by the local parish, the Virginia Negro slave faced a harsh world dominated by his master, and with little possibility of protective intervention and support from an outside institution.

While the relationship of the Church to the slave was only one of several relationships, it was probably the most important non-planter one available. Because of this, the success or failure of the Anglican or Catholic Church to mold the life and soul of the Negro slaves had a profound impact on the personality, social organization and even eventual assimilation of the Negro into Cuban and Virginian society.

HERBERT S. KLEIN
University of Chicago

$\mathcal{N}otes$ and $\mathcal{D}ocuments$

Fertility Differentials between Slaves in the United States and the British West Indies: A Note on Lactation Practices and Their Possible Implications

Herbert S. Klein and Stanley L. Engerman

RECENT studies of the Atlantic slave trade by Philip Curtin and others have demonstrated that the United States received a relatively small share of the total African migration to the Americas.[1] Yet, the United States emerged by the end of slavery with a black population comparable in size to those of the Brazilian and West Indian slave societies which experienced much greater migrations of Africans. The causes of these differential rates of population growth have long been debated by contemporaries and by historians, and have been most frequently attributed to differing planter attitudes toward slave reproduction and material treatment, particularly as they were influenced by the opportunity to obtain new slaves from Africa.

We shall argue, however, that explanations resting solely on planter attitudes are insufficient, and, based upon available data, other forces must be considered. Interpretation of the data is made difficult by the fact that newly imported Africans formed greatly different proportions of the total slave population in these societies. Inferences drawn without distinguishing between these imported slaves and those Creoles born in the New World are apt to be highly misleading.[2] Nevertheless, even after allowing for these

Mr. Klein is a member of the Department of History at Columbia University and Mr. Engerman is a member of the Departments of Economics and History at the University of Rochester. Mr. Engerman was supported by the National Science Foundation.

[1] See, in particular, Philip D. Curtin, *The Atlantic Slave Trade: A Census* (Madison, Wis., 1969), 88-91.

[2] For a discussion of some of these difficulties see Herbert S. Klein and Stanley L. Engerman, "The Demographic Study of the American Slave Population" (forthcoming in the Proceedings of the 1975 International Colloquium on Historical Demography).

distinctions, there remains a marked difference between the rates of natural increase of slaves on mainland North America and those in the West Indies (and elsewhere), which is explained for the most part by the higher fertility of slaves on the mainland.[3] And, as will be argued, these fertility patterns can be explained, at least in part, as a result of differences in the period of childspacing. These variations in childspacing, like those in fertility, are often attributed to the behavior and decisions of slaveowners. High fertility in the United States has been considered the outcome of something called "slave-breeding" by masters, while lower fertility elsewhere has been attributed to malnutrition and overwork, as well as spontaneous abortion, miscarriage, and infrequent sexual intercourse due to the work regime. When lower fertility is considered to have rested on the decisions of slaves, as in the West Indies, emphasis is placed upon abortion and infanticide.

There was, however, another mechanism that may have affected slave fertility, breastfeeding. Direct evidence, as well as inferences drawn from patterns of childspacing, indicates that on the mainland of North America the breastfeeding interval was generally about one year, while for the West Indies it was typically at least two years. The existence of the differential between the United States and the West Indies seems amply documented from travelers' reports, plantation records, and other contemporary sources, but the cause and significance of this difference remain to be examined. Lactation practices can reflect differences in the diet, especially in the availability of milk and protein supplements. Because the longer nursing interval was similar to that observed in Africa, and the shorter period more similar to that of the white population in Europe and North America, there may also be implications for the discussion of the acculturation process and the extent of African "carryovers" and adaptations in various parts of the New World. In addition, given the effectiveness of lactation as a contraceptive, at least for limited periods and in conjunction with taboos on sexual intercourse, it is possible that this differential can explain a part of the fertility difference between the two areas. Since it is possible that, on the mainland, the lactation period was longer in the early eighteenth century than in later years, it may be that shortening of the period was related to the onset of high rates of fertility there. We do not claim that these differences in childnursing practices can alone account for the observed differences in slave

[3] See Klein and Engerman, "Demographic Study"; Stanley L. Engerman, "Some Economic and Demographic Comparisons of Slavery in the United States and the British West Indies," *Economic History Review*, 2d Ser., XXIX (1976), 258-275. hereafter cited as Engerman, "Some Economic and Demographic Comparisons," and Robert W. Fogel, "Recent Developments in the Demography of Slavery" (unpubl. MS, 1977). In the early 18th century the importance of mortality differences was greater, but even then fertility differences existed. While the following discussion is based upon a comparison of the United States and the British West Indies, most other slave societies in the Americas had a demographic pattern resembling that of the islands, and it is thought that similar explanations will account for differences between those areas and the United States.

fertility between North America and the British West Indies and that the other explanations are inappropriate. Rather, we wish to suggest a hypothesis for further study, as well as to indicate an important difference in slave patterns of behavior between the United States and elsewhere.

A useful framework for the study of differences in female fertility among populations would distinguish four components: the percentage of females who were childbearers, the age of mothers at the birth of the first child, the childspacing interval, and the age of mothers at the birth of the last child. Each could be affected by physiological conditions, diet patterns, work routines, master interference, and cultural mores. Recent discussions of the differences in demographic performance, as well as the debates among contemporaries, have tried to determine which of these influences was the primary determinant of observed patterns. By considering the components of female fertility individually, important differences can be detected that permit the distinguishing among possible causes. Thus, for example, we would expect a "slavebreeding" type of interference by masters, as sometimes posited for the United States, to lead to the highest possible percentage of females bearing children, an early age at first birth (with minimum lag between the onset of fecundability and childbirth), minimal childspacing, and a high age of last birth.[4] Poor diet, in combination with a rigorous work routine, could lead to relatively higher percentages of childless females, late age of onset of menarche and initial childbearing, prolonged intervals of childspacing, and early age of menopause and the cessation of childbearing. Cultural mores would affect the childbearing span, as well as childspacing. Thus if data on the physiological reproductive span were available, it would be possible to separate various physical and cultural impacts upon fertility.

At present we lack sufficient studies to generalize adequately about the components of differences in fertility among regions or over time. In addition to demographic data, we also require more information on differences in food intake and work arrangements. Yet, data are becoming available that permit us to understand the relevant issues better. In particular, we can examine some data relating to nineteenth-century West Indian-United States fertility comparisons, in conjunction with similar data for earlier periods, to see what can be said about the statistical components of fertility differentials and how these may be explained by the factors noted above.[5]

[4] For a recent argument as to the existence of "slavebreeding" in the U.S. see Richard Sutch, "The Breeding of Slaves for Sale and the Westward Expansion of Slavery, 1850-1860," in Stanley L. Engerman and Eugene D. Genovese, eds., *Race and Slavery in the Western Hemisphere: Quantitative Studies* (Princeton, N.J., 1975), 173-210; Richard Sutch, "The Treatment Received by American Slaves: A Critical Review of the Evidence Presented in *Time on the Cross*," *Explorations in Economic History*, XII (1975), 335-438, and the comments by Stanley L. Engerman in "Comments on the Study of Race and Slavery," in Engerman and Genovese, eds., *Race and Slavery*, 495-530. See also Fogel, "Recent Developments."

[5] The comparisons between the U.S. growth and the British West Indian decline

The fertility and mortality estimates for the United States in the nine-teenth century, when slave imports had ceased (and the heavy losses in seasoning that confound death rate comparisons no longer occurred), indicate a crude birth rate of about 50-55 per 1,000.[6] Given the observed rate of natural increase, the death rate fell in the range of about 25-35 per 1,000. While the different age compositions make precise comparisons difficult, the figures suggested by the parliamentary registration reports for Jamaica (be-fore adjusting for the undercounting of infant mortality) are birth rates of about 23 and death rates about 26, providing a net decrease in population of about 3 per 1,000.[7] Crude estimates made for the period 1817-1829 indicate

in slave population figured extensively in the British debates on abolition and emancipation, as can be seen from examining Parliamentary Papers as well as the pamphlet literature listed in Lowell Joseph Ragatz, comp., *A Guide for the Study of British Caribbean History, 1763-1834* (Washington, D.C., 1932). This pattern did, at times, present problems for critics who needed to offset the implication of good care for U.S. slaves. This is one of the points discussed in the fascinating pamphlet by Robert Dale Owen, *The Wrong of Slavery: The Right of Emancipation* (Phila-delphia, 1864). For a subtle probing of the implications of these differential popu-lation patterns for the study of the comparative treatment of slaves and related issues see C. Vann Woodward, "Southern Slaves in the World of Thomas Malthus," in his *American Counterpoint* (Boston, 1971), 78-106.

[6] These U.S. estimates are approximated from Warren S. Thompson and P. K. Whelpton, *Population Trends in the United States*, Demographic Monographs, IX (New York, 1933), 8 and 263. Estimates of birth rates and mortality under U.S. slavery are found in Ansley J. Coale and Norfleet W. Rives, Jr., "A Statistical Reconstruction of the Black Population of the United States, 1880-1970: Estimates of True Numbers by Age and Sex, Birth Rates, and Total Fertility," *Population Index*, XXXIX (1973), 3-36; Jack Ericson Eblen, "New Estimates of the Vital Rates of the United States Black Population during the Nineteenth Century," *Demography*, XI (1974), 301-319; Melvin Zelnik, "Fertility of the American Negro in 1830 and 1850," *Population Studies*, XX (1966), 77-83; Richard Steckel, "The Economics of U.S. Slave and Southern White Fertility" (Ph.D. diss., University of Chicago, 1977); Reynolds Farley, *Growth of the Black Population: A Study of Demographic Trends* (Chicago, 1970); and Robert Evans, Jr., "The Economics of American Negro Slavery, 1830-1860," in Universities-National Bureau Committee for Economic Research, *Aspects of Labor Economics* (Princeton, N.J., 1962), 185-243, hereafter cited as Evans, "Economics of American Negro Slavery." See also the various sources and discussions in Maris A. Vinovskis, "The Demography of the Slave Population in Antebellum America," *Journal of Interdisciplinary History*, V (1975), 459-467.

[7] See B. W. Higman, "The Slave Populations of the British Caribbean: Some Nineteenth-Century Variations," in Samuel R. Proctor, ed., *Eighteenth-Century Florida and the Caribbean* (Gainesville, 1976), 60-70, which compares the various British areas of the time. Even if one accepts the argument that infant mortality was excluded (and an examination of the Registration Reports suggests that at least some deaths of infants born in the three-year registration period were included), the fertility differentials would remain more important than those of mortality in explaining differential population change. Fogel, "Recent Developments," uses stable population models to adjust for undercounting in some of the data reported by

unadjusted Creole death rates in the range of 20 to 24, and Creole birth rates (unadjusted for infant mortality) of about 25-27, while the birth rates for the slave population as a whole had increased over time because of the increased share of Creoles in the population.[8]

Generalizations for the period before the closing of the slave trades in 1808 are somewhat more difficult because of the impact of geographic differences, as well as shifts over time as the result of the introduction of new crops.[9] Whereas, on the mainland, Virginia and Maryland apparently experienced rates of natural decrease down to the start of the eighteenth century, Peter Wood has argued that the South Carolina pattern was one of high natural increase in this period.[10] Moreover, for South Carolina, 1720 saw a shift to a period of apparent natural decrease (or, at the least, a lower rate of natural increase), because of the growing dominance of rice production, but this same period saw a shift to a high natural increase in Virginia, Maryland, and North Carolina.[11]

Higman, and concludes that this raises the birth rate from about 23 to 33, and the death rate by the same amount. See also B. W. Higman, *Slave Population and Economy in Jamaica, 1807-1834* (Cambridge, 1976) for extensive analysis of patterns of mortality and fertility in Jamaica in 1832. For an examination of slave population in the Caribbean neglected in the recent debate, see Alexander Moreau de Jonnés, *Recherches Statistiques sur L'esclavage Colonial* . . . (Paris, 1842).

[8] See Klein and Engerman, "Demographic Study," as well as Michael Craton, "Jamaican Slave Mortality: Fresh Light from Worthy Park, Longville and the Tharp Estates," *Journal of Caribbean History,* III (1971), 1-27, and "Jamaican Slavery," in Engerman and Genovese, eds., *Race and Slavery,* 249-284. Here again, adjustment for omitted infant mortality would raise both birth and death rates.

[9] It has frequently been argued that there was a shift to more favorable treatment of U.S. slaves in 1808, leading to greater paternalism there, as a result of closing the slave trade. As discussed in Engerman, "Some Economic and Demographic Comparisons," the basic demographic differences were not affected by the openness of the slave trade.

[10] For Maryland see Russell R. Menard, "Economy and Society in Early Colonial Maryland" (Ph.D. diss., University of Iowa, 1975) and "The Maryland Slave Population, 1658 to 1730: A Demographic Profile of Blacks in Four Counties," *William and Mary Quarterly,* 3d Ser., XXXII (1975), 29-54; Allan Kulikoff, "Tobacco and Slaves: Population, Economy, and Society in Eighteenth-Century Prince George's County, Maryland" (Ph.D. diss., Brandeis University, 1975); and Carville V. Earle, *The Evolution of a Tidewater-Settlement System: All Hallow's Parish, Maryland, 1650-1783* (Chicago, 1975). For Virginia see Wesley Frank Craven, *White, Red, and Black: The Seventeenth-Century Virginian* (Charlottesville, 1971) and Edmund S. Morgan, *American Slavery—American Freedom: The Ordeal of Colonial Virginia* (New York, 1975). For South Carolina see Peter H. Wood, *Black Majority: Negroes in Colonial South Carolina, from 1670 through the Stono Rebellion* (New York, 1974), 131-166.

[11] See Wood, *Black Majority.* These South Carolina comparisons are confounded by possible reexports to North Carolina and Georgia, but the general pattern of change seems clear. On blacks in pre-1750 Georgia see Robert V. Wells, *The Population of the British Colonies in America before 1776* (Princeton, N.J.,

Attempting to determine vital rates for the British West Indies in the eighteenth century is still more difficult because of the poor quality of the records and because of important inter-island differentials.[12] It does seem possible that in the initial years of settlement the rate of natural increase may have been higher than that which followed the development of the plantation sugar economy and the consequent large increase of slave imports.[13]

When looking at the eighteenth- and nineteenth-centuries rates of mortality for the native-born slaves, and possibly even post-seasoned African slaves, it would appear that in general death rates of slave populations moved at roughly the same rates, and in the same direction, as rates for the free population of all colors. There were, of course, regional variations in death rates. Thus while in the border states of Maryland and Virginia slave and free mortality rates were similar and moved together over time, in New England mortality rates for whites were considerably lower than those in the more southern states and in the British West Indies.[14] Studies suggest that comments that newly imported slaves were worked for seven hard years and then died of exhaustion are far from the mark. The phenomenon of high death rates for unseasoned slaves, reflected clearly in the comparative prices of Creoles and imported slaves, and of seasoned and unseasoned slaves (and servants), was most probably related to encounters with new diseases rather than to deliberate overworking or poor care.[15]

While the presence of imported slaves with high rates of death in seasoning obscures the fact, it seems clear that in the eighteenth and

---

1975), 169-171. For North Carolina, Harry Roy Merrens, *Colonial North Carolina in the Eighteenth Century* (Chapel Hill, 1964), 74-81, shows such a rate of high population increase later in the century that some imports from elsewhere must have taken place then, and possibly earlier.

[12] For discussions of the differences among the islands in demographic performance, and the possible causes, see Curtin, *Atlantic Slave Trade* and Higman, "Slave Populations," in Proctor, ed., *Eighteenth-Century Florida*, 60-70.

[13] See, in particular, Craton, "Jamaican Slavery," and Richard B. Sheridan, "Mortality and the Medical Treatment of Slaves in the British West Indies," in Engerman and Genovese, eds., *Race and Slavery*, 249-284 and 285-310, respectively; and Richard S. Dunn, *Sugar and Slaves: The Rise of the Planter Class in the English West Indies, 1624-1713* (Chapel Hill, N.C., 1972).

[14] In addition to sources in n. 16 below see Morgan, *American Slavery—American Freedom* and Kulikoff, "Tobacco and Slaves." Morgan (p. 299) further suggests that a similar mortality decline for slaves and servants would encourage the greater importation of slaves. While the impact would vary with the actual relation of the death rate to the length of time in Virginia and with the interest rate, the argument is quite plausible, because Virginia was a "price-taker" for both slaves and servants.

[15] On prices of seasoned vs. unseasoned servants and slaves see Morgan, *American Slavery—American Freedom*, 175 and 297. A Jamaica planter of the 18th-century commented that after a few years surviving imported slaves were as valuable as those Creole-born (Barham Papers, Clarendon Collection, Bodleian Library, Oxford).

nineteenth centuries the major differences in mortality were not between the southern United States and the Caribbean but above and below the Mason-Dixon line: the northern United States was considerably more healthy than either the southern United States or the Caribbean. The differences in mortality between the southern United States and the Caribbean, for blacks (and whites), seem considerably less dramatic.[16] The implication is that, for Creoles, differences in mortality explain less of the differential rates of population change than do differences in fertility.[17]

Even when allowance is made for differences in the age and sex structure of the relevant populations, there remains a large difference in fertility per female of childbearing age between the British West Indies and the United States.[18] One set of circumstances that might help explain the differences in measured fertility would be differences in the sex ratio of the populations, which might have led to variations in family patterns. However, while a relative lack of females might help account for relatively low fertility in a few areas (an imbalance that can initially be traced to the impact of the slave trade), even if allowance is made for age at the time of import, there were still fewer births per female in the British West Indies when the slave trade

[16] For comparisons of black and white mortality in the West Indies see Carl Bridenbaugh and Roberta Bridenbaugh, *No Peace Beyond the Line: The English in the Caribbean, 1624-1690* (New York, 1972); Dunn, *Sugar and Slaves;* and Frank Wesley Pitman, *The Development of the British West Indies, 1700-1763* (New Haven, Conn., 1917). For arguments about the Maryland pattern see Menard, "Maryland Slave Population," *WMQ,* 3d Ser., XXXII (1975), 29-54, and Lorena S. Walsh and Russell R. Menard, "Death in the Chesapeake: Two Life Tables for Men in Early Colonial Maryland," *Maryland Historical Magazine,* LXIX (1974), 211-227. See also Wells, *Population of the British Colonies.* The northern U.S. was clearly the healthiest of New World settlements and also the region with relatively the greatest percentage of whites.

[17] For data on slave-life expectation in Jamaica, British Guiana, and the U.S. see Klein and Engerman, "Demographic Study." While restricting the comparisons to Creoles means that the impacts of the slave trade on demographic performance are put aside (on these see *ibid.,* and Herbert S. Klein, *The Middle Passage: Comparative Studies in the Atlantic Slave Trade* [Princeton, N.J., 1978]), the concentration does permit us to isolate some important aspects of slave adjustments in various parts of the New World. Overall, given the high mortality in seasoning, the impact of differential mortality would rise in importance when differences in the growth of the total population are considered.

[18] Moreoever, differentials in infant mortality would not be sufficient to explain the differences in measured fertility. See, for example, the comparison in Richard S. Dunn, "A Tale of Two Plantations: Slave Life at Mesopotamia in Jamaica and at Mount Airy in Virginia, 1799 to 1828," *WMQ,* 3d Ser., XXXIV (1977), 32-65, hereafter cited as Dunn, "Tale of Two Plantations." Also compare the rates in Michael Craton, *Searching for the Invisible Man* (Cambridge, 1978), with those presented by Evans, "Economics of American Negro Slavery," 212, and William Dosite Postell, *The Health of Slaves on Southern Plantations* (Baton Rouge, La., 1951), 153-158.

was open, and these differences continued after the slave trade closed, when the sex ratios in most areas were generally equalized.[19]

Differences in fertility cannot, therefore, be directly attributed to the effect of importation. It is, of course, possible that lower fertility per female might have resulted from the long-run impact of initially skewed sex ratios upon sexual practices and family developments, and particularly on the importance of two-parent residence.[20] Two-parent slave households apparently had higher fertility than did single-parent households.[21] In the United States the need for cross-unit marriages generated by the relatively small size of agricultural units and the proportion of slaves on farms on which on-site "marriage" was therefore precluded, raises the possibility of higher frequency of nonmarried females than in other slave societies, or in the United

[19] See Higman, Slave Population, and "Slave Populations," in Proctor, ed., Eighteenth-Century Florida, 60-70, and material presented in "Report from the Select Committee of the House of Lords on the State of the West Indies Colonies," Great Britain, House of Lords, Sessional Papers, 1831-1832, CCVI, CCVII, 127. Even after the international slave trade closed, the birth rate of slaves who were born in Africa but who came to the West Indies before the onset of puberty remained lower than those of Creole-born slaves. The reasons for this seem unclear; even when weighting for fertility differentials by age and looking at age-specific rate, a fertility gap remains. Writing in the mid-18th century, Jean Barbot commented that few African women on the Gold Coast had over five or six children, while on the Slave Coast few had over three or four (A Description of the Coasts of North and South Guinea [London, 1732], 239 and 348). For a contemporary explanation of differences in the sex ratio among imports see Bryan Edwards, The History, Civil and Commercial, of the British West Indies, II (London, 1819), 138-140.

[20] For a discussion of the origin of Afro-American patterns of family in Maryland see Allan Kulikoff, "The Beginnings of the Afro-American Family in Maryland," in Aubrey C. Land et al., eds., Law, Society, and Politics in Early Maryland (Baltimore, 1977), 171-196. See also Herbert G. Gutman, The Black Family in Slavery and Freedom, 1750-1925 (New York, 1976).

[21] For fertility rates by household structure see B. W. Higman, "Household Structure and Fertility on Jamaican Slave Plantations: A Nineteenth-Century Example," Pop. Studies, XXVII (1973), 527-550; Robert W. Fogel and Stanley L. Engerman, "Why the U.S. Slave Population Grew So Rapidly: Fertility, Mortality, and Household Structure," (unpubl. MS, 1975); and Gabriel Debien, Les Esclaves Aux Antilles Françaises, XVIIe-XVIIIe Siècles (Basse-Terre, 1974), 349. Owners and observers at the time frequently claimed this pattern of higher fertility for two-parent households, and sometimes used it as explanation for the U.S.-British West Indian fertility differentials. See, for example, [Anon], Instructions for . . . the Treatment of Negroes (London, 1786), 87; Frank Cundall, ed., Lady Nugent's Journal (London, 1907), 117-118; Gilbert Francklyn, Observations . . . of the Slave Trade (London, 1789), 87; and Hector M'Neill, Observations on the Treatment of Negroes (London, 1788), 40-44. For similar observations in other slave societies see Alexander von Humboldt, Personal Narrative of Travels to the Equinoctial Regions of America during the Years 1799-1804, III (London, 1853), 254; Henry Koster, Travels in Brazil (London, 1816), and Abstract of the Evidence Delivered Before a Select Committee of the House of Commons in the Years 1790 and 1791 . . . (London, 1791), 105-111.

States itself after emancipation.[22] And while in the British West Indies there were more nuclear households than heretofore thought, these were less frequent than in the United States.[23] While studies have not yet sufficiently distinguished nuclear from extended families, nor allowed adequately for relationships among contiguous units, the existence of the nucleus to the family is important. It is true, of course, that most masters proclaimed an interest in that type of arrangement as a means of control, as well as a measure to provide for higher fertility. Thus the specific familial development context is unclear, given our limited knowledge of African and white southern patterns.[24] It is important to note that work by Richard S. Dunn on early Barbados, and Gabriel Debien on the French West Indies suggests a pattern of purchases that permitted (if not encouraged) two-parent households, but Dunn and Debien argue that this encouragement altered with the expansion in imports resulting from the sugar boom.[25] Thus, it may be that the presumed absence and instability of families in the West Indies was a transient phase between intervals of somewhat more equal sex ratios and family stability.[26] Nevertheless, fertility differences persisted between slaves in the British West Indies and in the United States even when the same household types are compared.

[22] Nevertheless, it is possible that fertility was not markedly lower on these units than on units on which males and females were coresident (see Fogel and Engerman, "Why the U.S. Slave Population Grew So Rapidly"). This possibility is suggested also by the apparent high fertility in Virginia and North Carolina, states in which cross-owner marriage must have been quite prevalent. Steckel, "Economics of U.S. Slave and Southern White Fertility," indicates that the percentage of slave females bearing children was actually higher on small units than on larger plantations.

[23] See B. W. Higman, "The Slave Family and Household in the British West Indies, 1800-1834," *Jour. Interdis. Hist.*, VI (1975), 261-287; Michael Craton, "Hobbesian or Panglossian? The Two Extremes of Slave Conditions in the British Caribbean, 1783 to 1834," *WMQ*, 3d Ser., XXXV (1978), 324-356, on the West Indies; and Gutman, *Black Family*, and Fogel and Engerman, "Why the U.S. Slave Population Grew So Rapidly," on the U.S.

[24] These issues are raised in Kulikoff, "Beginnings of the Afro-American Family," in Land *et al.*, eds., *Law, Society, and Politics*, 171-196, and Gutman, *Black Family*. On slave family patterns see also Eugene D. Genovese, *Roll, Jordan, Roll: The World the Slaves Made* (New York, 1974), 450-523.

[25] See Dunn, *Sugar and Slaves*, 251 and 316, and Debien, *Les Esclaves*, 350-351. Although Richard Ligon in *A True and Exact History of the Island of Barbadoes* (London, 1673 [orig. publ. 1657]), 46-47, emphasized the "need" to purchase females, his discussion did not preclude the practice of polygyny.

[26] While it is often argued that West Indian concern with fertility did not arise until the closing of the slave trade, J. Harry Bennett, Jr., in *Bondsmen and Bishops: Slavery and Apprenticeship on the Codrington Plantation of Barbados, 1710-1838*, University of California Publication in History, LXII (Berkeley and Los Angeles, 1958), points to the introduction of an amelioration program on the Codrington estates in 1793, while George W. Roberts, *The Population of Jamaica* (Cambridge, 1957), 234-237, notes the importance of the Jamaican Act of 1792 in reflecting changing attitudes toward reproduction. Since the New World price of slaves began

Variations in fertility can be explained by physiological and diet conditions, as well as by cultural mores. The statistical framework presented above can help analyze the importance of these factors. For example, it had been argued by contemporaries that differences in sex ratios had led to familial instability and "promiscuity" among West Indian women, and that owing to more frequent intercourse and/or the higher potential of venereal disease fewer slave women were fertile.[27] But the study of West Indian plantation records shows insufficient recorded incidence of venereal disease to have so broad an impact on fertility, and the proportion of women who produced children in the West Indies under slavery seems to have been as high as two-thirds of total potential female childbearers, a figure below the four-fifths or more figure for United States slave women, but still too high to support the argument that substantial infertility can account for the observed pattern.[28]

It has also been argued that the combination of poor diet and the extensive work routine on sugar units caused lower West Indian fertility.[29] A poor diet would show up in later ages of menarche and earlier ages of menopause, thus cutting deeply into a potential period of childbearing, as well as causing prolonged intervals of childspacing. These dietary conditions,

---

rising about the middle of the 18th century, such a pattern of encouragement (or acceptance) of fertility might have begun even earlier. See the U.S. Bureau of the Census, *Historical Statistics of the United States* (Washington, D.C., 1976), II, 1174.

[27] The numbers of slaves in both areas who did not bear children were apparently in excess of the presumed rates of biological sterility. See, for example, Frank Lorimer, *Culture and Human Fertility* (Paris, 1954), 41-44, and sources cited there for a later period. For a discussion of infertility in parts of post-World War II Africa, raising many similar questions, see A. Romaniuk, "Infertility in Tropical Africa," in John C. Caldwell and Chukuka Okonjo, eds., *The Population of Tropical Africa* (New York, 1968), 214-224. While some connection is observed between infertility and venereal disease, it is not clear that these can explain the magnitude of fertility differences. For a critique of Farley's argument that fertility declines among 20th-century U.S. blacks were due to an increase in venereal disease see Joseph A. McFalls, Jr., "Impact of VD on the Fertility of the U.S. Black Population, 1880-1950," *Social Biology*, XX (1973), 2-19.

[28] The rates for the B.W.I. are based on slave lists for plantations in the Newton Papers (University of London Library), for Worthy Park in the Phillips Papers (Sterling Library, Yale), for Amity Hall Plantation in the Surrey Record Office (County Hall, Kingston-upon-Thames), and for the Island Plantation in the Barham Papers, Clarendon Coll. The first is in Barbados, the others Jamaica. For a lower figure for a Jamaica plantation, but one still above 50%, see Dunn, "Tale of Two Plantations," and for a more detailed analysis of Worthy Park see Craton, *Searching for the Invisible Man*. The U.S. data are from Steckel, "Economics of U.S. Slave and Southern White Fertility," and also James Trussell and Richard Steckel, "The Age of Slaves at Menarche and Their First Births," *Jour. Interdis. Hist.*, VIII (1977), 477-505. For a Virginia unit at the start of the 19th century see Dunn, "Tale of Two Plantations." Data for the childless rate among the first generation of emancipated slaves—under 10%—are in Irene B. Taeuber and Conrad Taeuber, *People of the United States in the 20th Century* (Washington, D.C., 1971), 378.

[29] See, most recently, Dunn, "Tale of Two Plantations."

indeed, could create a dual impact of increasing infant deaths and reducing the number of potential children. However, in comparing the United States and the British West Indies, the ages of mothers at the birth of their first child, while probably somewhat different, do not themselves explain the full fertility difference.[30] The age at which childbearing began, on average, was probably earlier on the mainland—somewhere about twenty to twenty-one for the United States (depending on sample and procedures) and at least a year or two later for the West Indies. Less is known about the age at which childbearing ended, but again, it is doubtful that the differentials were large enough to explain fertility differences.[31] The necessary detailed physiological information is lacking, and since the differences between ages of menarche (and subfecundity) and the birth of first children, and between menopause

[30] For the U.S. see ages at first birth in Steckel, "Economics of U.S. Slave and Southern White Fertility"; Robert W. Fogel and Stanley L. Engerman, *Time on the Cross: The Economics of American Negro Slavery* (Boston, 1974), I, 137-138, and the adjusted calculations presented in Fogel and Engerman, "Why the U.S. Slave Population Grew So Rapidly," and in Trussell and Steckel, "Age of Slaves at Menarche," *Jour. Interdis. Hist.*, VIII (1977), 477-505. For lower ages, based on a different sample and different procedures, with biases pointed out by Trussell and Steckel, see Herbert G. Gutman, *Slavery and the Numbers Game: A Critique of Time on the Cross* (Urbana, Ill., 1975), 147. Estimates for years in the 18th century are presented in Dunn, "Tale of Two Plantations" and Kulikoff, "Tobacco and Slaves." The Maryland estimates for the early 18th century are of an age below those for the later 18th century presented by Dunn, and the Steckel, Gutman, and Fogel and Engerman estimates for the 19th century. Clearly there is more need for detailed study, but it should be noted that if the 18th century estimates are accurate they contain implications for the age of menarche possible in the North American slave population. A useful source to estimate the age of menarche for United States slave females after 1808 is described in Stanley L. Engerman, "The Height of U.S. Slaves," *Local Population Studies*, XVI (Spring, 1976), 45-50, and used by Trussell and Steckel, "Age of Slaves at Menarche," *Jour. Interdis. Hist.*, VIII (1977), 477-505, to provide an estimate of menarche at age 15. Data on height by age and sex of slaves in Trinidad and those Africans on ships captured by the British squadron in the late 1820s are now being processed to be compared with this U.S. data.

Ages at first birth for West Indian units are calculations from the Barham Papers, and, for surviving first births, from samples in the slave Registration Reports for Trelawny Parish, Jamaica, and Trinidad. For ages of mothers on a rapidly growing Bahama unit see Craton, "Hobbesian or Panglossian?" *WMQ*, 3d Ser., XXXV (1978), 324-356, and for information on French West Indian units see Debien, *Les Esclaves*, 349, and Jacques Adelaide, "Demography and Names of Slaves of Le Moule 1845 to May 1848," in Woodville K. Marshall, ed., *Papers Presented at the 3rd Annual Conference of Caribbean Historians* (1971), 86-90. The ages of fertility figured extensively in the British abolition debates, as part of the search for the causes of the demographic performance there.

[31] There are no systematic data on this point, but inferences may be drawn from fertility patterns by age shown in Craton, "Hobbesian or Panglossian?" *WMQ*, 3d Ser., XXXV (1978), 324-356, and *Searching for the Invisible Man*, and age-specific fertility patterns in Higman, "Household Structure," *Pop. Studies*, XXVII (1973).

and last child, may be owing not only to diet but may reflect influences such as cultural and social mores as well, considerably more data from plantation records will be needed to help settle these issues. Nevertheless, childspacing remains of some importance in explaining the fertility differentials in the period after the slave trade closed. Differences for the earlier years are harder to analyze using present data, but it might be expected that similar influences would have been important.

Those studies of plantation records which have been undertaken to date suggest that in the United States the spacing between surviving children was about 2.9 years, while the interval for the British West Indies ranged between three and four years.[32] These differences in spacing could explain part of the measured difference in fertility rates between the British West Indies and the United States.

Having proposed spacing as a possible explanatory factor, it should be noted that this effect could be attributed to several influences. It might be the result of dietary deficiencies that imposed infertility, or of factors such as prolonged lactation, which reduced the probability of conception. And, if the pattern were influenced by prolonged lactation, it would be possible that the lactation period might reflect maintained customs or was a response to the diets provided by masters.[33] Since diet has been the more widely discussed, we wish to explore the social factor in more detail. Here we would raise the

527-550, and Steckel, "Economics of U.S. Slave and Southern White Fertility." However, Dunn in "Tale of Two Plantations" implies that the difference in age at the time of last birth would be an important determinant, since there were large differences in the numbers of females with only one child. He relates this to crop-mix. On fertility by crop in Jamaica see Higman, *Slave Population*, 118-138, which suggests little difference in fertility by crop produced. In the U.S., in the mid-19th century, counties producing sugar had slave fertility levels below the U.S. average, but not different from those of Louisiana cotton-producing counties. (See Engerman, "Comments," in Engerman and Genovese, eds., *Race and Slavery*, 530).

[32] The U.S. data are from Steckel, "Economics of U.S. Slave and Southern White Fertility," 103. The West Indian data are calculated from the Barham Papers and the Gale-Morant Papers (University of Exeter Library), and this spacing is consistent with the adjusted age-specific fertility rates based upon Higman, "Household Structure," *Pop. Studies*, XXVII (1973), 527-550. For data on spacing on a high-fertility Bahama plantation see Craton, "Hobbesian or Panglossian?" *WMQ*, 3d Ser., XXXV (1978), 324-356. Dunn, "Tale of Two Plantations," estimates childspacing of over three years on the low fertility Mesopotamia plantation in Jamaica. The major difference between the two units studied was the frequency of females with zero and one birth in Jamaica, which leads Dunn to emphasize the importance of diet and work routine, rather than customs, in explaining fertility differentials. Hopefully more work on other units will permit a determination of the relative importance of these different forces. The Bahama unit's high fertility is of interest because, as Craton notes, it produced cotton, not sugar, and also it was settled by slaves from East Florida after the American Revolution.

[33] On the relationship between diet and prolonged lactation see W. Brass, "Introduction: Bio-social Factors in African Demography," in R. P. Moss and

possibility that we are dealing with two different patterns of childnursing. In contemporaneous European and white North American society lactation was usually reduced to a period of about one year.[34] In the eighteenth century (indeed even at the present day) in African societies, the period of lactation was generally two to three years.[35] From the limited evidence of the plantation reports it would appear that nineteenth-century North American slave

---

R. J. A. R. Rathbone, eds., *The Population Factor in African Studies* (London, 1975), 87-94. A relationship between weaning and child mortality is noted by Anatole Romaniuk, "The Demography of the Democratic Republic of the Congo," in William Brass, *et al.*, *The Demography of Tropical Africa* (Princeton, N.J., 1968), 293 and by Pierre Cantrelle, "Mortality: Levels, Patterns, and Trends," in John C. Caldwell, ed., *Population Growth and Socioeconomic Change in West Africa* (New York, 1975), 108-109. Also of interest, in this regard, are the connections between nursing habits and the presence of cattle (see Joseph Boute, "Zaire," in Caldwell, ed., *Population Growth*, 606) and the possible impact of lactose intolerance among blacks (see Kenneth Kiple and Virginia Kiple, "Slave Child Mortality: Some Nutritional Answers to a Perennial Puzzle," *Journal of Social History*, X [1976], 284-309). Thus the differences in cattle-raising between the U.S. and the B.W.I. may play a part in explaining these adjustments.

[34] On childspacing in New England in the 17th and 18th centuries see Robert V. Wells, "Quaker Marriage Patterns in a Colonial Perspective," *WMQ*, 3d Ser., XXIX (1972), 415-442. It should be noted, however, that in some areas of the South, and particularly among lower-class whites, the nursing periods may have been longer. On this see, for example, the remarks of Frances Anne Kemble, *Journal of a Residence on a Georgian Plantation in 1838-1839* (New York, 1863), 253-254, and Frederick Law Olmsted, *A Journey in the Back Country* (New York, 1860), 199; while for an upper-class family, see Robert Manson Myers, ed., *The Children of Pride* (New Haven, Conn., 1972), 508, where a child was weaned at about 16 months. Kemble noted that the length of nursing might be longer for births which occurred in winter or spring and also, to her great surprise, that a second child could be born while the first was being breast-fed. Steckel, "Economics of U.S. Slave and Southern White Fertility," 103, estimates that the interval between births of surviving children was about 2.8 years for whites (slightly less than it was for slaves).

[35] For lactation periods in various parts of Africa at this time see Ronald Miller, ed., *Mungo Park's Travels in Africa* (London, 1969), 203; Thomas Winterbottom, *An Account of the Native Africans in the Neighbourhood of Sierra Leone . . .* (London, 1803), II, 218; John Matthews, *A Voyage to the River Sierra-Leone* (London, 1788), 98-99; Willem Bosman, *A New and Accurate Description of the Coast of Guinea* (London, 1814 [orig. publ. 1705]), 388; Capt. William Snelgrave, *A New Account of some parts of Guinea and the Slave Trade* (London, 1734), Introduction; Barbot, *Description of the Coast of Guinea*, 37, 243; and Archibald Dalzel, *The History of Dahomy, an Inland Kingdom of Africa . . .* (London, 1793), xix, among the travelers of the 18th century. That a two to three year period of lactation persisted in Africa well into the 20th century is noted by Lorimer, *Culture and Human Fertility*, 86-88. Lorimer points to the relation of such prolonged lactation and the presence of polygyny, which apparently avoids problems arising from taboos against intercourse during nursing. For recent discussions of current African practices as to childnursing and related sexual taboos see several of the studies in Caldwell, ed., *Population Growth*, particularly Hilary Page, "Fertility Levels: Patterns and

women were in fact breastfeeding for about one year, while in the West Indies the period was two years at the minimum.[36] It is important also that one study of early eighteenth-century Maryland suggests a childspacing pattern consistent with prolonged lactation, while the evidence for later years is consistent with a shorter period.[37] Thus it is possible that these shortened spacing intervals might help explain the initial upsurge in United States slave population growth, as well as the differences in fertility between the United States and the British West Indies.

Could this spacing differential be due to the need for West Indian slaves to nurture their children for longer periods because of differences in diet?

Trends," 52; John C. Caldwell, "Fertility Control," 64; Cantrelle, "Mortality," 109; Robert W. Morgan, "Fertility Levels and Fertility Change," 205-206; Barbara Harrell-Bond, "Some Influential Attitudes about Family Limitation and the Use of Contraceptives among the Professional Group in Sierra Leone," 484; John C. Caldwell and Barbara Thompson, "Gambia," 522-523; and Boute, "Zaire," 606.

[36] For the U.S. such a one-year period of nursing is consistent with the child-spacing intervals presented in Steckel, "Economics of Slave and Southern White Fertility, and is the period prescribed by planter journals. For a detailed discussion of lactation practices on a South Carolina cotton plantation see the plantation manual for the Hammond plantation (typescript at South Carolina Historical Society, Charleston). For a study of the length of nursing and the impact upon female labor productivity, see Robert William Fogel and Stanley L. Engerman, "Explaining the Relative Efficiency of Slave Agriculture in the Antebellum South," *American Economic Review*, LXVIII (1977), 275-296, which analyzes the data for the plantation of F. T. Leak. For the B.W.I. see, for example, the comments of [Dr. Collins], *Practical Rules for the Management and Medical Treatment of Negro Slaves in the Sugar Colonies* (London, 1811), 146; Thomas Roughley, *The Jamaica Planters' Guide* (London, 1823), 118; [Dr. James Grainger], *An Essay on the More Common West India Diseases* (London, 1764), 17; Francklyn, *Observations*, 52, and the discussion on p. 604 in Frank Wesley Pitman, "Slavery on British West India Plantations in the Eighteenth Century," *Journal of Negro History*, XI (1926), 584-668. Information in the Barham (list of June 1802 and birth registers) and Codrington (Gloucester Record Office) papers (slave lists) on "suckling infants" indicates the longer period of lactation in the West Indies than the U.S. It should be noted that Owen, *Wrong of Slavery*, 109, commented that differences in lactation periods "could" be enumerated as one among the most influential causes which went to produce the great variance of results as to increase of slave population in the West Indies and in the United States.

It might also be noted that some West Indian discussions in the 19th century do seem to suggest some reduction in nursing intervals to below two years, which could be consistent with points made by Dunn, "Tale of Two Plantations." If so, it would be important to determine the relative impacts of the shifting Creole-African mix as well as the possible improvements in slave diet.

An 1864 tract by D. José Ferrer de Couto cites a Cuban law of 1842 to the effect that children under three years of age be sold with mothers because "mothers are obliged to suckle and nurse them until they attain that age" (*Enough of War!* [New York, 1864], 71).

[37] See Menard, "Maryland Slave Population," *WMQ*, 3d Ser., XXXII (1975), 29-54.

While diet seems to have had some limited impact on the other demographic indices (and may explain in part differences in nursing customs), we do not expect such a phenomenon to account fully for the spacing differentials. More work on the British West Indian diet remains to be undertaken, since it has been argued (most strongly by Dunn) that the dietary factor may have directly contributed to forces producing such a difference in number of children. That planters themselves did not regard the period of lactation as fully explained by diet is indicated by the positive inducements, in terms of material rewards, which were apparently offered by several planters to West Indian slave women to encourage them to reduce the periods of lactation.[38]

In the general literature at the moment there seems to be some agreement that lactation, at least in the early post-pregnancy period, does in fact offer some limited contraceptive protection. How long this protection lasts is currently in dispute.[39] But from contemporary African evidence we also know that strong sexual taboos existed concerning abstinence in the lactation period.[40] It could be argued that the phenomenon of lactation, either by its direct physiological impact or by its social one, was sufficient to act as a constraint on the potential for pregnancy.

If lactation practices can be accepted as one factor in the differences in childspacing (whether owing to the natural or the social impact of nursing), the causes for this variation, given the differences in African and European practices, may have been influenced by the varying extents of cultural adaption. As in many other social and cultural patterns, West Indians retained more elements of African culture than did the North American slaves. The more intensive experience of the slave trade, and the much higher rates of African participation within the total population in the West Indies, marked a strong contrast between the two areas. For example, at about 1770

[38] See the comments of Baille and Clare in "Report from the Select Committee," House of Lords Papers, *Sess. Papers 1831-1832*, CCVI, CCVII, 51 and 282, and the comments contained in a 1785 letter contained in the Codrington Papers. See also the discussion in Pitman, "Slavery," *Jour. of Negro Hist.*, XI (1926), 604.

[39] On this relationship see Rose E. Frisch, "Demographic Implications of the Biological Determinants of Female Fecundity," *Soc. Biology*, XXII (1975), 17-22. For current studies of the relationship between lactation and fertility see, for example, Anrudh K. Jain *et al.*, "Demographic Aspects of Lactation and Postpartum Amenorrhea," *Demography*, VII (1970), 255-271; Robert Hinshaw, Patrick Pyeatt, and Jean-Pierre Habicht, "Environmental Effects on Child-Spacing and Population Increase in Highland Guatemala," *Current Anthropology*, XIII (1972), 216-230; Masri Singarimbun and Chris Manning, "Breastfeeding, Amenorrhea, and Abstinence in a Javanese Village: A Case Study of Mojolama," *Studies in Family Planning*, VII (1976), 175-179; and Jeroen K. Van Ginneken, "Prolonged Breastfeeding as a Birth Spacing Method," *ibid.*, V (1974), 201-206.

[40] See, for example, Winterbottom, *Account of Native Africans*, I, xxvii; Matthews, *Voyage to the River Sierra-Leone*, 99, and Barbot, *Description of the Coasts of Guinea*, 37. For a similar observation about slaves in Surinam see R. Van Lier, "Negro Slavery in Surinam," *Caribbean Historical Review*, III-IV (1954), 140. For a discussion of taboos in Africa today see n. 35 above.

TABLE I
SHARE OF BLACKS IN TOTAL POPULATION, UNITED STATES AND
BRITISH CARIBBEAN, 1700 TO C. 1830

	1700	1770	c. 1830
Northern United States [a]	3.6%	4.4%	2.3%
Southern United States [a]	21.1	39.3	37.9
British Caribbean [b]	77.7	90.6	90.8

Sources: [a] U.S. Bureau of the Census, *Historical Statistics of the United States* (Wash-
ington, D.C., 1976), II, 1168 (1700, 1770), and I, 22 (1830).
[b] John James McCusker, Jr., "The Rum Trade and the Balance of
Payments of the Thirteen Continental Colonies, 1650–1775" (Ph.D. diss.,
University of Pittsburgh, 1970), 712 (1700, 1770); Robert Montgomery
Martin, *Statistics of the Colonies of the British Empire* (London, 1839).

in the United States, the African-born represented only 30 percent of the
black population, while in Jamaica they numbered over 70 percent.[41]
Equally, even in the "black belt" section of the South, few areas achieved the
shares of black population domination that occurred in the British West
Indies (see Table I). Moreover, there were considerably higher numbers of
slaves per plantation in the West Indies than in North America, and
therefore a lessened day-to-day interaction with white society (see Table II).
Given the limited contact with white society in the West Indies, and the
higher concentrations of blacks within larger units, a stronger residue of
cultural practices from Africa could have remained.[42] While the research is
still only in its infancy, recent work seems to suggest some retentions of

[41] The U.S. data are from Fogel and Engerman, *Time on the Cross*, I, 23. The
Jamaica data are from Craton, "Jamaican Slave Mortality," *Jour. of Caribbean
Hist.*, III (1971), 1-27, and "Jamaican Slavery," in Engerman and Genovese, eds.,
Race and Slavery, 249-284. For 1830 the shares were about 90% and 75%, respec-
tively.
[42] For a discussion of cultural retentions in the B.W.I. see, for example, Orlando
Patterson, *The Sociology of Slavery: An Analysis of the Origins, Development and
Structure of Negro Slave Society in Jamaica* (London, 1967). For a discussion of
other aspects of the development of Creole society in Jamaica see also Edward
Braithwaite, *The Development of Creole Society in Jamaica, 1770-1820* (Oxford,
1971). Acculturation in the U.S. is discussed in Wood, *Black Majority* and Gerald
W. Mullin, *Flight and Rebellion: Slave Resistance in Eighteenth-Century Virginia*
(New York, 1972). See also Melville J. Herskovits, *The Myth of the Negro Past*
(New York, 1941) for the classic discussion of African patterns in the New World.
Winthrop Jordan has suggested that the Sea Islands area of the U.S. could provide a
useful test case. The ratio of children under five to females 15-39 in the 10 leading
rice counties of Georgia and South Carolina was less than four-fifths that of other
counties in those states in both 1850 and 1860. See U.S. Bureau of the Census, *The
Seventh Census of the United States* (1850) (Washington, D.C., 1853), and U.S.
Bureau of the Census, *Population of the United States . . . in 1860; . . . of the Eighth*

TABLE II
PERCENTAGES OF SLAVE POPULATION ON LARGE PLANTATIONS

Area	Date	"Threshold" Size (Number of Slaves)	Percent of Slaves
Barbados	1680[1]	60	54.3%
Maryland	1658–1710[2]	21	27.9
	1721–1730[3]	21	43.7
	1790[4]	20	37.2
South Carolina	1726[5]	50	38.0
	1790[4]	50	38.0
United States	1790[6]}	20	43.7
		50	15.7
	1850[7]}	20	50.6
		50	21.6
	1860[7]}	20	52.8
		50	24.9
Jamaica	1832[8]	51	75.7
Jamaica	1831[9]	30	80.5
Barbados	c.1831[9]	30	66.8
All West Indian Areas	c.1831[9]	30	74.0

Sources: [1] Richard S. Dunn, *Sugar and Slaves: The Rise of the Planter Class in the English West Indies, 1624–1713* (Chapel Hill, N.C., 1972), 96.

[2] (Four counties), see Russell R. Menard, "The Maryland Slave Population, 1658 to 1730: A Demographic Profile of Blacks in Four Counties," *William and Mary Quarterly*, 3d Ser., XXXII (1975), 29–54.

[3] (Two counties), see *ibid.*

[4] Lewis C. Gray, *History of Agriculture in the Southern United States to 1860*, I (Washington, D.C., 1933), 531.

[5] (One parish), Peter H. Wood, *Black Majority: Negroes in Colonial South Carolina from 1670 through the Stono Rebellion* (New York, 1974), 160–161.

[6] (Four states), Gray, *History of Agriculture*, I, 531.

[7] (Total South), *ibid.*, I, 530.

[8] B. W. Higman, *Slave Population and Economy in Jamaica, 1807–1834* (Cambridge, 1976), 70.

[9] "Classified Statement of Numbers of Proprietors . . . ," Aug. 1834, T. 71/1629, Public Record Office.

Census (Washington, D.C., 1864). On this area see also William R. Bascom, "Acculturation among the Gullah Negroes," *American Anthropologist*, XLIII (1941), 43-50, and Dale Evans Swan, *The Structure and Profitability of the Antebellum Rice Industry, 1859* (New York, 1975). Fertility levels in another area of heavy black concentration, the sugar counties of Louisiana, were slightly below those of the rice-growing areas (see n. 31 above).

kinship arrangements of possible African origins—at least in regard to marriage customs—even within North American society.[43] These can be assumed to have been greater in the West Indies, and we would expect more clearly defined and more widespread residues there.

Admittedly, the argument remains highly speculative. Nevertheless, the similarity in nursing practices between white and black North American women, and the apparent difference between black West Indians and North American slaves, seem to offer support for the conjectures we have raised. Equally, it is useful to note that the West Indian planters often seemed as desirous of a high rate of reproduction as the planters in the United States, particularly in the nineteenth century. This desire for infants is consistent with the positive prices of infant slaves in both areas. And, indeed, it was the West Indies planters who offered a greater degree of explicit incentives, both personally and through their legal codes, to encourage reproduction.[44] Moreover, in examining the United States we find that southern slave and southern white fertility were similar, although first births to slave mothers occurred at an earlier age than for whites. Patterns of childspacing were also similar, although whites may have had slightly shorter intervals between births. Thus the higher slave fertility in the United States does not appear to reflect an attempt at "breeding." While the mechanism of fertility decisions and controls in both areas remain unclear, research is suggesting a more active role for the slaves, and a greater consideration of the patterns maintained, adapted, and adopted by the enslaved. Thus, studies of childraising practices and changes in them over time are of great interest, and, of course, for a much wider set of issues than just the explanation of fertility differences.

[43] On various aspects of kinship arrangements see, for the U.S., Kulikoff, "Beginnings of the Afro-American Family," in Land *et al.*, eds., *Law, Society, and Politics*, 171-196, and Gutman, *Black Family;* for the B.W.I., Higman, "Slave Family," *Jour. Interdis. Hist.*, VI (1975), 261-287.

[44] On these points see Engerman, "Some Economic and Demographic Comparisons."

Tocqueville on Slavery, Ancient and Modern

Peter Augustine Lawler

The United States was the first regime to be founded consciously on rational principles. Perhaps the most important of these "modern" principles is egalitarian: no human being has the natural or divine right to rule over other human beings.[1] Scientific inquiry into natural necessity demonstrates the truth of the American belief that "each man at birth receives the faculty to rule himself and that nobody has the right to force his fellow man to be happy."[2] Every "enlightened" human being is aware that the only principle legitimating the power of government is the consent of the governed, and a rational human being consents to be ruled only to protect rights that all human beings share and that he himself can affirm as consistent with his individual self-interest.

It is a fundamental anomaly for such a regime to tolerate the existence of human slavery.[3] The American founders were well aware of this anomaly and some condemned slavery's injustice. They viewed it as an unfortunate inheritance from the colonial period, before Americans were in a position to deliberate freely and rationally about the

PETER LAWLER *teaches political science at Berry College in Georgia. He has published articles in journals of philosophy, theology, education, and political science.*

South Atlantic Quarterly 80:4, Autumn, 1981. Copyright ⊙ 1981 by Duke University Press.

1. Thomas Jefferson gives the most memorable statement of the principle: "The general spread of the light of science has already laid open to everyone the palpable truth, that the mass of mankind has not been born with saddles on their backs, nor a favored few, booted and spurred, ready to ride them legitimately, by the grace of God." *The Writings of Thomas Jefferson*, ed. P. C. Ford (New York, 1892–99), Vol. X, p. 391. An admirable contemporary statement is provided by Paul Eidelberg: "The Declaration proclaims that all men are created equal, meaning that all men are subject to the same moral law, as a consequence of which no group of men can rightly rule other men as if they were an inferior species." *On the Silence of the Declaration of Independence* (Amherst, 1976), p. 31.

2. Alexis de Tocqueville, *Democracy in America*, ed. J. P. Mayer, trans. G. Lawrence (New York, 1969), p. 363. Hereafter, page numbers in the text refer to this text.

3. "The fundamental cause of the civil war was not slavery as such. It was slavery in a nation *dedicated to the proposition that all men are created equal.* From the moment of that dedication, slavery as a permanent and hereditary condition of any class of human beings within the American polity became an unbearable anomaly." Harry Jaffa, *How to Think About the American Revolution,* (Durham, N.C., 1978), p. 62.

character of their regime. Nevertheless, the founders also concluded that immediate abolition was impossible, and they allowed slavery to continue to exist while carefully withholding moral approval from it. It was their not wholly unreasonable hope that a diverse commercial republic founded on liberal principles would gradually destroy slavery through popular enlightenment concerning both its injustice and its unprofitability. As long as slavery continued to exist, they also realized, it would be a serious threat to the regime's integrity.[4]

An unusually penetrating analysis of the effects of slavery on the integrity of the American and of any other modern, egalitarian regime (pp. 18–19) is provided by Alexis de Tocqueville in the eighteenth chapter of volume 1 of his *Democracy in America*. Not only does he bring to light with unparalleled clarity the effects of slavery on the antebellum South, but he also provides a comprehensive comparison of ancient and modern slavery. Thinking through this comparison allows Tocqueville's readers, especially those of aristocratic temperament or breeding, to appreciate the necessarily monstrous, destructive, and futile character not only of the attempt to preserve modern slavery but also of any attempt to establish and preserve any aristocratic regime after the diffusion of Christian and enlightenment egalitarianism (pp. 12–13).

According to Tocqueville, ancient and modern slavery had an important common feature: they were both foundations for aristocracies. He shows how this was true through his analysis of the distinctiveness of the American southerner's character. For the most part, Americans are typical inhabitants of modern civilization: free, equal, and hard at work in constant pursuit of materialistic goals (pp. 345–47, 375–76, 403–4). But the habits of mastery had "modified the character of the southerners and given them different customs." The effect of slavery on the South was to transform it into an "ancient" or aristocratic civilization. Accordingly, the South had "the tastes, prejudices, weaknesses and grandeur of every aristocracy" (pp. 346–47, 374–76).

The southern impetus toward grandeur was rooted in the aristocratic opinion that man's primary purpose was to perform noble deeds and cultivate his soul. The southerner understood himself to be free from the demands of useful work; he left such slavish activity to slaves. He thought that a real man did not concern himself with material cares. This contempt for merely brute nature was evidence that it is possible to establish one's own human particularity by refusing to identify oneself as essentially matter in motion. Consequently, the southerner

4. For an elaboration of these points, see Herbert Storing, "Slavery and the Moral Foundations of the American Republic," *The Moral Foundations of the American Republic*, ed. Robert Horwitz, (Charlottesville, Va., 1977), pp. 214–34.

loved his idleness above all; having to work implied material neediness and finally mortality (pp. 346, 375). He would be calling into question his own humanity if he were to imitate the northerner by constantly striving to master nature in pursuit of material well-being. The southerner understood himself to be free of the northerner's slavish fear of brute nature; he had conquered fear through his intransigent pride and his noble deeds (p. 347). In the South, writes Tocqueville, "it is nature that seems active and alive, whereas man is idle" (p. 345).

Tocqueville considers the southerner to be idle in the sense that he eschewed useful work, but far from purposeless or motionless. Compared with the slave or the slavish materialist, he pursued "wider and less defined objectives" (p. 375). He was drawn to the various forms of immaterial greatness. According to Tocqueville, he achieved considerable success in this effort. Tocqueville concludes that the southerner really did tend to be a man of moral and intellectual excellence. "The southerner is more spontaneous, witty, open, generous, intellectual, and brilliant" than his northern, or what we might call his bourgeois, counterpart (p. 376). If the purpose of a regime is to bring into being a few remarkable individuals who possess a plenitude of human excellence, slavery might appear to be justifiable. This "ancient" argument for the primacy of excellence is not finally endorsed by Tocqueville, but he allows the reader to see its strength. Indeed, he describes and praises the southerner's excellence, but he refuses to praise the South's regime.[5] For reasons which will become clear, Tocqueville refuses to give any moral and intellectual support for slavery, especially under modern circumstances. While he recognized that slavery per se is an evil and angrily condemns the founders of modern slavery, he is not blind to the grandeur of its human product (pp. 363, 340).

In Tocqueville's view, the passionate source of aristocratic greatness is pride experienced as a result of one's own recognition of one's own distinctive human excellence. The other characteristic of aristocratic passion is anger directed against anyone or anything that would threaten the status of the aristocrat's proud self-understanding. But unreasonable anger, derived from objectively illegitimate pride, is the aristocrat's characteristic weakness. To illustrate this point, Tocqueville traces the southern desire to secede from the Union not to an objective conflict of interest with the North but to aristocratic indignation. The South felt itself injured because its place or status within the American regime was on the decline and especially because there was insufficient political recognition of the manifest injustice of this decline. Proud, angry men are characteristically unable to develop the patience necessary

5. Consider the favorable impression Tocqueville gives us of aristocratic science. *Democracy in America*, pp. 459–65.

to undertake the rational calculation required to pursue their self-interest. Instead, their "ardent and irascible" passions causes them to strike out without reflection. Tocqueville asserts that experience showed that most human conflict is caused not by a clash of material interests but by aristocratic unreasonableness. Yet this same unreasonableness, he concludes, leads men to many of the forms of human greatness (pp. 375, 382–83).

At this point, it should come as no surprise to learn that Tocqueville traces the South's decline relative to the bourgeois North, in part, to the aristocrat's proud refusal to calculate and act on what was best for his material well-being. Although many southerners were perfectly aware of the economic disadvantages of slavery, they refused to allow this "modern" truth to alter their "ancient" understanding of themselves and of nature (pp. 348–49, 361). The purpose of the slave system after all was not to pursue limitless profit but to free the master for the performance of great deeds. Economic activity was not an end in itself; its purpose was to provide a context in which the good life could be lived. From this point of view, the southerner tended to think that slavery was indispensable. The places of master and slave, soul and body, freedom and necessity must remain sharply delimited if the aristocrat was to sustain his proud and angry defense of his humanity. If maintenance of such distinctions required attachment to a lost cause, so be it. Tocqueville shows that slavery would inevitably be "a fatal influence in the well being" of the southern master (p. 379). Hence the master acted irrationally by remaining attached to it. We are compelled to admit, however, that there is something admirable and distinctively human in such attachments.

Although ancient and modern slavery were both foundations for aristocracies, and to understand the southerner means primarily to understand the typical characteristics of aristocrats everywhere and at all times, Tocqueville's emphasis is actually on the differences between ancient and modern slavery. In antiquity, "slavery existed throughout the civilized world, only some barbarian peoples being without it." Hence the ancients argued "that slavery was natural and would always exist" because it was impossible to conceive of a civilized society without it (pp. 348, 439). They viewed slavery simply as an enslavement of body, and, at least in principle, bodily enslavement was understood not to be a reflection on the character of the slave's soul (his moral and intellectual qualities). Consequently, they "bound the slave's body, but left his spirit free and allowed him to educate himself"; indeed the slave was often "his [master's] superior in education and enlightenment." Tocqueville reports that "several of the most celebrated authors of antiquity were or had been slaves" (pp. 361, 341). Enslavement, indeed, was not thought to be especially appropri-

341

ate or inappropriate for any particular type of human being; it was simply the product of chance. The fortunes of war caused the enslavement
of both barbarians and "very civilized men" (p. 341n).

Ancient slavery, as Tocqueville presents it, was a positive legal
condition rooted simply in force. A slave was a human being who
found himself in unfortunate bodily circumstances. A change in these
legal circumstances could mean that a human being could be a slave
one day and "*free and equal* to his master" the next (p. 361). Because
the only basis of the distinction between master and slave was legal,
once the slave was legally emancipated there was nothing to keep them
apart. At least in principle, this change in legal circumstances indicated
nothing about the moral or intellectual quality of the human beings involved.

In antiquity, Tocqueville suggests, the merely conventional distinction between master and slave was straightforwardly justified as necessary for the cultivation of human excellence. The slave himself was
aware that he was not a slave by nature; he accepted his lot only as a
response to the threat of physical force (p. 362). There was no attempt
to justify why he in particular was enslaved while other, perhaps essentially similar human beings, were not. Slaves were needed; he had the
bad luck to be one. The fact that the slave was allowed to retain his
spiritual and intellectual freedom suggests a large measure of integrity
and even humanity in the ancient argument defending slavery.

Now Tocqueville acknowledges that this description must be qualified; legal distinctions could not help but effect mores. He saw a "natural prejudice [which] leads a man to scorn anybody who has been his
inferior, long after he has become his equal." The aristocratic side of
human nature causes a human being to crave and to hold tightly to any
evidence of superiority over his fellows, even if he is compelled to acknowledge in principle that the distinction in question had merely legal
or conventional roots. Because the impetus to prejudice was perfectly
natural, changes in law which abolished slavery in antiquity were followed by "an imagined inequality rooted in mores." But this "imagined inequality" was temporary; "the freedman was so completely like
the man born free that it was soon impossible to distinguish between
them." Because there was no natural (physical) difference between
master and slave and because masters did not force slaves to give up
their spiritual or intellectual freedom, any "secondary effects" brought
into being by the memory of legal distinctions could not sustain themselves indefinitely once legal emancipation had occurred. Slavery did
not in any sense permanently degrade any particular class of human beings (p. 341).

Ancient slavery, Tocqueville asserts, was destroyed by Christianity. Christianity both insisted on the slaves' rights and attacked the in-

stitution "as unjust" (pp. 363, 348). Having declared all men equal in God's eyes, Christianity brought forth "general truths" which overturned any basis for making radical distinctions among human beings. Spiritual equality was incompatible with bodily slavery; no aspect of human freedom ought to be denied to any member of the "multitude" under God. Christianity appears to have been the basis of the formation of the doctrine that it is unjust for some human beings to deny the bodily freedom of other human beings in the name of their own excellence. Although Tocqueville does not state this, perhaps the Christian teaching that the genuinely human spiritual potential is such that it can be achieved without the need of slaves was at the root of this doctrine. Eventually Christianity proved itself to be compatible with a "hierarchy of ranks" among human beings; it supported the medieval aristocracy. Its initial appearance in the Roman empire, however, was in support of the equality of all men, and this egalitarian thrust never totally disappeared (pp. 446, 439).

Modern slavery came into being in this egalitarian Christian context. "Christianity had destroyed servitude, the Christians of the sixteenth century reestablished it" (p. 341). Fundamentally "modern" in their acceptance of the Christian argument against the legitimacy of ancient slavery, they viewed the reestablishment of slavery as "an exception in their social system, and they were careful to restrict it to one of the races of man." The Christians of Europe "took their slaves from a race different from their own, which many of them consider inferior to the other human races" (pp. 341, 362). The reestablishment of slavery in Christian times could be justified only by a tacit denial of the humanity of the slaves, a denial made plausible by the visible sign of racial distinctiveness. Given the Christian belief that it is illegitimate for some human beings to enslave others on the basis of purely legal distinctions for any purpose, the Christian European was drawn to the conclusion that there must be a natural distinction between master and slave. According to Tocqueville's argument, modern slavery began with an illusory principle supporting human degradation absent from the conscious legal positivism underlying ancient slavery.

This tacit postulation of radical racial inequality "inflicted a smaller wound on humanity" than did ancient slavery, Tocqueville contends, because most human beings are thought to be exempted permanently from enslavement by right. But it is a wound "much harder to cure," because certain human beings are thought to be marked by their racial characteristics as slaves by nature. By reestablishing slavery on the basis of conclusions drawn from permanent and obvious physical distinctions, the Europeans tacitly "assumed that slavery would be eternal" (p. 362).

According to Tocqueville, the European consciously refused to deny explicitly the humanity of the black race. Nevertheless, he denied it in practice by treating the black in every respect as a beast of burden. Tocqueville states that "the European is to men of other races what man is to the animals." In another place, he reports that the European "almost takes him [the black] for some intermediate between beast and man" (pp. 317, 342). He can almost maintain the distinction between man and black as he does between man and beast, but not quite. None of the offspring of his beasts are fathered by him, and he cannot see the resemblance between himself and these offspring (p. 361). Blacks are "hardly recognized as sharing the common features of humanity", but the white cannot escape such recognition entirely (p. 342). This recognition is the source of profound despair for the white; he must on occasion deny his own children's humanity in order to deny that of his slaves. In his most candid moments, he must admit that such a denial is a monstrous illusion.[6]

Tocqueville contends that the southerner also recognized the black's humanity, although again he does not admit it, by engaging in "spiritualized despotism and violence." The ancients physically constrained their slaves but never denied their moral and intellectual freedom. They allowed them to develop spiritually as men. On the other hand, the southerner attempted to prevent his slaves from developing any specifically human qualities. He undertook to destroy their moral and intellectual potential. In particular, he made every effort to keep them from thinking the thoughts of free men (p. 361). The theory was that the black was naturally unable to think such thoughts, but the southerner, Tocqueville insists, contradicted this theory in practice by a constant effort to prevent the possibility of their thinking such thoughts.

Tocqueville concludes that this project of intellectual and moral degradation had achieved considerable success. The American black, he reports, "has reached the ultimate limits of slavery"; he "almost believes" himself to be an inferior being, a slave by nature, and "the habits of servitude have given him the thoughts and ambitions of a slave. . . ." He sees "a trace of slavery in [his] every feature." He is almost completely devoid of personal pride; he is almost unable to recognize his own humanity; hence "he holds himself in contempt." This self-contempt or shame is the obverse side of the master's pride. It is also an indication that he is indeed a human being; shame and pride are both distinctively human passions stemming from the same roots. Because he possesses the uniquely human ability to distinguish human from subhuman, and because he "almost" accepts the white's natural,

6. Ibid., pp. 362–63. "Among Americans of the South, nature sometimes, reclaiming her rights, does for a moment establish equality between white and black" (pp. 343–44).

human superiority, "he admires the tyrant even more than he hates him and finds his joy and pride in a servile imitation of his oppressors." Because the black slave "almost believes" he is essentially no more than a beast of burden to be directed by his human masters, "the very use of thought seems to him an unprofitable gift of providence." He "almost" agrees with his master that it is not useful or perhaps even possible for him to develop his specifically human capabilities. As a result, the modern slave, unlike his ancient counterpart, is almost totally unfit to live the life of a free man. Once freed, the black "often feels independence as a heavier burden than slavery itself" (pp. 317–19).

The shift from ancient to modern theory, in short, brought into being a change in the slave's character: the modern slave, according to Tocqueville's argument, is really not only legally but morally and intellectually degraded. A change in the law would not suffice to allow him to assume his place in the ranks of free men. Unlike most southerners, Tocqueville does not think that this radical racial degradation is necessarily permanent. The slavish characteristics attributed to the black race are not really natural and thus not really hereditary, and environmental damage could be remedied by environmental change. If whites should begin to treat blacks as free and equal human beings, they would become free and equal human beings. But the change in treatment must precede the change in black's capabilities, and the theory of permanent racial inferiority underlying modern slavery makes this course of events very unlikely (p. 341n.).

Tocqueville demonstrates that the southerner's determination to keep his slaves permanently in an abysmally ignorant and almost amoral state conflicted with the spiritual egalitarianism of Christianity and the secularization of this Christian perpective in modern philosophy. The great materialistic and egalitarian truths of modern philosophy are accepted dogmatically by virtually all Americans, northerners and southerners alike. According to modern philosophy, the locus of human freedom is in the maintenance of bodily independence. Each human being by natural right possesses absolutely the products of his bodily labor; to deny a man this right is to deny his essential humanity. The ancients, Tocqueville suggests, were in principle dualistic; they argued that it was possible both to be enslaved bodily and to be morally and spiritually free. Modern philosophy denied the truth of this dualism, because all beings, including human beings, are essentially body. Any definition of humanity grounded in immaterial distinctions such as qualities of soul is ultimately untenable (pp. 429–41).

Tocqueville, in describing the extremity of the black slave's plight, asserts that the slave had "lost even ownership of his own body" (p. 318). According to Tocqueville, although this loss characterized both ancient and modern slavery, the significance of the loss changed after the enlightenment produced by modern philosophy. In antiquity, it was thought that one could justly enslave a human being without denying his humanity; in a regime informed by the modern theory of materialistic egalitarianism, the enslavement of any human being is considered both unjust and fundamentally dehumanizing. In order to sustain the white's own sense of moral well-being and to keep slaves from recognizing the extent of their degradation, modern slaves had to be divested as completely as possible of all human characteristics. The only legitimate human assertion of mastery could be against nonhuman nature.

Tocqueville's central argument is, then, that modern slavery is necessarily destructive of human nature in a way that ancient slavery did not have to be. The preservation of modern slavery could be accomplished only through a brutalization of the slave's soul. For reasons already given, the natural distinction between white and black must be asserted to be akin to that between man and brute nature. Such a distinction could never be eradicated by merely legal or customary changes. Indeed, on the contrary, the southerner must maintain a constant program of destruction of the black's humanity in order to make an assertion concerning the natural distinctions between races plausible. The preservation of the southerner's illusion required "desperate" means of "unprecedented atrocity," which, to Tocqueville, indicates "some profound disturbance in humanity's laws" (p. 361).

Thus, Tocqueville contends, the only alternative the white had to keeping the black "as close to the beasts as possible" was to raise him to his own level (p. 361). The southern white refused to consider the possibility of raising up the black, however, because in doing so he would throw his own humanity into question. His humanity was sustained by the proud assumption that there was a radical difference between his own and brute nature, and that the black was all but a brute. Any effort to show the essential equality between white and black angered the southerner. It might open the possibility that the remainder of his asserted distinction between human and brute was merely conventional (p. 357). The modern white's resistance to reason in this respect is understandable; the logic of modern philosophical materialism does tend to blur the differences between man and brute.[7]

Tocqueville predicts that the white in America will never recognize the black as a fully human being. He is convinced that all whites, even those in the North, shared a racial pride derivative of the almost universal human pride in being human, and that they would never "mingle" with the "degraded race." To prevent an indiscriminate homogenization, custom rigidly isolated the black in those parts of the United

7. See Tocqueville's angry attack on theoretical materialism in ibid., pp. 543–46.

States where the law asserted that he was free. In truth, the custom of racial separation functioned to protect Americans from what was thought to be a threatening natural fact (pp. 342–43, 356).

Tocqueville finds it necessary to conclude, at this point, that there was no possibility of an amicable relationship between emancipated blacks and the dominant whites: "being unable to become the equal of whites, they [the blacks] will not be slow to show themselves their enemies" (p. 360). In the North, the number of free blacks was insignificant; they were not in a position to assert themselves. But the huge and constantly increasing number of blacks in the deep South presented a fundamental danger to the whites; only total ignorance and abject servitude prevented them from having the enlightenment and will necessary to attempt to kill the whites (pp. 355, 360). Consequently, although Tocqueville refuses to justify the principle of black slavery, he concedes "that all those who formerly accepted this terrible principle are not now equally free to get rid of it." Accepting the impossibility of complete racial equality, mere self-preservation forced even a calculating southerner to resort to complete racial brutalization. Any "intermediate measure" would terminate, Tocqueville predicts, "in the most horrible of civil wars and perhaps in the extermination of one or the other of the two races" (pp. 360, 354). The fact that even moderate human beings must eschew moderation shows, to Tocqueville, to "what excesses men may be driven once they abandon nature and humanity" (p. 340n). Because the aristocratic illusions maintaining modern slavery could not sustain themselves forever in a time of egalitarian enlightenment, Tocqueville concludes "that sooner or later in the southern states whites and blacks will come to blows" (p. 357). The South was aware that the days of slavery were numbered, and it was pervaded by a profound, silent fear. Not only the good life but mere life was threatened by the spectre of inevitable racial war (p. 358). No wonder Tocqueville begins his analysis by asserting "[t]he most formidable evil threatening the future of the United States is the presence of blacks on their soil" (p. 340).

Thus, according to Tocqueville's argument, the two strongest passions, pride and fear, worked together in inducing the southerner to preserve modern slavery. His attachment to the South's distinctive regime, it turns out, was not simply that of a proud aristocrat choosing to scorn the bourgeois concern for material prosperity; it was also firmly grounded in the material necessity of self-preservation. His aristocratic self-understanding was deficient; he was not free from concern with bodily well-being. But, in his case, "modern" enlightenment concerning aristocratic vanity was powerless to compel him to abandon his "ancient" regime. He was aware that a regime based on free labor and bourgeois equality would produce greater material strength; hence, he also knew that the South was undergoing a "fatal" weakening in comparison with the North. The option of becoming a modest egalitarian materialist in the name of burgeoning prosperity, however, was not open to him. Indeed, it was precisely his "modern" concern with mere self-preservation that was the basis for a calculated defense of his "ancient" regime.[8]

It is clear that Tocqueville wants us to reach this conclusion: The establishment of slavery on a natural and permanent basis—a monstrous synthesis of ancient or aristocratic pride and modern or egalitarian philosophy or science—begot both an illegitimate and humanly destructive racial pride and a desperate fear of being held accountable for the terrible injustice it produced. The genuinely human excellence manifested by some southerners was not sufficient justification for this wholesale destruction. Thus, we ought to consider not only the plight of the slave but the moral incoherence and despair at the heart of the southerner's superficially ennobled soul.

More generally, Tocqueville's analysis of the distinctiveness of modern slavery strongly suggests that any attempt to establish an aristocratic regime within the horizon of thought established by Christianity and modern philosophy is compelled to culminate in a theory of scientific racism. For all human beings who accept the "self-evident truth" that men are fundamentally equal for political purposes and hence that no human being has the right to enslave or otherwise lord it over another human being for any purpose, the only way to justify such a regime is to argue that those who are not aristocrats are not human beings.

Tocqueville's description of the tacit justification of modern slavery in the antebellum South points to a scientific argument for the existence of a master race. Harry Jaffa has shown that such an argument was first comprehensively articulated by the Confederacy's most brilliant defender, Alexander Stephens, in his "Corner Stone" speech.[9] It is Jaffa's conclusion that

. . . the Confederate states of America represented the first time in human history that a doctrine of a master race was fully and systematically set forth as the ground of a regime. More precisely, it was the first time that such a doctrine was set forth *on the authority of modern science*. It was this authority that made it so persuasive, and so pernicious.[10]

---

8. Ibid., "For the masters in the North, slavery was a commercial and industrial question; in the South it is a question of life and death" (p. 360).
9. Jaffa, *American Revolution*, pp. 155–59.
10. Ibid., p. 160.

Tocqueville shows us why the Confederacy's and other modern attempts to justify aristocracies, such as the various forms of Fascism, must ground themselves in such a uniquely pernicious and objectively unwarranted synthesis of ancient (master) and modern (scientific) principles. For this reason, it is dangerously imprudent for anyone, however profound, to arouse aristocratic longings in modern times. One thinks here of Nietzsche, Heidegger, and on a much lower level, the American literary "Agrarians" and their disciples.[11] Only if modernity could be transcended entirely could a decent aristocracy be established, and the lesson of "National Socialism" is that we do well to assume that such transcendence is impossible. It is to Tocqueville's great credit that he never suggested the possibility or desirability of any radical effort to overcome somehow the merely "middle class" (p. 376) character of modern man.

11. On the relevance of Nietzsche, Heidegger, and Fascism to Tocqueville's analysis, see Harry Neumann's remarkable review of Bernard Magnus, *Nietzsche's Existential Imperative, Independent Journal of Philosophy* 3 (1979): 139–41.

8

British Caribbean and North American Slaves in an Era of War and Revolution, 1775–1807

by Michael Mullin

In *Common Sense* (1776) Thomas Paine accused Great Britain of inciting American slaves "to destroy us." In Virginia, where rebellion existed for more than a year before the publication of Paine's pamphlet, the last royal governor raised the king's standard at Norfolk and proclaimed liberty for slaves who would join the war against their masters. Lord Dunmore was his sovereign's personal representative, and his strategy, which unleashed the dread specter of a general servile war, was unprecedented and terrifying. But Virginia Negroes during the Revolution never rebelled, although several thousand did resist as solitary, unorganized fugitives who joined whichever army— British, American, or French—seemed to offer them the most favorable prospects of freedom.[1]

Elsewhere in the Chesapeake the planter's authority was more fragile, and slaves reacted more dangerously than in Virginia. In Dorchester County, Maryland, authorities in 1776 broke up a meeting of blacks and confiscated eighty guns, bayonets, and swords; and later on the Eastern Shore Negroes fought alongside Tory partisans.[2]

Blacks in South Carolina should have been even more dangerously rebellious than were Chesapeake slaves. Low-country Negroes, the most African of all North American slaves,

235

had a fearsome tradition of organized resistance going back to the great Stono River rebellion of 1739. Although the evidence is inferential and sketchy (Charleston Police Board Minutes during the British occupation, loyalist claims, and correspondence of such military commanders as Sir Guy Carleton, Thomas Pinckney, and Nathanael Greene), South Carolina blacks apparently did not take advantage of their owners' predicament during the Revolution, nor did lowcountry planters exhibit the anxiety about their slaves' loyalty manifested by Maryland and Virginia slaveholders.[3]

At the close of the Revolution, North American planters realized that somehow a great disaster had been averted and praised slaves for their loyalty in the face of innumerable opportunities to act otherwise. The scion of the powerful Carroll family of Maryland wrote: "I think our negroes on the island have given proof of their attachment. . . . They might have gone off if they had been so disposed." When General William Moultrie returned to his South Carolina plantation in 1782, he was deeply affected by his slaves' reception. Each came forward, took his hand, and said, "God Bless you, massa! we glad for see you, massa! . . . The tears stole from my eyes and ran down my cheeks. . . . I then possessed about 200 slaves, and not one of them left me during the war, although they had great offers."[4]

Further south in the British Caribbean, planters, who encountered potentially even more destructive forces and events than the Americans did, also were fortunate to escape unscathed during years of war and revolution. In the sugar islands slaves outnumbered whites ten to fifteen to one; and maroonage (armed mountain villages of runaway Negroes) was a continual source of danger to whites and an inspiration to some lowland blacks. During this era of fundamental change in West Indian slavery, planters also faced increasing bankruptcies, declining profits, the revolution of former slaves in Santo Domingo (Haiti), British abolitionism, and their slaves' insistence that the end of the trade would be followed quickly by the abolition of slavery itself. Dissenting preachers, empire loyalists from America, and royalist emigrés from nearby French colonies—torn by civil wars and racial strife—came into the English islands and contributed to the atmosphere of crisis.

Behind this unnerving, kaleidoscopic scene loomed an even greater revolution in France, "by Men," the Jamaican assembly memorialized to the king, "who after overturning the Constitution of their own Country, and murdering their Sovereign, wished to carry their principles of Anarchy and Confusion, throughout the World." For planters the European dimension of the great French Revolution was sufficiently demoralizing, but when the "Levelling *Influenza*" threatened to "spread thro' the ruder Multitudes on This Side of the Western Ocean," their reactions were feverish—and not unreasonable. For the French Revolution was a shattering reality in the Caribbean, where the urbane governor of Guadaloupe, Victor Hugues, was busy deploying bilingual mulatto brigands, mountain fighters, in the British islands to incite maroons and plantation Negroes. Throughout the 1790s and Napoleonic era, then, a familiar image that sprang to mind whenever planters faced even the most inconsequential slave conspiracy was the ghastly possibility that it might become a "second St. Domingo War."[5]

These profoundly troubled reactions to the threat of a general servile uprising, however, came only from Jamaica—England's "jewel" of empire, staging area for counterrevolution against black and white jacobinism in the Caribbean, and an island with the largest and apparently the most dangerous slave and maroon communities in plantation America. But slaves elsewhere in the islands reacted differently to the crises of the era, as they had done in the American Revolution. Barbadians throughout the late eighteenth century, for example, praised their slaves' "quiet & well disposed" behavior, their "patriotism" and "tranquility."[6]

In retrospect the views of relatively peaceful slaves in wartime Barbados and South Carolina are more accurate and informative about those of all Anglo-American slaves during the era than are the words of Paine, the Virginians, and Jamaicans who thought blacks would "destroy" them. There never was a "second St. Domingo War" in any British or American plantation society at this time. To understand why this was so the following examination of the two major kinds of resistance that did take place—African uprisings and Creole conspiracies—also probes the question of why Africans and native American slaves seldom were able to overcome their ethnic and acculturative differences to cooperate as slaves had done in Haiti. While viewing slave rebels in their settings—mountains, plantations, and towns—on the one hand, and their varying rates of cultural change, on the other, I try as best I can to view the era from the slaves' vantage point by concentrating on what concerned them most: in the society at large, urbanization, accelerated by the endemic wars of the era; the French and Haitian revolutions, which meant much more to blacks than the American Revolution; and, on the plantations, the slaves' households and property, which they sometimes had to defend against other Negroes (maroons and French brigands, principally) as well as against whites. Essentially this essay is a proposal that Anglo-American slavery be examined in a comparative, hemispheric perspective on the basis of the slaves' varying rates of acculturation; this process depended upon the degree to which their owners and white supervisors participated in plantation management and the extent to which slaves controlled such vital resources as provision land and markets. In the islands plantation sanctions and values—partially of the slaves' own making—were based on the considerable control slaves exercised over food, markets, polygynous households, and heritable property. Upon this base Caribbean slaves created a Creole culture that was strongly African and achieved a degree of cultural autonomy unequaled on the mainland, particularly in Virginia, where the persistent, dominating presence of the master figure undercut the sources of slave authority (so prevalent in the islands) and encouraged slaves to assimilate to a culture that was largely not of their own making.

British and American slaves during this era participated in essentially two types of rebellion, actual insurrections and conspiracies. Different kinds of slaves with different strategies and objectives characterized each type. Insurrectionists and maroons were usually native Africans, many of whom were "new Negroes," men and a few women who only recently had been enslaved and imported to the new world. They followed the cultural sanctions of their African tribal ways and used the wild and formidable island interiors and the frontier areas of mainland America to establish either remote and relatively self-sufficient villages or camps for mounting raids on lowland plantations. Conspirators, on the other hand, were usually the sons and daughters of native Africans (called Creoles in the islands and country-born or American-born on the mainland), whose nonfield jobs as artisans and domestics, and situation as town Negroes accelerated their assimilation and made them unaccustomed and temperamentally unsuited to the maroons' techniques of wilderness survival and hit-and-run warfare. Creoles directed their elaborate schemes and ambitions at the whites' forts and port towns.

Maroons, who were ubiquitous throughout the mountainous islands, may be characterized in several ways: they were armed and organized; they lived either in camps or in more permanent villages with fairly stable economic and political arrangements around their root crops and small stock, headmen, conjurors, and obeahmen; they were not isolated from the plantations below, where they had wives and traded (wild hog meat for gunpowder and shot on one occasion); and they lived in relatively inaccessible mountain fastnesses. Comparatively flat, treeless, and dry islands like Barbados and Antigua had no reported instances of maroonage in the eighteenth century.[7]

By the 1760s, for example, maroons in Dominica—a wild, heavily forested, precipitous island—had built sturdy houses, planted gardens, raised poultry and hogs, fished in bountiful streams and the sea, and traded with plantation Negroes. They lived "very comfortably," wrote Thomas Atwood, a contemporary planter and historian, and they were "seldom disturbed." They also kept to themselves and never killed a white until 1778, when during the French occupation of the island their occasional nighttime forays became daytime raids of arson and pillage to the outskirts of Roseau, the capital city, with "conk shells blowing and French colours flying."[8]

In 1785 and 1786 the English used black soldiers, trackers, and spies to dismantle the major runaway settlements. In one camp of twenty or thirty they captured both English and French Negroes, including two women (one the governor's slave, Mary), and Monsieur Garshett, who had been in the woods for twenty years. They also killed Balla, a headman, probably by torture. Calling out to his tormentors to cut off his head because he could not be killed, Balla, the governor reported, "only . . . expressed much anxiety" about his obeah or charm, which he wanted buried, and his little five-year-old son whom "he bid to remember, the Beckys or White Men had killed his father."[9]

Armed and organized uprisings and maroonage in North America were virtually unknown at this time. The few instances of significant rebellion are described only in South Carolina sources (after the Revolution) and with none of the richness or depth of comparable Caribbean evidence. In December 1782, for instance, a Goose Creek planter wrote about fifty to one hundred "Black Dragoons who have been out four times within the last ten days plundering & robbing . . . last night they came as high as Mrs. Godins where they continued from 11 oclock till 4 this morning, & carried off everything they could . . . all her Cattle, Sheep, Hogs [and] Horses."[10]

When the British evacuated Charleston and Savannah some black irregulars chose to remain behind. Calling themselves "the King of England's soldiers," they raided at night and disappeared during the day into Savannah River swamps, and into a fortified encampment that was half a mile long, four hundred feet deep, with twenty-one houses and fields of crops surrounded by a four-foot breastwork of log and cane pilings. In May 1786 a combined force of militia and Catawba Indians defeated them, but a year later a very sparse governor's message to the legislature mentioned serious depredations of armed Negroes, "too numerous to be quelled by patrols," in the southern part of the new state.[11]

Even earlier, when most slaves were native Africans and the frontier was nearer at hand, maroonage in North America never matched its extent and intensity in the islands. On the American frontier armed and dangerous frontiersmen and land speculators and Indians, particularly the Over-the-hill Cherokees in the Carolinas—who had no equivalent in the Caribbean—fought runaway slaves for access to the wilderness.

As North American slaves lost tribal ways they seldom resisted slavery cooperatively. During the eighteenth century, few ran off in groups to establish remote settlements. While in the islands fugitives could join large and self-sufficient maroon villages on the ridges above their plantations, new Negroes in North America usually sat before smoldering fires in lonely camps in the woods alongside tobacco and rice pieces; and sometimes in the evening hours they came in to be fed at the doors of slave cabins and kitchens.[12]

These pictures of maroon and plantation blacks are somewhat misleading as they represent slavery in this era incompletely. The most significant changes in Anglo-American plantation societies took place in cities—not the countryside— and among free people of color (called freedmen or free Negroes in North America) and varieties of town slaves—domestics, artisans, dock roustabouts, watermen, and sailors. Whites throughout the mainland and islands overreacted to city slaves as they never had either to the plantation folk or the maroons, whose ways of resisting slavery were soon outmoded by the economic and cultural dvelopments that were pushing urban conspirators to the fore.

Endemic warfare after 1763 accelerated the growth of Anglo-American cities and the nonplantation (usually wartime) industries they incorporated. Slaves and free people of color were indispensable workers in mines and forges, munition and textile manufactories, and salt and rope works. These urban industries increased slave literacy and knowledge of colonial culture generally, while breaking down old and familiar patterns of plantation authority that traditionally had controlled slaves fairly well.

Varieties of documents from Baltimore to Bridgetown, Barbados—borough regulations, grand jury presentments, newspaper notices, and letters to the editor—make similar points regarding the expanding urban process and scene at this time: towns were rapidly getting out of control, and new police and regulations were needed to help identify and restrict city slaves and keep watch on their activities. In 1780 citizens in Augusta, Georgia, demanded more effective policing of slaves "rambling from place to place without written permits." In 1784 the captain of the James Street Fire Company in Bridgetown, Barbados, requested parish representatives to "suppress & abate such sheds & low houses erected & now erecting by negro & mulatto slaves & free negroes, which are not only public nuisances but afford fuel to spreading flames." Georgetown, South Carolina, citizens in 1790 asked for a stricter regulation of bread, liquor, and billiard licenses and an end to liquor sales to slaves aboard ships in the harbor. In Chatham County, Savannah, Georgia, in 1793 and 1796 whites demanded that Negro cartmen wear identification badges and insisted on better regulation of house rentals to Negroes and of dram shops, as their use of the latter encouraged them to steal. In Kingston, Jamaica, in 1797, a newspaper notice warned, "House-keepers cannot be too careful in seeing their doors & gates locked at this season of the year; & it is the duty of the Constables to take up all Negroes" in the streets after nine o'clock in the evening.[13]

Officials soon recognized that cities generated new kinds of organized resistance by slaves whose ways had become like the whites', but who were culturally even more threatening than the Africans. The solution of the Jamaica assembly was to keep slaves "constantly at home," while striking at the essentials of their potentially insurrectionary rites and associations—"disarm them, prevent caballing, drumming, sounding Conches & Horns, securing Rum & strong liquors, and also ammunition."[14] A contemporary historian, John Poyer of Speightstown, Barbados, warned in 1806 that "the coloured tribe not content with having their Balls, Routs & assemblies have established places of public rendezvous for Cockfighting & other Species of Gaming & in their general conduct have assumed an insolent & provoking deportment towards the legitimate inhabitants of the Island."[15] Poyer saw the rapid urbanization of large numbers of blacks in postwar Anglo-America as a contest between two cultures (his being the "legitimate" one) for control of Bridgetown. In Charleston, Henry Laurens, struggling in 1776 to rent and hire out his brother's town houses and black servants, finally threw up his hands and described urban slavery: "Your Negroes in some measure," he said, "govern themselves"—a contemporary view of urban blacks whom Ira Berlin appropriately has called "slaves without masters."[16]

In this context the rebellions designed by Anglo-American Creoles were similar regardless of their respective society's stage of development. St. George Tucker's account of Gabriel Prosser's conspiracy in Richmond, Virginia, in 1800—the largest and most ambitious up to that time in North America—is a most useful introduction to the origins and character of Creole conspiracies at the end of the century. "Nothing can stop the prodigious advancement of knowledge" among "this class of Negroes" (native Americans) whose new values and attitudes he attributed to the "unexampled rapidity" in the growth of wealth, population, and towns. Learning, "the vast march of mind," he added, "is the principle agent in evolving the spirit [the love of freedom] we have to fear" and had brought a change in Creole consciousness. The difference between Dunmore's black soldiers and Prosser's men was essentially ideological—in 1775, Negroes "sought freedom merely as a good, now they also claim it as a right."[17]

But urban conspirators, caught up in their "Balls, Routs & assemblies," their "caballing [and] drumming," never became insurrectionists—if that was ever their real intention. They no longer possessed the economic base, military leadership, athletic prowess, and ritual life of the runaway camps and maroon villages. "How should we think of such a thing," cried a conspirator under torture on Montserrat in 1768. "We have no arms! No powder! No camp, no any thing!" As incipient forms of black associationism, Creole conspiracies were based on towns, dancing, and music, elaborate oaths of initiation and allegiance, and overly ambitious plans of attack that included either seeking refuge outside or receiving help from outsiders. These common features warrant description in the slaves' own words to underline the conspiracies' remarkably consistent patterns from one colony or new state to another.[18]

Conspirators were typically among the least oppressed of nonfield slaves: our "most valuable Negroes on the Estate. . . . [The] most sensible of the Slaves" (Hanover Parish, Jamaica, 1776); coopers and boilers (St. Kitts, 1778); "Drivers and Head People" (St. Thomas in the East Parish, Jamaica, 1807); and blacksmiths, waitingmen, and town Negroes (Richmond, Virginia, 1800).[19]

Compared to the maroons' spartan existence in the mountains, urban conspirators, according to whites, aspired to or already lived the good life: once the capital of Richmond was taken, "on the day it should be agreed to [Gabriel] would dine and drink with the merchants of the City" (Virginia, 1800); "Their tables were covered with hogs, Guinea fowls, ducks and other poultry"; "they were not only in possession of the Comforts, but even the Luxuries of Life" (Tobago, 1801); and, "they arrived about Midnight & found a supper of fowls, bread, wine & rum. . . . One day when there was a dinner at Baptistes, he [the deponent] saw a great Cake at the table of Kings and Generals. But he was not admitted of the Party" (Trinidad, 1805).[20]

At their parties and rituals Creoles often talked about the French who were heroes to a great number of Negroes throughout the Americas. "They would drive the white people into the Sea [and] give the Country to the French" (St. George Parish, Jamaica, 1806); "Frenchmen were very good Masters for Negroes"; "As soon as the French came they [would] fight for them against the English"; and "they wanted to follow the example of Guadaloupe and St. Domingo . . . in the Chief's house was a print representing the Execution of the King of France" (Tobago, 1801); and "that the Negroes in the French Country (such is their Expression) were Men" (Clarendon Parish, Jamaica, 1791). The French were discussed more often in Gabriel Prosser's conspiracy than in any other. The Prosser organizers said Frenchmen were not to be killed because they were friends of liberty; the French would land at South Key and fight with them; a Frenchman at Corbin's in Middlesex County had first instigated the rebellion; and Jack Bowler, a leader, had received two kegs of gunpowder from a Frenchman.[21]

At the end of the century, as revolution swept through Europe and the islands, and whites for the first time employed regular Negro soldiers (the West Indian regiments), conspiracies became military in character, and Creole associations moved from gardens and barbeques to makeshift parade grounds. Simon Taylor, a leading Jamaican planter and politician, wrote a nervous letter about Negroes in St. Thomas in the East Parish who "had formed themselves into Society—that they mustered with wooden Swords, and wooden Guns and had appointed their Officers from Generals, to Sergeants and Corporals."[22]

When in 1805 dancing societies in Trinidad became military organizations, calling themselves "regiments" instead of "convoys," the authorities stepped in and uncovered the most significant conspiracy to date. The association, on plantations as well as in town, and with African as well as Creole members, had synthesized the major elements of this multinational island— Spanish, French, English official titles, and the ritual of the Catholic mass with wine and wafers as the flesh and blood of whites—into their rituals of rebellion. But this conspiracy bogged down in endless discussions and more planning than action, so it too was finally uncovered; and scores of men and women were executed or beaten severely, mutilated, or transported.[23]

Around their camp fires, the maroons spoke bluntly about giving whites a belly full or fighting them in broad daylight on the king's high road. At their entertainments Creoles talked in much greater detail about what they would do to whites—once the revolution began. But the Trinidad conspiracy of 1805 was as close as Anglo-American slaves came to organizing slaves of different nationalities and at different levels of cultural change. Unlike the Haitian revolutionaries, Boukman, the witch doctor, and the assimilated military leaders, Toussaint L'Ouverture and Henri Christophe, Anglo-American slaves in this era of revolution never were able to combine African traditions and Creole aspirations—tribal and assimilated styles of resistance—to free themselves. The following sections examine the slaves' material conditions that sharpened rather than synthesized their cultural differences.

Where a planter lived and his presence or absence from the estate helped define the nature of plantation organization, the degree to which master and slave participated in and controlled plantation authority and management, and the extent to which slaves achieved an economic base—provision grounds, markets, and heritable property—sufficiently strong to allow them to remain African in outlook and ways. But absenteeism was not as much a question of whether the planter lived on his estate as of the degree to which he came and went and the extent to which the plantation was his base of operations. This variable was intimately tied to the question of how slaves lived, where, with whom, and how they were fed or fed themselves.[24]

In the islands wealthy planters usually lived elsewhere (most often at "home" in England). Their slaves, who lived in villages of one hundred or more around the large, costly, and immobile sugar works, were the most permanent features on the estates. In North America, however, a vast continent with apparently endless vistas and resources, tobacco and rice required little capital equipment; slaves, particularly in tobacco regions, were spread out across the land in comparatively small and isolated settlements, and masters usually lived on their plantations.

Tobacco planters settled slaves on tracts of land called quarters where blacks lived in makeshift huts suitable for the area's migratory and often wasteful agricultural practices (George Washington, a "scientific planter," even used prefabs). Each quarter was worked by about ten or fifteen full hands under white overseers. Each slave lived in an environment that encouraged him to change his tribal ways quickly; that is, plantation authority in North America was personal and informal. In Virginia, owners were exceptionally and intensely patriarchal and close to each slave, who was known individually by the master and his family.[25]

An extensive network of navigable rivers in Virginia, a chronic absence of town life, and the gentry's desire to be "independent on every one but Providence," scattered settlers far into the interior of a vast country, where they built large and relatively self-sufficient plantations. Determined to be autonomous, tobacco planters encouraged slaves to change their traditions because their tanneries, blacksmith, and carpentry shops required educated (that is, Christianized) and skilled artisans. Virginia plantations were organized around the master's highly personal, indivisible, and unchallenged leadership. Planters as fathers, patriarchs who referred to slaves as "my people," the "black members of my family," carried their culture into the slaves' cabins, as they rode about their estates directly and persistently supervising the plantations' diverse routines and operations, while doctoring , advising, putting slaves into their varied tasks, intervening in their domestic spats and love affairs, and enforcing their own morality and values. Patriarchs as a matter of course provided slaves with their houses, fed them, and jealously regarded all plantation property and markets as their own.

The dynamic personalism that infuses the rich plantation records of such tobacco patriarchs as Landon and Robert Councillor Carter and George Washington is nowhere evident in comparable records for rice plantations. In the Carolina lowcountry, settled more than fifty years later than Virginia by Barbadians and Englishmen of the Restoration Era, a different kind of river system, a much higher percentage of unassimilated and untrained Africans among all slaves, and one of the largest cities in plantation America produced both different relationships between the land and its organization into plantations and different views about the desirability of changing African ways. Carolinians, like West Indians, believed that African ethnicity prevented serious security problems, that slaves who could read and write were dangerous.

Rice also made so much more money than tobacco (the weed's market declined sharply after about 1750), that by mid-century the lowcountry had the highest per capita income in America and what has been estimated as the fastest growth rate in the world. In structure South Carolina was a West Indian colony characterized by a well-defined export area, great fortunes, and capital, expertise and labor concentrated on the production of the cash crop with little attention paid to the kind of diversification (and hence self-sufficiency by means of slave acculturation and training) practiced by the rural Virginia aristocracy.[26]

Wealthy lowcountry planters were suburban aristocrats—like Sir Lewis Namier's English gentry, they were
equally at home in town or country. Concentrated on a plain of
sea islands and marsh that was extremely desirable agriculturally
but most unhealthy, they raised rice (and some indigo, corn,
potatoes, and livestock) and often traveled the year round from
their plantations to sea island and northern resorts, to Europe, or
more often to Charleston (especially during the mosquito-
malaria season from May to November), the source of the urban
goods and services that tobacco planters had to create on their
own plantations. Lowcountry slaves lived in denser, larger
settlements than did slaves in the Chesapeake, worked in gangs
of thirty or more supervised by black drivers, and participated in
work routines that were freer than those of either sugar or
tobacco Negroes. The lowcountry task system allowed slaves to
set their own pace and leave the fields—sometimes in the early
afternoon—when they were done. After a slave completed his
task "his master feels no right to call on him," wrote a St. Mary's,
Georgia, physician to his New England parents in 1806. Slave
"rights"—a familiar concept in rice and sugar areas—were
unheard-of in the Chesapeake. Through time Carolina and West
Indian slaves built up "rights" because their owners were
elsewhere and could not do much about them.[27]

In Caribbean societies where large slaveholders were
often absentees, plantation authority was managerial, imper-
sonal, and more highly rationalized than on the mainland.
Absentees directed their representatives in the islands to make as
much money for them as possible and left the details of everyday
decisions to a variety of specialists in a comparatively well-
defined hierarchy of command—from town agents and attor-
neys, off the plantation, to resident managers, overseers, white
tradesmen, bookkeepers, and black drivers, on the plantation.
These men, who were far more transient than the more permanently situated slaves, in turn, found it most expedient and
profitable to allow plantation Negroes to do as much for them-

selves as possible with regard to building their own homes, raising small stock and provisions, and even marketing their considerable surpluses. Absenteeism became a vital part of the plantation existences of West Indian slaves (and not necessarily a negative feature of their lives as it is often presented). Island slaves used the income from the sale of surplus food to sustain such African traditions as polygynous and extended households and a family property estate, as well as elaborate cosmological beliefs and practices—witchcraft, ancestor worship, and elaborate funeral rites—vital expressions of authority within slave plantation communities that I have discussed elsewhere.[28]

Many West Indian slaves grew their own food and accumulated considerable property over time. Slaves throughout the islands owned flocks of fowl and small stock, such as pigs and goats. With other salable products—firewood, fruit, vegetables, and fish—they created large slave markets that became the internal marketing systems for most islands.[29]

Slaves supplied the king's ships with wood and water. A planter from Nevis testified in 1788 before the parliamentary slave trade hearings that slaves also sold grass and other kinds of fodder and cut wood. At his own table, he continued, "at least" half and "perhaps" three-fourths of the fresh provisions consumed were supplied by Negroes. Another witness said that half of the specie in his island was controlled by slaves. And another mentioned that three-quarters of all the poultry and pork eaten by planters (and all of that consumed by slaves) was produced by slaves and purchased from the master's own or someone else's Negroes. John Luffman, who has left an excellent traveler's account of Antigua in the 1780s, noted that the slaves' "attention" to their pigs, goats, and fowl "prevented" whites from starving when ships could not come in safely to St. Johns.[30]

Negro markets were extremely lucrative, and many slaves used their earnings to purchase salt provisions, furniture, utensils, and clothing. Some Negroes were known to "possess from £50 to £200 at their death; and few among them, that are at all industrious and frugal," wrote the Jamaican historian and planter Edward Long, "lay up less than £20 or £30 . . . which they gain by sale of their hogs, poultry, fish, corn, fruits, and other commodities, at the markets in town and country."[31]

In North American plantation societies land was comparatively cheaper and much more abundant and the weather was more consistently seasonable than in the islands; consequently, planters usually incorporated the growing of provisions into the slaves' daily tasks and carefully controlled the distribution of food. On the mainland, where slaves were usually fed allowances, they had very little property and quasi-official Negro markets did not develop. Only occasionally is there a glimpse of some solitary, unorganized market activity. A Maryland fugitive in 1777 was described as "a great trader with other Negroes." A Virginia slave told his master before he ran away a second time that while previously free he had "dealt freely in Williamsburg in the oyster and fish way, in their seasons." Evidence from plantation account books indicates that some slaves traded for money with whites. Henry Ravenel's daybook, one of the very few surviving accounts from an eighteenth-century lowcountry plantation, includes such entries as: "paid Amy £4 for a hog" (October 1764); "p[ai]d Chelsea's Negroes £2.15 for fowls" (15 December 1764); "p[ai]d Hector for a hog and rice £3.3.0" (9 January 1765). Other slaves were paid for baskets, trees, rails, corn, myrtlewax, beef, rice, and hogs. There were about as many entries for women as for men.[32]

North American slave property and markets were so meager that they are scarcely comparable to West Indian equivalents. Consequently, a Polish poet's description of the slave quarters of one of the wealthiest planters in North America may be representative. At George Washington's Mount Vernon, the visitor was startled by the general poverty of slave homes and food.

> We entered some Negroes' huts—for their habitations cannot be called houses. They are far more miserable than the poorest of the

cottages of our peasants. The husband and his wife sleep on a miserable bed, the children on the floor. A very poor chimney, a little kitchen furniture amid this misery—a teakettle and cups. . . . A small orchard with vegetables was situated close to the hut. Five or six hens, each with ten or fifteen chickens, walked there. That is the only pleasure allowed to the negroes: they are not permitted to keep either ducks or geese or pigs.[33]

By the end of the century slave property and how it was disposed of had become a conspicuous feature of West Indian family life, and it is described in a variety of sources with essentially two messages—black women were prominent as market Negroes and traders generally, but men seemed to control profits and used property as a kind of heritable family estate. Slaves, moreover, openly resisted interference with this custom, which was an indispensable part of the cultural and "political" autonomy they had achieved by the end of the century.

Planters from Jamaica and the Ceded Islands—mountainous with abundant provision grounds, plaintain walks, and largely undeveloped interiors by as late as 1800—left the richest evidence concerning the relationship between slave food, family, and inheritances. A Tobagan planter told Parliament in 1788 that while Negroes "certainly have no particular right to any property they may acquire because they cannot defend it by law against their Masters . . . opinion which is stronger than Law gives them that right in their acquirements that I do not know that it is ever violated." In fact, the Negroes' "peculium [private property] is so sacred," he continued, "that though it may amount to a considerable sum they always take it away and carry it to the plantation which they are purchased to the very doors, the window shutters of their Houses they have perhaps framed themselves even though the master's property has been taken in execution." A large Grenadian planter, who once was a St. Kitts attorney, said that he owned slaves worth "40, 50, 100" and "even a few" worth £200 sterling, and that the slaves' "property is regularly conveyed from one generation to another without any interference whatever." Edward Long, a contemporary Jamaican historian, was even more explicit about the slaves' property estate:

the black grandfather, or father (as they are called) directs in what manner his money, his hogs, poultry, furniture, cloaths, and other effects and acquisitions, shall descend, or be disposed of, after his decease. He nominates a sort of trustees, or executors, from the nearest of kin, who distribute them among the legatees, according to the will of the testator, without any molestation or interruption, most often without the enquire of their mother.[34]

Caribbean slaves were as determined to maintain customary courtship and marriage practices as they were to protect the property in land and markets that allowed them to maintain African patterns of domesticity. The sum of the evidence of various kinds is that the slaves' practice of having plural wives was African in origin and extremely difficult to modify according to both the whites' Christian morality and their gradual awareness at the end of the century that the slaves' courtship practices ("connexions," "Licentious behaviour") depressed birth rates, ruined their health by spreading venereal disease, and left them exhausted in the fields after a night of "rambling." "A West Indian," author of the best demographic study of that time, said that slaves may have no objection to being baptized, but "marriage is quite another thing." The master may advise a slave which of two women to take as his wife, but if he interferes directly this "leads to acts of poisoning & obeah." During the parliamentary hearings on the slave trade, the former manager of the Society for the Propagation of the Gospel's Barbados plantation mentioned that naturally planters wished to curtail slaves' "rambles" because they were debilitating, "but he is afraid to interfere too much in it."[35]

In North America planters were not "afraid to interfere" in their slaves' domestic lives. In Virginia, as we have seen, owners personally involved themselves in the most intimate details of their slaves' lives, including mate selection, placing black youngsters in nonfield jobs, and attending slaves who were ill. In South Carolina, however, the relationships among owners, overseers, and blacks concerning slave households are not as clearly delineated as they are in comparable island and Virginia documents. An invaluable picture, provided in 1740 by an Anglican commissary, describes a unique mainland slave community—a separate "Nation within a Nation."

Among us Religious Instruction usually descends from Parents to Children, so among them it must first ascend from Children to Parents, or from young to Old.

    There are as 'twere a Nation within a Nation. In all Country Settlements, they live in contiguous Houses and often 2, 3 or 4 Famillys of them in One House. . . . They labour together and converse almost wholly among themselves.[36]

    The commissary's picture of the Carolina slaves' dense, unassimilated "Country Settlements" provides tantalizing clues to the sources of the Gullahs' isolated existences, which Alexander Garden associated with compact households and a patois or dialect that left them talking only among themselves. The image of a "Nation within a Nation" is powerful and was evoked in much the same way in Jamaica—but at the other end of the century. In a searching analysis of birth and death rates on his two plantations in a speech to the House of Commons on Chinese contract labor immigration to the West Indies, John Foster Barham, a prominent Jamaican absentee, concluded that moving his slaves from a lowland to a healthier mountain plantation would be impossible: "to interfere in their domestic lives" would be "dangerous and ineffectual" and could be accomplished only by altering their "political state."[37]

    By the end of the eighteenth century the West Indian slaves' "political state," based on an elaborate system of food resources, kinship, and markets, had generated an irreversible body of traditional rights that gave slaves considerably more leverage and bargaining power than blacks had on the continent. On larger Caribbean estates authority was consensual and dispersed among supervisors and slaves; the latter made plantation organization work for them in ways we will never understand very well. In some cases, moreover, the British system of shared authority extended to entire societies—particularly if they were geographically peripheral and essentially nonstaple-producing. In the society of adventurers, turtlers, and logmen of the Bay of Honduras, nearly all of the five hundred whites lived on offshore islands, and most of their five thousand slaves lived on widely dispersed mainland plantations, some of which were more than 250 miles upriver. This type of settlement, however, did not produce runaway villages of bush Negroes as occurred in a very similar setting in Dutch Guinea; nor did Indians (as they did somewhat in South Carolina) keep slaves close to home; one report said Indians on the bay were "negligible."[38]

While at first view the weight of the evidence on slave households and property could lead to arguments that Caribbean slavery merely coopted Negroes, a closer examination indicates that in practice the system was complex. The contradictions inherent in the island provisioning system and the divided authority it entailed are exposed in the same documents. Alexander Campbell, a large property owner in the Ceded Islands, told Parliament in 1788 that the more money a slave received from his grounds, the more "firmly attached" he was to the estate. But it also "becomes the greatest consequence to the inhabitants," he added, "that all Negroes are properly supported." What he meant (on a Ceded Island beset by maroons, black Caribs, and French settlers from within and French squadrons from without) was that it was a "universal custom" for the nine hundred slaves on his fourteen plantations to have one afternoon off a week in which to grow crops on their own land and that Grenadan Negroes were usually given passes to visit relatives and to attend churches and markets. If these practices were not followed, whites feared slaves would rebel.[39]

Three years later, Negroes rose up on the neighboring island of Dominica because of problems involving many of the

issues referred to in Campbell's testimony. Accounts of the
rebellion demonstrate the extent to which estates—and even the
tactics used to contain the insurrection—revolved around slave
participation in organization and routines. The plantation runaway dimension of the 1791 Dominican insurrection (principally a
war between English militia and French brigands from Mar-
tinique and Guadaloupe) began among slaves in the French
quarter of St. Patrick Parish and concerned a disagreement
between managers and slaves regarding a trade-off—additional
slave holidays for shorter slave provisions. When the lieutenant
governor looked back at the rebellion's inception, he said the
French planters "ha[d] in a great degree brought this on themselves." Before they could actively pursue the brigands, the
English realized that they first had to pacify the plantation
people. Commanders and militia therefore were ordered to
assemble the slaves and to discuss the issue of holidays (an
irresponsible rumor); they were to show "no manner of resent-
ment," nor to speak at all to the slave women, so as "to give
them cause to complain, or raise jealousy" in the Negro men.
They were not to mention punishments, and they were to
pardon all slaves who returned from the hills, even those who
were armed (suspected murderers excepted)![40]

The subtle nuances and shadings of authority *within* the
slave community—sources and expressions of authority that
were diverse and often conflicting—are even more difficult to
explain, but illustrations are useful. The island provisioning
system created paradoxes for both slave and free. Owners left
slaves to themselves to grow and market their own food, only to
realize sooner or later that their Negroes were far more autonomous than they wanted them to be. But slaves found that
the rights that gave them more control over their plantations
often made other Negroes their most immediate enemies, and
these were Negroes who came onto the plantations to free them.
While they marched unchecked, the Dominican maroons of 1791
sometimes announced to plantation slaves (whom we may

imagine were suitably impressed) upon which plantation they would dine the ensuing evening. They dined that year in some of the largest, most elegant plantations on the island. Once they descended, drove the whites out, ordered the Negroes to kill a beef, which they ate with mutton and brandy, before inviting the slaves to join the feast. The next morning, the maroons distributed the food they did not want to carry away. But their inferred message—"look who is feeding you now!" "we are dining in your master's kitchen, where is your protection, join us!"— usually was ignored by plantation slaves who fled with the whites, "sulked" in the cane, or actually joined parties of militia as "confidential negroes"—the baggage men, trackers, and (later in the century) soldiers who pursued maroons.[41]

In the 1790s, during uprisings on Dominica, Grenada, and Jamaica, large numbers of slaves refused to leave plantations vacated by whites. Earlier, more than 250 slaves were left on Barham's plantation during an uprising in which most (if not all) of the white men, "and a great many of the ablest Negroes," were out two or three times a week in parties against the rebels. Meanwhile, on the estate a new, untried man, sent out under indentures, had replaced the overseer. But there was no sign of unrest, although the slaves were apparently without supervision—except their own—for more than a month.[42]

Antagonistic ethnic and tribal rivalries—another source of values and sanctions within the slave community—probably were all that kept Jamaica from becoming another Haiti. Uprisings often set blacks against blacks who were scouts, baggage men, or trackers—a situation dramatized during a 1798 uprising in Jamaica, when a rebel screamed at an African who was defending his master's property and identified him by his ritual face scars: "You d——d Chamba cut-fac'd Son-of-a B——h."[43]

Violence between plantation Negroes and organized runaways was sometimes awesome and probably stemmed either from tribal and ethnic rivalries or from competition between plantation Negroes and maroons for food and women—

the details will never be very clear. The runaways, as essentially unacculturated tribesmen, were experts in the psychology of terror generated by their hit-and-run raids. In Tobago, another Ceded Island, a Coramantee band in 1770 wounded a Negro watchman, twice failed to kill a head driver, and then successfully ambushed him on the public road. This party later entered the yaws house on the driver's plantation and killed three sick Negroes, including a mother and nursing infant. Balla, the Dominican maroon leader, descended onto a plantation in mid-July 1785, shot four whites, threw them into a fire while they were still alive, and shot their head Negro, before wounding—but not killing—the black man's wife and several children.[44]

The role of mainland Negroes in plantation sanctions and organization is described with little of the richness of comparable West Indian sources. But both sugar and rice regions used slave drivers extensively (who in North America before the antebellum era are described only in lowcountry documents), and the authority of South Carolina drivers was formidable. In practice their authority provides views of a slave community, a "Nation within a Nation," more like those in the islands than in the Chesapeake. In the antebellum era, Frederick Law Olmsted, whose traveler's accounts are unequaled, visited an old and established lowcountry rice estate and used words describing its policy—"consulted," "managed," "governed"—unheard-of in the land of the Carters and Byrds. Drivers, Olmsted observed, are often "*de facto* the managers." Usually the proprietor gave orders directly to them, "without the overseer's being consulted or informed"; and both owner and overseer "deferr[ed]" to the drivers about when to flood the fields. Overseers, moreover, who were "frequently" employed only "as a matter of form . . . consult the drivers on all important points, and are governed by their advice."[45]

The most revealing account of a rice driver's participation in a West Indian style of plantation community concerned the new state of Georgia's attempts to confiscate and use as a college

George Whitefield's (and heirs') Bethesda Orphanage and the plantation and slaves that supported it. When in the 1790s state officials moved in and arrested the caretaker parson, the struggle quickly spilled over into the community at large and uncovered local passions about overseas' philanthropy versus local control of slaves, loyalist property and local public acquisitiveness, high and low church. These issues, however, all stemmed from a confrontation on the plantation between the reverend and the slaves on one side, the sheriff's posse on the other, and the driver in the middle as makeweight and ultimate symbol of control at the orphanage. When the sheriff first rode in, he called out to the driver to hold the reins of his horse. "I countermanded it," the reverend noted, "& order'd another of the Negroes to do it." The sheriff's people remained; and in the evening, "about half past 8 . . . [they] went out in order to give the Driver orders for the next day." After his arrest the minister, in jail, heard that the slaves were "collected," but they had refused to obey the sheriff's command. A week later they were at work; either the driver, he suspected, had been bribed, or he was "overawed by Fear."[46]

These pictures of the field hands' and drivers' relative autonomy in rice and sugar areas ought to be compared to the patriarchal style of plantation organization in Virginia, where masters, who possessed nearly all of what West Indian slaves considered their own, still often failed to be all things to their plantation families.

The reactions of Anglo-American slaves to the opportunities and perils of the revolutionary era stemmed from the ways tobacco, rice, and sugar plantations were organized around resident or absentee owners and from the degree to which slaves participated in plantation management. The slaves' managerial role depended upon their control over food resources, markets, households, and heritable property.

On tobacco plantations authority was monopolized by an

apparently powerful master figure whose personal supervision
created considerable conflict among all members of the estate.
Letters among planters, stewards, and overseers were often
bitter, angry, and confused about who really was in charge. Such
confusion originated in the master's inability to divide and
delegate sufficient authority to those whom he expected to do
their jobs most effectively as the slaves' immediate supervisors.

When challenged by even the lowest field hands, planters
themselves were sometimes surprisingly ineffectual. Landon
Carter's confrontations with his people fill up a copious diary
and clearly indicate how shaky plantation organization on the
patriarchal model could be in practice. Robert Councillor Carter's
voluminous plantation records (which are at Duke University),
however, reveal a man who superbly executed the patriarchal
role, becoming the personal leader or chief of all of his four
hundred slaves. Carter scarcely complained about even the most
trivial day-to-day rebelliousness. But during the revolutionary
war, even Carter lost slaves who deserted to the British (after he
had made a personal appeal to them not to do so); for, like many
other tidewater planters, he was vulnerable and defenseless
before Lord Dunmore and the British fleet.[47]

Evidence of another kind, fugitive slave notices for new
Negro runaways, also suggests that the Virginia owner had to be
constantly and effectively present if all was to work smoothly.
Some Africans reportedly ran off immediately after their master
died; and a few, when recaptured and questioned, implied that
they felt the personal bonds (whatever their precise nature may
have been) vanished with an owner's death.

Once the patriarch's authority was challenged by someone who seemed as powerful as he was, or if he simply no longer
could defend his plantation, slaves often sensed that they were
on their own. But even then they had no place to go and
relatively little to fall back on by way of family and property in
plantation settings where the master owned and dominated
virtually everything. The most extensively documented reaction

of wartime rebellious slaves described disorganized fugitives who set out on the Chesapeake Bay in canoes or some other kind of open boat. Sometimes they were swamped, many drowned, and a few were reported picked up by the wrong ship—an American instead of a British one. This image conveys a sense of the relationship between plantation organization and authority in the Chesapeake and the wartime reactions of slaves, who as the least African and most thoroughly detribalized of all Anglo-American Negroes, had been cut adrift from the extended households, family estates, grounds, and markets that kept slaves together as a people further south in the lowcountry and Caribbean.[48]

South Carolina slaves during the Revolution are more difficult to characterize because surviving documents say little about them. But rebellious slaves there also seemed to have acted cooperatively as they had before the Revolution when in groups some joined friendly Indians, the Spanish in the Floridas, or the British evacuations of Charleston and Savannah. An unusually well-documented instance (which may be juxtaposed with the picture of wartime fugitives adrift on the Chesapeake Bay) told of thirty slaves—thirteen American-born and eleven African adults with six children—who followed British General Augustine Prevost's army toward Savannah before the "greatest part of them" split off and "followed" Creek Indians to a town "called Cawetta or Coweater."[49]

But most Carolina slaves remained behind on their plantations and within the relative security of their "Nation within a Nation," comprising compact settlements, crops, and an unusual tasking system of work. While I have argued that lowcountry slaves had much more to defend at home than did slaves in Virginia, many probably stayed where they were during the war simply for reasons of survival. While revolutionary Virginia was a remarkably tightly knit society, the civil war between Tories and patriots in South Carolina was ferocious and kept black and white backcountry folk close to home. Late in the war, for example, Savannah merchant John Habersham wrote General Nathanael Greene, hero of the long and bitter southern campaign, that Mulberry Grove plantation (given to Greene by a grateful southern people) could not be rented because "some object to its being too remote from Town, and consequently exposed to Murderers and Robbers."[50]

War and revolution swept through the islands more fiercely and for a much longer time than on the mainland, and slaves there were more conspicuously rebellious than were North American blacks. But African maroons and urban Creoles were unable to act in concert with the preponderant majority of plantation Negroes in an attempt to free themselves. In 1800 a leading Jamaican politician came as close as anyone to explaining the basis of shared authority on Caribbean plantations that often set black against black as well as against white. Henry Shirley wrote that after a season of fear about slave uprisings, good weather and abundant provision crops had brought Negroes substantial prices for their marketable produce, and slaves were now "happy and content."[51]

But to leave an impression of accommodated and acquiescent slaves in this era would be misleading. Even the Creoles, who were apparently so enmeshed in their owners' values, made their own decisions and tried to construct their own norms and ways in new urban settings. As conspirators they made their choices before the different revolutionary traditions of the late eighteenth century and showed a clear preference for the French and Haitian examples. Even the Prosser conspirators, the most assimilated of Creoles anywhere, chose to spare those whites—Quakers, Methodists, poor white women, and especially Frenchmen—who were outside the mainstream of our Revolution.[52]

Compared with the maroons, the Creoles come off badly. The runaways in the mountains were doing something about slavery, while Creoles down below only talked about it. Creoles thought about taking white wives after the slaughter; maroons

had their wives with them in the hills; and so on. But the Creoles'
task as revolutionaries was much more difficult than was the
maroons'. Using their conspiratorial associations as meeting
places for blacks of different nationalities, they were able to
radicalize men such as Harold, a Trinidadian dancing convoy
chief. He was a carter, not a field slave, a Christian born in Africa
(of the Soso nation); he had bought his freedom and been a chief
of the St. George convoy since Spanish times, and his association was called Grenada, after that island's mode of dancing.
Behind the Creole's bluster, vacillating inaction, pomp, and
pageantry there persisted in all of their conspiracies from
Richmond, Virginia, to Port of Spain, Trinidad, a design to
bridge formidable ethnic and acculturative barriers among men
like Harold whose urban work had led them from the old values
and sanctions of the historically isolated plantation Negroes and
maroons into new, modern lives.

The outbreak of Creole associations of a distinctively
military character in the early nineteenth century may be seen as
an effort to use old ways of music and dance to secure a more
natural and human culture within the inhumane economic
system of white oppressors. Authorities know well this kind of
countercultural warfare, they fear it, and respond accordingly.
Even today in Jamaica some reggae songs are outlawed as
subversive. In the stunning Jamaican film, *The Harder They Come*,
the narcotics detective temporarily cuts off the country people's
livelihood, the ganga (marijuana) trade to city markets, in order
to suppress a song recorded by their folk hero whom the
detective is trying to capture or kill. But Mister Hilton, a
stereotypical capitalistic media mogul, reminds him, "no grass,
no hit tunes mean no law and order—anarchy!" The political
meaning and thrust of Afro-American culture in Third World
cities like Kingston still has not crystallized; and whether it will
tend to be assimilationist or revolutionary is unclear—
reminiscent of Gavin Stevens's remark in William Faulkner's
Intruder in the Dust, "The Past is never dead. It's not even past."[53]

Notes

1. Moncure D. Conway, ed., *The Writings of Thomas Paine*, 3 vols. (New York, 1894–96), 1:100. I wish to thank members of the Johns Hopkins University Departments of Anthropology and History Seminar in Atlantic History and Culture, and Rhys Isaac, in particular, for their helpful comments (17 October 1975) on this essay. The following proposal will be much more useful when monographs are completed about the issues I raise. I am currently preparing for Oxford University Press a book titled *Negro Slavery in the Old British Empire and North America during an Era of War and Revolution, 1750–1834.*

2. Ronald Hoffman, *A Spirit of Dissension: Economics, Politics, and the Revolution in Maryland* (Baltimore, 1973), pp. 147–48, 152–53, 184–85, 201, 204.

3. This section is based on conversations with Ron Hoffman, who is reading the extensive Nathanael Greene correspondence at Duke University and elsewhere while writing a book on the social and political dimensions of southern military campaigns during the Revolution. See also *Calendar of the Sir Guy Carleton Papers, Report on American Manuscripts in the Royal Institution of Great Britain*, 4 vols. (London, 1904–9); *Calendar of the General Otho Holland Williams Papers in the Maryland Historical Society* (Baltimore, 1940), esp. pp. 19–72; Thomas Pinckney's wartime letters to his sister Harriott, Blue Box No. 1, 1781–1782, Pinckney Papers, Library of Congress; Charleston (British) Police Board Proceedings, 1780–81; and South Carolina Loyalist Claims, South Carolina Department of Archives and History, microfilms of Public Record Office originals; see also, Bernard A. Uhlendorf, ed., *The Siege of Charleston . . . Diaries and Letters of Hessian Officers* (Ann Arbor, Mich., 1938).

4. Quoted in Benjamin Quarles, *The Negro in the American Revolution* (Chapel Hill, N.C., 1961), p. 121.

5. Jamaica Assembly Address to the King, 28 Nov. 1793; Council Address to Lieutenant Governor Williamson, both enclosed in Williamson to the Secretary of State, 30 Nov. 1791, Public Record Office, Colonial Office, London, 137/90 (hereafter cited as CO); extract of a letter from William Greene to Messrs. Aspinal and Hardy, Good Hope, Jamaica, 13 May 1798, CO 137/99 (some CO volumes have folio numbers, some do not).

6. Governor Cunningham to the Secretary of State, 22 Jan. 1781, CO 28/58; Seaforth to Lord Hobart, Pilgrim, Barbados, 6 June 1802, CO 28/68, f. 55; see also, Governor D. Parry to Lord Grenville, Barbados, 23 May 1791, CO 28/63.

7. The following is based on a paper I delivered at the Organization of American Historians Meeting (Boston, April 1975) entitled "Slave Resistance in an Age of Revolution: Major Insurrections and Conspiracies in the Old British Empire and North America, 1760–1807."

8. Thomas Atwood, *History of the Island of Dominica* (London, 1791), chapter 12.

9. Governor Orde to Sydney, Roseau, Dominica, 16 April 1786, CO 71/10, f. 21.

10. Thomas Bee to Governor John Mathews, Goose Creek, 9 Dec. 1782, Thomas Bee Papers, South Caroliniana Library, Columbia, S.C.

11. March 1787 letters from militia commanders and representatives for St. Peters Parish in a South Carolina Archives Miscellaneous file, Slavery before 1800, in which documents are now being reorganized according to their provenance (for example, Governor's Messages, Senate and Assembly Committee Reports). This material is in correspondence to the governor and a House Committee Report, 19 March 1787; see also Adele S. Edwards, ed., *Journals of the Privy Council, 1783–1788* (Columbia, S.C., 1971), pp. 186, 203–4; Quarles, *Negro in Revolution*, p. 174; and Reverend William B. Stevens, *A History of Georgia . . .*, 2 vols. (Philadelphia, 1859), 2:376–78.

12. Gerald W. Mullin, *Flight and Rebellion: Slave Resistance in Eighteenth-century Virginia* (New York, 1972), pp. 34, 40, 43–45, 55–57.

13. *Barbados Mercury* (Bridgetown), 14 Feb. 1784, Bridgetown Public Library microfilm; Augusta, Georgia, March 1780, Grand Jury presentment in Lilla M. Hawes, ed., *Papers of Lachlan McKintosh, 1774–79, Collections of the Georgia Historical Society* (Savannah, Ga., 1957), 12:88; Legislative petition from the Inhabitants of Georgetown, 19 Jan. 1790, South Carolina Archives; *Georgia Gazette*, 3 Jan. 1793, [n.d.] Oct. 1796; *Royal Gazette, Supplement*, 28 Oct. 1797, West Indian Reference Library, Kingston, Jamaica.

14. Stephen Fuller to Henry Dundas, 30 Oct. 1791, CO 137/89.

15. John Poyer to Governor Seaforth, 22 June 1806, "AN OPEN LETTER," reprinted in the *Journal of the Barbados Museum and Historical Society* 6 (May 1939): 163.

16. Henry Laurens to James Laurens, Charleston, Jan. 1776, Laurens Papers, Roll 13, South Carolina Archives microfilm. See Ira Berlin, *Slaves without Masters: The Free Negro in the Antebellum South* (New York, 1975).

17. [St. George Tucker], *Letter to a Member of the General Assembly of Virginia on the Subject of the Late Conspiracy of the Slaves, with a Proposal for their Colonization* (Richmond, Va., 1801), Virginia State Library microfilm.

18. "A Natural, Civil, and Religious History of MONTSERRET in the West-Indies, Including a Particular Account of the Struggles of the Free Coloured Inhabitants . . . by a Wesleyan Missionary who Resided Five Years in the Island," pp. 46–47, Ms., Biographical/West Indies, Box 1, Methodist Missionary Society, London.

19. "Extract of a letter from Sir Simon Clark to Benjamin Lyon Lucea, Jamaica, 23 July 1776; John Grizell to Lieutenant Governor Keith, Hanover, 27 July 1776, CO 137/71, f. 256v, ff. 262–63; CO 152/58, ff. 32–36v; Simon Taylor to Thomas Hughan, Kingston, 7 Jan. 1807, CO 137/120.

20. Mullin, *Flight and Rebellion*, p. 158; *Tobago Gazette, Extraordinary*, 1 Jan. 1802, enclosed in Governor Joseph Robley to Lord Hobart, Tobago, 2 Jan. 1802, CO 285/8; Council Minutes, Trinidad, 10 Dec. 1805, CO 298/2, f. 108.

21. Further Examination of Frank, Orange Vale, Jamaica, 8 Jan. 1807, CO 137/118; Brigidier General Hugh Lyle Carmichael's Report, 25 Dec. 1801, CO 285/8; Extract of a letter from Spanish Town, Jamaica, 6 Nov. 1791, CO 137/89; Mullin, *Flight and Rebellion*, pp. 143, 151–52.

22. Simon Taylor to Thomas Hughan, Kingston, Jamaica, 7 Jan. 1807, CO

137/120; Mullin, *Flight and Rebellion*, pp. 143, 148; Major General Adam William-son to Secretary of State Dundas, Jamaica, 18 Sept. 1791, CO 137/89; Taylor to Hughan, Kingston, Jamaica, 7 Jan. 1807, CO 137/120.

23. I examined the Trinidad conspiracy more closely in a paper for the New York Academy of Sciences Conference on Slavery in the Americas (May 1976); the proceedings will be published. The conspiracy is in CO 298/2, ff. 97–148v.

24. This section is based on paper presented to the Southern Historical Association Meeting (Dallas, November 1974), "Slave Property, Families and Plantation Authority in the Old British Empire."

25. Descriptions of eighteenth-century Virginia plantation life are based on *Flight and Rebellion*, esp. chapters 1 and 2.

26. On the rice planters' wealth, see M. Eugene Sirmans, *Colonial South Carolina: A Political History, 1663–1763* (Chapel Hill, N.C., 1966), p. 226.

27. Daniel Turner to his parents, St. Mary's, Georgia, 13 Aug. 1806, Daniel Turner Papers, Georgia State Archives microfilm.

28. I have begun to explore the most important basis for authority among plantation slaves—the spiritual dimension—in a paper, "Obeah and Christianity in Four Eighteenth-century Anglo-American Plantation Societies" [Virginia, South Carolina, Jamaica, and Antigua], presented at the annual meeting of the American Historical Association (New Orleans, 1972).

29. Cf. Sidney W. Mintz and Douglas Hall, "The Origins of the Jamaican Internal Marketing System," *Yale University Publications in Anthropology*, No. 57 (New Haven, 1960), pp. 3–26; Richard Sheridan, *Sugar and Slavery: An Economic History of the British West Indies* (Baltimore, 1973), pp. 259–60; Richard Pares, *A West-Indian Fortune* (London, 1950), chapter 6–7.

30. James White to Bishop Gibson, Vere, 23 April 1724, Fulham Palace Papers, West Indies, vol. 17, f. 185; House of Commons Sessional Papers, Accounts and Papers (1790), pp. 84, 106, 262, 307 (hereafter cited as Sessional Papers). John Luffman, *A Brief Account of the Island of Antigua . . . in the Years 1786, 1787, 1788* (2d ed., London, 1788), p. 94; Atwood, *History of the Island of Dominica*, pp. 178–79.

31. Edward Long, *The History of Jamaica . . .* , 3 vols. (London, 1774, reprint ed., 1970), 2:410–11.

32. Dunlop's *Maryland Gazette or Baltimore Advertiser*, 4 Nov. 1777, William Bond advertiser; *Virginia Gazette* (Rind), 26 Sept. 1768; J[ame]s Mercer to Battaile Muse, 3 April 1779, Muse Papers, Duke University Library; G. Francklyn, *Observations . . . Shewing, the Manner in which Negroes are Treated in the West-Indies* (London, 1789), p. 32; Daybook of Henry Ravenel of Hanover, South Carolina Historical Society, Charleston.

33. Quoted in Paul Leland Haworth, *George Washington: Farmer* (Indianapolis, 1915), pp. 196f.

34. "Copy Evidence of Mr Franklyn 13th March 1794," p. 19, Minutes of Evidence on the Slave Trade, House of Lords Record Office, London; Long, *History of Jamaica*, 2:410.

35. [A West Indian], *Notes in Defense of the Colonies* (London, 1826), pp. 34, 37; "1826—Barbados—Codrington College, Remarks on Codrington Estate & Treatment of Slaves," Series C, West Indies, Box 8, Society for the Propagation of the Gospel, London.

36. Garden to the SPG Secretary, 6 May 1740, cited in Frank J. Klingberg, *An Appraisal of the Negro in Colonial South Carolina* (Washington, D.C., 1941), p. 106.

37. "Subjects Particular Respecting the Negroes in Reply to Mr. J. Sinclair," Miscellaneous Political Papers of John Foster Barham, Bundle 2, C. 381, Barham Papers, Clarendon Deposit, Bodleian Library, Oxford.

38. [?] to Lieutenant Governor Dalling, Kingston, 3 Sept. 1779, CO 137/75, f. 1.

39. Sessional Papers, 29, 141–42.

40. James Bruce to Lieutenant Governor Sir John Orde, Castle Bruce, 15 Jan. 1791; 3 Feb. 1791, Order to Lord Grenville; Thomas Beech to Orde, Widcombe, 16 Jan. 1791; Charles Bertrant to [the Governor ?], 18 Jan. 1791, CO 71/19.

41. Arthur Bertrand, Andre Botro, and Gruand to Lieutenant Governor Orde, Point Mulatre, 19 Jan. 1791, CO 71/19.

42. Daniel Barnjum to John Foster Barham, 23 Dec. 1760, Barham Papers, Clarendon Deposit.

43. The Deposition of Henry Paulett and Alexander Steel, planters of Trelawney Parish, Jamaica, 18 April 1798, CO 140/84.

44. "An Account of the Insurrection among the Cormantee Slaves at Tobago," 21 Nov. 1770, Papers of Captain Francis Reynolds, Gloucestershire Record Office; Minutes of the Tobago Council, 27 Nov. 1770, CO 288/2; Governor Orde to the Secretary of State, Government House, Dominica, 15 Dec. 1785, CO 71/9, f. 324.

45. Frederick Law Olmsted, *A Journey in the Sea Board Slave States in the Years 1853–1854*, 2 vols. (New York [1856], 1904), 2:66–67.

46. John Johnson, "Official Journal" (1791–92), Johnson Papers, Georgia Historical Society, Savannah.

47. Mullin, *Flight and Rebellion*, p. 133 and chapter 4.

48. Ibid.

49. "List of Negroes the Property of William Reynolds Sr., December 12, 1783," Miscellaneous file, Slavery before 1800, South Carolina Archives.

50. Ron Hoffman led me to this document, Habersham to Greene, "Private," Savannah, 1 Nov. 1782, Nathanael Greene Papers, Duke University Department of Manuscripts.

51. Shirley to Edward Shirley, Kingston, 21 May 1800, CO 137/104.

52. Mullin, *Flight and Rebellion*, pp. 143, 151–52, 200n.

53. Quoted in C. Vann Woodward, *The Burden of Southern History* (New York, 1961), p. 36.

INTERPRETATIONS OF SLAVERY:
THE SLAVE STATUS IN THE AMERICAS

Recent interpretations of slavery in the United States suggest that we may be entering a new phase of scholarship on slavery as new approaches and categories are introduced by historians, and as anthropologists and sociologists again take up the study of an institution that was of such concern to their nineteenth century predecessors.

As an assessment of these interpretations, the concern of this essay is with those aspects of the legal status of the slave which appear as problematic or neglected. The purpose is to reformulate, refocus, and clarify rather than to introduce an alternative interpretation or to present new materials.[1]

Although the scholarship on slavery has tended to shift away from the strong moral bias as well as the categories of analysis carried over for so long from the pro-slavery and anti-slavery debates, those aspects of the slavery system traditionally at issue also constitute the problematic aspects in the more recent interpretations. These are the legal status of the slave, the relations of masters and slaves, and the relationship between these two facets of the institution.[2]

I

The concept of slavery covers a considerable variety of social phenomena, but it is generally thought of as the practice of bringing strangers into a society for use in economic production and legally defining them in terms of the category of property. The complete subordination of the slave to the will of the master is regarded as a main defining feature of the institution.

Subordination implies and is an aspect of authority. Authority is the socially recognized right to direct, control or manage some or all of the affairs of a per-

---

[1] The author wishes to acknowledge his obligations to M. I. Finley, John Hope Franklin, Robert Freedman, and Richard Robbins, among others, who have read and criticized this paper, and to the Research Council of Colgate University for a generous research grant.
[2] See Stanley Elkins, *Slavery* (Chicago, 1959), Chap. I: Kenneth Stampp, "The Historian and Southern Negro Slavery", *American Historical Review*, LVII (April, 1952), pp. 613-24; Richard Hofstadter, "U. B. Phillips and the Plantation Legend", *Journal of Negro History*, XXIX (April, 1944), pp. 109-25.

son, or group, or thing. In this sense there is an overlap between property as a bundle of rights over things and the authority which is invested in some person over others as their slaves, with the result that such types of authority are treated as property at law.[3]

Slavery involves the "legal assimilation of interpersonal rights to the norm of property rights over things".[4]

This definition of the legal status of the slave has been taken in many studies as a basis for an interpretation solely in terms of the property component in the status.[5] Thus although the interpretations of slavery in the United States to be discussed in this essay involve both the historical and comparative methods and an emphasis on economic as well as ideological forces, they arrive at a similar conception of the legal status of the slave as property. This conception obscures significant differences between the property and racial components in the status, and circumvents critical evidence pertaining to the personal component in the status.[6]

In this essay an attempt is made to distinguish between the property and racial components in the status of the ante-bellum slave through a comparison with Roman slavery where the status involved a property but not a racial component. This is followed by a consideration of the evidence for a personal component in the definition of the slave status in the United States. The essay concludes with some re-examination of the status of the slave in Latin America in terms of the three components.

The interpretations of Frank Tannenbaum [7] and Stanley Elkins [8] exemplify the shift away from the moral approach to the institution of slavery and the introduction of new methods and categories. The treatment in both is comparative. Why did slavery in the United States differ in form and consequences from the kind of servitude developed in the Latin American colonies of Spain

---

[3] M. G. Smith, "Slavery and Emancipation in Two Societies", *Social and Economic Studies*, III, Nos. 3 and 4 (1954), pp. 245-46.

[4] *Ibid.*, p. 246.

[5] The classic account is H. J. Nieboer, *Slavery as an Industrial System* (Rotterdam, 1910).

[6] Wilbert Moore, "Slave Law and the Social Structure", *Journal of Negro History*, XXVI. (April, 1941), pp. 171-202.

[7] *Slave and Citizen* (New York, 1947).

[8] *Slavery*. Chap. 2. This discussion is limited to his treatment of the legal status of the slave. Elkins proposes an alternative to the established approach to slavery in the United States which, taking its stance from the debates over slavery, has been concerned mainly with the rightness or wrongness of the institution considered in terms of categories pertaining to the health and welfare of the slaves. The historical study of slavery has alternated over the years between a pro-slavery and an anti-slavery position, but the purpose and the categories of analysis have remained unchanged. The result has been a continuing confusion of the historical study of slavery with moral judgments about slavery. Elkins proposes discarding this approach and adopting instead the method of comparison as followed by Tannenbaum. Slavery as an evil is taken for granted. Elkins' treatment of slavery as analogous to the concentration camp in its effects on Negro personality is discussed in Earle E. Thorpe, "Chattel Slavery and Concentration Camps", *The Negro History Bulletin*, XXV (May, 1962), pp. 171-76.

and Portugal? According to Tannenbaum, there were at least three traditions or historical forces in Latin America which prevented the definition of the slave there solely as property; namely, the continuance of the Roman law of slavery as it came down through the Justinian Code, the influence of the Catholic Church, and the long familiarity of the Iberians with Moors and Negroes.[9] Tannenbaum puts his emphasis on whether, "The law accepted the doctrine of the moral personality of the slave and made possible the gradual achievement of freedom implicit in such a doctrine" and on a universalistic religion, i.e. Catholicism, in preventing the definition of the slave solely as property.[10] In the United States slavery developed in a legal and moral setting in which the doctrine of the moral personality of the slave did not affect the definition of his status in the society. "Legally he was a chattel under the law, and in practice an animal to be bred for market." [11]

In comparing North American and Latin American slavery, Elkins adds to Tannenbaum's earlier treatment. The legal status of the slave in "the liberal, Protestant, secularized, capitalist culture of America" is contrasted with that of the slave in "the conservative, paternalistic, Catholic, quasi-medieval culture of Spain and Portugal and their New World colonies".[12] Elkins concludes that in the absence of such restraining institutions in the United States the search for private gain and profit was unlimited, and the law of slavery developed in such a way as to eliminate the slightest hindrance to the authority of the slaveholder over his slaves. The legal status of the slave developed exclusively in terms of property as the result of the demands of an emerging capitalism. Slavery in the United States was "a system conceived and evolved exclusively on the grounds of property".[13]

For Elkins and Tannenbaum the definitive feature of the legal status of the ante-bellum slave was the centrality of the property component. The rights of personality were suppressed by the law, and the legal subordination of the slave to the authority of the master in the areas of parentage and kinship, property and other private rights, and police and disciplinary power over the slave was developed to such an extent as to make slavery in the United States a unique system.[14] The entire institution became integrated around the definition of the slave as property.

Kenneth Stampp's *The Peculiar Institution* [15] has been viewed as one of the most important and provocative contributions since Ulrich B. Phillips' *American Negro Slavery*.[16] Although it is organized essentially in terms of the

[9]   Tannenbaum, pp. 43-65.
[10]   *Ibid.*, p. 8.
[11]   *Ibid.*, p. 82.
[12]   Elkins, p. 37.
[13]   *Ibid.*, p. 55.
[14]   *Ibid.*, p. 52. These categories are taken from Elkins, but they are also used by Stampp and Tannenbaum in describing the status of the slave.
[15]   (New York, 1957).
[16]   (New York, 1918).

categories used by Phillips and other earlier students of slavery, Stampp's study exceeds the earlier work in comprehensiveness, in presenting the response of the slave to the institution, and in its use of the available scientific evidence regarding race. In contrast to Elkins and Tannenbaum, Stampp takes up the social organization of slavery as well as its legal structure. His interpretation of the legal status of the slave is mainly in terms of economic values, and stresses the property component as do Elkins and Tannenbaum.[17] Unlike Elkins and Tannenbaum, however, he finds that the status also contained a personal element, which made for a certain degree of ambiguity in the status.[18]

In these interpretations, the initial status of the Negro is taken as having been neither that of a slave nor that of a member of a racial group against which discrimination was practised. The status of the Negro as a slave and his status as a member of a racial minority apparently developed concurrently, since there was no tradition of slavery or of racial discrimination in the colonies to inform the initial status of the Negro. The causal connection implied between slavery and racial discrimination is a widely held conception and needs to be reconsidered in the light of recent historical investigation and comparative evidence.

Much more difficult to grasp is the effect of racial discrimination on the definition of the slave status. Elkins refers to "the most implacable race-consciousness yet observed in virtually any society" as affecting the definition of the status, but the stress on economic values in his interpretation obscures any distinction that may have been intended between the property and racial components in the status.[19] Similarly, although Stampp refers to the fact "that chattel slavery, the caste system, and color prejudice" were a part of custom and law by the eighteenth century, no clear distinction is made between those features of the status which are to be attributed to the definition of the slave as property and those which are the consequence of racial discrimination.[20]

Tannenbaum is clearly concerned with the consequences of racial discrimination for the legal status of the Negro as slave and as freedman. He stresses the fact that slavery in the United States meant Negro slavery. In contrast to Latin America, slavery in the ante-bellum South involved "caste", "by law of nature", or "innate inferiority".[21] Slavery systems can be distinguished in terms of the ease and availability of manumission and the status of the freedman, as these indicate whether or not the law denied the moral personality of the slave.[22] In the United States the conception of the slave as a racial

---

[17] Stampp, Chap. 5.
[18] *Ibid.*, pp. 192-93.
[19] Elkins, p. 61.
[20] Stampp, p. 23.
[21] Tannenbaum, pp. 55-56.
[22] *Ibid.*, p. 69. See also William L. Westermann, *The Slave Systems of Greek and Roman Antiquity* (Philadelphia, 1955), p. 154.

inferior led to severe restrictions on manumission and to a low status for free Negroes. At the same time, however, it is readily apparent from Tannenbaum's comparison with slavery in Latin America that in his view the conception of the ante-bellum Negro as innately inferior affected all the legal categories defining his status: the extent of the assimilation of his rights to property in law as well as manumission and the status of the freedman.[23] Racial discrimination accentuated the legal definition of the slave as property.

The slave as property is taken as the primary or exclusive component in these interpretations of the legal status of the slave in the United States. For Elkins and Stampp this is the consequence mainly of economic forces, while for Tannenbaum ideological forces are basic. The focus on the definition of the slave as property results in a tendency to fuse the property and racial components, and in a failure to consider the evidence bearing on the personal component in the legal status.

II

While the assimilation to property in law of the rights of slaves was common to slavery in classical antiquity and the United States, slavery in ancient society "was a type unfamiliar to Europeans and Americans of the last two centuries. It had no color line. (Therefore, *pace Aristotles*, it had no single and clearly defined race or slave caste.)" [24] Moreover, the law of slavery in ancient society did not deny the moral personality of the slave as, according to Roman law, the institution of slavery was of the *Ius Gentium* but at the same time contrary to the *Ius Naturale,* for all men were equal under natural law.[25] A comparison with slavery in Rome where slaves were defined as property in law but did not constitute a separate caste in the society, and where the legal suppression of the personality of the slave, as expressed in the attitude toward manumission and the status of the freedman, did not occur, thus provides a method for distinguishing between the property and the racial components in the definition of the legal status. Since the categories of marriage and the family, property and other rights, and police and disciplinary powers over slaves are used by Elkins, Tannenbaum and Stampp in describing the status of the slave as property in the United States, these will guide the comparison with Rome.[26]

---

[23] Tannenbaum, p. 69.

[24] William L. Westermann, "Slavery and Elements of Freedom in Ancient Greece", *Bulletin of the Polish Institute of Arts and Sciences in America,* I (Jan., 1943), p. 346. See also M. I. Finley, "Beween Slavery and Freedom", *Comparative Studies in Society and History,* VI (Apr., 1964), p. 246.

[25] Westermann, *The Slave Systems,* pp. 57, 80; W. W. Buckland, *The Roman Law of Slavery* (Cambridge, 1906), p. 1. The consequent ambiguity in the status of the slave as property and as a person in ancient society is discussed at a later point.

[26] Materials for the description of the legal status of the ante-bellum slave are standard and taken from Elkins, Chap. 2; Stampp, Chap. 5; Tannenbaum, p. 69ff; and Helen T.

As to marriage and the family in the ante-bellum South, marriages between slaves had no legal standing. "The relation between slaves is essentially different from that of man and wife, joined in lawful wedlock . . . with slaves it may be dissolved at the pleasure of either party, or by the sale of one or both, depending on the caprice or necessity of the owners." [27] The denial of legal marriage meant, in conjunction with the rule that the child follow the condition of the mother, that the offspring of slaves had no legal father, whether the father was slave or free. The duration of the union between slaves depended on the interests of the master or those of the slaves. The union was subject at any time to being dissolved by the sale of one or both of the slaves. The children of these "contubernial relationships", as they were termed, had no legal protection against separation from their parents. In the law there was no such thing as fornication or adultery among slaves. A slave could not be charged with adultery, and a male slave had no legal recourse against another slave, free Negro, or white person for intercourse with his "wife". Nor could the slave present this abuse as evidence in his defense in a criminal charge of assault and battery, or murder.

Roman slaves were also legally incapable of marriage. Any union between slaves or between slaves and free persons was differentiated as *contubernium* as opposed to *conubium*. A marriage was terminated if either party became enslaved. Infidelity between slaves could not be adultery. Although a slave could be guilty of adultery with a married free woman, it was not possible for an enslaved female to commit the offense, or for it to be commited with her. The inheritance of slavery followed the rule that the child follow the status of the mother, whatever the position of the father. A child born of a free father and a slave mother was a slave and the property of the owner, while the child of a slave father and a free mother inherited the free status of the mother. The children of slaves were the property of the owner of the mother, and, since the economic use of slaves during the Republic was at the discretion of the master, slaves were bought and sold without regard for their families. "There was nothing to prevent the legacy of a single slave away from his connexions." [28]

According to the legal codes of the ante-bellum South, a slave "was unable to acquire title to property by purchase, gift, or devise".[29] A slave might not make a will, and he could not, by will, inherit anything. Slaves were not to hire themselves out, locate their own employment, establish their own residence, or make contracts for any purpose including, of course, marriage. A

Catterall, *Judicial Cases Concerning Slavery and the Negro* (Washington, 1926). Those for the Roman Republic are taken from the standard work by Buckland; R. H. Barrow, *Historical Introduction to the Study of Roman Law* (Cambridge, 1932); and Rudolph Sohm, *The Institutes* (Oxford, 1907).

[27] *Howard v. Howard*, 6 Jones N.C. 235, December 1858. Catterall, II, p. 221.
[28] Buckland, p. 77.
[29] Stampp, p. 197.

slave "can do nothing, possess nothing, nor acquire anything but what must belong to his master".[30] He could engage in financial transactions, but only as his master's agent. A slave could not be a party to a suit, except indirectly, when a free person represented him in a suit for freedom. Slaves might only be witnesses in court in cases involving slaves or free Negroes. When the testimony of a slave was allowed, he was not put under oath as a responsible person. Teaching slaves to read and write was prohibited, and instruction in religion was also subject to legal restrictions.

"Of the slave's civil position", in Rome, "it may be said that he had none." [31] A slave could not make a contract, he could be neither creditor nor debtor, he could not make a will, and if he became free, a will made in slavery was void. Slaves could in no way be concerned in civil proceedings which had to be made in the name of the master. A judgment against a slave was null and void and the pact of a slave was likewise void.

As to his participation in commerce, "his capacity here is almost purely derivative, and the texts speak of him as unqualified in nearly every branch of law".[32] Although the Roman slave could acquire possessions for the master, "the will of the slave and, in fact, his mental faculties in general, operate, in principle, where they operate at all, for the benefit of the master".[33] Legally the slave did not have possessory rights in the property acquired by him or granted to him. The *peculium* assigned to him by the master, to which the slave might add by investment, earnings, gift, interest, produce, or wages existed by the authority of the master and was subject to partial or total recall at the slaveowner's wish. The *peculium* was not alienable by the slave any more than other property. The *peculium* did not change the legal position of the slave. He was still a slave. No legal process which was closed to a slave without *peculium* was available to him if he had one. The *peculium* did not go with the slave upon manumission unless expressly given by the master.

Slaves were legally incapable of prosecution as accusers either on their own behalf or on behalf of others. As a general rule the evidence of slaves was not admissible in court, and when it was taken it was taken by torture, for it could not be received in any other form from slaves. Slaves were excluded from giving testimony on behalf of their masters.

The slave codes of the South supported the "full dominion" of the master in matters of policy and discipline. The slave's relationship with his master was expected to be one of complete subordination. Generally, homicide was the major crime that could be committed against an enslaved individual. The owner of a slave, however, could not be indicted for assault and battery on

[30] The Civil Code of Louisiana quoted in John C. Hurd, *The Law of Freedom and Bondage in the United States* (Boston, 1858), II, p. 160.
[31] Buckland, p. 82.
[32] *Ibid.*, p. 82.
[33] *Ibid.*, p. 82.

his own slave. "The power of the master must be absolute to render the submission of the slave perfect." [34] Furthermore, the master was not held responsible for the death of a slave as a consequence of "moderate correction", for "it cannot be presumed that prepensed malice (which alone makes murder felony) should induce any man to destroy his own estate".[35] The master was to recover damages caused by an assault or homicide against his slave.

During the Roman Republic there was no legal limitation on the power of the slaveowner: "his rights were unrestricted".[36] "Except in cases of revolt which endangered the government the Roman state left the problem of the discipline and punishment of slaves to their masters." [37] Sohm writes that as against his master, "a slave had no legal rights whatsoever".[38] In dealing with the offenses of slaves the owner's powers of punishment included corporal punishment, confinement in chains, confinement in the ergasulum, banishment from Rome and Italy, and the death penalty. Slaves, as possessions of value, were protected from mistreatment by persons other than their masters. In case of injury done to a slave "the master had cause of action for damages against the perpetrator".[39] If a slave was enticed into escaping or forcibly removed the owner might resort to both criminal and civil action.

These comparisons suggest that, on the legal evidence which defines the authority of the master in the areas of parentage and kinship, property and other rights, and police and disciplinary power over slaves, there is nothing sufficiently distinctive to distinguish the legal status of the slave as property in the United States from that in Rome.

Arnold Toynbee refers to the "Negro slave immigrant" as having been "subject to the twofold penalization of racial discrimination and legal servitude".[40] A society may extensively assimilate to property in law the rights of slaves, as indeed many have, but yet not restrict the status of slavery to members of a particular group for whom slavery is defined as natural, inevitable, and permanent as occurred in the United States. This was the introduction of caste into the status of the ante-bellum Negro, slave or free.[41] The Negro as

---

[34] *State v. Mann*, 2 Deveroux 263, (N.C.), December 1829, Catterall, II, p. 57.
[35] Virginia Act of 1669, Hurd, I, p. 232.
[36] Buckland, p. 36.
[37] Westermann, p. 75.
[38] Sohm, p. 166.
[39] Westermann, p. 83.
[40] Arnold J. Toynbee, *A Study of History* (Oxford, 1934), II, p. 218.
[41] There has been considerable disagreement as to whether the term "caste" is applicable to the American case. It has been insisted that it should be limited to India. The present writer agrees with Everett Hughes who writes: "If we grant this, we will simply have to find some other term for the kind of social category into which one is assigned at birth and from which he cannot escape by action of his own: and to distinguish such social categories from classes or ranked groups, from which it is possible, though sometimes difficult, to rise." Everett C. Hughes and H. MacGill Hughes, *Where Peoples Meet* (Glencoe, 1952), p. 111. Berreman has recently defined the term as to be useful cross-culturally. He defines a caste system "as a *hierarchy of endogamous divi-*

slave occupied both a slave status and a caste status.[42] He was subject to disabilities in addition to those connected with the legal categorization of him as property, and these disabilities continued to define his status as a freedman. Caste law as well as slave law governed the status of the Negro.

The restriction of slavery to the Negro rested on the legal principle that it was a status properly belonging to the Negro as an innately (racially) inferior being. If slavery was a status attaching to a racial inferior, then it was inheritable even where one parent was white. Intermarriage between Negro slaves and whites was prohibited. Racial inferiority, legalized inheritance, and endogamy were related to another principle; namely, that slavery was the presumptive status of every Negro or person of color. The slave status was to follow naturally and inevitably from Negro ancestry.[43]

Although the slave and caste statuses were coextensive for the preponderant majority of ante-bellum Negroes, there were free Negroes in the North and South who, however, continued to be members of the lower caste. Caste was inclusive of the slave and free status. Thus the rule that the child follow the condition of the mother made slaves of the majority of Negroes and members of the lower caste of all Negroes. Negroes, slave or free, were legally prohibited from intermarrying with members of the dominant group. All members of the lower caste were presumed to be slaves unless they could establish that they should be legally free. There was a definite strain in the legal structure to establish slavery and caste as coextensive for all Negroes. The status of the free Negro is evidence of this strain. Although legally no longer an object of property rights, he was legally and socially a member of a lower caste and as such his life chances, whether he lived in the North or South, were held within narrow limits.[44]

Slavery in Republican Rome was not restricted to any particular group who ought properly to occupy the legal status of slaves. The legal restrictions on intermarriage of slave and free, on manumission, and on the status of freedmen, though at times severe, were not the consequence of a conception of the slave or former slave as innately inferior. Those who were enslaved in

---

sions in which membership is hereditary and permanent. Here hierarchy includes inequality both in status and in access to goods and services. Interdependence of the subdivisions, restricted contracts among them, occupational specialization, and/or a degree of cultural distinctiveness might be added as criteria, although they appear to be correlates rather than defining characteristics." Gerald D. Berreman, "Caste in India and the United States", *American Journal of Sociology*, LXVI (Sept., 1960), pp. 120-21, cf. Louis Dumont, "Caste, Racism, and 'Stratification', Reflections of a Social Anthropologist", *Contributions to Indian Sociology*, V (Oct., 1961), pp. 20-43.

[42] Moore, pp. 177-9.

[43] *Ibid.*, 184-88. See also Winthrop D. Jordan, "American Chiaroscuro: The Status and Definition of Mulattoes in the British Colonies", *William and Mary Quarterly*, XIX, No. 2 (April, 1962), pp. 183-200.

[44] John Hope Franklin, *The Free Negro in North Carolina* (Chapel Hill, 1943); Leon F. Litwack, *North of Slavery* (Chicago, 1961).

Rome did not constitute a caste in the society for whom the proper and permanent status was conceived to be slavery.[45]

It is not surprising that the highly perceptive Alexis de Tocqueville should have noticed this essential difference between slavery in antiquity and the United States. However, observing that discrimination against the Negro persisted in those parts of the United States where slavery had been abolished, he concluded that slavery must have given "birth" to "prejudice".[46] A causal relationship between slavery and racial discrimination is also implied in the interpretations under discussion.

Setting aside the conventional question as to "why slavery produced discrimination?" Carl Degler has separated the two elements, and, still treating the question historically, asks rather "which appeared first, slavery or discrimination?" His main argument is that from the beginning "the Negro was treated as an inferior to the white man, servant or free".[47] Caste or elements of caste antedated slavery, and as the legal status evolved "it reflected and included as a part of its essence, this same discrimination the white man had practiced against the Negro" from the outset in New England as well as the South.[48]

The colonists of the early seventeenth century not only were well aware of the distinction between indentured servitude and slavery, but they had ample opportunity to acquire the prejudicial attitudes and discriminatory practices against Negroes through the slave trade and from Providence, Bermuda, Barbados, Jamaica, and the Spanish and Portuguese colonies.[49] Moreover, there was the inferior status ascribed to the non-Caucasian Indians and even their enslavement almost from the beginning of English settlement.

The evidence summarized by Degler indicates that Negroes were being set aside as a separate group because of their race before the legal status of slavery became fully crystallized in the late seventeenth century. There was legislation (1) preventing inter-racial marriages and sexual union; (2) declaring that the status of the offspring of a white man and a Negro would follow that of the mother; and (3) establishing civil and legal disabilities applying to Negroes either free or in servitude.[50] As to the situation of the Negro in the North, "from the earliest years a lowly differentiated status, if not slavery

[45]   Westermann, p. 15, 23.
[46]   Alexis de Tocqueville, *Democracy in America* (New York, 1948), I, pp. 358-60.
[47]   Carl N. Degler, "Slavery and the Genesis of American Race Prejudice", *Comparative Studies in Society and History*, II (Oct., 1959), p. 52. Cf. Oscar and Mary F. Handlin, "Origins of the Southern Labor System", *William and Mary Quarterly*, 3rd. Ser., VI (April, 1950), pp. 199-222; Winthrop D. Jordan, "Modern Tensions and the Origins of American Slavery", *Journal of Southern History*, XXVII (Feb., 1962), pp. 18-33.
[48]   Degler, p. 52.
[49]   *Ibid.*, pp. 53-56. See also Winthrop D. Jordan, "The Influence of the West Indies on the Origin of New England Slavery", *William and Mary Quarterly*, XVIII (April, 1961), pp. 243-250.
[50]   *Ibid.*, pp. 56-62. See also Moore, pp. 177-86.

itself, was reserved and recognized for the Negro — and the Indian, it might be added".[51] Degler concludes that "long before slavery or black labor became an important part of the Southern economy, a special and inferior status had been worked out for the Negroes. . . . it was a demand for labor which dragged the Negro to American shores, but the status he acquired cannot be explained by reference to that economic motive." [52]

Turning now to the personal component in the status of the ante-bellum slave, it is apparent that a conception of a legal relationship between persons or groups of persons is implied in the definition of slaves as a caste in the society. As we have seen, the ante-bellum slave was not uniformly regarded in the law as a person. There were certain situations and relationships, however, in which he was not regarded solely as property.

Kingsley Davis has observed that "slavery is extremely interesting precisely because it does attempt to fit human beings into the category of objects of property rights . . . . Always the slave is given some rights, and these rights interfere with the attempt to deal with him solely as property." [53] Westermann found this to be a "constant paradox" in Greek and Roman antiquity, and "inherent in the very nature of the institution". "Theoretically", the slave was a chattel and subject only to the laws pertaining to private property, and in "actuality" he was "also a human being and subject to protective legislation affecting human individuals".[54] Isaac Mendelsohn refers to "the highly contradictory situation" in the slavery systems of the ancient Near East "in which on the one hand, the slave was considered as possessing qualities of a human being, while on the other hand, he was . . . regarded as a thing".[55] Under the law in Greek, Roman, and Near Eastern society the slave had an ambiguous status: he was both an object of property rights and a rudimentary legal person.

As to the personal component in the status of the slave in the United States, Elkins argues that as a consequence of the requirements of capitalistic agriculture "to operate efficiently and profitably", through the rational employment of slaves as economic instruments, any ambiguity in the legal status of the slave as property could not be tolerated.[56] Any rights of personality that remained to the Negro at the end of the seventeenth century had been suppressed by the middle of the eighteenth.[57] However they may differ as to causation, Elkins and Tannenbaum are in agreement that the status of the slave was determinate as property. For Tannenbaum the "element of human

[51] Degler, p. 62.
[52] Ibid., p. 62. Jordan, *The Influence of the West Indies*, pp. 243-44, 250.
[53] *Human Society* (New York, 1949), p. 456.
[54] Westermann, p. 1.
[55] *Slavery in the Near East* (New York, 1949), p. 64.
[56] Elkins, p. 49, 53.
[57] Ibid., p. 42.

personality" had been lost in the definition of the slave in the United States.[58] Stampp, on the other hand, found a "dual character" in the legal codes. The legal authorities "were caught in a dilemma whenever they found that the slave's status as property was incompatible with this status as a person".[59] In a much earlier and very careful treatment of the personal component, Moore found that initially the question as to whether a slave was a person or a piece of property was involved in the difficult issue as to the status of the slave after conversion and baptism. Allowing the slave the privilege of salvation implied a recognition of him as a Christian person, and, by implication, as a legal personality. The idea that conversion and baptism altered the status of the slave as property was not easily changed, and the settling of the difficulty in favor of continued enslavement does not appear to have finally disposed of the matter.[60] "The persistence of this indeterminacy arising out of religious status", concludes Moore, "must be regarded as at least one source of the continued legislative and judicial declarations of the personality of the slave, despite other definitions and implications to the contrary." [61]

There are three aspects to be considered in taking up the matter of the doubtful status of the slave before the law. The most obvious, of course, is that the dual quality is inherent in the status itself. Slaves are conscious beings defined as economic property. On the one hand, the definition of the legal status conceives of them as objects of economic value. On the other hand, the slave as an item of economic value also remains a social object. The values he possesses as a conscious being can be utilized by the master, namely, his body, his skill, and his knowledge. The definition of the slave as a physical object overlaps that of the slave as a social object, since only social objects can perform and have intentions. The value of a slave as property resides in his being a person, but his value as a person rests in his status being defined as property.[62]

The second aspect involves the recognition in the law not only of the humanity of the slave, but also that he may be the subject of rights of his own. In this connection, Stampp has noted a significant juxtaposition of two clauses in the legal code of Alabama in 1853. The first defines the status of the slave as property and establishes the owner's rights to the slave's "time, labor, and services", as well as the slave's obligation to comply with the lawful demands of the master. The second contains the personal element and states the master's obligation to be humane to his slaves and to provide them with adequate food, clothing, and with care during illness and old age.[63]

---

[58] Tannenbaum, p. 97.
[59] Stampp, pp. 192-93.
[60] Moore, pp. 195-96.
[61] *Ibid.*, p. 196. See also Charles Sellers, "The Travail of Slavery", in Charles Sellers, ed., *The Southerner as American* (Chapel Hill, 1960), pp. 40-71.
[62] Talcott Parsons and Neil J. Smelser, *Economy and Society* (Glencoe, 1956), p. 12.
[63] Stampp, pp. 192-93. The following discussion is not intended to be comprehensive.

Similarly a Kentucky court ruled in one case that "a slave by our code, is not a person, but (negotium) a thing", while in another case in the same state the court considered "slaves as property, yet recognizes their personal existence, and to a qualified extent, their natural rights".[64]

Cases clearly affirming that the slave was a person were also numerous during the ante-bellum period. One judgment in Tennessee held:

A slave is not in the condition of a horse ... he is made after the image of the Creator. He has mental capacities, and an immortal principle in his nature ... the laws ... cannot extenguish his high born nature, nor deprive him of many rights which are inherent in man.[65]

That the slave as an object of property rights was protected by law and by remedies the law provided whereby an owner could recover damages done to his property has already been discussed. A slave was also entitled in his own right to protection from malicious injury to his life and limb. The courts ruled that manslaughter against a slave "exists by common law: because it is the unlawful killing of a human being";[66] that a slave is "a reasonable creature in being, in whose homicide either a white person or a slave may commit the crime of murder or manslaughter";[67] and that "Negroes are under the protection of the laws, and have personal rights, and cannot be considered on a footing only with domestic animals".[68] The justification of the legal principle that a crime could be committed against an enslaved individual tended to shift, and in many cases revealed the ambivalence between the conception of the slave as property, and as a person. In a judgment acknowledging that an indictment for an assault upon a slave could be made, a Louisiana court ruled that "Slaves are treated in our law as property, and, also, as persons ...."[69] As stated earlier, however, generally homicide was the major crime that could be committed against a slave, and the owner of a slave could not be indicted for assault and battery on his slaves.

Many of the laws also implied that a slave was a legal person in that he was capable of committing crimes and could be held to trial. Cases involving slave crimes were very numerous and frequently they turned on the conception of the slave as a person. In the judgment of a Georgia court in 1854:

... it is not true that slaves are only chattels, ... and therefore, it is not true that it is not possible for them to be prisoners ... the Penal Code ... has them in

---

For a detailed treatment of the definition of the slave as a person see Moore, pp. 191-202.
[64] *Jarman v. Patterson*, 7 T.B. Mon. 644, December 1828, (Ky.) Catterall, I, p. 311. See also *Catherine Bodine's Will*, 4 Dana 476, Oct. 1836, (Ky.) *Ibid.*, I, p. 334-35.
[65] *Kennedy v. Williams*, 7 Humphreys, Sept., 1846 (Tenn.) *Ibid.*, II, p. 530.
[66] *Fields v. State*, I Yerger 156, Jan., 1829 (Tenn.) *Ibid.*, II, p. 494.
[67] *Hudson v. State*, 34 Ala. 253, June 1859, *Ibid.*, III, p. 233.
[68] *State v. Cynthia Simmons and Laurence Kitchen*, I Brevard 6, Fall 1794 (So. Car.), *Ibid.*, II, p. 277.
[69] *State v. Davis*, 14 La. An. 678, July 1859, *Ibid.*, III, p. 674.

contemplation ... in the first division ... as persons capable of committing crimes; and as a ... consequence ... as capable of becoming prisoners.[70]

Another court held that a white man could be indicted and convicted as an accessory to a murder commited by a slave. The judgment stated that "Negroes are under the protection of the laws, and have personal rights .... They have wills of their own — capacities to commit crimes; and are responsible for offences against society."[71]

Again, however, there were limits on the extent to which the personality of the slave was recognized, and in defining these limits the courts frequently expressed the indeterminate character of the status:

Because they are rational *human beings*, they are capable of committing crimes; and, in reference to acts which are crimes, are regarded as *persons*. Because they are *slaves*, they are ... incapable of performing civil acts; and in reference to all such, they are *things*; not persons.[72]

That slaves were held to some of the responsibilities usually expected of persons in society and few of the privileges is further illustrated by the fact that slaves were persons who could abscond and commit capital crimes, but if killed or maimed in capture or put to death by law, the slaveowner was reimbursed for the loss of his property.

The third aspect pertains to the cases of manumission by will, deed, and legislative action; the instances of successful suits for freedom; and the cases of self-purchase — all of which implied evaluation of the slave as a person with some legal capacity:

They may be emancipated by their owners; and must, of course, have a right to seek and enjoy the protection of the law in the establishment of all deeds, or wills, or other legal documents of emancipation; and so far, they must be considered as natural persons, entitled to some legal rights, whenever their owners shall have declared ... they ... be free; and to this extent the general reason of policy which disables slaves as persons, and subjects them to the general reason of mere brute property, does not apply.[73]

Moreover, the presence of free Negroes in the population from the beginning; manumission; suits for freedom; and self-purchase indicated that slavery did not follow naturally and inevitably from Negro ancestry. The intrusion of the values of liberty and individual achievement into the legal structure meant that race and slavery were not coextensive for all Negroes. The law sanctioned the possibility of slaves legitimately aspiring to and attaining in attenuated form the culture goals of the enslaving group having to do with freedom and individual achievement. The status of the free Negro was real and

---

[70]   *Baker v. State*, 15 Ga. 498, July 1854, *Ibid.*, III, p. 35.
[71]   *State v. Cynthia Simmons and Laurence Kitchen*, I Brevard 6, fall 1794 (So. Car.), *Ibid.*, II, p. 277.
[72]   *Creswell's Executor v. Walker*, 37 Ala. 229, January 1861, *Ibid.*, III, p. 247.
[73]   *Catherine Bodine's Will*, 4 Dana 476, October 1836, (Ken.), *Ibid.*, I, pp. 334-35.

symbolic evidence of the indeterminacy resulting from the attainment of goals that were presumably denied to Negroes and applicable only to whites.[74]

III

In the interpretations of Elkins, Tannenbaum, and Stampp much has been made of the legal status of the slave as property and the extent to which the rights of slaves were assimilated to property in law. As the preceding discussion has indicated, in the United States where slaves were conceived of as innately inferior they constituted a caste in the society and their rights were extensively assimilated to property in law. In Republican Rome where slaves were not conceived of as innately inferior to the enslaving group and did not form a separate caste an equally extensive assimilation of their rights to property occurred. In contrast to the United States, manumission was easily available to the Roman slave, and the freedman could look forward to assimilation into Roman society.

Although the slave status in Rome was not justified in terms of the innate inferiority of the slave, the assimilation of ownership in slaves to property was comparable to that in the United States. Roman law respected the moral personality of the slave, as reflected in the rules governing manumission and the status of the freed slave, but this did not prevent the assimilation of his rights to property in law.

In so far as the legal categorization of the slave as property is concerned we are dealing with a common social form in Rome and the United States. Caste produced the contrast between the legal structures of the two systems of slavery. The consequence of racial discrimination for the legal structure of ante-bellum slavery was the creation of a hereditary, endogamous and permanent group of individuals in the status of slaves who, moreover, continued as members of a lower caste in the society after freedom. Although the conception of the slave as innately (racially) inferior to the enslaving group had important consequences for manumission and for the status of freedmen, as Tannenbaum has indicated, the comparison with Rome suggests that it did not accentuate the assimilation of ownership in slaves to property. Racial discrimination does not appear to have affected the legal status of the slave as property.

Now slavery in Rome was not a single social phenomenon historically. Not until the first two centuries of the Empire did significant changes occur in the authority of the master over the rights of slaves. "In their ultimate legal for-

[74] Wilbert Moore and Robin Williams, "Stratification in the Ante-bellum South", *American Sociological Review*, VII (June, 1942), pp. 343-51. Cf. Douglas Hall, "Slaves and Slavery in the British West Indies", *Social and Economic Studies*, II, No. 4 (December, 1962), pp. 305-18.

mulation the changes found expression in the Codes of Theodosius and Justinian." [75] Up to that time, although Roman law respected the moral integrity of the slave, the subordination of the slave to the authority of the master was comparable to that in the United States. The slave law that came down through the Justinian Code to influence the Iberian law of slavery, later to be transferred to Latin America, contained not only the doctrine of the moral personality of the slave, but also embodied those changes in later Roman law which had "loosened the strict controls by which the slave element had formerly been bound to the will of the master group".[76]

According to the interpretations of slavery in Latin America by Tannenbaum and Elkins, it was this body of law in conjunction with certain traditions and institutional arrangements that functioned to protect the slaves both from an extensive assimilation to property in law and from a caste status. Some reference will be made in the concluding portion of this essay to the need for a revision of this interpretation on the basis of more recent research.

Considerable variation occurs among slavery systems in the extent to which the slave is assimilated to property in law. Variations in this component are generally taken to be related to "the level of technical development and the accompanying institutional apparatus, including the economic system".[77] Where slavery was a domestic system, as in China and the Near East, the assimilation of the slave to property in law was less extensive than in Rome and the United States where slavery was an industrial system.[78]

The property component in the status of the ante-bellum slave was undoubtedly related to economic values and the labor needs of an emerging capitalism, as Elkins and Stampp have emphasized, but the entire status cannot be derived from the operation of economic values. On the one hand, the extensive assimilation to property in law of the Roman slave did not generate a conception of him as innately inferior and create a caste of slaves and freedmen. On the other hand, the absence of certain institutions and traditions embodying values respecting the moral personality of the slave does not account for the conception of the Negro as inherently inferior and for caste. If these were absent, then the assimilation of ownership in slaves to property in law must have caused racial discrimination and caste. The historical evidence indicates rather that discrimination against the Negro occurred before the slave status was fully defined and before Negro labor became pivotal to the economic system.[79]

---

[75] Westermann, p. 140.

[76] *Ibid.*, p. 140.

[77] Sidney W. Mintz, Review of *Slavery* by Stanley Elkins, *American Anthropologist*, 63 (June, 1961), p. 580.

[78] G. Martin Wilbur, *Slavery in China During the Former Han Dynasty* (Chicago, 1943), p. 243; Mendelsohn, pp. 121-22.

[79] That the essential features of a caste status for the Negro may have preceded the full development of the slave status does not alter the widely accepted proposition that the initial status of the Negro was not that of a slave but rather that of an indentured

In the conception of the legal status of the slave as determinate in terms of property the slave has neither a juridical nor a moral personality. The values of the dominant group in the United States that had a bearing on the law of slavery were, on the one hand, those which legitimatized slavery and the rigid system of stratification, and on the other hand, those values pertaining to freedom and individual dignity and worth. Although there was no complex of laws, traditions, and institutions pertaining to the institution of slavery as such that embodied these latter values, a significant element in the general value system of the South was an ethical valuation of the individual. The legal evidence indicates that these extra-legal values of the society were expressed in the legal definition and conception of slavery. The law of slavery shows the existence of an ethical norm, however vague and rudimentary, attaching value to the individual.[80]

The interpretation of the legal status of the slave primarily or wholly in terms of property has implications as well for the conception of the pattern of relations between masters and slaves. In discussing the connection between the legal structure and the master-slave relationship, David Potter has observed that "the human relationship within this legal context was complex and multiple". The relation between masters and slaves had "two faces — a paternalistic manorial one and an exploitative commercial one".[81]

In the interpretations of Tannenbaum, Elkins, and Stampp there is a close correspondence between the legal structure and the pattern of the master-slave relationship. Since, according to these writers, the slave status was governed by instrumental and economic values and not affected by the religious and ethical convictions of the dominant group attaching value to the individual, there was nothing to impede the rational use of slaves as economic instruments. The exploitative commercial pattern was expected to be followed

---

servant or free man. Some aspects of caste appear to have developed later than others, but the main defining features were fixed early and before the complete development of the status of slavery. Racial segregation, although obviously foreshadowed in the status of the free Negro, did not appear as a part of the caste system until the late nineteenth and early twentieth centuries. The system of restricted contacts between Negroes and whites, clearly based on the long-standing assumption of the innate inferiority of the Negro, was simply the latest feature of caste to develop. See C. Vann Woodward, *The Strange Career of Jim Crow* (New York, 1957).

[80] Moore, pp. 201-02. For another discussion of the alternative value systems and the resulting conflicts within Southern society and within individuals see Sellers, pp. 51-67. A similar ambiguity existed in connection with slavery in ancient society. In Roman law "slavery is the only case in which, in the extant sources..., a conflict is declared to exist between the *Ius Gentium* and the *Ius Naturale*". Buckland, p. 1. "No society", writes Finley, "can carry such a conflict within it, around so important a set of beliefs and institutions, without the stresses erupting in some fashion, no matter how remote and extended the lines and connections may be from the original stimulus." M. I. Finley, "Was Greek Civilization Based on Slave Labour?", in M. I. Finley, ed. *Slavery in Classical Antiquity* (Cambridge, 1960), p. 162.

[81] David M. Potter, Review of *The Peculiar Institution* by Kenneth Stampp, *Yale Review*, 46 (Winter, 1957), pp. 260-61.

in organizing the relations of masters and slaves. It was normatively and numerically the predominant pattern in the South.

Given this conception of the connection between the legal structure and the relations of masters and slaves, the paternalistic manorial pattern can only be interpreted as a deviation from the expected and approved pattern of the master-slave relationship. It is not interpreted as an equally recognized and approved mode of organizing and managing the relations of masters and slaves, but rather as the result of fortuitous circumstances. It is attributed to the smallness of the plantation or to the "personal factor".[82] According to this interpretation there was nothing in the law to sanction the paternalistic manorial pattern, while the commercial exploitative pattern was clearly compatible with the instrumental use of slaves as sanctioned in the definition of the slave as an object of property rights. Yet, the paternalistic manorial pattern was widespread in the South as an accepted and approved mode of organizing the master-slave relationship and represented, as did the personal component in the legal status, the intrusion of the valuation of the individual into a categorized relationship.[83]

IV

Since the contrast with slavery in Latin America is central to the interpretations of slavery in the United States by Tannenbaum and Elkins, some reference may be made to the more recent studies of slavery and race relations in Latin America and the implications for a comparison with North America. The results of these studies appear to be consistent with those of this essay.

In connection with the interpretations of slavery in Latin America by Elkins and Tannenbaum, Mintz questions whether slavery in Latin America

---

[82] Elkins, pp. 137-38.

[83] The pattern of the master-slave relationships continues to be one of the most problematic and debated aspects of ante-bellum slavery. The exploitative commercial pattern tends to be taken as the predominant pattern and in accordance with the normative prescriptions of ante-bellum society, while the paternalistic manorial pattern is generally treated as the result of the intrusion of non-normative factors, and usually attributed to smallness of size. However, Franklin has pointed out that the bulk of the slaves were on small plantations. If so, then the paternalistic manorial pattern must have been exceedingly widespread. On the other hand, it has also been suggested that this pattern was to be found on the larger holdings. Phillips had this conception of the master-slave relationship on large plantations. It seems likely that both patterns were normative; that is, accepted and approved ways of organizing the master-slave relationship. If this was the case, then further investigation must be directed at ascertaining the determinants of these patterns on the concrete level. Size would be one among several determinants. See John Hope Franklin, *From Slavery to Freedom* (New York, 1952), pp. 185-86. Needless to say, the pattern of the master-slave relationship is significant for the impact of slavery upon the personality of the Negro. If the paternalistic manorial pattern was widely institutionalized in the ante-bellum South, then a very significant number of Negro slaves were able to escape the tendency for the system to absorb the personality. Cf. Elkins, pp. 137-138.

can be treated as a single phenomenon historically.[83a] He points out that once slavery became a part of the industrial plantation system in Cuba and Puerto Rico, for example, an extensive assimilation to property in law of the rights of slaves occurred in spite of an institutional framework protecting the moral personality of the slave. Slavery in Cuba "dehumanized the slave as viciously as had Jamaican or North America slavery".[84] Much the same thing happened in Puerto Rico. Between 1803 and 1873 repressive laws were passed "more and more limiting the slaves' legal, social, economic status".[85] In connection with slavery on the sugar plantations and in the mines of Portuguese Brazil, E. R. Boxer writes that the widely accepted "belief that the Brazilian was an exceptionally kind master is applicable only to nineteenth-century slavery under the Empire" and not to the colonial period.[86] At the same time, however, "one of the few redeeming features in the life of slaves ... was the possibility of their buying or being given their freedom at some time, a contingency which was much rarer in the French and English American colonies".[87]

As to the racial component in the slave status, investigations of race relations in Brazil, where most of the work has been done, indicate that during the colonial period slavery also involved a caste system between whites and Negro slaves, "based on white supremacy and the institutionalized inferiority of colored slaves".[88] Concubinage was widely practiced, but inter-marriage was rare, "as the system demanded the separation of the two castes and the clearcut distinction of superiors and inferiors".[89] Colonial legislation discriminated against the free Negroes who "were often coupled with enslaved Negroes in the laws".[90] They were prevented from acquiring possessions or participating in activities in the society "which might tend to place them on a level with whites".[91] Mulattoes who attained positions of importance in Brazil "did so in spite of the official and social prejudices which existed against them throughout the whole of the colonial period".[92]

[83a] Useful summaries are to be found in Juan Comas, "Recent Research on Race Relations — Latin America", *International Social Science Journal*, XIII, No. 2 (1961), pp. 271-99; Oracy Nogueira, "Skin Color and Social Class", *Plantation Systems of the New World* (Washington, 1959), pp. 164-83; Roger Bastide, "Race Relations in Brazil", *International Social Science Bulletin*, IX, No. 4 (1957), pp. 495-512.

[84] Mintz, p. 581.

[85] *Ibid.*, p. 583, See also O. A. Sherrard, *Freedom from Fear* (London, 1959), p. 75.

[86] *The Golden Age of Brazil* (Berkeley, 1961), p. 173. Gilberto Freyre's *The Masters and the Slaves* (New York, 1946), on which much of the existing conception of slavery in Brazil is based, wrote mainly about domestic slaves.

[87] Boxer, p. 177.

[88] Harley Ross Hammond, "Race, Social Mobility and Politics in Brazil", *Race*, IV, No. 2 (1962), p. 477. See Charles Wagley, "From Caste to Class in North Brazil", in Charles Wagley (ed.), *Race and Class in Rural Brazil* (New York, 1963), pp. 142-156.

[89] *Ibid.*, p. 4.

[90] Boxer, p. 17.

[91] *Ibid.*, p. 17.

[92] *Ibid.*, p. 17.

It is readily apparent from these studies that a much greater similarity existed between slavery in the United States and Latin America than here-to-fore suspected. The status of slaves in Latin America, as well as in Rome and the United States, indicates that whether or not the law respected the moral personality of the slave, an extensive assimilation of his rights to property in law occurred under slavery as an industrial system. Moreover, contrary to the widely held conception, racial discrimination was present in Latin America and had the consequence of creating a duality in the status of the slave as property and as a member of a racial caste.[93] These elements were apparently combined to some extent with a respect for the moral personality of the slave in the law.

Further comparative study of slavery in the United States and Latin America will enable us to delineate more precisely the differences and similarities in the property, racial, and personal components of the slave status in these societies. We may also expect such study to reveal, as this essay has attempted to do, that economic and ideological forces were not mutually exclusive in their consequences for the legal structure of slavery.

ARNOLD A. SIO
Colgate University

---

[93] Nogueira, pp. 167-176, has attempted to distinguish race prejudice in Brazil from that in the United States. With reference to the origin of race prejudice in Brazil, James G. Leyburn, in his discussion of Nogueira's paper, questions whether it was slavery which produced prejudice. *Ibid.*, p. 181.

CAPITALISM, SLAVERY AND IDEOLOGY *

RELATING SLAVERY TO CAPITALISM IS A TASK WHICH, OVER THE YEARS, has exercised a good many minds. Some of the reasons for this are fairly obvious. From the point of view of those concerned with the mainstream of Western social and economic development slavery is apt to appear an anomaly. Morally and socially it seems regressive — an anachronism, a throw-back to the beliefs and practices of earlier times. Yet there is substantial evidence that, as a method of production, it was often very successful, providing both cheap goods and a high level of profits. It is thus a phenomenon which it is remarkably hard to categorize, an awkward exception to the rules. For this reason not only historians but economic theorists and social philosophers have kept coming back to it to see how this aberrant institution can, or just conceivably might, be related to the general pattern of Western development.

I do not intend to rehearse all their arguments, but I would like to begin by looking at some of them to see which methods of approach look profitable and which do not. And I propose to begin with what has been said about the origins of slavery, partly because this enables us to proceed chronologically, but mainly because here at least there exists a broad area of agreement.

In accounting for the rise of New World slavery historians have almost invariably drawn attention to the important role played by market forces. They have explained that in circumstances such as those prevailing in the Americas, where alternative forms of labour were scarce, resources plentiful, and the markets for goods elastic, the attractions of slavery were too compelling to be ignored. Often, indeed, these economic motives have been seen as so compelling as to render any further explanation superfluous. Given a choice between employing slaves and toiling for long hours in debilitating climates — or, indeed, in *any* kind of climate — settlers generally chose slaves.[1] Others have suggested that the explanation may not be quite so simple. After all, not every society is governed by, or even parti-

* An earlier version of this paper was presented to the Anglo-American Conference of Historians held at the University of London in July 1975. I should like to thank Roger Anstey, Michael Craton, Seymour Drescher and Stanley Engerman for their helpful comments on that draft.

[1] This is the explanation given in most standard textbooks: see, for example, Samuel Eliot Morison, Henry Steele Commager and William E. Leuchtenburg, *The Growth of the American Republic*, 6th edn., 2 vols. (New York, 1969), i, p. 46; John Blum *et al.*, *The National Experience* (New York, 1963), pp. 50-1; Harold F. Williamson, *The Growth of the American Economy*, 2nd edn. (Englewood Cliffs, N.J., 1951), p. 69.

cularly susceptible to, market forces. It took a particular set of cultural assumptions, along with appropriate economic and social structures, to make men act as they did. So in explaining the rise of slavery these historians have been apt to note the appearance, first in Europe and later — often in more clearly defined forms — in the Americas, of societies committed to exploiting a new ideology and a new method of life based on what we would now call capitalism. What was remarkable about this new way of life, we are told, was its ruthless commitment to rational calculation, to the control of nature and, above all, to the pursuit of profit. So there was nothing at all surprising in the fact that men thus possessed of the entrepreneurial spirit, finding themselves in a new land where no other forms of culture were solidly established, should have turned to slavery. Freed from the traditional usages and customs of Europe they adopted whatever new institutions appeared suited to their needs.[2]

Now there are objections to this view. It may be argued, for example, that American settlers were not quite as uniformly ruthless and self-seeking as is here suggested. The capitalist spirit was not Europe's only gift to the Americas. We know that New World settlers were often as remarkable for their anxiety to retain Old World customs as for their willingness to throw them off. And there were limits to the rapacity of even the most materialistically-minded colonists. How else are we to explain the all but universal distinction made between Indians and Africans who were regarded as susceptible to chattel slavery and Europeans who were not? Yet even when these objections are taken into account, the case for regarding slavery as a peculiarly capitalistic enterprise — a response to particular circumstances based on calculations of individual self-interest — remains a compelling one. Slavery might be socially regressive but economically it made sense.[3]

Yet if we regard the rise of slavery as largely due to market forces how are we to account for its demise? Well, one way of beginning would be to envisage situations in which there would have been

[2] Lewis Cecil Gray, *History of Agriculture in the Southern United States to 1860*, 2 vols. (Washington, 1933), i, p. 303; Stanley Elkins, *Slavery: A Problem in American Institutional and Intellectual Life* (Chicago, 1959), pp. 43-52; C. Duncan Rice, *The Rise and Fall of Black Slavery* (London, 1975), pp. 1, 44-6, 61-2. For a perceptive comment on the role of "capitalism" in New World settlement, see Lewis Mumford, *The Human Prospect* (Boston, 1955), pp. 191-201.

[3] Of course Europeans were subjected to various forms of more limited bondage, such as indentured servitude, but there was a great difference between these and chattel slavery which, at least in the Americas, was confined strictly to non-Europeans. It is, however, notable that even those historians who emphasize racial and cultural factors do not deny the importance of economic motives; see, for example, Winthrop D. Jordan, *White Over Black: American Attitudes Towards the Negro, 1550-1812* (Chapel Hill, N.C., 1968), p. 47.

equally strong economic motives for wanting to get rid of it. This might happen in the event of the supply of labour exceeding the demand to such an extent that the trouble and expense of maintaining a servile labour force no longer seemed worthwhile. Or it could happen in the opposite situation where the need for labour outran the supply so that employers either began poaching on one another by encouraging runaways, or alternatively joined together in a general act of manumission in the hope of attracting free labour.[4] Historically speaking, there are many examples of just such situations arising.[5] The difficulty is that, by and large, this is not what happened in the Americas. It is tempting to speculate as to whether, in the course of time, such situations *would* have arisen there. Modern predictions that, regardless of political circumstances, the days of slavery were numbered, are mostly based on some such calculation.[6] But for present purposes this is beside the point. The fact is that with notably few exceptions what ended New World slavery was not the beneficent working of economic forces — the invisible hand of Adam Smith — but the intervention of the state.

This does not, obviously, mean that economic considerations played no part in the process. Nevertheless, it does make the task of proving that they did exceedingly difficult. Not only must we first identify the economic motives for attacking slavery but we must further show how in practice these were translated into political actions and finally into specific legislative acts.

It also raises, in an unusually intractable form, the problem of distinguishing between different kinds of motive. As Roger Anstey has recently shown with respect to the 1806 Act abolishing the British slave trade to foreign and captured territories, humanitarians

[4] Stanley Engerman, "Some Considerations Relating to Property Rights in Man", *Jl. Econ. Hist.*, xxxiii (1973), pp. 43-65.

[5] W. L. Westermann, *The Slave Systems of Greek and Roman Antiquity* (Philadelphia, 1955), p. 120; Marc Bloch, "The Decline in Slavery", in *Cambridge Economic History of Europe*, i, 2nd edn. (Cambridge, 1966), pp. 246-53; Maurice Dobb, *Studies in the Development of Capitalism* (London, 1946), pp. 48-70. In the case of Cuba, the cutting off of the American slave trade after 1865 encouraged slaveholders to free their capital to invest in labour-saving machinery and in coolies. Similar changes were also, apparently, occurring in Brazil. In both instances, however, the transition from a slave to a free labour system was accompanied by political turmoil. Herbert S. Klein, *Slavery in the Americas: A Comparative Study of Virginia and Cuba* (Chicago, 1967), pp. 256-8; Rice, *op. cit.*, pp. 370-5. For an example of a peaceful transition occasioned by the demand for labour outrunning the supply, see Baron F. Duckham, "Serfdom in Eighteenth-Century Scotland", *History*, liv (1969), pp. 178-97.

[6] "In the absence of the Civil War, slavery in the United States could have lasted only a few more years. For, in a relatively short time, industrialization and rising living standards in the North, together with improving communications, would have made it increasingly difficult to keep the slaves in the fields": John Kenneth Galbraith, *The New Industrial State* (Harmondsworth, 1969), p. 142.

were capable of being just as devious as their opponents.[7] (What they did on that occasion was deliberately to suppress the moral argument side of their case and play up the national interest side.) This was by no means an isolated instance. Once the issue of slavery ceased to be a matter of reckoning profit and loss and became a struggle over government policy, the protagonists, not surprisingly, began using whatever arguments came to hand. As anyone familiar with the debates will testify, it is no more unusual to find humanitarians using economic arguments than to find their opponents using humanitarian ones.

But if we cannot decide the issue simply by totting-up arguments we can perhaps get somewhere by identifying the groups involved. Here what we find is that virtually without exception the principal defenders of slavery were, in fact, the slaveholders themselves. By contrast, those who spearheaded the attack on slavery were almost invariably men with no direct economic stake in the institution. On examination, a very high proportion of these turn out to have been Quakers or members of other religious groups which preached the exercise of disinterested benevolence as a means of bringing about necessary social reforms. And if we look at the careers of these individuals we are apt to find that although slavery was often their principal reform interest it was seldom their only one. This was the case not only in Britain and the United States but also in France, Denmark, Holland and even Brazil. Typically they belonged to interlocking networks of organizations devoted to temperance, women's rights, penal reform, peace, hydropathy — in fact to benefiting mankind in almost every way imaginable.[8]

These abolitionists had few doubts as to the nature of the contest in which they were engaged. It was a struggle between morality and entrenched economic interest. They were acting from disinterested motives, their opponents, the slaveholders, from motives of self-interest. It was so obvious there was no call for discussion. And in retrospect they saw no need to discuss it. The success of their movement represented the triumph of high moral principles over narrow sectional interests. The moral David had slain the economic Goliath.[9]

[7] Roger Anstey, *The Atlantic Slave Trade and British Abolition, 1760-1810* (London, 1975), pp. 364-90. For other examples of political disingenuousness, see Howard Temperley, *British Antislavery, 1833-1870* (London and Columbia, S.C., 1972), pp. 137-61, 176-82.

[8] Anstey, *op. cit.*, pp. 157-235; Temperley, *op. cit.*, pp. 66-84, 184-91; David Brion Davis, *The Problem of Slavery in Western Culture* (Ithaca, N.Y., 1966), pp. 291 ff.; G. H. Barnes, *The Anti-Slavery Impulse, 1830-1844* (New York, 1933), pp. 3-58; D. L. Dumond, *Antislavery: The Crusade for Freedom in America* (Ann Arbor, 1961), pp. 158-203.

[9] Thomas Clarkson, *A History of the Rise, Progress and Accomplishment of the Abolition of the African Slave Trade*, 2 vols. (London, 1808); W. P. and F. J. Garrison, *William Lloyd Garrison, 1805-1879*, 4 vols. (New York, 1885-9).

It is easy to see why they should have believed this. It is also easy to see why, for so long, historians were prepared to accept their explanation. It is, to begin with, an admirably straightforward explanation. It was also one that fitted in remarkably well with the assumptions of the Whig school. Economic interests built up the slave systems; the application of enlightened principles destroyed them.[10]

Yet it is not without its problems. After all, it was not the abolitionists who destroyed slavery but their governments. Even admitting, as on the whole we must, that abolitionists were acting for the reasons they claimed, it by no means follows that those who controlled the affairs of these governments were acting from the same motives. Doubts on this score are reinforced if we look at other policies adopted by these bodies, which were not generally unmindful of the need to foster entrepreneurial activity. If the abolition of slavery represented the triumph of the heart over the head this was by no means characteristic of the policies adopted by these governments generally.

The paradox is sharpened if we look at these struggles in historical perspective. One way of defining a capitalist society is to say that it is a society in which ordinary social functions are subordinated to the laws of the market. Judged by this standard the slave societies of the New World rank among the most thoroughgoing capitalist societies of which we have record. Not only was labour a commodity but so indeed were the labourers themselves. What needs to be explained is why this system should have come under attack precisely at a time — the latter part of the eighteenth century — when, so we are told, the market ethic was emerging triumphant and Western society as a whole was itself becoming an appendage of the market.[11] Moreover, if we look at the countries primarily concerned we find that they were precisely those at the forefront of this capitalist revolution and further that, within these countries, it was the middle classes, in other words those who are seen as the protagonists of the nascent market economy, who were leading the attack.

Considerations such as these have led, over the years, to a succession of revisionist accounts. It is true that these have not, generally speaking, presented the matter in quite such global terms. The idea that the individual national struggles constituted, in some sense, a broadly based international contest is, historiographically speaking, a recent development, although the idea that this was what

[10] Reginald Coupland, *The British Anti-Slavery Movement* (London, 1933), pp. 111, 250-1; G. M. Trevelyan, *English Social History* (London, 1942), pp. 495-7.
[11] For a description of these changes, see Karl Polanyi, *The Great Transformation* (New York, 1944), pp. 40-1, 71, 128-9, 133.

was happening was familiar enough to the participants themselves. Nevertheless, the fact that they chose to describe the question in national rather than international contexts did not prevent revisionists from drawing general conclusions. So, as early as 1903, we have the American Marxist critic, A. M. Simons, putting the issue in terms of rival economies seeking dominance:

> By 1850 a class began to appear, national in scope, compact in organization, definite in its desires and destined soon to seize the reins of political power. This was the capitalist class .... Once that capitalist class had wrested the national government from the chattel slave holders there was nothing for them [the slaveholders] to do but to secede. The margin of profits in chattel slavery was already too narrow to permit its continuance in competition with wage slavery unless the chattel slave owners controlled the national government. The Civil War therefore was simply a contest to secure possession of the "big stick" of the national government.[11]

A generation later, Charles and Mary Beard presented a non-Marxian version of the economic argument by translating the struggle over slavery into a conflict between aggressive Northern industrialism and Southern agrarianism, which had the rather paradoxical effect of making the slavemasters appear to be fighting on the side of democracy:

> ... the southward pressure of the capitalistic glacier ... conspired to assure the ultimate triumph of what orators were fond of calling "the free labour system". This was a dynamic thrust far too powerful for planters operating in a limited territory with incompetent labour on soil of limited fertility. Those who swept forward with it, exulting in the approaching triumph of machine industry, warned the planters of their ultimate subjection.[13]

Perhaps because the slavery issue was of less central concern to the British, a revisionist interpretation of the struggles over West Indian slavery was longer in coming but, when one finally did arrive, with the publication of Eric Williams's *Capitalism and Slavery* (1944), its message was no less emphatic:

> The capitalists had first encouraged West Indian slavery and then helped to destroy it. When British capitalism depended on the West Indies, they ignored slavery or defended it. When British capitalism found the West Indian monopoly a nuisance, they destroyed West Indian slavery as a first step in the destruction of West Indian monopoly.[14]

Thus baldly stated, Williams's thesis was even simpler than that of the traditionalists. Where they had seen two elements in conflict— the economic interests which supported West Indian slavery and the humanitarian interests which were attacking it — he saw only one. "The very vested interests which had been built up by the slave system now turned and destroyed that system .... The rise and fall of mercantilism is the rise and fall of slavery".[15]

[11] A. M. Simons, *Class Struggles in America* (New York, 1903), pp. 62-7.
[13] C. A. and M. R. Beard, *The Rise of American Civilization*, 2 vols. (New York, 1927), ii, pp. 6-7.
[14] Eric Williams, *Capitalism and Slavery* (Chapel Hill, N.C., 1944), p. 169.
[15] *Ibid.*, p. 136.

Considering that these accounts relate to two societies for which the slavery struggle had very different implications it is remarkable how many features they have in common. One is a deliberate playing down of the abolitionists and of the humanitarian side of the struggle generally. According to Simons, the Republican "indictment is never of slavery, but always of the South as a ruling section". According to the Beards the abolitionist creed was held in such low esteem that: "Nobody but agitators, beneath the contempt of the towering statesmen of the age, ever dared to advocate it". According to Williams the importance of the abolitionists had "been seriously misunderstood and grossly exaggerated".[16]

Secondly, they were much impressed by the growing power of "the new industrial interests" which "reached down into the Mississippi Valley", the "economic structure of machine industry" which "towered high above agriculture", the Lancashire Gulliver that the West Indian "Lilliputians could not hold down". By contrast, they saw the old-fashioned slave regimes as already in decline. Even in the United States it was a question of "the margin of profits", "diminishing fertility" and "incompetent labour", while in the West Indies the system had become "so unprofitable that for this reason alone its destruction was inevitable".[17]

Yet, in spite of this, none of the three regarded industrial capitalism and slavery as inherently antagonistic. The real issues were railroads, homesteads, bounties, subsidies and, above all, tariffs. Basically it was a struggle between a rising bourgeoisie and a declining plantocracy. Given a willingness on the part of the slaveholders to concede at the outset what the bourgeoisie wanted, there was no logical reason why they should not have been allowed to keep their peculiar institution. Of the three, Williams is the one who comes closest to assigning an independent role to the abolitionists when he credits them with speaking "a language that the masses could understand". Yet even he categorically denies that they would have succeeded "but for the defection of the capitalists from the ranks of the slaveholders and slave traders".[18]

Waiving for the moment the very big question of whether this was actually what these struggles were about it may be noted that in one respect the revisionists scored over the traditionalists in that they did at least try to relate the controversy over slavery to what they took to be the major economic developments of the day. Yet on closer examination their case turns out to be altogether less impressive than

---

[16] Simons, *op. cit.*, pp. 62-7; Beard, *op. cit.*, p. 38; Williams, *op. cit.*, p. 178. In fact, antislavery was one of the few issues on which the Republicans *were* united. See Eric Foner, *Free Soil, Free Labor, Free Men: The Ideology of the Republican Party before the Civil War* (New York, 1970), p. 304.

[17] Simons, *op. cit.*, pp. 62-7; Beard, *op. cit.*, pp. 6-7; Williams, *op. cit.*, p. 135.

[18] *Ibid.*, p. 136.

their rhetoric suggests. Certainly anyone hoping for some cosmic explanation of why slavery disappeared will be disappointed. For what in the end we are left with are mostly familiar chestnuts — tariffs, bounties and so on. Many of these were minor issues and some were not issues at all.

Williams is particularly vulnerable. For him the great issue was the West Indian sugar monopoly. "When British capitalism found the West Indian monopoly a nuisance, they destroyed West Indian slavery as a first step in the destruction of West Indian monopoly". Yet Williams's evidence that monopoly was regarded as a nuisance comes entirely from the period *after* slavery had been destroyed. In the debates over the emancipation bill the issue of monopoly was raised only once, by E. G. Stanley, who effectively disposed of it by pointing out that the West Indians did not have an effective monopoly:

> The quantity of sugar now imported annually into this country exceeds the demand by 1,000,000 cwt., and the consequence necessarily is, that the monopoly is practically and in effect a dead letter. The price in our markets is determined by the price they can obtain for the surplus abroad.[19]

This was a perfectly fair statement of the case. In the early 1830s sugar prices on the London market were lower than at any time in living memory. The difference between British West Indian and Cuban prices never amounted to more than a few percentage points and sometimes, as in 1829 and 1832, the British article was actually cheaper. British consumers had no reason for complaint. Monopoly only became an issue when, as a result of abolition, production declined, sales to the continent ceased and prices rose. By 1841 the British were buying their sugar at more than double the world market price. It was not the attack on monopoly that led to the attack on slavery, but the attack on slavery that led to the attack on monopoly.[20]

The claim that Northern capitalists in the United States found the political influence of Southerners a nuisance is less easily disposed of, since, quite plainly, some did. Yet it requires a certain act of faith, as well as a high degree of selectivity, to maintain that tariffs, internal improvements and the price of Western lands, rather than slavery, were the major issues, or even the major *underlying* issues, of the ante-bellum years. And against such inconvenience as Northerners suffered as a result of Southern policies must be set the substantial advantages which they derived from their connections with the South, a fact to which Southerners themselves bore eloquent testimony. Northern cotton manufacturers were dependent on Southern plantation agriculture for their raw materials. New

[19] *Hansard*, 3rd ser., xvii, col. 1,210 (14 May 1833).
[20] *Return of the Quantities of Sugar Imported into the United Kingdom from 1800 to 1852*, Parliamentary Papers, 1852-3 (461), xcix, pp. 567-9.

York finance houses provided Southerners with much of their capital and reaped their reward in interest. New England shippers carried the South's cotton to the factories of Europe and the North. According to Jefferson Davis the North was living like a vulture on the prosperity of the South. High on the South's list of grievances against the North was a belief that it was doing altogether too well out of its Southern connection.[11]

Not least among the advantages which Northerners enjoyed was the fact of being linked to what we have often been told was a highly profitable system of agriculture, which gave the United States something close to a monopoly (80 per cent) of the world production of raw cotton — a monopoly which she lost as a result of the Civil War and never wholly regained. Although scholars may argue about the cost-efficiency of this system as compared with Northern farming, few would nowadays doubt that the return on investment was generally enough, and often more than enough, for it to remain economically viable. On this point at least, Fogel and Engerman and their critics are agreed.[12] Now if these scholars are correct about American plantation agriculture, what about other slave systems? In a forthcoming study of British West Indian trade, Seymour Drescher of the University of Pittsburgh argues that historians have been quite wrong to assume that the importance of the West Indies to the mother country began to decline around the time of the American Revolution.[13] Using official trade figures he shows that quite the opposite was the case. Far from declining, trade with the West Indies continued to increase up to 1807 and even beyond. This was reflected in both import and export figures and represents not simply an absolute growth in West Indian commerce but an increase relative to British overseas trade as a whole. In short, the whole idea of West Indian decline is a myth, at least as it has been applied to the period up to 1820. Drescher does not carry

[11] Thomas P. Kettell, *Southern Wealth and Northern Profits* (New York, 1860); Charles S. Sydnor, *The Development of Southern Sectionalism, 1819-1848* (Baton Rouge, 1948), pp. 144-56, 177-221; Avery O. Craven, *The Growth of Southern Nationalism, 1848-1861* (Baton Rouge, 1953), pp. 246-82. For Northern views of the matter, see Philip S. Foner, *Business and Slavery: The New York Merchants and the Irrepressible Conflict* (Chapel Hill, N.C., 1940).

[12] Kenneth M. Stampp, *The Peculiar Institution: Slavery in the Ante-Bellum South* (New York, 1956), pp. 383-418; Alfred H. Conrad and John R. Meyer, *The Economics of Slavery and Other Studies in Econometric History* (Chicago, 1964), pp. 43-92; Robert William Fogel and Stanley L. Engerman, *Time on the Cross: The Economics of American Negro Slavery*, 2 vols. (Boston, 1974), i, pp. 59-70. A useful guide to the debate over slave profitability is Hugh G. J. Aitken, *Did Slavery Pay: Readings in the Economics of Black Slavery in the United States* (Boston, 1971). For a brief survey of the cost-efficiency issue, see Thomas L. Haskell, "The True & Tragical History of 'Time on the Cross' ", *New York Review of Books*, xxii (2 Oct. 1975), pp. 33-9.

[13] Seymour Drescher, *A Case of Econocide: Economic Development and the Abolition of the British Slave Trade* (Pittsburgh, 1977). I am extremely grateful to Professor Drescher for allowing me to consult this work in manuscript.

his study significantly beyond that date. However, using his figures in conjunction with D. Eltis's figures on the inter-colonial slave trade a wholly new picture emerges.[14] The economic problems of the West Indies, it begins to appear, were not the result of the inherent weakness and inefficiency of the slave system but of external influences brought to bear on it. Specifically, they were the consequences of a declining labour force brought about by the 1807 abolition of the slave trade and of the subsequent imposition of restrictions which prevented planters from transferring those slaves they had from the older colonies to the virgin lands of Trinidad and Guiana. In short, it begins to look as if Britain's planters found themselves in very much the position American planters would have been in had their labour force declined and had they been compelled to confine their operations to the eastern seaboard.

Pursuing the same line of argument we may note just how catastrophic the drop in West Indian sugar production actually was in the years following emancipation. This drop did not occur immediately because for the first four years, from 1834 to 1838, the freedmen were employed as apprentices — a status which, as the abolitionists were quick to point out, did not differ in any of its essentials from slavery, except that the hours of labour were somewhat reduced. During these four years total sugar production declined by only 10 per cent. But thereafter it declined very sharply indeed. Comparing production in the years 1839-46 with production in 1824-33, the overall drop was 36 per cent. On some of the smaller islands where there was no alternative but to work on the plantations the decline was less marked than in the larger colonies. In Barbados and Antigua it actually increased. But in Jamaica, where the freedmen were able to drift away into the mountains, production dropped by 50 per cent.[25]

If British statesmen were surprised by these developments, they had no right to be. This was what the planters had all along said would happen. Once the discipline of slavery was removed the Negroes would cease to labour, or at best would labour only intermittently. The immediate consequence of this was that the price to British consumers would go up and actual consumption would go down. Alexander Baring, head of the financial house of Baring Brothers and Co., was in no doubt that the effect of abolition:

> would be to double, nay to treble the price of sugar on the home market. Pray, were they prepared to treble the price of sugar to the people of England? Was the country prepared to pay 6,000,000l. annually ... for the pleasure of performing costly experiments in humanity?[26]

[14] D. Eltis, "The Traffic in Slaves between the British West Indian Colonies, 1807-1833", *Econ. Hist. Rev.*, xxx (1972), pp. 55-64.

[15] P. D. Curtin, *Two Jamaicas: The Role of Ideas in a Tropical Colony* (Cambridge, Mass., 1955), pp. 104-9.

[16] *Hansard*, 3rd ser., xviii, col. 493 (7 June 1833).

The same point was made by many other speakers, including Sir Richard Vyvyan, M.P. for Bristol, who went on to draw the obvious conclusion that if, in the future, the British people wanted sugar they would have to turn elsewhere, "the consequence [of which] would be a bounty upon the slave labour of foreign colonies, such as the Brazils and the Spanish islands".[27] In the Lords, the duke of Wellington expressed himself with characteristic bluntness:

> It was impossible not to apprehend serious evils from immediate emancipation .... If the West-India trade were abandoned, whence could we get sugar? Only from slave colonies, which were at this moment carrying on the slave trade .... It would seem we were going to do this, to sacrifice slaves and masters, and colonies, at an expense of losing 7,000,000l. of revenue. Such conduct appeared to him to be little, if at all, better than insanity.[28]

What is so striking reading the 1833 debates, and the same applies to the 1806-7 debates over the slave trade, is how often the opponents of abolition were in the event proved right. To be sure, some of their more alarmist claims proved wide of the mark. The blacks did not rise up in rebellion as in Santo Domingo. But on the specifically economic consequences of government policies events more often than not bore them out. British withdrawal *did* lead to an increase in the foreign slave trade from which the colonies of Britain's rivals *did* profit; the abolition of slavery *did* lead to a drastic falling off in production, prices *did* rise, consumption *did* decline, and in the end Britain *did*, despite strenuous protests from the abolitionists, turn to Cuba and Brazil, whose imports of slaves from Africa *did*, in consequence, rise.[29]

It is not possible to attribute quite the same degree of percipience to American slaveholders since in the event abolition was the result not of measured deliberation but of war. Nevertheless, the idea that the slavery issue, if taken up and pressed far enough, would lead to war was commonly held by men of all sections.[30] We also find, for example in Southern responses to West Indian emancipation, accounts of what might happen to the South if ever similar measures were applied there which accord very closely with what actually did happen. In 1848 a committee of Southern Congressmen pictured a broken and impoverished South governed by an alliance of

[27] *Ibid.*, col. 123 (30 May 1833).
[28] *Ibid.*, 3rd ser., xvii, col. 838 (2 May 1833).
[29] Temperley, *British Antislavery*, pp. 43-9, 137-67, 270; W. L. Mathieson, *Great Britain and the Slave Trade, 1839-1865* (London, 1929), pp. 1-27, 75-113; Christopher Lloyd, *The Navy and the Slave Trade: The Suppression of the African Slave Trade in the Nineteenth Century* (London, 1949), pp. 1, 24-7, 101-3; P. D. Curtin, *The Atlantic Slave Trade: A Census* (Madison, 1969), pp. 31-49, 231-64, 265-73.
[30] Lorman Ratner, *Powder Keg: Northern Opposition to the Anti-Slavery Movement, 1831-1840* (New York, 1968), pp. 35-64; Sydnor, *Development of Southern Sectionalism*, pp. 130-2; John Hope Franklin, *The Militant South* (Cambridge, Mass., 1956), *passim*.

Northern radicals and freed blacks.[31] Altogether the slavery issue had much more catastrophic implications for Americans than it could conceivably have had for the British.

So we are left wondering why responsible men, men with their nation's economic and political interests at heart, were prepared to go along with the abolitionists. The economic arguments for attacking slavery were, as we have seen, remarkably flimsy. Far from being on the point of collapse, it appears to have been as hale and hearty as ever. The economic historians have thus effectively removed one leg of the revisionist argument. The other leg, the notion that *somehow* industrial capitalism was hostile to slavery, never amounted to much since the revisionists were prone to exaggerate the extent to which interests conflicted while ignoring the degree to which they were mutually supportive. The burden of my remarks so far has been to suggest that they conflicted surprisingly little and that, by providing cheap raw materials, slavery actually served industry very well. So what can have possessed Parliament and Congress?

One possible explanation is that the traditionalists have been right all along and that abolition had nothing to do with economics except in so far as economic interest was a factor to be overcome. Yet if this is the explanation it points to other conclusions which are, to put it mildly, a little odd. Here we have a system — a highly successful system — of large-scale capitalist agriculture, mass producing raw materials for sale in distant markets, growing up at a time when most production was still small-scale and designed to meet the needs of local consumers. But precisely at a time when capitalist ideas were in the ascendant, and large-scale production of all kinds of goods was beginning, we find this system being dismantled. How could this happen unless "capitalism" had something to do with it? If our reasoning leads to the conclusion that "capitalism" had nothing to do with it the chances are that there is something wrong with our reasoning.

This may, indeed, be so. Looking back on the discussion so far you will see that, like the revisionists, I have been using the terms "capitalism" and "economic interest" as though they were interchangeable. This may or may not have been justified, but it is certainly not the only way of defining capitalism. The word itself did not enter English usage until the 1850s, so we do not have any contemporary usages to which we can refer back. But since then it has acquired a great variety of meanings. Often it is applied to any modern society which is not emphatically socialist. In a recent review

[31] Thomas Hart Benton, *Thirty Years View: or, A History of the Working of the American Government . . ., 1820–1850*, 2 vols. (New York, 1857), i, pp. 734-5.

of Raymond Williams's *The Country and the City*, E. P. Thompson
goes even further by arguing that over the last four centuries:

> Capitalism, like sin, is ever present; and if field laborers may escape the
> moralist's lash, since they are always in the last analysis the exploited,
> every other class, and its culture, becomes in some way contaminated by its
> covert or overt association with sin.[21]

Generally speaking, however, the term is used in a more limited way.
First, it is commonly used to describe the workings of a free market
economy — buying low, selling high, investing private capital and
effort wherever they will produce the most profit. Secondly, it is
used to describe the ideology or system of beliefs of those who believe
in the encouragement of such activities. Associated with it we
commonly find notions about minimal government, a common system
of law, the promotion of individual self-interest and the removal,
so far as the proper maintenance of social order will allow, of all
restrictions which might prevent men from benefiting themselves
and, incidentally, benefiting society, by making free use of their
capital and labour. Finally, capitalism is a term used to describe
the kind of society which, in the eyes of its critics, those beliefs and
practices actually produced — wage slavery, unemployment, the
cash nexus as the ultimate arbiter in human affairs, the ruthless
subordination of some classes to others.

If we are to get to grips with the issue of capitalism and slavery an
obvious first essential is to decide which of these definitions we are
using. So far I have used only the first, the free market economy
version. But if we look at the second, and think of capitalism as an
ideology, a whole new range of possibilities comes into view.[22]

The obvious place to start is with the works of the classical
economists. They, after all, were the theoreticians of capitalism.
I do not mean that they invented it, for what produced capitalism
was the march of events. What the economists did was to describe
and, in a sense, to legitimize something which had already been
going on for a long time. For present purposes, what is important

---

[21] *New York Review of Books*, xxii (6 Feb. 1975), p. 36.
[22] Some of these are described in David Brion Davis's *The Problem of Slavery
in the Age of Revolution, 1770-1823* (Ithaca, N.Y., 1975). Following on from
his *The Problem of Slavery in Western Culture*, this is by far the best account
there is of the intellectual origins of the antislavery movement. Yet it appears
that Davis is not quite certain in his own mind which definition of capitalism he
is using. In his precise and brilliant exposition of the views of individual
thinkers, many of which were highly idiosyncratic, he is plainly using the second
version. But to the extent that he accepts Antonio Gramsci's notion of "class
hegemony" and attributes British concern over slavery to unconscious guilt
aroused by labour conditions at home (which he sees as being "psychologically
displaced in a concern for the 'unfortunate slave' "), he is using the third, or
Marxist, version. Like all theories which depend heavily on psychological
inference these are hard either to prove or disprove. Davis, *The Problem of
Slavery in the Age of Revolution*, pp. 254, 348-50, 361-2, 366, 384, 421.

about them is what they reflected rather than what they taught, although in the long run that was important too.

Now one of the things they reflected was a general hostility towards slavery. According to Adam Smith: "The experience of all ages and nations ... demonstrates that the work done by slaves, though it appears to cost only their maintenance, is in the end the dearest of any".[34] This is patently untrue. At least it is patently untrue unless we imagine some other form of labour which, given the circumstances, was neither available nor in prospect. Thus Smith's statement is not only at odds with what modern scholarship has revealed about Negro slavery — and, incidentally, about other more recent systems of coerced labour[35] — but fails to accord with facts perfectly well known at the time he was writing. So what can have led him to make such an assertion?

If we look at the evidence he cites one thing is immediately clear: it is not based on any sort of cost analysis. This is surprising because elsewhere in *The Wealth of Nations* he shows himself perfectly capable of reckoning profit and loss. The evidence he actually cites is of two kinds. First, he provides a series of rather vague references to Russia, Poland, Hungary, Bohemia, Moravia, ancient Greece and Rome, and medieval Europe, as well as to the British West Indian and North American colonies. For an eighteenth-century scholar this is not surprising. What is more than a little curious, however, is the way he lumps all these systems together as though they were the same thing. To be sure he does say that sugar and tobacco cultivation could be profitable. But they are profitable only because of the intrinsic value of the product, rather as someone who found a mountain of gold would manage to make a profit by digging into it although he employed only octogenarians. Nowhere is there any indication that he distinguishes in his own mind between the expanding capitalist systems of the Americas and the still largely feudal systems of eastern Europe.

The second type of evidence he cites helps to explain *why* he failed to make this distinction. Slave labour was expensive because:

> A person who can acquire no property, can have no other interest but to eat as much, and to labour as little as possible. Whatever work he does beyond what is sufficient to purchase his own maintenance, can be squeezed out of him by violence only, and not by any interest of his own.[36]

This is a general theory of human motivation, and it goes far towards explaining why the classical economists were hostile to slavery. In fact it is quite wrong. There were many reasons why slaves should

[34] Adam Smith, *The Wealth of Nations*, ed. Edwin Cannan, 2 vols. (London, 1904), i, p. 364.
[35] See, for example, Edward L. Homze, *Foreign Labour in Nazi Germany* (Princeton, 1967), pp. 262-3, 308-9.
[36] Smith, *op. cit.*, i, p. 364.

work, apart from the application of external forms of coercion. In large part they were the same reasons which people have for labouring under any system — an ambition to raise themselves in their own estimation and that of others and a desire for whatever benefits, in the form of material reward or status, the system allowed. Under slavery the benefits for which it was reasonable to aim might be very severely circumscribed, but plainly they existed. Also, the fact that rewards are limited does not mean that men will not compete enthusiastically — or desperately — for them. All this Adam Smith ignores. Instead he gives us a crude theory which singles out one factor, the desire to acquire property, as the principal motive for labour.

Yet it was a theory on which, particularly because of its emphasis on property, eighteenth- and early nineteenth-century economic thinkers set great store. This does not, however, fully explain why, with the evidence of planter fortunes around them, they should have accepted such a notion. After all, there was no law which said that tobacco and sugar had to be produced by slaves. If it could have been produced more cheaply by free labour then, presumably, some-one would have set about doing so. Why was not this taken into account?

The explanation lies in the classical economists' assumption that freedom and prosperity went hand in hand. This happy conjunction existed because the most favourable conditions for creating wealth were those which gave men the greatest freedom to invest their energies in those activities which would earn them the highest rewards and which allowed them the most security in the enjoyment of those rewards once they had been earned:

> The natural effort of every individual to better his own conditions, when suffered to exert itself with freedom and security, is so powerful a principle, that it is alone, and without any assistance, not only capable of carrying on the society to wealth and prosperity, but of surmounting a hundred impertinent obstructions with which the folly of human laws too often incumbers its operations.[37]

This had been the British experience. Enjoying a larger measure of liberty than other people they had also attained a higher degree of wealth. It had also been the experience of Britain's North American colonists who, being freer to go their own way, had in due course outstripped their French, Spanish and Portuguese rivals. And it had also been the experience of other nations throughout history which, to the extent that they had encouraged initiative and provided security, had seen their material prosperity increase. The same laws that governed the affairs of nations also applied to individual enterprises. The greater the freedom allowed, the higher the likeli-hood of success. Although slavery was the dearest form of labour its

[37] *Ibid.*, ii, p. 43.

expense diminished to the degree that slaves were accorded the privileges of free servants. Thus Smith's hostility to slavery was a natural extension of his general belief in economic freedom, the beneficent effects of which could be observed in all societies at all levels.[38]

For abolitionists to turn such notions to polemical use was not difficult. Although they rejected the belief that it was self-interest rather than benevolence that made men labour for the benefit of others there was much in the new economic thought that they found congenial. They too were impressed by the growing prosperity of England. Whatever the sufferings of England's poor they hardly compared with those occasioned by slavery. According to James Stephen in *Dangers of the Country*, a work specifically designed to promote parliamentary support for the general abolition bill of 1807, Britain's treatment of Negroes was intolerable because:

> For our plenty we give them want; for our ease, intolerable toil; for our wealth, privation of the right of property; for our equal laws, unbridled violence and wrong. Science shines upon us with her meridian beams; yet we keep these degraded fellow-creatures in the deepest shadows of ignorance and barbarity. Morals and manners have happily distinguished us from the other nations of Europe; yet we create and cherish in two other quarters of the globe an unexampled depravity of both.[39]

That the British enjoyed such good fortune was by no means unconnected with the fact that they possessed what, earlier in the same passage, he describes as an "unexampled portion of civil liberty". In the past the British too had languished in poverty under tyrannous regimes but those days were happily gone. Freedom, and with it wealth and happiness, had prevailed.

This was very much what Adam Smith had said. It was also the message which, in debate after debate, the abolitionists hammered home. Freedom meant prosperity; freedom meant progress; freedom meant having willing workers as opposed to unwilling ones. Abolish the slave trade and the planters, no longer able to treat their bondsmen as expendable, would be compelled to behave more humanely; this, in turn, would cause production to rise so that, stage by stage, greater liberality being followed by larger yields, piecemeal and ultimately complete emancipation would occur.[40] Needless to say, nothing of the sort happened. This did not, however, disconcert the abolitionists, who put it down to the intransigence of the planters and their inability to recognize where their real interest lay.[41] In the 1833 debates, James Silk Buckingham, the new M.P. for Sheffield, provided the House with:

[38] *Ibid.*, pp. 73, 88.
[39] James Stephen, *The Dangers of the Country* (London, 1807), p. 195.
[40] Clarkson, *History of the Abolition of the Slave Trade*, i, pp. 284-6.
[41] Thomas Clarkson, *Thoughts on the Necessity of Improving the Conditions of the Slaves in the British Colonies* (London, 1823).

proofs, which were ample and authentic, of the perfect practicability and entire safety of the immediate transition from slavery to freedom, and of the superior productiveness and efficiency of free labour over slave labour wherever it had been tried.[42]

If anyone doubted this, then let him look to Britain. If anyone doubted that the Negroes would work let him note the British experience that love of wealth became "more and more intense in proportion to the amount of the property possessed". Freedom would encourage them to acquire knowledge, which would stimulate new material needs (including a desire for British manufactures) and so spur them on to greater effort. In due course "all the arts and elegances of life would progressively be substituted for the rude materials now in use among them".[43] A number of speakers, including several unconnected with the West India lobby, regarded this as wishful thinking. For the benefit of these, abolitionists did not hesitate to employ another weapon drawn from the armoury of the classical economists. "If the negro became an idler", declared Daniel O'Connell, "let him share the fate of the idler — let him perish".[44]

The persistence of these beliefs, despite accumulating evidence of the freedmen's capacity to withdraw their labour without perishing, is remarkable. From the abolitionists' point of view the facts could hardly have been more embarrassing. What made them particularly disconcerting, however, was their bearing on two other issues. One of these was the plan to make the West Indies a philanthropical show-piece in order to persuade other countries — and, in particular, the United States — to follow Britain's example. American abolitionists were continually demanding reassurance that emancipation was proving a success.[45] Of more pressing concern, however, was the growing demand in the country, now that British West Indian sugar was becoming prohibitively expensive, for the cheaper Cuban and Brazilian variety. This was something which, because of its implications for the Atlantic slave trade, the London Committee opposed. As a result, letters poured into the office from correspondents who wanted to know why, instead of free labour driving slave labour off the market, exactly the opposite was happening. Many of these, it turned out, were from provincial supporters

[42] *Hansard*, 3rd ser., xviii, cols. 475-6 (7 June 1833).
[43] *Ibid.*, cols. 476, 482 (7 June 1833).
[44] *Ibid.*, col. 314 (3 June 1833).
[45] Temperley, *British Antislavery*, pp. 114-19. When the British failed to provide reassurance American abolitionists did not hesitate to invent evidence to prove that emancipation *was* a success. See Ralph Waldo Emerson, *An Address Delivered in the Court House in Concord, Massachusetts, on the 1st August, 1844, on the Anniversary of the Emancipation of the Negroes in the British West Indies* (Boston, 1844), pp. 4, 30; William Lloyd Garrison, *West Indian Emancipation: A Speech Delivered in Abingdon, Massachusetts, on the First Day of August 1854* (Boston, 1854), p. 40.

who had genuinely believed that emancipation would promptly be followed by a massive increase in production. Yet despite the evidence, the London Committee never abandoned its belief in the superior efficacy of free labour. Initially it ascribed the decline in sugar production to bad weather conditions; later, when weather conditions improved, to necessary readjustments, unenlightened management, exhausted soils and other exceptional circumstances.[46] One suspects that had staple production ceased altogether this fact would not have been thought to reflect on the general proposition that free labour was more efficient than slave labour.

That the British public had not lost faith in this proposition either is suggested by the enthusiastic reception given to J. E. Cairnes's *The Slave Power: Its Character, Career, and Probable Designs*, first published in 1862. Professor Cairnes was an economist of the classical school and a disciple of John Stuart Mill, to whom he dedicated his work. Although the popular interest it aroused owed much to its topicality, this was not the aspect which most impressed reviewers. "In selecting the subject of North American slavery", he wrote in his preface, "I was influenced in the first instance by considerations of a purely speculative kind — my object being to show that the course of history is largely determined by the action of economic forces".[47] What is most interesting, however, is his account of his method, not so much for what it shows about his own attitudes as for what it reveals about the scholarly tradition which he represented:

> The comparative anatomist, by reasoning on those fixed relations between the different parts of the animal frame which his science reveals to him, is able from a fragment of a tooth or bone to determine the form, dimensions, and habits of the creature to which it belonged; and with no less accuracy, it seems to me, may a political economist, by reasoning on the economic character of slavery and its peculiar connexion with the soil, deduce its leading social and political attributes, and almost construct, by way of *a priori* argument, the entire system of the society of which it forms the foundation.[48]

There is no reason for supposing that contemporaries regarded this statement as remarkable. They saw its author as being — as indeed he was — an intelligent and erudite scholar, well-versed in the literature of his subject, and thus exceptionally well-placed to give an informed opinion. It appears to have occurred to none of the reviewers that, given his method, the outcome was bound to be a work not of fact but of fiction.[49]

[46] Temperley, *op. cit.*, p. 148.
[47] John Elliot Cairnes, *The Slave Power: Its Character, Career, and Probable Designs: Being an Attempt to Explain the Real Issues Involved in the American Contest*, 2nd edn. (London, 1863), p. vii. [48] *Ibid.*, p. 69.
[49] For a discussion of the response to Cairnes's work, see A. N. J. den Hollander, "Countries Far Away — Cognition at a Distance", *Comparative Studies in Society and History*, ix (1967), p. 364, and Adelaide Weinberg, *John Elliot Cairnes and the American Civil War: A Study in Anglo-American Relations* (London, [1970]), pp. 32-56.

Although the portrait of the South given in *The Slave Power* bears little relation to reality, it is, nevertheless, a very accurate description of what, according to the precepts of the classical school, the South *ought* to have been like. South of the Mason Dixon Line there extended a vast, thinly populated region of exhausted soils and abandoned dwellings. Holding sway over it was a small planter oligarchy which owed its position to its control over the only labour force available, which consisted of slaves. Their labour, however, being extracted by coercion, was reluctant, unskilled and wanting in versatility. Meanwhile, the great mass of the Southern population, the white trash, numbering around four millions, constituted "a promiscuous horde, who, too poor to keep slaves and too proud to work, prefer a vagrant and precarious life spent in the desert to engaging in occupations which would associate them with the slaves whom they despise". Although in many ways an embarrassment to the planters, these poor whites were nevertheless an instrument which, in times of conflict, they could use to further their ambitions.[50]

One thing that can be said about this account is that it is internally consistent and admirably well-rounded. It also fitted in very neatly with the presuppositions of his readers and for this reason attracted lavish praise. Harriet Martineau "agreed so entirely with almost every line in this volume" that "our way of seeing the facts is more like the action of one mind than two". In Stanley Jevons's view it was a "nearly or quite irrefragable piece of reasoning". The *Economist* described it as "masterly" and singled out for particular praise "its discriminative instinct, which arranges the different elements of the subject, by a sort of natural perspective in their true proportions and mutual relations". The *Spectator* also described the work as "masterly"; the *National Review* as "a compact and truthful analysis"; the *Northern Whig* as "a permanent contribution to economical science".[51] Such adverse comment as there was concerned details rather than the author's method or overall assessment.[52] Not least among Cairnes's admirers was Karl Marx, whose own views on the South, expressed in his articles for the *New York Daily Tribune*, the Vienna *Presse*, and in his letters to Engels, corresponded closely with those outlined by Cairnes.[53] For the

[50] Cairnes, *op. cit.*, pp. 44, 81-3, 95-8. In the first edition the "white trash" population had been put at five millions, but in response to American criticism he reduced it in the second edition to four: den Hollander, *op. cit.*, p. 366.

[51] These and other comments will be found in den Hollander, *op. cit.*, p. 364, and Weinberg, *op. cit.*, pp. 32, 39-41. For a recent analysis of Cairnes's economic views, see Fogel and Engerman, *Time on the Cross*, i, pp. 181-90.

[52] den Hollander, *op. cit.*, p. 364.

[53] ". . . the number of actual slaveholders in the South of the Union does not amount to more than three hundred thousand, a narrow oligarchy that is confronted with many millions of so-called poor whites, whose numbers constantly grew through concentration of landed property and whose condition is

(cont. on p. 113)

remainder of his life he continued to cite *The Slave Power* as his principal authority on all matters relating to North American slavery.[54]

Not surprisingly *The Slave Power* was also well received in the Northern United States, although it caused less of a stir there since Americans were already familiar with most of the arguments it contained. In fact, there was very little in Cairnes which had not been heard from political platforms or on the floors of Congress many times over. In large part, indeed, he was merely repeating what had come to be regarded as part of the official ideology of the Republican party, although many of the ideas it encompassed can be traced back to the Federalists at the beginning of the century.

As Eric Foner has recently shown, Republican ideology was very much the product of Northern culture, which is to say of a society composed of farmers and small entrepreneurs and of those who aspired to become farmers and entrepreneurs.[55] It stressed the value of hard work, competition, ingenuity, frugality, honesty and sobriety — all those qualities, in short, to which Northerners had traditionally attributed the expansive, dynamic character of their society. At its heart lay a belief in the dignity of labour and the right of the individual to acquire property, both as a reward for his effort and as a guarantee of his future economic well-being. By hard work men improved their conditions and contributed to the general welfare of the community. In other words, Republican doctrine was very much a capitalist ideology, allowing always that it applied to a society which still held out substantial promise that individual effort would be appropriately rewarded.[56]

That Republicans were able to make a political platform out of values which Northerners had hitherto taken largely for granted was the result of the sectional struggle over Western lands and a growing conviction that Southerners did not share the same values. Traditionally Americans had justified the practices of their society

---

(note 53 cont.)
only to be compared with that of the Roman plebeians in the period of Rome's extreme decline": article for the Vienna *Presse*, 20 Oct. 1861, in Karl Marx and Frederick Engels, *The Civil War in the United States*, 3rd edn. (New York, 1961), pp. 68-9. Marx was also under the impression that the South was "an oligarchy where the whole of the productive labour falls on the Negroes and the four millions of "white trash" are filibusters by profession": Marx to Engels, 10 Sept. 1862, in *ibid.*, p. 255. Unlike many later Marxists, Marx was in no doubt that the Civil War was "in the true sense of the word a war of conquest for the extension and perpetuation of slavery". The North he saw as responding "reluctantly, sleepily, as was to be expected with its higher industrial and commercial development": *ibid.*, pp. 79, 165.

[54] Karl Marx, *Capital*, 3 vols. (London, 1970 edn.), i, pp. 191, 254, 314, and iii, p. 376.

[55] Foner, *Free Soil, Free Labor, Free Men*, pp. 11-18.

[56] *Ibid.*, pp. 11-72.

by referring to a supposed Europe-America antithesis. Needless to say, the image of "Europe" employed bore little relation to reality, being conjured up simply to demonstrate the superiority of American virtue and achievement.[57] With the sharpening of sectional tensions in the 1840s and 1850s, however, Northerners and Southerners increasingly employed the same technique with regard to one another. That the South was backward was no new idea. Patriotic Northerners had long regarded it as an embarrassing exception to virtually everything that was said about American enlightenment and progress. What was new, however, was a political hostility based on the widespread belief that the South stood for everything that the North was not. While the North represented democracy, energy and prosperity, the South stood for privilege, lethargy and decay. The reasons for this were not far to seek. "Enslave a man", declared Horace Greeley, "and you destroy his ambition, his enterprise, his capacity. In the constitution of human nature the desire of bettering one's condition is the mainspring of effort".[58] Yet blighting though slavery was to all it touched, the disease was readily susceptible to cure. Abolish slavery, argued Hinton Rowan Helper, and Southern land values would increase fourfold overnight.[59]

It is, of course, difficult to draw a line between belief, wishful thinking and a willingness to use whatever arguments seem best designed to serve a purpose. Yet even if we accept that much of what was said falls into this last category, it is plain that capitalist ideology served the abolitionists well. This fact was acknowledged by the most able of the Southern polemicists, George Fitzhugh, who made an attack on the principles of the classical economists the centre-piece of his argument. The economists' "fundamental maxims, laissez-faire and *pas trop gouverner*" were in his view "at war with all kinds of slavery, since they in fact assert that individuals and peoples prosper most when governed least".[60]

[57] See, for example, Daniel J. Boorstin, *America and the Image of Europe* (New York, 1960), and W. R. Brock, "The Image of England and American Nationalism", *Jl. Amer. Studies*, v (1971), pp. 225-45.

[58] Quoted in Foner, *Free Soil, Free Labor, Free Men*, p. 46.

[59] Hinton Rowan Helper, *The Impending Crisis of the South: How to Meet It* (Baltimore, 1857). For a discussion of Helper's economic views, see Fogel and Engerman, *Time on the Cross*, i, pp. 161-9. *The Impending Crisis* was the most elaborate contemporary exposition of the economic case against slavery and was extensively used by Republicans as campaign propaganda. In 1859, for example, a group of Republican Congressmen joined together in distributing 100,000 copies of the work. What is interesting about Helper's figures, however, is not so much that they were wrong but that, as Stanley Engerman has recently shown, much better figures were available and were ignored: Stanley Engerman, "A Reconsideration of Southern Economic Growth, 1770-1860", *Agric. Hist.*, xlix (1975), pp. 355-7.

[60] George Fitzhugh, *Sociology for the South: or, The Failure of Free Society* (Richmond, Va., 1854), p. 1.

Such notions had a particular appeal for men with little knowledge or practical experience of the world. Adam Smith, the father of the movement, was in his estimation a perfect example of this type:

> For writing a one-sided philosophy no man was better fitted than Adam Smith. He possessed extraordinary powers of abstraction, analysis and generalization. He was absent, secluded and unobservant. He saw only that prosperous and progressive portion of society whom liberty and free competition benefited, and mistook its effects on them for its effects on the whole world.[61]

For the merchants and manufacturers of Scotland and England and their counterparts in the North this was no doubt an admirable philosophy. They, after all, were the ones who profited from the system, the "vampire capitalist class"[62] which preyed on the rest. For what Adam Smith and his disciples did not acknowledge, either because they did not choose to or because they themselves were blind to the consequences, was that their system of universal liberty was merely a recipe for allowing the astute, the avaricious and the mendacious to exploit the ignorant, the poor and the weak. Thomas Hobbes had maintained that a state of nature was also a state of war. This was untrue because man was naturally an associative animal; but it was emphatically the case with capitalist society which set man against man and class against class.[63]

Two points that are commonly made about Fitzhugh are that his attack on capitalist society was more persuasive than his defence of slavery and that to a remarkable degree it paralleled that of the Marxists. There is, however, another aspect of his thought which is less frequently commented on but which is highly relevant to the issue in hand. This is his view of the slavery struggle as an attempt by a metropolitan culture to impose its values on to a provincial society. This idea was by no means unfamiliar to British defenders of slavery who had argued that the Reform Act of 1832, which had enfranchised the middle classes, had also, by abolishing the rotten boroughs, disenfranchised the colonies, whose spokesmen had traditionally looked to them for seats. As a result, Sir Richard Vyvyan had declared: "the House of Commons had assumed to itself a metropolitan power unenjoyed by ancient Rome".[64] The implications of this, however, were more elaborately and subtly described by Fitzhugh. According to him, the culture that was being imposed was capitalist culture. It owed its dominance to its undoubted success in harnessing energy and technology and, although the wealth thereby created had been monopolized by the few, those few had, largely

---

[61] *Ibid.*, p. 10.
[62] George Fitzhugh, *Cannibals All!: or Slaves Without Masters* (Richmond, Va., 1857), p. 175.
[63] Fitzhugh, *Sociology for the South*, p. 32.
[64] *Hansard*, 3rd ser., xviii, cols. 113-16 (30 May 1833).

because of their wealth, been able to impose their standards on the
rest of mankind.   This was evident not only in matters of dress and
language but in the realm of ideas also.   Unfortunately, Southerners
had gone along with this process, not realizing where it was leading:

> We of the South teach political economy, because it is taught in Europe.
> Yet political economy, and all other systems of moral science, which we
> derive from Europe, are tainted with abolition, and at war with our
> institutions.   We must build up centres of trade, of thought and fashion at
> home.   We must become national, nay, provincial and cease to be
> cosmopolitans.[64]

In short, it was time for Southerners to make a stand against the
cultural imperialism of Europe and the North and to reaffirm the
values of their own society.   In particular, it was time for them to
make known their "change of policy and opinion, and to throw Adam
Smith, Say, Ricardo and Co., in the fire".[65]

That it took the defenders of slavery so long to come up with an
effective critique of the classical economists is not entirely surprising.
After all, the European socialists did not manage much better and the
classical economists themselves, given the degree to which society
had already been transformed by precisely those processes which
they set out to describe, were remarkably belated in their discoveries.
Yet until they had evolved effective ways of countering the arguments
derived from economic theory the defenders of slavery were at a
serious disadvantage.   They were particularly handicapped because,
as Fitzhugh was ultimately to show, these arguments were derived
from values deeply rooted in a dominant metropolitan culture.

What made the metropolitan ideology of the late eighteenth and
early nineteenth centuries a capitalist ideology was not, of course,
any iron law of economics.   Slavery and related systems of forced
labour can be highly profitable.   There is no logical reason why
Negro slaves should not have been turned into factory workers.
Occasionally this happened.[67]   But by and large it did not happen,
and since men tend to generalize from their own experience it came
naturally to those in the metropolis to suppose that freedom and the
adoption of more efficient modes of production went together.   In
vain the slaveholders argued that the colonies, the Southern states,
were different, that abolition meant *less* efficient production, that it
was simply unrealistic to generalize about the world on the basis of
what went on in Britain or Massachusetts.   In the end, as we have
seen, Southerners were able to evolve a critique of "free" society no

[64] Fitzhugh, *Cannibals All!*, p. 88.
[65] *Ibid.*, p. 89.
[67] Prior to the Civil War about 5 per cent of Southern slaves were employed
in manufacturing industry.   Most of these enterprises were profitable and
slave labour was generally found to be more economical than other forms of
labour available.   R. S. Starobin, *Industrial Slavery in the Old South* (New
York, 1970), p. xii.

less incisive than the Northern critique of slave society, but this was a late development. In the meantime they had the solid weight of the conventional wisdom with which to contend.

I am not suggesting that this "explains" the attack on slavery or even that it modifies to any substantial degree what the traditionalists have told us about the humanitarian and religious impulses which went into the making of the antislavery movement. What I am saying is that if the object is to relate capitalism and slavery this is one important way in which they were related. And I would go somewhat further and say that it offers a solution to a problem which has puzzled many historians — namely, how could a philosophy which extolled the pursuit of individual self-interest have contributed, in the absence of any expectation of economic gain, to the achievement of so praiseworthy an object as the abolition of slavery. For although an examination of capitalist ideology may not tell us much about the motivation of the abolitionists it does go a fair way towards explaining why men of independent judgement who did not share the abolitionists' moral repugnance were prepared, on occasion, to go along with them. It did not, of course, prevent them from acting in other ways on other occasions — accepting Brazilian and Cuban sugar, acquiescing in a massive trade in coolie indentured labour, or turning a deaf ear to the pleas of the American freedmen. On these occasions they behaved as capitalists are supposed to behave: they weighed their own interests and acted accordingly.

The idea that late eighteenth- and early nineteenth-century capitalist ideology was a libertarian creed may strike some as surprising. Were not the capitalists busy grinding the faces of the poor? Was not this the high point of capitalist oppression of the working classes? Well, yes they were, and yes it was. We now know that early industrial capitalism was often a peculiarly ruthless system of exploitation capable of producing appalling misery. But this is not how it appeared to most middle-class people of the period. It is dangerous to project later ideas backwards and to attribute them, in the form of unconscious guilt or hostility, to people of the time. One of the most important contributions of both the Southern and Marxist critics of capitalism was to demonstrate that its defenders were themselves genuinely unaware of the practical implications of their philosophy.[68] James Stephen's comments are indicative of

[68] Fitzhugh, for example, pictures them as sleep-walkers, so entranced by the abstract beauty of their notions that they failed to notice that labourers in their own society had become "slaves without masters" — that is, slaves of the state and as such available for corporate exploitation by the middle classes. Fitzhugh, *Sociology for the South*, pp. 44-7; Fitzhugh, *Cannibals All!*, p. 117. This is also, presumably, what Engels means by "the bourgeois illusion of the eternity and finality of capitalist production", which he cites as an example of "false consciousness"; Engels to F. Mehring, 14 July 1893, in Karl Marx and Frederick Engels, *Selected Works*, 2 vols. (Moscow, 1951 edn.), ii, pp. 451-2.

this, and he had known poverty and seen the inside of a debtors' prison. In fact capitalism was not seen as a "system" at all in the sense that slavery or feudalism were systems. Rather it was an emancipation from traditional restraints, a liberation of energies, a letting go.

To men whose eyes were set on this utopian vision, as to many modern scholars, slavery appeared an anachronism. And, again like modern scholars, finding that it did not fit in with their beliefs about the way the world was developing, they jumped to the conclusion that, being morally and socially regressive, it must also be economically inefficient and that they would be better served by a freer system. Not everyone believed this but enough did substantially to affect the issue. The cause of humanity, we are often told, is best served by truth; but sometimes, it would seem, it may be even better served by error.

University of East Anglia   *Howard Temperley*

THE SPECTER OF CRISIS: Slaveholder Reactions to Abolitionism in the United States and Brazil

*Robert Brent Toplin**

IN A PAPER READ BEFORE THE Southern Historical Association's 1970 meeting Professor Thomas E. Skidmore closed a comparative study of race relations in the United States and Brazil with an interesting suggestion. He recommended that historians begin related research by asking first about the similarities between conditions in the two countries rather than asking about the differences. Whether the subject is slavery, abolition, or race relations, this proposal seems helpful. Too often comparative studies begin with an *a priori* observation that the conditions in the two countries were noticeably distinct, leading the sudent into a web of difficulty in defining the sources of contrast. By first examining the similarities between the United States and Brazil, the contrasts can more readily be placed where they belong.[1]

In a more extended analysis it would be worthwhile to compare several aspects of the abolition controversy in the two countries with a view toward both similarities and differences. We would want to compare the ideologies of the abolitionist movements, the disagreements among abolitionists regarding gradualism and immediatism and moderate and radical tactics, the presence of racism in both the pro and antislavery camps, the extent to which proprietors manumitted their slaves, and

* An earlier version of this paper was read before the 1971 meeting of the Southern Historical Association. The author is grateful for financial assistance from a Younger Humanist Fellowship from the National Endowment for the Humanities and a Ford Grant in the Humanities.

1 Thomas E. Skidmore, "Comparative Race Relations Since Emancipation—The United States and Brazil: How Different?," presented at the Southern Historical Association Meeting in Louisville, Kentucky, Nov. 12, 1970. Much of the confusion has resulted from efforts to expand on the implications of contrasts suggested in Frank Tannenbaum, *Slave and Citizen: The Negro in the Americas* (New York, 1946) and Stanley M. Elkins, *Slavery, A Problem in American Institutional and Intellectual Life* (Chicago, 1959), pp. 52-139. Two important studies which do much to clarify the problems involved in contrasting slavery and race relations in the United States and Latin America are: David Brion Davis, *The Problem of Slavery in Western Culture* (Ithaca, 1966), pp. 223-288; Carl N. Degler, *Neither Black Nor White: Slavery and Race Relations in Brazil and the United States* (New York, 1971).

129

their reactions to programs for gradual, compensated emancipation.[2] The present study is limited in that it addresses one major theme, yet a theme that can suggest approaches to the aforementioned topics. By beginning with an emphasis on similarities, the study asks: To what extent did the abolitionist movements in the United States and Brazil represent real threats to slaveholders in the two countries, threats not only in the form of applying pressure toward long-term emancipation but also immediate dangers? An understanding of the Brazilian experience will shed more light on the perspective of those American slaveholders who saw secession as an answer to their problems.

In many ways the reasons slaveholders gave for their opposition to emancipation in the United States and Brazil reflected similar patterns of argument. Some of the most important concerns are immediately obvious. Simple pecuniary interest in the security of property would be one. Men who had invested heavily in servile labor would not want to see this investment suddenly decreed worthless. The threat to a whole life-style would be another primary concern of slaveholders facing an abolitionist challenge. Slaveholding generated a social and political world which would be altered radically if the fundamental institution on which it rested were destroyed. A fear of race adjustment in the post-emancipation society also troubled the slaveholders. This problem is well documented regarding American history, but we should also be cognizant of the virulent forms of racism that pervaded Brazilian slaveholding society. The language of anti-abolitionist propaganda in Brazil in the 1880's became so laden with hostile stereotypes that the country's most famous black abolitionist, José do Patrocínio, thought, "prejudice against colored people can prolong slavery indefinitely." In both countries racism served as an obstacle to emancipation.[3] Less obvious are the potential dangers which slaveholders saw in the *process* of abolition. They genuinely feared the mischief abolitionism could cause if it successfully encroached upon the ostensibly stable order of slavery. The substance of this fear deserves analysis in greater detail, first in terms of the developments in Brazil which forced a settlement of the abolition issue in 1888 and, second, in view of the fearful predictions made by southern secessionists in the United States.

Brazilian slaveholders actually *experienced* many of the nightmares that troubled American slave proprietors. For decades before the 1880's, Brazilian planters warned that antislavery agitation could eventually reach the slave-quarters, exciting bondsmen with the idea of escape and, possibly, igniting the powder-keg of servile revolt. Whether by fleeing or fighting, slaves would surely respond to abolitionist propa-

[2] The author is preparing a book which will deal with these and related subjects.
[3] *Gazeta da Tarde*, Sept. 18, 1885, p. 1; *Vinte e Cinco de Março*, No. 1, May, 1884. Robert Brent Toplin, "From Slavery to Fettered Freedom: Attitudes Toward the Negro in Brazil," *Luso-Brazilian Review* (Summer, 1970), 3-12; Robert Brent Toplin, *The Abolition of Slavery in Brazil* (New York, 1972), Chs. V and VI.

ganda should they come in contact with it. From the perspective of slave-holders, it was essential to bar the bondsmen from communication with the activities of the antislavery movement. Slaves were relatively manageable when resigned to a lifetime in bondage, but once stirred by hopes of freedom, their attitude could become rebellious.[4]

It is significant that a series of reforms which liberalized the conditions of the bondsman in the last years before abolition in Brazil did much to weaken slavery's institutional props and raise the captives' hopes for freedom. Between 1885 and 1888 various senators, government ministers, and local political and judicial reformers succeeded in winning legal guarantees for better treatment of the slaves. New laws prohibited proprietors from flogging their bondsmen, public authorities began to receive the complaints of slaves and act on their grievances, and judges, living in urban centers where abolitionism had made significant gains, increasingly delivered decisions in favor of freeing litigant captives. In a variety of cases involving the legal status of slaves, the burden of proof suddenly fell on the masters.

These changes challenged what *senhores* called their "moral authority"—their ability to determine their own rules. Despite the presence of various laws to protect bondsmen and help emancipate them, proprietors had traditionally operated with minimal imposition from outside authorities. Ordinarily the *senhor* was final arbiter on his estate, a condition essential to his dominion over servile workers. The system was based on *evasion* of formal laws, not their execution. Effective control depended on the power of masters to interpret regulations according to their own interests and to exclude themselves from rules they found undesirable. Senator Silveira Martins identified the problem with sharp insight when he said, "The servile regime is an exception. When the exceptional laws disappear, slavery is finished." Developments in the 1880's showed that slavery could not be liberalized effectively and remain viable. The institution rested on coercion; liberalization undermined its foundations.[5]

Once radical abolitionists won popularity and freedom of movement in major Brazilian cities, they were able to exploit the deterioration of slaveholder control. Pockets of abolitionist agitation appeared proximate to the principal plantation areas. Major cities became asylums for runaway slaves. Unlike the American slaveocrats, the Brazilian slave-

---

[4] For examples of this fear, see: *Congresso Agricola: Collecão de documentos* (Rio de Janeiro, 1878), pp. 47, 248-249; *Rio News*, (Oct. 15, 1880, pp. 3-4; Feb. 5, 1882, p. 3; *Gazeta do Povo*, Jan. 12, 1888, p. 1; Malvino da Silva Reis, *Situação econômica do Brasil: Exposição apresentada à commisão especial nomeda pela assembléa geral da Associação Commercial em 2 de maio de 1884* (Rio de Janeiro, 1884), p. 21.

[5] *Annaes da Câmara* (1886), Sept. 29, p. 288; Sept. 30, p. 289; Oct. 11, pp. 307-308; Oct. 13, p. 482; *Annaes do Senado* (1886), Sept. 29, p. 288; *Província de São Paulo*, July 19, 1887, p. 1; *Rio News*, June 24, 1887, p. 4; *Gazeta do Povo*, Nov. 4, 1887, p. 2.

holders could not contain abolitionist activities geographically. Despite serious repressive efforts, they were not able to crush discontented ele-. ments or localize them effectively. The hour was too late; neither cajoling nor coercion could check the growing urban antislavery movement inspired by both intellectual and economic concerns.

Slaveholders found troublemakers in their own backyards. Abolitionists, including many Negro freedmen, worked their way into the slave quarters at night, urged captives to flee, then slipped back into their places of refuge before daybreak. Bondsmen lost their fear of punishment as they became aware of the legal restraints on their masters' power and the new opportunities for escape. How could slavery be maintained under such conditions, asked a leading slaveholder? By the ignorance or resignation of the slaves? Hardly. In 1887 and early 1888 thousands of bondsmen made rapid exit. Many fought their way to freedom, producing firearms, slaying overseers and masters and engaging in bloody combat when police troops tried to pursue them. By early 1888 Brazilian slavery seemed to be collapsing in a wave of upheaval, violence, and chaos.[6] Unless political leaders checked the breakdown by announcing the complete abolition of slavery, it appeared the situation would continue to deteriorate into more dangerous forms of anarchy and social revolution. Understandably, the leaders chose an emancipation decree, announcing the famous Golden Law on May 13, 1888. Making political hay of a necessary act, they hailed it as "the work of humanity, of foresight and of progress."[7]

The substantial danger of slave violence in antebellum America has not been accorded the serious treatment that it deserves. As in Brazil, the reality of the problem is often underrated in historical interpretations. Descriptions of slavery in the United States often minimize the danger of revolt by emphasizing that references to it in antebellum sources really reflect super-sensitivity and emotionalism concerning slavery, racist attitudes, or a failure of the slaveowner to realize that the shoring up of slavery's institutional controls after the Nat Turner rebellion secured the proprietors against further threats of serious, collective uprisings. Even in some of the finest works of scholarship, historians show reluctance to deal with the danger at face value. After offering considerable evidence for the excitement abolitionism could stir within the slave population, scholars often identify the slaveholders' protestations as examples of hysteria, irrational perception, or race anxieties.[8]

[6] *Annaes da Câmara* (1888), June 7, p. 93. Robert Brent Toplin, "Upheaval, Violence, and the Abolition of Slavery in Brazil: The Case of São Paulo" *Hispanic American Historical Review* (Nov., 1969), 639-655; Richard Graham, "Causes for the Abolition of Negro Slavery in Brazil: An Interpretive Essay," *ibid.*, (May, 1966), 123-137.

[7] *Relatório* of the Minister of Agriculture, Commerce and Public Works, Rodrigo Augusto da Silva, 1889, p. 5.

[8] See, for example, David M. Potter, "John Brown and the Paradox of Leadership Among American Negroes," *The South and the Sectional Conflict* (Baton Rouge,

An assessment of the slaveholders' anxieties and the substance of their fears raises several questions. Was a latent readiness to revolt really a condition of the slave population? Could abolitionist literature be judged truly incendiary, as many southerners considered it? Could an abolitionist movement have eventually developed within the South itself? From the perspective of the slaveholder, were censorship and repression rational responses to a real threat? These questions lead to other queries concerning the movement toward secession. Did the Republican victory in 1860 represent a real and imminent threat to slavery? Did the slaveholders actually have much to gain by secession, assuming that independence could be achieved easily?

The fear of servile revolt persisted, as manifested in southern speech-making and writing throughout the antebellum period. To be sure, slaveholders did not enjoy discussing the topic, as they believed that open debate on such a volatile matter might reach the ears of the bondsmen.[9] Also, they feared that abolitionists would view affirmation of a real threat as tantamount to admitting that the South controlled freedom-loving blacks through force and coercion. When the Missouri debates brought congressmen into one of the early, frightening confrontations on the slavery issue, Edward Colston of Virginia expressed his fear that slaves might be listening to the exchanges in the galleries, and Georgia's Thomas W. Cobb warned that the antislavery challenge could kindle a fire "which seas of blood can only extinguish."[10] Indeed, James Tallmadge, Jr., the outspoken anti-extensionist whose amendment prompted the famous debates, admitted that conditions which allowed easy social intercourse between free blacks and slaves could open the way to servile war.[11]

1968), pp. 203-217; C. Vann Woodward, "John Brown's Private War," *The Burden of Southern History* (rev. ed., Baton Rouge, 1968), pp. 61-68; Roy F. Nichols, *The Disruption of American Democracy* (New York, 1948), pp. 513-517; Allan Nevins, *Ordeal of the Union* (New York, 1947), I, 282, 507. Two outstanding recent studies which focus on South Carolina also reveal some surprisingly ambivalent statements about the problem of violence, observations which contradict the thrust of the books' evidence. See William W. Freehling, *Prelude to Civil War: The Nullification Controversy in South Carolina, 1816-1836* (New York, 1968), pp. 49, 64, 358; and Steven A. Channing, *Crisis of Fear: Secession in South Carolina* (New York, 1970), pp. 22-55, 78, 266-268, 289. It should be noted that Professor Freehling has refined and clarified his position on the issue. See "Paranoia and American History," *The New York Review of Books*, Sept. 23, 1971, p. 36.

[9] *Annals of Congress*, 16 Cong., 1 sess., House of Representatives (1820), 1023-1024.

[10] Horace Greeley, *A History of the Struggle for Slavery Extension or Restriction in the United States from the Delcaration of Independence to the Present Day* (New York, 1856), p. 9.   Reports on the Denmark Vesey slave conspiracy of 1822 indicated that some of the plotters had become inspired to revolt against slavery through reading excerpts from the congressional debates on the Missouri Compromise. Robert S. Starobin (ed.), *Denmark Vesey: The Slave Conspiracy of 1822* (Englewood Cliffs, 1970), pp. 71, 84, 90, 100.

[11] Greeley, *A History of the Struggle for Slavery Extension*, pp. 9-12.

In Thomas R. Dew's famous tract of 1832 which signaled a significant hardening of proslavery attitudes, the theme of potential insurrection flows throughout. Dew used large italics in his book for the first time on page 78—specifically for the word "insurrections."[12] In the years to follow, many leading defenders of slavery would recite the major points of his interpretation. As Dew put it, slavery was well under control as long as outside agitators did not disturb it. The blacks were usually content in their condition and loyal to their masters. In more than two centuries of slavery in the United States, there had been only a few significant attempts at insurrection. If slavery's critics should meddle in master-slave relationships, poisoning the bondsmen's minds with heinous thoughts, the tranquil African could be transformed into a "midnight murderer." Antislavery agitation was loaded with hidden deviltry. Even seemingly moderate appeals could be dangerous. Imprudent philanthropists did not understand that experimenting with the idea of emancipation could spread unrest among the slave population. The murders and destruction that attended revolts in Haiti and Virginia should not be forgotten.[13]

It is not surprising that Alfred Iverson of Georgia referred to similar dangers when he addressed the Senate in 1861 to explain his farewell to the Union and his state's intention of joining the secession movement. Iverson predicted that Lincoln's presidency would open the mails to incendiary abolitionist literature and establish an environment conducive to more raids like John Brown's—conditions which would induce poisonings, murders and revolts on an unprecedented scale. In Iverson's view, the necessary step was clear. "We believe," he said, "that the only security for the institution to which we attach so much importance is secession and a southern confederacy."[14]

Just as in Brazil then, the fear that abolitionist agitation could spark a potentially explosive slave population was *fundamental* to the arguments of southern slaveholders. Racist attitudes figured in the thinking of both groups of slaveholders, but the practical problem of preventing a dangerous polarization of relationships between slaves and masters represented their primary concern. Moreover, it is clear in the Brazilian case that the concern of slave proprietors was not based on unrealistic, emotional fears. In the 1880's their slaveholding order began to collapse in the face of new gains by the antislavery forces. Whether the fears of American slaveholders were as well-founded remains to be considered.

[12] Thomas R. Dew, *Review of the Debate of the Virginia Legislature of 1831 and 1832* (Richmond, 1832), p. 78.

[13] *Ibid.*, pp. 5, 8, 63, 110, 114-125. Also, see William Drayton, *The South Vindicated from the Treason and Fanaticism of the Northern Abolitionists* (Philadelphia, 1836), pp. 254-275, 280-281, 299; Thomas R. R. Cobb, *An Inquiry into the Law of Negro Slavery in the United States of America* (Philadelphia and Savannah, 1858), pp. clxxv, clxxvi, ccvix, ccxi-ccxii; Chancellor Harper in *The Pro-Slavery Argument* (Philadelphia, 1853), pp. 74-76.

[14] *Congressional Globe*, 36 Cong., 2 sess., Senate (1860), 11.

It is a question that cannot be answered precisely because the events of the Civil War precluded a settlement of the emancipation issue by other means. Nevertheless, those other possibilities ought to be explored. Certainly the proprietors were cognizant of the diverse contingencies before them.

The shocking news of John Brown's raid on Harper's Ferry helped to crystallize secessionist thought. Southerners reacted severely not only to the John Brown raid but also to the way many northerners praised it.[15] Even William Lloyd Garrison, the pacifist, the non-resistant, sounded disturbingly receptive to Brown's violent acts. While maintaining his allegiance to pacifist principles and insisting that Brown's rifles and spears were meant only for the slaves' self-defense, he asserted that Brown was justified in trying to strike a blow for freedom. Garrison gave his blessing for "Success to every slave insurrection at the South, and in every slave country," and said, "Rather than see men wear their chains in cowardly and servile spirit, I would, as an advocate of peace, much rather see them breaking the head of the tyrant with their chains."[16] Actually, Garrison's accommodation to radical, daring, attacks on slavery was mild compared to the sanction for militant, even violent action given by many other leading abolitionists in the late 1850's.[17] An environment propitious for slave escape and rebellion seemed fast developing.

The scenario of a troubled future which greatly worried southerners resembled the crisis which Brazilian masters feared and eventually experienced in the last years of slavery. A few of the major parallels can be mentioned. For example, Southern slaveholders felt increasingly isolated in a world growing ever more hostile to their civilization; Brazilian slaveocrats lost many of their closest allies under the pressure of new currents of thought which branded slavery as anachronistic and hailed the concept of a free labor system. Southern slaveholders worried that even passage of moderate proposals to promote emancipation could open a Pandora's box of troubles; Brazilian slaveocrats discovered that gradual, reformist measures to facilitate manumission only excited

---

[15] Thomas Ricaud Martin, *The Great Parliamentary Battle and Farewell Addresses of the Southern Senators on the Eve of the Civil War* (New York and Washington, 1905), pp. 113, 156, 173; Allan Nevins, *The Emergence of Lincoln: Prologue to Civil War, 1859-1861* (New York and London, 1950), II, 20, 127; Avery Craven, *Edmund Ruffin: A Study in Secession* (Baton Rouge, 1966), p. 171. David Brion Davis points out that many southerners viewed John Brown's raid as the fulfillment of an old prophecy, namely, that despite the abolitionists' claims of non-violence, they really intended to stir slaves into rebellion. See *The Slave Power Conspiracy and the Paranoid Style* (Baton Rouge, 1969), pp. 34-35.

[16] George M. Fredrickson (ed.), *William Lloyd Garrison* (Englewood Cliffs, 1968), pp. 59-62.

[17] See, for example: George M. Fredrickson, *The Inner Civil War: Northern Intellectuals and the Crisis of the Union* (New York and Evanston, 1965), pp. 36-44; Carleton Mabee, *Black Freedom: The Non-Violent Abolitionists from 1830 Through the Civil War* (New York and London, 1970), pp. 318-332; Peter Brock, *Radical Pacifists in Antebellum America* (Princeton, 1968), pp. 221-239.

the expectations of abolitionists, forcing the proprietors to try desperately to prevent reform from snowballing. Southerners worried that related issues developing out of the slavery controversy, such as the concern for civil liberties and the fugitive slave law, could stimulate antisouthern feeling among people who had been largely apathetic on the question of abolition; Brazilian slaveholders saw their efforts to silence antislavery speakers and recapture fugitives backfire to the point of making the defense of slavery seem outrageous to many of the free population, an attitude which stirred them into active support of the abolitionists. In addition to these parallels, there are others which directly concern threats to the internal stability of the slaveholding society. Southerners feared that the urban centers could become hubs for abolitionist activities and asylums for fugitive slaves, that merchants and travelers would act as emissaries of the abolitionists, and that black freedmen would join forces with their brothers in bondage in the event of a crisis. All of these problems were prominent features of the breakdown of the slaveholding order in Brazil in the 1880's.

In the American South by 1860-1861 the sound of secessionist argumentation had a comforting and logical ring to the ears of weary slaveholders who were well aware of the trends of history. They came to recognize the foresight of John C. Calhoun whose strident voice of defiance they could not accept fully in earlier years. Were not Calhoun's prophesies borne out when the newly elected President, considered only a *moderate* Republican, had plainly stated that sooner or later slavery had to be put on the course toward ultimate extinction?[18] Once the slavery extension issue was resolved, would not Republicans turn their eyes toward that task?[19] Even the passage of very modest laws to promote emancipation might dangerously excite the slaves' expectation of freedom. And what did the Republicans have in mind as a blueprint for further political success? If the Republican leaders had any political acumen, they would certainly try to stretch their influence southward to break away from the sectional party image. Was not this thought behind the decision of sixty-eight Republican congressmen to endorse Hinton Rowan Helper's incendiary book? Had not Helper boldly tried to drive a wedge between the slaveholding and non-slaveholding whites of the South? As Helper explained, "a freesoiler is only a tadpole in an

[18] Robert W. Johannsen (ed.), *The Lincoln-Douglas Debates* (New York, 1965), pp. 14, 16, 55.

[19] Martin, *The Great Parliamentary Battle*, pp. 116-117, 155-168; *Congressional Globe*, 36 Cong., 2 sess., Senate (1860), 187; (1861), 267, 271; David Christy, "Cotton Is King, Or Slavery in the Light of Political Economy," *Cotton Is King and Pro-Slavery Arguments* (Augusta, 1860), p. 218; Margaret L. Coit (ed.), John C. Calhoun (Englewood Cliffs, 1970), pp. 46-47; James Williams, *Letters on Slavery from the Old World* (published by the Confederacy—Middle District of Tennessee, 1861), reprinted 1969, Miami, Florida, p. viii.

advanced state of transformation; an abolitionist is a full and perfectly developed frog."[20]

How could Republicans begin to challenge slavery internally? To many southern secessionists the trick could be accomplished easily—without radical abolitionist legislation and without violent appeals for revolution. Republicans could eat away at slavery subtly without drawing great attention through blatant acts. They could make government patronage jobs available to abolitionists, insure that abolitionist literature could be mailed to southern communities, appoint antislavery leaders to the federal courts and pass new forms of taxation which would be applied specifically to property in chattel labor.[21] Even as a minority party, the Republicans could greatly capitalize on their growing popularity and their control of the governmental machinery. The southerners who made their influence felt in national politics during the 1850's must have been keenly aware of the way a minority could wield disproportionate power in the government.

The secessionists came close to pulling off what the Brazilian slaveocrats had much less chance of achieving, that is, establishment of an independent slaveholding nation that could be free of abolitionist threats for its immediate future. It is not surprising that prominent Brazilian defenders of slavery often described themselves as "the John C. Calhoun of Brazil," and hoped to resist new challenges more successfully than the South had been able to do.[22] The Brazilians could not check the growing threat, however, because they were unable to isolate the opposition geographically and, perhaps most important, the hour in history was too late for effective resistance against the antislavery forces. On the other hand, for the American secessionists of 1860-1861, independence seemed feasible, especially if it could be achieved peaceably. One after another, the southern senators made dramatic appeals in their farewell addresses, asking that their states be allowed to depart from the Union without bloodshed.[23]

Thus, a review of the Brazilian experience suggests that there may have been considerable substance behind the fears of American slaveholders. To be sure, we are dealing with a futuristic concern when dis-

[20] *Congressional Globe*, 36 Cong., 2 sess., Senate (1860), 4; Channing, *Crisis of Fear*, pp. 255-256; Hinton Rowan Helper, *The Impending Crisis of the South: How to Meet It* (New York, 1860), pp. 25-27, 113, 116.

[21] Eric Foner, *Free Soil, Free Labor, Free Men: The Ideology of the Republican Party before the Civil War* (New York, 1970), pp. 5, 118-123, 134, 207-213, 313-316; Greeley, *A History of the Struggle for Slavery Extension*, p. 5; Helper, *The Impending Crisis*, pp. 156, 178; *Congressional Globe*, 36 Cong., 2 sess., Senate (1860), 3-4, 11, 202-203; Hans L. Trefousse, *The Radical Republicans: Lincoln's Vanguard for Racical Justice* (New York, 1969), p. 104.

[22] Martinho Campos and Andrade Figueira were especially outspoken among the pro-slavery leaders who identified themselves with the ideals of John C. Calhoun. *Annaes da Camara* (1880), IV, 445-446; (1887), V, 72.

[23] *Congressional Globe*, 36 Cong., 2 sess., Senate (1860), 4, 11-13, 29, 33-34, 73, 189, 217; Martin, *The Great Parliamentary Battle*, pp. 179, 218.

cussing the southern leaders' fears, and the fact that many of these predictions turned into reality in Brazil does not *necessarily* indicate that the same kinds of problems eventually would have developed in the United States. Moreover, the fear of internal agitation from abolitionists and slaves was not the only motivation for secession. But let us not conclude by retreating from where this analysis has been leading. If we may believe that southern secessionists meant what they said and, indeed, that Republican ideologues meant what *they* said, then the case for secession looks strong.[24] From the point of view of the slaveholder who worried about his future security, it made good sense to try to establish peaceful secession. However, from the point of view of the present-day historian who applies moral criteria to his analysis, the case for secession obviously does not look strong. The moral side of the issue is most certainly a legitimate consideration, but it can be applied more effectively once the uncomfortable ironies of the story are recognized.

[24] Foner, *Free Soil, Free Labor, Free Men*, passim; J. G. de Roulhac Hamilton, "Lincoln's Election an Immediate Menace to Slavery in the States?," *American Historical Review* (July, 1932), 700-711.

Acknowledgments

Richard R. Beeman, "Labor Forces and Race Relations: A Comparative View of the Colonization of Brazil and Virginia," *Political Science Quarterly* 86 (1971): 609–36. Reprinted by permission of the *Political Science Quarterly*.

David Brion Davis, "Slavery," in C. Vann Woodward, ed., *The Comparative Approach to American History* (1968): 121–34. Reprinted by permission of Basic Books.

Carl N. Degler, "Slavery in Brazil and the United States: An Essay in Comparative History," *American Historical Review* 75, No. 4 (1970): 1004–28. Reprinted by permission of the *American Historical Review*.

Seymour Drescher, "Brazilian Abolition in Comparative Perspective," *Hispanic-American Historical Review* (1988): 429–60. Reprinted by permission.

Richard S. Dunn, "A Tale of Two Plantations: Slave Life at Mesopotamia in Jamaica and Mount Airy in Virginia, 1799–1828," *William and Mary Quarterly*, 3rd Ser., 34, No. 1 (1977): 32–65. Reprinted by permission of the *William and Mary Quarterly*.

Stanley M. Elkins, "Cultural Contacts and Negro Slavery," Proceedings of the *American Philosophical Society* 107 (April, 1963): 107–09. Reprinted by permission of the *Proceedings of the American Philosophical Society*.

Stanley M. Elkins and Eric McKitrick, "Institutions and the Law of Slavery: The Dynamics of Unopposed Capitalism," and "Slavery in Capitalist and Non-Capitalist Culture," *American Quarterly* 9 (Spring, 1957 and Summer, 1957): 3–21, 159–79. Reprinted by permission of *American Quarterly*.

M.I. Finley, "Between Slavery and Freedom," *Comparative Studies in Society and History* 6, No. 3 (1964): 233–49. Reprinted with the permission of Cambridge University Press.

M.I. Finley, "The Idea of Slavery," *New York Review of Books* 81 (January 26, 1967): 6–10. Reprinted with permission from *The New York Review of Books*. Copyright (c) 1967 Nyrev, Inc.

Eugene D. Genovese and Elizabeth Fox-Genovese, "The Slave Economies in Political Perspective," *Journal of American History* 66 (June, 1979): 7–23. Reprinted by permission of the *Journal of American History*.

Eugene D. Genovese, "Materialism and Idealism in the History of

Negro Slavery in the Americas," *Journal of Social History* 1 (1968): 371–94. Reprinted by permission of the *Journal of Social History*.

Richard Graham, "Slavery and Economic Development: Brazil and the United States South in the Nineteenth Century," *Comparative Studies in Society and History* 23, No. 4 (1981): 620–55. Reprinted with the permission of Cambridge University Press.

Herbert S. Klein, "Anglicanism, Catholicism and the Negro Slave," *Comparative Studies in Society and History* 7 (April, 1966): 295–327. Reprinted with the permission of Cambridge University Press.

Herbert S. Klein and Stanley L. Engerman, "Fertility Differentials Between Slaves in the U.S. and the British West Indies: A Note on Lactation Practices and Their Possible Implications," *William and Mary Quarterly*, 3rd Ser., 35, No. 2 (April, 1978): 357–74. Reprinted by permission of the *William and Mary Quarterly*.

Peter Augustine Lawler, "Tocqueville on Slavery, Ancient and Modern," *South Atlantic Quarterly* 80, No. 4 (Autumn, 1981): 466–77. Reprinted by permission of the *South Atlantic Quarterly*.

Michael Mullin, "British Caribbean and North American Slaves in an Era of War and Revolution, 1775–1807," in Jeffrey J. Crow and Larry E. Tise, eds., *The Southern Experience in the American Revolution* (1978): 235–67. Reprinted by permission of the University of North Carolina Press.

Arnold A. Sio, "Interpretations of Slavery: The Slave Status in the Americas," *Comparative Studies in Society and History* 7 (April, 1965): 289–308. Reprinted with the permission of Cambridge University Press.

Howard Temperley, "Capitalism, Slavery, and Ideology," *Past and Present* 75 (1977): 94–118. Reprinted by permission of *Past and Present*.

Robert Brent Toplin, "The Specter of Crisis: Slaveholder Reactions to Abolitionism in the United States and Brazil," *Civil War History* 18 (June, 1972): 129–38. Reprinted by permission of *Civil War History*.